"TO SEE OURSELVES AS OTHERS SEE US"

Scholars Press
Studies in the Humanities

Publication of this volume was made possible with the
assistance of the Alexander Kohut Memorial Foundation of
the American Academy for Jewish Research.

"TO SEE OURSELVES AS OTHERS SEE US"

Christians, Jews, "Others" in Late Antiquity

Edited by
Jacob Neusner
and
Ernest S. Frerichs

Literary Editor:
Caroline McCracken-Flesher

Scholars Press
Chico, California

"TO SEE OURSELVES AS OTHERS SEE US"
Christians, Jews, "Others" in Late Antiquity

Edited by
Jacob Neusner
and
Ernest S. Frerichs

© 1985
Scholars Press

"The Way and the Ways" by A. H. Armstrong was originally published in *Vigiliae Christianae* 38 (1984) 1–17 and
is reprinted by permission.

Library of Congress Cataloging in Publication Data
Main entry under title:

"To see ourselves as others see us."

(Scholars Press studies in the humanities)
Includes index.
1. Judaism—Controversial literature—History and
criticism—Congresses. 2. Christianity and other
religions—Judaism—History—Congresses.
3. Judaism—Relations—Christianity—History—Congresses.
4. Judaism—History—Talmudic period, 10–245—
Congresses. 5. Church history—Primitive and early
church, ca. 30–600—Congresses. I. Neusner, Jacob,
1932–   . II. Frerichs, Ernest S. III. McCracken-Flesher,
Caroline. IV. Series: Scholars Press studies in the
humanities series.
BT1120.T6 1985   296.3'872'093   85–2488
ISBN 0–89130–819–9 (alk. paper)
ISBN 0–89130–820–2 (pbk. : alk. paper)

BT
1120
.T6
1985

Printed in the United States of America
on acid-free paper

For

MERTON STOLTZ

Brown's great provost,
whose leadership made
its mark, long beyond
his term of office

A salute from the editors,
who remember
and appreciate

CONTENTS

Contents

Preface

It is an essential part of human behavior to divide the world into ourselves and the rest. The ancient Middle East had known many such divisions—kinsmen and strangers, Jews and gentiles, Greeks and barbarians, citizens, metics, and aliens, as well as others. A classification already familiar to Jews and Christians was between believers and unbelievers. In Islamic times this came to be by far the most important line of division, overshadowing all others.

Bernard Lewis
The Jews of Islam
(Princeton, 1984),
pp. 19-20.

Looking backward upon the formative centuries of Christianity and Judaism, we focus upon how insiders thought about themselves by what they said concerning "others." The reason is that, from the perspective of our own day, the critical issue of world civilization, the principal and generative tension in the life of humanity, emerges from that protean concern: who am I? who is the one different from me? who are we? who are those different from us? We take the measure of the matter by its capacity to come to full expression in nearly every dimension of society and culture, politics and collective existence, and religion. The theory of the other expresses the sense of self. The lines of structure mark out, to begin with, insider from outsider. From parturition to death, the individual takes shape through successive separations and unions. From center to frontier, societies discover themselves by signifying difference and stipulating what difference difference makes. So, in all, in the heart and center of the study of humanity we take up the divided heart, the uncertain vision, the off-center perspective, that, in the eye of the beholder, tells a person who is like, and who is unlike.

For that study, religion forms the single richest field of investigation. For in the religious dimension one sector of humanity proves at once most like and most unlike all the other sectors. On the one side, religions speak of pretty much the same things in heaven and on earth, natural and supernatural. On the other, religions commonly turn out to be talking about different things to different people, with little, or no, shared set of topics or even common frame of reference. And, it remains to note, where sense for difference proves acute, it is within, in that shared, therefore most contested, turf of religious traditions claiming to emerge from a single point of origin: Judaism, Christianity, Islam. As Lewis points out, what that vast portion of human civilization framed by Islam and Christianity shares—the Western hemisphere and most of the Eastern as well—is the sense that people are what they are because of belief or unbelief. That definitive trait of the bulk of human civilization comes to the West, and to the world, out of late antiquity, specifically, out of the Judaic and Christian worlds of late antiquity. As Lewis says, it is that point of division—belief, unbelief—that Islam then brought to the world unaffected by Christianity and (all the more so) Judaism. So when we ask about how religious groups defined themselves through what they said about the other, we investigate one of the principal traits of much of the civilization of humanity, and, it goes without saying, of the whole of the civilization of the West.

When we reach that ancient world of the Greco-Roman Mediterranean in the first seven centuries of the common era ("A.D."), the matrix of Western civilization as we know it, we find a world in which "the other" bears diverse definitions. These definitions emerge only from the character and perspective of the group from whose perspective the "other" is other, that is, different or not normal. Taking the exemplary case of how the other appears in the writings of the ancient rabbis who defined Judaism as we know it, we find the search for a single criterion for otherness somewhat elusive. "The other" of course is the gentile, different from the Israelite. But gentiles play no role in the system. What "other" matters? Among Israelites these others may be an Israelite unbeliever, by reason of heresy; an Israelite of a different order, such as a Samaritan; an Israelite bearing traits that distinguish that person from the norm, for instance, a woman, who, because of her gender, is seen as abnormal, and so as other, by the men who wrote the books; the Israelite who does not keep the law; the Israelite who keeps the law but not in the way the writers prescribe; the Israelite who keeps the law in the way the writers prescribe, but not everywhere and all the time; not to mention the minor, the slave, and so on. And then, within the "us" were others, who differ on opinion within the accepted agenda of difference. Such a catalogue tells us that the world fundamentally consisted of "others," beyond the self. So when we ask, "Who, to you, is different or strange," we had best summon the patience to sit for a rather considerable answer. It goes without saying that equivalent catalogues of "others" serve equally well within the diverse families of religious communities we call, all in all, Christianity.

That is why we begin with Judaism and Christianity our analysis of the place and role of "the other". These two groups contended with one another for the same turf, the title of "Israel," and standing as God's first love and Scripture's authentic heir. It is not that the families of Christianity and the families of Judaism provide the only or the best example of the role and place of thought about the outsider in the systems of late antiquity. Rather, these families attract our interest for two reasons. First in today's world most people interested in the formative age of Christianity and Judaism turn out to be Christians or Jews. Second, even if they bore no claim to relate to the past under study, that past did, and does, define the West as we have known it. Accordingly, if we wish to ask how a given group expressed its sense of itself through its doctrine of the outsider, we find ourselves well-served by the ancient founders and framers of our world: the Christians and Jews who, for good or ill, made us what we are.

Let us elaborate on this point. In the first seven Christian centuries, the two great religious traditions of the West, Christianity and Judaism, took the measure of one another. In so doing, each tradition framed a theory of the other and so, in the process, also reached a definition of itself. For the issue of explaining the other also provoked thought about the frontiers between the self and the other, marking out the limits of the inside and delineating the lines of structure beyond. Now what makes the inquiry into the reciprocal conceptions of Judaism and Christianity in these formative centuries critical? It is the simple fact that the developing theories of the other left a legacy, for both medieval and modern Western civilization, of not only intolerance but also restraint, not only a quest for universal conformity but also a capacity to sustain difference. Our ultimate reward, long in the future, will be to find such roots of theories of pluralism as may be uncovered in the formative centuries of Judaism and Christianity: the foundations of pluralism in two traditions that lay claim, against one another, to a single and universal truth.

Judaism and Christianity in late antiquity present histories that mirror one another. When Christianity began, Judaism was the dominant tradition in the Holy Land and framed its ideas within a political framework until the early fifth century. Christianity there was subordinate and had to work against the background of a politically definitive Judaism. From the time of Constantine onward, matters reversed themselves. Now Christianity predominated, expressing its ideas in political and institutional terms. Judaism, by contrast, had lost its political foundations and faced the task of working out its self-understanding in terms of a world defined by Christianity, now everywhere triumphant and in charge of politics.

Within the stated theme, the volume at hand takes up a single problem: How do the religious traditions of Judaism and Christianity, in their formative centuries, take up the problem of the outsider? Both traditions confronted the issue of defining themselves. This demanded definition not only of who is within and who is without. It also required the formation of a mode of thinking about the outsider. Both traditions framed a theory of the outsider within the large systematic framework of their religious world-views. Both theology and social policy within formative Christianity and Judaism therefore took up, and made detailed statements about, "the other." Viewed systematically these statements explained, first, who is the other, second, how does the other fit into the way of life and world view of the faith, and third, and most relevant to our own day, upon what basis is one sort of outsider to be tolerated, and another to be banned and, if possible, exterminated. The final issue, flowing from the first three, then takes up practicalities and concrete actions, specifically, what in late antiquity did the two nascent traditions actually do, as distinct from what they would like to have done, in the confrontation with difference, particularly of the disagreeable kind.

The program of the volume in general encompasses two traditions and two aspects of the theory of the other in each: First, general theories of the outsider, and second, specific theory about the other. Thus we take up Judaism on the gentile world in general, the Christian world in particular; and Christianity on the outside world in general, the Judaic world in particular. Clearly, each tradition deemed the other to be special and apart from the world at large. But what difference did the distinction make, between Judaism and the rest of the unbelieving world, when it came to framing social policy and effecting it, for instance in the Theodosian code? And how differently did the sages of the rabbinic canon of writings treat Christianity from the otherwise undifferentiated world of "paganism?" These two questions exemplify the specific problem before us. The papers of this book then may fall within the grid just now described.

What do we hope to achieve, as we inaugurate an on-going exercise in learning how two closely related religious communities thought about one another in particular and the world at large in general? It is to gain a measure of perspective on each of the two communities, to understand what they have been, so that we may frame a vision of what each may become in time to come. To compare one thing to another, we provide an account of likeness and difference, just as much as, in our studies in this book, we establish comparisons on how each group sorted out points of likeness and difference. We propose to compare and contrast because we postulate a fundamental commonality between the families of Christianity and the families of Judaism. We propose to compare because we perceive a basic point of difference, too, that bears significance. We are able to compare Judaisms and Christianities because we find in common a shared language and mode of discourse concerning a single holy book and doctrine. The two congeries of religious worlds exhibited in common points worth fighting about. So as is now clear, in the exercise at hand we ask how the two groups dealt with a single question. It is a legitimate question because both groups not only addressed that question but, as we said at the outset, expressed their understandings of themselves in whom they identified as, and what they said about, outsiders. To state matters simply: Judaism and Christianity invite comparison and contrast because they stand close enough to seek mutual intelligibility and (therefore) to conduct vigorous and protracted argument with one another.

The book at hand moves across a variety of Judaic and Christian writings, from the Apocrypha and Pseudepigrapha of the Hebrew Scripture ("the Old Testament"), to the New Testament, patristic writings in Syriac and Greek, the Mishnah, Tosefta, the two Talmuds, and rabbinic compilations of exegeses of Scripture called "midrashim," and on into the study of the law and politics of the Byzantine world and the earlier centuries of the medieval Latin West. We do not know many books that propose to join together so many presently-discrete fields of learning, history, philosophy, theology, religion, and literature; Greek, Hebrew, Latin, Aramaic, Syriac; the formative history of Christianity; Roman law and Latin Church history, and onward. If the book succeeds, readers will find it possible to read the papers as a group, not merely consult them individually for the research they contain. If the book fails, it will have provided a forum for what we believe to be distinguished and substantial research, that alone. We leave it to the reader and to the future to issue a verdict on our work. We hoped to talk together about a common, large question. Whether or not we have succeeded in doing so in this book is something only time—and research generated here—will tell. Our conviction is simply that the work has proved illuminating and suggestive, and that we have learned a great deal in the doing of it.

Because of its fundamental importance, the editors chose to reprint A. H. Armstrong, "The Way and the Ways: Religious Tolerance and Intolerance in the Fourth Century A.D.," which originally appeared in *Vigiliae Christianae* 1984, 38:1-17, and which was first read at the International Patristic Conference at Oxford on September 9, 1983. We are grateful to the author, and also to the publisher, E. J. Brill, for granting permission to us to reprint this paper. The author is thanked, also, for reviewing the paper and making some minor corrections.

Finally, the editors note with thanks the support for the conference, August 6–10, 1984, at Brown University, entitled "To see ourselves as others see us," accorded by the National Endowment for the Humanities, with matching grants of the Lilly Endowment, Indianapolis, Indiana, and the Nancy Harris Fund for Judaic Studies at Brown University. Additional support in organizing the conference came from the Alperin Family Foundation of Rhode Island, the Jewish Federation of Rhode Island Endowment Fund, and the Max Richter Foundation. As for all things that we do, so for this project too, the greatest source of support, both material and intellectual, came from Brown University. Whatever contribution this volume makes both to learning and to the attainment of deeper understanding among the families of Western civilization accrues to the credit of these worthy friends and supporters of this project and, indeed, of all the projects and enterprises of the editors.

We state—with much pleasure—that nothing we do could ever prove of worth if we did not enjoy the everyday counsel and solid advice of our colleague, Wendell S. Dietrich, and of our other friends and colleagues in the Program in Judaic Studies at Brown University.

J. N.
E. S. F.

Program in Judaic Studies
Brown University
Providence, Rhode Island

September 26, 1984
29 Elul 5744

Abbreviations

AB	Anchor Bible
ANRW	*Aufstieg und Niedergang der römischen Welt*
Ant.	Josephus, *Jewish Antiquities*
Aphrahat, *Dem.*	Aphrahat, *Demonstrations Against the Jews*
APOT	R.H. Charles, ed., *The Apocrypha and Pseudepigrapha of the Old Testament*, 2 vols., (Oxford: Clarendon, 1912).
ATR	*Anglican Theological Review*
A. Z.	Abodah Zarah
B.	Babylonian Talmud
Barn.	Epistle of Barnabas
BASOR	*Bulletin of the American Schools of Oriental Research*
B.C.E.	Before the Common Era (= B.C.).
BCH	*Bulletin de Correspondance Hellénistique*
BEvT	Beiträge zur evangelischen Theologie
Bekh.	Bekhorot
Bib	*Biblica*
BM Add.	British Museum, Additional Manuscript
B. Q.	Baba Qama
BZ	Biblische Zeitschrift
CBQ	*Catholic Biblical Quarterly*
CD	Cairo (Genizah text of the) Damascus (Document). Published by S. Schechter. *Fragments of a Zadokite Work*, Rev. ed. by J. A. Fitzmyer. (New York: KTAV, 1970); Translation by Vermes, *Scrolls*, pp. 95-117
Chron. Pasch.	Chronikon Paschale
Chrysostom, *Homilies* (or) Chrys. *Jud.*	*John Chrysostom's Eight Homilies Against the Judaizers*, trans. P. W. Harkins, *The Fathers of the Church*, vol. 68 (Washington, D.C.: 1979).
CSCO	Corpus Scriptorum Christianorum Orientalium

C. Th.	*Codex Theodosianus*. English translation with commentary by C. Pharr (Princeton: 1952).
Dem.	Demai
Deut.	Deuteronomy
Didascalia	Didascalia Apostolorum
DJD(J)	Discoveries in the Judaean Desert of Jordan. (Oxford: Clarendon, 1955-)
Ep. Diog.	Epistle to Diognetus
Epiph. *Haer*	Epiphaniua, *Panarion Against All Heresies*
Eus. *H.E.*	Eusebius, *Historia Ecclesiastica*
Eus. *Life of Const.*	Eusebius, *Life of Constantine*
E. T.	English translation
EvT	*Evangelische Theologie*
Ex.	Exodus
ExpT	*Expository Times*
FRLANT	Forschungen zur Religion und Literatur des Alten und Neuen Testaments
Fs.	Festschrift (jubilee or memorial volume)
Git.	Gittin
HeyJ	*Heythrop Journal*
Hist.	Gregory of Tours, *Historiae/Histories*, in MGH, vol. I (1885).
HR	*History of Religion*
HTR	*Harvard Theological Review*
HTS	Harvard Theological Studies
HUCA	*Hebrew Union College Annual*
Hul.	Hullin
IDBS	*The Interpreter's Dictionary of the Bible: Supplementary Volume.* (Nashville: 1976).
Ign. *Phil.*	Ignatius, *Epistle to the Philadelphians*
Interp	*Interpretation*
JBL	*Journal of Biblical Literature*
JBLMS	Journal of Biblical Literature Monograph Series
JJS	*Journal of Jewish Studies*
Jn	John
JRS	*Journal of Roman Studies*
JSJ	*Journal for the Study of Judaism in the Persian, Hellenistic, and Roman Period*
JSNT	*Journal for the Study of the New Testament*
JTS	*Journal of Theological Studies*
Just. *Dial.*	Justin, *Dialogue with Trypho the Jew*

JW	Josephus, *Jewish Wars*
Kil.	Kilayim
M.	Mishnah
Matt	Matthew
Meg.	Megillah
MGH	*Monumenta Germaniae historica*, Wilhelm Arndt and Bruno Krusch, (Hannover).
MPG	See PG
MPL	*Patrologia Latina*, Ed. J. P. Migne (Paris: 1844-55).
Mt	Matthew
Murray, *Symbols*	Robert Murray, *Symbols of Church and Kingdom* (London: 1975).
NovT, N.T.	*Novum Testamentum*
NTS	*New Testament Studies*
Num	Numbers
OC	Oriens Christianus
OTP	J. Charlesworth, ed., *The Old Testament Pseudigrapha*, (Garden City: Doubleday, 1983-).
Par.	Parah
Pe.	Peah
Pes.	Pesahim
PG	*Patrologia Graeca*. Ed. J.P. Migne. (Paris: 1857-66).
PIBA	Proceedings of the Irish Biblical Association
1QH	Hymn Scroll. Published by E. Sukenik. *The Dead Sea Scrolls of the Hebrew University*. (Jerusalem: Magnes, 1955); Translation by Vermes, *Scrolls*, 149-201
Qoh.	Qohelet, Ecclestiastes.
1QpHab	Habakkuk Commentary. Published by M. Burrows. *The Dead Sea Scrolls of St. Mark's Monastery* 1. (New Haven: American Schools of Oriental Research, 1950); Translation by Vermes, *Scrolls* 235-41.
4QpNah	Nahum Commentary. Published by J. Allegro, DJDJ5:37-42. Translation by Vermes, *Scrolls*, 231-35
4QpPs[a]	Psalms Commentary. Published by J. Allegro. DJDJ5:42-50. Translation by Vermes, *Scrolls*, 243-45.

1QS	Rule of the Community (Manual of Discipline). Published by M. Burrows. *The Dead Sea Scrolls of St. Mark's Monastery* 2. (New Haven: American Schools of Oriental Research, 1951); Translation by Vermes, *Scrolls,* 71-94
RB	*Revue Biblique*
REJ	*Revue des études juives*
SANT	*Studien zum Alten und Neuen Testament*
SBLDS	SBL Dissertations Series
SBLSBS	Society of Biblical Literature Sources for Biblical Study
SBLSCS	SBL Septuagint and Cognate Studies
SBT	Studies in Biblical Theology
Shab.	Shabbat
Sheb.	Shebiit
SJLA	Studies in Judaism in Late Antiquity
SNTSMS	Society for New Testament Studies Monograph Series
SR	*Studies in Religion/Sciences religieuses*
SUNT	Studien zur Umwelt des Neuen Testaments
SVTP	Studia in Veteris Testamenti Pseudepigraph
T.	Tosefta
TAPA	Transactions of the American Philological Association
TDNT	*Theological Dictionary of the New Testament*
Toh.	Tohorot
TMos	Testament of Moses
TS	Theological Studies
TU	Texte und Untersuchungen
VC	*Vigiliae christianae*
Vermes, Scrolls	*The Dead Sea Scrolls in English,* Geza Vermes, (London: Penguin Books, 1962). 2nd ed. 1975.
Y.	Palestinian Talmud

ONE
The Problem of the Other

1

What A Difference A Difference Makes

Jonathan Z. Smith
University of Chicago

"The discourse of difference is a difficult one." T. Todorov, *La conquête de l'Amérique: La question de l'autre* (Paris, 1982).

"To See Ourselves as Others See Us: The Theory of the Other in the Formative Age of Christianity and Judaism." What a formidable topic to set before an international gathering of scholars as the focus for a summer's week-long period of papers and reflections! Only the title's points of chronological reference to the first centuries strike me as bearing a measure of self-evidence. Quite rightly, they have supplied the skeletal outline for the proceedings of our conference. Abstaining from the question of the referent for "Christianity" or "Judaism," what is by no means clear is what was intended by the framers of our topic when they employed the portentous phrase "the theory of the other." I take it to be the obligation of one charged to give a "keynote" address to inquire into this most general aspect of our subject.

For this reason, in what follows I shall not dwell at all on the stated chronological period, nor venture to anticipate the welter of historical particularities and exempla concerning Christians and Jews which the full program promises. Rather, I shall direct my inquiries toward that phrase "the theory of the other," and attempt to discern several senses in which the "other" can be framed as a theoretical issue. That is to say, I shall want to ask, from the perspective intellectual history, what difference does difference make? My point of entry into this difficult matter has been supplied by the poetic apostrophe in our conference's title.

I

"There is no settling the point of precedency between a louse and a flea." Dr. Johnson.

I would like to believe it was far from accidental that our conveners chose to introduce our topic with a line from the conclud-

ing stanza of a poem by Robert Burns. First published in the historic
Kilmarnock edition of 1786, it has, detached from its context, since
become a piece of proverbial lore.

> O wid some Power the giftie gie us
> To see oursels as ithers see us!
> It wad frae mony a blunder free us,
>   An' foolish notion:
> What airs in dress an' gait wad lea'e us
>   An' ev'n devotion![1]

In quoting Burns's lines, we have already gained an initial
purchase on our topic. What language was the poem written in? The
language seems not-quite-English, yet, is it different enough to be
classified as "other"? To quote one distinguished scholar of Scottish
literature on Burns:

> Though all of this is still unmistakably Scots, only a small change of
> spelling is required to make these couplets visually indistinguish-
> able from English...[but] they have to be pronounced with a
> Scottish accent. Thus they fall within the compass of Scottish speech
> and the language employed in them cannot strictly be called 'Eng-
> lish;' perhaps it should rather be termed 'near-English.'[2]

It may be fairly asked, how "near" is near? How "far" is far? How
different does difference have to be to constitute "otherness"? Under
what circumstances, and to whom, are such distinctions of interest?

The question of interest reminds us of yet another facet to our
theme, one that is contained within the original sense of "interest" as
continued in legal and economic usage. Difference is rarely something simply to be noted; it is, most often, something in which one has
a stake. Above all, it is a political matter. As the proximate historical
setting of Burns suggests, following after the Union of the Crowns in
1603 and the Parliamentary Union of 1707, and contemporary with the
establishment in Edinburgh of a "Select Society for the Promoting of
the Reading and Speaking of the English Language," what appears
from a linguistic point of view to be "near," appears from a political
vantage to be exceedingly "far."[3] How far might be measured by

---

[1] Robert Burns, *Poems Chiefly in the Scottish Dialect* (Kilmarnock: 1786), 192–4, esp. 194.
[2] K. Wittig, *The Scottish Tradition in Literature* (Edinburg: 1958), 201.
[3] The social and political settings of Scottish vernacular have been well studied by D. Craig, *Scottish Literature and the Scottish People* (London: 1961). I have taken the detail of the "Select Society" from D. Murison, "The Language of Burns," in D. A. Low, ed., *Critical Essays on Robert Burns* (London: 1975), 56.

comparing Burns's self-consciously vernacular poems with the equally self-conscious classic English prose of his Scottish contemporary, Adam Smith. Difference is seldom a comparison between entities judged to be equivalent. Difference most frequently entails a hierarchy of prestige and the concomitant political ranking of superordinate and subordinate.

Yet, as the Scottish example illustrates, such distinctions are usually drawn most sharply between "near neighbors." For a Scotsman to opt for either Scottish or English (both being Anglo-Saxon dialects) is a more politically striking decision than to have chosen to speak either French or Chinese.[4] The radically "other" is merely "other"; the proximate "other" is problematic, and hence, of supreme interest.

But there is more. The choice of our conveners proved to be of even greater prescience. For the poem that contains the line "to see ourselves as others see us" is entitled "To a Louse: On Seeing One on a Lady's Bonnet at Church." Perhaps this will seem an unsuitable topic; it has appeared so to many of Burns's deepest admirers. But the louse has provided the subject for a wide variety of poets and painters,[5] although it has been eclipsed in this regard by the equally parasitic flea[6] in the works of poets ranging from John Donne to Roland Young, in operatic works by Mussorgsky and Ghedini, and not forgetting its place in the anonymous Victorian pornographic novel, *Autobiography of a Flea, told in a Hop, Skip and Jump, and recounting all experiences of the Human and Superhuman Kind, both Male and Female; with his Curious Connections, Backbitings and Tickling Touches.*[7] Burns's poem will not repay further study—it's lousy; but its pediculine subject will.

There is, perhaps, no scientific area of scholarship in which more

---

[4] For the ideological issues and their relation to continental theories concerning language, see F. W. Freeman, "The Intellectual Background of the Vernacular Revolt before Burns," *Studies in Scottish Literature*, 16(1981), 160–87.

[5] See the study by H. Meige, *Les pouilleux dans l'art* (Paris: 1897). For a catalogue of old, scientific illustrations, see G. H. F. Nuttall, "The Systematic Position, Synonymy and Iconography of *Pediculus humanus* and *Phthirus pubis*," *Parasitology*, 11(1919), 329–46, esp. 337–9.

[6] For a study of the flea in literature, see B. Lehane, *The Compleat Flea* (New York: 1969).

[7] Title page, *Autobiography of a Flea* in the edition published by the Erotica Biblion Society (New York: 1901). The first edition, published for the Phlebotomical Society, London, bears the date 1789. This is false. The *Autobiography* is clearly a work of Victorian England. For a bibliography devoted to the special topic of the flea in erotic literature, see H. Hayn and A.N.Gotendorf, *Floh-literatur (de pudicibus) des In- und Auslandes vom XVI Jahrhundert bis zur Neuzeit* (Dresden [?], 1913).

sustained attention has been devoted to the taxonomy and definition
of "otherness" than parasitology. Rare for biology, here is a sub-dis-
cipline devoted not to a natural class of living things, but rather to a
relationship between two quite different species of plants or animals.
It is the character of the difference and the mode of relationship which
supplies both the key characteristics for classification and the central
topics for disciplinary thought. This is especially apparent in the
literature of the last half of the nineteenth century, while parasitology
was achieving status as an independent field of inquiry.[8] Observations
about some of the larger parasites on animals and man may be found
throughout antiquity.[9] However, awareness of parasitism's ubiquity
had to await the late seventeenth-century development of the microscope.[10] This resulted in a decisive shift of intellectual interest to the
scientific, philosophical and literary topos of the intricately small.[11]
Even after this point, despite the enormous increase in data,[12] theo-

---

[8] I know of no good history of parasitology. For the present, W. D. Foster, *A History of Parasitology* (Edinburgh and London: 1965) remains the most serviceable.

[9] R. Hoeppli, *Parasites and Parasitic Infections in Early Medicine and Science* (Singapore: 1959) is a rich repertoire of ancient sources (especially valuable for its inclusion of Chinese materials). There are a series of comprehensive notes on the Greco-Roman parasitological literature in F.Adams, *The Seven Books of Paulus Aegineta* (London: 1844–47), 1–3, esp. 2:139–53.

[10] See, in general, A. N. Disney, et al., *The Origin and Development of the Microscope* (London: 1928), R. S. Clay and T. H. Court, *The History of the Microscope* (London: 1932). The introductory material to the English translation of Leeuwenhoek's writings by C. Dobell, *Antony van Leeuwenhoek and His "Little Animals"* (London: 1932) is invaluable. It will be recalled that an early term for microscope was "louse-lens."

[11] Much work remains to be done on the topos, "small is more interesting than large." While such a notion is as old as Pliny (*Historia naturalis* 11.1), it became a dominant motif only after the fashioning of lenses, both for the telescope and, most especially, for the microscope. For the former, one thinks of Galileo's encomium to the "little moons" of Jupiter which concludes with a defense of and hymn of praise to tiny things (Galileo, Letter of May 21, 1611, in P. Dini, *Epistolario Galilei* [Leghorn: 1872], 1:121–2). The latter is summarized, at a late stage of its development, in the wellknown dictum in Emerson's essay, "On Compensation": "The microscope cannot find the animalcule which is less perfect for being little," (R. L. Cook, ed., *Ralph Waldo Emerson: Selected Prose and Poetry* [New York: 1950], 109). The fundamental study of this topos is M. Nicolson, *The Microscope and English Imagination* (Northhampton, Mass.: 1934), in the series, *Smith College Studies in Modern Languages*, 16.4, which should be read in conjunction with her analogous studies of the telescope, "The Telescope and the Imagination," *Modern Philology*, 32(1935), 233–60; "The New Astronomy and the English Literary Imagination," *Studies in Philology*, 32(1935), 428–62, cf. Nicolson, *The Breaking of the Circle: Studies in the Effect of the "New Science" Upon Seventeenth Century Poetry*, 2nd ed. (New York: 1960). For other studies of this topos, see A. Lovejoy, *The Great Chain of Being* (Cambridge, Mass.: 1936), 236–40; A. Gerbi, *The Dispute of the New World* (Pittsburgh: 1973), 16–20.

[12] It is the special merit of E. Mayr, *The Growth of Biological Thought* (Cambridge,

retical issues with respect both to taxonomy[13] and "spontaneous generation" had to be settled before the discipline of parasitology could emerge.[14]

While the majority of biology's historians have focused their attention on the aetiological issues associated with the theory of "spontaneous generation" (*generatio aequivoca* or "abiogenesis"), it was, in fact, the taxonomic implications that were more serious for our theme. Until the stunning monograph by J. J. S. Steenstrup (1842),[15] it was by no means clear that many parasites go through both free-living and parasitic stages of development (at times, with sex changes) that bear no resemblance to each other and often with an invariant sequence of hosts. It is the generation of parasitologists that immediately followed upon this discovery that developed the classificatory systems of most interest to us.[16] It was first thought that one biological

---

Mass.: 1982), 1:134–40, to place the increase in knowledge about the number of parasitic species within the context of the general 18th century increase in the knowledge of the number and diversity of animal and plant species. The article by P. Geddes, "Parasitism, Animal," *Encyclopaedia Britannica*, 9th ed. (1875–89), is an eloquent witness to the perception of parasitism's ubiquity: "we observe not only the enormously wide prevalence of parasitism—the number of parasitic individuals, if not indeed that of species, *probably exceeding that of non-parasitic forms*—but its very considerable variety in degree and detail" (18: 260, emphasis added).

[13] For some of the taxonomic implications, see F. B. Churchill, "Sex and the Single Organism: Biological Theories of Sexuality in the mid-19th Century," *Studies in the History of Biology*, 3(1979), 139–77.

[14] For an overview, see J. Farley, *The Spontaneous Generation Controversy from Descartes to Oparin* (Baltimore: 1977). (Pages 18–9, 34–8, 58–66 focus on parasites). I have been much helped by the treatment in E. Guyénot, *Les sciences de la vie au XVIIᵉ et XVIIIᵉ siècles* (Paris: 1941, 211–19. With particular reference to parasites, see R. Hoeppli and I. H. Ch'iang, "The Doctrine of Spontaneous Generation of Parasites in Old-Style Chinese and Western Medicine," *Peking Natural History Bulletin*, 19(1950–1), 375–415, reprinted with revisions in Hoeppli, *Parasites and Parasitic Diseases*, 113–56.

[15] J. J. S. Steenstrup, *Über den Generationswechsel oder die Fortpflanzung und Entwicklung durch abwechselnde Generationen, eine eigenthümliche Form der Brutpflege in den biederen Thierklassen* (Copenhagen: 1842). This German translation (by C. H. Lorenzen) is the first publication of Steenstrup's manuscript, *Om Fortplantning og Udvikling gjennem vexlende Generationsraekken*. An English translation was rapidly published by the John Ray Society, *On the Alternation of Generations or the Propogation and Development of Animals through Alternate Generations* (London: 1845). On Steenstrup and his contributions, see E. Lagrange, "Le centenaire d'une découverte: Le cycle evolutif des Cestodes," *Annales de Parasitologie*, 27(1952), 557–70.

[16] A. W. Meyer, *The Rise of Embryology* (Stanford: 1939), 43, supports the notion that the decisive generation in parasitology was the period, 1840–70. In what follows, I have surveyed the following widely used texts: J. Leidy, *A Flora and Fauna within Living Animals* (Washington, D.C.: 1853); F. Küchenmeister, *Die in und an dem Körper des*

class could contain all zoological parasitic forms, and so the older
nomenclature of external form which presented the parasite as "worm-
like" (whether expressed through the Greek, *helminth,* or the Latin,
vermis) yielded to a neologism of relative position, the *Entozoa*
(animals who live within).[17] This was a major shift in taxonomic
strategy, creating a class of animals joined together by their "mode of
existence" even though, judged by other criteria, they belonged to
different zoological classes.

Regardless of what biological class the individual parasitic species
belonged to, they might be classified qua parasites by the mode of
their relationship to their hosts. From this point of view, parasitology
is not the study of parasites, it is the study of the host-parasite
relationship. Parasites are classified by their relationship to the
"other," by the modes and degrees of "otherness."

The initial move in this complex taxonomic endeavor was to
attempt a general definition of "parasitism" within the animal kingdom. (Plant parasitism posed a different set of issues). A "parasite"
was defined as an organism of one species that obtained benefits (most
usually food) from an organism of another species with whom it was in
direct contact and which served as "host." It was understood that this
definition was both relative and non-reciprocal. The definition was
relative in that the parasite must be smaller than its host (e.g. the leech
which, when it preys on smaller animals, is properly termed a
"carnivore," is rightly called a "parasite" when it attaches itself to
larger animals). It was non-reciprocal in that the host must derive no
benefit from the parasitic association. Indeed, most usually the association is detrimental to the host. This latter, non-reciprocal criterion
is understood to imply that the negative effect must be the direct
result of the benefit derived by the parasite (e.g., the destruction of the
host's cells by feeding) and not indirect, such as in the case of diseases
transmitted to the host by the parasite.[18]

---

lebenden Menschen vorkammenden Parasiten (Leipzig: 1855), 1–2; C-Davaine, *Traité
des entozoaires et des maladies vermineuses de l'homme et des animaux domestiques*
(Paris: 1860) T. S. Cobbold, *Entozoa, An Introduction to the Study of Helminthology*
(London: 1869); P.-J. van Beneden, *Les commensaux et les parasites dans la règne
animal,* 2nd ed. (Paris: 1878); R. Leuckart, *Die menschlichen Parasiten,* 2nd ed.
(Leipzig: 1879–86), 1–2. For contrast to the 'newer' parasitology, C. Rudolphi, *Entozoo-
rum sive vermium intestinalium historia naturalis* (Amsterdam: 1808–10), 1–2 was
employed.
[17] This process of changing nomenclature may be illustrated by the compound titles in
the works by Davine, Cobbold and Rudolphi in note 16, above.
[18] This last distinction creates a new series of definitional issues still unresolved in the
literature. From one point of view, every disease produced by a microorganism might

Concealed within such late nineteenth-century attempts at a generic definition of "parasitism" were a set of thorny taxonomic distinctions. If attention was focused on the criterion of "benefit," then the attempt was made to distinguish the non-reciprocal benefit to the parasite from closely related phenomena such as "symbiosis" (a term invented in 1879 by A. de Bary) in which both species derived necessary mutual benefits from their association, "mutualism" (a term introduced by Beneden in 1876) in which one species derived benefit without affect on the other and "commensalism" (likewise created by Beneden) in which one species lives on or in another without apparent benefit or harm to either.[19]

Note that such taxonomic distinctions, by virtue of their concern for matters of association, are explicitly political. The definitions are based on hierarchical distinctions of subordination and superordination, on mapping structures of benefits and reciprocity. Such political interests are continued in those taxonomic distinctions made with respect to the nature and character of the direct relationship between host and parasite which constitute a virtual typology of "otherness."

Perhaps the most influential of these was that developed by R. Leuckart in *Die menschlichen Parasiten* (first edition, 1863–76). His first distinction was between what he termed "ectoparasites" (or "epizoa") and "endoparasites" (or "entozoa"). Ectoparasites "live on" their hosts; endoparasites "live in" their hosts. Both may be further subdivided into two classes on the basis on the basis of whether the relationship of parasite to host is "temporary" or "permanent."

In general, ectoparasites are temporary. They seek their hosts in order to obtain food or shelter, and leave them when they have been satisfied. They tend to inhabit the surface of their host's body, or its immediately accessible orifices. Their bodily form is little modified by their parasitic habit when compared with closely related non-parasitic forms.

In general, endoparasites are more complex. They tend to have both parasitic and non-parasitic life stages, the former being highly modified when compared with the latter. In their parasitic stages, the relation to their host is stationary. They more usually inhabit the internal organs of their host.

With primary reference to endoparasites, Leuckart introduced a

---

be considered a parasitic disease. In practice, parasitic diseases are more narrowly defined, but the criteria remain unclear.

[19] To these distinctions were added others chiefly derived from botany, such as "epiphytism," in which one species derives physical support but not nourishment from another species. (For example, mistletoe is a parasite; English ivy is not).

further set of classificatory differentia based on "the nature and duration of their strictly parasitic [stage] of life." (1) Some have "free-living and self-supporting" embryos which become sexually mature only after they have reached their hosts. (2) Others have embryos which are parasitic but "migratory," moving either (a) to a "free life," (b) to another part of their host, or (c) to a different host, before becoming sexually mature. (3) Others are parasitic during every stage of their lives, having no migratory embryonic stage and passing their entire lives on a single host.[20]

In the above, it should be noted that Leuckart's entire classificatory project is based on the differing forms of relationship between parasite and host. It is a relativistic, political system which does not follow the traditional anatomical/morphological criteria for taxonomy.

Before continuing, it may be well to pause and to make explicit what considering this brief history of late nineteenth-century parasitology has contributed to the question of a "theory of the other."

Perhaps the most important point is that reiterated by Leuckart: "no broad line of demarcation can be drawn between parasites and free-living animals."[21] That is to say, "otherness" is an ambiguous category. This is so because it is necessarily a term of interrelation. "Otherness" is not so much a matter of separation as it is a description of interaction. As the taxonomy of parasitism makes clear, the relation to the "other" is a matter of shifting temporality and relative modes of relationship. There are degrees of difference, even within a single species.

While at one level the taxonomy of parasites (and, hence, of "otherness") appears to be reducible to the ancient legal question, *Cui bono*? at another level the distinctions between "parasitism," "symbiosis," "mutualism", "commensalism," "epiphytism" and the like are distinctions between types of exchange. A "theory of the other" must take the form of a relational theory of reciprocity. "Otherness," whether of Scotsmen or lice, is a preeminently political category.

It might have been thought that I would go on and attempt to make a further contact with this symposium's theme by cataloguing

---

[20] I stress that the above is a summary of an influential late-19th century taxonomy. For the current state of the question: (1) the most significant work on the *theory* of parasitism has been done by Russian scientists. Their work has been made available in the English translation of V. A. Dogiel, *General Parasitology* (New York: 1966) with rich bibliography. (2) For a review of the complex contemporary state of the question with regard to *taxonomy*, see the distinguished collection edited by G. D. Schmidt, *Problems in the Systematics of Parasites* (Baltimore: 1969).

[21] Leuckart, *Die Parasiten des Menschen*, 1:3.

the varied roles parasites have played in western religions[22]—not forgetting the Roman deity, Verminus.[23] Indeed, parasites, and most particularly the louse, have supplied a variety of Christian theological conundrums ranging from the justification for their existence in terms of natural law (a matter still raised by Immanuel Kant)[24] to ticklish questions as to whether Adam and Eve had lice in Paradise prior to the Fall (I remind you that what is alleged to be the shortest poem in the English language reads, in full, "Adam Had 'em"),[25] whether Eve contained in her body not only the seed of all future human beings but also of all future human parasites,[26] and whether lice and other parasites found a place on Noah's Ark.[27] Nor should we ignore Charles Bonnet's triumphant demonstration of the Virgin Birth's scientific credibility when he observed parthenogenesis in plant lice.[28] But I have another sort of connection in mind.

It would appear that the term "parasite" came into technical discourse as a generic category only in the last decades of the nineteenth century. A search of lexica, encyclopaedia, and earlier scientific works reveals that it was in common use in botany at the beginning of the century,[29] and was taken over only at a later stage by zoologists, replacing, as we have seen, "entozoa," and "helminths."[30]

[22] For a wide-ranging survey, see the chapter, "Parasites and Parasitic Infections in Religion," in Hoeppli, *Parasites and Parasitic Infections, 396–409.*

[23] Verminus is known from only one Latin inscription, *Corpus Inscriptionum Latin-arum,* 7.1: no. 3732= H. Dessau, *Inscriptiones Latinae Selectae* (Berlin: 1892–1916), 2.1: no. 4019. See E. Buchner, "Verminus," *Real-Encyklopädie der classischen Alter-thumswissenschaft,* 2.8: 1552–3; Hoeppli, *Parasites and Parasitic Infections,* 397–8.

[24] I.Kant, *Allgemeine Naturgeschichte und Theorie des Himmels* (1755) in P. Mesiger, ed., *Kant: Populäre Schriften* (Berlin: 1911), 127.

[25] Leuckart, *Die Parasiten Des Menschen,* 1.35; A. W. Meyer, *The Rise of Embryology,* 67; H. Zinsser, *Rats, Lice and History* (Boston: 1935), 182; Hoeppli, *Parasites and Parasitic Infections,* 401; Guyenot, *Les sciences de la vie,* 218–9. For the poem, Lehane, *Compleat Flea,* 96–7.

[26] Meyer, *Rise of Embryology,* 66.

[27] D. C. Allen, *The Legend of Noah* (Urbana: 1963), 72, 185; Hoeppli, *Parasites and Parasitic Infections,* 401

[28] B. Glass, et al., *Forerunners of Darwin: 1745–1849* (Baltimore: 1959), 51.

[29] "Parasite" is standard in English as a botanical term in the early 18th century. See, for example, *Chamber's Encyclopaedia* Edinburgh: 1727–41), s.v. "parasite." For its massive use in an influential, early botanical work, see A. P. de Candolle, *Physiologie végétale* (Paris: 1832), vol.3, *Des parasites phanerogames.*

[30] I have been unable to locate the first self-conscious use of the term "parasite" as a zoological term. It gained early currency among the first generation of parasitologists as the result of the comprehensive article by the distinguished biologist, Carl von Siebold, "Parasiten," in R. Wagner, ed., *Handwörterbuch der Physiologie* (Brunschweig: 1844), 2: 641–92, but there is no explicit reflection on the name. (Siebold's article was a major influence in the acceptance of Steensrup's work, op.cit. 646–7). From a review of the

This is not the first time the word "parasite" has replaced a previous set of terms. Such a substitution had occurred once before, in ancient Athens during the first half of the fourth century (BC). This earlier shift established "parasite" as bearing a cultural connotation. And this sense persisted through the middle of the nineteenth century as the prime meaning of "parasite," while laying the ground for the later European scientific usage.[31]

As is well known, the figure of the fawning Parasite was a stock character in ancient Greek comedy. The type is archaic, going back at least to the first half of the fifth century and the play *Hope or Riches* by the Sicilian, Epicharmus. But while the character is old, its name, "Parasite," is at least a century younger. It first appeared in Alexis' play by that name (c. 360-50 BC), and replaced the older names for this stock figure, the "Flatterer" (*kolax*) and the "Sycophant."

Much ink has been expended on this name change by modern scholarship,[32] but the issue was posed centuries earlier in a lengthy

---

citations in the early works cited above (note 16) and a survey of the titles in J. Ch. Huber, *Bibliographie der klinischen Helminthologie* (Munich: 1895), it would appear that F. Küchenmeister, *Die in und an dem Körper des lebenden Menschen vorkommenden Parasiten*, 1st ed. (Leipzig: 1855) was the first comprehensive work to use "parasite" in its title. Again, I can find no explicit meditation on the use of the term. This was strengthened in the title of the English translation of the 2nd edition, *On Animal and Vegetable Parasites of the Human Body* (London: 1857), 1–2. As best as I can determine, the *Zeitschrift für Parasitenkunde* (Jena: 1869–75) was the earliest journal to employ "parasite" in its title.

[31] In this regard, the articles on "Parasiten" in J. Ersch and T. Gruber, eds., *Allgemeine Encyklopädie der Wissenschaften und Kunst* (Leipzig: 1838), 3.2: 417–23 are revealing. There is a brief, one-paragraph article consisting of two sentences which provides a botanical definition of "parasite" by A. Sprengel (423a). This is preceded by a long article of seven pages (thirteen columns) on the social meaning of parasite by M. H. E. Meier—a brief treatment of its cultic use (417a–418a), and a long essay on the figure of the Parasite in ancient comedy (418b–423a). This proportion has been reversed by the turn of the century. For example, in the 11th edition of the *Encyclopaedia Britannica* (1910–11), there is an anonymous one-paragraph article on the cultic and literary sense of "parasite" (20: 770a–b), followed by a twenty-two page article on "parasitic diseases" (20: 770b–793b) and a five page article on botanical and zoological "parasitism" (20: 793b–797b).

[32] The fundamental study remains O.Ribbeck, *Kolax: Eine ethologische Studie* (Leipzig: 1883) in the series, *Abhandlungen der Königl. Sächsischen Gesellschaft der Wissenschaften*, Phil.-hist. Klasse, 9.1: 1–113. See further, M. H. E. Meier, "Parasiten," in Ersch-Gruber, *Allgemeine Encyklopädie*, 3.2: 418–23; J. E. B. Mayor, *The Thirteen Satires of Juvenal* (London: 1901), 1: 271–2; A. Giese, *De parasiti persona capita selecta* (Kiel: 1908); F. M. Cornford, *The Origin of Attic Comedy* (London: 1914—I cite the new edition edited by T. H. Gaster, Garden City: 1961), 143–5; J. O. Lofberg, "The Sycophant-Parasite," *Classical Philology*, 15(1920), 61–72, cf. Lofberg, *Sycophancy at Athens*, diss. University of Chicago (1917); M. E. Dilley, *The Parasite: A Study in Comic Development*, diss. University of Chicago (1924), J. M. G. M. Brinkhoff, "De

(now lost) lexicographical work preserved in excerpted form by the third-century AD rhetorician, Athenaeus.[33]

The relevant passage, in a manner typical of Athenaeus, is in the form of a quotation within a quotation.

> Plutarch said, The name, parasite, was in earlier times a dignified and sacred name. Take, for example, what Polemon[34] writes about parasites. . . . Parasite is nowadays a disreputable term, but among the ancients we find it used of something scared, equivalent to companion [*synthoinos*, "messmate"] at a sacred feast. (6. 234d)

Six examples are given to illustrate this archaic, cultic use of the term "parasite" before a series of quotations are marshalled to illustrate its transformation into a comedic term of opprobrium.[35] It is the first cultic example which is of greatest interest to us—that of the annual celebration of Herakles at Kynosarges, outside Athens.

The gymnasium at Kynosarges[36] was open to membership by Athenian residents lacking the status of full citizens, most particularly, since the law of Pericles in 451-50,[37] the children of mixed marriages (*nothoi*) between Athenian males and foreign women.[38] According to

Parasiet op het romeinsche Toneel," *Neophilologus* 32(1948), 127–41; L. Ziehen, E. Wüst and A. Hug, "Parasitoi," *Real-Encyklopädie der classischen Alterthumswissenschaft,* 18: 1377–1405; T. B. L. Webster, *Studies in Late Greek Comedy* (Manchester, 1953), 63–5; W. G. Arnott, "Studies in Comedy (1): Alexis and the Parasite's Name," *Greek, Roman, and Byzantine Studies*, 9(1968), 161–8.

[33] Athenaeus, *Deipnosophistae*, 6. 234d–248c, in the edition and translation by C. B. Gulick in the *Loeb Classical Library* series (Cambridge, Mass.: 1929), 3: 54–119. That Athenaeus was dependent on a lost lexicographical work was argued by V. Rose, *Aristoteles Pseudepigraphus* (Leipzig: 1863); 457–9.

[34] On Polemon, fragment 78 (Preller)= Jacoby, *Fragmente der griechischen Historiker*, 3: 137–8, see L. Preller, *Polemonis periegetae fragmenta* (Leipzig: 1838), 115–23.

[35] On the cultic term, *parasitos, parasitoi*, in addition to the works cited above, note 32, each of which devote some pages to the subject, see A. von Kampen, *De parasitis apud Graecos sacrorum ministris* (Göttingen: 1867), A. Tresp, *Die Fragmente der griechischen Kultschriftsteller* (Giessen: 1914), 209–11; R. Schlaifer, "The Cult of Athena Pallensis, "*Harvard Studies in Classical Philology*, 54(1943), 141–74, esp. 152; L. Ziehen, "Parasitoi (1)," *Real-Encyklopädie der classischen Alterthumswissenschaft*, 18.3: 1377–81; H. W. Parke, *Festivals of the Athenians* (Ithaca, N.Y.: 1977), 51.

[36] On Kynosarges, see J. E. Harrison, *Mythology and Monuments of Ancient Athens* (London: 1890), 216–9; W. Judeich, *Topographie von Athen*, 2nd ed. (Munich: 1931), 422–4.

[37] For the Periclean law, see Aristotle, *Constitution of Athens*, 26.3. See further, the excellent discussion of this law in relation to the *nothoi* in A. Diller, *Race Mixture Among the Greeks Before Alexander* (Urbana: 1937), 91–100, in the series, *Illinois University Studies in Language and Literature*, 20.1–2.

[38] For the *nothoi* in Athens—which means a person of mixed descent instead of its more usual meaning, "bastard"—in connection with Kynosarges, see Demosthenes, *Ora*

Polemon, the Herakleion at Kynosarges possessed a stele with a law
from Alcibaides:

> The priest shall sacrifice the monthly offerings in company with the
> parasites. These parasites shall be drawn from men of mixed descent
> [ek tōn nothōn] and their children according to ancestral custom.[39]
> And whoever shall decline to serve as parasite, the priest shall charge
> him before the tribunal. (6. 234e)

In addition to their monthly sacrificial duties, the chief annual cultic
activity of the parasites was to eat a meal, during the month, Metagei-
tnion, together with Herakles—hence the derivation of "parasite"
from *para* + *sitos*, (to eat) grain beside (another).[40]

With this last piece of information on the most archaic use of the
term "parasite," we may briefly come to rest. The earliest use of the
term referred to a rule-governed, legally required relationship of
commensality between representatives of a community of not-quite-
Athenians (the *nothoi*) and a cult figure (Herakles) who was neither
quite-hero nor quite-god.[41] To think about parasites, whether in the
most ancient or most modern sense of the term, is to think about
reciprocal relations of relative "otherness."[42]

Before attempting a fresh start on the question of a "theory of the
other," it might be well to collect and restate the conclusions that
might be drawn from this first set of reflections on the topic which
began with an eighteenth century poem by Robert Burns and ended
with an archaic cult law, after rapidly passing through the history of
late nineteenth-century parasitology.

In this first state of our inquiry, even though three quite different
sorts of data were explored, the conclusions drawn were symmetrical.

---

tions, 23. 216. See further, U. E. Paoli, *Studi di diratto attico* (Florence: 1930), 272–6;
K. Latte, "Nothoi," *Real-Encyklopädie der classischen Alterthumswissenschaft*, 33:
1066–74, esp. 1069–71.

[39] The requirement that the *parasitoi* be chosen *ek tōn nothōn* appears to be bur-
lesqued in the fragment from Diodorus of Sinope, *The Heiress*, quoted in Athenaeus, 6.
239d–e (= T. Kock, *Comicorum Atticorum Fragmenta* [Leipzig: 1880–88], 2: 420).

[40] The *parasitoi* of Herakles are mentioned in Athenaeus's citations of fragments from
Kleidemus (6. 235a) and Philocorus (6. 235d). Other mentions include: Aristophanes,
Daitales (Kock, *Comicorum Atticorum Fragmenta*, 1: 438) and Alciphron, *Parasites*,
3.42. For a collection of testimonia concerning the cult of Herakles at Kynosarges, see
S. Solders, *Die ausserstädtischen Kulte und die Einigung Attikas* (Lund: 1931), 78–80.

[41] There is, thus, an irony in P.-J. van Beneden's attempt to distinguish between *les
commensaux* and *les parasites* in his work by that title. (See above, note 16). The former
is synonymous with the latter.

[42] While this would take us far from our theme, see the important monograph by D.
Whitehead, *The Ideology of the Athenian Metic* (Cambridge: 1977) for another aspect
of "relative otherness" in Athens.

"Otherness," it is suggested, is a matter of relative rather than absolute difference. Difference is not a matter of comparison between entities judged to be equivalent, rather difference most frequently entails a hierarchy of prestige and ranking. Such distinctions are found to be drawn most sharply between "near neighbors," with respect to what has been termed the "proximate other." This is the case because "otherness" is a relativistic category inasmuch as it is, necessarily, a term of interaction. A "theory of otherness" is, from this perspective, essentially political. That is to say, it centers on a relational theory of reciprocity, often one that is rule-governed.

While I shall return to this set of contentions in my conclusion, it seemed useful to inquire as to whether there was a stronger "theory of the other" than the political; that is to say, were there situations that led to a more radical theory of "otherness"? It is to this essentially anthropological question that I turn by way of making a second start on our theme. Such a theory, we shall see, is essentially a project of language.

II

The Sioux have a saying, 'With all beings and all things we shall be as relatives.' Our Hillel said, 'Separate thyself not from the community.' Mazel Tov to Rabbi Glaser and his excellent programs linking Judaism to brothers and sisters of Indian cultures and for reminding us that we are all members of one tribe. "Letter to the Editor," *Reform Judaism*, 12.4(1984): 32.

The social and cultural awareness of the "other" must surely be as old as humankind itself. "Cultures are more than just empirically comparable; they are intrinsically comparative."[43] As Robert Redfield has argued, the world-view of any people consists essentially of two pairs of binary oppositions: MAN/NOT-MAN and WE/THEY.[44] These two oppositions are often correlated, i.e., WE = MAN; THEY = NOT-MAN. Indeed, the distinction between "us" and "them" is present in our earliest written records.[45] It is an omnipresent feature

---

[43] J. A. Boon, *Other Tribes, Other Scribes: Symbolic Anthropology in the Comparative Study of Cultures, Histories, Religions, and Texts* (Cambridge: 1982): 230.
[44] R. Redfield, "Primitive World View," *Proceedings of the American Philosophical Association*, 96(1952), 30–36, reprinted in Redfield, *The Primitive World and Its Transformations* (Ithaca: 1953), 84–110. Passage quoted: 92.
[45] See the Sumerian materials in S. N. Kramer, *The Sumerians* (Chicago: 1963), 275–88. Cf. R. Labat, *Manuel d'epigraphie akkadienne* (Paris: 1948), nos 60 and 74 for the terminology. A particularly instructive example is provided by G. Buccellati, *The Amorites of the Ur III Period* (Naples: 1966), 92–5. Cf. M. Liverani, "Per una considerazione storica del problema amorreo," *Oriens Antiquus*, 9(1970), 22–6.

of folk taxonomies.[46] The distinction is most ubiquitous in the complex rule-governed matter of kinship in institutions such as endogamy, exogamy, and the incest taboo.[47] Likewise, it is universal in the
detailed etiquette and laws concerning "the stranger,"[48] as well as in
those devoted to its less studied opposite, "the friend."[49] Social and
cultural awareness of the "other" is also the centerpiece of the most
persistent ethnographic traditions.[50] As times, cultural differences
appear merely to have been noted (for example, as "curiousities" in
travel reports). More frequently, "difference" supplied a justificatory
element for a variety of ideological postures, ranging from xenophobia
to exoticism, from travel, trade and exploration to military conquest,
slavery and colonialism. The "other" has appeared as an object of
desire as well as an object of repulsion; the "other" has rarely been an
object of indifference.

---

[46] While the literature on this subject has become vast in the past several years (see
H. C. Conklin, *Folk Classification: A Topically Arranged Bibliography* [New Haven,
1972]), the most useful essay, from our perspective, is B. E. Ward, "Varieties of the
Conscious Model: The Fishermen of South China," in M. Banton, ed., *The Relevance
of Models for Social Anthropology* (London: 1965), 113–37.

[47] See the important remarks on "true endogamy" in C. Lévi-Strauss, *The Elementary
Structures of Kinship* (Boston: 1969), 46–7. The close relationship of social sanctions
with respect to sexuality and "otherness" is made starkly plain in the title of the
published proceedings of the 12th Conference of French Jewish Intellectuals (1971),
edited by J. Halpérin and G. Lévitte, *L'Autre dans la conscience juive: Le sacré et le
couple* (Paris: 1973). "Otherness" and "sacrality" are reduced to questions of intermarriage!

[48] See the famous "Exkurs über den Fremden" in G. Simmel, *Soziologie*, 3d ed.
(Leipzig: 1923), 509–12. This is developed in M. M. Wood, *The Stranger: A Study in
Social Relations* (London: 1934). For an excellent collection of 33 essays which focus on
the legal relations to the "stranger," see the collective volume, *L'Étranger* (Brussels:
1958), 1–2 which appeared as volume 9 in the series, *Recueils de la Société Jean Bodin.*
The definitional article by J. Gilissen (1: 5–57) is of particular merit. There are vast
collections of data regarding "strangers" from an anthropological perspective—e.g. J. G.
Frazer, *The Golden Bough*, 3d ed. (London: 1935), 3: 101–16; P. J. Hamilton-Grierson,
"Strangers," in J. Hastings, ed., *Encyclopaedia of Religion and Ethics* (Edinburgh:
1921), 11: 883–96. A. van Gennep, spatializing the "stranger" gained the generative
model for *Rites de Passage* (Paris: 1909). There are a set of important theoretical notes
in Lévi-Strauss, *Elementary Structures of Kinship*, 60, 402–3. P. Gauthier, *Symbola: les
étrangers et la justice dans les cités grecques* (Nancy: 1972) provides a model
monograph for the study of the topic in an ancient society.

[49] From an anthropological perspective, this theme has been a consistent object of
attention by Africanists. See, among others, M. Wilson, *Good Company* (London: 1951),
and D. Jacobson, *Itinerant Tribesmen: Friendship and Social Order in Urban Uganda*
(Menlo Park: 1973).

[50] M. Duak-M'bedy, *Xenologie: Die Wissenschaft vom Fremden und die Verdrängung
der Humanität in der Anthropologie* (Munich: 1977) collects much interesting data in
the service of an unsatisfying and confused thesis.

On rare occasions, meditation on cultural difference, on "others," itself became one of a culture's dominant features. Such was the case in fifth-century BC Ionia[51] and in the Chinese periods of the T'ang and Southern Sung,[52] and such may be inferred from the pre-conquest court of Moctezuma with its remarkable zoological collections of all types of birds and animals and human forms.[53] This living museum appears to be quite similar to that all but contemporary "human zoo" maintained by Cardinal Ippolito de Medici which consisted of "a troop of barbarians who talked no fewer than twenty different languages and were all of them perfect specimens of their races."[54]

As this last example hints, the cultural meditation on difference received its most massive institutionalization in the vast modern western enterprise of anthropology: a xenological endeavor which began with the savants of the Renaissance and Enlightenment was fueled by the discoveries of the "Age of Reconnaissance" and continued into the present. Indeed, the most distinctive feature of modern anthropology is its relatively recent requirement that the anthropologist have living experience of the "other." It is fieldwork which makes anthropology a distinctive enterprise among the human sciences.[55] Because of this, anthropology may be described as the science of the "other." As Claude Lévi-Strauss bluntly states:

> Anthropology is the science of culture as seen from the outside. . . .
> Anthropology, whenever it is practiced by members of the culture it

---

[51] The standard monographs remain K. Trüdinger, *Studien zur Geschichte der griechisch-römischen Ethnographie* (Basel: 1918) and L. Pearson, *Early Ionian Historians* (Oxford: 1939).

[52] See the various studies by E. H. Schafer, including: *The Golden Peaches of Samarkand: A Study of T'ang Exotics* (Berkeley: 1963); *The Vermilion Bird: T'ang Images of the South* (Berkeley: 1967); *Shore of Pearls: Hainan Island in Early Times* (Berkeley: 1970).

[53] Cortés "2nd Dispatch," in D. Enrique de Vedia, *Historiadores Primitivos de Indias* (Madrid: 1918), 1: 34b–35a in the series, *Biblioteca de Autores Españoles*, 22. Translation in I. R. Blacker and H. M. Rosen, *Conquest: Dispatches of Cortes from the New World* (New York: 1962), 60–1.

[54] J. Burckhardt, *The Civilization of the Renaissance in Italy* (New York: 1929), 291–2.

[55] For the history of fieldwork, see A. I. Richards, "The Development of Field Work Methods in Social Anthropology," in F. C. Bartlett, ed., *The Study of Society* (London: 1939), 272–316; P. Kaberry, "Malinowski's Contribution to Fieldwork Methods and the Writing of Ethnography," in R. Firth, ed., *Man and Culture*, 2nd ed. (London: 1960), 71–91, esp. 72–6; G. W. Stocking, Jr., ed., *Observers Observed: Essays on Ethnographic Fieldwork* (Madison: 1983), in the series, *History of Anthropology*, 1. See further, P. C. W. Gutkind and G. Sankoff, "Annotated Bibliography on Anthropological Field Work Methods," in D. G. Jongmans and P. C. W. Gutkind, eds., *Anthropologists in the Field* (New York: 1967), 214–71.

endeavors to study, loses its specific nature [as anthropology] and becomes rather akin to archaeology, history and philology.[56]

That is to say, anthropology holds that there is cognitive power in "otherness," a power that is removed by studying the "same." The issue, as Lévi-Strauss has phrased it in the passage quoted above, is not the sheer distance of the object of study,[57] but rather the mode of relationship of the scholar to the object. In anthropology, the distance is not to be overcome, but becomes, in itself, the prime focus and instrument of disciplinary meditation.[58]

To be sure, even within contemporary anthropology, "otherness" remains a relative category in at least two important senses. First, unlike parasitism, the "other" is of the same species. Despite wide variation, it is man studying man; it is *Homo sapiens* and not some Martian which is the object of attention. (It may be noted that, since 1970, the American Anthropological Association has sponsored a section at its annual meeting on the issues raised by the possibility of the future study of extra-terrestrial beings. However to date, such matters have been better explored by science fiction writers, for example, the profound work of Michael Bishop).[59]

Matters with respect to this first qualification are, in fact, more complex. Anthropologists have at times explored other cultures (or particular institutions within them) in such a way as to suggest that they might be conceived of as "limiting cases,"[60] that they represent so extreme a development of something known and familiar that they appear to be radically "other."[61] More usually, they have insisted on just the opposite: in some often unspecified way, the "other" is to be seen as "typical." While the field encounter is most frequently described as an extremely traumatic, disorienting kind of experience,

---

[56] C. Lévi-Strauss, *Structural Anthropology* (New York: 1976), 2: 55.

[57] History, to take up Lévi-Strauss's example, treats the temporally remote at least to the same degree as anthropology treats the spatially remote.

[58] Such is most explicitly the case in C. Lévi-Strauss, *Tristes Tropiques* (Paris: 1955) and J.-P. Dumont, *The Headman and I: Ambiguity and Ambivalence in the Field-working Experience* (Austin: 1978).

[59] For a collection of papers from the 1974 meeting on "Cultural Futuristics," see M. Maruyama and A. Harkins, eds., *Cultures Beyond the Earth: The Role of Anthropology in Outer Space* (New York: 1975). For science fiction novels which make extra-terrestrial anthropology their central theme, see, among others, the sophisticated works of Michael Bishop, *Transfigurations* (Berkeley: 1979) and Chad Oliver, *Unearthly Neighbors* (New York: 1960).

[60] For the notion of "limiting case," see L. Dumont, *Homo Hierarchicus*, 2nd ed. (Chicago: 1979), 24–7.

[61] Colin Turnbull's novelistic study of the Ik would be an extreme example, *The Mountain People* (New York: 1972).

the result, as reported in the monograph, reads as an encounter with "Everyman." Edmund Leach has characterized this quixotic element with precision:

> When we read Malinowski we get the impression that he is stating something which is of general importance. Yet how can this be? He is simply writing about Trobriand Islanders. Somehow. . .he is able to make the Trobriands a microcosm of the whole primitive world. And the same is true of his successors; for Firth, Primitive Man is a Tikopian, for Fortes, he is a citizen of Ghana.[62]

Second, anthropological investigation is, by nature, relational. What an anthropologist reports is almost always solely based on his or her interaction with a particular people. For this reason, anthropology has tended to develop and embrace theories that factor out time and the historical, that eliminate all past before the fieldworker's presence.[63] Hence, the evolutionism of the late nineteenth-century "armchair" anthropologists was jettisoned by workers in the field in favor of a functionalism which depended on the observation of a given society at time "t," or, later, in favor of the atemporalism of a variety of structuralist approaches. For this reason, as well, the anthropological report, no matter how great a period of time had elapsed between the field experience and publication, is almost always written in the "ethnographic present," in what Jan Vansina has called the "zero-time fiction."[64]

The effect of these two qualifications (and there are more) has been to relativize "otherness" in anthropological discourse—if not in experience. Anthropology has become largely an enterprise of "decipherment," attempting to "decode" an encrypted message from "another" with the firm prior conviction that, because it is human, it will be intelligible once it is "broken."[65] That is to say, anthropology is essentially a project of language with respect to an "other," which concedes both the presence of meaning and the possibility of translation at the outset. Indeed, without these two assumptions, "all the

---

[62] E. R. Leach, *Rethinking Anthropology* (London: 1961), 1.

[63] For a profound meditation on this theme, see J. Fabian, *Time and the Other: How Anthropology Makes Its Object* (New York: 1983).

[64] J. Vansina, "Cultures Through Time," in R. Naroll and R. Cohen, eds., *A Handbook of Method in Cultural Anthropology* (Garden City, N.Y.: 1970), 165. See further, Fabian, *Time and the Other*, 80–97, and the shrewd characterization of the "functionalist monograph" in J. Boon, *Other Tribes, Other Scribes*, 13–4.

[65] For a profound meditation on "decipherment," see M. V. David, *Le Débat sur les écritures et l'hiéroglyphique aux XVIIᵉ et XVIIIᵉ siècles et l'application de déchiffrement aux écritures mortes* (Paris: 1965).

activities of anthropologists become meaningless."[66] As such, contemporary anthropology is to be seen as part of the Anglo-American philosophical tradition which has tended to view "otherness" as a problem of communication in contradistinction to the Continental philosophical tradition which has tended to conceive of the "other" in terms of transcendence and threat.[67]

This contemporary anthropological viewpoint stands in sharp contrast to the classical ethnographic tradition where, from Herodotus on, there is rarely the perception of an opacity to be overcome. Difference is, itself, utterly transparent. The "other" is merely different and calls for no exegetical labor. Within the classical ethnographic sources, differences may be noted; at times, differences may be compared, but they are most frequently set aside. Difference is insignificant—that is to say, difference signifies nothing of importance and therefore requires no decipherment, no hermeneutical projects. In classical ethnography, the "other" does not speak. This topos can be illustrated from traditions as far apart as the notion that the "other" is a "barbarian," i.e. one who speaks unintelligibly[68] (or, in stronger form, one who is mute),[69] and the conventions of "silent trade."[70] For

---

[66] E. R. Leach, *Political Systems of Highland Burma*, 2nd ed. (Boston: 1965), 15.

[67] This distinction between the Anglo-American tradition of the "other" and the Continental deserves further study. For the present, D. Locke, *Myself and Others: A Study in Our Knowledge of Minds* (Oxford: 1968) may be taken as an exemplary review of the Anglo-American tradition: M. Theunissen, *Der Andere: Studien zur Sozialontologie der Gegenwart*, 2nd ed. (Berlin: 1977) may be taken as an exemplary review of the Continental.

[68] One need do no more than appeal to the onomatopoeic derivation of *barbaros* from "ba! ba! ba!," i.e. unintelligible, stammering, animal- or child-like speech (already in the *Iliad* 2. 867). See, among others, the semaisiological study by A. Eichhorn, *Barbaros quid significaverit* (Leipzig: 1904). The same notion is found in the sparse Israelitic ethnographic tradition (e.g.. Ezekiel 3.5–6; Isaiah 33. 4–19; Psalm 114.1), and underlies narratives such as Judges 12.5–6. Compare the Meso-american analogue. "The Indians of this New Spain derive, according to what is generally reported in *their* histories, from two diverse peoples; they give to the first the name, Nahuatlaca, which means '*People who explain themselves and speak clearly,*' to be differentiated from the second people, at the time very wild and uncivilized, concerned only with hunting, to whom they give the name, Chichimecs, which means, 'People who go hunting'." Juan de Tovar, *Historia de los indios mexicanos*, in the edition and French translation by J. La Faye, *Manuscrit Tovar: Origines et croyances des Indiens de Mexique* (Graz: 1972), 9, emphasis added.

[69] See the collection of examples in T. Todorov, *The Conquest of America* (New York: 1984), 76. A variant of this is to treat the "other" as a "parrot" with no native language, but imitating European speech. See, for example, the report by Bernardino de Minaya cited in L. Hanke, "Pope Paul III and the American Indians," *Harvard Theological Review*, 30(1937), 84.

[70] L. Olschki, *Marco Polo's Precursors* (Baltimore: 1943), 4–5 and note 9 citing the

the classical ethnographer, the labor of learning an "other's" language would be sheer folly.[71] Classical ethnography manipulated a few basic explanatory models to account for "others." Briefly put, similarity was, above all, to be explained as the result of a temporal process: common descent and genealogy in remote times; contact, borrowing and diffusion in more recent times. Difference was, above all, to be explained as the consequence of a spatial condition, preeminently climate. This would later become known as "environmental determinism."

To be sure, there were perturbations, encounters with "others" that appeared to present cognitive shocks—the Greek experience of Egypt; the thirteenth century "Mongol Mission"—but these were rapidly assimilated to the prevailing models. However, there was one perturbation that was not so readily assimilable, that of the so-called "discovery" of America. It is here that the anthropological issue of the "other" as preeminently a project of language most clearly begins.[72]

If there was one cosmographical element that could be taken for granted in the West prior to the "voyages of discovery," it was that the inhabitable world, the *oikoumenē*, was divided into three unequal parts.[73] It was this tripartition, Ovid's *triplex mundus*, that allowed the classical traditions to be so readily merged with the biblical. For most

---

earlier literature. See further, H. Hart, *The Sea Road to the Indies* (New York: 1951), 2ln. and P. Wheatley, *The Golden Khersonese: Studies in the Historical Geography of the Malay Peninsula before AD 1500* (Kuala Lumpur: 1961), 130–1.

[71] The observations of A. Momigliano, *Alien Wisdom: The Limits of Hellenization* (Cambridge: 1975), 7–8, 91–3, et passim. may be generalized. Note further the observation that, even with an interpreter, the barbarian may prove unintelligible, as in Hanno, *Periplus*, 11, in the English translation by R. Harris (Cambridge: 1928), 26.

[72] Of the many formulations, that by W. Franklin, *Discoverers, Explorers, Settlers: The Diligent Writers of Early American* (Chicago: 1979), 7 is most useful for our theme. "More than anything else, the West became an epistemological problem for Europe. . . .It was simply the fact of 'another' world which most thoroughly deranged the received order of European life. The issue was not merely an informational one. It involved so many far-reaching consequences that the very structure of Old World knowledge—assumptions about the nature of learning and the role of traditional wisdom in it—was cast into disarray. . . .Faced with a flood of puzzling facts and often startling details, the East was almost literally at a loss for words. Having discovered America, it now needed to make a place for the New World within its intellectual and verbal universe."

[73] For a brief overview of the classical conception of the *triplex mundus*, see F. Gisinger, "Geographie," *Real-Encyclopädie der classischen Alterthumswissenschaft*, suppl. vol. 4: 521–685, esp. 552–6. See further, the standard histories: E. H. Bunbury, *A History of Ancient Geography* (London: 1879), 1: 145–6; H. Berger, *Geschichte der wissenschaftlichen Erdkunde der Griechen*, 2nd ed. (Leipzig: 1903), 82–90; H. F. Tozer, *A History of Ancient Geography*, 2nd ed. (Cambridge: 1935), 67–70.

of western history, Pliny and Genesis 10 contained all that was
necessary for both anthropological and geographical theorizing.[74] If
there was one cosmographical element that became increasingly
apparent to the West after the impact of the "voyages of discovery," it
was that there were additional inhabitable land masses, and that
neither the classical nor the biblical traditions could be easily harmonized with this new world view. To Europe, Asia and Libya/Africa
must now be added the neologism, "America"[75]—the *quarta orbis
pars*.[76] This "fourth part," eventually recognized as what the ancients
had theoretically termed an *orbis alterius*,[77] for the first time in
western intellectual history raised the theoretical issue of the "other"

---

[74] For Pliny's centrality, see E. W. Gudger, "Pliny's Historia naturalis: The Most
Popular Natural History Ever Published," *Isis*, 6(1924), 269–81 which provides a
census of printed editions from 1469–1799. Of direct relevance to our topic, see
Columbus' copy of Pliny with his annotations in C. de Lollis, *Scritti di Cristoforo
Colombo* (Rome: 1894), 471–2 in the series, *Raccolta di Documenti e Studi Pubblicati
dalla R. Commissione Columbiana*, 1.2. In the early "New World" scientific and
historical literature, Pliny serves as the standard of classical knowledge, e.g. E. Alvarez
López, "Plinio y Fernández de Oviedo," *Annales de Ciencias naturales del Instituto J.
de Acosta* (Madrid: 1940), 1: 46–61 and 2: 13–35.

On Genesis 10, see the commentary and full bibliography in the magisterial work of
C. Westermann, *Genesis* (Göttingen: 1966–), 662–706. From our perspective, the most
useful work is G. Hölscher, *Drei Erdkarten: Ein Beitrag zur Erforschung des hebrais-
ches Altertums* (Berlin: 1948), esp. 45–56.

[75] The origin and derivation of the name, "America," remains a matter of some
controversy. J. A. Aboal Amaro, *Amérigho Vespucci: Ensayo de bibliografía crítica*
(Madrid: 1962) provides a representative summary of the various proposals. See pp. 15,
18, 20, 31, 53, 55, 56, 60, 61, 64, 65, 66, 67, 68, 71, 79, 89, 90–4, 123, 124–5, 127–8, 129,
131, 134–5, 136, 144–5, 147–8, 148, 149. See further the important study by C. Sanz, *El
Nombre América: Libros y mapas quo lo impusieron* (Madrid: 1959) and the review of
scholarship by J. Vidago, "América: Origem e evolucão deste nome," *Revista Ocidente*,
67(1964), 93–110.

The figure of "America" as a "fourth" entity was developed through a process of
experimentation. This is seen most clearly in the development of "America's" iconography. See, among others, J. H. Hyde, "L'iconographie des quatres parties du monde
dans les tapisseries," *Gazette des Beaux Artes*, 66(1924), 253–72; C. Le Corbeiller,
"Miss America and Her Sisters: Personifications of the Four Parts of the World,"
Metropolitan Museum Bulletin, n.s. 19–20(1960), 209–23. On the general theme, see E.
Köllmann, et al., "Erdteile," *Reallexikon zur deutschen Kunstgeschichte* (Munich:
1967), 5: 1107–1202.

[76] The first occurrence of this phrase is in M. Waldseemüller[?], *Cosmographiae
Introductio* (St. Dié: 1507), a iii. See the facsimile edition by J. Fischer and F. von
Wieser (reprint, New York, 1969), xxv.

[77] The theme of the *orbis alterius* was first developed at length in Pomponius Mela, *De
situ orbis*, 1.4; 3.7 (in the edition of G. Parthey [Berlin: 1867]). See, in general, A.
Rainaud, *Le continent austral* (Paris: 1893).

as a project of language and interpretation. For this reason, we must pause and examine this cosmographical shift more carefully.

The classical cosmography may be summarized in terms of four elements.

(1) The earth, most usually thought of as spherical, was pictured as a great terraqueous globe, divided into northern and southern hemispheres. The earth's most distinctive feature was a large island in the northern hemisphere—the *orbis terrarum*.[78]

(2) Of greater significance than the division into hemispheres was the marking off of the terrestrial globe into "zones" (most usually five) in which only the intermediate (temperate) zones were presumed inhabitable.[79] That is to say, the extreme northern and southern (polar) zones and the middle (equatorial) zone were judged too severe to support human life in any recognizable form.[80] Habitation was possible only in the northern and southern temperate zones.

(3) The distinction as to habitability became central and was expressed by the term, *oikoumenē*.[81] Geographically, the *oikoumenē*, the "inhabitable world," was that portion of the northern earth-island south of the Arctic Circle, north of the Tropic of Cancer, bounded on the east and west by Ocean, that was known to be inhabited. Theoretically, the possibility was entertained that there might be a corresponding "inhabitable land" in the southern hemisphere—a possibility most usually advanced for reasons of geometric symmetry.[82] If

---

[78] As in well-known, there was a conceptual debate as to whether water or land was primary—the former (and most widely held view) gave rise to the picture of land as insular; the latter reduced the oceans to land-locked lakes. See A. Norlind, *Das Problem des gegenseitigen Verhaltnisses von Land und Wasser und seine Behandlung im Mittelalter* (Lund-Leipzig: 1918) in the series, *Lunds Universitets Årsskrift*, n.s. 1.14.2.

[79] The "zonal" division is attributed either to Parmenides (Strabo, 2.2.2) or Pythagoras (Aetius, *De placitis philosophorum*, 3.14.1). Both attributions have been the subject of debate. See, among others, W. A. Heidel, *The Frame of the Ancient Greek Maps* (New York: 1937), 76, 80, 91, in the series, *American Geographical Society Research Series*, 20; W. Burkert, *Lore and Science in Ancient Pythagoreanism* (Cambridge, Mass.: 1972); 305–6. The division by *zonai* must not be confused with the division into *klimata* (which were later correlated with the Ptolemaic parallels). See, E. Honigmann, *Die sieben Klimata und die POLEIS EPISEMOI* (Heidelberg: 1929), 4–9, 25–30.

[80] Posidonius, fragment 28 (Jacoby) in Strabo, 2.2.3.

[81] See, in general, F. Gisinger, "Oikoumenē," *Real-Encyclopädie der classischen Alterthumswissenschaft*, 17.2: 2123–74. From our perspective, the most useful study is J. Partsch, *Die Grenzen der Menscheit(1): Die antike Oikoumene* (Leipzig: 1916) in the series, *Berichte über die Verhandlungen der König. Sächsischen Gesellschaft der Wissenschaften zu Leipzig*, Phil.-hist. Kl. 68(1916), 1–62.

[82] For an influential form of this argument, see Macrobius, *Commentarius in Ciceronis Somnium Scipionis*, 2.5.9–36 in the translation by W. H. Stahl, *Macrobius: Commentary on the Dream of Scipio* (New York: 1952); 200–6. Note that the view that the

so, it would be "another world. . .an other *oikoumenē*. . .not inhabited by ones such as us" but by other species of men.[83]

(4) The northern *oikoumenē* was divided into three lobes:[84] Europe, Asia, and Libya/Africa.[85] These were most frequently distinguished from one another by river boundaries.[86]

In time, these four essential classical cosmographic elements

---

southern temperate zone "is also inhabited *is inferred* solely from reason" (2.5.17, emphasis added). This symmetrical argument goes back to the speculation of Krates that the northern *oikoumenē* is but one of four inhabited land masses. See, H. J. Mette, *Sphairopoiia: Untersuchungen zur Kosmologie des Krates von Pergamon* (Munich: 1936), 76–7.

[83] Strabo, 2.5.13. Cf. 2.5.34; 2.5.43. Strabo here denies that such "other worlds" are part of the study of geography, confining geography to "our *oikoumenē*." For an important discussion of this limitation, see C. van Paassen, *The Classical Tradition of Geography* (Groningen: 1957), 4–31. This limitation persisted on the part of some geographers even after the "discovery" of America, e.g. the "Preface" by Johannes Cochlaeus to the 1512 edition of Pomponius Mela, *De situ orbis*: "In our lifetime, Amerigo Vespucci is said to have discovered that new world. . .[that] is quite distinct from [Africa] and bigger than our Europe. Whether this is true or a lie, it has nothing. . .to do with Cosmography or History. *For the peoples and places of that continent are unknown and unnamed to us. . . .Therefore, it is of no interest to geographers at all.*" (emphasis, added). The passage has been quoted in E. P. Goldschmidt, "Not in Harrisse," in *Festschrift Lawrence C. Wroth* (Portland: 1951), 133–4 and J. H. Elliott, "Renaissance Europe and America: A Blunted Impact," in F. Chiappelli, ed., *First Images of America* (Berkeley: 1976), 1:14. Both Goldschmidt and Elliott have drawn negative conclusions from the passage rather than setting it within the context of the Strabonian limitations on "geography."

[84] It is important to avoid the anachronism of imposing our insular notion of "continent" on this tripartition. I have not been able to locate a history of the term, but it would appear that it referred to a contiguous (*continens*) land mass, e.g. W. Cunningham, *The Cosmographical Glasse* (London: 1559), 113, "Continens [margin: continent] is a portion of the earth which is not parted by the seas asounder." Thus Waldseemüller, in 1508, distinguished between the traditional three contiguous land masses which made up the northern earth-island and the newly discovered "island" of "America": *et sunt tres prime partes continentes, quarta est insula* (Fischer and Wieser facsimile edition, p. xxx). The application of the term "continent" to all of the major land masses occurs only in the late 16th century. F. Gagnon, "Le thème médiéval de l'homme sauvage dans les premières représentations des Indiens d'Amérique," in G. H. Allard, ed., *Aspects de la marginalité au Moyen Age* (Quebec: 1975), 96 attempts to discern an evaluative opposition in the early iconography of the "Indies"—"la terre ferme européenne est opposée à l'île primitive."

[85] While the division of the world-island into three land masses is already presumed by Herodotus (e.g. 2.16), it was, perhaps, implied by the arrangement of Hecateus's *Periodos* into two books (Europe and Asia) with Libya as an appendix. See, F. Gisinger, *Die Erdbeschreibung des Eudoxus von Knidos*, 2nd ed. (Amsterdam: 1967), 14–18, 35–6.

[86] See, R. von Scheliha, *Die Wassergrenze im Altertum* (Breslau: 1931), esp. 34–42, in the series, *Historische Untersuchungen*, 8.

received distinctively Christian interpretations. Combining the speculations of the Greco-Roman geographers and Genesis 10, the three lobes of the world-island became identified with the three sons of Noah who repopulated the *oikoumenē* after the Flood.[87] In turn, the tripartition became identified allegorically with a range of specifically Christian elements ranging from the Trinity[88] and the "Three Wise Men"[89] to the triple papal tiara (the *triregnum*).[90]

Such a view, with its striking monogenetic implications, made all but impossible Christian belief in the existence of other inhabited worlds apart from the northern, tripartite *oikoumenē*. As Augustine declared of the monstrous races as described by encyclopaedists such as Pliny, so, too, of "other worlds":

> Either the written accounts of certain races are completely unfounded; or, if such races do exist, they are not human; or, if they are human, they are descended from Adam.[91]

---

[87] This is graphically depicted in the Noachic "T-O" maps. The study by M. Destombes, *Mappemondes A.D. 1200–1500* (Amsterdam: 1964), in the series, *Monumenta Cartographica Vetustioris Aevi*, 1 supercedes all previous publications.

[88] E. g. Hrbanus Maurus, *De Universo*, 2.1 (*MPL* 111:54); 12.2 (111:353–4). See, also, the expanded edition of the *Glossa ordinaria* ad Mt 2.11 (Venice: 1603), 5:62. This identification is not found in the *Glossa* as printed in *MPL* 114:75.

[89] The identification depends on first identifying the unnumbered magi of Mt 2 as "three kings" (Leo, *Sermon* 33 [*MPL* 54:235] is an early example) and then identifying the three kings with the three continents. See [pseudo] Jerome, *Expositio Quatuor Evangeliorum* ad Mt. 1.2 (*MPL* 30:537); Hrbanus Maurus, *Commentariorum in Matthaeum* ad Mt 1.2 (*MPL* 107:760); [pseudo] Bede, *In Matthaei Evangelium exposito* ad Mt 1.2 (*MPL* 92:113); Michael Scot, *Liber introductorius* (MS. Bodleian 266), f.3 (as cited in L. Thorndike, *A History of Magic and Experimental Science* [New York: 1923], 2:318). J. Duchesne-Guillemin, "Jesus' Trimorphism and the Differentiation of the Magi," in E. J. Sharpe and J. R. Hinnells, eds., *Man and His Salvation* (Manchester: 1973), 97, asserts, in passing, that the identification is as old as Augustine, but I have not located a reference. On the identification, see in general, H. Kehrer, *Die "Heiligen Drei Könige" in der Legende und in der deutschen bildenden Kunst* (Strassbourg: 1904), 23 and H. Baudet, *Paradise on Earth: Some Thoughts on European Images of Non-European Man* (New Haven: 1965), 17–8.

[90] The triple tiara appears to be a 14th century innovation, most usually explained as symbolizing the Pope's authority over heaven, earth, and hell (see J. Braun, "Tiara," *Encyclopaedia Britannica*, 11th ed., 26: 911–12). However, Pedro Simón, *Primera parte de las noticias historiales de las conquistas de Tierra-Firme en las Indias Occidentales* (Cuenca: 1627), 1: 9 suggests that a fourth crown be added to symbolize the Pope's authority over "America"—the other three crowns being associated with the traditional tripartition. As this latter suggests, the numerical symbolism can be dazzling, e.g. Gregory Horn, *Arca Noe* (Leiden-Rotterdam: 1666), 35, 183, et passim., who attempts to correlate the three sons of Noah, the four "world empires," and the five "continents."

[91] Augustine, *Civitate Dei*, 16.8 (in the *Loeb Library* edition and translation). Being

That is to say, either "other worlds" do not exist, or, if they exist, they are uninhabited, or, if they are inhabited, then they must (somehow) be descended from Adam and have been populated by the sons of Noah. All Christian discussion of "antipodes" and "austral" land masses took place within the framework of this logic.[92]

With this brief sketch, the stage for the emergence of our theme has been set: how to make room for an "other world," for an inhabited fourth part of the globe, a "world," an *oikoumenē*, unanticipated by either the Greco-Roman or the biblical traditions?

It is simple, in retrospect, to appreciate the impact of the "discovery" of America, and to sense its challenge to both biblical and classical world views.[93] But this is anachronistic. What was apparent by the middle of the sixteenth century was by no means clear half a century earlier.[94] It is a distinctly modern voice that we hear in the

---

"human" means, above all, having reason—as in Augustine, *De Trinitate*, 7.4.7. (*Corpus Christianorum*, 50:255).

[92] In addition to Rainaud, *Le continent austral*, see W. Wright, *The Geographical Lore of the Time of the Crusades* (New York: 1925), 157–65 and P. Delhaye, "Le théorie des antipodes et ses incidences théologiques," which appeared as note "S" in his edition, *Godfrey de Saint-Victor: Microcosmus* (Lille-Gembloux: 1951), 282–6. The arguments against the inhabitability of the austral island or the antipodes are elegantly summarized in Pierre d'Ailly, *Imago Mundi*, 7 (in the edition of E. Buron [Paris: 1930] and the English translation by E. F. Keever [Wilmington, N.C.: 1948]).

From our perspective, the most interesting argument (in terms of the Augustinian options) is that: while the *orbis alterius* is real, its inhabitants are not. This is already implied by the influential encyclopaedia of Isidore of Seville, *Etymologiae*, 14.5.7 (*MPL* 82:512); cf. 9.2.133 (82:341). For Isidore's view, see, G. Boffito, "La leggenda degli antipodi," *Festschrift A. Graf* (Bergamo: 1903), esp. 592 and n.4. Isidore's view of the antipodes found graphic representation in the 'Beatus" maps—see, K. Miller, *Mappae Mundi* (Stuttgart: 1895–8), 1: 58; T. Simar, *Le géographie de l'Afrique centrale dans l'antiquité au moyen age* (Brussels: 1912), 150–8 and J. Marquis Casanovas, et al., *Sancti Beati a Liebana in Apocalypsin Codex Gerundensis* (Olten-Lausanne: 1962), ff. 54v–55r. Note, however, that in the later figures which are attached to Isidore's discussion of the "zones" in *De natura rerum* 1.10 (*MPL* 83:978–9 with figs.), two inhabitable "zones" are shown. (See the discussion of this in E. Brehaut, *An Encyclopedist of the Dark Ages: Isidore of Seville* [New York: 1912], 50–54). Furthermore, the outline of Isidore's geographical section in the *Etymologiae*, appending a section on islands after sections on the tripartite *oikoumenē* suggests yet a third pattern (see Wright, *Geographical Lore*, 259, 460, n.12).

[93] The issue of the geographic impact has been often studied since the pioneering work of K. Kretschmer, *Die Entdeckung Amerikas und ihre Bedeutung für die Geschichte des Weltbildes* (Leipzig: 1892).

[94] This issue has been the special burden of the important and controversial works by Edmundo O'Gorman which have been fundamental to my construction of this section. See, especially, *La idea del descubrimiento de América: Historia de esa interpretacion y crítica de sus fundamentos* (Mexico City: 1951) and the similarly titled, though quite

remark of the sixteenth century Florentine historian, Francesco Guicciardini:

> Not only has this navigation confounded many affirmations of former writers about terrestrial things, but it has given some anxiety to the interpreters of the Holy Scriptures.[95]

A voice echoed by his contemporary, the Parisian lawyer, Étienne Pasquier:

> It is a very striking fact that our classical authors had no knowledge of all this America which we call 'new lands.'[96]

A voice so modern that it has called forth recent reinterpretations of the very words "discovery"[97] and "conquest"[98] as they appear in the fifteenth-and sixteenth-century literature. But the earlier voices are less clear. The anthropological perception of the "other" had yet to occur and to find its voice.

For the cognitive issue of the "otherness" of America to emerge, America first had to be perceived as truly "other." Despite an emerging vocabulary of "otherness" (from Columbus's *otro mundo* to Vespucci's *un altro mondo,* or *mondo nuovo* and Peter Martyr's *nova tellus, alter* or *alius orbis, novus orbis,* and *de orbe novo*),[99] the moment at which this perception first emerged in intellectual discourse is far from clear.

It is tempting to place the emergent perception no later than the point at which Balboa first saw the Pacific (September 25, 1513),[100] or the point at which the reports of the survivors of the Magellan

---

different work, *The Invention of America: An Inquiry into the Historical Nature of the New World and the Meaning of its History* (Bloomington: 1961).

[95] F. Guicciardini, *Storia d'Italia* (1561) in the edition of C. Panigara (Bari: 1929), 2:130–1 as cited in H. Honour, *The New Golden Land: European Images of America from the Discoveries to the Present Time* (New York: 1975), 84.

[96] E. Pasquier, *Les oeuvres* (Amsterdam: 1723), 2:55 as cited in J. H. Elliott, *The Old World and the New: 1492–1650* (Cambridge: 1970), 8.

[97] W. E. Washburn, "The Meaning of 'Discovery' in the Fifteenth and Sixteenth Centuries," *American Historical Review,* 68(1962–3): 1–21. Note that this article is conceived as a fundamental attack on O'Gorman's work (note 94, above).

[98] C. Gibson, "Conquest and the So-Called Conquest in Spain and Spanish America," *Terrae Incognitae,* 12(1980): 1–18.

[99] See the useful collection of such terms in Kretschmer, *Die Entdeckung Amerikas,* 360–9.

[100] There are no primary sources. See, J. Toriboio Medina, *El Descubrimiento del Oceano Pácifico* (Santiago: 1914) for a thorough review of the early historians who mention Balboa's discovery, none of whom appear to emphasize its cosmographic implications.

trans-Pacific circumnavigation of 1517–21 became available.[101] But this is by no means certain. It can be no earlier than the report of the first voyage of Columbus (April, 1493).[102] But this is premature. There can be no doubt that Columbus interpreted all of his sightings and land-falls in terms of the classical, tripartite *oikoumenē*, perhaps expanding, in theory, only the classical limits of inhabitability to all five "zones" of the world-island.[103] From the first to the last, he was convinced that he had reached the Asian coast, the easternmost boundary of the *orbis terrarum*.

---

[101] The best reviews of the complex Magellan literature are M. Torodash, "Magellan Historiography," *Hispanic American Historical Review*, 51(1971): 313–35, esp. 313–26, and F. Leite de Faria, "As primeiras relacões impressas sobre a viagem de Fernão de Magalhães," in A. Teixeira de Moto, ed., *A Viagem de Fernão de Magalhães e a questo de Molucas* (Lisbon: 1975): 473–518, in the series, *Estudos de cartografia antiga*, 16. Surprisingly, while the older sources relate the drama and novelty of the circumnavigation, none of them draw cosmographical implications. (1) Fugger Newsletter: *Eine schöne Newe zeytung so Kayserlich Mayestet ausz getz nemlich zukommen sind* (Augsburg: 1522), 8 (in C. Sanz, *Ultimas Adiciones to H. Harrisse, Biblioteca Americana Vetustissima* [Madrid: 1960], 2:909–12). (2) Maximilian of Transylvania, *De Moluccis Insulis* (Cologne: 1523), on which see Faria, "As primeiras relacões", 479–500. See esp., in the English translation by J. Baynes printed in Ch. E. Nowell, *Magellan's Voyage Around the World: Three Contemporary Accounts* (Evanston: 1962), 274, 275–6, 277, 279–80, 291–2, 309. (3) Antonio Pigafetta, *Primo viaggio intorno al mundo*, written c. 1523. On the complex history of this text, see Faria, "As primeiras relacões", 506–16. The earliest printed version, in French (Paris: 1525) is now available in a facsimile edition and translation by P. S. Paige, *The Voyage of Magellan* (Ann Arbor: 1969), esp. 20. See also the Ambrosian manuscript in Nowell, *Magellan's Voyage*, 64. (4) *Roteiro* of the anonymous "Genoese Pilot," in H. E. J. Stanley, *The First Voyage Round the World by Magellan* (London: 1874), 9.

The earliest work that I can find that appreciates the cosmographic implications of the circumnavigation is Richard Eden's paraphrastic translation of Peter Martyr's, *Decadas—The Decades of the Newe Worlde or West India* (London: 1555), facsimile edition (New York: 1966), 214r–215r who sets the reports of Maximilian, Pigafetta and Peter Martyr in the context of the classical tripartition ("the hole globe or compase of the earth was dyvyded by the auncient wryters into three partes") and concludes with a clear statement of novelty ("the antiquitie had never such knowledge of the worlde. . .as we have at this presente by th'industrye of men of this oure age").

[102] Columbus's first report, *Epistola de Insulis Nuper Inventis* (dated, February 15, 1493) was first printed prior to Columbus's arrival at Barcelona (between April 15–20, 1493). There were 11 printed editions by 1497. See C. Sanz, *La Carta de Colón* (Madrid: 1958) for facsimiles of the first 17 printed editions. Cf. Sanz, *Bibliografía general de la Carta de Colón* (Madrid: 1958). See further, the useful tabulation in R. Hirsch, "Printed Reports on the Early Discoveries and Their Reception," in F. Chiappelli, ed., *First Images of America*, 2:537–52 and appendices 1–3 (unpaginated).

[103] It is reported by his son that Columbus wrote a *Memoria anotacion para probar que las cinco zonas son habitables*, c. 1490. If so, it is now lost. Ferdinand Columbus, *Vida del Almirante Don Cristóbal Colón*, chap. 4, in the English translation by B. Keen (New Brunswick, N.J.: 1959), 11.

His persistence was remarkable and unrelenting. The day after his first landfall at San Salvador (October 14, 1492), he wrote that "in order not to lose time" he will set off immediately to "see if I can find the island of Cipango [Japan]."[104] In a letter dated July 7, 1503, at the conclusion of his fourth and final voyage, he wrote that he was only nineteen days journey westward from "the river Ganges."[105]

Throughout his writings, what was in fact new and previously unknown was translated endlessly and effortlessly by Columbus into what was old and well-known. For example, on November 26 and again on December 11 1492, having "understood"[106] the Arawaks to speak of a nearby man-eating tribe which they feared, "the *Cariba*," Columbus misunderstood them to have pronounced the name as *Caniba*—a misunderstanding we perpetuate every time we utter the word "*cannibal*." This misperception was further compounded by being placed within Columbus's preexistent interpretative scheme. *Caniba* sounded to him like the familiar *cane*, "dog." Therefore, Columbus concludes, the *Caniba* must be the cynocephalic monsters of European travel lore, associated especially with India.[107] Alterna-

---

[104] The *Journal* written by Columbus during his first voyage has had a complex history. The document itself has been lost. It was massively excerpted in Bartolomé de las Casas, *Historia de las Indias*, book 1, chaps. 35–75, a work composed between 1527 and 1560, but not published in full until the Madrid edition of 1875–6. (There are excerpts as well in Ferdinand Columbus, *Vida* which permit some cross-checking). The *Columbus Journal* was first printed separately by M. Fernández de Navarrete, *Colección de los viajes y descubrimientos que hicieron por mar los españoles desde fines del siglo XV* (Madrid: 1825–37), 1: 1–166. C. Sanz, *Diario de Colón* (Madrid: 1962), 1–2 has published a facsimile edition of the Las Casas manuscript (Madrid MS.V.6, n.7). For the distinction between Columbus and Las Casas, see A. Vásquez, "Las Casas' Opinions in Columbus' Diary," *Topic*, 11 (1971), 45–56. I cite the convenient edition by G. Marañon, *Diario de Colón* (Madrid: 1968) and the English translation by C. R. Markham, *The Journal of Christopher Columbus* (London: 1893). Passage quoted, Marañon, *Diario*, 29; Markham, *Journal*, 40.

[105] The so-called *Lettera rarissima*, addressed by Columbus to the king and queen, July 7, 1503. Text and translation in R. H. Major, *Christopher Columbus: Four Voyages to the New World, Letters and Selected Documents* (London: 1847; reprint: New York: 1961), 169–203. I have combined two separate figures: Ciguane is "nine days journey westward" (Major: 175), the "river Ganges" is "ten days" from Ciguane (Major: 176).

[106] It must be recalled that Columbus could not "speak" with the natives, despite his frequent (and, sometimes lengthy), translations of what they said. He communicated with them in "signs."

[107] Marañon, *Diario*, 81; Markham, *Journal*, 87. For the appearance of man-eating cynocephali in the Orient in a book owned by Columbus, see H. Yule and H. Cordier, *The Book of Ser Marco Polo*, 3d ed. (London: 1921), 2: 309. The argument by D. B. Quinn, "New Geographical Horizons: Literature," in F. Chiappelli, *First Images of America*, 2: 637, that Columbus elicited the information concerning the cynocephali by

tively, *Caniba* reminded him of the word, *"Can"* (i.e. Khan), therefore, he declared, "Caniba is nothing else but the great Can who ought
now to be very near."[108]

At only one juncture does Columbus's confidence appear shaken
and the easy verbal translations and associations seem to falter.
During his third journey, on August 5, 1498, Columbus became the
first European to set foot on the South American mainland, on the
Paria peninsula on the coast of what is now called Venezuela.
Although he first believed the peninsula to be another island, by
August 15th, he correctly interpreted the physical evidence as requir-
ing the land mass to be "a great mainland, of which nothing has been
known until now."[109] Remarkably, Columbus was able to fit even this
"discovery" into the tripartite schema in its Christian interpretation.
For concealed within the Christian topography was a "wild card"—an
option hitherto of merely theoretical status, that, in addition to the
tripartite world-island, there was a terrestrial Paradise.[110] It is this
mythic land mass that Columbus understands himself to have discovered, in the process altering the commonly accepted view of the globe
as spherical into something rather more eccentrically bulbous. The
letter to the Spanish court of October 14, 1498, is devoted almost
entirely to this remarkable proposition.[111]

Columbus begins his Letter with a sort of preamble, summarizing
his accomplishments in all three voyages and making plain his
conservative intention to place his "enterprise. . .which was foretold
in the writings of so many trustworthy and wise historians" (including
Isaiah!) within the context of the "sayings and opinions of those
[ancients] who have written on the geography of the world."[112]
Nevertheless, the land of which he will now write is "another world
[*otro mundo*] from that which the Romans, and Alexander, and the
Greeks made mighty efforts. . .to gain possession of."[113] What does
this portentous phrase, "another world," mean?

---

showing "pictures to his Arawak informants" from illustrated editions of Marco Polo
and Mandeville is without evidence.

[108] Marañon, *Diario*, 103; Markham, *Journal*: 106.

[109] Excerpt by B. Las Cass from the Columbus *Journal* of the 3d voyage in *Raccolta di
documenti e studi publicata dalla R. Comisione Columbiana* (Rome: 1892–6), 1.2: 22.

[110] While most frequently placed in the east, there was a speculative tradition that
Paradise lay beyond the earth-island, inaccessible to man. See J. K. Wright, *Geographical Lore of the Time of the Crusades*, esp. 262.

[111] *Raccolta*, 1.2: 26–40; text and translation in R. H. Major, *Christopher Columbus*,
104–46.

[112] Major, *Christopher Columbus*, 105–6.

[113] Major, *Christopher Columbus*, 109, cf. 143.

In the body of the letter, two interpretative options are proposed. The land mass is either "an immense tract of land situated in the south" (i.e. a new austral world-island), or it is "terrestrial paradise." Columbus opts for the latter interpretation. Citing the opinions of patristic authorities, he states, "the more I reason on the subject, the more I become satisfied that the terrestrial paradise is situated on the spot I described."[114]

From our perspective, it would appear that rather than opting for the "correct" choice—that he had indeed discovered a previously unimagined land mass—Columbus persuades himself of the opposite.[115] He does so by arguing for an essential difference between the two hemispheres. The southern is not spherical like the northern,[116] for "Ptolemy and the others who have written on the globe had no information respecting this part of the world which was then unexplored, they only established their arguments with respect to their own hemisphere."[117] In a bizarre image, Columbus declares:

> I have come to another conclusion concerning the world, namely that it is not round as they describe, but is in the form of a pear, which is very round except where the stalk grows, at which point it is most prominent; or like a round ball, upon one part of which is a prominence, like a woman's nipple.[118]

At the height of this nipple-like protrusion is:

> the spot of the earthly paradise whither none can go without God's permission, but this land which your Highnesses have now sent me to explore is very extensive, and I think there are many others [countries] in the south [otras muchas en el austro] of which the world has never had any knowledge.[119]

In this manner, Columbus had it both ways. All of the lands previously sighted and explored in his voyages were part of the "Indies"—part of the Asian lobe of the tripartite *orbis terrarum*. This newly discovered *otro mundo* was not contained within the bounds of the tripartite division, but it was not an *orbis alterius*. Rather, it was the only possible exception within Christian topography—terrestrial

---

[114] Major, *Christopher Columbus*, 142.
[115] The most remarkable instance of this "persuasion" is the oft-cited *Información y testimonio acerca de la exploración de Cuba* printed in Navarrete, *Colección*, 2: no. 76.
[116] Major, *Christopher Columbus*, 129–30, 133.
[117] Major, *Christopher Columbus*, 131.
[118] Major, *Christopher Columbus*, 130. The image is repeated twice, Major, 131 and 137.
[119] Major, *Christopher Columbus*, 137 (in revised translation); cf. 135, 136, 142, 145.

paradise.[120] It was an "old" land in terms of biblical tradition; a "new" land in terms of Spanish possession.[121] Peter Martyr's nearly contemporary verdict (1501) will suffice: *fabulosa mihi videantur.*"[122]

To understand the Columbian "fantasy," it is insufficient to characterize him as possessing a "medieval mind," as many recent commentators have done,[123] or to depict him as being deluded through an extreme case of wish fulfillment—an interpretation as old as his early chronicler, Las Casas, who, writing of Columbus' fixation on establishing his proximity to the courts of the Khan, comments: "How marvellous a thing it is how whatever a man strongly desires and has firmly set in his imagination, all that he hears and sees at each step he fancies to be in its favor."[124] What we must see in Columbus is primarily a failure of language, the inability to recognize the inadequacy of his inherited vocabulary and the consequent inability to project a new. At best, there is a muddle. Things are either "like" or "unlike" Spain, but nothing is "other." In a manner similar to the classical ethnographers', Columbus recognizes nothing that requires "decipherment"; all is sheerly transparent.

We must leave, then, the explorer and turn to the scholar for our purposes, the towering figure of Peter Martyr whose *De Orbe Novo* represents the first, systematic, historiographical reflection on the Columbian "discoveries" by a non-participant.[125]

---

[120] This distinction between two types of land—the "Indies" and the "Paradisical"—is maintained in two other documents associated with the 3d voyage: the *Letter* to Dona Juana de la Torres (1500) in Navarrete, *Colección*, 1, esp. 267–8; and the so-called *Papal Letter* (February, 1502) in *Raccolta*, 1.2: 64–6.

[121] See Major, *Christopher Columbus*, 143. The Spanish Crown appears to have taken up Columbus's rejected option. As they had doubted his earlier identification of the newly discovered islands with the "Indies" (see the texts cited in O'Gorman, *Invention*, 81–2, 157, n.18), settling on the ambiguous phrase, "islands and firm land. . .in the western part of the Ocean sea, toward the Indies [*versus India*]," (Papal Bull, *Inter Caetera* [May 3, 1493] in Navarrete, *Colección*, 2: no. 17), so, now, they inferred the existence of a large southern land mass and dispatched no less than six expeditions during the period 1499–1502 to make territorial claims (O'Gorman, *Invention*, 104).

[122] Peter Martyr, *De Orbe Novo*, 1.6. *Opera*, 64; MacNutt, 1:139 (see note 125, below for bibliographical references).

[123] E.g. C. O. Sauer, "Terra firma: Orbis novus," in A. Leidlmair, ed., *Festschrift Hermann von Wissmann* (Tubingen: 1962), 258, 260, 263; T. Todorov, *The Conquest of America*, 12–3, et passim.

[124] Bartolomé de las Casas, *Historia de las Indias*, 1.44. I cite the edition published in Madrid, 1927(?), 1: 224.

[125] The major work of Peter Martyr, *De Orbe Novo*, has had a complex history which affects its interpretation. The first *Decade* devoted to Columbus and Martin Alonso Pinzón was completed (with the exception of book 10) between 1493 and 1501. An Italian version, which survives in only two copies, was published (most probably

The most striking element in Peter Martyr's earliest writings on Columbus's "enterprise" between 1493 and 1495 is an absence: he scrupulously avoids the term "Indies," and, hence, the Columbian identification.[126] This is apparent, already, in his earliest reaction. In May, 1493, less than two months after Columbus's return from his first

---

without Martyr's consent) by P. Trevesan under the title, *Libretto de tutta la navigatione de Re des Spagna de le isole et terreni nouvamente trovati* (Venice: 1504)—now available in a facsimile edited by L. C. Wroth (Providence: 1930). It is uncertain whether this text is an abridgement of Martyr's first *Decade* as eventually published, or an accurate copy of Martyr's first version which he later expanded. The *Libretto* received wide circulation when it was incorporated as Book 4 of Francanzano Montalboddo's collection, *Paesi Novamente Retrouati* (Venice: 1507), which rapidly went through 15 editions. (See D. B. Quinn, "Exploration and Expansion of Europe," in the *Rapports* of the 12th International Congress of Historical Sciences [Vienna: 1965], 1: 45–59).

The first *Decade*, in Martyr's final version, was first published in a collection of his works, *P. Martyris Angli Mediolanensis Opera: Legatio babylonica, Oceani Decas, Poemata, Epigrammata* (Seville: 1511), d–f. The first three *Decades* were published under the title, *De Orbe Novo Decades* (Alcala: 1516). The fourth *Decade* was published under the title, *De Insulis nuper repertis simultaque incolarum moribus* (Basle: 1521). All eight *Decades* were published posthumously, *De Orbe Novo Petri Martyris* (Alcala: 1530)—now available in a facsimile edition by the Akademische Druck- und Verlangsanstalt, *Petrus Martyr de Angleria: Opera* (Graz: 1966), 35–273. Until this facsimile (which I cite), the full text of *De Orbe Novo* was most readily available in the edition by Richard Hakluyt (Paris: 1587).

An English translation of the first four *Decades* was made by Richard Eden, *The Decades of the Newe Worlde or West Indies* (London: 1555)—facsimile edition (New York: 1966), 25–161. An English translation of the entire work was first made by M. Lok, *De Orbe Novo or The Historie of the West Indies* (London: 1612). The standard English translation (which I cite with minor revisions) is that by F. A. MacNutt, *De Orbe Novo* (New York: 1912; reprint New York: 1970), 1–2.

A more difficult question is the correlative use of the extensive correspondence, first published as *Opus Epistolarum Petri Martyris* (Alcala: 1530)—facsimile edition, *Opera* (Ganz: 1966), 275–707, which are available in the important Spanish translation by J. López de Toro, *Epistolario de Pedro Mártir de Angleria* (Madrid, 1953–7), 1–4, in the series, *Documentos inéditos para la historia de España*, 9–12. A selection of the *Letters* which relate to the "new world" were published in French translation by P. Gafferal and l'Abbé Louvot, *Lettres de Pierre Martyr Anghiera relatives aux découvertes maritimes des espagnols et des portugais* (Paris: 1885).

The evidence of the *Letters* must be used with extreme caution. While their authenticity has been challenged, this seems unlikely. It is certain that their chronology is unreliable; many appear to have been backdated. See, among others, J. Bernays, *Petrus Martyr Anglerius und sein Opus Epistolarum* (Strassburg: 1891).

For the relative chronology of the individual books of the various *Decades*—a matter crucial for their interpretation—I have followed that given by E. O'Gorman, *Cuatro historiadores de Indias* (Mexico City: 1972), 43–4.

[126] This is, quite rightly, insisted upon by C. O. Sauer, "Terra Firma: Orbis Novus", 260–1; 262, n.7.

voyage—if the epistolary record is to be credited[127]—he refers to Columbus as having travelled to the "western antipodes."[128] In September, 1493, he augments this description by locating the "western antipodes" in the "new hemisphere of the earth." Here, novelty clearly refers to their previously unknown status; the islands have been "hidden since Creation."[129]

By November, 1493, Martyr reports (in the first book of the first *Decade*) the existence of "recently discovered islands in the western ocean,"[130] but he remains ambivalent as to their identification. He knows that Columbus understands this "unknown land" to consist of "islands which touch the Indies,"[131] but he is not convinced. He suggests that they are a previously unknown group of westerly Atlantic islands, thoroughly analogous to the long-familiar Canaries.[132] Furthermore, when reporting on "Hispaniola," he notes that Columbus believes it to be the rediscovered ancient Solomonic site of Ophir (an identification, like terrestrial paradise, which shows forth Columbus's attempt to locate his "enterprise" within the framework of biblical cosmography). Martyr rejects the identification, suggesting instead the legendary western Atlantic islands, the Antilles.[133] All three of Martyr's interpretations (the "western antipodes," the analogy with the Canaries, and the Antilles) show Martyr as rejecting Columbus's oriental fantasy. All three place his discoveries in the western Atlantic, in terms which recall Greco-Roman geography.

There is, however, a hint in this 1493 account of something more. Columbus claims to have found "indications of a hitherto unknown *alterius terrarum orbis.*"[134] Martyr will later report, in 1501, that Columbus believes it to be "the continent of India"—an identification that Martyr firmly rejects.[135] But for now, Martyr supplies no identification.

---

[127] On the problems attendant on using the *Epistles*, see above, note 125.
[128] *Epistle* 130. *Opera*: 360; *Epistolario*, 1: 236. The term *antipodes* recurs in *Epistles* 134 (September, 1493); 140 (January, 1494); 144 (October, 1494).
[129] *Epistle*, 134. *Opera*: 361; *Epistolario, 1: 244.*
[130] *De Orbe Novo*, 1.1. *Opera*: 39; MacNutt, *De Orbe Novo*, 1: 57.
[131] *De Orbe Novo*, 1.1. *Opera*: 41 and 39; MacNutt, *De Orbe Novo*, 1: 65 and 57.
[132] *De Orbe Novo*, 1.1. *Opera*: 39; MacNutt, *De Orbe Novo*, 1: 58.
[133] *De Orbe Novo*, 1.1. *Opera*: 40; MacNutt, *De Orbe Novo*, 1: 61, cf. 1: 87, 114 et passim. For this claim, see Columbus's *Papal Letter* (February, 1502) in *Raccolta*, 1.2: 472 and Columbus, *Libro de las Profecías* (1501–2), in *Raccolta* 1.2: esp. 150–6. The identification persists through the early literature. See the important study by G. Gliozzi, *Adamo e il nuovo mondo* (Florence: 1976), 147–74.
[134] *De Orbe Novo*, 1.1. *Opera*: 41. MacNutt's translation (1: 65) is inadequate at this point.
[135] *De Orbe Novo*, 1.4. *Opera*: 54; MacNutt, *De Orbe Novo*, 1: 105, cf. 1: 92, 139–40, 178, 330 et passim. Compare further, *Epistles*, 135 and 142.

In November, 1493, Peter Martyr employs a different terminology, one for which he will become famous. In a letter to Cardinal Sforza, he writes of a *novus orbis* that Columbus has discovered.[136] Again, we must inquire as to the meaning of this portentous phrase.

Martyr's earliest usage of the term *novus orbis* is closely akin to his even earlier phrase, "the new hemisphere of the earth" (*novo terrarum hemisperio*). It means newly discovered parts of the familiar globe. When Martyr writes of the *novus orbis*, he is not identifying a new geographic entity in the sense we are familiar with when we capitalize the "New World" as the Americas in contradistinction to the "Old World." Martyr's *novus orbis* is neither Columbus's *otro mundo* (which he understands, as we have seen, to be terrestrial paradise), nor Vespucci's *mundus novus* (which he understands to be a previously unknown extension of Asia),[137] but like these terms, it

---

[136] *Epistle*, 138. Opera: 360; *Epistolario*, 1: 250. The phrase recurs in *Epistles* 142 (October 20, 1494) and 154 (February 2, 1494).

[137] For the Asian extension, see Vespucci, 1st *Letter* (July 18, 1500) in R. Levillier, ed., *El Nuevo Mondo: Cartas relativas a sus viajes y descubrimientos* (Buenos Aires: 1951), 277, cf. 299.

The term "new world" occurs only 5 times in Vespucci's writings, only in the letter now entitled, *Mundus Novus* (n.p., n.d.—c. 1502–4). See the summary bibliography in J. A. Aboal Amaro, *Amérigho Vespucci*: 99–111. Its most important occurrence is in the first paragraph: "On a former occasion I wrote to you at some length concerning my return from those *new regions* which we found and explored with the fleet. . . .And these we may rightly call a *new world*. Because our ancestors had no knowledge of them, and it will be a matter *wholly new* to all those who hear of them." (English translation by G. T. Northup, *Mundus Novus* [Princeton: 1916], 1, (emphasis added), in the series, *Vespucci Reprints, Texts and Studies*, 5). The phrase, *"quasque novum mundum appellare licet"* may be taken as indicating the author's self-consciousness at coining a term, but what does it mean? The context makes plain that *novus* refers to the fact that the lands were unknown and unexpected, i.e. (a) that they could not be harmonized readily with any of the lands described by the ancient authorities, and (b) that they occurred in the southern hemisphere which, according to the ancients, was entirely Ocean. *Mundus* refers to the fact that the lands were inhabited, i.e. that they constituted a "world" in the sense of *oikoumenē*. The question of whether they were a previously unknown extension of the familiar tripartite *oikoumenē* or constitute a "new" geographical entity was not raised in the *Mundus Novus*.

However, extreme caution must be used in evaluating this text. "Vespucci's writings have had a strange and complicated history. They have suffered at the hands of translators, copyists, printers. . . .The texts on which we base our judgements are *vastly different* from those which left the author's hand." (G. T. Northup, *Amerigo Vespucci: Letter to Pietro Soderini* [Princeton: 1916], 1, in the series, *Vespucci Reprints, Texts and Studies*, 4 [emphasis added]). While it may be too extreme to label the *Mundus Novus* and the *Soderini Letter* "forgeries" as has been done by F. J. Pohl, *Amerigo Vespucci:Pilot Major* (New York: 1944), esp. 144–67, C. O. Sauer, "Terra Firma: Orbis Novus", 268, n.19 and 269; R. Iglesia, *Columbus, Cortés, and Other Essays* (Berkeley: 1969), 253, among others, they are most certainly not, in their printed form, by

does not challenge the old world view. This will not occur in explicit fashion until the *Cosmographiae Introductio* of 1508 with its declaration that Vespucci had discovered a previously unsuspected "fourth part of the world."[138]

At any rate, Martyr does not employ the phrase "new world" in his *Decades* until those portions of the work composed after 1514.[139] Here, it may well carry the connotation of an *orbis alterius*, but only after the period of the initial responses, when the notion of the inadequacy of the tripartite *oikoumenē* had become commonplace in intellectual discourse.

What has been learned thus far from the first explorer and the earliest interpreter of that exploration is the difficulty in conceptualizing "otherness." Something "different" has been sensed, but has as yet gained no distinctive voice. Rather, the old language has been stretched to accomodate it. Perhaps this "stretching" is what was meant by the curious phrase the sixteenth-century historian Hernan Pérez de Oliva used to describe the Columbian "enterprise." He speaks of an enterprise in which Columbus "sought to unite the world and give to those strange lands the form of our own."[140] The "other" emerges only as a theoretical issue when it is perceived as challenging a complex and intact world view. It is only then that the "different" becomes the problematic "alien." The incapacity of imag-

---

Vespucci. They represent Latin versions by anonymous translators that probably ill accord with Vespucci's original. See A. Magnaghi, *Americo Vespucci: Studio critico* (Rome: 1924), 1–2; the careful textual and philological study of the *Soderini Letter* by Northup (op.cit.), and the review of the current state of the question in R. Levillier, *Américo Vespucci* (Madrid: 1966), 339–62.

Regardless of authorship (or the original meaning), the phrase took on independent power and was widely disseminated, shifting, in time, from a preeminently geographical to a social-political context. See, on this, C. Ginzburg, *The Cheese and the Worms: The Cosmos of a Sixteenth Century Miller* (Baltimore: 1980), 81–6.

In letters subsequent to *Mundus Novus* attributed to Vespucci, the term does not recur. The phrase is dropped in favor of the less suggestive "new lands" in the conventional sense of lands of which there was previously no knowledge. See Levillier, *El nuevo mundo*: 201, 203, 204–5, 233, 251, 259, et passim.

[138] Martin Waldseemüller, *Cosmographiae Introductio* (St. Dié, 1507): a iii—facsimile edition by J. Fischer and F. von Weiser (reprint: New York: 1969), xxv. I am aware in giving the traditional attribution, that many authorities consider the *Introductio* to be the work of Matthias Ringmann. See the excellent review of the state of the question by F. Laubenberger, "Ringmann oder Waldseemüller?," *Erdkunde*, 13 (1959), 163–79.

[139] The first use of the term is in *De Orbe Novo*, 3.1. *Opera*, 105; MacNutt, *De Orbe Novo*, 1: 281, written in 1514. Here, as elsewhere, the term occurs in the dedication. The term appears as the title for the first three books in the Alcala edition of 1516.

[140] H. Pérez de Oliva, *Historia de la Invención de las Yndias*, in the edition of J. Juan Arrom (Bogota: 1965), 53–4 as quoted in J. H. Elliott, *The Old World and the New*, 15.

ination exhibited by Columbus and Peter Martyr stands as eloquent testimony to that intactness. Yet, once the question is admitted, once alienation is even fleetingly glimpsed, it cannot be silenced or ignored. It will give rise to thought as expressed in speech. What was inconceivable in the last decade of the fifteenth century became commonplace, for some, by the first decade of the sixteenth. The "Americas" were, as the 1508 *Introductio* named and described them—in an act of language, not of exploration—a "fourth part" of the world. Like us, in that it was inhabited; unlike us, in its geographical form. For the familiar three parts were contiguous land masses (i.e. continents); the newly discovered "fourth part" was discontinuous, it was understood to be an island surrounded by a vast expanse of water.[141] It was the insular nature of the unexpected "discovery" of a "fourth part" of the "world" that gave rise to the more intense debate over "otherness"—that respecting the land's inhabitants: its humans, animals and plants.

For Columbus, knowing that he was in the "Indies," the presence of human inhabitants, of animals and plants which seemed both familiar and strange, presented no major intellectual problems. True, the naked men and women did not resemble the high civilization of the "great Khan" that Marco Polo and Toscanelli had led him to expect. But, no matter. As he endlessly repeats, he has heard that the capitol of the Khan is just a short journey away. Because he is in what he believes to be both a contiguous and an unfamiliar land, he can recognize differences and impose similarities without giving these matters a second's thought. Because he cannot speak directly to the natives, except through ambiguous "signs," he can impose his language on whatever or whomever he encounters without impediment.[142] He "gives to these strange lands the form of our own" precisely because he did not know what Oliva knew decades later, that in some profound fashion, the lands were truly "strange." The most obvious example of this is also the most enduring: six days after landing, Columbus was able to easily and unquestioningly call the indigenous population "*Indios.*"[143]

Less often noted, but, in fact, far more massive a feature of Columbus's writings is his constant Europeanization of the indige-

---

[141] *Cosmographiae Introductio*, facsimile edition: xxx, "*et sunt tres prime partes continentes, quarta est insula.*" See above, note 84.

[142] In his marginal notations to Columbus's *Journal* of his first voyage, Las Casas frequently comments on Columbus's linguistic limitations. See, J. A. Vásquez, "Las Casas' Opinions in Columbus' Diary", esp. 53–4.

[143] Marañon, *Diario*, 37; Markham, *Journal*, 48.

nous flora and fauna.[144] Take, for example, the matter of the nightingales (the common name for a group of small Eurasian thrushes of
which no species is to be found in the Americas). Even before making
land-fall, Columbus found one night on board ship so agreeable that,
according to Las Casas, "the Admiral said that nothing was wanting
but to hear the nightingale."[145] Columbus was not to be disappointed.
On at least three occasions after landing in the "Indies" he heard "the
singing of the nightingales and other birds of Castile."[146]

For all the unconscious humor that might be found in these and
other examples,[147] the point as to "Indians," "nightingales," and the
like is far more serious. As Terrence Hawkes reminds us, "a colonist
acts essentially as a dramatist. He imposes the 'shape' of his own
culture embodied in his speech on the new world, and makes that
world recognizable" and, hence, "habitable" for him.[148] So long as
Columbus and the other early explorers were successful in giving "to
those strange lands the form of our own," the lands could not emerge
as truly "strange"; they could not be perceived as objects of thought;
there could be no language, and hence, no theory of the "other."

The early records must therefore be searched for moments of
heightened self-consciousness, for crises of confidence in the sheer
translatability of "here" to "there," of "old" to "new," of "familiar" to
"strange." Such moments are difficult to find and to pinpoint with
chronological precision. Nevertheless, a set of such essentially lin-

---

[144] Rarely, Columbus recorded native names for useful or edible species, e.g. *aje, aji, cazave*, although some of these may be interpolations by Las Casas (Vásquez, "Las Casas' Opinions", 51–2). At times, Columbus does recognize difference, but in a somewhat casual manner. For example: "The trees are as unlike ours as night from day, as are the fruits, the stones, and everything. It is true that some of the trees bore some resemblance to those in Castile, but most of them are very different, and some were so unlike that no once could compare them to anything in Castile." Marañon, *Diario*, 38; Markham, *Journal*, 49. See, in general, L. Hughes, *L'opera scientifica di Cristoforo Colombo* (Turin: 1892).

[145] Marañon, *Diario*, 16; Markham, *Journal*, 30.

[146] Marañon, *Diario*, 100, cf. 62, 106; Markham, *Journal*, 103, cf. 71, 109. On the significance of this see Menéndez Pidal, "La lengua de Cristóbal Colón," *Bulletin hispanique*, 42(1940), 27 and n.1, criticizing the important essay by L. Olschki, "Il lusignuolo di Colombo," in Olschki, *Storia letteraria delle scoperte geografiche* (Florence: 1937), 11–21. See further, Gerbi, *The Dispute of the New World*, 161, n. 12 and index, s.v. "nightingales."

[147] Compare the incident of the nutmegs and cinnamon, Marañon, *Diario*, 58–9; Markham, *Journal*, 67.

[148] T. Hawkes, *Shakespeare's Talking Animals* (London: 1973), 211. Barry Holstun Lopez, in his short story, "Restoration," makes effective use of this motif. Lopez, *Winter Count* (New York: 1982), 1–14, esp. 8–12.

guistic "turns" can be discerned—although a determination of their contemporary influence must remain problematic.[149]

The "issue of the Indians," that is to say, the question of how the "New World" came to be populated[150] was, as best as can be determined, first raised in interrogatory form[151] in a play printed c. 1519 and attributed to John Rastell, brother-in-law of Sir Thomas More. Rastell, a minor Tudor poet and major early English printer had himself attempted a journey to the "New Founde Lands" in 1517.[152]

In the play *A New Interlude and a Mery, of the Nature of the iiij Elementis, declarynge many proper poyntys of philosophy naturall and of dyvers straunge landys,*[153] the author, in the guise of describ-

---

[149] See the wise comments on the difficulty of establishing criteria for "impact" and "influence" in J. H. Elliott, "Renaissance Europe and America: A Blunted Impact?" in F. Chiappelli, ed., *First Images of America*, 1: 11–24.

[150] This question was made infinitely more complex by the encounter with the "high" civilizations of Mesoamerica. See, for an overview, the important monograph by B. Keen, *The Aztec Image in Western Thought* (New Brunswick, N.J.: 1971).

[151] So, L. E. Huddleston, *Origins of the American Indians: European Concepts, 1492–1729* (Austin: 1967), 8, 110, in the series, *University of Texas, Latin American Monographs*, 11. Huddleston's survey of the topic is the finest to date.

[152] For biographical information on Rastell, see A. W. Reed, *Early Tudor Drama* (London: 1926), 1–28, 187–223. For the attempted 1517 voyage, see the summary account in D. B. Quinn, *England and the Discovery of America* (London: 1974), 162–9.

[153] The text survives in only a single, imperfect printed copy in the British Museum. It lacks a title page and other introductory material, hence neither its author, date or place of publication are beyond dispute. The play was first attributed to Rastell in 1557. The attribution has been accepted by all scholars. The date is more controversial. Estimates range from 1517–1530, with the majority of scholars suggesting 1519–20.

I have not seen the facsimile edition in the series, *Tudor Facsimile Texts* (London: 1908). I have used the recent edition by R. Axton, *Three Rastell Plays* (Totowa, N.J.: 1979), 29–68, esp. 48–52. The more familiar edition is that by J. O. Halliwell, *The Interlude of the Four Elements: An Early Moral Play* (London: 1848), esp. 27–33, in the series, *Percy Society: Early English Poetry, Ballads and Popular Literature in the Middle Ages*, 22. It is accessible, as well, in E. Arber, ed., *The First Three English Books on America* (Westminster: 1895), xx–xxi. (In 1971, a modernized and abridged form of the play was performed at Cambridge University. See R. E. Coleman, ed., *The Four Elements as Performed at the University Printing House* [Cambridge: 1971]; B. Critchley, ed., *Siberch Celebrations, 1521–1971* [Cambridge: 1971], 83–131, esp. 106–11).

There has been considerable scholarship devoted to the cosmographical elements in the play. See, G. P. Park, "The Geography of The Interlude of the Four Elements," *Philological Quarterly*, 17(1938), 251–62; M. Borish, "Source and Intention of The Four Elements," *Studies in Philology*, 35(1938), 149–63; E. M. Nugent, "The Sources of John Rastell's The Nature of the Four Elements," *Publications of the Modern Language Association*, 57(1942), 78–88; G. P. Park, "Rastell and the Waldseemüller Map," ibid. 58(1943), 572–4; J. Parr, "More Sources of Rastell's Interlude of the Four Elements," ibid. 60(1945), 48–58; H. C. Porter, *The Inconstant Savage: England and the North American Indian, 1500–1660* (London: 1979), 34–7.

ing a globe, knows that there is a single mass of "new landes. . . westwarde. . . that we never harde tell of before thus/by wrytnge nor other meanys."[154] It stretches from the "north parte" where "all the clothes/That they were is but bestis skins" to the "south parte of *that contrey*" where "the people there go nakyd alway/the lande is of so great hete."[155] The poet immediately goes on to pose the query:

> But howe the people furst began
> In that contrey or whens they cam,
> For clerkes it is a questyon.[156]

The first explicit attempt to answer this question,[157] to go beyond narrative and description to the level of explanation, was Gonzalo Fernández de Oviedo y Valdés' encyclopaedic work,[158] *Historia general y natural de las Indias islas y Tierra Firme del Mar Oceano*, specifically, in those parts published in 1535.[159] Oviedo offers two hypotheses: (1) the land had been populated by the ancient Carthaginians[160] (2) his more persistent argument, that the lands were ancient Spanish possessions (identified with the Hesperides) associated with the mythical Spanish king Héspero, who was alleged to have reigned c. 1680 B.C.[161] Thus for Oviedo, there was no "new discovery," or

---

[154] Axton, *Rastell*, 49 (lines: 737–8).

[155] Axton, *Rastell*, 51 (lines: 811–15). Emphasis, added.

[156] Axton, *Rastell*, 51 (lines: 817–19).

[157] Huddleston, *Origins*: 15–16.

[158] On the encyclopaedic nature of this work, see Enrique Alvarez López, "Plinio y Fernández de Oviedo," *Annales de Ciencias naturales del Instituto J. de Acosta* (Madrid: 1940), 1: 46–61; 2: 13–35; D. Turner, "Oviedo's *Historia*. . .The First American Encyclopedia," *Journal of Inter-American Studies*, 5(1960), 267–74.

[159] Oviedo, *Historia general y natural de las Indias islas y Tierra-Firme del Mar Oceano*, 1st ed. (Seville: 1535) containing the "Prologue," Books 1–19 and Book 50.1–10. The bulk of the *Historia* remained in manuscript until the edition of José Amador de los Ríos (Madrid: 1851–55), 1–4. See the careful account of the publication history in D. Turner, *Gonzalo Fernández de Oviedo y Valdés: An Annotated Bibliography* (Chapel Hill: 1966), 7–13. I cite the edition by J. Pérez de Tudela, *Historia general y natural de las Indias* (Madrid: 1959), 1–5, in the series, *Biblioteca de Autores Españoles*, 117–21, which reproduces the 1851–55 text.

[160] *Historia*, 2.3; Pérez de Tudela, 1: 17. See, G. Gliozzi, *Adamo e il nuovo mondo*, 247–58. The Carthaginian tradition is based on an altered version of Aristotle, *Mirabiles auscultationes*, 84 (see, A. Giannini, *Paradoxographorum Graecorum* [Milan: 1965], 258–9).

[161] *Historia*, 2.3; Pérez de Tudela, 1: 17–20. See G. Gliozzi, *Adamo e il nuovo mondo*, 28–30. This identification is based on the pseudo-Berossus forgeries of Annius of Viterbo, *Commentaria super opera diversorum auctorum de antiquitatibus* (Rome: 1498), on which see, D. C. Allen, *The Legend of Noah*, 114–5. Ferdinand Columbus, *Historie*, 10 (Keen: 28–34) responds with heat to both of Oviedo's contentions.

problematic population; "through the agency of Columbus, God had returned the Indies to their [original and] rightful owner—the Spanish Crown."[162]

While attempts persisted to deny "otherness" by arguing, in one form or another, that the "new" land was in some sense rediscovered "old" land that was a part of the tripartite *oikoumenē* and a part, as well, of classical geographical lore, these would remain minority positions.[163] More usually, given the monogenetic interpretations of Genesis 1-10, three kinds of theoretical options were proposed. (1) The new land was not wholly insular. It was connected (most usually by a land bridge) to the tripartite *oikoumenē* and thus, though an "other world" geographically, it was populated by an overland migration of familiar peoples. It should be noted that this remains, today, the leading explanation. (2) There was a "second Ark"—one not recorded in Scripture, with all that implied. (3) There was some form of miraculous intervention—the *locus classicus* being Augustine, *De Civitate Dei,* 16.7, which posed the hypothesis that angels transported animals to remote islands after the Flood.

These interpretative options were taken up and systematically reviewed for the first time by Joseph de Acosta in his remarkable, *Historia natural y moral de las Indias,* a work begun c. 1580.[164] Acosta rejected the hypotheses of the "second Ark" and of angelic intervention,[165] while supporting in a sophisticated manner the hypothesis of a land bridge or a narrow strait separating the "Indies" from the "old world."[166] He rejected all attempts to deny difference: the "Indies" were not Ophir or Atlantis; the "Indians" were not Hebrews.[167] His understanding of the process of population was complex and sugges-

---

[162] Huddleston: 16. Cf. O'Gorman, *La idea del descubrimiento:* 80–3.

[163] The most popular version of this thesis identified the new lands with Atlantis. See I. Rodríguez Prampolini, *La Atlantida de Platón en los cronistas del siglo XVI* (Mexico City: 1947), Gliozzi, *Adamo e il nuovo mondo,* 177–246.

[164] The first two books of Acosta's *Historia,* those most relevant to our interests, were begun c. 1580 and published in Latin as *De natura novi orbis libri duo* (Salamanca: 1589). Acosta translated these two books into Spanish, added 5 others, making up the whole, *Historia natural y moral de las Indias,* 1st ed. (Seville: 1590), 2nd ed. (Barcelona: 1591), 3d ed. (Madrid: 1608). The *Historia* was translated into Italian, French, Dutch, German and Latin by 1602. An English version was prepared by E. G. [= Edward Grimston], *The Naturall and Morall Historie of the East and West Indies* (London: 1604). I cite the critical edition by E. O'Gorman, *Historia natural y moral de las Indias* (Mexico City: 1940) and C. R. Markham's reedition of Grimston's translation, *The Natural and Moral History of the Indies* (London: 1880), 1–2.

[165] *Historia,* 1.16. O'Gorman, *Historia,* 61; Markham, *History,* 1:45.

[166] *Historia,* 1.20–1. O'Gorman, *Historia,* 75–81; Markham, *History,* 1: 57–64.

[167] *Historia,* 1.22–3. O'Gorman, *Historia,* 83–88; Markham, *History,* 1: 64–9.

tive. The inhabitants of the "new world" came over from the "old" at different times in the past. They gradually lost their previous cultures and developed their own indigenous ones, becoming first hunters, then agriculturalists.[168] Therefore, there will be cultural similarities between the "new" and the "old," but these similarities are the result of similar development, and may not be used, in themselves, as clues to origin.[169] Finally, note must be taken of the publication in 1607 of the first book wholly devoted to the question of the Indians' origins, Gregorio García's *El origen de los indios de el Nuevo Mundo, e Indias occidentales*. It is a massive, five hundred and thirty-five page review of all possible interpretative options.[170]

The concomitant issue, the origin of the flora and fauna and their similarities and differences to those of the "old world," was largely addressed by the same sort of theorizing as attended the human. But there was one difference. Given the monogenetic interpretations of Genesis 1-10, the "Indians," if identified as human (and, there is little evidence that they were not),[171] could never be absolutely "different." Animals and plants could be so perceived. Thus, it is in their naturalistic observations and writings that we find the clearest early statements of "otherness" framed in terms of the linguistic implica-

---

[168] *Historia*, 1.24. O'Gorman, *Historia*, 89–90; Markham, *History*, 1: 69–70.

[169] In addition to the valuable preface in O'Gorman's edition (reprinted in O'Gorman, *Cuatro historiadores*, 165–248), see Th. Hornberger, "Acosta's *Historia*. . .A Guide to the Source and Growth of the American Scientific Tradition," *University of Texas Studies in English*, 19(1939), 139–62; Gliozzi, *Adamo e il nuovo mondo*, esp. 371–81; Huddleston, *Origins*, 48–59.

[170] García, *El origen de los indios de el Neuvo Mundo, e Indias occidentales* (Valencia: 1607). This 1st ed. is exceedingly scarce. The 2nd ed. (Madrid: 1729) is most commonly cited. It contains extensive notes by its editor, Andres González de Barcia Carballido y Zúñiga. Unfortunately, these have not always been distinguished from García's words in subsequent scholarship. A facsimile of the 2nd ed. has been edited by F. Pease (Mexico City: 1981), in the series, *Biblioteca Americana*. Pease's introduction is of great value. Huddleston, *Origins*: 60–76 gives an overview.

Huddleston's overall conclusion deserves notice. "Two clearly distinguished traditions [as to the origin of the Indians in the period, 1492–1729] have emerged from my investigations: the Acostan and the Garcian. The first, marked by a skepticism with regard to cultural comparisons, considerable restraint in constructing theories, and a great reliance on geographical and faunal considerations, is named for Joseph de Acosta, who gave it its earliest clear expression. . . .The Garcian tradition, named for the author of the *Origin de los Indios*. . .is characterized by a strong adherence to ethnological comparisons, a tendency to accept trans-Atlantic migrations, and an acceptance of possible origins as probable ones." (Huddleston, *Origins*, 13).

[171] The various writings by Lewis U. Hanke have been crucial in gaining perspective on this matter. See, among others, "Pope Paul II and the American Indians," *Harvard Theological Review*, 30(1937), 65–102; *Aristotle and the American Indians* (Chicago: 1959); *The Spanish Struggle for Justice in the Conquest of America* (Boston: 1965).

tions of "difference."[172] I shall content myself with citing three telling examples from the rich, sixteenth-century Spanish naturalistic literature. First, perhaps the earliest and most extreme statement of "otherness," from a work by Oviedo published in 1526, which describes what appears to be a jaguar.

> In my opinion, these animals are not tigers, nor are they panthers, or any other of the numerous known animals that have spotted skins, nor some new animal [of the "old world"] that has a spotted skin and has not [yet] been described. The many animals that exist in the Indies that I describe here, or at least most of them, could not have been learned about from the ancients, since they exist in a land which had not been discovered until our own time. There is no mention made of these lands in Ptolemy's *Geography*, nor in any other work, nor where they known until Christopher Columbus showed them to us. . . . But, returning to the subject already begun. . .this animal is called by the Indians, *ochi*.[173]

This last sentence is of crucial importance. Given the stated inadequacy of "old world" taxa, Oviedo self-consciously shifts to native terminology. Our second example is Acosta's protest against the imperialism of names (as in Columbus and the nightingales).

> The first Spaniards gave many things found in the Indies Spanish names taken from things which they somewhat resembled. . . when, in fact, they were quite different. Indeed, the difference between them and what are called by these names in Castile are greater than the similarities.[174]

Finally, Acosta makes a complex, theoretical statement concerning "difference."

> What I say of the *guanacos* and *pacos* I will say of a thousand varieties of birds and fowls and mountain animals that have never

---

[172] To insist on the importance of the naturalistic materials has been the special contribution of A. Gerbi, *The Dispute of the New World* (Pittsburgh: 1973) and *La natura delle Indie nove da Cristoforo Colombo a Gonzalo Fernandez de Oviedo* (Milan: 1975). I have also profited from observations in C. E. Chardon, *Los naturalistas en la américa latina: Los siglos XVI–XVIII* (Cuidad Trujillo: 1949), 1.

[173] Oviedo, *De la natural hystoria de las Indias*, 1st ed. (Toledo: 1526), 11--facsimile edition (Chapel Hill: 1969), 37–9; English translation by S. A. Stoudemere, *Natural History of the West Indies* (Chapel Hill: 1959), 47–8. This work, frequently called the *Sumario*, must not be confused with Oviedo's larger and later, *Historia general de las Indias* (see above, note 159). A parallel passage does occur in the *Historia*, 1.12.10, Pérez de Tudela, 2, 39–42, esp. 40.

[174] Acosta, *Historia*, 4.19. O'Gorman, *Historia*, 275. The Grimston translation is not useful at this point.

been known [previously] by either name or appearance, nor is there
any memory of them in the Latins or Greeks, nor in any nations of our
[European] world over here. . . . It is well to ask whether these
animals differ in kind and essence from all others, or if this difference
be accidental. . . . But, to speak bluntly, any one who in this way
would focus only on the accidental differences, seeking thereby to
explain [away] the propogation of the animals of the Indies and to
reduce them [to variants] of the European, will be undertaking a task
that he will not be able to fulfill. For, if we are to judge the species
of animals [in the Indies] by their [essential] properties, they are so
different that to seek to reduce them to species known in Europe will
mean having to call an egg a chestnut.[175]

The "new world" is not merely "new," not merely "different"—it is
"other" *per essentiam*. As such, it calls forth an "other" language.

As this review has suggested, although slow to start, the theoretical issues posed by the "otherness" of "America" were raised in
sharp form as a project of language by the end of the sixteenth century.
But they could not be solved—not for want of data, but because theory
was inadequate. This deficiency at the level of theory persisted for
centuries. The nineteenth century finally established the principle of
polygenesis—above all, through that major contribution to anthropological theory now improperly discredited, the notion of "race". The
nineteenth century also contributed an early understanding of genetic
variation's processes and the procedures for polythetic classification.
It is only in the last decades, following upon the long and arid debates
over independent variation versus diffusion, that we are beginning to
develop adequate theories and well-formulated criteria for diffusion.[176]

III

"Few questions have exerted so powerful a grip on the thought of
this century than that of the "Other". . . .It is difficult to think of
another topic that so radically separates the thought of the
present. . .from its historical roots." M. Theunissen, *Der Andere*, 2nd
ed. (Berlin, 1977).

In the first part of this essay, in relation to the notion of "parasite,"
attention was focused on what might be termed the political aspects of

---

[175] Acosta, *Historia*, 4.36. O'Gorman, *Historia*, 325–6. The Grimston translation is not
useful at this point.
[176] For an important overview of the present state of the question, see the monograph
by A. Laming-Emperaire, *Le problème des origines américaines* (Lille: 1980), in the
series, *Cahiers d'archéologie et d'ethnologie d'Amérique du Sud.*

a "theory of the other." That is to say, we were largely concerned with the figure of the "proximate other," with questions of the relativity of "otherness," of its modes and degrees,[177] often perceived hierarchically. We were led to postulate that "otherness," by its very nature, required a relational theory of reciprocity (in other words, politics), and that a "theory of otherness," in this sense, must be construed as a rule-governed set of reciprocal relations with one socially labeled an "other."

In the second part of this essay, that concerned with the "discovery" of "America," we shifted to what might be termed the linguistic aspects of a "theory of the other."[178] In the same way that, according to one historian of science, "Ptolemy's model of the earth was the weapon by which the real earth was conquered intellectually,"[179] so, too, here. The "conquest of America," for all of its frightful human costs, was primarily a linguistic event.[180] Once recognized (in the face of an intact, linguistically embedded world view), "otherness" was on the one hand a challenge to "decipherment"; on the other hand, it was an occasion for the "stretching" of language—both for the creation of

---

[177] For an interesting attempt to describe "relative otherness" with more precision, see E. S. Bogardus, "A Social Distance Scale," *Sociology and Social Research,* 17(1933), 265–71. J. C. Mitchell, *The Kalela Dance* (Manchester: 1956), 22–8, in the series, *Papers of the Rhodes-Livingstone Institute,* 27 has adapted the scale for a tribal context with interesting results for our theme.

[178] By emphasizing in separate sections the political and linguistic aspects of a "theory of the other," I do not mean to imply their separation. As is well known, especially in matters of colonialism, the two go hand in hand. This is well illustrated in an incident that has become emblematic for historians of the period. "In 1492, in the introduction to his *Gramática* [*de la lengua castellana*], the first grammar of a modern European language, Antonio de Nebrija writes that language has always been the partner [*compañera*] of empire. And in the ceremonial presentation of the volume to Queen Isabella, the bishop of Avila, speaking on the scholar's behalf, claimed a still more central role for language. When the Queen asked flatly, 'What is it [good] for?' the Bishop replied, 'Your Majesty, language is the perfect instrument of empire.' " (S. J. Greenblatt, "Learning to Curse: Aspects of Linguistic Colonialism in the Sixteenth Century," in F. Chiappelli, *First Images of America,* 2: 562). The story is told in a variety of historical works including: J. B. Trend, *The Civilization of Spain* (London: 1944), 88; L. Hanke, *Aristotle and the American Indian,* 8 and 127, n.31; D. Lach, *Asia in the Making of Europe* (Chicago: 1977), 2.3: 504; T. Todorov, *The Conquest of America,* 123.

[179] J. Leighly, "Error in Geography," in J. Jastrow, ed., *The Story of Human Error* (New York: 1938), 92–3.

[180] It is in this sense that E. O'Gorman is quite right to insist on *la invención de América.* (See above, note 94). Cf. H. B. Johnson, "New Geographical Horizons: Concepts," in F. Chiappelli, ed., *First Images of America,* 2: 623, "[in early German reports] the fourth part of the world was always *erfunden* not *endeckt.*"

new linguistic entities ("new world" and the like) and the attempt, through discourse, to "give to these strange worlds the shape of our own."[181] "Otherness" is not a descriptive category, an artifact of the perception of difference or commonality. Nor is it the result of the determination of biological descent or affinity.[182] It is a political and linguistic project, a matter of rhetoric and judgement.

It is for this reason that in thinking about the "other," real progress has been made only when the "other" ceases to be an ontological category. That is to say, "otherness" is not some absolute state of being. Something is "other" only with respect to something "else." Whether understood politically or linguistically, "otherness" is a situational category. Despite its apparent taxonomic exclusivity, "otherness" is a transactional matter, an affair of the "in-between."[183]

In our historical review, this situational and transactional character loomed large through the notion of the "proximate other." That is to say, absolute "difference" is not a category for thought, but one which denies the possibility of thought. What one historian has stated about the concept, "unique," may be applied as well to the notion of the "wholly other" (with the possible exception of odd statements in even odder Continental theologies):

> This word 'unique' is a negative term signifying what is mentally inapprehensible. The absolutely unique is, by definition, indescribable.[184]

---

[181] For an important attempt to describe the "grammar" of such discourse, see B. Bucher, *Icon and Conquest: A Structural Analysis of the Illustrations of de Bry's Great Voyages* (Chicago: 1981), 24–45.

[182] See, from a quite different perspective, the arguments by F. Barth, "Introduction," in Barth, ed., *Ethnic Groups and Boundaries: The Social Organization of Cultural Difference* (Boston: 1969), esp. 9–15. Barth's theoretical work is of crucial importance for our topic.

[183] While I place no confidence in the probative force of etymological arguments, it is, perhaps, of interest to note that *an, the hypothetical root of the Germanic-English, "other," contains the notion of duality: the second or other member of a pair, e.g. Anglo-Saxon, ōðer. (J. Pokorny, *Indogermanisches etymologisches Wörterbuch* [Bern-Munich: 1959–69], 1:37–8). *Al, the hypothetical root of the Greco-Roman *alien* and the Germanic-English, "else," contains the notion in extended form, the other of more than two (Pokorny, *Wörterbuch*, 1: 24–6).

[184] A. J. Toynbee, *A Study of History* (Oxford: 1961), 12: 11. Cf. the delicious comment in H. W. Turner's *Commentary on Otto's Idea of the Holy* (Aberdeen: 1974), 19, "when Otto describes this experience of the Numen as 'Wholly Other,' he cannot mean *wholly* 'Wholly Other.' "

The "otherness" of the common housefly can be taken for granted, but it is also impenetrable. For this reason, its "otherness" is of no theoretical interest.[185] While the "other" may be perceived as being either LIKE-US or NOT-LIKE-US, he is, in fact, most problematic when he is TOO-MUCH-LIKE-US, or when he claims to BE-US. It is here that the real urgency of a "theory of the other" emerges. This urgency is called forth not by the requirement to place the "other," but rather to situate ourselves. It is here, to invoke the language of a theory of ritual, that we are not so much concerned with the drama of "expulsion," but with the more mundane and persistent processes of "micro-adjustment."[186] This is not a matter of the "far," but, preeminently, of the "near." The problem is not alterity, but similarity—at times, even identity. A "theory of the other" is but another way of phrasing a "theory of the self."

In the examples discussed above, the parasite was the object of intense theoretical interest not merely because it was "there," but because it invaded intimate human space. The parasite was apart from and yet a part of our personal bodily environment.[187] So too, with the "Indian"—although matters here are neccessarily more complex. The aboriginal Amerindian became a figure of high theoretical interest only when he was gradually thought of as being "in-between"— neither the well-known though exotic citizen of the fabled "Indies," nor a separate species of man (as in Linnaeus's remarkable proposal to establish the types: *Homo americanus, Homo monstrosus patagonici,* and *Homo monstrosus plagiocephali* to describe three forms of Amerindians).[188] Rather, especially in the latter half of the eighteenth century, he became a figure of intense and long-lasting speculation precisely to the degree that Amerindian culture was seen as revelatory

[185] See, however, the stunning exception in the work of the biologist, Johannes von Uexküll. In his work (published with the collaboration of the artist, G. Krizat), *Streifzüge durch die Umwelten von Tieren und Menschen: Ein Bilderbuch* (Berlin: 1934), he begins with a "tick's eye view of the world" (pp. 1–2, 8–9) and procedes to present several pictures as they would appear *für die Menschen* and *für die Fliege* (fig. 11c [p. 24], fig. 15 [p. 29], fig. 31 [p. 58], fig. 32 [p. 62]).

[186] I owe the phrase, "micro-adjustment," to C. Lévi-Strauss's formulation of ritual as processes of *micro-péréquation,* in *La pensée sauvage* (Paris: 1962), 17.

[187] This intimacy is well symbolized by two closely related folk beliefs, that of the "heart worm" carried in each individual's heart from birth; and the worm which serves as "life-index," when it dies, its human host dies as well. See, H. Pagenstecher, *Vermes* (Leipzig: 1878–93), 1: 38; R. Hoeppli, *Parasites and Parasitic Infections,* 64, 160.

[188] C. Linnaeus, *Systema natura,* 10th ed. (Holmiae: 1758) as cited in T. Bendyshe, "On the Anthropology of Linnaeus," *Memoirs of the Anthropological Society of London,* 1 (1863–4), 424–5.

of the European's own past.[189] "In the beginning," to cite John Locke, "all the world was America."[190]

By way of conclusion, this may be pressed in a direction closer to the explicit theme of this conference. Due to the emergent disciplines of anthropology, history of religions and the like, we know of thousands of societies and world views which are "different," but in most cases, their "remoteness" guarantees our indifference. By and large, Christians and Jews qua Christians and Jews have not thought about the "otherness" of the Kwakiutl or, for that matter, of the Taoist. The bulk of Christian theoretical thinking about "otherness" (starting with Paul) has been directed toward "other Christians" and, more occasionally, towards those groups thought of as being "near-Christians," preeminently Jews and Muslims. Today, as in the past, the history of religious conflicts, of religious perceptions of "otherness" is largely intraspecific: Buddhists to Buddhists, Christians to Christians, Muslims to Muslims, Jews to Jews. The only major exceptions occur in those theoretically unrevealing but historically common moments when "proximity" becomes more a matter of territoriality than of thought.

A "theory of the other" rarely depends on the capacity "to see ourselves as others see us." By and large, "we" remain indifferent to such refractions. Rather, it would appear to imply the reverse. A "theory of the other" requires those complex political and linguistic projects necessary to enable us to think, to situate, and to speak of "others" in relation to the way in which we think, situate, and speak about ourselves.

---

[189] This has been the special burden of the important monograph by R. L. Meek, *Social Science and the Ignoble Savage* (Cambridge: 1976).
[190] This quotation, from the second of John Locke's *Two Treatises of Government* (P. Laslett, ed. [New York: 1965], 343) appears as a major theme in Meek's book, cited above.

2

Otherness Within: Towards A Theory Of Difference in Rabbinic Judaism

William Scott Green
University of Rochester

In his book *Primordial Characters* Rodney Needham notes that "it is a frequent report from different parts of the world that tribes call themselves alone by the arrogant title 'man,' and that they refer to neighboring peoples as monkeys or crocodiles or malign spirits."[1] At first glance, this widespread ethnographic fact might seem to reduce any society's theory of others to a declaration of its superiority over and its separation from surrounding peoples, to a means of affirming that "we" are completely human, but "they" are not. Many cultural theories of the other surely do serve the purposes of self-affirmation and boundary building, but even brief reflection should suggest that the problem of conceiving the other is more complex than that. Indeed, with some slight exegesis, Needham's statement itself can serve as a useful template for that complexity.

First, that peoples universally entitle themselves and others points to an important semantic component in any theory of the other. The very act of naming, "the capacity to nominate others as equal or unequal, animate or inanimate, memorable or abject, discussor or discussed," is evidence of a society's sense of its singularity.[2] The language a society uses and the terminology it invents to describe and classify those besides itself, along with the social action such language entails, are primary clues to its self-understanding. Second, that the peoples designated as "them" are so often neighbors highlights the component of social proximity in any society's conception of the other. Devising a notion of the other is clearly requisite to the establishment of any society and is as much a matter of imagination as of confrontation; as James Boon observes, ". . . any culture requires its actors to counterdistinguish themselves, irreducibly segmented, from others:

---

[1] Rodney Needham, *Primordial Characters* (Charlottesville, Va.: 1978), p. 5.
[2] David Parkin, "Introduction," in *Semantic Anthropology*, ed. David Parkin (London: 1982), p. xlvi.

other worlds (divine, extraterrestrial), other eras (past idylls, future utopias), other languages, other cultures."[3] But when multiple groups inhabit the same or adjoining space and when they are too much alike, the specification of difference is an urgent necessity. The most critical feature of otherness thus presupposes familiarity and reciprocity, and perhaps resemblance, between and among groups. Finally, the terms "monkeys, crocodiles, and malign spirits" suggest that any theory of the other is an exercise in caricature. The neighboring peoples, after all, are not really crocodiles (any more than the ones who call them that are really "man"), but some trait of their collective life makes the label fitting and plausible to those who invent it.

A theory of the other can represent at best only a partial vision and a feat of exaggeration, but it also constitutes, dialectically, an act of appropriation. The neighboring peoples do not establish themselves as others; they do not call themselves "crocodiles." Rather, they are so contrived by someone else. A society does not simply discover its others, it fabricates them by selecting, isolating, and emphasizing an aspect of another people's life and making it symbolize their difference. To evoke the significant disparity of which otherness is composed, the symbol must correspond powerfully to the naming society's sense of its own distinctiveness. In the terms of our example, "crocodile" is not, and cannot be, a neutral or arbitrary label. To be revealing and meaningful, it must reach inside the culture of the people who employ it, correlate to some piece of themselves that they believe prominently displays who they are, and induce response, perhaps fear or disgust, but also perhaps envy or respect. The construction of a theory of the other thus involves a double metonymy and a double distortion. In creating its others, a society confuses some part of its neighbor with its neighbor, and a piece of itself with itself, and construes each in terms of the other. Although designed to mark and certify divergence and discontinuity, such correspondences can forge enduring reciprocal patterns of the inside and the outside. They can reshape the naming society's picture of itself, expose its points of vulnerability, and spark in it awareness of, or reflection about, the possibility or the reality of otherness within. The boastful proposition "we are men and they are crocodiles" implies that "we were, or could have been, or might yet be crocodiles too."

It therefore is an oversimplification to suppose that theories of the other serve merely or mainly to erect cultural boundaries and maintain social distance, that they are designed, so to speak, to keep the

---

[3] James A. Boon, *Other Tribes, Other Scribes: Symbolic Anthropology in the Comparative Study of Cultures, Histories, Religions, and Texts* (Cambridge: 1982), p. 232.

"crocodiles" out. A nuanced reading suggests that such theories also are means by which societies explore their internal ambiguities and interstices, experiment with alternative values and symbols, and question their own structures and mechanisms.[4] Envisioned in this way, our query about theories of the other in rabbinic Judaism should encourage us not to loiter lengthily or to scratch aimlessly around the historical outside, but to inquire purposefully about the cultural inside of the people we study and to ask "how cultures, perfectly commonsensical from within, nevertheless flirt with their own 'alternities,' gain critical self-distance, formulate complex (rather than simply reactionary) perspectives on others, embrace negativities, confront (even admire) what they themselves are *not*."[5]

This approach provides an alternative to the persisting propensity in rabbinic studies to construe ancient Jewry, including its various subdivisions, as a single cultural entity whose members held a reasonably uniform, mutually applied self-understanding that decisively separated them from the definitive others, the non-Jews. Implicitly or explicitly, such work tends to ground ancient Judaic theories of the other in an analytical category that is best called "Jewish peoplehood." For example, a prominent rabbinic scholar asserts that what made a Jew an outsider "was not slackness in observing the [halakic] precepts, or even alienation from tradition, but the act of denying the election of the Jews: for that act destroys the conceptual basis on which the separate existence of the Jewish people is founded and endangers its survival."[6] Another specialist presses the notion further and argues that since "even the most virulent [sectarian texts from the Second Temple period] never accuse members of other groups of having left the Jewish community,"[7] all such groups probably identified one another as part of the same people. In his words, "Sinners they were, but Jews all the same."[8] Moreover, he suggests that in early rabbinism "no one could be excluded from the Jewish people and lose his Jewish status as result of any beliefs or

---

[4] Ibid., p. 114.

[5] Ibid., p. 19.

[6] E. E. Urbach, "Self-Isolation or Self-Affirmation in Judaism in the First Three Centuries: Theory and Practice," in *Jewish and Christian Self-Definition, Volume Two: Aspects of Judaism in the Greco-Roman Period*, ed. E. P. Sanders (Philadelphia: 1981), p. 292.

[7] L. H. Schiffman, "At the Crossroads: Tannaitic Perspectives on the Jewish-Christian Schism" in *Jewish and Christian Self-Definition, Volume Two. Aspects of Judaism in the Greco-Roman Period*, ed. E. P. Sanders (Philadelphia: 1981), p. 115.

[8] Ibid., p. 116.

actions."[9] Whatever their differences, these two sets of claims represent the position that most ancient Jews shared a common national or religio-ethnic self-definition, that ancient Judaism therefore manifested considerable tolerance of internal dissent, and that in such a context otherness meant being outside "the Jewish community," or bereft of "Jewish identity," or excluded from "the Jewish people." According to this model, one was either in or out; there appears no middle range, no place, as it were, for a Jewish "crocodile".

Of course, it would be foolish to deny that the extreme distinction between Israel and non-Israel, Jew and non-Jew, the pristine "us" and the utterly-beyond-the-pale "them," is a fundamental component of any Judaic theory of the other. Whether we encounter it as Israel *vs.* the nations or Jew *vs.* gentile, this opposition forms a necessary outer limit for, and thus is a constitutive element of, any culture or religion we choose to mark as Jewish. Had there been no nations, Israel would have had to invent them, for without "crocodiles" there can be no "man". But the possession of a fundamental principle of classification does not guarantee its application in a particular circumstance. In the study of culture or religion, as in the study of language, the determination of an underlying system of rules, or the elucidation of a foundational taxonomy, is just the beginning of the work. The story is not complete until we discover how the rules or taxa are used. And within a single culture, religion, or language, the degree to which constitutive rules or taxa become regulative and actually govern thought, speech, and behavior can vary enormously.[10] Different actors in different contexts can apply the rules and taxa with frequencies, subtleties, selectivities, and emphases of sufficient diversity to create the cultural and religious equivalents of dialects and to nearly preclude mutual intelligibility. Therefore, in the study of ancient Judaic theories of the other, it is no axiom that the classification "nations," or "gentiles," is the exclusive, or even the most significant, concrete instance of the general category "other" that every society requires for its own constitution. To revert to our earlier metaphor, although there may indeed be "crocodiles" out there in the swamp, more dangerous ones, camouflaged or hybrid, lurk close by, well inside the village.

This line of inquiry into rabbinic Judaism obliges us to revise or replace the analytical models we normally use to describe ancient rabbis and rabbinism. Categories such as "the Jewish people" are too analytically imprecise and too culturally specific to allow us to see rabbinic materials in terms of our larger and non-rabbinic question,

---

[9] Ibid., p. 139.
[10] Parkin, op. cit., pp. xix-xx.

and the terms we frequently import from the social sciences, such as "sect" or "elite," are too analytically specific and too culturally imprecise to allow ancient rabbis to speak in their own terms. In place of these we require a model that is sufficiently general to place our data in a comparative context, sufficiently explicit to be analytically revealing, and sufficiently flexible to conform to the evidence we have, in the form that we have it. Any scholarly model of rabbis or rabbinism that ignores or denies the documentary divisions within rabbinic literature, that depicts all rabbinic writings as a single, seamless composition, and that requires us to read through or beyond the documents as if they were not there, is suspect.

The evidence for rabbinic Judaism, as we have it, is literary and documentary, comprised of numerous highly technical halakic or exegetical compositions, each with a discrete agenda, discourse, and world-view, but all of which are anonymous, collective, and insular. Even this briefest of sketches precludes the possibility that rabbinic writing is representative of or addressed to "the Jewish people," undifferentiated and broadly construed. Rather, the documents' scholastic shorthand, their numerous and disputatious rabbinic authorities, and their nameless discursive and narrative voices evoke what Brian Stock calls a "textual community."[11] In Stock's exposition, a textual community consists of a relatively small group of literati whose fellowship and communal life is based not on ethnic heritage or doctrinal confession, but on a shared devotion to—perhaps an obsession with—an authoritative text or set of texts. In the life of the community, the text both "structure[s] the internal behavior of the group's members and . . . provide[s] solidarity against the outside world."[12] For the group, the text constitutes a definitive "reference system for both everyday activities and for giving shape to many larger vehicles of explanation."[13] As the "nexus of thought and action,"[14] the text shapes the members' perceptions of social relations, encourages the acting out of specific, textually supported roles, and "edits" their experience.[15] Within such communities, the texts are conceived as vehicles to "complete understanding and effortless communication with God."[16]

Although the textual community is necessarily literate, its foun-

---

[11] Brian Stock, *The Implications of Literacy: Written Language and Models of Interpretation in the Eleventh and Twelfth Centuries* (Princeton: 1983).
[12] Ibid., p. 90.
[13] Ibid., p. 3.
[14] Ibid., p. 101.
[15] Ibid., p. 91.
[16] Ibid., p. 90.

dational document usually is sufficiently well known and assimilated
to obviate the need for its perpetual rehearsal and citation at length.
Even without repetition, and even if physically absent, the text can
continue to regulate the community's life. "As a consequence," Stock
explains, "interaction by word of mouth could take place as a superstructure of an agreed meaning, the textual foundation of behavior
having been entirely internalized. With shared assumptions, the
members were free to discuss, to debate, or to disagree on other
matters, to engage in personal interpretations of the Bible or to some
degree in individualized meditation and worship."[17] Finally, the
textual community defines itself not solely in terms of its possession of
its text, but equally in terms of its particular reading and application of
it.[18]

   This model has two important implications for our inquiry. First,
it suggests that from within a textual community, otherness can be
plotted on a continuum of what we might call "textual proximity"—
not to be confused with geographical proximity—and calculated in
terms of literacy and textuality. At the far end of the spectrum would
be the illiterate, who have no text at all, and at the near end are other
literati who read the community's text improperly or deny its authority altogether. The former are the most dissimilar and the least
troublesome. The latter, however, are the least alien but the most
dangerous, and the community's specification of their otherness thus
should be a primary preoccupation. The second implication concerns
the question of tolerance. Whether a real or putative document, the
text at the center of the community is conceived as a material object.
Our model specifies that the community's members use the text to
structure their behavior and to provide solidarity against the outside
world. By making the limits of its world coextensive with the limits of
the text, and by using the text as a template for perception, understanding, and meaning, a textual community attempts to objectify
knowledge, social relations, indeed, all experience. This process
renders subjectivity implausible or incredible, deflects internal dissent from primary to secondary issues, and makes it nearly impossible
for the community or its members to conceive of themselves as apart
from the text. In a crucial sense, then, textual communities cannot—
and indeed do not want to—see either themselves as others see them
or others as they see themselves. The result is a unidirectional,
irreversible vision that objectifies both the self and others and,
consequently, justifies and encourages neither mutual intelligibility

[17] Ibid., p. 91.
[18] Ibid., p. 88.

among groups nor tolerance of difference.[19] We therefore should expect the worlds of textual communities to be populated with others.

Implicitly and explicitly the literary remains of rabbinic Judaism point to the aptness of the textual community as a model for their analysis. Rabbinic documents, including those that particularly will concern us here (the Mishnah, Tosefta, and Palestinian Talmud), present themselves as the record, if not the work, of small literate communities. Each offers evidence of dispute and debate, and each is centered around and preoccupied with a particular text. For all its literary autonomy and conceptual novelty, the Mishnah "constitutes a vast and detailed account of what a group of men believed Scripture to say and mean."[20] It is, however, a work of creative and independent reflection," a statement *on* the meaning of Scripture, not merely *of* the meaning of Scripture."[21] Likewise, "nearly every discourse" of the Palestinian Talmud "addresses one main point: the meaning of the Mishnah."[22] For the framers of the Palestinian Talmud, the Mishnah was regarded as "constitutive, the text of ultimate concern.[23]. . . the authoritative law code of Israelite life, the center, the focus, the source. From it, all else flows. Beyond the Mishnah is only Scripture."[24]

If the traits just listed constitute implicit but *prima facie* evidence of a textual community, the later rabbinic elaboration of the textual symbol "Torah" provides an explicit ideology of one. At this point in the history of scholarship on rabbinic Judaism, it hardly is dramatic to claim that ancient rabbis understood Israel's possession of Torah (conceived at least as a material document), to be the mark of Israel's distinction among the nations, but regarded themselves as the Torah's sole reliable, and perhaps legitimate, guardians and guarantors. It may be less obvious that from the end of the second century, Torah, although never denoting less than a text, is made to contain a nearly comprehensive range of social and cultural connotations. In later rabbinism, Torah stands not only for a document and its contents, but also "for a kind of human being. It connotes a social status and a sort of social group. It refers to a type of social relationship. It further denotes a legal status and differentiates among legal norms. As

---

[19] Parkin, op. cit., pp. xli, xliii-xliv.

[20] Jacob Neusner, *Judaism: The Evidence of the Mishnah.* (Chicago: 1981).

[21] Ibid., p. 170.

[22] Jacob Neusner, *Judaism in Society: The Evidence of the Yerushalmi* (Chicago: 1983), p. 29.

[23] Ibid., p. 73.

[24] Ibid., p. 76.

symbolic abstraction, the work encompasses things and persons, actions and status, points of social differentiation and legal and normative standing, as well as 'revealed truth' ... Torah stood for salvation and accounted for Israel's this worldly condition and the hope, for both individual and nation alike, of life in the world to come."[25] For rabbinic Judaism, "the word Torah stood for everything. The Torah symbolized the whole, at once and entire."[26] In the terms of our model, this totalized application of a textual symbol constitutes and represents a labor of massive and overwhelming objectification.

Three pertinent implications follow. First, if Torah in rabbinic Judaism is construed as knowledge, and saving knowledge at that, then it will be difficult in a rabbinic context to imagine knowledge as a personal creation or a private possession. Rather Torah, as knowledge, will be conceived as an autonomous object or substance, a precious resource to be acquired, absorbed, and ingested, and then handed on in appropriate way to other appropriate persons. But the acquisition and passing on of Torah can be no casual exercise; it will require uncommon deliberation and unsullied attention. Second, it should follow that the distinction between the possessor of Torah and Torah itself, between subject and object, will be minimized, resulting in a near fusion of the two. On this point the Palestinian Talmud is explicit, for it presents the rabbi as equivalent to a scroll of Torah, "a material, legal comparison, not merely a symbolic metaphor."[27]

Third, seeing Torah as the objectification of knowledge helps to account for rabbinism's distinctive and, in historical context, peculiar discourse of orality and disputation. In the documents rabbis appear not as writers but as speakers; they engage one another face to face, and refer to Scripture and the Mishnah in half-verses and sometimes by allusion. Our model suggests that we understand this portrayal as neither evidence of nor a claim for an oral culture, but as the oral superstructure of a profoundly literate one. This, in turn, allows us to construe the rabbis' contentiousness not as license for dissent, but rather as a means of their intense engagement with one another and with their text. Their rigorous examination of Torah and their often fierce and harsh disagreements about a wide range of halakic and exegetical matters can occur only because of unquestioned and unquestionable shared assumptions about the ultimacy of their text.

---

[25] Jacob Neusner, "Torah: From Scroll to Symbol, *The Case of the Mishnah*," in *Approaches to Ancient Judaism VI*, ed., W. S. Green, (Chico: 1985) [forthcoming].
[26] Ibid.
[27] Neusner, *Judaism in Society*, p. 205.

In rabbinic Judaism, rabbis are expected to reflect continuously and rigorously on their text, to probe deeply into it, but not to think their way out of it.

From this description of Torah as a vehicle of objectification it follows, as our model stipulates, that rabbinic Judaism will manifest little tolerance for alternatives and, in its real or imaginary forays into the world beyond its texts, will encounter a multiplicity of others. The earliest writings of rabbinic Judaism, the Mishnah and its companion-commentary Tosefta, suggest at least this much. Even a cursory survey of those documents reveals not a term or two, but a virtual lexicon of titles employed or devised by rabbis to designate those besides themselves, those, that is, whom they could not trust or whose presence they could not abide. A comprehensive register of such terms would include all those named in Mishnah Sanhedrin Chapters 7-9 and 11 who qualify for execution, whether by stoning, burning, beheading, or strangling—a list of at least thirty items. Most of these terms—including murderer, blasphemer, idolater, Sabbath-violater, beguiler, sorcerer, and so forth—derive from Scripture, the center of the Mishnaic textual community. Whether such figures were present or not, they constitute a part of the Mishnah's semantic universe and are objects of both reflection and legislation. A more conservative and pertinent listing would include those with whom rabbis claim to have had social interaction or those whom they exclude from what we know to be a rabbinic but non-scriptural locative category, the one realm rabbis were certain they controlled, "the World to Come." The former would include the *am haaretz* and the Samaritan (often designated as *kuti,* to emphasize foreign origin). The latter, first from Mishnah Sanhedrin 10:1, are the following: the denier of resurrection of the dead, the denier that the Torah is from heaven, the Epicurean, the reader of outside books, the reciter of charms over wounds, and the pronouncer of God's name with the proper letters. A comparable list, in Tosefta Sanhedrin 13:5, is rather more elaborate. It includes *minim* (usually translated as "heretics" or "sectarians"), *meshummadim* (usually translated as "apostates"), informers, Epicureans, deniers of Torah, separaters from the community, deniers of resurrection from the dead, and sinners who cause the public to sin.

Scholars have attempted to account for several of these titles by seeking evidence of historical—that is, real flesh-and-blood—groups to which these names should be attached.[28] Any serious advance on

[28] For example, see Alan Segal, *Two Powers in Heaven* (Leiden: 1977), Reuven Kimelman, "*Birkat Ha-Minim* and the Lack of Evidence for an Anti-Christian Jewish Prayer in Late Antiquity," in Sanders, op. cit., pp. 226-244, S. Katz, "Issues in the

that research is unlikely. But the work of theorists such as Saussure, Foucault, Levi-Strauss, and Leach[29] has taught us that words are not necessarily representative of things or persons. That insight allows us to understand early rabbinism's lexicon of otherness not simply as a reaction to external political pressures, but as a consequence of internal cultural preoccupations.

Our theory holds that conceiving the other entails a double metonymy, seeing a part of "them" in terms of an essential piece of "ourselves," and our model of textual community makes literacy and textuality the principal determinants of otherness. We therefore ought to be able to understand all or most of the titles on our list of early rabbinism's excluded others in terms of textual proximity. A preliminary effort reads as follows: The *am haaretz*, perhaps the rabbinic equivalent of the medieval *idiotes*, has no text and cannot be trusted.[30] The Samaritan surely has the wrong text, and must be watched. The outsiders write their own texts, and have no part in "us". The Epicurean discards the text. The deniers of resurrection and Torah deny the text. Those who utter charms over wounds, and those who pronounce the name, use the text improperly. The informers expose the text to inappropriate others. The apostates violate the text,[31] and some sinners cause other Jews to do so. Finally, the *minim*, who wear phylacteries,[32] offer sacrifices,[33] and write and read Torah,[34] appropriate our text and pretend to be "us". The *minim* appear to be too close for comfort, and it is hardly accidental that for them early rabbinism reserved the following uncharacteristic and bitter fury:

> The sacrifice of a *min* is idolatry. Their bread is the bread of a Samaritan, and their wine is deemed the wine of idolatry, and their produce is deemed wholly untithed, and their books are deemed magical books, and their children are *mamzerim*. People do not sell anything to them or buy anything from them. And they do not take wives from them or give children in marriage to them. And they do

[29] For useful introductions, see Terence Hawkes, *Structuralism and Semiotics* (Berkeley and Los Angeles: 1977), John Sturrock, ed., *Structuralism and Since* (Oxford: 1979), and Edmund Leach, *Culture and Communication* (Cambridge: 1976).
[30] Stock, op. cit., pp. 27-29.
[31] Tosefta Horayot 1:5.
[32] Mishnah Megillah 4:8.
[33] Tosefta Hullin 1:1.
[34] Tosefta Shabbat 13:5, Tosefta Sanhedrin 8:7. Also Schiffman, op. cit., pp. 153-4 and Katz, op. cit., pp. 56-63.

not teach their sons a craft. And they do not seek assistance from
them, either financial or medical.[35]

In all, it seems that the presence of the *minim* was especially
intolerable, both in this world and the next.

A final point about this list of excluded others merits attention. All
who are denied a place in the World to Come are Jews.[36] That such
status failed to moderate the judgment of their ultimate fate raises
serious doubt about the pervasiveness and power of "Jewish identity"
and "Jewish peoplehood" in early rabbinic Judaism. The materials
considered above, in fact, demonstrate that early rabbis were preoccupied with fixing the boundaries of their own group and that they
devoted extensive linguistic energy to a remarkably detailed elaboration of their own periphery. The precision of that elaboration is
especially telling when contrasted with the documents' failure to
differentiate among gentiles.[37] In the semantic universe they created
for themselves, early rabbis do not appear as leaders or devotees of
"the Jewish people," religiously or ethnically construed, but rather as
a wary and watchful group of Jewish textualists, surrounded from
within. This is the legacy of otherness inherited by the framers of later
rabbinic writings.

We have considered a theory of difference and an analytical model
of rabbinism, and have explored both against a sample of early
rabbinic literary data. To complete this exercise, it will be helpful to
do the same for a specimen of later rabbinic writing. A useful example
is the talmudic picture of Elisha ben Abuyah, an alleged second
century Palestinian rabbi who is characterized in the scholarly literature as the sole rabbinic heretic. Elisha's pertinence to this inquiry,
however, derives not from scholarly interpretation but from native
rabbinic classification. In most rabbinic texts he is called by the
sobriquet *Aher*, "Other". A rabbi labelled by other rabbis as different
is particularly appropriate to any study of the problem of otherness in
rabbinic Judaism. The two principal accounts of Elisha occur in the
Palestinian Talmud (Tractate Hagigah 2:1, beginning at 77b), and in
the Babylonian Talmud (Tractate Hagigah, beginning at 14b). This
paper considers only the first of these. It reads as follows:

A. Four entered a garden.
B. One looked and died; one looked and was smitten; one looked and cut
   the shoots; one entered safely and went out safely.

---

[35] Tosefta Shehitat Hullin 2:20-21.
[36] To be sure, the documents contain discussions of the fate of gentiles, but gentiles are
not included in the lists under discussion. See Tosefta Sanhedrin, 13:2.
[37] See the papers by Porton and Neusner in this volume.

C. Ben Azzai looked and was smitten.

D. Concerning him Scripture says, *If you have found honey, eat only your fill [lest you become filled with it, and vomit]* (Prov. 26:16).

E. Ben Zoma looked and died.

F. Concerning him Scripture says, *Precious in the eyes of the Lord is death to his saints* (Ps. 116:15).

G. Aher looked and cut the shoots.

H. Who is Aher?

I. Elisha ben Abuyah, who would kill the masters of Torah.

J. They say, "Every disciple whom he would see praised in Torah, he would kill him.

K. "And not only that, but he would enter the house of meeting, and he would see young men before the teacher. He would say, 'What are those sitting and doing here? This one's profession [will be] a builder; this one's profession a carpenter; this one's profession a fowler; this one's profession a tailor.'

L. And when they would hear [him speak] so, they would depart from him [their teacher] and go to them [the professions]."

M. Concerning him Scripture says, *Do not let your mouth bring flesh into sin [and do not say before the angel that it is an error; why should God become angry at your voice and ruin your handiwork.]* (Eccl. 5:5).

N. —for he ruined the handiwork of that very same man [= his own].

O. Even in the hour of persecution they [the Romans] would make them [the Jews] carry burdens [on the Sabbath].

P. And they [the Jews] intended [that] two would carry one burden, on account of [the principle that] two who perform a single labor [on the Sabbath are exempt from a sin-offering].

Q. He said, "Make them carry them singly."

R. They [the Romans] went and made them carry them singly.

S. They [the Jews] intended to deliver them [their burdens] in a *karmalit*, so as not to [violate the Sabbath law and] bring [something] out from the private domain to the public domain.

T. He said, "Let them carry them straight through [from the private to the public domain]."

U. They [the Romans] went and made them carry them straight through.

V. R. Aqiba entered safely and went out safely.

W. Concerning him Scripture says, *Draw me, let us run after you; [the king has brought me into his chambers.]* (Song 1:4).

1. R. Meir was sitting expounding in the house of study of Tiberias.

2. Elisha, his master, passed, riding on a horse on the Sabbath day.

3. They came and said to him, "Behold, your master is outside."

4. He stopped his exposition and went out to him.

5. He said to him, "What were you expounding today?"

6. He said to him, "*And the Lord blessed the end of Job's life more than the beginning* (Job 42:12)."

7. He said to him, "And how did you begin it?"

8. He said to him, "*And the Lord doubled all Job's possessions* (Job 42:10)—for he doubled all his property."
9. He said, "Alas for what is lost and not found.
10. "Aqiba your master would not have expounded so, rather,
11. "*And the Lord blessed. . .*(Job. 42:12)—By the merit of the commandments that were in his hand from his beginning [= that he performed from the beginning of his life]."
12. He said to him, "And what more have you been expounding?"
13. He said to him, "*The end of a thing is better than its beginning* (Eccl. 7:8)."
14. He said to him, "And how did you begin it?"
15. He said to him, "To a man who begat children in his youth, and they died, and in his old age they were replaced [for him], lo, *The end of a thing is better than its beginning* (Eccl. 7:8).
16. "To a man who produced goods in his youth, and lost [them], and in his old age profited, lo, *The end of a thing is better than its beginning* (Eccl. 7:8).
17. "To a man who studied Torah in his youth and forgot it, and in his old age recovered it, lo, *The end of a thing is better than its beginning* (Eccl. 7:8)."
18. He said, "Alas for what is lost and not found.
19. "Aqiba your master would not have expounded so, rather,
20. "*The end of a thing is better than its beginning* (Eccl. 7:8)—when it is good from its beginning.
21. "And to me the [following] incident [occurred]:
22. "Abuyah, my father, was among the notables of Jerusalem.
23. "On the day that came to circumcise me, he invited all the notables of Jerusalem and seated them in one house,
24. "And R. Eliezer and R. Joshua in one house.
25. "And when they had eaten and drunk, they began to clap hands and dance.
26. "Said R. Liezer to R. Joshua, 'Since they are occupied with theirs, let us be occupied with ours.'
27. "And they sat and occupied themselves with the words of Torah,
28. "from the Torah to the Prophets, and from the Prophets to the Writings.
29. "And fire descended from heaven and surrounded them.
30. "Abuyah said to them, 'My masters, have you come to burn [down] my house upon me?'
31. "They said to him, 'Heaven forfend! Rather, we were sitting and reciting the words of Torah,
32. "from the Torah to the Prophets, and from the Prophets to the Writings,
33. "and the words were as bright as at their delivery from Sinai.'
34. "And the fire lapped them as it lapped them from Sinai."
35. "And the origin of their delivery from Sinai [is that] they were delivered only in fire,
36. "*And the mountain burned with fire to the heart of heaven* (Deut. 4:11).

37. "Abuyah, my father, said to them, 'If such is the power of Torah, if this son survives for me, I [will] dedicate him to Torah.'

38. "Because his intention was not for the sake of heaven, therefore they [the words of Torah] were not established in that man [= me, Elisha]."

39. He said to him, "And what else did you expound?"

40. He said to him, "*Gold and glass cannot be compared to it, nor can it be exchanged for work of fine gold* (Jb. 28:17)."

41. He said to him, "And how did you begin it?"

42. He said to him, "The words of Torah are as difficult to acquire as vessels of gold and as easy to lose as vessels of glass.

43. "And just as vessels of gold and vessels of glass, if they are broken, he [their owner] can return and make them vessels as [they were] at the outset, so a disciple who forgot his learning, he can return and study it as at the beginning."

44. He said to him, "Enough, Meir, until here is the Sabbath limit."

45. He said to him, "How do you know?"

46. He said to him, "From the hoofs of my horse, for I have been counting, and he has gone two thousand cubits."

47. He said to him, "And you have all this wisdom, and you do not return?"

48. He said to him, "I cannot."

49. He said to him, "Why?"

50. He said to him, "For once I was passing before the House of the Holy of Holies, riding on my horse, on the Day of Atonement that fell on the Sabbath, and I heard a *bat qol* go out from the House of the Holy of Holies, and it says, "Return, O children!—except for Elisha ben Abuyah,

51. 'who knew my power and rebelled against me.' "

52. And whence did all this come to him [= How did all this happen to him?]

53. Rather, once he was sitting and studying in Bikat Ginisar and he saw one man go up to the top of the palm tree and take a dam [from] upon the fledglings, and he [the man] descended from there in peace.

54. The next day he saw another man who went up to the top of the palm tree and take the fledglings and send the mother away, and he came down from there, and a serpent bit him and he died.

55. He said, "It is written, *You shall surely send the dam away and take the fledglings for yourself, so that it may be good for you and lengthen your days* (Deut. 22:7).

56. "Where is the good of this?

57. "Where is the length of days of this?"

58. And he did not know that R. Jacob had expounded before him,

59. . . . *so that it may be good for you* (Deut. 22:7)—[This refers] to the World to Come, which is wholly good.

60. . . . *and lengthen your days* (Deut. 22:7)—[This refers] to the future [world], which is wholly long.

61. And there are those who say [that it was] because

62. he saw the tongue of R. Judah haNahtom, dripping blood, in the mouth of a dog.

63. He said, "This is Torah, and this is its reward?

64. "This is the tongue that would give forth words of Torah flawlessly.

65. "This is the tongue that was concerned with Torah all its days.

66. "This is Torah, and this is its reward?

67. "It seems that there is no reward and no resurrection of the dead."

68. And there are those who say [that]

69. his mother, when she was pregnant with him, was passing by temples of idolatry and smelled [the smell of their] kind [of incense], and the odor penetrated her body like the venom of a snake."

70. After several days, Elisha became ill.

71. They came and said to R. Meir, "Behold, your master is ill."

72. He went, wanting to visit him, and found him ill.

73. He said to him, "Do you not repent?"

74. He said to him, "And if they repent, are they received?"

75. He said to him, "Is it not written, *You return man to dust* (Ps. 90:3)?— Until the soul is crushed, they accept [repentance]."

76. In that very hour Elisha wept, and departed [from the world], and died.

77. And R. Meir was happy in his heart.

78. And he said, "It seems that in the midst of repentance my master died."

79. After they buried him, fire descended from heaven and burned his grave.

80. They came and said to R. Meir, "Behold, the grave of your master is on fire."

81. He went out, wanting to visit it, and found it on fire.

82. What did he do?

83. He took up his prayer cloak and spread it upon it.

84. He said, "*Sleep through the night, and in the morning, if he redeems you, well, let him redeem you; and if he does not want to redeem you, I swear by the Lord, I will redeem you* (Ruth 3:13).—

85. "*Sleep* (Ruth 3:13)—in this world, for it resembles night.

86. "*in the morning* (Ruth 3:13)—This is the World to Come, which is wholly morning.

87. "*If he redeems you, well, let him redeem you* (Ruth 3:13)—This is the Holy One, Blessed be He, for he is good,

88. "for it is written of him, *The Lord is good to all, and his mercies are over all his works* (Ps. 145:9).

89. "*And if he does not want to redeem you, I swear by the Lord, I will redeem you* (Ruth 3:13)."

90. And it [the fire] was extinguished.

91. They said to R. Meir, "If they say to you in that world, whom do you want to bring near, your father or your master, [what will you do]?

92. He said to them, "I [will] bring my master first and my father afterwards."

93. They said to him, "And will they listen to you?"

94. He said to them, "And have we not learned thus:

95. "They save the book chest with the book, the phylactery bag with the phylacteries?

96. "They save Elisha, Aher, by the merit of his Torah."
97. After [several] days, his [Elisha's] daughters went to collect charity from Rabbi.
98. Rabbi decreed [no], and he said, *"Let there be no one to extend him kindness, and let no one be generous to his orphaned offspring* (Ps. 109:12)?"
99. They said to him, Rabbi, do not look at his deeds, look at his Torah."
100. At that very hour Rabbi wept and decreed that they be supported.
101. He said, "If this is what one who labors at Torah not for its own sake produces—one who labors at Torah for its own sake—how much the moreso!"

The text is long, interesting, and quite rich, and a comprehensive textual, literary, and historical analysis is impossible here. The following remarks concentrate on those elements that address the question of theories of the other in rabbinic Judaism. For that purpose, we need to explore the text with four questions in mind: What, from the point of view of the text, made Elisha into an outsider, an "other," an *aher*? How does the text account for him? What are the consequences of his "otherness"? Finally and most important, why is the story told at all?

At the outset, one brief literary observation is apposite. The passage easily can be divided into two large segments, which are differentiated below by letters and numbers. There is good reason to suppose that the segment I-U, which is interpolated into the well known passage of Tosefta Hagigah 2:3-4, was composed independently of the lengthy narrative of 1-101.[38] Although perhaps not a pristine unity, that narrative clearly has received considerable editorial attention. But since the long narrative of 1-101 assumes that Elisha is known to the reader, since I-U constitutes an explicit introduction of him, and since the two segments are presented in direct sequence, it is plausible to suppose that some redactor expected them to be read together, as a piece. Let us now turn to the text.

At I-J, Elisha is baldly cast as a murderer, a killer of masters and disciples of Torah. At K-L he dissuades young men from the study of Torah and urges them into practical professions. M appears to take this as an act of leading others into sin, and N assures the reader that Elisha was the principal victim of his own behavior. Since the Palestinian Talmud understands the rabbi as "Torah incarnate,"[39] in I-N Elisha is also the destroyer of the text, the wrecker of Torah's

---

[38] For a full analysis of the Toseftan passage, see David J. Halpern, *The Merkabah in Rabbinic Literature* (New Haven: 1980).

[39] See Neusner, *Judaism in Society*.

present and its future. Then at O-U Elisha is depicted as an informer, who exposes the details of Torah to the Romans and thus forces the Jews into serious acts of Sabbath violation.

The long narrative that attempts to account for Elisha's treachery and to describe his fate begins at line 1. It is introduced at lines 1-4 with the curious image of Rabbi Meir interrupting his Sabbath sermon to accompany his teacher Elisha and engage in exegetical discussion. Elisha passes the house of study riding a horse, an act that, if not strictly prohibited in all Palestinian rabbinic circles, surely is starkly unconventional for anyone trained in Torah. The exchanges between them at lines 5-21 accomplish two purposes. First, they set the stage for Elisha's autobiographical account of his circumcision at lines 21-38 by having Elisha insist that a good end depends on a good beginning. Of equal significance, they begin to establish Elisha's own expertise in Torah, for at lines 10 and 19 he chides Meir for forgetting or not knowing what his teacher, Aqiba, taught. Since in rabbinic imagination Aqiba is a much admired figure, the association of him with Elisha is hardly trivial.

At lines 21-38 Elisha recounts the story of the day of his circumcision and his father's disingenuous dedication of him to Torah. Interestingly, Eliezer and Joshua, the two rabbis, are seated separately from the other notables and at line 26 they engage one another and their text while the rest of the company rejoices at the circumcision. The distinction between the rabbinic "us" and the laymen's "them" is explicit at line 26, and is underscored by Abuyah's incomprehension of the heavenly sign of delight in the rabbis' Torah at line 30. For our purposes, however, the important point comes at line 38, which blames Abuyah's impure motives for the failure of Torah to take root in his son.

Lines 39-43 contain another exegetical exchange, but now the focus has shifted from the question about the beginning of life to a concern about its end, and at line 43 Meir raises the theme of return to, and recovery of, Torah.

The brief exchange at lines 44-46 exhibits a stunning reversal. While urging his teacher to return to and reacquire Torah, Meir forgets it himself and must be prevented by Elisha from violating the Sabbath limit. Meir's question at line 45, "How do you know?", is thus at least as defensive as it is curious. Elisha's answer betrays irony because his horse, the very instrument of his unrabbinic behavior, is the means he uses to defend the sanctity of the Sabbath day.

Meir's question at line 47 could not be more fitting: "And you have all this wisdom, and you do not return?" Elisha's answer is straightforward. Because he knew God's power and rebelled against him—in rabbinic terms, because he knew Torah and deliberately violated it—even the possibility of his repentance is definitively foreclosed by Heaven.

Line 52 introduces the Talmud's attempt to understand Elisha's alienation from Heaven, and lines 53-69 offer three explanations. At lines 53-60 Elisha witnesses an unmistakable and concrete disconfirmation of a scriptural promise.[40] Lines 61-67 present a comparable circumstance, and Elisha implicitly denies the power of Torah and explicitly denies resurrection of the dead. Both segments offer cases in which experience contradicts Torah and leads Elisha to think his way out of the text and to renounce its efficacy. By contrast, lines 68-69 depict his alienation from Torah as the result of his mother's accidental encounter with idolatry.

At lines 70-89 we turn to the consequences of Elisha's behavior. He becomes ill, and Meir arrives to urge his repentance and to affirm its attainability (lines 73-75). Whether or not Elisha actually repents at line 76 is unclear, but Meir takes his tears as evidence of a decisive change of heart (ll. 77-78). It makes no difference in any case, because Heaven's negative judgment, which we saw at line 51, is confirmed when fire descends to consume Elisha's grave (line 79). The scene at lines 79-90 must constitute one of the most poignant passages in rabbinic literature. In a gesture of unremitting loyalty to his teacher, and a clear demonstration of ancient rabbis' conception of their own power, Meir contravenes heaven's verdict. Through an exegesis of Ruth 3:13, which he allows to speak for him without elaboration at line 89, he vows that if God refuses to do so he himself will redeem Elisha in the World to Come. At line 90 the heavenly sentence is lifted.

Lines 91-101 explain both the reason for Meir's action and for Heaven's decision. In answer to a question about whom he would save first in the World to Come, Meir replies, in standard rabbinic fashion, that his teacher would precede his natural father. His questioners are incredulous, and he answers them with a citation of Mishnah Shabbat 16:1. Elisha is likened to a container of Torah books or of phylacteries. Since on the Sabbath they are saved from fire because of their contents, so Elisha is brought into the World to Come on account of his. The same rationale is repeated in the exchange between Judah the Patriarch and Elisha's daughters at lines 97-101. Despite his willful misdeeds, Elisha is saved, not on account of repentance, but because of the Torah that is in him.

[40] See Mishnah Hullin 12:1-5 and Tosefta Shehitat Hullin. Lines 54-60 resemble Tosefta Shehitat Hullin 10:16.

We saw earlier that the framers of the Palestinian Talmud inherited from the Mishnah and Tosefta an elaborate set of categories for marking otherness. In the narrative Elisha falls into at least three, and probably four of them. He is an informer, a sinner who causes others to sin, a denier of resurrection from the dead, and probably a denier of Torah. Any one of these should prohibit him from a place in World to Come; any one would represent a definitive sign of otherness. But, while Elisha richly earns the label "other," the framers of the text refuse to apply it to him. He is an "other," but the Talmud will not let him occupy that status. The problem now is to understand how and why the text accomplishes this remarkable result.

According to our theory and model, the members of a textual community possess a flat and one-dimensional vision of the world beyond their text; they have no "thick" perception. Their text shapes, limits, and objectifies their experience of the outside and establishes categories of otherness that can never be more than caricatures. A denier of Torah is only that, and no more. The "other" is only a "crocodile;" nothing else about him needs to be known. The outsider merits neither understanding nor appreciation, just proper indentification and labelling. To overcome this perceptual barrier, the received textual categories must be upset and the expectations they generate thwarted. Our text achieves that goal with Elisha ben Abuyah in two ways.

First, it offers no consistent picture of him. He is both a committer of heinous crimes and a master of Torah. He interrupts a Sabbath sermon, yet teaches Torah to his student. He violates Torah, yet ends in the World to Come. In all, he hangs in the interstices of rabbinism, sometimes in and sometimes out. In some cultural settings such liminality might make Elisha a witch or a trickster. But in the context of the rabbinic textual community, this figuration serves to reveal more than one side of him and to enhance his subjectivity.

This fuller vision is especially evident in the text's incapacity to provide a uniform explanation of Elisha's deviance. Two of the accounts, as we saw, place the responsibility squarely on Elisha. His experience belies the Torah, and he reasons his way to a rejection of the text. But the two other accounts present him as a victim. His mother, quite by accident, affects him in the womb. His father, through improper designs, guarantees before the fact that Elisha will follow another path. So Elisha is both accountable and not, deserving of rejection and not.

Second, the text highlights Elisha's subjectivity by presenting his circumstance not only from the textual point of view, but also from his

own. The unusual autobiographical story of the day of his circumcision and his telling of the *bat qol* that denies him the possibility of
repentance both depict him as he sees himself. These accounts, along
with his repeated exchanges with Meir, make him an interesting,
somewhat complex, and even sympathetic character.

But a textual community would prefer not to manipulate its
categories and not to undercut its texts, so the reasons for doing so
must be pressing indeed. Again, we must return to our model.
However closely bound its members are to one another and to their
text, a textual community is not a tribe. Ethnicity will not serve to
define it or defend it. The text, to be sure, is conceived as a material
object. It stands at the center of the community and also delimits its
periphery. To remain authoritative, it must be a source of continual
study, reflection and intellectual engagement. If one can enter the
community through its text, however, one can depart from it in the
same way. The walls of a textual community are, in principle, scalable
and vulnerable. But if one can depart from the text, and the text, once
acquired, can depart from him, then the text's ultimacy, primacy, and
constitutive character are corrupted and diminished. It is one thing to
declare as "other" someone who is outside the text to begin with. It is
quite something else to declare that one who had the text from the
beginning can be on the outside. To do so makes the text a victim of
subjectivity, reduces its stature, and destroys it as the community's
center. This can explain why talmudic narrators are prepared to
relativize Elisha, to humanize him, but ultimately revert to the model
of Torah as objectified knowledge. In Meir's response to his questioners, he likens Elisha to a chest of books or a bag of phylacteries—
hardly a personal image. Likewise, Elisha's daughters urge Rabbi to
forget their father's deeds, to ignore the behaviors that made him
distinctive, and to remember instead his Torah, knowledge that is
hardly peculiar to him.[41]

Thus, Elisha ben Abuyah, whose deeds make him an outsider, is
preserved by talmudic narrators as an insider because the consequences of letting him out are too severe. And because they keep him
inside, they can use him as a vehicle to test the boundaries of their
textual community and to sort out the internal ambiguities of their
own culture. Whatever the historical reality of this figure, this talmudic account of Elisha ben Abuyah answers the question, "What

---

[41] For other analyses of this passage see A. Büchler, "Die Erlosung Elisa b. Abujahs aus
dem Hollenfeuer" *MGWJ* 76 (1932), 412-56, and A.P. Hayman "Theodicy in Rabbinic
Judaism" in *Transactions of the Glasgow University Oriental Society* 26 (1978), 28-43.

would happen if . . . .?" It is an experiment of intellect and emotion that explores a most dangerous, destructive circumstance and renders it nugatory. A necessary cultural exercise, it allows the textual community, from inside the safety of the text, to experience the most threatening kind of otherness, the otherness within.[42]

---

[42] My thanks are due to Professors Jonathan Z. Smith, F.J. Poole, Gary G. Porton, Ayalah Gabriel, Gerald Bond, and Jacob Neusner for their critical comments and observations.

TWO
Defining Difference: The First Century

3

Revealed Wisdom as a Criterion for Inclusion and Exclusion: From Jewish Sectarianism to Early Christianity

George W. E. Nickelsburg
University of Iowa

My topic touches on one of the ironies in the history of Western religions. Christianity arose as a relative latecomer among the sects and groups in post-Exilic Judaism; however, within a few decades the churches, which were now composed largely of gentiles, were claiming that they alone were the true embodiment of the Israelite religion that had given birth to them. The irony is twofold. A young, upstart group whose membership had rapidly and radically changed was asserting that it was more authentic than its parent group. And this attitude of superiority and exclusivism was derived, in part, from ideas and attitudes already present in the parent body.

In this paper I shall discuss two issues. The first is a matter of authority: the early Christians, and some Jews before them, based their exclusivistic stance on the claim that they had received divine revelation. The second issue relates to the conclusions drawn from this claim: divine authority could not be controverted; people who held a contradictory position were ipso facto wrong and, hence, excluded from the community of the saved.

My paper divides into two parts. First, I shall discuss Jewish texts in which revelation or revealed wisdom is a criterion for inclusion and exclusion from the community of the saved. In the second part I shall survey a selection of New Testament texts that reflect a similar viewpoint. The Jewish and Christian texts express this viewpoint not by means of a single word or root (e.g., ἀποκαλύπτω), but through a variety of words and expressions which we shall note.[1]

---

[1] See Morton Smith ("On the History of APOKALYPTO and APOKALYPSIS," in David Hellholm, ed., *Apocalypticism in the Mediterranean World and the Near East: Proceedings of the International Colloquium on Apocalypticism, Uppsala, August 12—17, 1979* [Tübingen: J. C. B. Mohr, 1983] 9—20), who rightly contests the idea that the

A. Jewish Literature

1. Torah, Wisdom, and the Wise Teacher in Ben Sira

We can profitably discuss claims of revealed divine authority in the context of Joshua ben Sira's wisdom theology. In chapter 24, he asserts that divine Wisdom is resident in the Torah and is the source of Life—the blessing of the covenant. For Ben Sira, this Wisdom is channeled to the pious Israelite through the teaching of sages like himself, and he likens such teaching to prophecy (vv. 32—33). In chapter 39, Ben Sira stresses the crucial role of the sage. He devotes himself to the study of the Torah, the wisdom of the ancients, prophecies, and parables (vv. 1—3). When he prays and makes proper confession of his sins, the Lord "fills him with a spirit of understanding" so that he can "pour forth words of wisdom (σοφία)" (vv. 5—7). Thus, he will "reveal (ἐκφανεῖ) instruction in his teaching" of "the Law of the Lord's covenant" (v. 8). In short, life-giving Wisdom resides in the Torah, and God reveals this to his people through his inspired sages.

2. Revealed Wisdom According to the Books of Enoch

a. The Epistle of Enoch

The collection of writings known as 1 Enoch is also concerned with divinely revealed wisdom, but there are crucial differences from Ben Sira's theology. I shall begin with the last major division of 1 Enoch, the so-called Epistle of Enoch (chapters 92—105). This section was composed either in the early decades of the second century B.C.E., around the time of Ben Sira, or around the end of the century during the reign of John Hyrcanus or Alexander Janneus.[2] In either case, we can determine in some detail the kind of historical circumstances that formed the context of this work. The author depicts a sharp division in Israel with social, economic, and religious dimensions. The rich and the mighty, called "the sinners," are oppressing the poor, whom the author designates "the righteous." Serious religious differences also divide "the righteous" and "the pious" from their opponents. This latter situation is of interest to us here.

In chapters 98:9—99:10, the author contrasts two types of people:

Greek words, (ἀποκαλύπτω) and ἀποκάλυψις, have a technical meaning referring to divine revelation.

[2] On the date, see George W. E. Nickelsburg, *Jewish Literature Between the Bible and the Mishnah* (Philadelphia: Fortress, 1981) 149-50. My analysis of the Epistle here is, in part, a condensation of my article, "The Epistle of Enoch and the Qumran Literature, *JJS* 33 (1982; Fs. for Yigael Yadin) 333—48.

the "fools . . . do not listen to the wise," and they will be damned
(98:9); others "listen to the words of the wise . . . and do the
commandments of the Most High . . . and they will be saved" (99:10).
In opposition to the wise sages of the author's own persuasion are the
false teachers. They "alter the words of truth and pervert the eternal
covenant and consider themselves to be innocent" (99:2). They
"annul the words of the righteous" (98:14) and they "write lying
words and words of error. . . and lead many astray with their lies"
(98:15). Their activity is tantamount to idolatry (99:1). The issue in
this religious controversy is the interpretation of divine Law. At stake
are the salvation and damnation of the respective groups, for the
differences in interpretation are matters of Truth and Falsehood, true
religion and idolatry.

The situation described by the author of the Epistle is placed in
historical and eschatological perspective in the Apocalypse of Weeks
(93:1—10; 91:11—17). After the Exile, in the seventh week, "a
perverse generation arises." At the end of this week, the elect are
chosen from Israel, the chosen root. "Sevenfold wisdom and knowledge is given to them (hkmh wmd' ttyh[b lhwn])," and they execute
judgment, uprooting the foundations of violence and the structure of
deceit that characterize the perverse generation. Here several things
are noteworthy. The time is in some sense "the end"; it is the seventh
week. The perversity of this generation parallels the activity of those
who "alter" the truth. "Wisdom" is revealed and is salvific in function; it is given by God to "the chosen" for the purpose of defeating
the falsehood or deceit that damns.

What is the content of this revealed wisdom? To begin with, the
author appears to be making reference to opposing interpretations of
the Mosaic Torah. Precisely what laws the false teachers allegedly
pervert and misinterpret, and how they do so, we do not know. The
author speaks only of the fact of this misinterpretation, not of its
content.

Although revealed wisdom includes the true interpretation of the
Mosaic Torah, such wisdom is epitomized in the Enochic corpus
itself. According to 104:10—13, which is an interpretation of the
Apocalypse of Weeks, Enoch knows two mysteria, two revealed
secrets about the end time.[3] Sinners will pervert the words of truth.
The books of Enoch and their wisdom (tebab) "will be given"
(δοθήσονται) to the righteous and pious, who will believe in them and
rejoice in the salvation they offer. The Enochic books are the source of

---

[3] See Raymond E. Brown, "The Semitic Background of the New Testament Mysterion,"
Bib 39 (1958) 426—48; 40 (1959) 70-87.

life-giving wisdom in at least two ways. First, the astronomical book reveals information about the structure of the universe and the divinely ordained solar calendar (chaps. 72-82) Second, the Epistle is itself a deposit of wisdom (*tebab*) which Enoch has compiled for his children and their latter-day spiritual descendants (92:1). Its central message about the coming judgment encourages the righteous to keep faith and cling to the hope of salvation, and it warns the sinners that they will be judged and damned for their wicked words and deeds.

If the Enochic books are revealed wisdom, how has this wisdom been given? Here it is important to understand the literary function of the Epistle. These chapters comprise a series of addresses that are based on the revelations recounted in the earlier parts of 1 Enoch. According to chapters 12-16, Enoch ascended to the heavenly throne-room. There he learned of the judgment of the watchers. Subsequent chapters recount his journeys through the cosmos. The function of these journey narratives is evident in the visions that constitute their goal. Enoch sees the places of punishment (chaps. 17—19; 21; 26—27), the place of the dead (chap. 22), and Jerusalem and Paradise (chaps. 28—32). Then he is shown the heavenly tablets. These contain a record of human deeds and their rewards and punishments (81:1-4). Against the background of these cosmic journeys and visions, and in light of the dream visions Enoch had received earlier (chaps. 83-84; 85-90), the angels command him to compile a testimony for his children and their spiritual descendants (81:5-82:3). He does this in chapter 91 and in the Epistle. Enoch guarantees the reality of eternal blessings by referring to his own inspection of the heavenly tablets (103:1—3; cf. 81:1—4). The certainty of the judgment, which is denied by some of the author's enemies,[4] is attested by the existence of the places of judgment and punishment that he saw in his journeys. Since the Enochic works are pseudonymous, we cannot be certain whether the real author is claiming that he himself experienced such visions. In any case, this author validates his message by an appeal to visionary revelation.

Although the author of the Epistle bitterly condemns those who disagree with him and reject the authority of his revelations, he does indicate an openness to outsiders who repent, and he encourages his readers to share his testimony with "the sons of the earth" (105:1; 100:6; cf. 91:14). A similar openness to the gentiles is evident in both

---

[4] See George W. E. Nickelsburg, *Resurrection, Immortality, and Eternal Life in Intertestamental Judaism* (HTS 26; Cambridge/London: Harvard University/Oxford University, 1972) 125—28.

the Book of the Watchers (10:21) and Enoch's second dream vision (90:37—38)[5].

A brief comparison of the theologies of Ben Sira and pseudo-Enoch will underscore their differences. For Ben Sira, the sage mediates life-giving Wisdom through his inspired interpretation of the Torah. However, Ben Sira does not contrast this interpretation with other interpretations that lead to damnation. For the author of the Epistle, on the other hand, such a contrast is essential. Moreover, unlike Ben Sira, who takes a dim view of dreams and visions (34:1-8), pseudo-Enoch asserts the indispensability of the cosmic and calendrical revelations that are central to the Enochic corpus. Those who deny or contradict these interpretations and revelations are courting certain damnation. Finally, Enoch's wisdom has an eschatological dimension. It is God's gift in preparation for the end. One's response results in final and eternal salvation or damnation.

b. 1 Enoch 1—5

1 Enoch 1—5 was probably composed in the third century B.C.E. as an introduction to an early form of the Enochic corpus. Using phrases and forms from the Balaam oracles (esp. Num. 24:15—17) and the Blessing of Moses (cf. Deut. 33:1-2), and making reference to Enoch's heavenly visions and their angelic interpretations, this section announces the coming theophany and the great eschatological judgment that will divide between the sinners and the righteous and chosen.

In language and viewpoint, these chapters parallel the Epistle, especially the Apocalypse of Weeks. The author cites the heavenly bodies and the elements of nature as a paradigm of order. They obey God's created order and do not alter their works. The sinners, by contrast, have changed their deeds and spoken proud and hard words against God's majesty (cf. chap. 101).[6] The reference to the heavenly bodies may indicate that the sinners do not subscribe to the Enochic calendrical views. Concerning the chosen we are told,

---

[5] In his paper for this conference, John J. Collins discusses texts in which observance of the Torah does not appear to be a condition for the salvation of the gentiles. Such observance seems to be presumed in our texts, however, at least in 91:14 and probably in 10:21.

[6] The occurrence of the verbs ἀλλοιόω and ἐξαλλοιόω in chaps. 1—5 and 92—105 is noteworthy in the context of the discussion in this conference. Jonathan Z. Smith notes that one is threatened mainly by "the other" who is not totally different. The use of verbs denoting change suggests that the heart of the criticism lies in the belief that one's opponent has altered what once was held in common. The perceived danger is that the opponent claims to be the authentic representative of the tradition (cf. 99:2).

Then wisdom will be given (δοθήσεται...σοφία) to all the chosen,
   and they will all live;
and they will sin no more
   through wickedness or pride.
And in the enlightened man there will be light,
   and in the wise man, understanding. (5:8)

As in the Epistle, eschatological, God-given wisdom leads to salvation.

c. The Parables of Enoch

The Enochic Book of Parables, chaps. 37-71, is introduced as
eschatological wisdom which Enoch received when he ascended to
heaven and saw visions depicting events relating to the final judgment. The book of eschatological wisdom is now given to the righteous who live in the end time.

The author of the parables is not especially concerned with
religious conflicts among the Jewish residents of Palestine. His
interest parallels a different concern of the Epistle, the coming
judgment. The villains in the Parables are "the kings and the mighty,"
who oppress the houses of the congregations of the righteous and
elect (46:8), reject the sovereignty of their Lord (46:5), and deny the
heavenly realm. The wisdom which Enoch transmits is a heavenly,
eschatological secret, now revealed to the righteous and chosen on
earth.[7] In the "Chosen One" or "son of man," who now stands before
God, they have a heavenly champion, an eschatological savior. He
will deliver them when he sits on the glorious divine throne to judge
the kings and the mighty, and after that they will dwell with him in
eternal joy and glory. Although the author of the Parables focuses on
the conflict between the chosen and righteous and their oppressors,
he does make reference to the repentance of certain "others," who are
evidently not part of this conflict (50:1—3). It is not clear whether
these are other Jews or gentiles.

To summarize my discussion of the books of Enoch with respect
to the focus of this conference, let me repeat that the insiders are the
righteous, the pious, the chosen. Their status is related to their
possession of revealed, eschatological wisdom about God's Law and
the imminent judgment. In part, this wisdom has been revealed

---

[7] See the discussion of the Parables in John J. Collins, "The Heavenly Representative:
The 'Son of Man' in the Similitudes of Enoch," in John J. Collins and George W. E.
Nickelsburg, ed., *Ideal Figures in Ancient Judaism* (SBLSCS 12; Chico, Ca.: Scholars,
1980) 111—33. Specifically on the Son of Man being revealed and on his relationship to
wisdom, see 1 Enoch 48:1—7.

through visions and cosmic journeys. The outsiders reject this wisdom as invalid and act accordingly. In the judgment, God will reward the insiders for their faithfulness and deliver them from the oppression of the outsiders. He will also punish the outsiders for their rejection of divine wisdom and their oppression of the insiders. Yet the conflict between insiders and outsiders notwithstanding, the authors expect that some of the outsiders will be converted and saved.

3. The Qumran Scrolls

At many points the documents unique to the Qumran library reflect a mentality similar to that of the Enochic authors.

a. The Damascus Document

The historical prologue to the Damascus Document recalls the description of the seventh week in the Apocalypse of Weeks (CD 1; 1 Enoch 93:10). The post-exilic period was marked by widespread sin, characterized as blindness and error. God created a small remnant called "a plant root" (1:7; cf.1 Enoch 93:10). Their repentance and salvation involved revelation and knowledge:

> "And they *perceived* (*wybynw*) their iniquity, and *recognized* (*wyd'w*) that they were guilty men" . . . .And so "God . . . raised up for them a *Teacher* of Righteousness to guide them in the way of his heart. And he *made known* (*wywd'*) to the latter generations that which God had done to the latter generation, the congregation of traitors. . ." This was "when the Scoffer arose, who shed over Israel the waters of *lies*."
>
> (1:8—15, Vermes)

Here revelation and knowledge have two aspects familiar to us from 1 Enoch. The Teacher of Righteousness makes known both God's Law and God's eschatological judgment. His opposite number, the Scoffer, teaches falsehood.

b. The Commentaries

The Habakkuk commentary takes note of the two aspects of the Teacher's activity. The eschatological interpretation of Habakkuk 2:1-2 concerns "the Teacher of Righteousness, to whom God made known (*hwdy'w*) all the mysteries of the words of his servants the prophets" (7:1—4). Habakkuk 2:4 refers to "all those who observe the Torah . . . whom God will deliver . . . because of their affliction and their faith in the Teacher of Righteousness" (8:1—3). Similarly, the author contrasts the Teacher of Righteousness and the Man of Lies, who despised the Torah (5:8—12). The issue of true and false teaching, probably as it relates to the interpretation of the Torah, recurs in several passages in the commentaries on Nahum and the Psalms (4QpNah 2:8; 3:4; 4QpPs[a] 1:18—19).[8]

c. Hymns of the Teacher

Several of the *hodayoth* treat the relationship between the teacher and his disciples. Especially noteworthy is 4:5ff. This hymn contrasts truth and falsehood, knowledge that saves and folly that damns. These are spelled out with reference to Law and prophecy; the hymn distinguishes the teacher's interpretation of the Law from that of his opponents and speaks of false seers in contrast to the teacher's knowledge of divine mysteries. Moreover, the author anticipates the judgment of the false teachers and prophets.

d. The Community Rule

According to the Community Rule, proper observance of the Torah—which is necessary for salvation—presupposes the revealed interpretation of the Law which is to be found only in the Community. Thus when one joins the Community, one leaves on the outside those who are perverse and damned and one enters the covenant of God (5:7—20). This involves conversion (*šûb*, 5:1, 8, 14) to "the Law of Moses according to all his commands. . . , following all that is revealed (*kwl hnglh*) of it to the sons of Zadok" (5:8—9).

This viewpoint is also reflected in two hymns among the *hodayoth* which add an eschatological dimension (3:19-36; 11:3-14). When one enters the community, one is raised up from the death and damnation that characterize the world as the realm of Satan, and one is brought into the realm of eternal life, where one shares the knowledge (*d't, bynh*) of the angels.[9]

e. Summary

The Essenes believed that their group was the eschatological community of salvation. The insiders were the true Israel, the chosen who would be saved; the outsiders were damned. The salvation of the insiders involved their possession of revealed knowledge. This included the Essene interpretation of the Torah and the belief that they were living in the end time, in anticipation of God's judgment. Moreover, to judge from evident references to wrong feasts (1QH 4:12), the citation of the *Book of Jubilees* (CD 16:2—4), and the

---

[8] See Nickelsburg, "Epistle," 337.
[9] See Heinz-Wolfgang Kuhn, *Enderwartung und Gegenwärtiges Heil* (SUNT 4; Göttingen: Vandenhoek & Ruprecht, 1966); and Nickelsburg, *Resurrection*, 152—56.

contents of their library, they also viewed some of the Enochic literature as part of their revealed wisdom.[10]

The Teacher of Righteousness was also an early source of their revealed knowledge. In part, this revelation was derived from the interpretation of Scripture (1QpHab 7:1—4). Though different from Ben Sira's interpretation, the Teacher's was an eschatological interpretation. References to false seers and a passage such as 1QS 11:3 ("My eyes have beheld his marvellous deeds, and the light of my heart, the mystery to come," Vermes) may indicate that visionary activity was not foreign to the Essene community, although we have no example of an apocalypse that was surely created at Qumran.

The Essenes' attitude toward outsiders seems to have varied from time to time. 1QS 8 and CD 4:9—12 suggest that there was a time when they welcomed outsiders. Other passages in the Community Rule counsel the insiders to hate the outsiders and to conceal saving knowledge from them (1QS 9:16—17; 10:19-25).

4. Fourth Ezra

I conclude this section of my paper as I began it, with brief reference to a work whose theology of wisdom lacks the exclusiveness of 1 Enoch and the Qumran literature, viz. 4 Ezra.

Although 4 Ezra is replete with dialogues and visions that are related to the kind of apocalyptic material we have been discussing, its attitude toward this literature is ambivalent. At the very least, this author mildly disparages the kind of visionary accounts that are typical, e.g., of 1 Enoch.[11]

Of special interest to the present inquiry is the Ezra legend recounted in chapter 14. Ezra and his scribal colleagues are the recipients of two kinds of revealed wisdom. The twenty four books of the Hebrew Scriptures contain what is necessary for salvation, and therefore they are to be published openly. The seventy remaining books contain esoteric knowledge, which is to be hidden and made available only to the wise. Unlike the Enochic authors and the Essenes, "Ezra" does not believe that the possession of this revealed, esoteric wisdom creates an exclusive community of the saved.[12] Rather like Ben Sira, he esteems the Torah as the source of the

---

[10] On the Qumran manuscripts of parts of 1 Enoch, see J. T. Milik, *The Books of Enoch* (Oxford: Clarendon, 1976). On the other calendrical materials at Qumran, see idem, *Ten Years of Discovery in the Wilderness of Judaea* (SBT 26; London: SCM, 1959) 107-13.

[11] See Michael E. Stone, "Lists of Revealed Things in the Apocalyptic Literature," in F. M. Cross et al., ed., *Magnalia Dei*, Fs. G. Ernest Wright (Garden City, N.Y.: Doubleday, 1976) 420.

[12] See Michael A. Knibb, "Apocalyptic and Wisdom in 4 Ezra," *JSJ* 13 (1983) 560-74.

wisdom that leads to salvation. I have used these two texts to bracket
my study of the sectarian and apocalyptic literature in order to contrast
two types of wisdom-oriented literature that flourished in Judaism
during the time when Christianity was born. I shall now turn to some
examples of early Christian theology that chose the sectarian option.

B. The Literature of Early Christianity

In this part of my paper I shall argue three points. 1) The belief
that salvation is bound up with revelation is more prevalent in the
New Testament than is generally recognized, and it often coexists
with other kinds of soteriology. 2) This viewpoint has much in
common with the Enochic and Qumranic texts I have discussed. (I do
not argue direct derivation, but parallel usage.) 3) Like the authors of
the Jewish texts, many of the teachers, preachers, and writers of the
first century Christian Church drew the conclusion consonant with
their viewpoint: persons who rejected the revelations on which the
Christian proclamation was based were excluded from the community
of the saved.

Because my thesis involves a quantitative factor (the widespread
occurrence of the claim of revelation), my discussion will cite examples from a large number of texts: John, "Q", Mark, Matthew,
Luke-Acts, Paul, and Revelation. Of necessity, my treatment of these
texts will be cursory. Space does not permit a detailed discussion of
the nuances in the various claims of revelation and in the functions of
those claims.

1. The Gospel According to John

The Fourth Gospel provides the best known New Testament
example of a revelatory soteriology. Although there are occasional
references to Jesus' death for others (10:11, 15; 11:49—52; 15:13—14),
the primary soteriological event in the Gospel is the descent of Jesus
the revealer.[13]

This soteriology of revelation is related to the kind of Wisdom
theology found in Sirach 24.[14] For Ben Sira, Wisdom descends to earth
and pitches its tent (κατασκηνόω, v. 8) among humans by being

---

[13] For an excellent discussion of John's theology of descent and ascent and its social
setting, see Wayne A. Meeks, "The Man from Heaven in Johannine Sectarianism," *JBL*
91 (1972) 44—72.

[14] The relationship between John's christology and Jewish wisdom theologies is widely
recognized. See, e.g., Rudolf Bultmann, *The Gospel of John: A Commentary* (E.T.;
Philadelphia: Westminster, 1971) 22—24; F. -M. Braun, *Jean le Theologien* 2 (Paris: J.
Gabalda, 1964) 113-35; Raymond E. Brown, *The Gospel According to John* 1 (AB 29;
Garden City, N.Y.: Doubleday, 1966) cxxii-cxxv.

embodied in the Torah. In John, the Wisdom figure, called Logos or Son, descends and pitches its tent (σκηνόω, v. 14) among humans by becoming incarnate in Jesus of Nazareth. For Ben Sira, the Wisdom resident in the Torah offers life to those who accept and follow it and death to those who reject it. According to John, those who believe in Jesus by accepting him as the revealer have eternal life. Those who reject his claims are damned.

The functional equivalence of Torah and Jesus, or the sage and Jesus the teacher, is not accidental. John underscores both the parallel and the contrast between his theology and traditional Jewish wisdom theology: "the Law was given (ἐδόθη) through Moses; grace and truth came through Jesus Christ" (1:17). The contrast is underscored in stories about Jesus' controversies over the Torah (see 5:9—18; 7:16—24; 9:13—34). The contrast has another striking facet. In 1 Enoch and the Qumran texts, the authority of revelation is invoked to support one interpretation of the Torah against other interpretations. In John and other texts we shall discuss, Jesus the revealer challenges the authority of the Torah itself.

In the Fourth Gospel, Jesus is the unique revealer, and in this respect, the evangelist approximates the theology of 1 Enoch and Qumran. When God "gave" his son (ἔδωκεν, 3:16), this was an eschatological event parallel to the giving of wisdom in 1 Enoch and the revelations received by the Teacher of Righteousness. Its eschatological quality is evident in Jesus' claim to be "the resurrection and the life" 11:24—26, the one through whom one has passed from death to eternal life (5:24). This formulation of a "realized" eschatology is, moreover, reminiscent of the Qumran *hodayoth* that describe entrance into the community as resurrection from the sphere of death to the realm of eternal life.

Because Jesus is the eschatological revealer, positive or negative response to him involves *eternal* life or damnation. In the Fourth Gospel, the term "the Jews" is a veritable synonym for those who do not believe in him and who are, therefore, lost. Several times, the evangelist notes ironically that these Jews are especially culpable because they do not recognize in Jesus the unique fulfilment of their own religious tradition (see esp. 5:30—47).

2. The Wisdom Theology of "Q"

In the document "Q", the hypothetical written source of the teaching material unique to Matthew and Luke, the authority of Jesus' teaching lay in his status as the presence of divine wisdom, or, at least,

84 George W.E. Nickelsburg

her unique spokesman.[15] The prayer of Jesus recorded in Matthew 11:25—27 and Luke 10:21—22 is especially relevant to our discussion. It is sometimes called the "Johannine thunderbolt" in the midst of the Synoptic tradition. In form and wording it is also reminiscent of the Qumran *hodayoth*.

> I give thanks to you, Father, Lord of heaven and earth,
> that you have hidden these things from the wise and prudent
> and have revealed (ἀπεκάλυψας) them to the babes.
> Yea, Father thus it is your gracious will.
> All things have been delivered to me by my Father,
> and no one knows the son except the Father,
> nor does anyone know the Father except the Son
> and anyone to whom the Son wishes to reveal (ἀποκαλύψαι) him.

Salvation is revealed knowledge, and Jesus the Son is the unique revealer of the Father. There are two groups of people: those who know the Father and those who do not. Although the Matthean form of this text does not explicitly state that Jesus the unique revealer is the eschatological revealer, such an interpretation is clear in the Lukan form of the pericope, where Jesus interprets the passage privately to his disciples:

> Blessed are the eyes that see the things that you see;
> For I say to you that many prophets and kings desired
>   to see what you see and did not see,
> and to hear what you hear and did not hear. (10:23—24)

3. The Gospel According to Mark

To the casual reader, Mark's christology is miles apart from John's. Mark's Jesus proclaims the coming of the kingdom and never speaks at length of his own function as the revealer. Nonetheless, in his activity as teacher and preacher, Mark's Jesus may well be filling the role of Wisdom or Wisdom's spokesman. Moreover, in Mark, as in John, much turns on people's ability or inability to recognize who Jesus is.[16]

In any case, Jesus' revelatory activity is central in one passage that is noteworthy for our discussion. In chapter 4 Jesus teaches the crowd

---

[15] On the place of wisdom speculation in "Q," see M. Jack Suggs, *Wisdom, Christology, and Law in Matthew's Gospel* (Cambridge: Harvard University, 1970) 5—97. On the relationship between "Q" and Jewish wisdom literature, see James M. Robinson, "*LOGON SOPHON*: On the Gattung of Q," in *Trajectories Through Early Christianity* (Philadelphia: Fortress, 1971) 71—113.
[16] See George W. E. Nickelsburg, "The Genre and Function of the Markan Passion Narrative," *HTR* 73 (1980) 175—76.

through the use of parables. Later, when they are alone, the disciples ask him about the meaning of the parables. He responds:

> To you has been given the mystery of the kingdom of God,
>   but for those on the outside everything is in parables;
>   so that, "they may indeed see, but not perceive,
>   and they may indeed hear but not understand,
>   lest they turn against and be forgiven." (4:11—12)

The pattern is familiar. Jesus' proclamation involves a *mysterion*, an eschatological secret. Like the wisdom mentioned in 1 Enoch and the Wisdom present in the Johannine Jesus, the explanation of the secret has been *"given"* (δέδοται) to the disciples. They are the inside group, who are saved by their knowledge.[17] "Those on the outside" hear only the riddle of the parable, and due to their lack of insight and understanding, they are not forgiven.[18]

4. The Gospel According to Matthew

Jesus' relationship to the history and traditions of Israel is of the essence of Matthew's gospel. The narrator repeatedly cites the biblical passages that are fulfilled through Jesus' activity.[19] Within the narratives, Jesus often relates his teaching to the Torah. Although there is ambiguity in Matthew's presentation of this relationship, and scholarly opinions differ concerning the extent to which the Matthean Jesus sets aside the authority of the Torah, the primacy of Jesus' teaching is clear.[20] This is most explicit in the antitheses in the Sermon the Mount: "You have heard it said by the men of old. . . but I say to you. . ." (5:21—48). The crucial significance of Jesus' teaching is also stressed in the closing words of the Sermon (7:24—27). The person who hears Jesus' words and does them is like a wise man who builds his house on a rock so that it withstands torrential rains and

---

[17] As the plot of Mark's gospel develops, the disciples show themselves to be as ignorant as the outsiders here described (cf. esp. 8:17—21). Nonetheless, Mark's reference to the distinction between insiders and outsiders is noteworthy.

[18] See, however, Vernon K. Robbins (*Jesus the Teacher* [Philadelphia: Fortress, 1984] 137—38), who cites a statement attributed to Socrates.

[19] For passages introduced by formulae indicating "fulfillment," see 1:22; 2:15, 17, 23; 4:14; 8:17; 12:17; 13:35; 21:4; 27:9; cf. also 3:15; 5:17; 26:54, 56.

[20] See, e.g., Gerhard Barth, "Matthew's Understanding of the Law," in Günther Bornkamm, Gerhard Barth, and Heinz Joachim Held, *Tradition and Interpretation in Matthew* (Philadelphia: Westminster, 1963) 58—164; Charles E. Carlston, "The Things that Defile (Mark VII. 14) and the Law in Matthew and Mark," *NTS* 15 (1968) 75—86; and the summaries of literature in Joachim Rohde, *Rediscovering the Teaching of the Evangelists* (Philadelphia: Westminster, 1968) 90ff., and Daniel J. Harrington, "Matthean Studies Since Joachim Rohde," *HeyJ* 16 (1975) 387.

winds. The one who does *not* do them is like the fool whose house collapses because it is built on sand. In this doubly structured allusion to the doubly structured oracle in Isaiah 28, salvation and damnation are tied to one's response to "my words" rather than to the Torah. This same shift from the Mosaic Torah to Jesus' teaching is evident in the apostolic commissioning at the conclusion of the Gospel (28:16—20). The apostles are to make disciples who will "observe everything that I have commanded you," i.e., who will obey the dominical teaching contained in the Gospel. A similar shift to the first person singular occurs in Jesus' commissioning of Simon in 16:18: "you are Peter, and upon this rock *I* shall build *my* Church." The *qahal Yisrael* has become *ekklesia mou*.

These audacious moves to "christologize" the Torah and the community of the faithful are related to Matthew's understanding of Jesus' identity or, better, his several identities. According to M. J. Suggs, in the Gospel of Matthew the "I" of Jesus' teaching is Wisdom herself.[21] In chapter 16, Jesus commissions Simon after he has confessed that Jesus is the Christ. The *ekklesia* is the messianic community. In 28:16—20, Jesus speaks as the risen and exalted one. He commissions apostles (rather than God commissioning prophets) because, in words reminiscent of Daniel 7, "all authority in heaven and earth has been given to me." That authority, granted to the risen one, undergirds all of the teaching that Matthew has ascribed to the earthly Jesus.[22]

Not only does Matthew stress *Jesus'* authority as the teacher who is, at once, the voice of Wisdom, the Messiah, and the exalted Lord, he also deals with the secondary question of *apostolic* authority, and he roots this authority in revelation. When Simon voices the confession of the Church that Jesus is the Christ, he does so because "flesh and blood have not revealed (ἀπεκάλυψεν) it to you, but my Father who is in heaven." When the apostles proclaim the Gospel and teach the commands of Jesus, they do so in response to a commissioning vision in which the risen and exalted Lord played the role of God himself and they took the place of the prophet.[23]

The theological consequences of Matthew's christology are well

---

[21] Suggs, *Wisdom*, 99—127.
[22] The commissioning at the end of the Gospel is the christological key by which one is to read the entire Gospel; see Otto Michel, "Der Abschluss des Matthäusevangeliums," *EvT* 10 (1950) 22-22; and Wolfgang Trilling, *Das Wahre Israel* (SANT 10; Munich: Kösel, 1964) 11—51.
[23] On the relationship of Matt 28:16—20 to prophetic commissioning accounts, see Benjamin J. Hubbard, *The Matthean Redaction of a Primitive Apostolic Commissioning* (SBLDS 19; Missoula, MT: Scholars, 1974).

known. He depicts the Pharisees in particular and "all the people" in general as rejecting both Jesus' authority as teacher and his status as Messiah as well as the belief in the resurrection, which confirms these. On the grounds of this rejection, Matthew maintains they have lost their place in the convenantal community.[24]

5. Luke-Acts

Divine revelatory activity plays a central role in Luke-Acts. In the first two chapters of the Gospel, angelic visions and the activity of the Holy Spirit confirm the significance of the events surrounding the births of John and Jesus. At his baptism, Jesus becomes the bearer of the Spirit at whose prompting he will carry on his healing and preaching ministry. In Acts the apostolic ministry is also a function of the Spirit.

Acts 6—7 provides a different kind of example. Filled with wisdom and the Spirit, Stephen comes into conflict with elements of the Jewish community who accuse him of preaching that Jesus will abolish Temple and Torah.[25] Standing before the Sanhedrin, Stephen recites the history of Israel as the repeated rejection of the prophets, whom God nevertheless vindicated, and he cites the crucifixion and resurrection of Jesus as the crowning example of this pattern of rejection and vindication. As confirmation of this claim, the Spirit gives Stephen an ecstatic vision of the risen Lord exalted at the divine throne. The son of man spoken of by Enoch is identified with Jesus the Christ. The Sanhedrin, however, rejects Stephen's claim of revelation and executes him for blasphemy.[26]

This is but one of many occasions in Acts where Luke depicts "the Jews" rejecting the divinely commissioned and inspired activity of the apostles. Another instance occurs in chapter 22, where the Jews reject Paul's account of the vision in which the risen and exalted Lord commissioned him as an apostle to the gentiles. The Book of Acts ends as Paul quotes Isaiah 6 (quoted in Mark 4:11—12, cited above) to describe the Jews' rejection of the gospel and its consequences: they do not perceive or understand, and so they cannot turn and be healed (28:23—29).

---

[24] See especially Matt 21:28—22:14 and 27:24—26 and the discussion by Trilling, *Das Wahre Israel*.

[25] Cf. Luke 21:14—15 and Jesus' promise to "give" his disciples wisdom with which to answer their adversaries.

[26] Luke has cast the story of Stephen's martyrdom into the same mold as the passion narrative (on the genre, see Nickelsburg, "Genre and Function"). It is noteworthy that at the point in the story where Jesus refers to the exaltation of the Son of Man (Luke 22:69), Stephen has a vision of the exalted Son of Man as confirmation of his speech.

6. The Apostle Paul

Several times in his epistles, the Apostle Paul refers to his
apostolic commissioning. The Epistle to the Galatians provides an
important example for our purposes. Here Paul argues that one is
justified not by the observance of the Torah, but through faith in Jesus
the Christ. This Jesus is the incarnate Son, whom God has sent at the
end time to redeem people from the curse that falls on those who seek
but cannot find salvation in the Torah (4:4—5). According to Paul, the
Christ event is mediated through the gospel, which is the eschatological proclamation of the event. In chapter 1, he clarifies the authority
of this gospel: God "revealed" his Son in Paul (ἀποκάλυψις,
ἀποκαλύπτω vv. 12, 15—16). Because of the revelatory character of his
commissioning, Paul curses anyone who proclaims a gospel contrary
to his own (specifically a gospel in which the observance of the Torah
is necessary for salvation, vv. 6—9), even if such a person claims
angelic revelation as the source of authority for their gospel.

For Paul, as for John, the incarnation of Jesus parallels the Jewish
idea of the descent of Wisdom (cf. 4:4—5 with Rom 8:3—4). Different
from John, Paul does not focus on Jesus' teaching or revelatory
activity, but on his death and resurrection as the eschatological event
of salvation. Nonetheless, the proclamation participates in the event
and is construed as an eschatological revelation. One's positive or
negative response to this revealed message results in salvation or
damnation.

Although in Galatians Paul is primarily concerned with the
salvation of the gentiles, in Romans he broadens the picture to include
Jewish responses to the gospel. According to chapters 1—3, both Jews
and gentiles stand under divine indictment and can be justified only
through faith in Jesus Christ. In chapters 9—11 he addresses the
problem that many Jews have rejected the gospel. One is "saved" by
confessing that Jesus is Lord and "believing" (πιστεύω) in the resurrection (10:9). In 11:20 Paul contrasts such faith on the part of the
gentiles and the unbelief of many Jews (πίστις, ἀπιστία), but he
anticipates the salvation of those who do not persist in their unbelief
(11:23).

In 1 Corinthians 1:17—2:16, Paul uses the term "wisdom" (σοφία)
to describe the gospel. Although as a preacher he eschews the use of
human rhetorical wisdom, he finds divine wisdom in the folly of the
cross, the eschatological secret (μυστήριον) which confounded the
demons and shocks the religious sensibilities of Jews and gentiles
alike. The gospel is the proclamation of this wisdom which God has
now revealed (ἀπεκάλυψεν, 2:10).

7. The Revelation to John

I conclude my discussion with brief reference to the New Testament Apocalypse. The risen and exalted Christ appears to John of Patmos as an eschatological revealer, who commands the seer to record and publish what is revealed to him. The main part of the book is an account of heavenly visions of events related to the imminent divine judgment, and in this respect its form parallels the Parables of Enoch. The theological viewpoint of the book is reminiscent of the Qumran Scrolls. Both the Roman Government and the author's religious opponents are described as operatives of Satan.[27] Like other apocalyptic works, the Book of Revelation has an exhortative function, which is explicit in the letters to the seven Churches that preface it. According to these letters, one's salvation or damnation turns on one's response to the revelation recorded both in the body of the book and in the letters.

C. Summary and Conclusions

An important constituent in the literature of early post-biblical Judaism is the belief that revelation and revealed wisdom play a significant role in human salvation. In this paper I have focused attention on sectarian literature, such as the books of Enoch and the Qumran Scrolls, where wisdom is mediated through an eschatological revelation possessed by the chosen. Outsiders are damned because they lack or reject the revelation that enables them properly to observe divine Law and to read the signs of the times. This sectarian viewpoint, however, was not typical of Judaism, as the examples of ben Sira and 4 Ezra indicate. On other issues, too, and even with respect to the question of Jews and gentiles, one finds early Jewish texts that have a broad perspective as to who will be saved.[28] And this perspective continues to appear in the later writings of rabbinic Judaism, where the salvation of the gentiles is not tied to God's revelation in the Mosaic Torah.

In early Christianity the situation is more complex and, in a way, paradoxical. On the one hand, the early Church is marked by an increasing openness to the gentiles. On the other hand, the Church appears, from its inception, to have adopted the sectarian Jewish approach that asserted the validity of its position by claiming divine revelation. Salvation was tied exclusively to the person and activity of Jesus of Nazareth.

Precisely how the revelation relates to Jesus varies from text to

---

[27] See the conference paper by Adela Yarbro Collins.
[28] See the conference paper by John J. Collins.

text. In some cases, Jesus himself is perceived as the eschatological revealer or, indeed, the eschatological presence of Wisdom itself.[29] In other texts, the gospel about Jesus is construed as the proclamation of the eschatological events of the incarnation, death, and resurrection of Jesus, a proclamation which has been validated through visions or revelations of Jesus the exalted eschatological savior. In either case, sectarian arguments about the right and salutary interpretation of the Torah have been replaced by the belief that Jesus himself and/or his teaching have replaced or fulfilled the Torah. As in the Jewish texts, however, the rejection of these revealed claims leads inevitably to damnation.

At the beginning, Christian sectarian claims functioned like the Enochic and Qumranian claims. Christians were not anti-Jewish, much less anti-Semitic. To the contrary, they were Jews who asserted that other Jews were excluded from the community of the saved if they did not accept the revelation of the gospel. However, as the Church became a predominately gentile group, this ironic situation developed: former outsiders had become insiders, and they used arguments developed by their predecessors on the inside in order to claim that they, the former outsiders, were now exclusively the insiders.

In recent decades, we have had reason to rethink this situation. The cruel and barbarous events of twentieth century European history and the insights of the social sciences, among other things, have led to some healthy introspection into the origins and dynamics of Christian exclusivism. Historians of early Christianity and Christian theologians have pointed out that the roots of much Christian anti-Judaism and anti-Semitism can be traced back to the New Testament itself.[30] This fact constitutes a major problem for Christian theologians concerned with these issues. However, it is the gist of my argument that the problem is even more radical than is sometimes suggested. The theological crux is not just *present* in the canonical Scriptures of the Church, where it creates an embarrassment for those who take seriously the authority of these Scriptures. Rather, the crux is to be found precisely in places where early Christian preachers and teachers are making claims of revelation. The exclusivism that has

---

[29] Space does not permit a discussion of the early Christian creeds and hymns that describe Jesus as the descending Wisdom figure.

[30] See, e.g., Rosemary Radford Ruether, *Faith and Fratricide: The Theological Roots of Anti-Semitism* (New York: Seabury, 1974) 64—116; Samuel Sandmel, *Anti-Semitism in the New Testament?* (Philadelphia: Fortress, 1978); and Charlotte Klein, *Anti-Judaism in Christian Theology* (Philadelphia: Fortress, 1978). See also the conference papers by Wayne A. Meeks and Sean Freyne.

bred anti-Judaism is supported and defended by appeals to revelation. Indeed, the exclusivistic viewpoint itself is explicitly affirmed as revealed truth.

The Christian theologian who wishes to deal responsibly with this situation finds himself or herself in a real dilemma. One rightly seeks new constructions that break down the old barrier that has been seen to exclude the people of Israel from their own heritage. However, in attempting these new constructions, one strikes at those very points where the religious tradition is claiming divine authority on essential matters. To change the metaphor, this is radical surgery on a vital organ of the faith. One dare not give the impression that one is simply pulling a little theological splinter that has been the source of great irritation, or that one is making some minor theological adjustments in a new, wiser, and more loving and ecumenical age. In a religious tradition that prizes a catholic identification with its past, honesty is a sine qua non within the community of faith. And in this particular case, honesty requires the admission that the shape of the kerygma may be very different from what has been transmitted as the apostolic faith. The Christian theologian must build wisely, responsibly, and with love both for those within the immediate community of faith and for those within the broader community whose existence has so long been denied.

4

Breaking Away: Three New Testament Pictures of Christianity's Separation from the Jewish Communities

Wayne A. Meeks
Yale University

We have now become accustomed to say that earliest Christianity was a sect of Judaism. This is useful language: it helps us avoid some kinds of anachronism, and it may assist Christians to approach the painful history of Jewish-Christian relations with appropriate humility. Moreover, there is ancient support for this terminology. It was Josephus who depicted the "Jewish philosophy" as made up of three or four "sects" (*haireseis, Ant.* 13.171; *Vit.* 10–12; *B.J.* 2.162; their members *hairetistai, B.J.* 2.119, 124; cf. *Ant.* 18.11 *philosophiai*). And the book of Acts, which like Josephus speaks of Pharisees and Sadducees as *haireseis*, also has outsiders occasionally speak of Christians as a *hairesis* (Acts 24:5, 14; 28:22).

However, there are some problems with the phrase. After all, in writing as he did, Josephus had an apologetic purpose for which we have to make allowance. We should not fall into the trap of thinking that all, or even the majority, of Jews in Josephus' time belonged to one of the "sects" he named, any more than a majority of non-Jews were Stoics, Platonists, or Epicureans. Further, while it may be appropriate to translate his *hairesis* as "sect," what he and Acts called by this term is not necessarily the same as what a modern sociologist means by "sect." To make matters more difficult, the sociologists have not had an easy time agreeing on a definition of the latter category. Finally, the book of Acts, too, had apologetic aims, and the picture its author drew of early Christianity may be distorted, or, at best, may not represent the whole movement.

For all these reasons, a fresh look at the evidence may be timely. In order to take account of some of the diversity of viewpoint present in the early Christian literature while still keeping the inquiry within reasonable bounds, I propose to examine three sets of documents: the Fourth Gospel, the letters of Paul and his disciples, and the Gospel of Matthew. All these are most likely earlier than Acts, and, of the

Christian writings of the first century, they are the ones most inten-
sively concerned with the question of Christianity's relationship to
Israel. Each of them gives some reason for affirming that Christianity
indeed *had* been a sect of Judaism, but we shall find that each looks
back at that connection from a point just *after* a decisive break has
occurred..The following questions may help to focus our inquiry: (1)
With what kind of Judaism was each of these writers or groups of
writers concerned? (2) What was the relation between the author's
Christian community and that variety of Judaism? (3) In what social
context was this interaction taking place?

The Johannine Groups and "the Jews"

Although the Fourth Gospel is certainly not the earliest of our
sources, it is a convenient place to begin, because despite the
occasional obscurity of its symbolic language, it portrays the Jewish-
Christian issue starkly and with peculiar intensity. The rupture
between the followers of Jesus and "the Jews" is at the center of
attention; it has manifestly shaped the Johannine groups' language
and their perception of the world. These features of the Johannine
universe have become so widely recognized in recent scholarship that
there is no need for me to rehearse the evidence.[1]

Even in the synoptic gospels there are predictions that Jewish
authorities, among others, will persecute Jesus' followers (for example, Mark 13:9–13 and parallels). The comparable prediction in John
16:2, however, is rather different. On the one hand, the expected
hostility is intensified—"the hour is coming when everyone who kills
you will think he is offering a service to God." On the other, instead
of general chastisement by "councils" (*synedria*) and "synagogues,"
Jesus here tells the disciples that "they will make you *aposynagōgoi.*"
This peculiar expression occurs also in 9:22, where we are told that
"the Jews had already decreed that if anyone confessed him [sc.
Jesus] as Messiah, he would become *aposynagōgos*," and 12:42,
where the "many" leaders [*archontes*] who believed in Jesus did not
confess that belief "on account of the Pharisees, lest they become
aposynagōgoi." Those fearful leaders are exemplified in this gospel
by Nicodemus (3:1–21; 7:48–52; 19:39). The positive countertype is
the blind beggar healed by Jesus in chap. 9; he boldly refutes "the

---

[1] See Wayne A. Meeks, " 'Am I a Jew?'—Johannine Christianity and Judaism," in Jacob
Neusner, ed., *Christianity, Judaism, and Other Greco-Roman Cults: Studies for
Morton Smith at Sixty* (Leiden: Brill, 1975) 1:164-185; for more recent literature, see
F. F. Segovia, "The Love and Hatred of Jesus and Johannine Sectarianism," *CBQ* 43
(1981) 258-272.

Jews" (not otherwise identified) who interrogate him about Jesus, whereupon they "put him out" (9:34).

Louis Martyn's ingenious "two-level reading" of John 9 and other conflict stories in this gospel has been widely accepted in its general outline if not in all its details.[2] There is a broad consensus today that many aspects of the confrontation between Jesus and the Jewish authorities are projections into the narrative from the experience of the Johannine community. The evangelist has not only made Jesus prophesy such experiences, he or she has also adapted the stories circulating among these Christian groups into vignettes that provide *exempla* of good and bad faith. Consequently, we can use the dialogues and stories in John to learn something about the separation sometime in the last quarter of the first century between these particular Christian groups and the Jewish communities. It would help if we knew exactly where this took place, but unfortunately we have no direct evidence. Further below I shall make a tentative suggestion about the Johannine locale.

The Fourth Gospel has a great deal to say—much but by no means all of it negative—about *hoi ioudaioi*, which modern translations ordinarily render as "the Jews." A fair amount has been written about this usage, for it is puzzling in several respects.[3] There are places, like John 7:1, where *hoi ioudaioi* is primarily a geographical term, and there is a strong contrast, which apparently carries some symbolic weight, between "the Galileans" and "the Judaeans." It will not do, however, to treat the term as always merely geographical.[4] Phrases like "the festival of the *ioudaioi*," referring to festivals in which "Greeks" from the Diaspora and Galileans (including Jesus) participate, require us to think of the term as designating something like a religious community. Anachronism may trip us up, however; it is important to remember that our concept "a religion" can hardly be expressed in Greek or Latin, for the religious pluralism that was characteristic of the Roman empire was structured in a quite different way from our kind of pluralism. Cults traveled principally by the

---

[2] J. Louis Martyn, *History and Theology in the Fourth Gospel* (2nd ed.; Nashville: Abingdon, 1979).

[3] Most recently, see U. C. von Wahlde, "The Johannine 'Jews': A Critical Survey," *NTS* 28 (1982) 33-60; cf. my "Am I a Jew?" cited above, n.l.

[4] Against C. J. Cuming, "The Jews in the Fourth Gospel," *ExpT* 60 (1948-49) 290-292; M. Lowe, "Who were the IOUDAIOI?" *NovT* 18 (1976) 101-30; see criticism by Klaus Wengst, *Bedrängte Gemeinde und verherrlichter Christus: Der historische Ort des Johannesevangeliums als Schlüssel zu seiner Interpretation* (Biblisch Theologische Studien 5; Neukirchen: Neukirchener Verlag, 1981) 40.

migration of people,[5] and they tended to be identified by their place
of origin: "the Syrian goddess" and the like.[6] It may help to remind us
that neither of our categories "religion" and "race" had been invented
in antiquity if we translate *ioudaioi* as "Judaeans," keeping in mind
that "Judaeans" may refer either to people residing in Judaea or to a
diaspora city's community of resident aliens whose origin was in
Judaea, and who preserved their identity by means of characteristic
religious customs. In either case, the term is one more likely to be
used by an outsider looking in than by a member of the community
speaking within the group.

These considerations do not yet solve the problem of people like
the blind man in John 9 who is indubitably both a "Jew" and a
resident of Judaea, but who is, along with his parents, distinguished
from the *ioudaioi*. Von Wahlde argues that in such passages "the
Judaeans" are to be understood as "the [Jewish] authorities," and that
all of the hostile references to "the Judaeans" in John *may* be so
understood.[7] With what would this usage correspond in the real
world? It is hard to imagine a situation in which someone resident in
Judaea would say, "The Judaeans put me out of the synagogue." In a
diaspora city, say Ephesus or Antioch, it is somewhat more plausible,
since we may think of a Jew speaking to non-Jews.

Von Wahlde's survey focuses narrowly on the use of the term "the
Judaeans," so that he does not help us much to understand the
dialectic between those so designated in John and other groups,
especially "the Galileans" and "the Samaritans." It is that dialectic,
however, which determines the meaning of these terms in the
structure of the Johannine narrative. Jouette Bassler has made that
particularly clear in her analysis.[8] Correcting earlier work (including
my own) which observed these symbolic oppositions but concentrated one-sidedly on the places so represented, Bassler points out
that it is groups more than places in which the fourth evangelist is
interested. "Galileans [and on one occasion Samaritans] symbolize

---

[5] See Ramsay MacMullen, *Paganism in the Roman Empire* (New Haven and London:
Yale, 1982), pp. 113-115.
[6] Cf. my remarks in "Am I a Jew?" 182, and note the comments by Alf Thomas Kraabel,
"Judaism in Western Asia Minor under the Roman Empire" (unpublished Th. D.
dissertation, Harvard: 1968) 30f. An inscription of benefactors of Smyrna, ca. 125 C.E.,
includes a group called *hoi pote Ioudaioi;* Kraabel argues this refers to recent
immigrants from Judaea, recalling Dio Cassius 37.16.5-17.1.
[7] Von Wahlde, "The Johannine 'Jews'," passim.
[8] Jouette M. Bassler, "The Galileans: A Neglected Factor in Johannine Community
Research," *CBQ* 43 (1981) 243-257.

those who receive the Word, Judeans symbolize those who reject it."[9]
Bassler also points out the inconsistency in the reconstructions of
Johannine community history by R. E. Brown and J. L. Martyn who
"have exhaustively combed the Gospel (and letters) for allusions to
groups that figured [negatively] in the community's history", but who
nonetheless reject suggestions that "the Galileans" or "Samaritans" in
the narrative prefigure real groups in the church's experience. Any
reconstruction of the setting and history of the Johannine Christians
must offer some explanation for the special and positive place accorded both the Galileans and the Samaritans in this Gospel.

There are a few more peculiarities of John's story which we
should keep in mind before we try to deduce its geographical and
social setting. First, the boundaries of the story are the boundaries of
Israel. While *ioudaioi* is frequently used in a hostile sense, *Israel* is
always used positively in this Gospel, which can describe Jesus'
mission as to "gather into one the children of God who are scattered"
(11:52). Now because the context makes it clear that these children
include more than the *ethnos* of the Judaeans, the reader may jump to
the conclusion that gentiles are included. Yet in fact there is hardly a
hint of a specifically gentile mission in John. We do hear of "Greeks,"
but it is the *"diaspora* of the Greeks" (7:35) and "certain Greeks of the
pilgrims who came to worship at the festival" (12:20). That is, it is
Greek-speaking Jews who are meant.[10]

Second, the imagery and structure of the Johannine argument are,
despite contrary appearances, profoundly Jewish. The author of the
Gospel, the community traditions he employed, and presumably his
audience, if they understood what was being said, were intimately
familiar with scripture and with a variety of interpretive traditions. To
be sure, the evangelist uses the Jewish traditions in a way that Jews
would regard as perverse, but his transformation of them presupposes
familiarity.[11]

Preliminary answers to our first two questions emerge from the
clues we have recalled so far. What kind of Judaism is represented by
the hostile "Judaeans" of the Fourth Gospel? We cannot identify

[9] Ibid. 253.
[10] These "Greeks" may of course have been Jewish proselytes or *theosebeis*, as most of
the commentaries suggest, but that requires that John observed a rigorous distinction
between *hellēnes* and *hellēnistai*, of which we cannot be sure. Hans Windisch observes
that *hellēnes* can sometimes refer to "Hellenized Orientals" but insists that it cannot
refer to Greek-speaking Jews (*TDNT* 2:509f.). Were the latter not "Hellenized Orientals"? In any case, if the *hellēnes* in John were meant to refer to a mission to gentiles, the
passages in question are a strangely muted way to do so.
[11] See "Am I a Jew?" and the literature referred to there.

these Judaeans with any of the various "sects" of Israel that we hear about in ancient sources. The Pharisees, for example, do have a leading role in the opposition to Jesus, but they seem a conventional group here, without distinguishing characteristics—in contrast to the situation in Matthew. This counts against an assumption that the Johannine communities took shape primarily vis à vis the formative rabbinic movement at Yavneh. Also against that assumption is the fact that the controversies in John do not turn centrally on practice, but on beliefs. Christian beliefs about Jesus seemed blasphemous to the Judaeans of John's gospel. This emphasis on beliefs does not mean that the traditions used in John do not retain a memory of controversy about practice. For example, the story of Jesus healing a paralytic (5:1–8) has at some point been converted into a controversy story by adding the note, "It was the sabbath that day" (5:9c–16). The controversy, however, does not lead to a pronouncement about what is the proper way to observe the sabbath, as for example the stories of Matthew 12:1–14 do. Instead, it leads to the much more severe accusation that Jesus "made himself equal to God" (5:17) and to a discourse on Jesus' relationship to "the Father." This observation does not help us much to discover just which group of Jews may have been in mind, however, for probably most Jews would have agreed that it was blasphemy for any human being to be called "God" in the sense the Johannine Christians meant when speaking of Jesus (10:33).[12]

If there are no grounds for identifying the opposing "Judaeans" of John with "normative Judaism" or its "formative" predecessors at Yavneh, nevertheless we must recognize that, in the eyes of the Johannine community, the "Judaeans" and their *archontes* were people who exercised power. The locus of their power, moreover, was in the synagogues, and it was sufficient to expel persons from membership, even to threaten their lives.

The relationship of the Johannine Christians to "Judaism," then, was a relationship with organized Jewish communities centered in synagogues. By the time the Fourth Gospel was written, these Christians were no longer connected with those communities. By the time when the three Johannine letters were written, there was no sign of any direct interaction with the synagogues, nor even of any interest

---

[12] See W. A. Meeks, "The Divine Agent and His Counterfeit in Philo and the Fourth Gospel," in Elisabeth Schüssler Fiorenza, ed., *Aspects of Religious Propaganda in Judaism and Early Christianity* (Notre Dame and London: University of Notre Dame Press, 1976) 43-67.

in the issue of separation.[13] Yet when the Gospel was written, the rupture with the synagogue remained in the sect's memory as the all-important crisis which had shaped the groups' identity and helped to shape their christology. One might say that "the world" of the Fourth Gospel, in more than one sense, is the world of Judaism. It would be more accurate, however, to say that it is a world in which groups identified as "Judaeans," "Samaritans," and "Galileans" interact. If we assume, for reasons mentioned above, that the Gospel's world is not a purely artful creation but reflects in some measure the real context in which the Johannine groups took their distinctive shape, then it is worth asking whether we can think of a place or at least a kind of place where the Johannine fictions would correspond with reality.

External evidence does not take us very far. By late in the second century, some traditions connected the Fourth Gospel's author with Ephesus, but most recent students of John have been skeptical of these traditions. Even if we take them quite seriously, they do not answer the question of where the formative break between the Johannine communities and the "Judaean" synagogues took place. We are left with the internal evidence, that is, the peculiarities of the Johannine narrative. Is it more plausible to think of it as having been produced in an urban, diaspora environment, or somewhere in the Land of Israel? Attempts to argue for a Palestinian or other bilingual provenance on the basis of a putative Aramaic *Vorlage*, which were popular a generation ago, have not been successful.[14] The language of the evangelist and of the tradition upon which he immediately depended was Greek, and there is no reason to believe that Greek had not been the language of the Johannine groups for some time. Hence the chances are stong that we should look to some *polis* for the origin of this work. Martyn takes this for granted when he speaks of the events mirrored in the Gospel's stories as taking place in "the Jewish Quarter of John's city."[15]

Would controversies among "Judaeans," "Samaritans" and "Galileans" have an immediate meaning to residents of a polis like Ephesus or Antioch? The more we learn from archaeology of the immigrant communities' organization in the Graeco-Roman cities, the

---

[13] Pace J.A.T. Robinson, "The Destination and Purpose of the Johannine Epistles," *NTS* 7 (1960-61) 56-65.

[14] See the literature discussed in "Am I a Jew?" and note the remarks by Klaus Beyer, *Semitische Syntax im Neuen Testament* (Göttingen: Vandenhoeck & Ruprecht, 1962) 1:17f.

[15] Martyn, *History and Theology in the Fourth Gospel* (rev.ed.; Nashville: Abingdon, 1979) 30.

more plausible such scenes appear. Especially, the existence of a substantial Samaritan Diaspora side by side with the Jews seems more and more certain. Tombstones found in Thessalonica have shown that there was a Samaritan community in that city as late as the second century C. E., and we know that there was a large Jewish community there.[16] Just recently, inscriptions from the island of Delos dated to the second century B.C.E. have revealed a community who called themselves "Israelites of Delos, who offer first fruits at sacred Har Garizim."[17] Their community center, if Philippe Bruneau is right, was less than one hundred meters from the Judaean synagogue.[18] The question whether "in this mountain" or "in Jerusalem" was the place to honor God (John 4:20) was evidently a question that could be argued on Delos as well as in Palestine, and presumably in any city where there was an organized Jewish as well as a Samaritan community.[19]

The "Galileans," however, pose more of a problem in such a setting. To be sure, it is possible that "Galileans" had already become a nickname for Christians, as it would be for the emperor Julian three centuries later and perhaps already in Epictetus (*Diss.* 4.7.6). Yet the "Galileans" in John are not simply identified with those who become Jesus' disciples. They are rather those who are receptive to the signs and word of Jesus. It is possible that the evangelist hit upon the symbolic use of the term by an ingenious blending of such an outsiders' nickname with reflection on the geographical setting of Jesus' career, but his work in that case would seem extraordinarily artificial. It is more straightforward to assume that "Galileans" as well as "Judaeans" and "Samaritans" were known entities in the formative milieu of the Johannine community. It is not impossible that an association of immigrants from Galilee might have existed and been called "the Galileans" in one or another Mediterranean city in the

---

[16] B. Lifshitz and J. Schiby, "Une synagogue samaritaine à Thessalonique," *RB* 75 (1968) 368-378.

[17] Philippe Bruneau, " 'Les Israélites de Délos' et la Juiverie délienne," *BCH* 106 (1982) 465-504.

[18] Bruneau 488; some caution is necessary, for the Jewish inscriptions discovered so far are dated to the first century C.E. The Samaritan and Jewish evidence does not therefore overlap in time, and it is a conjecture, though a reasonable one, that both communities were continuous over a long period. See Bruneau's careful discussion, 495-499.

[19] Whether the temple on Gerizim destroyed by John Hyrcanus in 128 B.C.E. (Josephus, *Ant.* 13.256; the parallel in *B.J.* 1.63 mentions Hyrcanus' defeat of the "Cuthaeans," but not the destruction of the temple) was subsequently rebuilt, ancient sources do not reveal. That Mt. Gerizim remained a cultic center for the Samaritans, however, is clear.

Roman age, but I am aware of no evidence for such. A setting somewhere in Palestine thus seems more plausible.

There is one further aspect of the Gospel's imagery that speaks in favor of a Palestinian setting. If the primary Johannine milieu had been a large, cosmopolitan city, then it is strange that we hear no whisper in the Fourth Gospel about a dominant, pagan society. There is only the Roman governor who plays his necessary role. For those who picture the "Jewish Quarter of [a Graeco-Roman] city" after the model of the mediaeval ghetto, that may not seem surprising, but in fact Jewish life in Alexandria, Antioch, Sardis, Miletus, and Aphrodisias was nothing like that.[20] Yet for the Johannine Christians, as late as when the Gospel was written, "the world" into which they were sent, but to which they belonged no more (John 17:14–18), was a world dominated by the "Judaeans."

The symbolic importance of Galilee and Samaria and the presence of what seem to be old local traditions from these areas in John some years ago prompted me to posit a Galilean provenance for the Gospel.[21] My argument was simplistic in some respects, yet there are still good reasons for considering whether the Johannine groups took shape in Galilee even though we shall probably never be certain. The recent explorations by Eric Meyers and others show that some areas of Lower Galilee in particular might well provide just the socio-cultural mix which my analysis of the symbolism in John requires: the towns were both urbanized and hellenized; the community could relate closely with Samaria, Judaea, and "the Diaspora of the Greeks"; strong Jewish communities were prepared to exercise firm discipline; and there was, of course, a quite positive sense for "the Galileans."[22]

---

[20] This point has now been repeatedly made; Kraabel's observations are exemplary. See, besides his dissertation cited above, A. T. Kraabel, "Paganism and Judaism: The Sardis Evidence," in André Benoit et al., eds., *Paganisme, Judaïsme, Christianisme . . . Melanges offerts à Marcel Simon* (Paris: Boccard, 1978) 13-33; "The Diaspora Synagogue: Archaeological and Epigraphic Evidence since Sukenik," *ANRW* II.19.1 (1979) 477-510; "Social Systems of Six Diaspora Synagogues," in Joseph Gutmann, ed., *Ancient Synagogues: The State of Research* (Brown Judaic Studies 22; Chico, CA: Scholars, 1981) 79-91.

[21] On local traditions in John, see the recent article by C. H. H. Scobie, "Johannine Geography," *SR* 11/1 (1982) 77-84.

[22] E. M. Meyers, J. F. Strange, and Dennis E. Groh, "The Meiron Excavation Project: Archaeological Survey in Galilee and Golan, 1976," *BASOR* 230 (1978) 1-24; Eric M. Meyers and James F. Strange, *Archaeology, the Rabbis, and Early Christianity* (Nashville: Abingdon, 1981). See also the impressive collection of literary evidence in Sean Freyne, *Galilee from Alexander the Great to Hadrian; 323 B.C.E. to 135 C.E.* (Wilmington and Notre Dame: Michael Glazier and Univ. of Notre Dame, 1980) and Freyne's observations in "Galilean Religion of the First Century C.E. against its Social

An alternative localization is that proposed by Klaus Wengst.[23] His analysis, though more detailed than mine can be here, parallels mine in most respects. There are two weaknesses. First, he does not pay adequate attention to the symbolism of the interaction among "Galileans," "Samaritans," and "Judaeans" in the Johannine narrative which I have stressed above. However it would only strengthen the conclusions he reaches. Second, and more troublesome, he assumes that a "uniform, pharisaically defined Judaism" became normative in Palestine instantly after 70 C.E., and that it was that kind of Judaism the Johannine Christians confronted (Wengst, 42). Jacob Neusner's research argues persuasively that it was not until the Bar Kochba crisis that the thoroughgoing reinstitutionalization of life in the land of Israel began,[24] and I have argued above that the Johannine controversies do not seem essentially "halakhic."[25] Further, Wengst assumes a village rather than an urban setting, and one sufficiently uniform that exclusion from the synagogues would mean effective exclusion from social and economic life. There is nothing in the Fourth Gospel, however, which speaks directly of economic pressures. The Johannine Christians evidently were able to sustain their independent and increasingly sectarian existence. A *polis*, though not a very cosmopolitan one, as explained above, seems more plausible than a circle of villages. Finally, Wengst has assumed too quickly, with many students of John, that the expulsion from synagogues is explained by the imposition of the *birkat ha-minim* (Wengst, 52-57). It is time to recognize that the *birkat ha-minim* has been a red herring in Johannine research. Not only do questions remain about its date

---

Background," *PIBA* 5 (1981) 98-114. Freyne gives very short shrift to archaeological evidence, ignores the Meyers-Strange thesis of Galilee's two cultural regions, and asserts that "the overall Galilean ethos was rural and peasant," with no significant hellenistic influence, "despite the circle of the cities" (1981, 107f.). The statement seems a priori rather than a conclusion from evidence.

[23] See above, n. 4.

[24] The foundations of Jacob Neusner's position were laid in his studies of traditions associated with particular named sages, especially *Eliezer ben Hyrcanus: The Tradition and the Man* (SJLA 3,4; Leiden: Brill, 1973), built up through the long series of historical and redactional studies of Mishnaic traditions by Neusner and his students (most of them published in the Brill SJLA series), and confirmed in his *Judaism: The Evidence of the Mishnah* (Chicago and London: Univ. of Chicago, 1981).

[25] Against Wengst's analysis on p.63, which is not altogether self-consistent. Wengst cites Severino Pancaro's observations about "Law" as center of controversy (*The Law in the Fourth Gospel: The Torah and the Gospel, Moses and Jesus, Judaism and Christianity according to John* [NovTSup 42; Leiden: Brill, 1975]). However, Pancaro may have misled Wengst, for *nomos* in John usually refers to the books of Moses or scripture in general, i.e., "Torah," not *halakha*. See further my review of Pancaro in *JBL* 96 (1977) 311-314.

and the earliest form of its wording—not to mention questions of where and when it would have been effective after it was promulgated[26]—the more fundamental issue for interpreting John 16:2 and John 9's depiction of the healed blind man's expulsion is whether these scenes have anything to do with the way the *birkat ha-minim* would have worked in practice. John does not speak of people who do not go to synagogue services because they cannot conscientiously say the prayers. It speaks of being put out of the synagogue. All we have to assume is that the *archontes* of the Jewish community in John's location had simply made up their minds to get rid of these troublemaking followers of a false Messiah.

Nevertheless, Wengst's proposal for the geographical setting of the formative (perhaps not the final) stage of the Fourth Gospel is attractive. He proposes the southern part of the kingdom of Agrippa II, especially the western portion around Bathyra in Batanaea. The factors present in the larger towns of Lower Galilee would be present there as well.

Whichever of these three possibilities we prefer—Galilee, Batanaea, or some small *polis* elsewhere with a relatively large presence of Judaean, Galilean, and Samaritan immigrants—the Johannine Christians had formed their lives in a society dominated by the Jewish community. In response, they had taken on the characteristics of a *sect* in the modern sociological sense.[27] Significantly, the social formation which they developed by the time the Johannine letters were written depended upon that institution so characteristic of Christianity in its early spread through the cities of the Mediterranean basin, as of other migratory cults: the Graeco-Roman household.[28] Traumatically divorced from the synagogues, Johannine Christians made a new life for

---

[26] Reuven Kimelman, "*Birkat Ha-Minim* and the Lack of Evidence for an Anti-Christian Jewish Prayer in Late Antiquity," in E. P. Sanders, ed., *Jewish and Christian Self-Definition*, vol. 2: *Aspects of Judaism in the Graeco-Roman Period* (Philadelphia: Fortress and London: SCM, 1981) 226-244.

[27] I proposed this interpretation in "The Man from Heaven in Johannine Sectarianism," *JBL* 91 (1972) 44-72, and it is now widely accepted. See, e.g., the recent article by F. F. Segovia (above, n.1).

[28] See A. J. Malherbe, "The Inhospitality of Diotrephes," in Jacob Jervell and Wayne A. Meeks, eds., *God's Christ and His People: Studies in Honour of Nils Alstrup Dahl* (Oslo: Universitetsforlaget, 1977) 222-232; reprinted with an addendum in *Social Aspects of Early Christianity* (2nd ed.; Philadelphia: Fortress, 1983) 92-112. See also W. A. Meeks, *The First Urban Christians: The Social World of the Apostle Paul* (New Haven and London: Yale, 1983), esp. chap. 3. For a massive collection of evidence on the use of households in the establishment of Jewish, Christian, and other Graeco-Roman cults, see L. Michael White, "Domus Ecclesiae, Domus Dei" (Ph.D. Diss. Yale Univ., 1982).

themselves within private houses, starting anew just as Jewish or
Samaritan immigrants in Diaspora cities had often done when they
first arrived.

Pauline Christianity and the Jews

In contrast with the Fourth Gospel, the Pauline letters provide us
with a wealth of specific information about the places and social
settings where existed the Christian groups founded by Paul and his
co-workers.[29] I have called the setting "urban" for convenience, but
that adjective may tempt us to commit anachronisms. It is important to
distinguish the village and rural setting presupposed by most of the
gospel stories about Jesus from the culture of the Graeco-Roman
towns, but we must not confuse the latter with our post-industrial
notion of a city. I mean by the term "urban" that Pauline Christianity
was at home in the Greek *poleis* of the eastern Roman provinces.

One characteristic of that setting was "pluralism," if I may be
permitted yet another deliberate anachronism. There was no officially
sanctioned "religion" of the empire.[30] Both the hellenistic and the
Roman cultures tended to be quite tolerant of different kinds of
religious practices—so long as they did not endanger public order or
infringe upon common decency, and so long as they seemed to have
some ancient pedigrees. Specifically, the national cult of the resident
aliens was ordinarily not only tolerated but even protected—even if it
was a little bizarre in Roman eyes, as was the case with Judaeans. But
a new superstition without any national basis, like the Christians', was
something else again, and likely to attract suspicion or disdain.[31]

This pluralist context which is so strikingly absent from the
Fourth Gospel is always lurking at the edges of the Pauline letters.
Take, for example, the characterization of the converts in 1 Thessalonians 1:9 as those who "turned from idols to serve the living and true
God," or Paul's concern about interaction between the Christian
community and pagan culture as he answers questions about eating
"meat offered to idols" in 1 Corinthians 8–10, or his warning not to let

---

[29] I have analyzed the sociographic information of the Pauline letters in *The First
Urban Christians* (see previous note). For the evidence underlying the following
summary, I refer the reader of that work, and to the large literature cited there.
[30] MacMullen, *Paganism*; emphasized by also Nikolaus Walter, "Christusglaube und
heidnische Religiosität in paulinischen Gemeinden," *NTS* 25 (1979) 422-442, and Gerd
Theissen, *Psychologische Aspekte paulinischer Theologie* (Göttingen: Vandenhoeck &
Ruprecht, 1983) 46.
[31] Cf. the comments by E. A. Judge, "Christian Innovation and its Contemporary
Observers," in Brian Croke and Alanna M. Emmett, eds., *History and Historians in
Late Antiquity* (Sydney et al.: Pergamon, 1983) 13-15, and Robert L. Wilken, *The
Christians as the Romans Saw Them* (New Haven and London: Yale, 1984).

charismatic phenomena get out of hand, lest outsiders think the Christians were indulging in a Dionysiac orgy (1 Cor 14:23). Paul not only recognizes, as does the fourth evangelist, that it is not possible to "go out of the world" (1 Cor 5:10), he also is concerned that "the outsiders" should think well of the Christians' behavior (e.g. 1 Thess 4:11f.).

In further contrast to the Fourth Gospel, we hear very little about "the Jews" or "the Judaeans." The only place where Paul sounds like John is in 1 Thessalonians 2:14–16, and a number of commentators have suggested that all or part of that passage is an interpolation.[32] There is otherwise remarkably little in the Pauline letters to suggest any continuing contact between the Christian groups and the organized Jewish communities in their cities. Paul himself ran into conflict with Jewish authorities from time to time (2 Cor 11:24f.), but the real and potential conflicts he treats and anticipates in the congregations he addresses are either internal or between the Christian groups and the pagan society of the city.

This state of affairs is surprising on two counts. First, the book of Acts would have us believe that Paul always began his mission in the synagogue. That, however, is clearly a later idealization, although it cannot be entirely false in view of Paul's reported conflict with synagogue authorities, just mentioned, and his statement in 1 Corinthians 9:20. Nevertheless, his retrospective accounts of his missionary career assert that he saw himself commissioned entirely as "apostle of the gentiles" (Gal 1–2; Rom 15:15–21; cf.11:13f.). Accordingly, we have to set aside the Acts picture of the earliest mission in order to understand the separation of Pauline Christianity from the synagogues.

The second reason why the rarity of allusions to the Jewish communities in Pauline letters is surprising, however, has to do with

---

[32] Birger A. Pearson, "1 Thessalonians 2:13-16: A Deutero-Pauline Interpolation," *HTR* 64 (1971) 79-94; Daryl Schmidt, "1 Thess 2:13-16: Linguistic Evidence for an Interpolation," *JBL* 102 (1983) 269-279; other literature cited by both. The case for interpolation has been rebutted, most recently by Karl Paul Donfried, "Paul and Judaism: 1 Thessalonians 2:13-16 as a Test Case," *Interp* 38 (1984) 242-253, though I find his construal of the text strained. If commentators would stop to ask whether *hypo tōn ioudaiōn* in 2:14 should be translated "by the Jews" or not rather "by the Judaeans," I believe it would be obvious that vss. 13-14 fit quite well into the pattern of the letter and of Paul's thought elsewhere. Vss. 15-16, on the other hand, require the word to refer to "the Jews" in a global sense and import into the letter the kind of anti-Jewish polemic found in later Christian literature, especially in interpretations of the fall of Jerusalem. Donfried would make these verses an older tradition quoted by Paul; it ssems to me more likely they were added later by a reader whose conception of Paul's mission was rather like that of the author of Acts. Cf. *First Urban Christians* 227, n.117.

a central element in Paul's theology. The question of the continuing
validity in the Christian groups of such *miṣvot* as circumcision and
kashrut, and the broader issue of the relation between Israel's hopes
and traditions and Christianity (between "Jew and Greek"), were
vigorously debated in the Pauline circles. Paul and some of his
disciples made them the touchstone for understanding the radical
innovation entailed in accepting the gospel of the crucified Messiah.
Furthermore, there are several indications in Paul's letters that his
relationship to his own past and to "Israel according to the flesh"
continued to exercise his deepest feelings (e.g. Rom 9:1–5). Nevertheless, the locus of these conflicts is altogether different from that
reflected in the Fourth Gospel.

The main difference is this: the great issue in Pauline Christianity
is not between "the synagogue" and the sect of the Christians, but
within the Christian movement. The social context of Pauline groups
is the private household provided by various patrons in each city. That
form of organization does not become visible in the Johannine
communities until the later phase marked by the Johannine letters.
The household may have served as the location of those Christian
cells, too, by the time the Fourth Gospel was written, but the Gospel
provides no evidence for it. Instead, the identity of the groups is
largely determined by their reaction to the synagogues and the
synagogues' attitudes toward them. For Pauline Christians the case is
quite different. Like the fourth evangelist, Paul wants to claim the
name and hopes of Israel for the followers of Messiah Jesus.[33]
Theologically it is correct to say that the scriptures and traditions of
Judaism are a central and ineffaceable part of the Pauline Christians'
identity. *Socially,* however, the Pauline groups were never a sect of
Judaism. They organized their lives independently from the Jewish
associations of the cities where they were founded, and apparently, so
far as the evidence reveals, they had little or no interaction with the
Jews.

Paul's own reflection on Israel's "disbelief" and destiny in God's
plan is unique in early Christian literature (Rom 9–11). Even this
discussion, however, does not arise from any active engagement

---

[33] Much has been written about the phrase, "the Israel of God," in Gal 6:16. I think
myself that Paul uses it here with deliberate ambiguity. It certainly includes the
addressees, the Christian groups of Galatia, and it certainly is not limited to "Jewish
Christians." Yet, in the light of Paul's fuller exposition of his thinking about Israel not
too many years later in Rom 9-11, we are justified in thinking that "Israel" here includes
not only the "remnant" who follow Messiah Jesus (Rom 11:5), but also the entire
people, "all Israel," which would be reconciled in Paul's eschatological vision (Rom
11:26).

between either the Pauline groups or the various Christian groups in
Rome and the Jewish communities. This homily by Paul is the climax
of the entire letter, as commentators in the past few years have
belatedly recognized.[34] It belongs to Paul's reflection on the purpose
and meaning of his own mission, and that, in turn, is an integral part
of his protreptic discourse on the nature of the Christian life by which
he introduces himself to the Roman Christians.[35] It is thus, again, the
Christian community's internal dynamics and beliefs, rather than real
interaction with Jews, that evokes this discussion.

At least some of Paul's disciples understood the significance of his
preoccupation with unity of Jew and gentile in "the Israel of God."
The encyclical letter we know as Ephesians develops the grand idea
of one "household of God" uniting Jew and gentile 2:11–22). This can
be regarded as a kind of cosmic projection of an idealized Pauline
house church.[36] Yet in this letter there is no hint of any relation a
Christian might have with the majority of the Jews meeting in the
synagogue down the street. Ephesians' sublime disregard of that issue
is testimony that Pauline Christians in Asia Minor had gone their own
way without much contact with the strong, well placed Jewish
communities which existed in the cities of that region. The pseudonymous but more particular epistle to the Colossians points in the same
direction, despite the fact that it attacks a syncretistic movement
among the Christians which seems to involve a Jewish festival
calendar, sabbath observance, some dietary rules (2:16) and perhaps
Jewish mystical practice of some kind (2:18).[37] Even here the author
does not say anything about contact between the Christians and the
Jewish community of Colossae.

There is thus a certain paradox about Pauline Christianity. The
apostle himself was deeply concerned about the relation between
Christianity and "the Israel of God." Yet he and his associates had
created an organized movement that was entirely independent of the

---

[34] See especially Nils A. Dahl, *Studies in Paul* (Minneapolis: Augsburg, 1977) 137-158.
Also Krister Stendahl, *Paul among Jews and Gentiles and Other Essays* (Philadelphia:
Fortress, 1976) 4.

[35] Stanley K. Stowers, *The Diatribe and Paul's Letter to the Romans* (SBLDS 57; Chico,
CA: Scholars, 1981).

[36] On Ephesians' idealization of the church, see N. A. Dahl, "Cosmic Dimensions and
Religious Knowledge (Eph 3:18)," in E. Earle Ellis and Erich Grässer, eds., *Jesus und
Paulus; Festschrift fur Werner Georg Kümmel zum 70. Geburtstag* (Göttingen: Vand-
enhoeck & Ruprecht, 1975) 72f.

[37] See the various proposals represented in Fred O. Francis and Wayne A. Meeks, eds.,
*Conflict at Colossae: A Problem in the Interpretation of Early Christianity Illustrated
by Selected Modern Studies* (rev.ed., SBLSBS 4; Missoula, MT: Scholars, 1975).

Jewish communities in the cities of the northeastern Mediterranean basin. The scriptures and traditions from Judaism played a major part in the beliefs and practices of Pauline Christianity, yet the identity of the Pauline groups was not shaped by having once been within a Jewish context. However much Paul's own identity may have been formed by the trauma of what we call his conversion, there was no comparable trauma for the communities which he founded. Unlike the Johannine groups, the Pauline congregations were not composed of people who had become *aposynagōgoi.*

Matthew Against the Scribes and Pharisees

The combination of strong Jewish traditions with rejection of Jewish institutions is as fiercely ambivalent in Matthew as in John. The terms of the argument, however, are quite different. It is not always easy to determine exactly what is at issue in Matthew, and scholarly opinions have diverged widely on the question of the Matthean community's relationship to Judaism. Only in rather recent years have scholars recognized the full import of the question of precisely what kind of Judaism confronted the Matthean Christians and in what way. The recent comment by Graham Stanton is accurate: "Scholarly interest in many aspects of first-century Judaism is considerable and significant advances are being made, especially by J. Neusner and his pupils. Few Matthean specialists have yet taken these advances sufficiently seriously."[38] What would it mean for our three questions if we did take those advances seriously? First, it would mean keeping constantly in mind the diversity of both the forms of Judaism and the forms of Christianity in the first century. That point, however, is now generally conceded, at least in principle. Second, we would have to try more rigorously than has usually been the case to avoid anachronisms when comparing first-century documents with those produced by the rabbinic schools of the second century and later. Third, we would have to acknowledge that the means by which groups of Jews and Christians established their own cohesion, identity, and boundaries were not always the same. Christian scholars tend to think of group identity in terms of theological systems or "confessions," and in spite of our best intentions, we almost inevitably ask Christian theological questions of Jewish documents.[39] As a corrective, when we look through Matthew's eyes at the

---

[38] Graham Stanton, *The Interpretation of Matthew* (Issues in Religion and Theology 3; Philadelphia: Fortress and London: SPCK, 1983) 17.
[39] Jacob Neusner's criticism of E. P. Sanders, *Paul and Palestinian Judaism, HR* 18

Jewish groups he opposed, it will be well to begin with clues to more external aspects of the groups' life, which do not imply a systematic theology.

The opponents in Matthew are preeminently "the scribes and the Pharisees," and the Pharisees are particularly odious to the writer. There are other groups, too, which are mentioned as Jesus' opponents, but for the most part they seem to be relics of the remembered tradition and no longer to have sharp contours.[40] Matthew can, for example, simply merge the Sadducees with the Pharisees, even though he knows from Mark, if nowhere else, that they were distinct sects (Matt 3:7; 16:1,6,11,12 and Mark 22:34). The Pharisees and scribes of Matthew's acquaintance "like . . . to be called 'Rabbi' " (23:6f.), and the prohibition of this and other titles in the Christian community identifies "rabbi" with "teacher" (23:8–10). All of this fits admirably Neusner's reconstruction of the institutionalization that occurred at Yavneh, in which leaders from the sect of the Pharisees joined with members of the professional guild of scribes to create a new thing: the rabbinic academy and, eventually, the rabbinic court.[41] It has long been recognized that the issues at stake in the Matthean controversy stories have more similarity in both form and substance with parallels in rabbinic literature than do pre-Matthean forms. W. D. Davies especially, in his pioneering work on the Sermon on the Mount, argued eloquently for seeing the work of the Christian scribes in Matthew's community as "a parallel task" to that of the rabbis at Yavneh.[42] Neusner's work requires revision of Davies' at many points, but it tends to reinforce this fundamental insight.

Even if we accept the proposition that Matthew's "scribes and Pharisees" refer to the emerging rabbinate of Yavneh, however, a number of puzzles remain. Where and in what form did the Christian community encounter Yavneh's rabbis? From the typical setting of the controversy stories, we may gather that the main location was in "their [i.e., the Jews'] synagogues." There the rabbis have or want to have "the first seats" (23:6). That they also are said to like wide phylacteries

---

(1978) 177-191, is valid at precisely this point, though I think that on the whole he treats Sanders' important contribution rather too severely.

[40] Sjef van Tilborg, *The Jewish Leaders in Matthew* (Leiden: Brill, 1972) has sorted out the evidence conveniently, although his analysis is not particularly illuminating.

[41] Elaborated in many places, Jacob Neusner's reconstruction is conveniently summarized in "The Formation of Rabbinic Judaism: Yavneh (Jamnia) from A.D. 70 to 100," *ANRW* II/19.2 (1979) 3-42; cf. " 'Pharisaic-Rabbinic' Judaism: a Clarification," *HR* 12 (1973) 250-270.

[42] *The Background of the Sermon on the Mount* (Cambridge: University Press, 1964) 315.

and long "hems" (presumably *ṣiṣit* 23:5) does not help us to be more specific, but the whole passage implies that the rabbis enjoy considerable prestige in public (in the *agorai,* at banquets) as well as in the synagogues. The problem is the more difficult because we know so little about the extent of the Yavneh academy's power and prestige outside its immediate circle. Because the majority of Matthean scholars think, though without absolutely convincing evidence, that Matthew was written in Antioch on the Orontes, we would like very much to know whether representatives of the Yavneh school, or a diaspora equivalent similarly constituted, could have exercised power in that metropolis at so early a date. Unfortunately, the prospects are slim for answering these questions definitively.

We turn then to our second question. What connections were there between the Christian groups out of which and for which Matthew was written, and the emerging new form of rabbi-led Judaism? Scholars who have pursued this question in recent years have come to dismayingly opposite conclusions. Either Matthew's Christians were a "Jewish-Christian" sect which, however alienated from the rabbinic leadership, still belonged to the "union of synagogues" (as Hummel puts it),[43] or they had no connections at all and existed in a purely pagan environment (Van Tilborg, for example). What leads serious scholars to such incompatible conclusions is a real ambivalence in the evidence in the First Gospel itself. We must decide how the "Jewish" elements in Matthew are to be reconciled with the "anti-Jewish" elements, a problem similar to that in the Fourth Gospel. The "redaction-historical" method that has come to prevail in such studies, despite the discouraging lack of agreement in results, does give promise of a solution along lines similar to those found in recent Johannine scholarship. A consensus is emerging that the Matthean community went through several stages of interaction with the Jewish communities close to it, and that these stages have left fossils in the strata of tradition and redaction.[44] A quick summary of the evidence will show the direction in which an answer to our question must be sought.

---

[43] Reinhart Hummel, *Die Auseinandersetzung zwischen Kirche und Judentum im Matthäusevangelium* (BEvT.33, 2nd ed; Munich: Kaiser, 1966).

[44] For example, W. G. Thompson, *Matthew's Advice to a Divided Community* (Analecta Biblica 44; Rome: Pontifical Biblical Institute, 1971); summarized in "An Historical Perspective in the Gospel of Matthew," *JBL* 93 (1974) 243-262; Douglas R. A. Hare, *The Theme of Jewish Persecution in the Gospel According to St. Matthew* (SNTSMS 6; Cambridge: University Press, 1967; John P. Meier, *The Vision of Matthew: Christ, Church and Morality in the First Gospel* (Theological Inquiries; New York, Ramsey, Toronto: Paulist, 1979).

There is much in Matthew that sounds like intra-Jewish, sectarian debate. To begin with, there are the learned arguments from scripture which have led Von Dobschütz and others to identify the evangelist with the "scribe discipled to the Kingdom of Heaven" of 13:52. Then there is the concern with "commandments" that crops up throughout Matthew, culminating in the "Great Commission" of 28:20. The Sermon on the Mount reads like the ethic of a Jewish sect. Jesus speaks here as the authoritative teacher of Israel. The crowds are astonished at his teaching for he has authority, unlike *their* scribes (Matthew has added the pronoun to the Marcan phrase; 7:29). Here and elsewhere in this gospel we could say that Jesus is the authoritative interpreter of *halakha* (for example, in the Sabbath controversies of chapter 12.) Yet only rarely does the form of these controversies approximate the forms typical of the debates transmitted in rabbinic tradition's early strata.[45] The Matthean debates are much broader and less stylized, and they question more fundamental issues of Jewish identity.

Jesus' authority in Matthew is that of the Messiah of Israel, the son of David, who has come to "save his people" (1.21). In illustration of this, the crowds repeatedly bring their sick to Jesus for healing, for, as Messiah, he "bears away" the diseases of Israel (8:17; citing Isa 53:4). Matthew inserts one of his summaries to this effect into the Temple Cleansing pericope: "They brought him blind and lame *in the Temple,* and he healed them" (21:14). In these passages and elsewhere, Jesus is well received by the "crowds" (*ochloi*), but rejected by the formal leaders of Israel.[46] In Mark it was the leaders of Israel— there identified as the high priests and scribes and elders (Mark 11:27)—who "recognized that it was against them that he spoke the parable" of the vineyard (12:12); Matthew connects this remark with the parable of the two sons also, and changes the leaders to "the high priests and the Pharisees" (Matt 21:45).

From such texts we get the impression that the Matthean prophets and disciples were an integral part of one or more of the Jewish communities in Matthew's environment, challenging the leaders on their own ground. In support of such a reading, one could observe that 23:2f. seems to accord some authority to the teaching of the scribes and Pharisees, even while sharply challenging their integrity and

---

[45] A number of important points are still to be found in Morton Smith, *Tannaitic Parallels to the Gospels* (JBLMS 6; Philadelphia: SBL, 1951); for more extended analysis of the early rabbinic forms, see Jacob Neusner, *The Rabbinic Traditions about the Pharisees before 70* (Leiden: Brill, 1971).

[46] See Van Tilborg 142-165.

sincerety (contrast 16:5–12!). This sounds indeed like a sectarian
dispute between two schools, both of which construe the faithful life
in similar terms, but which disagree about the locus of authority and
the form of internal community life. So also, Matthew retains the
Q-saying that the disciples will "sit on twelve thrones judging the
twelve tribes of Israel" (19:28). It is easy to imagine a time when
Christian missionaries actually believed that they could win over the
allegiance of masses of Jews from their constituted leaders. Perhaps,
adopting part of W. D. Davies' suggestions in *The Background of the
Sermon on the Mount,* we could even think of an active competition
between representatives of the new "rabbinic" academy at Yavneh
and missionaries of the Jesus movement.

Yet there are many indications in the First Gospel that the
connections with organized Jewish communities cannot have been so
close when the gospel was written. If the Matthean Christians once
held such an optimistic view of their mission to the organized Jews in
their town, they have long since become disillusioned. In a remark
that betrays a distance quite as complete as that in John, they can
speak of a story about the disciples' faking the Resurrection, a story
"spread among the Jews until this day" (28:15). This gospel contains
a rising theme, climaxing in the trial and passion narrative, of the
alienation of "the whole people" from Jesus, their appointed Messiah.
The theme is clearly sounded in the healing of the centurion, for "in
no one in Israel" has Jesus found such faith (8:10), and he adds that
"many will come from East and West and recline at dinner with
Abraham and Isaac and Jacob, but the sons of the Kingdom will be cast
into outer darkness." The implication of this dark saying works its way
through the rest of the gospel: through the judgment pronounced in
10:14f. on towns of Israel which did not receive the apostles (emphasized by Matthew's placement of the judgment pericope from Q in
11:20–24 and the saying that no one can know the Father but the Son
in 11:27); through the parables of Two Sons, the Vineyard, and the
Banquet. Despite the modified Marcan statement in 21:45f. (quoted
above), these parables speak not merely of judgment on Israel's
leaders, but of replacing Israel by another *ethnos* (21:41, 43). Looking
back, we see that this replacement is foreshadowed by the curious
story of the "Canaanite" woman of 15:21–28, for Jesus' disclaimer that
he is sent only to "the lost sheep of the house of Israel" is but the
counterpoint to his receiving the faith of this gentile, just as the
identical phrase in the sending of the twelve (10:6) is prelude for
judgment on those who reject their message.[47] Thus not only is "the

---

[47] Cf. Meier 104.

whole sanhedrin" responsible for Jesus' condemnation (26:59), but "all the people" confirms it by the saying which would have such terrible and unforeseeable consequences, "His blood be on us and on our children" (27:25).

Like the Johannine community, then, the Matthean was shaped to a very large extent by the attempt to define the Christian groups' relation to Jewish traditions, Jewish expectations, and the organized Jewish communities. Unlike John, but rather like Paul, Matthew sees the Jewish self-definition primarily in terms of law and commandments and, more broadly, in the question of what it means to "do the will of God." Like Paul personally, but unlike the Pauline churches, Matthew's community has had to wrestle with that issue in a way central to its own development. However, all three are alike, finally, in seeing the ultimate issue and crisis to be defined by christology. Although the christologies of John, Paul, and Matthew are different from one another in many respects, the breaking point for each is in the question of Jesus' role as Messiah vis à vis Israel (and the world).

The Judaism from which Matthew has separated looks much more like that taking shape in the academy of Yavneh around the same time than does the Judaism from which the Johannine Christians were expelled. The "rabbis" who represented the Yavnean (or some analogous but otherwise unknown) merging of scribal profession with Pharisaic piety were important and prestigious people in Matthew's environment. Unfortunately there are few clues that would enable us to describe that environment with any specificity. "Their synagogues" and "banquets" and *agorai* sound like an urban setting, and Matthew's Greek and the knowledge of the LXX he presupposes speak for that as well. The early mission to "the lost sheep of the house of Israel" described in chap. 10, however, sounds like itinerancy among villages on Palestinian soil[48] (though some of Matthew's redactional touches make the scenery less rural; e.g. addition of *polis* in vss. 11, 14, 15). Did the Christian groups for which Matthew wrote, or some significant number of their members, originate as a sect of Galilean Jews before the war, later to join the already existing Christian household communities of Antioch? It is probably not possible to advance beyond conjecture. It is not even possible to say

---

[48] For a wide-ranging and suggestive discussion of the "ecology" of the early mission, see Gerd Theissen, "Wanderradikalismus: Literatursoziologische Aspekte der Überlieferung von Worten Jesu im Urchristentum," and "Legitimation und Lebensunterhalt: Ein Beitrag zur Soziologie urchristlicher Missionare," both reprinted in *Studien zur Soziologie des Urchristentums* (2d. ed., Tübingen: Mohr (Siebeck), 1983) 79-105, 201-230.

very much about the internal organization of the Christian groups, even though such passages as 16:18–20 and 18:15–20 imply a high degree of sectarian self-consciousness and self-discipline.

Concluding Observations

The three major witnesses from early Christian literature which we have considered show us three quite different circles of the movement, each profoundly shaped by its Jewish heritage and by the trauma of separation from Judaism experienced either by the sect as a whole or by some of its leaders. The path of separation, then, was not single or uniform. Taking these three paths as representative, it may yet be useful to ask, now, where were they leading for the future of Christianity and of Judaism? On the one hand, they were leading to a Christianity that could not allow itself to forget its origins in Judaism. That meant, preeminently, that in order to define itself Christianity would always in some way turn to the Jewish scriptures. Moreover, it inherited some of the Jewish ways of interpreting them. If Marcion's movement had endured, Christianity would have become a very different thing.

Nevertheless, by the end of the first century, and much earlier than that in the Pauline groups, the Christian movement was socially independent of the Jewish communities in the cities of the empire. That had little or nothing to do with formal measures like the *birkat ha-minim*, but much to do with the internal dynamics illustrated by the three corpora of documents we have surveyed and with the social setting of Jews and Christians in the Greek cities. There would continue to be interactions between Jews and Christians in various places; there would continue to be followers of Jesus who remained within synagogues here and there, down through at least the fifth century, despite disapproval by leaders on both sides; there would be Christians of pagan origin who continued to be attracted to the synagogue until at least the same period. These, however, were the exceptions. By and large the separation was complete by the beginning of the second century. For example in Antioch, the first bishop, Ignatius, betrays hostility toward "Judaism" but little evidence of any knowledge of the Jews. A later successor, Theophilus, could simply take for granted that the scriptures and central traditions of Israel now belonged to the Christians.[49]

---

[49] Ignatius, Mag 8:1-9:2; 10:3; Philad 6:1; 8:2; see also William R. Schoedel, "Ignatius and the Archives," *HTR* 71 (1978) 97-106, and Paul J. Donahue, "Jewish Christianity in the Letters of Ignatius of Antioch," *VC* 32 (1978) 81-93; Theophilus, *Ad Autol.* 2.33 et passim.

To Jews, claims like those of Theophilus must have seemed so preposterous and the Christian movement so remote or so minuscule that, save for a few local exceptions, they could ignore it altogether. That accounts for the sparse evidence about Christianity in Mishnah, Talmuds, and early midrashim. Too late, the Jewish leaders would be forced to recognize how dangerous the Christian movement was. Not even the post-Constantinian changes of the fourth century seem to have alerted them, portentous as those changes seem in retrospect. In places like Antioch, Sardis, and Aphrodisias, the Jewish communities remained secure and powerful, hardly troubled even as the legal and political mechanisms of Christian dominance were put into place. Yet what survives from those communities' glory is only what has lately been uncovered by the archaeologist's spade. In time, the Christians would dominate the cities and, in ways partly obvious and partly obscure, would choke off the growth of those Jewish communities. The living Judaism that survived, which we see taking shape as a "utopian" vision in the Mishnah and more practically in the two talmuds,[50] seems rather to have been a rural and small-town phenomenon. Thus the massive confrontation between "apostolic Christianity" and "normative Judaism," which even now haunts the imagination of students of Christian origins, never happened.

---

[50] Jacob Neusner, *Judaism: The Evidence of the Mishnah* (Chicago and London: University of Chicago Press, 1981; *Judaism in Society: The Evidence of the Yerushalmi* (Chicago: Univ. of Chicago, 1983).

5

Vilifying the Other and Defining the Self: Matthew's and John's Anti-Jewish Polemic in Focus

Sean Freyne
Trinity College, Dublin

The first and fourth gospels' Jewish character and concerns have often been contrasted with their strident anti-Jewish sentiments, prompting somewhat embarrassed Christian interpreters, at least in post-holocaust times, to find ways of softening the impact of their vituperative rhetoric. One favoured tactic has been to distinguish between the Jewish people, the crowds, who on the whole are sympathetic to Jesus, and the leaders, who are hostile and so the butt of the evangelists' condemnations. Yet even a casual perusal shows that such a distinction does not really hold up for either work as a whole, even if it does appear to fit certain individual episodes or comments. Another approach has been to ascribe the anti-Jewish remarks to an earlier stage of the tradition and thus to exonerate the final redactor. But this merely puts the problem back one stage. Moreover, the redactor cannot be entirely free of blame since he has, after all, included the offending material in his work.[1] Third, in the case of the Fourth Gospel, the Jewish hostility to Jesus has been identified with that of the world, which is then interpreted existentially, following Bultmann[2]. But such a solution to the problem does

---

[1] For a recent discussion of such attempts in regard to John, and with a proposal along the lines of different attitudes reflected at different level of the work, cf. C. J. Hickling, "Attitudes to Judaism in the Fourth Gospel" in *L'Évangile de Jean: Sources, rédaction, theologie* (Louvain: 1977), ed. M. de Jonge, 347-354; also J. von Wahlde, "The Johannine Jews," NTS 28(1982)33-60. For a discussion of Matthew's views on Judaism, cf. S. Legasse, "L'Anti-judaisme dans l'évangile selon Matthieu," in *L'Évangile selon Matthieu: Rédaction et Theologie* (Louvain: 1971), ed. M. Didier, 417-428; cf. also W. Pesch, "Theologische Aussagen der Redaktion von Matthäus 23," in *Orientierung an Jesus, Zur Theologie der Synoptiker. Festschrift für Josef Schmidt* (Herder: 1973), ed. P. Hoffman, 286-299; E. A. Russell, "The Image of the Jew in Matthew's Gospel" in *Studia Evangelica* VII, ed. E. A. Livingstone, T.U.126, (Berlin: 1982), 427-42.

[2] E. Grässer, "Die Antijüdische Polemik in Johannesevangelium," NTS 10 (1965) 74-90.

not consider that in John, the world is characterised precisely as
comprised of unbelieving Jews. The text itself drives us back to the
question of what caused this anti-Jewish polemic within the gospels,
and to what social matrix it belonged. Therefore, it would be a false
hermeneutic to try to escape the force of the Matthaean and Johannine
invective either by attempting to exonerate the masses of Jesus'
Jewish contemporaries from responsibility for this rejection, or by so
de-historicising the actual confrontation that it ignores the clear
import of our texts.

Our conference's overall theme has prompted the question which
may serve as a new key for exploring the polemics of these two works
and their intentions. It is a sad fact of everyday human experience,
both at the personal and social levels, that our most sharply worded,
slanted and in the end downright insulting statements are often
directed at those persons or groups who threaten us most and impinge
most directly on our own sense of identity by challenging our
self-esteem. Precisely, it would seem, because it touches the very core
of who we think we are, the threat which is posed by such "others"
provokes a primitive, even violent response. This violence expresses
itself in attempting to destroy the "other," at least at those points
where the perceived threat is most real.[3] This universal human
experience had been thematised in the Greco-Roman world of our
authors in a conscious set of rules for *vituperatio* which were learned
in the schools of rhetoric and aimed at destroying the social and
political *persona* of one's adversary.[4] The Palestinian Ben Sirach,
writing in the second century B.C.E., was equally conscious of the
social implications of vituperative speech, as he repeatedly reminds
his readers.[5] It does not, therefore, appear too presposterous to

---

[3] For a useful discussion of the literary expression of such ideas from an historical
perspective, cf. R. C. Elliot, *The Power of Satire, Magic, Ritual, Art*, Princeton 1960.
[4] Cf. M. A. Grant, *The Ancient Rhetorical Theories of the Laughable*, Madison, 1924;
D. L. Clark, *Rhetoric in Greco-Roman Education*, (New York: 1957). Aristotle, in his
Rhetorica (3.19,1 and 1.9.4,41), set the trend for subsequent treatment by giving the
following list of virtues that one should mention in a *laudatio*: justice, courage,
self-control, magnificence, magnanimity, liberality, gentleness, practical and speculative wisdom. An evil character is proved by the opposites. These criteria had been
developed at Rome by Cicero (*De Orat.* 2,43,182 and 2.11.45f) Cf. also the ps.-
Ciceronian treatise on rhetoric, *Ad Herrenium*, especially, 1.5.12f.
[5] Ben Sirach 5:11-6:17; 8:5-7; 28:14; 39:4.6.10. These admonitions to moderation in
one's speech and recognition of the social implications of the language of praise and
blame may be due to the court provenance of the wisdom tradition, but they could
equally well reflect Greco-Roman rhetorical conventions, given the deep penetration of
hellenistic culture into Judaism as reflected in this work according to Martin Hengel's
masterful analysis in *Judentum und Hellenismus*.

suggest that both Matthew's and John's vilification of Jews comes directly and immediately from their concerns to define the identities of the communities for whom they wrote. This contention could certainly look for support from recent studies of both works, stressing as they do the respective evangelists' strong community concerns and equally, their Jewish milieux. Their necessity to define 'a place on which to stand' within Judaism and to lay sole and privileged claim to it, would appear to offer an interesting vantage point for evaluating what we have called Matthew's and John's anti-Jewish rhetoric.

Choosing two early Christian writers for our exploration does not of course suggest that we are necessarily dealing with a common front against a common Judaism in these two works. There are at least some indications in each, especially in the treatment of the figure of Peter, that had they come into actual contact, the authors and their constituencies might have been only slightly more sympathetic to each other than they were to their respective Jewish opponents. Rather, the value of contrasting in the light of this paper's working hypothesis two early Christian communities which deal with similar, if not identical, social situations that touch them deeply, lies in illustrating the ways in which a common concern can work itself out giving rise to quite different perspectives both on the perceivers and on their opponents.

Community Building, in the sense of giving a group its distinctive identity within a larger tradition, has many different aspects. It must inevitably touch various levels of peoples' lives–the economic level, the cultural level, in the broad sense of values, attitudes and assumptions, and ultimately, the religious level. It is a commonplace of recent New Testament studies that these levels or perspectives interact with and influence each other, even if none of them should be collapsed into any or all of the others. For our present purposes it will be sufficient to concentrate on the following three aspects of this complex process. One, what role do the communities of Matthew and John ascribe to themselves as primary within the larger Jewish tradition? Two, within each group, how does this vision of its task shape the foundation myth in terms of its Jesus figure? Three, what typical attitudes are expected from the loyal adherents of each group, given the group's assumptions about itself and its origins?

1) Matthew

To state that Matthew thought of his community as having primarily a teaching responsibility seems like stressing the obvious when we consider the gospel's final commission "go make disciples of all the nations, *teaching* them ..." (Mt.28:19). Yet we need to specify this role more precisely. The disciples are to teach all that Jesus "has commanded" (*eneteilamēn*). This points to the considerable body of teaching that Jesus imparts throughout the gospel, focused particularly in the five great discourses that punctuate the story. While these collections of sayings embody many different types from a form-critical point of view, at the work's close they are all categorised in one particular way, namely, as commandments. They are not proverbs, beatitudes, apocalyptic utterances or prophetic speeches; they are *entolai,* commands.

That this characterisation of Jesus' teaching grows at once from the Matthaean community's own self-understanding and its perception of its various Jewish counterparts, emerges from a number of considerations of the work as a whole. The community has its own explicit rites of admission and rules for expulsion (28:19 and 18:15-19). These show considerable similarity to the Qumran and other sectarian halakha.[6] For instance, those who are *fully* discipled in the kingdom (*mathēteutheis*), and so capable of carrying out the final commission (cf.28:19), are twice designated as scribes (*grammateis,* 13:51 and 23:34) This designation is not found elsewhere for any Christian minister, but it is a characteristic description of a teacher in 2nd-temple Judaism. "Binding and loosing" (16:19 and 18:18), terms which have plenty of parallels in later rabbinic writing to describe an authoritative teaching role (but cf. already Mt.23.4), are used to describe the Matthaean church's understanding of its own authorisation to teach.[7] The community's piety has a distinctively Jewish spirit to it in its prayer, fasting and alms giving, yet it too is presented in terms of a set of commands defining Christian piety's specific character in terms of not doing what is done in the synagogues (6:2 and 5). The gospel's central notion, the kingdom of God (heavens), is itself the object of teaching and instruction (13:11 and 19). Knowledge of the kingdom defines the Christian scribe, "who can bring forth from his treasure the new and the old" (13:52). Matthew treats many of the disputes between Jesus and his Pharisaic and/or scribal opponents in such a way that, unlike Mark, his source, he vindicates not Jesus' authority but the Matthaean community rule. Indeed in one instance (Mt.19:9) he appears to opt quite deliberately for one of the current

[6] J. Gnilka, "Die Kirche des Matthäus und die Gemeinde von Qumran," BZ 7(1963) 43-63; C.-H. Hunzinger, "Spüren pharisäischer Institutionen in der frühen Rabbinishcen Uberlieferung," in *Tradition und Glaube, Festschrift für K. G. Kuhn* (Göttingen: 1971), 147-156
[7] G. Bornkamm, "Die Binde und Lösgewalt in der Kirche des Matthäus" in *Die Zeit Jesus. Festschrift für H. Schlier* (Freiburg: 1970), 93-107; P. Hoffmann, "Der Petrus-Primat in Matthäusevangelium," in *Neues Testament und Kirche. Festschrift für R. Schnackenburg,* ed. J. Gnilka, 94-114; cf. especially, 101f. n. 29.

halakhic opinions (at least as ascribed by later authorities) on the issue of divorce.[8] In these disputes, Jesus appears as the Jewish authorities' teacher. When they call his ruling into question, they are represented as not understanding the Scriptures (9:13; 12:3.5.7.; 21:16.42; 22:29.31). And on one occasion, they are represented as transgressing those Scriptures through their own tradition (15:3; ct. Mk.7:8).

This list, by no means exhaustive, should suffice to illustrate that Matthew's concern with teaching and his manner of categorising both Jesus and his disciples as teachers, arises directly from and is determined by other Jewish teachers' experience, the claims, piety and the mode of instruction, based on the common heritage of the Scriptures. But Matthew does not conceive of this teaching community as just one among many possible rivals; he wishes to make absolute claims for his Jesus figure and the community that is linked to him in its teaching mission. Jesus alone merits the designations "teacher" (*didaskalos*) or "master" (*katergētēs*). Others are not to aspire to any such title within the community, even if they can be known officially as prophets, wise men and scribes (Mt.23:8-10 and 23:34).

The reason for this apparent discrepancy (within the same chapter) with regard to suitable nomenclature for those variously engaged in a teaching ministry is best explained in the light of the earlier presentation at 11:25-30 and 16:16-20. The former passage is made up in part of a Q passage (vv.25-27,cf.Lk.10:21-22) and in part by special Matthaean material (vv.28-30) which by implication contrasts Jesus' teaching (his light yoke) with that of the wise and understanding (presumably the scribes and pharisees), who elsewhere are castigated for placing heavy and unsupportable burdens on men's shoulders (23:4). However, Jesus' disciples receive a special revelation from him concerning the Father.[9] Likewise, Peter's confession of Jesus as "the Son of the Living God" is based not on flesh and blood but on a revelation from the Father (16:17). With these claims, expressed in both wisdom and apocalyptic language, the Matthaean community lays claim to an intimate knowledge of the Father's will through its only teacher, 'the Christ'. Thus it seeks to invest its own teaching with special authority since its definitive instructor and guide is the

---

[8] R.Hummel, *Die Auseinandersetzung zwischen Kirche und Judentum im Matthäusevangelium* (Munich: 1963), 36-56.
[9] The polemical, anti-pharisaic and anti-scribal tendencies of the Matthaean redaction and location of this passage have been well demonstrated recently by G. Künzel, *Studien zum Gemeindverständnis des Matthäus-Evangeliums* (Stuttgart: 1978), 79-94.

mythical eschatological teacher.[10] Within such a perspective there is no place for teachers who might claim an authority based on learning or tradition. Matthaean teachers may indeed be called scribes, wise men or prophets, but by the nature of their community's founding myth, their task and function is inevitably seen as different from that of their counterparts in Judaism's other branches. Matthew, it seems, wants to make this point aggressively, and so the Christology of the work is developed to underpin its claims. Emmanuel, interpreted as "God with us", is the name of the child Jesus (1:21); he is present as guarantor of the community's decisions (18:20), and in the end, the teaching mission is based on his presence being continued to the close of the age (28:20).

From this founding myth of Jesus as the eschatological teacher whose messianic claims are authenticated through an appeal to the Scriptures at every stage of his ministry, Matthew draws very clear consequences for the teaching that is proposed in Jesus' name. Corresponding to the motif of Scripture's fulfilment throughout his career (which highlights its *heilsgeschichtliche* character), there is also the theme of the laws' and prophecies' fulfilment as God's revealed will (Mt.5:17), whose prophetic function is indicated by Mt. 11:15.[11]

Thus, Matthew seeks to build his teaching on the inherited tradition, yet at the same time to supercede it. The scribe of the kingdom can bring forth "the new and the old" (13:52; cf.9:17), thus providing a righteousness that is greater than that of the scribes and Pharisees and which alone is suited for entry into the kingdom (5:21). The Scribes' and Pharisees' authority is recognised at one level because they sit on Moses' seat (23:2), yet their teaching is declared inadequate for the new situation which Matthew believes Jesus' career to have inaugurated (7:28). To be "perfect" (*teleios*), a Matthaean solipsism among the Synoptics (5:38; 19:21), is the attainable ideal only for those who call God, Father (that is, the disciples of Jesus, cf.6:10), and who are prepared to follow Jesus' radical ideal no matter how meticulous their observance of the old may have been.

It is because of these claims to a higher ethical standard based on

---

[10] Cf. H. Teeple, *The Mosaic Eschatological Prophet*, JBL Monographs X, (Philadelphia: 1957), and more recently, T. Donaldson, "Moses Typology and the Sectarian nature of early Christian anti-Judaism: A Study of Acts 7" JSNT 12 (1981) 27-52, have highlighted the evidence for this understanding of Moses as the end-time teacher in Second-Temple Jewish literature of various strands.

[11] J. Meier's treatment of this passage from the point of view of Matthaean redaction seems the most satisfying to me. Cf. his *Law and History in Matthew's Gospel* (Rome: 1976), and more briefly, *The Vision of Matthew*, Paulist 1978, 222-229.

the eschatological-teacher myth in which its life and beliefs are grounded that the Matthaean community can make absolutist claims on its own behalf with regard both to the inheritance and the future of Israel. As we shall see, unlike John our author persists in using Israel as the designation for Judaism in a global sense during the actual ministry of Jesus (10:56; 15:24). But this is only to point up its failures and its tragedy; failure in fruit-bearing means the transference of the kingdom to another *ethnos* (21:43) and leads ultimately to the tragedy of an abandoned house that remains deserted (23:38f) as unrepentant Israel finds no place at the eschatological banquet with its own patriarchs (8:10f). Being a son of Abraham does not count now (3:9) since sons of the kingdom are recognised not by birth but by faith in Jesus as God's eschatological teacher that leads to doing the Father's will as he has defined it (cf.17:26; 12:50; 21:31). For Matthew, confirmation of this understanding of his community's substitution for Israel and so validation for its foundation myth is seen in the fact that Israel's official death-wish (27:25) has been confirmed in his own generation (23:34,36) by the king's destruction of his rebelious city (22:7).

2) John

When the first and fourth gospels are examined under the rubric of "Jewish concerns," of the many possible contrasts between them, the absence of detailed treatment of Jewish legal issues in the latter work is the most striking. Twice a sabbath healing is the occasion to trigger off a dispute between Jesus and his Jewish opponents. Yet that issue is very quickly passed over for the one central to the whole gospel, namely, Jesus' authority and theological claim to be equal to God (5:10f; 9:14; cf.7:19ff.).[12] It is all the more significant, therefore, to find it repeatedly stressed that Jesus' opponents are observant Jews in the strict sense and judge him accordingly—they claim he cannot be from God on the grounds that he does not observe the sabbath (9:10). In strict accordance with the Jewish law (cf. Lev 24:16; M.Sot 5:3; Ant IV,8.6) Jesus is to be stoned not for violation of the sabbath, but for blasphemy (10:30-34; cf.8:59; 11:8), and the people who are sympathetic to him are to be excommunicated from the synagogue (9:22; 12:42; 16:2). In the opponents' eyes there can be only this one explanation for such naivetè: "this people who do not know the law are accursed" (7:49). On the other hand, since the opponents have heard from the law that the Messiah lives for ever, how can Jesus say

---

[12] S. Pancaro, *The Law in the Fourth Gospel*, NT Suppl XLII (Leiden: 1975), especially 9-63.

that the Son of man must be raised up (12:34)? They have a law and according to that law Jesus should die (19:7), but they themselves cannot enter the Praetorium lest they become defiled and cannot celebrate Passover (18:28. cf.19:31). It is not that the disciples of Jesus are made to espouse an antinomian position against these opponents within the gospel. While the Johannine Jesus gives just one commandment (*entolē*), namely to love the brother (13:34), elsewhere (14:15.21; 15:10) this is designated by the plural (*entolai*), but these are nowhere spelled out, least of all by the development of a distinctive *halakha* as in Matthew.[13] Whatever the range of concerns covered by such commands, the author(s) of the Fourth Gospel show no desire to derive them from Scripture as a way of countering their opponents legal orientation. Yet such a holding back does not mean that the fourth gospel is totally removed from the sphere of Jewish concerns. Quite the contrary, as we shall see. What it does suggest, however, is that the Johannine community has adopted a strategy quite different to Matthew's in order to establish its own claims. It has no desire to define itself as an alternative to those branches of Judaism that were making or had made Pentateuchal law the corner store for their edifice. The silence is deafening; it is as though there is a conscious attempt to destroy the opponents' world by refusing to take it seriously.

The way the Johannine community has developed its own foundation myth, which Wayne Meeks has so impressively developed in relation to the group's attitude to "the world" as represented by the Jews, corresponds to this stance. However, it seems possible to take Meek's insight further by focussing on aspects of the Johannine Christ myth other than the ascent/descent motif. Meek's article touches on these but does not develop them.[14] Of course we are dealing with a highly complex picture. Strands of varying hues from various backgrounds—Jewish, Gnostic, hellenistic–are all interwoven to present a Christ myth that underpins a community that is turned in on itself, that has a high consciousness of its own identity, and which has separated itself from the world, from Judaism and, it seems, even from other Christian groups.[15] Nevertheless, by focussing on certain di-

---

[13] Pancaro (*Law*, 445-51), and others see here a conscious use of Deuteronomic legal terminology, especially the oscillation between *entolē* (singular) and *entolai* (plural). The absence of any specific legal enactments against such a background only helps to highlight the provocative nature of the assertions in Jewish ears.

[14] W. Meeks, "The Man from Heaven in Johannine Sectarianism," JBL 91 (1972) 44-72.

[15] G. McRae, "The Fourth Gospel and *Religionsgeschichte*," CBQ 32 (1970) 13-24; D. Moody Smith, "Johannine Christianity: Some Reflections on its character and delineation" NTS 21(1975) 222-248.

mensions of the Johannine Christ myth that can with some confidence be identified as Jewish, we should manage to detect the points at which the community wishes either to be reassured in its own claims or rejects those of rival groupings. As Nils Dahl reminds us, it is as "the Jews" that the Johannine community characterises the unbelieving world, particularly since it is excluded from the synagogue. There is an almost universal consensus that the Johannine writings took final shape within the context of a dispute with Jammia Judaism.[16]

Because John contrasts so strikingly with Matthew in the place it gives to the law in its community, it is particularly instructive to see John's treatment of Moses, (and indeed other figures of the ancient Scriptures, generally) in relation to the Christ figure. Unlike Matthew, John recognizes no law or prophets to be fulfilled. Rather, they are witnesses to Christ who can now be called in evidence to the great *krisis* that Jesus' ministry initiates. Already 1:16f. strikes a critical note of contrast between "law given to Moses" and "grace and truth through Jesus Christ," even if the *charin anti charitos* of the previous verse could arguably be taken to suggest a synthetic rather than an antithetic parallelism.[17] Subsequently, there is no independent value ascribed to the Mosaic law, least of all as a revelation of the divine will; the Scriptures are not a source of eternal life as the Jews think, but only a witness to Christ (1:45 and 5:39). Hence, there is no desire to develop a set of observances based on those Scriptures. Jesus' command is new, not a combination of the new and the old, and it is specifically his (cf.15:12). The law, on the other hand, is theirs. Since they have so badly misunderstood the Law (that is the Scriptures), Moses, as author of the Scriptures ("he wrote of me" 5:40), will be their accuser (5:45). So their appeal to him against "this man" as to one to whom God spoke is tragically pointless and mistaken (9:28f. Indeed, they so totally misunderstand Moses' role as witness to Christ that their refusal to believe in Jesus implies they never really shared

---

[16] The Johannine Church and History," reprinted in N. Dahl, *Jesus in the Memory of the Early Church*, Minneapolis, 1976, 99-119, especially 111. There is widespread acceptance of J. L. Martyn's conclusions about the influence of the expulsion from the synagogue on Johannine Christians, even when some reservations are expressed about certain aspects of his argument. Cf. his *History and Theology in the Fourth Gospel*, Rev. ed. (Nashville: 1979).

[17] H. Thyen, "Das Heil Kommt von den Juden," in D. Lührmann and G. Strecker, eds. *Kirche, Festschrift für G. Bornkamm*, 185-204, especially 173f, argues for a synthetic parallelism in line with the whole positive tone of his article in regard to the Johannine Jews; Pancaro, *Law* 539f argues for an antithetic understanding of law and gospel both in this verse and elsewhere in John.

in the Sinai revelation (5:37). On one occasion, it is conceded that Moses has given the Jews the law only to accuse these law-observant people of never having kept it (7:19)! Thus the authority of Moses and Abraham, Isaiah, Jacob and the prophets as representative figures in the Jewish tradition relates to their witnessing to Christ and authenticating his claims as the sole revealer of the Father. Consequently, any Jewish tradition that might seek to build itself on their foundation is seriously misled and can make no claim to the truth.[18]

In this exclusive and absolute role of the Johannine Christ figure within the Jewish tradition many different strands of that tradition—wisdom, cultic, mystical—are appropriated, sometimes positively, sometimes negatively. But it is in relation to the legal tradition as represented by Moses that one detects at once the most urgent, and therefore the most polemical thrust. Yet it is this very claim, based on a Christocentric view of history, that determines the community's own stance. It alone is Israel, not the new or the replacement Israel, but simply Israel (1:31.50; 3:10; 12:13; cf.1:48), the community of Jesus' disciples who have accepted him as the revelation of the Father's *doxa* (cf.2:11). Over against this community of believers are "the Jews," those who form a solid block of opposition to Jesus and to his community throughout the work and who, on one occasion, pointedly call themselves disciples of Moses (9:28).[19] Not that Jews are excluded from Israel; in the Johannine perspective, Jesus' redemptive death ensures that the whole nation will not perish (11:52). Moreover there are others who wish to come to Jesus but for "fear of the Jews" only secretly (7:13; 9:22; 11:7f; 19:38; 20:19).

Foremost among these is surely Nicodemus, a teacher in Israel (3:10) who comes to Jesus by night (3:2;19:39), shows an initial faith

---

[18] A more detailed investigation of the treatment of these central figures from Israel's history (Abraham, Jacob, Moses and Isaiah e.g. in the Fourth Gospel) would show that the colouring comes from Jewish traditions other than the legal one, ranging from dissident (Samaritan) to fringe (Merkavah), as has been shown by such a wide range of Johannine scholars as Moody Smith, Dahl, Meeks, Brown, Schnackenburg, and Thyen. However, this fact only highlights "the inherently conflictual situation" (Moody Smith, cf. note 15 above) that has been taken into a Christian context from Judaism and underlines the polemical intentions of John in regard to the legal traditions and its exponents.

[19] M. Lowe's attempt in "Who were the *IOUDAIOI?*" (NT 18[1976] 101-130) to give the term a purely geographical meaning of Judaeans is, in my view, unsuccessful in the end. Nor is the term used in a purely negative sense, *pace* Grässer, "Antijudaismus," 76f; S. Pancaro, "The Church and Israel in St. John's Gospel," NTS 21(1975) 396-405, especially 401, is more nuanced in distinguishing positive, negative and neutral uses of the term "the Jews" in John .

in him, but in the end seems to be on the wrong side of the sharp line separating Jesus' true believers from all those who can be designated as simply "the world". Nicodemus has a representative role for all those "Jews" (in a neutral sense), both leaders and ordinary people, who are sympathetic to Jesus but who earn the following highly ironic, yet negative judgment from the evangelist: "they preferred the respect (*doxa*) of men to the glory (*doxa*) of God" (12:43; cf.5:44). But it is Nicodemus' characterization that is particularly significant in our present context. Initially, he is described by the evangelist rather pleonastically and with some foreboding as "a man of the Pharisees" and a ruler (*archōn*) of the Jews. This suggests that "are you a teacher in Israel?" the question Jesus directs at Nicodemus has an ironic intention (cf.3:10). At 7:50-52 he is one of those Pharisees who pride themselves on their knowledge of the law. Yet he challenges his fellows to act according to that law by giving Jesus a hearing, only to have the derisive name 'Galilean' hurled at him. Then at 19:38-42 he accompanies Joseph of Aramathea (a crypto-disciple of Jesus) at the burial, ensuring that Jesus is buried according to Jewish custom (v.40), before the feast of the Jews (v.41). In short, Nicodemus is representative of a law–focused understanding of the Jewish tradition. So while portraying him as sympathetic may have been useful within the evangelists' overall purpose, John does not show that he made the transition necessary to be a Johannine Christian.[20] The suggestion is that consideration of Jesus from the perspective of the law, however well intentioned, will not lead to a proper appreciation of him; true understanding must be preceded by a rebirth through water and the Spirit (3:5).

The Johannine community has therefore firmly set its face against the legal tradition in Israel and found another "centre" to which it can give its undivided emotional and intellectual commitment,[21] in Jesus as revealer. The community's assurance about its own stance within the Jewish tradition and the claims it seeks to make for it are based on

---

[20] For the treatment of Nicodemus in the Fourth Gospel cf. M. de Jonge, "Nicodemus and Jesus. Some observations on Understanding and Misunderstanding in the Fourth Gospel," reprinted in *Jesus: Stranger from Heaven and Son of God*. (Missoula: 1977), 29-48; also Meeks, "Man from Heaven," 54f. R.E. Brown, *The Community of the Beloved Disciple* (New York: 1979), 72, n. 128 disagrees with the interpretation of Nicodemus as a crypto-Christian, but in my view, Brown is reading too much into his final appearance in the gospel, since it is only Joseph of Arimathea who publicly asks for the body (19:38f).
[21] Cf. F. Segovia, "The Love and Hatred of Jesus in Johannine Sectarianism," CBQ 43 (1981) 258-272.

the presence of the Paraclete who, as the Spirit of truth, has led them into this fulness of understanding about Jesus. Their sense of assurance is articulated by the repeated declaration that they have been chosen by the Father or by Jesus (6:39; 10;29; 15:19; 17:6.8.9.12.24; 18:9). Indeed it is this heightened sense of election that gives the community the courage to face a world whose hostility takes the form of persecution from fellow Jews of the synagogue (15:18; 16:2; cf.17:14). In the farewell discourses, the opposites of love and hatred and joy and sorrow at once typify the community's own inner affective life and the opposition which it encounters from those outside. These oppositions help to focus on the psychological experiences that give such a powerful impetus towards developing a strong sense of self-identity. Yet, as we have seen, these experiences only reinforced the community's resolve to locate that self-identity within, not outside Judaism. Johannine Christianity is convinced that salvation "is of the Jews" (4:22).[22]

It is perhaps significant that we are forced to such generalizations as "the Johannine community" and cannot point to any distinctive group within it (as for example the scribes in Matthew) as responsible for developing this highly distinctive portrait of itself and the equally distinctive negative protrayal of its opponents. This undifferentiated sense of community corresponds to the community's undifferentiated sense of its opponents, but is ultimately grounded in the community's structures and experience. The highly original forms which the articulation has adopted, especially the speeches of Jesus, and the claim that these are validated by the gift of the Spirit, points to a distinctive form of early Christian prophecy allied to a subtle literary skill as this development's germinal seed-bed.[23] Perhaps we should attribute the differences between Matthew and John—not merely in terms of their own self-definition within Judaism but also in their distinctive vituperative attacks on their opponents to this background. It is to this topic that we must now turn our attention with, I hope, a much better appreciation of the internal dynamics that generated and articulated anti-Jewish rhetoric in the first and fourth gospels.

---

[22] It is one of the challenging features of Thyen's important article, "Das Heil kommt von den Juden," (cf. note 17) that he takes this verse (Jn. 4:22) to have a positive, existential meaning for the Johannine community, which thus becomes the key for interpreting the treatment of the Jews in the work as a whole. For another perspective with the history of its interpretation in early Christianity, cf. I. de la Potterie, " 'Nous adorons ce que nous connaisons, car le salut vient des Juifs.' Histoire de l'exégese et interpretation de Jn. 4:22," *Biblica* 64(1983)74-115.

[23] This idea has been well developed, especially by D. Moody Smith, 'Johannine Christianity,' 232f.

II: The Rhetoric of Vituperation and Community Building

As a first step toward evaluating how anti-Jewish rhetoric functions within this perspective of community building, we must ask where the two communities stand in relation to their Jewish opponents. Today, there is almost universal agreement that both gospels come from the post-70 period, and the scholarly discussion has centred on the extent to which the decision of Jamnia affected their relations with an emerging, normative Judaism. However, as Peter Schäfer's careful evaluation of the evidence makes clear,[24] a note of caution is called for here that is not always observed, even by critical scholars. Indeed it is much better to stay with the perspectives which the texts offer, since a highly interesting contrast between the two works emerges from this angle of vision. In both works the Christian communities being addressed would appear to be in a less advantageous legal and social position than their Jewish opponents, since the former are represented as suffering at the hands of the latter. Yet the social settings are quite different. In Matthew, the Christian missionaries are under attack. Their suffering is explained in relation to the fall of Jerusalem which is seen as God's punishment for their ill-treatment (cf.10:23; 22:7; 23:34). Though cast in the form of prophecy on the lips of Jesus, this presumably relates to the past of the author, who is writing in the post-70 period.[25] In John, on the other hand, the persecutions and consequently, the "fear of the Jews," are directly related to expulsions from the synagogue (9:22f; 12:42; 16:2) and with the attendent loss of social and legal status within the larger Roman world. Thus, while Matthew looks back at a situation that the community has lived through, has had etched on its memory, but has subsumed into a vision of universal mission which will also bring its own suffering (28:16; cf.10:18), John, is speaking to a settled community situation in which lasting and deep divisions of the most intimate, familial kind can occur (9:20f).[26] It will be worthwhile to keep this

---

[24] P. Schäfer, "Der sogenannte Synode von Jabne," Judaica 31 (1975) 54-64 and 116-124, reprinted in the collection *Studien zur Geschichte und Theologie des Rabbinischen Judentums* (Leiden: 1978), 45-65.

[25] D. Hare, *The Theme of Jewish Persecution of Christians in the Gospel according to St. Matthew*, S.N.T.S. Monographs 6 (Cambridge: 1967).

[26] S. Brown, "The Matthaean Community and the Gentile Mission," NT 22 (1980); 193-221, argues that one of the gospel's purposes is to convince the Jewish element in Matthew's church of the need for a universal mission. The addition *kai tois ethnesin* at 10:18 suggests that a similar fate awaited the missionaries among the gentiles as had been experienced in the mission to Israel, but this would only have confirmed them in their ideas about the suffering prophet as part of God's plan, which was current in Judaism, and would have therefore consoled and confirmed the missionaries.

very real difference of social situation in view as we explore the anti-Jewish rhetoric in both works.

One obvious starting point for our exploration is the contrasting literary strategies of the two writers as they handle their Jewish opponents. As is well known, Matthew's narrative is punctuated by five lengthy discourses. Yet none of these, not even ch.23 with its bitter direct attack on the scribes and Pharisees, is addressed to the Jewish opponents.[27] True, the opponents do appear in the controversy sections of ch.12 (Beelzebul controversy) and ch.15 (discussion about purity and impurity), and while their presence is essential to the narrative, on both occasions there is a change of audience to the crowds (12:46), or to the disciples and crowd (15:10.12). In the Jerusalem section various Jewish opponents are addressed directly through three parables (21:28-22:14) and in the subsequent four controversy stories (22:15-46). Even here important instruction for the disciples is constantly interwoven.

The narrative would seem to require some form of direct confrontation between the protagonists in order to lead into the denouement of the plot in the trial and death of Jesus. By contrast in "the books of the Signs" (chs.1-12), John has the Jews present as Jesus' protagonists from the start. Thus the narrative tension is heightened and the central issue of Jesus' identity is clearly and repeatedly enunciated. By bringing both parties to the trial on stage, the author shows at once, in contrast with Matthew, how central the debate is for him and his church. At the same time, he clearly indicates the impossibility of any 'fusion of horizons' for the adversaries and, presumably, for their respective constituencies also.

Corresponding to these differing macro-strategies of the two compositions, differing approaches to vilification are adopted by both writers throughout their works. Matthew's most favoured strategy for denigrating his Jewish opponents is that of *synkrisis*, or unfavourable comparison, a highly fashionable technique among the school rhetoricians.[28] Matthew shows himself to be quite adept in this regard, but the effect is to distance himself and his community from opponents whose special position in regard to God's blessings only serves more

---

[27] P. Minear, "The Disciples and the Crowds in the Gospel of Matthew" (in *Gospel Studies in Honor of S. E. Johnson*, ed. M. Sheppard jr. and E. C. Hobbs, ATR Supplement Series III, 1974), has shown by his "audience criticism" approach that the addressees of these discourses are part of the Matthaean redaction.

[28] Hermogenes in his *Progymnasmata* states that "sometimes we draw our comparisons of equality . . . sometimes we put the one ahead, praising also the other to which we prefer it; sometimes we blame the one utterly and praise the other." *Rhettores Graeci*, vol. 2, ed. L. Spengel (Frankfurt: 1966), 14f.

forcibly to highlight their failures, especially when they are contrasted with the most unlikely characters from within and outside
Israel. The men of Niniveh and the Queen of the South responded
more generously to the preaching of Jonah and the wisdom of
Solomon than does this generation to Jesus, even though he embodies
in himself both prophetic and wisdom traditions to a far greater
degree than any of these scriptural figures (12:41-42). A gentile
centurion has greater faith than the sons of the kingdom (8;11); even
Tyre, Sidon and Sodom would have performed penance had they the
opportunity of Chorozain, Bethsaida and Caphernaum (Mt.11:20-24);
even the tax collectors and harlots will precede the Jewish leaders
into the kingdom because of their genuine repentance (21:31). With
the exception of the last example, all these have Q parallels. Yet either
by the location in which he places it, or by rounding it out Matthew
has highlighted the contrast. One does not have to look very far to see
why this is a most suitable rhetorical tactic for his purposes. In
juxtaposing greater to lesser to point up the failure of the former, the
contrast fits in with Matthew's salvation-history scheme of the replacement of Israel. At the same time, Matthew manages to underline
the necessity for moral performance from those who now have
preference and who, as we have seen, are his real audience.

John's dominant strategy in dealing with opponents is that of irony
which flows over into caricature and parody.[29] Thus Jesus' opponents
appear limited (ch.3), self-opinionated (ch.7-8) and finally, foolish
(ch.9). There is a gradual deterioration in their character which
reaches its nadir at the point where their behaviour is most threatening to John and his community, the expulsion from the synagogue.
The lowest point corresponds to their rejection, ironically, of the very
things they hold most dear, that is: Moses (6:30-31), Abraham
(8:52-53), the prophets (12:41) and finally, God himself. They cry to
Pilate "we have no king but Caesar" (19:15). For their part, despite
their constant concern with a rigid monotheism in rejecting Jesus'
claims (5:18; 8:59; 10:33), the Jews are made to respond in varying
derogatory ways founded in their Jerusalem-based legal perspective.
They call those who accept Jesus ignorant (7:49) or Galilean (7:52),
and call Jesus a Samaritan and possessed (8:48), or a threat to their
privileged religious and legal position (11:48). But from the superior
perspective of the writer and his implied readers, these intended
aspersions have a genuine element of truth and are not all derogatory.

---

[29] Alan Culpepper, *Anatomy of the Fourth Gospel. A Study in Literary Design*
(Philadelphia: 1983), especially 165-180, has a helpful treatment of the use of irony in
John.

Herein lies the irony of the opponents' failure and the limitation of their perspective, but also the strength of the author's case against them as far as his own readership is concerned. As Wayne Booth puts it, "the implied invitation to come and live on a higher and firmer location", an essential ingredient of irony also includes "a strong sense of rejecting a whole structure of meanings, a kind of world that the author himself rejects".[30] For John's ideal readership there could be no question of sharing a world-view with such blind and stupid people, or indeed of attempting to emulate their religious concerns with a "better righteousness." One senses that standing directly behind such rhetoric is an author and a community who are deeply troubled by the situation as represented by their opponents. If the community is to come through the trauma it is experiencing, it must discredit them in the way chosen.

Now we must turn to the specific charges in question and see how they are directed at supplying the needs of the respective authors as these have been defined in the first half of this paper. In general it can be shown, I believe, that two complementary motifs occur which are simply the reverse sides of the same concern, namely, that of community building. These are as follows: 1) discrediting the opponents at the points where particular and exclusive claims for one's own community need to be established, and 2) using the opponents' failures and inadequacies as a means of warning one's own community. We shall examine each aspect in turn.

1) Discrediting the opponents

While Matthew still retains certain distinctions between various known groupings within first-century Judaism, it does not seem possible to make any clear differentiation with regard to specific charges for different groups. The tendency seems to be to tar all the different groups with the same brush while nevertheless retaining some sense of their variety. It is difficult to decide whether this feature is attributable to the intentions of the redactor or is already part of the received tradition.[31] Our main concern is with the charges as they are formulated by the final redactor. These can be reduced to the following three: 1) a failure to understand the Scriptures adequately, especially in the area of attitudes towards the law; 2) hypocricy; 3) culpable blindness.

---

[30] Wayne C. Booth, *A Rhetoric of Irony*, The University of Chicago Press, (Chicago: 1974), 36.
[31] D. Garland, *The Intention of Matthew 23*, Suppl. NT LII, (Leiden: 1979), 43-46 and Appendix B, 218-221, has a discussion of the topic with reference to the recent literature and charts, which show clearly Matthew's use of various designations for the groups.

We can begin with the charge of blindness. The Pharisees (and the Scribes) are described three times as "blind guides" (15:14; 23:16 and 24) and three times as "blind" (23:17, 19 and 26). The description is directly related to the Pharisees' inability to interpret the work of God correctly since their own halachic interpretations about hand-washing, oath-taking, the cleansing of utensils and insistence on minutiae of the law of tithing, result in neglecting weightier matters such as mercy, justice and faith (15:6; 23:16-25). From the lack of fruits which they produce (cf.21:43), Matthew infers that there are direct moral overtones to this blindness. The seriousness of this condition is highlighted through the Beelzebul controversy at 12:22-45. In contrast to the possessed blind and dumb man who is cured, the Pharisees are left in a much worse condition. It is subtly suggested by means of a parable that they risk, not merely blindness but demonic possession because they have attributed Jesus' power of healing to Beelzebul and demanded a sign. They thus fail to recognize the true source of Jesus' power in the Spirit of God, or to acknowledge him as one "greater than Solomon", the wise teacher. Here their blindness is traced not just to a lack of judgment with regard to the Scriptures, but to an evil disposition that refuses to see God's presence in the ministry of Jesus or His wisdom in Jesus' teaching. This radical condemnation is all the more pointed because in mounting it, by way of immediate introduction, Matthew has reinterpreted a text from Isaiah as applied to Jesus in order to clearly establish the claim that his ministry is a fulfilment of Old Testament prophecy (Mt.12:18-21).[32] In such circumstances the Scribes and Pharisees' failure is all the more reprehensible, the argument goes. The implication is that Matthew himself is the true scribe who understands the correct import of the Scriptural text.

Closely related to the charge of culpable blindness is the designation "hypocrite", which is applied to the scribes and Pharisees seven times throughout the work (15:7; 23:13, 15,23,25,27,29). The usual understanding of the epithet is that it denotes a lack of correspondence between word and action on the part of the Scribes and Pharisees, especially in view of 23:3's warning 'For they say and do not". However this understanding does not fit the subsequent condemnations in the "woes" section of ch.23 (with the exception of vv.25-27—the concern about cleansing of externals with the inside still unclean). Indeed, its close association with the charge of blindness does not so much imply conscious dissimilation as faulty conclu-

---

[32] L. Cope *Matthew. A Scribe Trained for the Kingdom*, CBQ Monographs 5, (Washington: 1976), 32-35, and J. Neyrey, "The Thematic use of Is 42:1-4 in Mt 12," *Biblica* 63(1982) 457-473.

sions drawn from wrong premises. This consideration has led to the search for a broader field of reference for the term as Matthew uses it and to the suggestion that it may be related to the Qumran "seekers after smooth things". This possibility is intriguing, since in the Scrolls, this expression always occurs in contexts where the sectarians are in dispute with their opponents on a particular interpretation of the law—even when the note of ethical corruption is also implied, as it certainly is in Matthew.[33]

The suggestion that the charge of hypocricy relates to a failure of interpretation is linked to Matthew's third charge against the Scribes and Pharisees as listed above, namely their failure to interpret the Scriptures correctly. As we previously noted, this occurs repeatedly in contexts of dispute. Twice the opponents are told to go and learn the meaning of the Hosean statement "I desire mercy not sacrifice" in contexts in which explicit Christological claims are made to support the position that is being adopted (Hos. 6:6; cf. Mt.9:13 and 12:7). The ironic query "have you never read (in the law)?" is used to defend the Matthaean attitudes on sabbath observance and divorce (12:5; 19:4). It also serves to apply scriptural texts of condemnation to the opponents (21:16 and 42). The Sadducees too are said to err, "not knowing the Scriptures," when they object to the idea of resurrection from the dead (22:29-33).

These comments' clear polemical overtones, combined with the theme of Scripture's fulfilment in Jesus' career which is often achieved by appropriately adapting the actual biblical texts to the context, indicates that this is the heart of Matthew's attack on the Pharisaic and Scribal traditions. As we have seen, the charges of hypocrisy and blindness can be shown to be intimately related to the Scribes' and Pharisees' failure in this regard. We are therefore justified in concluding that Matthew's anti-Jewish polemic is directed towards establishing the claim that it is Christian scribes alone (whose authority derives from and is totally dependent on that of Jesus) who can interpret the Scriptures properly in the new situation of fulfilment brought by his coming. Since this is a matter of life and death, to establish such an audacious claim rival claimants must not merely be discredited, they must be destroyed. The rhetoric of *vituperatio* as was practised in the schools, or in the everyday affairs of men was not wholly adequate to the task, even when denigrating comments are

---

[33] For a full discussion cf. Garland, *The Intention*, 91-123, especially 104-111, on the possible similarities with the Qumran *dwryshy halqoth*; cf. also M. Gertner, "The terms *Pharisaioi, Gazarēnoi, Hyokritai*: their semantic complexity and conceptual correlation," BSOAS 26 (1963), 245-268.

made or sub-human epithets applied. Only a rhetoric that is inspired by apocalyptic hatred could achieve the desired effect, and Matthew certainly has his own highly developed repetoire to meet the panic-laden demands of the situation.[34] The language of annihilation not denigration is called for as the community seeks to establish its exclusive claims on the Jewish inheritance that its opponents also claim. Both want to appropriate the law and the prophets (seen both as the story of God's history with his people and the revelation of his will).

If we turn to John's detailed denigration of the opponents, we find there is no need to challenge their exegetical tradition as is the case in Matthew. As we have seen in the first part of our paper, John sought to establish a place in Judaism that was over against but not superior to the law-based position of the Jewish opponents. His tendency is not to differentiate various groups within Judaism, however loosely. But insofar as the generalising expression "the Jews" is not wholly adhered to, the Pharisaic element is the one singled out as constitut-ing the real opposition.[35] However, there is no debate about the Pharisees' understanding of the law or its implications. Simply, its premises are rejected and discredited as incapable of understanding God's sole revelation in Jesus.

Thus the charge of blindness, which also occurs in the context of the healing of a blind man (ch.9), is given an ironic twist that puts the matter in its proper Johannine perspective. "For an object of judg-ment (*eis krima*) I came into this world so that those who do not see might see and those who see might become blind," Jesus declares. The Pharisees retorted "surely you are not calling us blind?" To this Jesus countered "if you were blind you would not have sin; and now you say we see and your sin remains" (9:39-41). This brief dialogue brings the issue into the open. The Pharisaic opponents claim to be able to see, but their claim is allowed only to be followed by the worse charge of permanent sin. This makes the declaration of the purpose for Jesus' coming ("for an object of judgment") all the more ominous. In rejecting Jesus, the Pharisaic group unwittingly rejects the one who has been introduced to the ideal reader as he who takes away "the sin of the world" (1:29). So the group's members will die in their sins

---

[34] On the relation between perceived threat and apocalyptic rhetoric cf. the highly suggestive article of Amos Wilder, "The Rhetoric of Apocalyptic," in *Jesus' Parables and the War on Myths* (London: 1982), 153-168. Appendix A. below, p. 142 gives a list of the apocalyptic denunciations of opponents in Mt.

[35] Cf. 1:24; 3:1; 7:32.45.48; 9:16.40; 11:47.57; 18:3. Cf. notes 1 and 19 above on the question of the Jews in Jn.

(8:23f). Their condition, then, is irredeemable. It bears the ultimate consequences from the Johannine perspective.

The other expressions of the charge against the Jews are merely variants of this central theme in which the two protagonists are contrasted as inhabitants of two different spheres and shown to have an unbridgable chasm between them. Nicodemus and the Jews cannot understand because they are "from below" and "of the earth", whereas to understand the in-depth meaning of Jesus' signs which the Johannine community claims for itself (1:51; 2:11), one must be "born from above", or "born of the Spirit" (3:3 and 5; 6:63). They judge constantly by externals, that is, in terms that relate to this world; they know Jesus' family (6:42f), his place of origin (1:27) and his destiny (8:22f), but accurate as this knowledge may be in regard to this world, it prohibits them from penetrating the inner mystery which the Johannine group feels itself privy to, namely, that God is Jesus' Father, and that Jesus is from above and will return there (3:19; 6:62; 8:42). The ultimate condemnation is arrived at in the declaration that they are neither the children of God nor of Abraham, but rather the children of the devil (8:39-44).[36] To appreciate the force of this utterance within the Johannine perspective, it should be recalled that elsewhere the devil is described as the "prince of this world" who is "cast out" through Jesus' exaltation, an event which coincides with the judgment of this world (12:31). In an apparent allusion to the Genesis story, the devil is described as a destroyer of men from the beginning, a liar and the father of lies (8:44). By being characterised as his children, the Jews are declared to be irretrievably under his influence within the world, caught up in falsehood rather than the truth and, in the end, sharing the doom that the unbelieving world has merited. As it confronts the Johannine community in a hostile and unrelenting way, the group will no longer be cared for by Jesus or his Father (ch.17).

John rarely uses the language or imagery of apocalyptic annihilation in passing final sentence on the Jews. Rather he draws on his cosmic dualism to paint an unrelieved picture of confrontation and hostility between the Johannine Christians and their opponents. There is such an aura of inevitability and finality about the situation from the start that there would appear to be no place for any change of heart on the part of the opponents. Yet such a conclusion could obscure the fact that John sees the Jewish refusal to believe in Jesus as culpable, arising from an evil disposition. Those whose deeds are

---

[36] T. Dozemann, "Sperma Abraham in Jn 8 and related literature," CBQ 42(1980) 342-358.

evil do not want to come to the light (3:20); the Jews do not have God's word abiding in them (5:38); they have never kept the law of Moses (7:19); they seek honour from one another and not the glory that is from God (5:44; 12:43); they judge by externals (7:24; 8:15); they claim to be able to see, and so are guilty (9:40). By repeatedly drawing attention to the failures of Christianity's opponents, John avoids falling into the trap of total determinism that his cosmic dualism could so easily suggest. True, his own community has a heightened sense of its election as we have seen, yet its the opponents moral failures, however unspecified they remain in John's account, do have a bearing on the attainment of proper insight. In the end, "being of the world" or "being of God" is as much a choice as it is a given. That fact makes those who have chosen the latter all the more intolerant of those who have opted otherwise.

ii) Warning for one's own community

Our examination of the ways in which Matthew and John have chosen to discredit their opponents has shown that each has directed their attacks at those points where they themselves are seeking to make exclusive claims for their own communities. In Matthew the Jews are shown to have failed in understanding or expounding the law and the prophets as God's revealed will. In fact they have destroyed it by their own tradition. In John, on the other hand, the Jews lack the depth of vision to see or understand the reality of God in Jesus. In each, the strategies of vituperation are combined either with the vehemence of apocalyptic annihilation or the absoluteness of cosmic dualism. The result is two contrasting, yet equally unflattering portraits of Matthew's and John's respective opponents within a Jewish perspective. Yet there is another aspect to this extreme language that calls for attention also and which helps to relate it to our authors' social concerns: it serves at once to warn their own communities and to sharply define their tasks.

We have already noted in passing that Matthew ch.23, the high point of Matthaean anti-Jewish invective, is not addressed to the Scribes and Pharisees but to disciples and the crowds, that is, real and potential members of the community. Since this introduction is clearly attributable to Matthaean redaction, it should alert us to the act of communication that the author is engaged in with his own community. Even though the Scribes and Pharisees are granted a certain authority at the outset because they occupy the seat of Moses, they are rejected as authoritative guides. A very different model of teaching ministry is proposed; one which is linked with Jesus' servant ministry by the aid of two sayings Matthew has used elsewhere to express the

model for genuine discipleship (23:11-12; cf. 20:26; 18:4). It is only
after this general instruction that the woes against the Scribes and
Pharisees are uttered. Though the direct mode of address, "you," is
employed, the intention is not to change the audience but to adopt a
judicial tone for passing judgment on the guilty (cf. 11:20-24). They,
therefore, serve as a clear warning for Christian teachers who may
have attempted to adopt not just the name but the style and faults of
their Jewish counterparts, especially as they were possibly of Pharisaic origin themselves.[37] That there is this intimate connection in the
author's mind between attacking Jewish opponents and instructing
his own community is evidenced elsewhere in the gospel when the
author either introduces advice applicable to all (cf.12:33-37;
22:11-14), or leaves the initial controversy behind by way of introduc-
ing instruction for those sympathetic to Jesus (15:10-20; 16:5-12). In
each of these instances, attitudes that are typical of one or other of the
Jewish groups as presented by Matthew are castigated, and an
alternative or contrasting set of values is proposed.

However, closer examination of ch.23 shows a different, though
related pattern emerging. In all, eleven different unacceptable traits
of the scribes and Pharisees are listed. As appendix B (below, p. 143)
shows, all of these can be found elsewhere in Matthew as issues about
which the disciples require instruction or as attitudes which they are
warned to avoid (that includes the charge of hypocrisy). Thus
Matthew's concerns for his own community are couched in the very
terms which he uses to castigate the scribes and Pharisees. He applies
the same image, "fruit", to the moral conduct of both groups (3:10;
7:15-20; 12:33; 21:43); the same apocalyptic judgment is in store for
the failed disciple and the Jewish opponents alike, namely, exclusion
from the kingdom and condemnation to outer darkness where there
will be weeping and gnashing of teeth (8:12; 13:42 and 50; 22:13;
24:51). It is precisely because Matthew has attempted to define his
own group's identity in relation to that of Pharisaic Judaism, both in
terms of its tasks and rewards, that he can turn his anti-Jewish rhetoric
into warning for his own community. From the vantage point of a
scribe discipled in the kingdom, bringing forth what is new and old,
he can judge the failures of all other groups in Judaism and, in the
process of discrediting their claims, obtain a clearer perspective of the
challenge that faces his own group if its claim is to be sustained.

---

[37] The warnings of Mt 5:18f, for example, are clearly addressed to teaching practices in
his own community that are unacceptable. In particular the stress on "doing and
teaching" that is enjoined here recalls discussions about the priority of *midrash* over
ma'aseh at Jamnia.

Significantly, in view of the relationship with Judaism arising out of the experiences of the mission to Israel, one of the chief tasks is to develop a mission to "all nations." Matthew's group thereby lays claim to being the messianic people that mediates the blessings of Abraham to all (28:16; cf.3:9; 8:11), whereas its Jewish counterparts make their proselytes "sons of Gehenna, twice as much as themselves" (23:14).

John states the macro-purposes of his work at 20:31. He intends "that you might believe that Jesus is the Christ, the Son of God, and that believing, you may have life in his name." The precise address-ees of this declaration are presumably, in the first instance, his own community, represented throughout the work as the disciples. Yet in the narrative portrayal of this group, at least its inner core had grasped the true meaning of Jesus' presence from the start (1:51; 2:11) and remained constant even when some disciples walked no more with him (6:66-70). True, the farewell discourses (especially the prayer of ch.17) display anxieties about this group in a hostile world, especially in view of Jesus' absence (17:12f). The danger of disunity seems to be lurking in the background (17:21). Indeed the cosmic dualism of light and darkness, truth and falsehood, believers and world that has been used through the work to give this Johannine group a strong sense of identity and election, comes to a resounding climax in this, Jesus' final monologue (cf.17:6.9.11.24).[38] But the community has played its part also. Its members have kept the word of God that Jesus has given them, and they have received his message and have believed (17:6-9)—this in direct contrast to the Jews, whose failures have made them into the unbelieving world. This contrasting parallelism be-tween the inhabitants of the two spheres is carefully orchestrated by John to give his own group a greater assurance in its stance outside the synagogue. The Christians need not fear that their perception of the truth is any less secure because of what has happened to them, since those who represent the synagogue have rendered themselves inca-pable of understanding and are not any longer even the objects of the Revealer's or his Father's concern. Here vilification serves not so much to define but to confirm the self that finds itself cut off from its natural matrix and is attempting to see an alternative mission for itself by way of compensation (17:18.21).

That new-found sense of mission is directed in the first instance to those "others" who come into the Johannine purview and whose

[38] Cf. the recent detailed study of this chapter by H. Riss, *Das Gebet zum Vater. Zur Interpretation von John.17* (Stuttgart: 1979), especially 339-378 and 474ff.

relation to the disciples is not so clear, but for whom vilification of the Jews could have had rather different consequences. Raymond Brown may have pushed the evidence too far in suggesting three such separate social groups within the gospel, crypto-Christians (ch.9), Jewish Christians of inadequate faith (6:60-66; 7:3-5; 8:31; 10:12) and Christians of apostolic churches, as represented by the figure of Peter contrasted with that of the beloved disciple.[39] Yet there is no doubt that there are such borderline cases. To these may be added those Jews who believed in Jesus' name because of the signs which he gave, but who appear to receive a negative valuation (2:25-3:1), and the disciples of John the Baptist (3:22-6). We have already seen that Nicodemus is cast as a representative figure for such sympathetic Jews, and the question of his final allegiance appears to be left ambiguous, at least. The stories of the Samaritan Woman (ch.4) and the man born blind (ch.9) are deliberately constructed in such a way as to suggest stages in faith from a low to a high Christology. Thus the Johannine author indicates the possibility of transition from one sphere to the other for both Christian and Jewish sympathisers alike, since, as we have seen more than once, Johannine faith is in the end both a matter of choice and a gift. Without the predisposition of openness and good intention, no advance is possible. But even then, full blown faith is not assured. In such a context one can see the special role that the vilification of the Jews as unbelievers could play. Their blindness was culpable, but that need not or, indeed, should not preclude others from having the courage of their convictions to make an open and complete transition.

Conclusions

We have been attempting to understand the anti-Jewish rhetoric of Matthew and John in the light of their own community concerns, concerns for the authoritative definition of an independent and exclusive place within Judaism in line with the eschatological and messianic claims that early Christianity as a whole had sought to make for itself. A number of different approaches come to mind as possible heuristic devices for describing the phenomena we have uncovered. Social psychology, for example, might suggest the transference of fears into aggression; sociology could talk of sectarian rhetoric; cultural anthropology might see here a case of aggressive resymbolisation to meet social needs. Illuminating as all these approaches undoubtedly are, it would seem that some hermeneutical reflection

---

[39] *Community of the Beloved Disciple.* 71-88.

concerning the texts' contemporary meaning, is called for, especially in view of the long history of oppression of Jews by Christians to which these texts contributed, once they were taken as foundational documents by a dominant Christianity backed by the power and authority of the state.

For many Christians it would be a shocking, not to say a highly offensive suggestion, to state that their foundational documents are themselves documents of betrayal insofar as they concerned themselves exclusively with the question of their own identity and ignored the radical command to a universal and all-embracing love. Yet identity questions, both personal and social, would seem to be as essential to us as the very air we breathe. The search for and preoccupation with defining the self are symptoms of our condition, both Jewish and Christian—especially, it would seem, when we are confronted with the experience of a God who seeks to destroy such deep-seated longings within us! Therein lies the paradox that borders on the tragic in our situation. The Christological experience of God in early Christianity captured a few fleeting glimpses of the possibility of risking all by refusing to be identified (for example, Mark's portrayal of Jesus), just as Moses, Isaiah and Job had captured it briefly in their visions of a God who calls out, or who can bring all the nations to Mt. Zion, or who refuses to solve the intractable problem of evil and yet claims to be a good God. But living with such visions is highly dangerous. Hence the need to domesticate this God in the more familiar institutions of life and culture which we see in Matthew's adaptation of the Markan Jesus into the Messiah of Israel, using the attestation of the Scriptures.

The identity problem had beset Judaism, and indeed torn it apart, from the Babylonian captivity at least. Early Christianity was a good learner—in that regard it was thoroughly Jewish from the beginning and remains so to-day with its discussions and soul-searchings that have debased the word ecumenical. History can testify to other ways in which both Jews and Christians have sought to escape the identity question, namely the way of gnosis. But that way too had its hidden pitfalls especially, I would suggest, its desire to opt out of history since it constantly raises anew the question of identity in the tension between memory and hope, and the conflicting ideologies that these give rise to. We cannot turn our backs on such problems and proceed as though they do not exist, hidden as they are in the most innocent and sublime of visions (e.g. in the gospel of John with its inaugural picture of the universal Logos incarnate). It is only when we take seriously both the radical ambiguity of our common human situation and the distortions it has given rise to, even in our so called 'classic', foundational documents, both Jewish and Christian, that we have any hope of moving beyond the past and making a better future together.

Appendix A: Apocalyptic Denunciation of Opponents in Matthew

—'Already the axe is laid to the root of the unfruitful tree...They cannot hope to escape the coming wrath.
(3:7.10–Pharisees, and Sadducees).

—Those who follow their righteousness will never enter the kingdom of heaven. (5:20–Scribes and Pharisees).

—Instead of sharing the messianic banquet in the kingdom with the Patriarchs they, sons of the kingdom, will be cast out where there is weeping and gnashing of teeth. (8.11f. General)

—Those who blaspheme against the Spirit will receive no forgiveness either in this age or the age to come. (12.32, Pharisees).

—On judgment day the Ninevites and the Queen of the South will rise and condemn this evil generation.
(12:41.42 Scribes and Pharisees)

—Not having been planted by the heavenly Father they will be uprooted. (15.:13, Pharisees)

—The kingdom of God will be taken from them and given to a nation producing the fruits of it. (21:43, chief priests and Pharisees)

—As the King makes a marriage feast for his son he will kill the murderers and destroy their city. (22:7, General)

—They do not enter the kingdom of God themselves and they attempt to prevent others entering. (22:13, Scribes and Pharisees)

—They make proselytes sons of gehenna twice as much as themselves. (23:15, Scribes and Pharisees)

—They are full of lawlessness. (23:28, Scribes and Pharisees)

—They are filling up the measure of their forefathers' guilt, regarding the innocent blood that has been shed and responsibility for it will come on this generation. (23:32.36, General)

—Their house will be left deserted; no stone will be left upon another. (23:38;24:2, General)

Appendix B. Denunciations in Matthew 23 directed at Disciples elsewhere.

	Scribes & Pharisees	Disciples
1. Teaching but not doing	23:3	5:19; 7:21-23
2. Refusal to help those in distress	23.4	18:10; 25:41-45; (cf.10:40-42)
3. Seeking places of honour and respect before men	23:6.7 (cf.6:2.5.16)	6:1-19; 20:26f; (cf.23:8-11)
4. Hypocricy	23:13.15.23.25.27.29.	6:2.5.16; 7:5; 24:51
5. Lawlessness	23:28	8:23; 13:41; 24:12
6. Making somebody else a son of gehenna	23:15	18:6-10; 10:28 (cf.5:29-30)
7. False ideas about oaths	23:16-22 (cf.12:34: evil speech)	5:33.37
8. Neglect of *krisis, eleos, pistis*	23:23	7:1-5 (*krisis*) 5:7; 24:10; 25:42-46 (*eleos*) 14:31; 17:19-20 (*pistis*)
9. Blindness	23:16 (cf.15:14)	5:22-23 (cf.5:14-16)
10. Concern for externals but full of greed and lust	23:25	7:15; 6:24; 13:22
11. False respect for the dead.	23:29	8:21-22

6

The Jews as Seen by Paul and Luke

Etienne Trocmé
University of Strasbourg

I

If we accept that a majority of the thirteen letters in the New Testament canon attributed to the apostle Paul are actually his work, as seems most likely, and if we agree as most scholars do that the Gospel according to Luke and the Book of Acts were written by the same author (who may even have been called Luke), then the two writers this paper is about are doubtless the most prolific of all first-century Christian authors. Between them, they contribute one half of the New Testament and some of the best pages in that collection, including, on the one hand, the Lukan Infancy Narrative, the most moving parables (Good Samaritan, Prodigal Son, etc.), and masterpieces like Stephen's speech and Paul's conversion or shipwreck. On the other hand, they produced remarkable documents like the epistles to the Romans and the Philippians, or the well-known Hymn to Love in I Cor. 13.

All this would be a rather poor justification for the choice I made in this paper were it not that these two writers are the main advocates or early Gentile Christianity in the form that was to prevail later on–and also that the author of the Book of Acts is a zealous supporter of Paul, whom he claims implicitly as his master. Whether he actually was a faithful disciple of the apostle is another question altogether, which we may leave aside as it does not really touch the problem we are looking into here.

What is crystal-clear is that both men belong to the same circles, that the younger of the two wants to appear as the legitimate successor of the other, and that both writers have a problem with Judaism—a situation that will change soon, when Gentile Christians will all have become Marcionites of a kind.[1]

---

[1] The literature concerning Paul is so overwhelmingly large that I prefer to limit myself to one title only. J. Christiaan Beker's *Paul the Apostle, The Triumph of God in Life and Thought* (Edinburgh: 1980), I consider the best book on Paul's thought in recent years.

II

So, before we go any further, we must try to understand what the problem is in each case. Perhaps this conference's motif will help to express our findings: in relation to Judaism, Paul is the insider who tries to become an outsider, whereas Luke (if he bore that name) is an outsider who wants to appear as much of an insider as possible. The Jew who feels that God has chosen him to preach the Gospel to the Gentiles goes as far as he can to shake off the yoke of the Law, but his heart remains broken when he looks at his people and sees them rejecting the Gospel (Rom.9:1-5). However the Gentile who lives among Gentile Christians insists on the Jewishness of the Gospel and describes the Apostle of the Gentiles as the faithful Jew who never gave up his Jewish ways. A paradoxical state of affairs, indeed! We have no time now to analyse it fully, but we must take it into account since it colors the view the two men take of the Jews.

Paul's biography is reasonably well-known in parts. A native of Cilicia, he was a Greek-speaking Jew who doubtless had access to the Bible through the Septuagint. Although he had certainly had a Greek schooling, judging from his use of rhetorical devices in his writings, he was also familiar with some of the exegetical methods of the rabbis of his day. His understanding of Scripture was Jewish, even though he may have twisted the meaning of some texts in a highly personal way. He often preached in synagogues, because there only could he find a pre-trained audience that could understand his message (see Acts 17). In other words, Paul was firmly rooted in Judaism. Further, this was the Judaism of the time when the Jerusalem Temple was, so to speak, in full swing. Although the Jews had their difficulties even in those days, it is fair to say that the times were favorable to Judaism. Obviously, Paul knew that the diaspora synagogues were usually on good terms with the Roman authorities, and that Palestinian Judaism was influential and strong, with the Temple priestly hierarchy a highly prosperous concern.

Since personal reasons, circumstances and caution would have inclined Paul to remain within the Jewish community, his tendency to break away from Judaism can only be accounted for by other strong motivations to do so. As we all know, his main motive was a firm belief that God had chosen him to preach the Gospel to Gentiles. Obedience to a divine call was a stronger impulse than the desire to remain a

---

On Luke, what matters is the highly fruitful debate on his theology initiated in 1954 by Hans Conzelmann in *Die Mitte der Zeit* English trans. *The Theology of St. Luke* (1960). This can best be approached with the help of François Bovon, *Luc le théologien, vingt-cinq ans de recherches (1950-1975)* (Neuchâtel-Paris: 1978).

member of the community of his youth or the wish not to antagonize the synagogues. But it was not easy for Paul to make such a move. He was still emotionally a member of the Jewish people and felt great disappointment that they had not accepted the Gospel of Jesus Christ (see Rom.9:1-5). As a result, all the remarks Paul makes about the Jews have an emotional undercurrent and insist that God's election gives to the Jewish people a plus that cannot be lost, whatever happens. As a matter of fact, Paul is extremely proud of being a Jew, and he considers that his special ministry is nothing but the solution to Israel's unfulfilled vocation to make God known to all men—a solution made necessary by the Jews' refusal to fulfil their mission in spite of its urgency.

Luke was a Gentile by birth and shared Paul's Hellenistic culture. We know little about his life and his way to the Christian faith, but in spite of what has been said, there is no reason to deny that he must have been one of Paul's converts. However we can assume that his double book was not written before 80 or 85 C.E., much later than Paul. Luke-Acts is neither a second-century piece, nor an apologetic writing prepared with a view to Paul's appearance in the Emperor's court. A discussion of this dating would be too long and altogether out of place here. More to the point, as a result of our choice of date, we can note another important difference between Paul and Luke. The Judaism Luke has in mind, even when he tells us stories of past days, is much weakened in comparison to what it was in the fifties or sixties C.E.: Jerusalem is in shambles and the Temple is completely destroyed, so that no sacrifice can be held there any longer; Palestinian Judaism is in dire straits after years of a savage war on its soil; Diaspora Jews have not suffered in the same way, but their position within the Roman Empire is far less satisfactory than it was, say, thirty years earlier, and they have much to do to restore their image. At the same time, many Jews seem to have lost heart in those days (see 4 Ezra). What was their role in the world now that God had so severely punished them for their sins?

Strangely enough, Luke is keenly interested in that Judaism which has received a terrible blow and has not really recovered from it. Not only does he insist that the Bible is divinely inspired and that many of its prophecies have been fulfilled in the life of Jesus and events of the Early Church, what is more striking, he depicts Jewish persons and institutions as though he were directly connected with them. He puts the emphasis on the Jewishness of Jesus (who never leaves Jewish Palestine during his life-time, according to his Gospel), of all early Christians, and of Paul himself. He seems to assume that this reinforces the claims of the Gospel in the Gentile world. An outsider who had nothing at all to do with Judaism originally, he insists on every feature that shows how Jewish early Christianity was! He seems to have a vested interest in that bias at a time of strong anti-Jewish feeling among Gentiles! Just as Paul needed a strong motivation to break away from his Jewish background, Luke must have had a similarly forceful impulse to speak so much about Judaism and to give, on the whole, a rather good image of the Jews. We shall come back to that. For the time being, let us say simply that, even if Luke was not motivated as personally as Paul, he was nonetheless keen on the Jewish roots of Christianity in a fashion that implies some kind of personal commitment.

It is difficult to give here a full account of what this "commitment" might have been, because we have to do some guess-work based on as much evidence as is available. Let me summarize my conclusions and ask you to accept them as a working hypothesis. As we said earlier, at the time Luke wrote, Judaism was in difficult straits as a result of the Jewish War and the ruin of the Temple. But Gentile Christianity as Paul had established it around the Aegean Sea was also having a hard time as a consequence of Paul's untimely death in the sixties C.E., after his attempt at reconciliation with the Mother Church at Jerusalem had failed. Conversely, the Jewish Christian communities, particularly in the *diaspora*, were going through a period of optimism and growth thanks to James's death and to the end of the Jerusalem Church's crushing rule and the helpless confusion that prevailed in the synagogues between Jerusalem's Fall and the spreading of the Jamnia school's Reform movement. Witnesses to this phase of Jewish Christian expansion and appeal to all Jews are the epistle of James and the Gospel According to Matthew, both written to present their brand of Reform Judaism to Jews and Gentiles. Luke realized that the small group of churches which persisted in claiming a Pauline origin would be swallowed up by that conquering trend within Christianity if nothing was done to redefine their heritage so as to prove that it was as firmly rooted in Judaism as any of its competitors. He felt he could show as much without giving up the reference to Paul and the turn toward the Gentiles which were the original features of the Churches he was trying to rescue, because he was one of their leaders. Luke's approach to Judaism derived from his keenness to save Gentile Christianity from absorption into Jewish Christianity.

III

Having shown how existentially-based Paul's and Luke's understanding of Judaism was, we must now turn to what both writers actually say about Jews and the Jewish heritage.

Let us begin with Paul. It has been said again and again in the last thirty years that *Heilsgeschichte* was a typical feature of Luke's writings and a sort of watering-down of the original Pauline Gospel. There is an element of truth in that, but we should not forget that Paul's epistles include a number of passages which are *heilgeschicht-liche* interpretations of past, present or future events in the history of mankind, and, in the first place, in the history of the Jews. As a matter of fact, these passages are so important in the sections of the epistles devoted largely to Judaism that the best way of doing justice to Paul's approach to the religion of his forefathers is to follow the historical order of past, present and future.

Even Scripture is connected with that chronological succession. Of course, much of what is found in the Holy Book has eternal value, either as commandment or as analysis of human behavior in relation to God. But Scripture comes out of the past, informs us about the past, and thus helps us in our life today. Paul states just that in Romans 15:4, I Cor.10:6 and Gal.4:22-28, even if the words he uses vary (e.g. "instruction"; "example"; "allegory"). This all-important past, known to us through the records which God made possible, is the past of the Jews, "our fathers" (1 Cor.10:1). It is not altogether a glorious past, but it has had its hours of glory (2 Cor.3:9-10). Paul emphatically describes some of the heroes in that Jewish past as examples of the relation between God and man. Adam is mentioned occasionally, but of course he is not a Jew at all, and the mythical past he illustrates is not really part of the history of salvation (Rom.5:12ff; 1 Cor.15:45ff). Next comes Abraham, whose story with God is told in some detail in Rom.4 and Gal.3. And there are further allusions (Rom.9:7; 11:1; 2 Cor.11:22; Gal.4:22). One of the points Paul wants to make about Abraham, with a view of ruining the Jewish assertion that the righteous person is one who obeys the commandments of the Law, is of course that God granted him righteousness simply because he trusted in Him. Another is that Abraham was declared righteous even before he was circumcised and therefore is not simply the father of righteous Israel, but the father of all believers, whether they are circumcised or not. As a consequence, Abraham is an example for all men to look to and an encouragement for them all to trust in God to the extent of counting on miracles. According to Paul, Abraham's status thus remains somewhat ambiguous. He is indeed the father of all believers, but he is also the father of Israel as a people (see Gal.4:22ff.), although this in itself is not enough to ensure the election of all his physical offspring (Rom.9:6ff.). In fact in Romans 9-11, Paul seems to suggest that God selected at each generation those descendants of Abraham whom he wanted to favor. Only later, it seems, as a result of Israel's refusal to listen to his God (Rom. 9:30ff.), did the election of Gentiles instead of Jews appear. But it is only in addition to a Remnant of believing Israelites that the Gentiles are brought in (Rom.9:24-29; 11:1-11).

The next major figure in the Jewish past who interests Paul is Moses (Rom.5:14,9:15 and 10:5.19; 1 Cor.10:2; 2 Cor.3:7.13.15). Moses is first and foremost the writer of the Pentateuch. His utterances can be quoted in support of statements on important religious topics (Rom.9:15: the freedom of God to elect whom He will; Rom.10:5: justification by works of the Law; Rom.10:6-8: justification by faith, through the preaching of the Gospel; Rom.10:19: God will make His people jealous of another people; 1 Cor.9:9: the apostles' right to a livelihood). His writings are read "to this day" to Jews (2 Cor.3:15), but Moses himself said that they could not be properly understood since a veil was on the heart of the Jews (2 Cor.3:16ff.). As a writer, Moses is a figure of the past. But this is only a vague past, not an historical past. Yet Moses is also the historical leader who brought Israel out of Egypt through the Red Sea and under the Cloud in the desert (1 Cor.10:2). It was he who helped the Israelites to get those great gifts of God, the manna and the water from the Rock (1 Cor.10:3-4). And last but not least, it was Moses who received the Law on Mount Sinai (2 Cor.3:7), in an extraordinary dialogue with God that made his later relationship with the Jews a difficult one, because he then reflected the glory of God (2 Cor.3:13; see Gal.3:19-25). As a matter of fact, Paul considers this event as a major turning point of *Heilsgeschichte*. The relationship between God and humankind is changed because the sins of men are now taken into account (Rom.5:13-14; Gal.3:19-25); what matters even more, sins abound so that grace has to abound even more. Indeed, Christ's coming is rendered urgent (Rom.5:20-21).

Finally, Paul mentions David as one of the great leaders in Jewish history, but far less often than he mentions Abraham and Moses. Twice, Paul alludes to David as author of the Psalms, but he does not allude to him as king and founder of a dynasty (Rom.4:6-8; Rom.11:9). David is also mentioned in Rom.1:3 as the ancestor of Jesus-Christ. This means that Paul was conscious of at least some of the theories of Jewish Davidic messianism, and implies, of course, that he recognised David's historical role in Jewish history.

A few more names taken from Israel's past crop up here and there in Paul's letters. We can disregard these as unimportant allusions, apart, perhaps, from one. Romans 11:2-4 comprises Elijah's complaint to God, as the prophet finds himself completely isolated in his struggle against idolatry in Israel, and God's answer, with the news that a remnant exists which Elijah will lead. It refers to historical events in the Jewish people's past, and shows how God acts whenever Israel rebels against Him.

Of course, the main role in Israel's history is that of the people itself. As I mentioned earlier, Israel's election by God carries with it, in Paul's eyes, the consequence that at each generation some at least of the Jews will benefit from God's favor—given as it pleases God (see the examples of Isaac in Rom.9:6-9 and Gal.4:22.29-30, and of Esau and Jacob in Rom.9:10-13). So in spite of the people's rebellious behavior (see 1 Thess.2:15 on the killing of prophets), generation after generation, the "vessels of election" were taken from the ranks of the children of Israel, even if some were also called for that purpose from the Nations (Rom.9:24-26). In other words, the "Remnant of Israel" (the ὑπόλειμμα) always remained at the heart of the History of Salvation (Rom.9:27-29).

On the other hand, the example of Israel's past history must be read as a warning to the people of Paul's time, whether Jews or Gentile Christians. For they too can all be cast out by God if they rebel against Him like Israel in the desert (1 Cor.10:5-10), and discover too late that they do not belong to the Remnant!

This being said, a major theological problem is raised by Paul's understanding of the Jewish past. Paul himself is aware of it, though many of his commentators are not. If the giving of the Law has made man responsible for his sins, how are we to understand that the Jewish sinners (and perhaps also others) of former ages were not punished by God as the Law required? Is this fact compatible with the idea that God is a righteous God who stated clearly what proper behavior was and what the penalties were for not behaving? Paul wants it to be quite clear that God is righteous—otherwise how could he be gracious? He would be indulgent in the most despicable way. To evade this difficulty, Paul explains in Rom.3:25-26 that in order to disclose his full righteousness in Jesus Christ, God chose to be patient (ἀνοχή) and to close his eyes on the sins of men, particularly Jews, so long as the time of Christ's coming was not yet arrived (πάρεσις προγεγονότων ἁμαρτημάτων). This understanding of the Jewish past enlightens us in many ways about Paul's attitude to Israel: he implies that whereas the Israelites were rather well-treated in the past, they now have to be aware of the new stage in God's action.

All this concerned Israel's past. Let us now turn to what Paul has to say about the Israelites' present situation and attitude. The earliest remarks we find in Paul's letters about the Jews are in 2 Thess.2:14-16. Paul had had great difficulties in Thessalonica, and the Church he had founded there apparently had suffered Gentile hostility in the city. So to encourage the Christians there, he tells them that their suffering is to be compared with that of the Churches in Judaea, who were under attack from their fellow-countrymen, the Jews (or the Judaeans). At this point, Paul's language becomes particularly violent. It is as if he is asking "what do you expect? These people are wicked. They killed the prophets of old, and even the Lord." They had persecuted Paul and, as they had tried to prevent him from preaching the Gospel to the Gentiles, they could not please God or be considered friendly by others. It is not quite clear whether when he speaks about the obstacles the Jews put in his way, Paul means all the Jews or only those of Judaea. In any case, he is very harsh on "the Jews", although he does not deny he is one of them. The Jews are the enemies of God's representatives among them, to the extent of persecuting or even killing them. As many of the prophets said, they are a stiff-necked people who constantly rebel against the God who chose them and blessed them in so many ways.

Elsewhere, Paul uses more guarded language but says similar things. The Jews reject the Gospel of Jesus Christ (Rom.10:21). This is not the result of any lack of interest in God's will, but of a misunderstanding on their part about what that will is (Rom.10:2). They imagine they have to acquire righteousness through the Law and thus find themselves in a blind alley (Rom.9:31 and 10:3). The Jews' failure to please God is not, in Paul's eyes, tied to only their negative reaction to the Gospel. It is also visible in other fields. There are some interesting remarks to that effect in Romans, chapters 2 and 3. The antithesis Jew-Greek, which Paul frequently uses instead of the Jew-Gentile couple, simply because he is writing to Greek-speaking groups, appears several times in this context. It follows a long stretch of hostile comments on the ethical attitudes of "the bad" and "the good" in general (Rom. 1:18 to 2:8), and is meant here both as a theological classification (see the πρῶτον in 1:16 and 2:9.10) and as an ethnic characterization of the two "nations" as they co-existed in the Roman Empire (2:9.10 and 3:9). For Paul, in the cities of the Empire, where so many people mix, and especially in Rome, there are really only two nations, and the Jews are one of these. Is that a gross exaggeration on his part? To some extent, yes. But the Jews were quite numerous in all the main cities and, among the ethnic groups, were perhaps the one best organized for survival in those melting pots of Antiquity. Whether the righteous Gentiles alluded to in 2:14-16 are meant as Gentile Christians or, as is more likely, as all the Gentiles leading a virtuous life, their situation is seen as quite different from that of the Jews. God will judge them without the Law. In other words, as Hellenes and Romans knew very well, the Jews' specificity is attached to the existence among them of the Law of Moses. Paul insists that this is not simply a cultural reference, but a legislation which must be put into practice.

The Jews fail to do precisely this, in Paul's eyes. Just like the Gentiles, as a group they are under the yoke of sin (Rom. 3:9). So God's grace is wholly unmotivated. This might be a mere theological proposition, but Paul makes it more concrete and specific by accusing "the Jews," as a whole, of various misdemeanors. For example, they are arrogant, since they mean to teach the will of God to others and claim to be guides for the blind, light for those who live in darkness, etc. (Rom.2:17-20). Unfortunately, their actions contradict their theoretical attachment to the Law; they teach that stealing is wrong, but they steal; they denounce adultery while themselves committing that sin; they abhor idols and at the same time commit an act which our old translators rendered as "sacrilege" (ἱεροσυλεῖς) and which nowadays we do not really know how to translate. (No great loss, perhaps, as we do not have the slightest idea to what action it might refer.)

Perhaps it denotes misbehavior toward the Jerusalem Temple, like refusing to fulfil one's obligations of taxation, pilgrimage and so forth. Or perhaps it refers to some criminal behavior in relation with this or that Gentile Temple. In any case, Paul picks out some fields in which some Jews had a few crimes on their conscience and claims that it is enough to disqualify the whole Jewish people as a Law-obedient group. A strange reasoning indeed, but colored by Paul's conviction that, in terms of *Heilsgeschichte*, a people is a unit which has one and the same fate, unless some of its members break away from the majority in a deliberate way. This idea seems rather shocking to us at first, for it smacks of collective guilt, a concept we abhor although it has not vanished from our minds. But Paul sees the Jews as struck by God's anger at their refusal to obey the Law and listen to the Gospel (Rom.1:18ff is meant for them too). The punishment lies in the growth of awful sins among the Jews as well as among the Gentiles (see also 1 Thess.2:16, which means the same). Besides, Paul adds a remark which corrects his thesis to some extent. If the Jewish people is to be condemned for the misbehavior of some of its members, this is because they rob God of the honor due to him by not complying with His actual will. Through their fault, the Gentiles speak ill of God, who is ill-obeyed although He claims to rule the world. The Jews ought to be the best public relations agency for their Lord, but in fact their job is very poorly done because they tolerate among them sinners who should have been expelled long ago. Thus, the main failure of the Jews in Paul's time is not in their having refused to listen to the Gospel of Jesus Christ, but in their having rendered a weak witness to God among the Gentiles, neglecting their chief duty.

Finally, Paul has a few things to say about the Jews' future. He has met with too much resistance from his people to hope that he will see the day when they will accept his Gospel. Their "no" to justification by faith in Jesus Christ is too firm to be understood as a temporary accident which can be made good after a while. Indeed, it has been announced by the prophets and therefore is part of God's purpose (Rom.9:32-33 and 11:7-10). Nonetheless—and even apart from his personal feelings, which we described earlier—Paul prays for the salvation of his people (Rom.10:1). He knows that the Remnant of Israel gathered around him is a sign of hope, even for the people it was carved out of (Rom.11:1-6). Their stumbling does not necessarily end in falling (Rom.11:11a). Their ἥττημα (their "diminishing," their "reduction") meant riches for the Nations (Rom.11:12), so their πλήρωμα (their "fulness," their "all coming together") will work the same way—for the world, for sure, but for themselves in the first place.

Paul derives two consequences from these somewhat cryptic remarks. The first has to do with the near future. The apostle would consider it the crowning of his ministry among Gentiles to cause emulation among the Jews, who, after all, are also sent by God as witnesses for His glory to all nations (Rom.11:13-14a). That salutary feeling of having to think again in order not to be completely overtaken by a competitor will, Paul believes, lead to salvation for some of them (Rom.11:14b). This overcoming of the doubts of some Jews (Paul calls it "life from the dead" without further qualification, so that we are left guessing at its precise meaning) will have far-reaching results. Whatever the case, Paul considers that it is no use preaching the Gospel to the Jews. Evangelising the Nations is the only way to convince some Jews that this fulfils Israel's mission to the whole world. Therefore it has to be supported actively. A rather interesting interpretation of the Jews' attitude towards the Gospel!

The other consequence concerns the eschatological future. Romans 11:25-32, in which Paul discusses this, has been widely debated. Yet there is no consensus about its interpretation. Consider, for instance, Fr. Francois Refoulé's recent book *"Et ainsi tout Israël sera sauvé" (Romans 11, 25-32)*, (Paris: 1984). Refoulé insists that Πᾶς Ἰσραήλ in Rom.11:26 means "All the believers," including the believing Jews, and not the historical people of the Jews. Without entering into a full discussion of that passage, I want to make a few remarks about it. What Paul wants to reveal to his readers is a "secret," a "mystery" known to him, doubtless, by some direct revelation from Heaven (Rom.11:25). Of course it is based on Scripture, as 11:26-27, which combines material from Isaiah 59:20, Jeremiah 31:33-34 and Isaiah 27:9 tries to show. It emphasizes the promises of forgiveness and liberation given in these prophetic exhortations addressed to Israel. But Paul's mystery is certainly both more specific than the prophets' words and more closely applicable to the Jews' situation in his time. The hardening of the heart sent to a large part of Israel by God will be long; it will not end before the "fulness of the Gentiles" has "entered". These phrases are of course rather ambiguous. But they doubtless indicate that God, who chose to send a spirit of blindness to Israel in order to promote the evangelisation of the Gentiles, when "the fulness of the Gentiles" is gathered into the Church, will put an end to that situation and forgive his people for their refusal to accept his grace. This "fulness" may of course mean the pre-determined number of those who are to be saved, or a large majority, or all Gentiles. But it is God's own decision that Israel's "no" will finally be changed into a "yes". "And thus, the whole of Israel will be saved," adds verse 26a. There can be no question that this phrase (26a) echoes "the fulness of Gentiles" and "the fulness of Israel" (in the same chapter, vv.25 and 12). It could be that πᾶς Ἰσραήλ is meant to include the Gentiles who accepted the Gospel, but that is unlikely. Paul says in fact that Israel, including both Jews who accepted Jesus as Messiah **and** Jews who did not, but finally did away with their hostility to Gentiles entering the Covenant in large numbers, will benefit from God's grace at the End. The often-raised problem of the so-called "conversion" of the Jews to Jesus Christ is not at all present in Paul's mind. For him, what counts is that God's grace will be the deciding factor when God decides to open the hearts of the Jews to their Christian brethren from the Nations.

IV

Although we cannot but agree that Luke's theological thinking and his literary work are shot through with the theme of *Heilsgeschichte*, we must add that his understanding of the history of salvation is a good deal narrower in scope than Paul's. For instance, eschatology is far less important for Luke and so does not need to be discussed here. As for Israel's past history, Luke sees it in a narrower perspective than Paul does. The result is that when we study Luke, using an outline based on Israel's past, present and future is not adequate. It will be more suitable to base my remarks here on the two categories of Jews Luke distinguishes. These are Palestinian Jews on the one hand and diaspora Jews on the other, As we shall see, Luke views the two groups with rather different eyes.

Before we turn to these groups, however, we must make a few remarks on Luke's use of Scripture in relation to his ideas concerning the Jews. Heir to a rich tradition, both in his Gospel and in Acts, Luke is ready to accept scriptural quotations and even interpretations of important texts customary in the Early Church. In one example, Luke 4:21.23-27, borrows from tradition the commentary of Isaiah 61:1-2 and 58:6. This boils down to a harsh negation of any special right of the Jews to be the receivers of God's grace. It corresponds roughly to Luke's own ideas. But it is more brutal in its use of stories from Scripture to show that God's salvation is aimed at Gentiles (the widow of Sarepta and the healing of Naaman the Syrian). Again, the saying of Jesus recorded in Luke 11:29-32, which goes back to a very early tradition, comments on the stories of Jonas and of the Queen of Sheba to call on the Jews to listen to the Gospel instead of asking for signs from heaven. It fits well with Luke's own ideas, but it interprets Scripture in a way that sounds more anti-Jewish than Luke's own contributions. The same might also be said of Stephen's speech in Acts 7, the least likely of all the speeches in Acts to have been made up by Luke and the most violent in its attacks on the Jews of the Past.

Wherever we can spot the hand of Luke himself (e.g. in the other speeches in Acts, even though these are not free compositions), we find a much more conciliatory tone (see for instance the first part of Paul's speech at Pisidian Antioch in Acts 13:16-22). Although he is a Gentile Christian, Luke is certainly not one who would pick out the passages in Scripture that could be read in an anti-Jewish fashion. What interests him, in the Bible, is any passage that can be understood as a prophecy of the coming of the Messiah, Jesus, and of that event's far-reaching consequences. He shares this attitude with other Christians of his time, but, as the speeches in Acts 2, 3 and 13 show, he goes his own way, combining the quotation from Scripture, his commentary, the *kerygma* and the call to conversion. As an educated Greek, he has a view of Scripture which differs from Paul's in that it pays little attention to a close exegesis of every detail in the text.

Another feature of Luke's attitude to Scripture is worthy of attention before we move on. It is this: Luke was doubtless a constant reader of the Septuagint, and when he writes, he tends to imitate the style of the Greek Bible. Consider for instance the use of the phrase καὶ ἐγένετο in Acts. This has often been noted as a clear attempt at Biblical style. Several other features of his style, such as can be detected in Luke 1 and 2, contribute to a first-class *pastiche* of Biblical narrative. But Luke goes one step further. He occasionally writes a hymn very similar to Psalms or hymns of Scripture (see the *Magnificat* in Luke 1:46-55 and the *Benedictus* in Luke 1:68-79). In other words, to him, Scripture is not a closed canon. It can be extended, his own writings are already a "New Testament" to him—although it took the Churches more than a century to accept the idea. Scripture comprises not only venerable books from a distant past; it continues to grow in the hands of non-Jews who consider they are fully entitled to claim that Jewish heritage as their own.

If we now turn to what Luke has to say about Palestinian Jews, we of course see plenty of unpleasant remarks about the people who opposed Jesus and the Early Church. In order of appearance, these are the people of Nazareth (Lk.4:16-31), the "scribes and Pharisees" (Lk.5:17-26,5:29-39,6:6-11,7:29-30,11:44.53-54,14:3-6,15:1ff), the Pharisees taken by themselves (Lk.6:1-6,7:36-50,11:37-43, 12:1,14:1,16:14-18,18:10-14), the Samaritans (Lk.9:51-56), the Galilean cities (Lk.10:13-15), the lawyers and the scribes (10:25-37,11:45-52,20:39-47), the ruler of a synagogue (Lk.13:14), the people of Jerusalem (13:34-35), and finally, the chief priests, scribes and elders (Lk.20:1-8 and 19-26, 22:1-6.52ff.66ff,23:10.13ff,24:20). If we add the enemies of the Jerusalem Church mentioned in the first chapters of the Acts, we cannot but be very impressed by the hostility of so many Palestinian Jews towards Jesus. There is no doubt that Luke felt the Jews of Palestine had misunderstood the Master and that some of their leaders had done all they could to get him out of the way. Luke simply accepted an idea that was present in all layers of Christian tradition. But he modified it in order to adapt it to his own purpose, although it is at some points difficult to say what these modifications were and what their aim was. Luke makes a clear difference between the Pharisees, on the one hand, and the scribes or lawyers on the other (see for instance Luke 11:37-54, where a curse is thrown by Jesus on the two groups in succession). But he tends to combine the efforts of the two categories in a new way, as if he felt from his own experience that a rabbi was bound to be a Pharisee (as indeed became true as the Jamnia school acquired a growing influence within Judaism). Another combination of Jesus' enemies which Luke notes frequently and which is rare elsewhere in the Gospel is that of high-priests and scribes. It may reflect simply Luke's idea of the scribes' role in Palestinian Judaism.

What matters more is that some of Jesus' opponents mentioned in Luke are not simply groups with a common attitude, but groups that are divided, some of their members being hostile and others friendly. This applies both to the Pharisees and to the scribes in Luke's writings. As has often been noted, the Pharisees are not constantly inimical to Jesus in Luke-Acts. In the Gospel, they act as hosts to the Master, even if their conversation at table is a little tense (7:36-50,11:37,14:1); they warn him of impending danger (13:31-33); they ask pertinent questions (17:20-21). In Acts, a kind of complicity seems to exist on occasions between some Pharisees and the Chris-

tians in Jerusalem (5:34-40 and 23:6-9). Some Pharisees even became
Christians (Acts 15:5). As for scribes, they are not a unified group in
Luke. He calls them either γραμματεῖς, νομικοί or νομοδιδάσκαλοι,
and they have a reasonably friendly attitude on some occasions
(Lk.20:39; see Lk.10:25-37). In Acts, the Pharisees mentioned earlier
as having a fairly positive attitude to the Early Christians are also
scribes at the same time. It might even be noted that, although the
"high priests" are constantly hostile to Jesus in the Gospel and
opposed to the preaching of the Gospel in Acts (see for instance Acts
5:17ff.), "many priests" are said in Acts 6:7 to have decided to "obey
the faith", as the writer puts it. The same is not true of other groups,
like the Sadducees, but on the whole Luke-Acts is less violent than
the other Gospels in its attacks on the Jewish leaders in Palestine.

As we saw, the people of Jewish Palestine, and particularly of
Jerusalem, were not described as a constantly friendly group. But
Luke-Acts makes it clear that Jesus was well-liked by his people and
that this was a reason for his foes to fear him (Luke 22:1-2). After the
sentence passed on Jesus by Pilate with the consent of "the people"
(Luke 23:13 and 18), Luke is the only Evangelist to mention that "a
crowd of the people" followed Jesus to the place of his execution and
mourned about his death (Lk.23:27-31 and 48). In Acts the people of
Jerusalem are persistently offered salvation by the apostles and,
having repented their sins in general, or their attitude to Jesus, they
accept baptism in great numbers (Acts 2:41, etc.), becoming lasting
members of a large congregation (see Acts 21:20). Their attitude is that
of many Palestinian Jews from other cities and regions in that country
(5:16,9:31 etc). In other words, the Jews of Palestine were friendly to
the Christian cause for the most part; their leaders could not really
prevent them from accepting Jesus as the Messiah. Even those who
did not accept baptism were most respectful of "the faith" (see, for
instance, 5:13). Thus, nothing could stop the progress of the Gospel in
Jewish Palestine. The only weakness of the large Church gathered
there was that it did not understand Paul's action among Gentiles
(Acts 21:21), which was the future of the Christian Church (Acts
28:30f.). As a result, they had not helped their Jewish brethren in
Palestine to understand the Gentile mission as part of the witness of
Israel to the nations. So the Jerusalem crowd was easily aroused
against Paul (Acts 21:30, etc.).

According to Luke, Palestinian Jews were not only friendly to
Jesus and the Early Church whenever they were not influenced by
their leaders. They were also a pious people among whom there were
devout groups and individuals who waited for the coming of the
Kingdom of God. Various instance can be mentioned (Lk.7:2-9;7:36-

50,18:9-14.18:18-23,19:1-10.21:1-4,23:50-56, Acts 5:34-39,10:1ff.), but no better example exists than that of Lk. 1 and 2, where the reader is plunged into a warm atmosphere of piety at the time of the birth of John the Baptist and Jesus. Zachariah and Elizabeth, Mary and Joseph, the shepherds at Bethlehem, Simeon and Anna in the Temple, all are fine figures of religious Palestinian Jews, and Luke takes pleasure in emphasizing their significance so as to show how deep the roots of Christianity reach within Judaism.

Of course, this description of Palestinian Judaism, with some bad leaders but also some good ones, with some very pious groups and persons among them, and finally, with a great deal of goodwill and serious religion among the masses, suffers one great weakness; it describes a world that, after the War of the Jews and the Fall of Jerusalem, was to Luke quite dead. It is always easier to paint a rosy picture of a distant past than to show the lights and shadows of what no longer exists!

Turning now to Luke's description of the diaspora Jews, a group which the writer knew fairly well since he came across them almost constantly, we find a less optimistic view. The first feature of Acts that we should note is the presence of Jews wherever Christian missionaries go—in Syria, in the whole of Asia Minor, in Macedonia, in Greece and in Rome. That corresponds, as far as we know, to historical fact. The Jews had settled in most of the cities in the Eastern half of the Roman Empire and in at least some of those in the Western half, beginning with Rome. The existence of Jewish synagogues or, wherever that was not possible (Philippi!), of more informal gatherings, is understood by Luke as an asset for the Christian missionaries, who found no better *Anknüpfungspunkt* than those gatherings of people who shared their faith in the one God, Creator, Providence, Lawgiver and Judge. The "Greeks" who took part in those meetings and found it difficult to become proselytes were particularly open to the preaching of the Christian Gospel, but some of the Jews were also led to accept the message of salvation through Christ. It has been said quite often that Luke is too systematic in telling how Paul began his preaching at the synagogue wherever he went. But there is good reason to believe that Luke was right in most cases.

Throughout the Empire, the Jews occasionally had difficulties with the people and governments of the cities where they lived as well as with the Roman authorities. Luke is aware of this (Acts 18:2.12-17 and 19:33-34). But he emphasizes far more the cooperation between the Jews and Roman or civic authorities—a state of affairs which indeed corresponds to the needs of the delicately balanced situation of Jewish colonies throughout the region. As small minorities in the midst of populations that were usually attached to their local cults, the Jews had to be on good terms with those in power, or at least to have as much influence as possible on public opinion. They could achieve this through the "God-fearers" who were attracted to their faith. Luke gives us examples of this in Cyprus (13:6-8), in Pisidian Antioch (13:50), in Iconium (14:2-5), in Lystra (14:19), in Thessalonica (17:5-9), in Beroea (17:13), in Corinth (18:12ff) and probably also in Ephesus, since Paul cannot go back there on his way to Jerusalem (20:17). According to Luke, the Jews' influence at all those places was based mostly on the attraction synagogue-worship exerted on some of the best people everywhere (see Acts 13:42-50,14:1,17:4.12.17,18:4). But some Jews had also become influential through the use of various magic tricks (Acts 13:6-8,19:13-16.19). In spite of Luke's efforts to show the contrary, these must have seemed to the ordinary person very similar to Paul's exorcisms and healings (see Acts 19:11-12!).

To these diaspora Jews, Luke tells us, the Christian Gospel had a familiar ring owing to its Biblical roots. When Paul and his companions started preaching in a synagogue, there was always a period of a few hours to a few months when they were listened to or even were able to engage in serious discussion with the Jews. But only few Jews would become Christians, whereas many god-fearers did (13:42-45,14:1,17:4,17:10-12.17,18:4 and 19:8ff). Then, Paul and his fellow-preachers would be expelled from the synagogue and, if they were lucky, could carry on their work in the same city by finding another meeting-house, as in Corinth (18:7) and Ephesus (19:9). To the synagogue authorities' violent reaction Paul replied, according to Luke, by saying solemnly that he was now turning to the Gentiles—as he does also in the final scene of the book, in Rome (28:25-29). Interestingly enough, Luke does not describe the Jews as a united front. They have discussions or even violent quarrels between themselves about the Christian Gospel (17:10-11,18:17,19:9 and 28:24-25). The violent reaction that finally prevails in most places is connected with the idea that the Christian Gospel is a subversive ideology that spreads throughout the world and has to be fought against if the synagogue is to survive (see Acts 17:6,24:5 and 28:22).

Thus, there are nuances in the rather negative view Luke takes of the diaspora Jews. They are daily rivals and sometimes dangerous opponents for the Christian Church. One feels it in the picture given in the Book of Acts. This is a story of rejection, separation and painful competition, but the Jews are not ignored or despised. The image of them given by the Book of Acts remains a view, not a caricature.

V

To conclude, neither Paul nor Luke sees the Jews as the completely abstract theological concept of a "people of God" tied to a mythical past, or as the unacceptable evil community which ought to be suppressed, as did later Christian generations. To Paul and Luke, the Jews are still men and women who struggle with the Word of God and try to obey it, even though a majority of them make the wrong choice. The days of Pseudo-Barnabas and Marcion are not yet come.

7

A Symbol of Otherness: Circumcision and Salvation in the First Century

John. J. Collins
DePaul University

In Acts 15:1, we are told that some men came down from Judea to Antioch and were teaching the brethren that "unless you are circumcised according to the custom of Moses you cannot be saved," and that Paul and Barnabas had no small dissension and debate with them. The position of these Judeans is often regarded as archetypically Jewish. Circumcision, after all, was the sign of the covenant with Abraham: "This is my covenant which you shall keep, between me and you and your descendants after you: every male among you shall be circumcised. . . and it shall be a sign of the covenant between me and you" (Gen. 17:10-11). Its importance is amply attested by the events of the Maccabean era and by the forcible circumcisions of the Hasmoneans.[1] While the custom was not uniquely Jewish, it was virtually synonymous with Judaism in the Roman period. The satirist Persius could speak simply of "the sabbath of the circumcised" (*Sat.* 5.184). Tacitus held that Jews "adopted circumcision to distinguish themselves from other peoples by this difference. Those who are converted to their ways follow the same practice" (*Hist.* 5.2). Petronius, in a more derisive tone, says that "The Jew may worship his pig-god and clamor in the ears of high heaven, but unless he also cuts back his foreskin with the knife, he shall go forth from the people and emigrate to Greek cities and shall not tremble at the fasts of Sabbath imposed by the law" (*Frag.* 37).

There is no doubt that circumcision was widely perceived by Gentiles as a symbol of Judaism's otherness. The Pauline rejection of circumcision as a requirement for Gentiles was surely a significant factor in emergent Christianity's "breaking away" from its Jewish matrix. Yet Jewish views on circumcision and on the salvation of the Gentiles were not entirely uniform, so the conflict within the Chris-

---

[1] See R. Meyer, *"peritemnō," TDNT* 6(1968) 72-84.

\` tian community has been said to reflect an "internal Jewish debate."[2] In this paper I wish to review the spectrum of Jewish opinions in the Greco-Roman Diaspora, which was more diversified and generally less stringent than the homeland. I shall address three questions:

1. what did Jews demand of Gentiles, on the evidence of the so-called propaganda literature?
2. at what point was a Gentile considered to become a member of the Jewish community?
3. what can be said of the controversial category of "God-fearers" or Gentiles on the periphery of Judaism?

The answers to these questions may help clarify how far the Christian dispute reflected an internal Jewish debate, and how far it resulted from new factors which were intrinsic to Christianity itself.

I. The Jewish propaganda literature

By Jewish propaganda literature I mean those compositions which are ostensibly addressed to a Gentile audience. Whether these works were composed primarily for a Gentile audience or were rather intended to bolster the self-respect of the Jews has been disputed since Tcherikover's famous article.[3] This question does not seem to me to admit of an unequivocal answer. Propaganda is often most effective with the home constituency, and it is probable that most readers of these works were Jews. Yet they obviously seek and claim the respect of the Greeks, and what better way to bolster self-respect than by winning the respect of others?[4] Whatever the case, these works do provide some specific indications of what Diaspora Judaism wanted from the Gentile world. I will consider four examples: the third Sibylline Oracle and the Letter of Aristeas from the Ptolemaic period, and, from the Roman, Pseudo-Phocylides and the fourth Sibylline Oracle.

The main body of *Sib. Or.* 3 was composed in the second century BCE, probably in the reign of Ptolemy VI Philometor, who was exceptionally favorable to the Jews.[5] The oracles have a strong political and eschatological interest. They expect a decisive turning point in the reign of "the seventh king of Egypt from the line of the

[2] H. D. Betz, *Galatians* (Hermeneia, Philadelphia: Fortress, 1979) 89.
[3] V. Tcherikover, "Jewish Apologetic Literature Reconsidered," *Eos* 48(1956) 169-93.
[4] See further my discussion in *Between Athens and Jerusalem: Jewish Identity in the Hellenistic Diaspora* (New York: Crossroad, 1983) 8-10.
[5] J. J. Collins, *The Sibylline Oracles of Egyptian Judaism*, SBLDS 13, (Missoula: Scholars, 1974) 21-34; "The Sibylline Oracles," in *The Old Testament Pseudepigrapha* (ed. J. H. Charlesworth, Garden City: Doubleday, 1983) 1:354-57.

Greeks" (vss 193, 318, 608), most probably either Philometor himself or his expected successor Neos Philopator. This king is referred to in Egyptian idiom as "a king from the sun" who will stop the entire earth from evil war.[6] The sibyl does not look immediately for Jewish independence but for a favorable Gentile monarch under whose patronage "the people of the great God will again be strong" and will be "guides in life for all mortals."[7]

The oracles unabashedly praise the Jews as "a race of most righteous men" (219). Specific features which are singled out are rejection of astrology and superstition, practice of social justice (218-264) and avoidance of idolatry and homosexuality (573-600). These are presumably the ways in which they can serve as guides in life for all mortals. In a number of passages, however, the sibyl appeals directly to the Greeks: "To what purpose do you give vain gifts to the dead and sacrifice to idols? Who put error in your heart that you should abandon the face of the great God and do these things?" (547-549). The way for Greece to escape the din of war is "by offering the holocausts of oxen and loud-bellowing bulls. . .at the Temple of the great God." The sibyl does not expect immediate conversion: "you certainly will not sacrifice to God until everything happens," but "what God has planned will not go unfulfilled." (570-71).

The Egyptian Sibyllines (Books 3 and 5, but also 11-14) are exceptional in Diaspora Judaism by their lack of belief in a judgment after death or resurrection.[8] Salvation is to be sought in this world. For the Jews it is a peaceful life around the temple free from war (702-09). For Greeks it is also life free from war and subjection. It is a collective, political state, not a matter of individual conversion. The requirements are the abandonment of idolatry and offering sacrifice at the

---

[6] *Sib. Or.* 3:652. Collins, *The Sibylline Oracles*, 40-43. The phrase "king from the sun" also occurs in the Egyptian Potter's Oracle.

[7] *Sib. Or.* 3: 194-195. A. Momigliano, sees here an allusion to the Maccabean revolt, but nothing else in *Sib. Or.* 3 supports this suggestion; "La portata storica dei vaticini sul settimo re nel terzo libro degli Oracoli Sibillini," *Forma futuri: Studi in onore del Cardinale Michele Pellegrino* (Turin: Bottega d'Erasmo, 1975) 1077-84. *Sib. Or.* 3:767 would seem to imply that the Ptolemaic kingdom is an intermediate stage to be superseded finally by the kingdom of God.

[8] M. Hengel disputes this in "Messianische Hoffnung und politischer 'Radikalismus' in der jüdisch-hellenistischen Diaspora," in *Apocalypticism in the Mediterranean World and the Near East* (ed. D. Hellholm, Tübingen: Mohr, 1983) 656 n.2. He points to *Sib. Or.* 4:178-190 which speaks of resurrection, and *Sib. Or.* 3:705ff. *Sib. Or.* 4 cannot be assimilated to the same tradition as *Sib. Or.* 3 and 5, in view of their fundamentally different attitudes to temple worship. It is usually located in Syria or the Jordan valley. *Sib. Or.* 3:705ff does not speak of eternal life, but is concerned with the continuing generations of the Jewish people, as Hengel himself admits.

temple of the great God, presumably in Jerusalem. These requirements are filled out in a few other passages. In 624-634 the sibyl
appeals to the Gentiles to turn back and be converted—by offering
sacrifices to the immortal God and practising justice. In the eschatological time they will repent of idolatry, send to the temple and
ponder the law of the Most High (716-723). They are warned not to
attack Jerusalem (732-40), to "shun unlawful worship," and to avoid
adultery, homosexuality and infanticide (762-66).

The requirements for salvation, then, are partly cultic and partly
moral. While the salvation of the Gentiles is eschatological, the sibyl
may have expected it in the fairly near future. What is notable for our
present discussion is that the Greeks are never required to practise
circumcision, observe the more distinctive commandments, or become Jewish. The focal point of conversion is worship of the true God
in the Jerusalem temple.[9] Greek mythology is accommodated by an
euhemeristic explanation in which Cronos and Zeus are reduced to
human status (vss 110-115), but worship is restricted to "the most high
God" or "the great God" who may, however, be conceived in Greek
terms.[10]

The Letter of Aristeas is presented as a letter from one Greek to
another, although it is patently composed by a Jew.[11] Here there is no
appeal for conversion. Indeed conversion is unnecessary, since "God,
the overseer and creator of all things, whom they worship, is He
whom all men worship, and we too, your Majesty, though we address
him differently, as Zeus and Dis; by these names men of old not
unsuitably signified that He through whom all creatures receive life
and come into being is the guide and lord of all" (Ep. Arist. 16).[12] The
purpose of the Letter is not to convert, but to win sympathy and
admiration; it is full of expressions of praise for Jerusalem, the law and
the wisdom of the translators. The author does not avoid the distinctive, separatist aspects of Jewish law, but defends them by means of
allegorical interpretation. Moses fenced the people in so "that we
might not mingle at all with any of the other nations" (139). What this
means, however, is that they should be "free from all vain imagina-

---

[9] Compare the traditional Jewish hope in Isa 2:2-4.

[10] On the identification of the God of Judaism with Greek conceptions of God, see M.
Hengel, *Judaism and Hellenism* (Philadelphia: Fortress, 1974) 1:261-267. Compare
Artapanus, who adopts an euhermeristic explanation of Egyptian cults and claims that
Moses founded them, but appears to endorse the cults as useful. See Collins, *Between
Athens and Jerusalem*, 32-38.

[11] Collins, *Between Athens and Jerusalem*, 81-86.

[12] Compare Celsus in Origen, *Contra Celsum*, 1.24 and 5.41; Hengel, *Judaism and
Hellenism*, 1.262.

tions." This position can be appreciated by "leading Egyptian priests" who "call us men of God." This title applies to "those who worship the true God." The Epistle, like the sibyl, rejects polytheism and gives an euhemeristic explanation of its origin (128-138). In doing so, the author could hope to win the respect of philosophically oriented Gentiles.[13] Judaism is presented as a non-violent, non-aggressive philosophy (148). The sages selected for the work of translation are "men of the finest character and highest culture," versed in Greek as well as in Jewish literature (121). They "rejected a rough and uncouth manner. . . and never assumed an air of superiority to others" (122). They did not present themselves as members of an exclusive, chosen people. The attitude of the Epistle is well summed up by Hadas: "The theology premised is applicable to all mankind, not to the Jews alone, and God's providence is universal. It is not suggested that God will show special consideration for the Jews simply by virtue of their being Jews, nor is there any hint of proselytization. . . . The Jews follow their own traditional usage to attain a religious end; the same end may be attained by others by a different path."[14]

Both the sibyl and Ps. Aristeas praise Judaism explicitly. Ps. Phocylides does not even mention it. Jewish authorship is inferred from a few allusions to the Pentateuch. Since some of these concern relatively obscure points (e.g. 140: "If a beast of your enemy falls on the way, help it to rise") we might not expect a Gentile author to pick them out, but the issue is not beyond question.[15] Jewish authorship is supported by a reference to bodily resurrection (103-104) and by the extensive parallels between these sayings and the summaries of Jewish law in Philo's *Hypothetica* 7.1-9 and Josephus' *Against Apion* 2. 190-219, but while Philo and Josephus claim to be summarizing Jewish laws, Ps. Phocylides does not.[16]

The common material in Philo, Josephus and Ps. Phocylides concerns the network of family and social relations, and the characteristically Jewish polemic against adultery and homosexuality. Ps.

---

[13] M. Nilsson, *Geschichte der Griechischen Religion* (Munich: Beck, 1950) 2:546-52; G. Delling, "Monos Theos," *Studien zum Neuen Testament und zum hellenistischen Judentum* (Göttingen: Vandenhoeck & Ruprecht, 1970) 391-400; H. W. Attridge, *First Century Cynicism in the Epistles of Heraclitus*, HTS 29 (Chico: Scholars, 1976) 13-23.
[14] M. Hadas, *Aristeas to Philocrates* (New York: Harper, 1951) 62.
[15] See P. W. van der Horst, *The Sentences of Pseudo-Phocylides* SVTP 4 (Leiden: Brill, 1978) 70-76.
[16] J. E. Crouch, *The Origin and Intention of the Colossian Haustafel*, FRLANT 109 (Göttingen: Vandenhoeck & Ruprecht, 1972) 84-101; M. Küchler, *Frühjüdische Weisheitstraditionen* (Göttingen: Vandenhoeck & Ruprecht, 1979) 207-318; Collins, *Between Athens and Jerusalem*, 143-148.

Phocylides, however, lacks any polemic against idolatry; it even refers to the heavenly bodies as "blessed ones" (75, 163) and says that the dead will become "gods" (104). These allusions are not incompatible with monotheism, and the expression *heis theos esti sophos* (vs. 54) may be taken to affirm it, but monotheism is scarcely an issue in these sayings. There is no question here of conversion to a specific cultic practice or of rituals such as circumcision.[17] Salvation involves both the immortality of the soul and the resurrection of the body, but the only requirement that can be inferred is conformity to the ethic set forth in the sayings. In the public realm, too, we are told that "wisdom directs the course of lands and cities" (131). The Jewish law is an implicit contributor to this wisdom, but it is not explicitly acknowledged. There is no distinction here between Jew and Greek.

The purpose of Ps. Phocylides has puzzled commentators. It is evidently not a proselytizing work nor can it be taken as propaganda for Judaism at all. If it was written by a Jew, the author does not appear to have attached importance to that fact. Some scholars have suggested that we have here the work of a "God-fearer"—i.e. a Gentile on the threshold of Judaism, familiar with the Torah from the preaching of the synagogue.[18] The affinities with Philo and Josephus do indeed support a connection with the synagogue, but the identification of "God-fearers" is problematic, as we shall see later. If the work can stand as an example of Jewish preaching, it is remarkable for its lack of insistence on the distinctive aspects of Judaism.

Our final example of Diaspora literature ostensibly addressed to Gentiles is *Sib. Or.* 4. This document comes from the late first century of the common era and differs from the Egyptian Sibylline tradition of Books 3 and 5 in significant ways: it rejects temple worship and expects a resurrection of the dead.[19] The typical Sibylline review of history culminates with the threat of the destruction of the world by fire. This impending threat provides the context for the sibyl's preaching:

> "Ah wretched mortals, change these things, and do not lead the great God to all sorts of anger, but abandon daggers and groanings, murders and outrages, and wash your whole bodies in perennial rivers. Stretch out your hands to heaven and ask forgiveness for your

[17] Vs. 31 "Do not eat blood; abstain from foot sacrificed to idols," is an interpolation found in only one inferior manuscript. Another reference to "gods" in vs. 98 is unintelligible and must be emended.

[18] Van der Horst, *The Sentences,* 76.

[19] J. J. Collins, "The Place of the Fourth Sibyl in the Development of the Jewish Sibyllina," *JJS* 25(1974) 365-80; "The Sibylline Oracles," 381-83.

previous deeds and make propitiation for bitter impiety with words of praise; God will grant repentance and will not destroy" (*Sib. Or.* 4:162-69).

This appeal is addressed to humanity at large. In the aftermath of the Jewish revolt, the plea to abandon daggers and murders may be addressed primarily to Jews. The baptism which the sibyl calls for cannot be equated with proselyte baptism, but is a symbol of repentance for Jews and Gentiles. As such, it and may be compared to the baptism of John. There is no suggestion that those who wash their bodies in perennial rivers are thereby incorporated into the Jewish people. There is no appeal for circumcision of the Gentiles, or for proselytism at all. After the resurrection "as many as are pious" (*hossoi d'eusebeousi*) will live on earth again. This sibyl definitely rejects not only idolatry, adultery and homosexuality, but also animal sacrifice and even temples. Such a view of religion might appeal to philosophically sophisticated pagans, but it is at odds not only with popular pagan religion, but also with much of traditional Judaism. That it was written after the destruction of the temple is presumably a factor here, but other strands of Judaism, including *Sib. Or.* 5, did not renounce temple worship in principle at this time.

This brief sampling of Diaspora literature shows some variation, but also some dominant trends. What these Jews asked of Gentiles was primarily that they worship the one true God. This was usually thought to entail a rejection of idolatry. They also insisted on an ethical code with special emphasis on avoiding adultery and homosexuality.[20] The lack of reference to circumcision is impressive, even in contexts where we would expect to find it—e.g. Ezekiel the tragedian fails to mention it as a requirement for celebrating the Passover.[21] Most of the works which have been regarded as propaganda literature show little interest in proselytizing, but show a desire to share and be accepted in the more philosophically sophisticated strata of Hellenistic culture. Salvation is seldom restricted to membership of the Jewish people.[22] This literature may not represent all

---

[20] See the discussion of "the common ethic" in *Between Athens and Jerusalem* 141-168.

[21] J. B. Segal, *The Hebrew Passover from the Earliest Times* (London: Oxford, 1963) 24.

[22] In "The Covenant as a Soteriological Category and the Nature of Salvation in Palestinian and Hellenistic Judaism," in *Jews, Greeks and Christians*, essays in honor of W. D. Davies, ed. R. Hamerton-Kelly and R. Scroggs (Leiden: Brill, 1976) 34-38, E. P. Sanders identifies different levels of salvation in Philo. The highest level is the vision of the Logos. Sanders concludes that "only some will see, but all of those who see will be Jews or proselytes," but adds "(with the possible exception of a few wise Gentiles)." In *Prob.* 73-75, Philo includes in the small number of the wise the seven

strata of Jewish society, but it represents a substantial body of opinion nonetheless.

II. Conversion and proselytism

The literary remains of the Hellenistic Diaspora represent the views of well-educated Jews who saw themselves, in Philo's words, as "near to being citizens, because they differ little from the original inhabitants" (*Mos.* 1.35). Philo and Josephus claim that this form of Judaism was attractive to Gentiles. Philo claims that "not only Jews but almost every other people, particularly those which take more account of virtue, have so far grown in holiness as to value and honor our laws" (*Mos.* 2.17). We may assume some exaggeration here, but the claim is supported by Seneca's complaint that "the customs of this accursed race have gained such influence that they are now received throughout all the world. The vanquished have given their laws to the victors."[23] Both Philo and Seneca emphasize the observance of the sabbath. Philo presents the synagogues as schools of philosophy which stand wide open in every city on each seventh day, where the law is preached under two main "heads" of duty to God and to humanity (*Spec. Leg.* 2.62). Josephus claims that the Jews of Antioch "were constantly attracting to their religious ceremonies multitudes of Greeks, and these they had in some measure incorporated into themselves" (*JW* 7.3.3[45]). There is some evidence of active prose-lytizing in Rome. In 139 B.C.E. the Jews were allegedly expelled from Rome "because they attempted to transmit their sacred rites to the Romans."[24] The expulsion under Tiberius in 19 C.E. may have had a similar reason: "they were converting many of the natives to their customs."[25] Such active proselytizing is not well attested else-

---

sages of Greece, the Persian Magi, Indian Gymnosophists, as well as the Jewish Essenes.

[23] Seneca, in Augustine, *De Civitate Dei*, 6.11. M. Stern, *Greek and Latin Authors on Jews and Judaism* (Jerusalem: The Israel Academy of Sciences and Humanities, 1974) 1:431.

[24] Valerius Maximus 1.3.3. Three summaries of this text survive, one of which says that the Jews "attempted to infect the Roman customs with the cult of Jupiter Sabazius". A second does not mention the Jews, and the third does not mention Sabazius. In "Sabazius and the Jews in Valerius Maximus: A Re-examination," *JRS* 69(1979) 35-38, E. N. Lane argues that the Jews were expelled, but that the association with Sabazius is due to an error in the transmission of the text.

[25] Cassius Dio, *Hist Romana* 57.18.5a (Stern, *Greek and Latin Authors*, 365). Josephus blames this episode on four individuals who deceived a proselyte named Fulvia (*Ant.* 18.3.4-5[65-84]). See also Tacitus, *Annals*, 2.85.5, Suetonius, *Tiberius*, 36.1 and E. M. Smallwood, *The Jews under Roman Rule* (Leiden: Brill, 1976) 201-206.

where,[26] but Judaism attracted adherents throughout the Diaspora. The question that arises is at what point these people ceased to be "others" and were accepted as members of the Jewish people.

In the Talmud, there are three requirements for a proselyte: circumcision, baptism and sacrifice.[27] The requirements of baptism and sacrifice are not attested before the end of the first century. However circumcision of proselytes is clearly evidenced from the Maccabean era on, not only in the forcible circumcision of the Idumeans and Itureans by the Hasmoneans (*Ant* 13.9.1[257-58] and 13.11.1[318], but also in the story of Achior's conversion in Judith 14:10. The Herods required Gentiles to be circumcised before they married into the family; some accepted and some declined.[28] In the Roman Diaspora, the custom is attested by Tacitus (*Hist*. 5.2), Petronius (*Frag*. 37) and Juvenal (*Sat*. 14.99). Whether it was universally held as a requirement for conversion to Judaism has nonetheless been questioned from time to time.[29]

We may infer from Philo that there were some Jews in Alexandria who dispensed with the practice of circumcision. In his famous discussion of the limits of allegorical interpretation in *Migr. Abr.* 89-94, Philo says: "such men I for my part should blame for handling the matter in too easy and offhand a manner." He is in agreement with their allegorical understanding of circumcision as "the excision of

---

[26] Horace, *Sat*. 1.4.138-143, which is often cited in this context, does not necessarily refer to proselytizing at all, but may involve coercion for other purposes. See J. Nolland, "Proselytism or Politics in Horace, *Satires* 1.4.138-143," *VC* 33(1979) 347-55.

[27] B. J. Bamberger, *Proselytism in the Talmudic Period* (New York: Ktav, 1968, first published in 1939) 42-55; G. F. Moore, *Judaism in the First Centuries of the Christian Era* (New York: Scribners, 1971, first published in 1927) 331. S. J. Cohen, "Conversion to Judaism in Historical Perspective," *Conservative Judaism* 36(1983) 31-45, notes that the triple requirement is attributed to Rabbi Judah the Patriarch in Sifre Numbers 108, but does not appear anywhere in the Mishnah. In "At the Crossroads: Tannaitic Perspectives on the Jewish-Christian Schism," *Jewish and Christian Self-Definition*, ed. E. P. Sanders, A. I Baumgarten and A. Mendelson (Philadelphia: Fortress, 1981) 2: 115-156, L. H. Schiffman argues that proselyte baptism is pre-supposed by Christian baptism, but this is by no means necessary. There is some inherent probability that the practice of sacrifice by converts originated before the destruction of the temple, but neither requirement is attested in first-century stories of conversions such as *Joseph and Aseneth* and the story of Izates of Adiabene.

[28] *Ant*. 16.7.6(225):Syllaeus the Arab refused, saying that if he complied he would be stoned to death by the Arabs. *Ant* 20.7.1 (139); Epiphanes of Commagene declined but Azizus of Emessa consented, in order to marry Drusilla, daughter of Herod Agrippa. *Ant* 20.7.3 (145); Polemo, king of Cilicia, was circumcised in order to marry Bernice. When the marriage collapsed he abandoned Judaism again.

[29] Recently, N. J. McEleney, "Conversion, Circumcision and the Law," *NTS* 20(1974) 328-333.

pleasure and all passions, and the putting away of the impious conceit," but argues that literal observance is to the spiritual as the body is to the soul, and cannot be neglected. What is noteworthy, however, is the tolerant tone of his disapproval. He stops far short of denying that the allegorizers are authentic Jews or members of the covenant people. While he presents his view strongly, he presents it as simply his own opinion, and he was not in a position to impose his opinion on the whole Jewish community. Insofar as he shares their allegorical understanding, moreover, he may have felt more kinship with such people than with the literalists. The context of the discussion is the importance of good reputation. Philo comments that "very many, after coming to Virtue's feet with no counterfeit or unreal homage and with their eyes open to her genuine loveliness, through paying no regard to the general opinion have become the objects of hostility, just because they were held to be bad, when they were really good" (*Migr. Abr.* 86). If this refers to the allegorists, it would seem that Philo was rather sympathetic to them, while other elements in the Jewish community were far more hostile.[30]

Philo defends the need for literal observance of circumcision, but he does not simply affirm it as "a sign of the covenant." He is at pains to justify it in terms that will appear respectable to a Greek.[31] On the one hand, he emphasizes its hygienic value.[32] On the other, he accords primacy to its allegorical significance (the excision of pleasure and conceit).[33] He can even derive support from the Egyptians, "a race regarded as pre-eminent for its populousness, its antiquity and its attachment to philosophy" (*Spec. Leg.* 1.2), although elsewhere he calls them "a worthless breed, whose souls were infected with the poison and bad temper alike of the crocodiles and asps of their country" (*Leg. ad Gaium*, 166-70). Philo does not treat circumcision as

---

[30] P. Borgen, *Paul Preaches Circumcision and Pleases Men* (Trondheim: Tapir, 1983) 43,71, argues that there was some persecution of those who abandoned circumcision, and draws an analogy with Paul.

[31] For a summary of Philo's statements on circumcision, see J. Z. Smith, "Fences and Neighbors: Some Contours of Early Judaism," in *Imagining Religion: From Babylon to Jonestown* (Chicago: University of Chicago, 1982) 14.

[32] *Spec. Leg.* 1.4-7. Philo lists four allegedly traditional arguments in favor of circumcision: freedom from ulceration, cleanliness, assimilation to the heart and increased fertility.

[33] *Spec. Leg.* 1.8-11; *Quaest in Gen.* 3.46-52 (on Gen 17:10-14). The symbolic understanding of circumcision as circumcision of the heart was widespread already in the biblical period. Cf. Lev 26:41; Deut 10:16, 30:6; Jer 4:4, 9:25; Ezek 44:7,9. Also 1QS 5:5.

a central symbol of ethnic or religious identity,[34] but the extent of his apologia shows his awareness that it was widely so regarded (cf. also *Quaest in Gen.* 3.46-52). Philo's allegorical understanding of the significance of circumcision inevitably detracts from the importance of the physical rite, even though he defends that too. Philo could have agreed with Paul that "he is not a real Jew who is one outwardly nor is true circumcision something external and physical. He is a Jew who is one inwardly and real circumcision is a matter of the heart, spiritual and not literal" (Rom 2:28-29).

In view of Philo's comments on the allegorists, we must allow that there were some ethnic Jews who abandoned circumcision without repudiating Judaism, however much other Jews may have "blamed" them. Of course, this could also be said of the Hellenizers before the Maccabean revolt. However they were a rather different case because of their political ambitions. We do not know how numerous these allegorizers may have been, but their existence shows that the absolute link between circumcision and Judaism which Petronius rightly or wrongly perceived in Rome could not be presumed in all areas of the Diaspora.[35]

The question of circumcision is, of course, more likely to be controversial in the case of a convert than in the case of an ethnic Jew. Philo's pronouncements on the matter leave room for debate. In *Quaest in Ex.* 2.2, he argues that "in reality the proselyte is one who circumcises not his uncircumcision but his desires and sensual pleasures and the other passions of the soul. For in Egypt the Hebrew nation was not circumcised." The implication of this passage is surely that circumcision is not an essential prerequisite for membership of the Hebrew nation. Harry Wolfson saw here a reference to "spiritual proselytes" or "God-fearers," and contrasted them with the "full proselytes" to whom Philo refers elsewhere.[36] The other passages do

---

[34] J. Z. Smith, "Fences and Neighbors," 14: "For Philo, the practice seems to have little to do with either ethnic or religious identity."

[35] P. Borgen, "The Early Church and the Hellenistic Synagogue," in *Paul Preaches Circumcision and Pleases Men*, 68-69, finds "also in other writings hints... which suggest that there were Jews who ignored circumcision." The example which he cites from Ignatius, *Philad.* 6.1 discourages learning Judaism from the uncircumcised, but does not say that the latter are Jews (despite the interpretation offered by C. K. Barrett, "Jews and Judaizers in the Epistles of Ignatius," in *Jews, Greeks and Christians*, eds. R. Hamerton-Kelly and R. Scroggs, 234,242). Borgen also adduces Abot of Rabbi Nathan 26 and related rabbinic material, but again, this does not directly support his case. See also his "Debates on Circumcision in Philo and Paul," ibid., 15-32.

[36] *Spec. Leg.* 1.52; 308-309; *Virt.* 103,104. Wolfson, *Philo* (Cambridge, Mass: Harvard, 1948) 2:370. Compare also F. Siegert, "Gottesfürchtige und Sympathisanten," *JSJ* 4(1973) 123.

not mention a requirement of circumcision either, and the distinction
between two kinds of proselyte has no basis in Philo's terminology. In
view of the passage in *Migr. Abr.* 89-94, we may assume that Philo
would "blame" a convert who did not fulfil the literal commandments,
including circumcision, but the ritual is not an entrance requirement
and its omission does not necessarily exclude the proselyte from the
Jewish community, at least in theory.[37]

Philo's position here may be compared to that ascribed to R.
Joshua in the Babylonian Talmud (Yeb. 46a). R. Eliezer is said to have
held that one who is circumcised but not baptized is a convert, as in
the case of the Jews at the Exodus. R. Joshua maintained that one who
is baptized but not circumcised is a convert, like the Israelite women
at the Exodus. The sages insisted on both requirements. In the
Jerusalem Talmud (J. Kid. 3.14.64d), R. Joshua is said to have required
both circumcision and baptism. Bamberger argues that the Jerusalem
version is the "correct" one and that even the Babylonian text "cannot
mean that R. Joshua permitted conversion without circumcision," for
"how indeed could R. Joshua have flouted the direct written word of
the Torah?"[38] The issue, however, is not what R. Joshua actually held
but what was the view attributed to him, and this cannot be decided
by *a priori* considerations. Neither R. Joshua nor Philo is suggesting
that circumcision be abandoned. The question is simply at what point
a convert becomes a Jew, whether circumcision is a prerequisite for
entry, or a duty consequent on admission.[39] The view attributed to R.
Joshua in the Babylonian Talmud is the latter, and it was evidently not
accepted by the sages. Philo's position seems to be similar. Both
discussions are theoretical, and do not prove the actual existence of
uncircumcised proselytes, but they have at least potential significance
nonetheless.[40]

When Philo speaks of proselytes, he ignores the ritual aspect of
conversion and pays far greater attention to its social aspects. Prose-

---

[37] Borgen, "The Early Church," 67: "bodily circumcision was not the requirement for
entering the Jewish community, but was one of the commandments which they had to
obey after having received the status of Jews." Borgen compares the position of Hillel
in B Shabbath 31a, which does not, however, address this question directly. See also
N. J. McEleney, "Conversion," 328-29. J. Nolland, "Uncircumcised proselytes?" *JSJ*
12(1981) 173-79, against McEleney, infers from *Migr. Abr.* that Philo would have
insisted on circumcision.

[38] Bamberger, *Proselytism*, 46-52. Compare W. G. Braude, *Jewish Proselytizing in the
First Five Centuries of the Common Era* (Providence: Brown, 1940) 76.

[39] S. Bialoblocki, *Die Beziehungen des Judentums zu Proselyten und Proselytentum*
(Berlin: Nobels Kulturbibliothek, 1930) 15.

[40] Bamberger, *Proselytism*, 51.

lytes, he says, should be accorded every favor and consideration and equal rank with the native born because "they have left their country, their kinsfolk and their friends for the sake of virtue and religion. Let them not be denied another citizenship or other ties of family and friendship. . ."[41] Religion was an integral part of civic life in the Hellenistic and Roman cities. Jewish monotheism might win the respect of the philosophically sophisticated, but proselytes who abandoned the worship of pagan gods would thereby be cut off from many civic and social activities. Jews as a group did not enjoy full citizenship in Alexandria or other cities of the Diaspora in the first century,[42] and so the status of proselytes must have been ambiguous. Atheism, or refusal to worship the gods, was at least a scandal, perhaps a crime.[43] Jews were exempt from this charge (at least by custom), but the status of the proselyte was less clear.[44] Consequently, proselytes could on occasion be persecuted, as we know from the case of Flavius Clemens under Domitian, although this seems to have been exceptional.[45]

Quite apart from the legal ramifications, however, conversion to Judaism involved a major social transition. Philo explains Balaam's oracle "Behold, a people will dwell alone and among the nations it will not be reckoned," as follows: "not because their dwelling-place is set apart and their land severed from others, but because in virtue of the distinction of their peculiar customs they do not mix with others to depart from the ways of their fathers" (*Mos.* 1.278). Even Jews who minimized their observance of strange customs would still be set apart socially if they refused to worship the pagan gods. The objection against Jewish claims to citizenship, from Alexandria to Ionia, was that they did not worship the gods of their neighbors.[46] Practical monotheism, with its social consequences, was a more significant dividing line between Jew and Gentile than an individual ritual such

---

[41] *Spec. Leg.* 1.52. Cf. *Spec. Leg.* 1.308-309; *Virt.* 103,104.

[42] Smallwood, *The Jews under Roman Rule*, 227-230. The decisive evidence is found in the letter of Claudius. See also S. Applebaum, "The Legal Status of the Jewish Communities in the Diaspora," in *The Jewish People in the First Century*, Compendia Rerum Iudaicarum ad Novum Testamentum, eds. S. Safrai and M. Stern (Philadelphia: Fortress, 1974) 1:420-463.

[43] J. Juster, *Les Juifs dans l'Empire Romain* (Paris: Geuthner, 1914) 1:254-259. R. MacMullen, *Paganism in the Roman Empire* (New Haven: Yale, 1983) 62: "to deny the reality of the gods was absolutely unacceptable. You would be ostracized for that, even stoned in the streets."

[44] V. Tcherikover, *Hellenistic Civilisation and the Jews* (New York: Atheneum, 1970) 306: "there exists no document which exempts the Jews from participating in the worship of the gods."

[45] Smallwood, *The Jews under Roman Rule*, 378-83.

[46] For Alexandria, *Ag.Ap.* 2.65; for Ionia, *Ant.* 12.3.2 (126).

as circumcision. Conversion to Judaism involved joining a new community and being accepted as a member of a synagogue.[47] We may assume that synagogues would normally have insisted on circumcision, but in a place like Alexandria there may have been exceptions.

The most elaborate literary account of a conversion from the Diaspora is found in the romance *Joseph and Aseneth*. The portrayal of the conversion process here accords well with what we have seen in Philo. Aseneth is a representative or model proselyte.[48] In 15:6 she is told that in future she will be called "city of refuge," and those who attach themselves to the Lord through repentance will be protected by her "wall." Since she is a woman, the issue of circumcision does not arise, but the fact that the main literary portrayal of the proselyte experience from the Hellenistic Diaspora concerns a woman should perhaps warn us not to attach too much importance to circumcision. In fact, Aseneth's conversion is not marked by any ritual. The episode of the honeycomb describes a mystical experience of some sort, but it is not a repeatable rite.[49] The formulaic references to eating the bread of life, drinking the cup of immortality and anointing with the oil of incorruption are most satisfactorily explained as a reference to the entire Jewish way of life (8:5-6 and 15:4).[50] When Joseph first meets Aseneth, he tells her that it is not fitting for "a pious man (*andri theosebei*) who blesses with his mouth the living God and eats the blessed bread of life and drinks the blessed cup of immortality and anoints himself with the blessed oil of incorruption to kiss an alien woman who blesses dead and dumb idols with her mouth and eats from their table bread of strangling and drinks from their libations a cup of treachery and anoints herself with oil of perdition."[51] Since the eating and drinking are predicated of Joseph as a pious man, they cannot be a ritual of initiation but must refer to the habitual practice of the pious Jews. The point of distinction from Gentiles is, again, the rejection of idolatry and its attendant sacrifices and social functions.

---

[47] J. Z. Smith, "Fences and Neighbors," 15, notes that affiliation with a synagogue is one of the most common items noted in Jewish epitaphs from antiquity. Note also the rabbinic maxim that the rejection of idolatry is the acknowledgement of the whole law (Sifre Numbers 111, Deut 54, Megilla 13a, Moore, *Judaism* 1:325).

[48] C. Burchard, *Untersuchungen zu Joseph und Aseneth* (Tübingen: Mohr, 1965) 119; Collins, *Between Athens and Jerusalem*, 217.

[49] On the alleged affinities of Joseph and Aseneth with mystery religions see D. Sänger, *Antikes Judentum und die Mysterien* (WUNT 2/5; Tübingen: Mohr, 1980).

[50] Burchard, *Untersuchungen*, 86. M. Philonenko, *Joseph et Aséneth: Introduction, Texte Critique et Notes* (Leiden: Brill, 1968) 91, attempts to identify a ritual here.

[51] I follow the text of C. Burchard, "Ein vorläufiger griechischer Text von Joseph und Aseneth," *Dielheimer Blätter zum Alten Testament* 14(1979) 2-53.

Even before the encounter with Aseneth, we learn that Joseph does not eat with the Egyptians, although he is the ruler of all Egypt (7:1 and 20:9). The actual conversion of Aseneth takes place when she throws away the idols which she formerly worshipped (10:13). Her acceptance into the Israelite community takes place when Joseph embraces her—that is, admits her to the social intimacies from which she previously had been excluded. It is consolidated when she marries Joseph and acknowledges Jacob as her father. The network of social relations gives external expression to the conversion that has taken place inwardly.

Joseph and Aseneth is of course a fiction. It tells us an author's ideal, not the historical custom. It is very doubtful that a Jew in Egyptian service could remain as socially aloof as Joseph. Yet in the Ptolemaic era it was possible for Jews to rise in the government service without abandoning Judaism and probably without engaging in idolatry.[52] *Joseph and Aseneth* posits good relations between Joseph and the Egyptians. Pentephres is an Egyptian priest, and Joseph does not eat with him (7:1), but Pentephres is glad to give his daughter, and he blesses the God of Joseph (3:3; 20:7). Both he and the pharaoh might be taken to represent pagan sympathizers with Judaism, although neither observes any Jewish laws.[53] Whether such people can attain salvation (which for *Joseph and Aseneth* is immortality) is not really discussed. Aseneth was "dead" before her conversion, but then she was not especially sympathetic to the God of Israel at that point either.[54]

The best known story of an historical conversion to Judaism in the Diaspora is the story of the royal house of Adiabene recounted by Josephus (*Ant.* 20.2.3-4 [34-48]). A Jewish merchant named Ananias "visited the king's wives and taught them to worship God after the manner of the Jewish tradition." Through them he also won over Izates, the crown prince. In the meantime, his mother Helena had been converted by another Jew. When Izates wished to be circumcised, since he considered that he would not be genuinely a Jew otherwise, his mother tried to stop him "For, she said, he was a king; and if his subjects should discover that he was devoted to rites that were strange and foreign to themselves, it would produce much

[52] The priest Onias, founder of Leontopolis, was a general in the army of Philometor (Josephus, *AgAp;* 2.49). See P. M. Fraser, *Ptolemaic Alexandria* (Oxford: Clarendon, 1972) 1.83-84.
[53] See M. Philonenko, *Joseph et Aséneth*, 51.
[54] The conclusion of Sanders ("The Covenant as a Soteriological Category," 23) that "Outside of Judaism there is no salvation" seems to me more unequivocal than the text warrants.

disaffection and they would not tolerate the rule of a Jew over them."
Ananias supported her, partly out of self-interest, since he feared he
would be blamed if there was a revolt, but also because he held that
"he could worship God (*to theion sebein*) even without circumcision
if he had fully decided to be devoted to the ancestral customs of the
Jews, for this was more important than circumcision." He added that
God would pardon him if, constrained by necessity and by fear of his
subjects, he failed to perform the rite. Izates was persuaded for the
time being, but later another Jew, Eleazar, came from Galilee. He had
a reputation for being very strict about the law, and persuaded Izates
that circumcision was indeed necessary. His mother's fears of rebellion were not realized and indeed, Izates enjoyed divine protection.
He and his mother became renowned benefactors of Jerusalem.

This fascinating story gives rise to several problems. There is no
reason to doubt the report that the conversion took place in two stages,
but it is difficult to know how far the interpretative comments are
supplied by Josephus himself rather than by the characters to whom
they are attributed. Izates is in many ways an atypical proselyte. He is,
after all, about to become king, and so his case involves political
complications.[55] We know little of conditions in Adiabene and
whether they were at all similar to the western Diaspora. Yet some
conclusions can be drawn on the basis of Josephus' narrative.

Ananias justifies his position with a general theological principle—it is possible to worship God without circumcision. This is not
simply a matter of expediency.[56] Josephus must have been aware of
this principle. As we have seen, it had some support in Alexandria and
even in rabbinic Judaism.[57] This principle, however, is qualified here
in two respects. First, Izates' mother implies that his subjects would
not regard him as a Jew if he was not circumcised, and this accords
with Izates' own initial sentiment.[58] Second, the assurance the God
would pardon the omission suggests that it is normally culpable.
Izates is excused because of "necessity," just as a dispensation might
be given to a hemophiliac. The latter point, however, is compatible

---

[55] Jacob Neusner, *A History of the Jews in Babylonia: I. The Parthian Period*, Brown
Judaic Studies 62 (Chico California: Scholars, 1984, original publication Leiden: Brill,
1969) 61-67.

[56] Contra Bamberger, *Proselytism*, 51.

[57] Besides the dispute in the Babylonian Talmud noted above, see also the disagreement between R. Eliezer and R. Joshua as to whether Gentiles have a share in the world
to come (Tos. Sanhedrin 13.2). See Siegert, "Gottesfürchtige," 119-120.

[58] J. Nolland, "Uncircumcised Proselytes?" *JSJ* 12(1981) 173-194, argues that Izates
would be left "in sociological terms, something less than a Jew" (193).

with the view that circumcision is not an entry requirement but an obligation consequent to admission.[59]

The story is regrettably elliptical on Izates' status and practice after his conversion but before his circumcision. We are told that he read the law, but we are not told whether his devotion to the ancestral laws of the Jews extended to Sabbath observance or dietary laws, or whether he abandoned all worship of pagan gods. If he did, would this not have upset his subjects as much as circumcision? Further, while his subjects would not have regarded him as a Jew until he was circumcised, it is not clear how he was regarded by Ananias or by himself. It has been suggested that the expression "to worship God" (*to theion sebein*), is a play on the phrase *sebomenos ton theon*, and denotes a special class of "God-fearers" who observed the Jewish laws but stopped short of circumcision. But this is far from certain.[60] It would seem, however, that "to worship God" means to do all that is necessary and so, presumably, to ensure salvation (in whatever sense) whether it qualifies one as a Jew or not. The ambiguity of Izates' case is heightened by his peculiar situation. For him, to become a Jew is not to join a synagogue, as it would have been in Alexandria or Rome. Izates' case rests on his internal decision to an unusual degree.

The story of Izates corroborates the view that in popular perception circumcision was a major identifying sign of Judaism. It also shows that there was some difference of opinion within Judaism as to whether circumcision was necessary for salvation. What is not clear is whether Izates was for a time, by way of exception, an uncircumcised proselyte, or whether Ananias was affirming that one could worhsip God without converting to Judaism. In the peculiar case of Izates, where the usual social complications may not have held, the difference may not be of ultimate importance.

III. The "God-fearers"

The story of Izates raises the question of the existence of "God-fearers," a class of pious Gentiles who stopped short of full acceptance of the law. The description of this class in the Pauly-Wissowa article of Kuhn and Stegemann is typical: "they frequent the services of the synagogue, they are monotheists in the biblical sense, and they participate in some of the ceremonial requirements of the Law, but they have not moved to full conversion to Judaism through circumcision. They are called. . . sebomenoi or phoboumenoi ton theon."[61]

---

[59] Bialoblocki, *Die Beziehungen*, 15.
[60] Siegert, "Gottesfürchtige," 129.
[61] K. G. Kuhn and H. Stegemann, "Proselyten," *PWRE* Sup 9(1962) 1260.

Estimates of their number have been high ("perhaps millions").[62] Yet recently A. T. Kraabel has proclaimed their disappearance and argued that "at least for the Roman Diaspora, the evidence presently available is far from convincing proof for the existence of such a class of Gentiles."[63]

The issue has a number of aspects which should be distinguished. First, there is a question as to whether certain expressions such as *hoi phoboumenoi ton theon* are technical terms for a well-defined class. Second, whether there was a class of pious Gentiles interested in Judaism, and third, whether those Gentiles, if they existed, conformed to the description set out in Pauly-Wissowa.

The only undisputed technical name for pious Gentiles is the expression "fearers of heaven" in the Talmudic literature.[64] Even here it does not seem that a consistent code of behavior was implied. In the opinion of Saul Liebermann "all the 'fearers of Heaven' must have accepted monotheism and the moral laws, whereas in questions of religious ceremonies and ritual they may have widely differed."[65] There is also some difference of opinion as to whether these "fearers of heaven" would attain salvation after death. The story of the Roman senator who gave his life to protect the Jews in *Midrash Debarim Rabba* 2.24 clearly implies that he would not have been saved if he had not been circumcised.[66] By contrast, Rabbi is said to have told Antoninus that he could eat of leviathan in the world to come, but not of the Passover lamb, since he was not circumcised.[67]

Outside the rabbinic literature, the main body of evidence is found in Acts in the usage of *phoboumenoi* and *sebomenoi*. Even here it is questionable how far these are technical terms rather than ad hoc descriptions.[68] The non-technical sense is suggested in part by the strange distribution—*phoboumenoi* in the first half of Acts, *sebomenoi* in the second. The expression *tōn sebomenōn prosēlytōn* in Acts 13:43 makes it difficult to maintain that *sebomenoi* was a technical term for a class distinct from proselytes. Moreover, it is not clear

[62] *Encyclopedia Judaica*, 10:55.
[63] A. T. Kraabel, "The Disappearance of the 'God-Fearers,' " *Numen* 28(1981) 121.
[64] L. H. Feldman, "Jewish 'Sympathizers' in Classical Literature and Inscriptions," *TAPA* 81(1950) 208; Siegert, "Gottesfürchtige," 110.
[65] S. Liebermann, *Greek in Jewish Palestine* (New York: Jewish Theological Seminary of America, 1942) 81.
[66] Siegert, "Gottesfürchtige," 110-112.
[67] Liebermann, *Greek in Jewish Palestine*, 78-80.
[68] K. Lake, "Proselytes and God-Fearers," in *The Beginnings of Christianity: Part I. The Acts of the Apostles*, eds. F. J. Foakes Jackson and K. Lake (London: MacMillan, 1933) 74-96.

precisely what constitutes a *phoboumenos* or *sebomenos*, beyond some reverence for the God of Israel. Cornelius, who is certainly not a proselyte, shows his piety by almsgiving and prayer. In other cases the "God-fearers" are associated with the synagogues. In no case, however, are we told how far they kept the Jewish law or whether they were strict monotheists.

Supporting evidence for the terminology of Acts is rare indeed. No technical terms for such pious Gentiles are found in Hellenistic Jewish literature before Josephus. In *Joseph and Aseneth* it is Joseph, the Israelite, who is called *theosebēs* (8:5,6) and *phoboumenos ton theon* (8:5,6 and 8:9). Even in Josephus, only one passage uses *sebomenoi* in the supposed technical sense, *Ant* 14.7.2(110). This passage explains the wealth of the Jerusalem temple by reference to the contributions of *tōn kata tēn oikoumenēn Ioudaiōn kai sebomenōn ton theon*. Even in this case the interpretation is disputed. Kirsopp Lake argued that since *sebomenōn* does not have the article, it should be read as a further description of the Jews, so "all the Jews worshipping God throughout the world."[69] Against this, the presence of the *kai* and the analogy with Acts supports the view that the *sebomenoi* are distinct (e.g. Acts 17:17: "he spoke in the synagogue," *tois Ioudaiois kai tois sebomenois*).[70] Even if the reference in Josephus is to pious Gentiles, the use of the term is poorly supported.

Neither *phoboumenos ton theon* nor *sebomenos ton theon* occurs in inscriptions.[71] Debate has centered on the occurrence of the Greek term *theosebēs* and the Latin *metuens*. The term *theosebēs* is used by Josephus to refer to Poppaea, consort of Nero, who interceded for Jews on two occasions. She was not known for her piety, however, and there is no reason to infer from Josephus anything more than a general sympathy for the Jews.[72] Those, like Lifshitz, who find evidence for the "God-fearers" in the inscriptions, assume the existence of this class on the basis of Acts and Josephus and look for anything that could be interpreted as a reference to it.[73] The problem with this procedure was noted by Feldman.[74] Both *theosebēs* and *metuens* can

---

[69] Lake, "Proselytes and God-Fearers," 85.

[70] R. Marcus, "The Sebomenoi in Josephus," *Jewish Social Studies* 14(1952) 247-250; Siegert, "Gottesfürchtige," 127.

[71] Siegert, "Gottesfürchtige," 151.

[72] *Ant.* 20.8.11 (195); *Vit.* 16. She was implicated in the murder of Agrippina and the banishment of Octavia. See Siegert, "Gottesfürchtige," 160.

[73] B. Lifshitz, "Du Nouveau sur les "Sympathisants," *JSJ* 1(1970) 80: "Si donc ces demi-prosélytes sont indubitablement attestés chez Josèphe et dans le NT on les cherchait tout naturellement dans les inscriptions."

[74] Feldman, "Jewish 'Sympathizers'," 205.

be used in a pagan, polytheistic context.[75] When they are used in a Jewish context, they may simply refer to Jews. Until recently there was no clear instance of the use of *theosebeis* to refer to Gentile sympathizers with Judaism. Such an instance now seems to be provided by a late second- or early third-century CE inscription from Aphrodisias in Asia Minor. This inscription uses the term for a group that is distinguished from the Jews but associated with them.[76] Other occurrences must now be reconsidered in light of this: e.g., the problematic inscriptions from the Miletus theatre (*Eioudeōn tōn kai Theosebion*), where the word order initially suggests one group, the Jews, rather than two, and the Pantikapaion inscription which refers to the synagogue, *tōn Ioudaiōn kai theon sebōn*.[77] The import of the Aphrodisias inscription cannot be fully assessed until it has been published. It should be noted, however, that *theosebēs* is not in any case an unequivocal term. It may still, on occasion, refer to a Jew (as in *Joseph and Aseneth*), or, in a polytheistic context, to a pagan. The meaning of each occurrence must be judged from its context. The Aphrodisias evidence bears most directly on the use of the plural *theosebeis* to designate a group. Occurrences of the singular *theosebēs* in epitaphs or in the inscriptions from the Sardis synagogue remain quite ambiguous. Even in the Aphrodisias inscription it is not clear what qualifies a person as a member of the *theosebeis*.[78] Finally, it is well to remember that *theosebeis* is not the term used in Acts, and so it does not confer a technical sense on *sebomenoi* or *phoboumenoi*.

The case for a technical understanding of *metuens* rests largely on Juvenal's fourteenth satire, which refers to a Roman father who is *metuentem sabbata*.[79] In the same passage, however, the phrase *metuunt ius* refers to full proselytes. In the inscriptions, *metuens* is found in both pagan and Jewish epitaphs. There is no unambiguous occurrence for God-fearer, although that usage is not necessarily excluded.[80]

The terminology, then, shows some fluctuation. *Phoboumenoi*, *sebomenoi* and *theosebeis* can all on occasion refer to Gentiles who

---

[75] For *theosebēs* see G. Bertram, "*theosebēs, theosebeia*," *TDNT* 3(1965) 123-128. In the phrase *deum metuens, deum* may be genitive plural (Siegert, "Gottesfürchtige," 152).
[76] This inscription will be published by Joyce Reynolds.
[77] See L. Robert, *Nouvelles Inscriptions de Sardes* (Paris: Maisonneuve, 1964) 41, and the discussion in Rajak's article in this volume.
[78] See the comments of A. T. Kraabel in this volume.
[79] The argument was developed by J. Bernays, "Die Gottesfürchtigen bei Juvenal," *Gesammelte Abhandlungen von Jacob Bernays* (Berlin: 1885) 2:71-80.
[80] Siegert, "Gottesfürchtige," 152.

are associated with Judaism in some way, but none of these terms is unequivocal, and each occurrence must be interpreted in its own context.

The evidence for Gentile adherents of Judaism is not, however, limited to this terminology. We have already noted the statements of Philo and Seneca about the spread of Jewish laws and Josephus' claim that the Jews of Antioch partially incorporated Gentile admirers. Josephus further claims that "The masses have long since shown a keen desire to adopt our religious observances; and there is not one city, Greek or barbarian, nor a single nation, to which our custom of abstaining from work on the seventh day has not spread, and where fasts and the lighting of lamps and many of our prohibitions in the matter of food are not observed" (Ag.Ap. 2.282). This claim is corroborated by frequent allusions to Jewish customs in the Roman satirists from the time of Augustus.[81] Much of the Roman evidence suggests a rather superstitious curiosity, although it could lead in time to full conversion (cf. Juvenal's fourteenth satire, where the father observes the sabbath and the son is eventually circumcised). The distinction between the partially observant father and fully converted son is supported by Epictetus' reference to the type-figure who "is not a Jew but is only acting the part," as opposed to one who has been baptized.[82] Josephus claims that at the outbreak of the Jewish war, when the Syrians had rid themselves of the Jews, "still each city had its Judaizers, who aroused suspicion" (JW 2.18.2 [463]). These constituted "an equivocal element" which the Syrians regarded as alien, though evidently not as Jews.[83] Moreover, even if one regards the account of Paul's missionary activity in Acts as largely fictional, the fiction requires verisimilitude to establish plausibility. Luke would scarcely have given such prominence to a category that was not known to exist at all.

This evidence shows beyond reasonable doubt that Judaism in the

---

[81] On the Roman reception of Judaism see M. Stern, "The Jews in Greek and Latin Literature," in *The Jewish People in the First Century*, 2: 1101-1159; J. G. Gager, *The Origins of Anti-Semitism: Attitudes Toward Judaism in Paganism and Christian Antiquity* (Oxford: Oxford University, 1983). Even Augustus is said to have boasted that "not even a Jew, my dear Tiberius, observes the Sabbath fast as faithfully as I did to-day" (Suetonius, *Augustus*, 76). See also R. Goldenberg, "The Jewish Sabbath in the Roman World up to the Time of Constantine the Great," in *Aufstieg und Niedergang der römischen Welt* II.19.1, eds. H. Temporini and W. Haase (Berlin: de Gruyter, 1979) 414-447.

[82] Arrian, Diss. 2.9.19-21. Note that the point of transition here is not circumcision but baptism.

[83] Josephus also claims that the women of Damascus had with few exceptions become converts to the Jewish religion (JW 2.20.2 [560]).

Roman Diaspora did win adherents who stopped short of circumcision. It does not, however, corroborate the description of this class, as
we find in the Pauly-Wissowa article of Kuhn-Stegemann or in
Lifshitz's article. What we find is a broad range of degrees of
attachment, not a class with specific requirements or with a clearly
defined status in the synagogue. Juvenal's fourteenth satire illustrates
the range: first the father who observes the sabbath, then the son who
worships nothing but the clouds and the divinity of heaven, finally
circumcision. Not all so-called "God-fearers," even in Acts, were
necessarily monotheists or had necessarily quit the pagan community.[84] We should like to know more of the manner in which the Jews
of Antioch incorporated Greeks, or to know how far Philo identified
the *proselytoi* who have joined the new and godly commonwealth and
have equal rank with the native born (*Spec. Leg.* 1. 51-52) with the
proselytes who have circumcised not their uncircumcision but their
desires and pleasures (*Quaest in Ex.* 2.2). There was also a spectrum
of opinion on the Jewish side, as we can see from the story of Izates
and from the debate over allegorists in Alexandria.

   It has been said that the crucial question which confronted
first-century Judaism was that posed by the Gentile world.[85] This is
probably true in the sense that the very survival of Judaism depended
on working out a *modus vivendi* with the Gentile world. It is not true,
however, that first-century Judaism was greatly preoccupied with the
salvation of the Gentiles. That was ultimately a matter for the
eschatological age. In the meantime, the literature suggests a "self-
confident Judaism" in Kraabel's phrase.[86] There is relatively little
evidence of active proselytizing (despite Matt 23:15).[87] Jews were,
however, both willing and able to attract Gentiles to their synagogues
and Gentiles were eager to adopt Jewish customs. Diaspora Judaism
seems to have accepted a wide range of Gentile behavior (from
superficial interest to full conversion), and was not too greatly concerned to establish specific points at which one became eligible for
salvation.[88] Of course, the literary evidence may not give us the whole

---

[84] Contra Lifshitz, "Du Nouveau sur les 'Sympathisants,' " 80.

[85] W. D. Davies, "From Schweitzer to Scholem: Reflections on Sabbatai Svi," *JBL*
95(1976) 547.

[86] A. T. Kraabel, "Paganism and Judaism: The Sardis Evidence," in *Paganisme,
Judaïsme, Christianisme: Mélanges offerts à Marcel Simon*, eds. A. Benoit, M. Philonenko, C. Vogel (Paris: de Boccard, 1978) 21. Compare Gager, *The Origins of Anti-Semitism*, 99.

[87] Only 8 of 731 inscriptions from Italy mention proselytes (Kuhn-Stegemann, "Proselyten," 1264).

[88] In his "Paul and the Torah," in *Anti-Semitism and the Foundations of Christianity*

picture, but it suggests that full incorporation into the Jewish people was not generally considered essential for Gentiles to worship God in an adequate and acceptable way.

IV. The Christian debate on circumcision

The people who came from Judea to Antioch according to Acts 15 represent the stricter end of the spectrum of Jewish opinion. The position of Paul, however, cannot be equated with that of even the most liberal Hellenistic Jews. No Hellenistic Jew actively discouraged circumcision. According to Acts 21, Paul was accused of teaching all the Jews among the Gentiles to forsake Moses, telling them not to circumcise their children or observe the customs. Whether this charge was justified is disputed.[89] Paul was primarily concerned with Gentiles. Moreover, he told the Corinthians that any one who is already circumcised should not seek to remove the marks of his circumcision (1 Cor 7:18). Whether the children subsequently should be circumcised is not clear. Yet even with regard to the Gentiles, Paul goes much further than a Jew like the Ananias who converted Izates. While neither circumcision nor uncircumcision matters (and so might be expected to be optional), he tells his Gentile converts that if they have themselves circumcised, Christ will be of no advantage to them (Gal 5:2). The strength of his feelings on the subject is clear when he warns the Philippians against "the dogs. . . who mutilate the flesh" (Phil 3:2) or wishes that those who trouble the Galatians might mutilate themselves (Gal 5:12). These statements are made in polemical heat, to be sure, but they are worthier of a Roman satirist than of a Hebrew born of Hebrews.

Paul's vehement rejection of circumcision comes from the fact that he preached a new creation in which there was neither Jew nor Greek, circumcision nor uncircumcision (Gal 6:15). This new creation had its own theological basis—faith in Christ—and its own social reality with its distinctive rituals of baptism and the Lord's supper.[90] Paul's converts are not said to join the synagogue, even as "God-fearers," but formed their own new assembly. Circumcision symbolized a different social reality and a different way to salvation, hence the decisive rejection. Despite recent claims to the contrary,[91] Paul's

---

(New York: Paulist, 1979) 58, L. Gaston claims that legalism arose as a Gentile problem because God-fearers not under the covenant had to establish their righteousness by performance of certain works. I know of no evidence which would support this view.
[89] e.g. Gaston, "Paul and the Torah," 66; Gager, The Origins of Anti-Semitism, 211-12.
[90] E. P. Sanders, Paul, the Law and the Jewish People (Philadelphia: Fortress, 1983) 176, with reference to 1 Corinthians.
[91] So especially Gaston and Gager.

rejection of circumcision symbolized a rejection of the ultimate efficacy of the contemporary synagogue.[92] He did not of course reject the heritage of Judaism or deny that the Jews were heirs to the promises, and he certainly continued to regard himself as a Jew. Yet those Jews who did not believe in Christ were not "in Christ," and that was what mattered.

Paul's belief in the resurrection of Jesus and its eschatological implications distinguished him radically from Diaspora Jews such as Philo or Ananias. Prior to his conversion, he was probably at the stricter end of the spectrum in terms of the importance he attached to circumcision.[93] After his conversion he continued to attach greater importance to it than did many Jews of the Diaspora, but for largely negative reasons. It symbolized and facilitated the contrast between the new creation and the old. Diaspora Judaism, in general, had sought to emphasize points of similarity to its gentile environment. Paul was concerned to emphasize the novelty, and therefore the "otherness" of the new creation. The implied devaluation of the Jewish way of life stirred greater passions than was ever the case with the allegorists of Alexandria, and made for a crucial and fateful difference from the Jews of the Diaspora who also, in their way, extended the hope of salvation to the Gentiles.

---

[92] E. P. Sanders, *Paul and Palestinian Judaism* (Philadelphia: Fortress, 1977) 7: "In short, this is what Paul finds wrong with Judaism: it is not Christianity." While Paul would not have distinguished Judaism and Christianity in this way, Sanders' insight is essentially correct.

[93] Gaston, "Paul and the Torah," 61, suggests that Paul was a Shammaite, but specific correspondence is lacking. See Sanders, *Paul and Palestinian Judaism*, 138 n.61.

8

Insiders and Outsiders in the Book of Revelation and Its Social Context

Adela Yarbro Collins
University of Notre Dame

The aim of this essay is to clarify the attitudes toward outsiders reflected in the book of Revelation, the probable functions of those attitudes, and the conflicts they represent. This goal suggests temporal and geographical limits for the essay, namely, the first century C.E. and western Anatolia.

The notion of outsiders requires some comment. The judgment that some are insiders and others outsiders is obviously dependent on a particular perspective. It is relative to the self-definition of a particular group and to the criteria for membership in that group. In order to clarify the notions of insiders and outsiders as they will be inferred from the text of the book of Revelation, the first part of this essay will consider these notions in terms of the cultural diversity of western Anatolia toward the end of the first century of the Common Era.

Definitions of Insiders and Outsiders

During prehistoric times, in the Mediterranean region from Italy to Anatolia each extended family, the *gens* or *genos*, was an independent unit. Each had its own religious tradition and practice, its own political organization under the chief or patriarch, and its own means of economic survival. At that early stage, insiders included the other members of one's *gens* or *genos* and their dependents; all others were outsiders. The ancient cities were formed by coalitions of these extended families. They made laws to govern their common life (not their internal affairs). They had a common worship centering on one or more gods whose power and protective interest in the city they recognized. All free males in these families were citizens of the city. At that time, the insiders were citizens and their dependents. Citizens of other cities and foreigners—indeed all others—were defined as outsiders.[1]

The ancient city went through profound changes from about the eighth century before the Common Era until the Roman conquest. Perhaps the most significant change brought about by the Roman conquest was the definitive loss of autonomy by the individual cities. The primary protective deities of the cities became Roma and Caesar. Traditional laws were subordinated to the *imperium* of the Roman governor.[2] The Roman presence in Anatolia was thus a major factor in the perceptions of insiders and outsiders.

From the Perspective of Romans and Greco-Asiatics

The term "Greco-Asiatics" is intended to reflect that the citizens from cities in western Anatolia during the first century of the Common Era belonged to a culture which was shaped by local traditions deriving from a variety of ethnic groups and by their languages and cults, as well as by Greek language and culture.[3] From the perspective of the Romans and Greco-Asiatics, the most important criterion for defining insiders and outsiders was still citizenship. Because Rome was the most powerful city in the Mediterranean world at the time, Roman citizenship was highly desirable. At this time it was not yet a merely symbolic attribute, but carried real advantages with it. The title "Roman citizen" no longer carried with it political rights, but it did confer the right to be governed according to Roman laws, that is, civil rights.[4] In 90 B.C.E. Roman citizenship had been extended to all Italians. During the Principate, it was extended to entire municipal units in the western provinces in a process of Romanization.[5] In the East, where municipal traditions were already established, it was extended only to individuals, primarily prominent ones.[6]

Thus, in the cities of western Anatolia toward the end of the first century C.E., the ultimate insiders were the Roman citizens. This

---

[1] Numa Denis Fustel de Coulanges, *The Ancient City* (Baltimore: The Johns Hopkins University Press, 1980; originally published in 1864) 32-215.
[2] Ibid., 216-380.
[3] William M. Ramsay, *The Letters to the Seven Churches of Asia* (New York: Hodder and Stoughton, 1904) 128-29.
[4] Fustel de Coulanges, *The Ancient City*, 378.
[5] A. N. Sherwin-White, "Municipium," *The Oxford Classical Dictionary* (Oxford: The Clarendon Press, 1949) 582-83.
[6] William M. Ramsay, *The Social Basis of Roman Power in Asia Minor* (Aberdeen: Aberdeen University Press, 1941; reprinted, Amsterdam: Adolf M. Hakkert, 1967) 4, 6-7, 209-210.

group included the proconsul, quaestor,[7] and legates at the top of the pyramid of power, the resident Italians,[8] and the Greco-Asiatic aristocrats who had acquired Roman citizenship. The local aristocrats with Roman citizenship would have been the only locals eligible for the priesthood of the imperial cult.[9] They also would have dominated the executive boards in the cities. These boards assembled the Council and People, presented resolutions to them, and took the lead in the administration of civic affairs.[10] Technically speaking, all those who were not Roman citizens were outsiders from the point of view of Roman citizens. Nevertheless, the old Greco-Asiatic aristocracy, even those who did not achieve Roman citizenship until 212 C.E., had considerable wealth, some power, and social status.[11] Rather than speaking simply of outsiders and insiders, therefore, we can acknowledge a spectrum of social groups which occupy various points on a scale between the extremes of outsiderhood and insiderhood.

The local aristocrats who were not Roman citizens could not technically own land (*dominium*), but could possess it (*in bonis*). Thus they could derive income from the land, sell it, or dispose of it by will. They were, however, obliged to pay tithes and taxes to the Romans.[12] They probably served as local magistrates, though perhaps not the highest ones. Although they may not have been admitted to the executive boards of the cities, it is likely that they were members of the city Council (*boulē*).

Next on the scale, occupying more or less the middle, would be the Greco-Asiatic *dēmos*, the body of ordinary citizens (*politai*). These people had the right to vote in the Assembly (*ecclēsia*) of the city. Despising labor because of its servile connotations, some of the poor among them would have been likely to get involved in corruption or sedition.[13] Nevertheless suffrage did not mean much in western Anatolia at this time. The popular Assembly, once powerful, had become basically a confirmatory body. Its members did not introduce resolutions, but merely voted on those presented by the executive

---

[7] David Magie, *Roman Rule in Asia Minor*, 2 vols. (Princeton: Princeton University Press, 1950) 1. 159-60.

[8] Ibid., 1. 162-64.

[9] Ramsay, *The Social Basis of Roman Power in Asia Minor*, 6.

[10] Magie, *Roman Rule in Asia Minor*, 1. 643.

[11] Fustel de Coulanges, *The Ancient City*, 379-80; A. N. Sherwin-White, "Citizenship, Roman," *The Oxford Classical Dictionary*, 195.

[12] Fustel de Coulanges, *The Ancient City*, 371; Magie, *Roman Rule in Asia Minor*, 1. 157.

[13] Fustel de Coulanges, *The Ancient City*, 328-35; Magie, *Roman Rule in Asia Minor*, 1. 600.

board and Council. Moreover, the resolutions passed by the Assembly
had to be approved by the Roman governor.[14]

Beneath the ordinary citizens in terms of political and civil rights
were freedpeople, the former slaves.[15] These were often bound by
contract to supply certain services to their former masters, either with
no salary or a partial salary. They were thus bound and subordinate to
their wealthy patrons. On the other hand, they derived some security
and prestige from the association. Many of them were shopkeepers,
artisans and laborers. In terms of political, legal and social status,
these people were low on the scale. But they were insiders of a sort
insofar as they shared the culture and religion of their patrons. Lower
on the scale, but analogous to the freedpeople, were the slaves. Their
economic well-being and social status varied according to the status of
their owners and to their own ethnic background, education and
skills. Those who were best off were the city slaves and imperial
slaves.[16]

All of the groups discussed so far were insiders either in the sense
of having considerable power and prestige (Roman citizens) or in the
sense of belonging, even if with low status, to the traditional organization of an ancient city-state.

Another group, resident aliens, were by definition outsiders. At
first these people had no rights whatsoever. Since the laws applied
only to citizens, resident aliens could not claim the protection of the
local laws. In the first century, some resident aliens still had this
status, or rather lack of status. Gradually, however, laws relating to
resident aliens had evolved. At Athens there were three types of
foreigners: temporary visitors, permanent residents who had not
achieved the status of metics (*metoikoi*), and metics. Each metic had
to have a citizen sponsor (*prostatēs*), register in the deme in which he
or she lived, and pay an annual headtax (*metoikion*). They were not
allowed to marry citizens legally or to own land or houses. Sometimes
metics were given special privileges such as permission to own
property and to build houses, or to be released from financial obligations. The benefits of being a metic included the opportunity to share
in the common life of the city and the protection of the laws.[17] In
Ephesus and Pergamum resident aliens were called *paroikoi*.[18]

[14] Magie, *Roman Rule in Asia Minor*, 1. 640-41.
[15] Reginald H. Barrow, "Freedmen," *The Oxford Classical Dictionary*, 371.
[16] Barrow, "Slaves, II. 11. iv," *The Oxford Classical Dictionary*, 844; Magie, *Roman Rule in Asia Minor*, 1. 545, 568, 647.
[17] Jakob A. O. Larsen, "Metics," *The Oxford Classical Dictionary*, 563.
[18] Magie, *Roman Rule in Asia Minor*, 1. 149, 225; 2. 1037, 1503; according to A. H. M.

Within this group of resident aliens, therefore, was a range from rank outsiders (those with no legal status or privileges) to those close to becoming insiders (those with extensive privileges).

The Jews in the cities of western Anatolia constitute another distinct group. According to the book of Obadiah, there were exiles from Jerusalem in Sardis (Sepharad) at that time (verse 20).[19] Substantial evidence about Jewish communities in western Anatolia, however, is available only from the Seleucid period onward.[20] Not long after 213 B.C.E., Antiochus III had two thousand Jewish families moved from Babylonia and Mesopotamia to the fortresses and most important places in Lydia and Phrygia.[21] These families were military colonists or settlers (*katoikoi*). They were given certain privileges in return for their loyalty to the Seleucid regime and their willingness to provide military assistance if needed. Their privileges included the right to live according to their own laws, the grant to each of land for farming, for viticulture and to build a house, the exemption from tithes on produce for ten years, and royal financial support for their religious officials (*hypēretai*).[22] Under the Seleucid and Ptolemaic kings, Jews were settled as military colonists also in Osroene, Cyrenaica, Egypt, Syria and Parthia.[23] These settlements were part of the general movement toward establishing new cities and colonies initiated by Alexander and carried on by his successors. Greeks and non-Greeks served as military settlers.[24]

The subsequent legal and political status of Jews in western Anatolia is a complex question. Its clarification is related to the wider

---

Jones in his *The Greek City from Alexander to Justinian*, resident aliens in many cities were called *katoikoi* (Oxford: The Clarendon Press, 1940) 160.

[19] M. J. Mellink, "Sepharad," *IDB* 4 (1962) 272-73; Shimon Applebaum, "The Legal Status of the Jewish Communities in the Diaspora," *The Jewish People in the First Century*, Compendia Rerum Iudaicarum ad Novum Testamentum, Section One, 2 vols., ed. S. Safrai and M. Stern (Assen: Van Gorcum and Comp. B. V., 1974 and 1976) 1. 432.

[20] Menahem Stern, 'The Jewish Diaspora," *The Jewish People in the First Century*, 1. 143.

[21] Josephus *Ant.* 12. 3. 4(147-53), Applebaum, "The Legal Status of the Jewish Communities in the Diaspora," 431-32.

[22] Ibid.

[23] Osroene: Shimon Applebaum, "The Social and Economic Status of the Jews in the Diaspora," *The Jewish People in the First Century*, 2. 725; Cyrenaica: Applebaum, "The Legal Status of the Jewish Communities in the Diaspora," 425-26; Egypt: ibid., 426, 460; idem, "The Organization of the Jewish Communities in the Diaspora," *The Jewish People in the First Century*, 1. 466, 469; Syria: idem, "The Legal Status of the Jewish Communities in the Diaspora," 432-33; Parthia: idem, "The Organization of the Jewish Communities in the Diaspora," 470-72.

[24] Hans J. Wolff, "Hellenistic Private Law," *The Jewish People in the First Century*, 1. 537.

problem of their legal status outside Judea in the Hellenistic and Roman periods. The Jews' status under the Seleucid and Ptolemaic monarchies is particularly difficult to determine. Josephus claimed that the Hellenistic kings had given Jews citizenship in Alexandria and in cities of Asia, Cyrenaean Libya, and Syria, specifically Antioch.[25] He uses terms like *politeia, isopoliteia, isotimia, isonomia, isomoiria,* and *isoteleia.*[26] Of these, only *isopoliteia* and *isoteleia* are technical legal terms. Josephus does not, however, appear to use *isopoliteia* in its technical sense.[27] The others are general terms describing an ideal state of affairs.

Early in this century many scholars (for example, the learned William M. Ramsay) accepted Josephus' testimony at face value and concluded that in many Hellenistic cities, Jewish colonists and immigrants were enrolled as citizens in a body. Ramsay suggested that the Jewish community in a particular locality would have been organized as a tribe and thus have constituted one of the fundamental organizational units of the city.[28] The collective worship of each of these tribes would have been Jewish. The problem arises with regard to the collective worship of the city. Ramsay was acutely aware of the magnitude of this problem. Ancient citizenship was defined not only as a share in the city's constitution and laws, but also as a share in the worship of its gods. In the normal course of things, a Jewish tribe in a Hellenistic city would have been expected either to abandon their traditional religious faith and way of life or to combine it with the worship of the local deities. Ramsay solved the problem by conjecturing that many Hellenistic cities made an exception for the Jews and recognized their citizenship, even though they did not worship with their non-Jewish fellow citizens.[29]

The scholarly consensus has shifted considerably since a papyrus containing Claudius' rescript to the citizens of Alexandria has become widely known. It was discussed in H. Idris Bell's book *Jews and Christians in Egypt,* published in 1924. The papyrus version gives a quite different impression from Josephus' summary of Claudius'

---

[25] The relevant texts are cited by Applebaum, "The Legal Status of the Jewish Communities in the Diaspora," 435.

[26] *Politeia* and related terms: Josephus *Ant.* 12. 3. 1 (119); *isopoliteia*: ibid., 12. 1. 1 (8), 19. 5. 2 (281); *isotimia*: idem, *Ag. Ap.* 2. 4 (35), *Ant.* 12. 3. 1 (119); *isonomia*: idem, *Ant.* 16. 6. 1 (160); *isomoiria*: idem, *J. W.* 2. 18. 7 (487-88); *isoteleia*: idem, *Ant.* 16. 6. 1 (161).

[27] Applebaum, "The Legal Status of the Jewish Communities in the Diaspora," 436, 438-39.

[28] Ramsay, *The Letters to the Seven Churches of Asia,* 132, 146-47, 438-39 note 6, see also pp. 151-55.

[29] Ibid., 148.

ruling on the dispute between Greeks and Jews in Alexandria over the question of Jewish citizenship.[30] Claudius' rescript makes clear that at the time of writing, the Jews as a body were not citizens of Alexandria, but were resident aliens with certain privileges. Since Claudius, like Augustus and other Roman authorities before him, tended to confirm the status quo rather than to innovate, it seems that the Jews had never as a group possessed citizenship in Alexandria.

Recent studies of the problem, such as those by Mary Smallwood and Shimon Applebaum, have tended to conclude that the Jews as a group did not possess citizenship in any Greek city in the Hellenistic or early Roman period.[31] The history of the legal status of the Jews in the cities of western Anatolia should be reconstituted, therefore, along the following lines. At first they came to these cities as military colonists (*katoikoi*) or as resident aliens (*paroikoi*). In cities founded by Hellenistic kings, the Jewish colonists or residents were probably organized from the beginning in their own association, namely a colony or body of residents in a foreign city (*katoikia*), or a corporate body with its own organization and laws (*politeuma*).[32] Members of such an association would not technically have citizenship in the city as such, but they would have significant status and autonomy, at the same time constituting a recognized part of the city. Such an arrangement was feasible in these new cities since there were no well established municipal institutions, local aristocracy or traditional worship. Since all were newcomers, it was easier for the Jews to be placed on an equal footing with the Greeks and Greco-Asiatics.[33]

It is likely that Antiochus III and other Seleucid kings established Jews as colonists also in the older Greco-Asiatic cities of western Anatolia. If so, the Jews would have been given privileges at the time of settlement. Another possibility is that the Seleucid kings required the older cities to grant Jews already there as resident aliens the legal status of metics (or its equivalent, the status of *paroikoi*) and certain privileges, thus creating a counterforce or a check and balance to the local Greco-Asiatic citizens. Part of this process may have been the establishment of a Jewish *politeuma* in these older cities.

---

[30] The papyrus rescript: CII 153; the edict according to Josephus: *Ant.* 19. 5. 2 (280-85); see Victor Tcherikover, *Hellenistic Civilization and the Jews* (The Jewish Publication Society of America, 1959; reprinted, New York: Atheneum, 1970) 313-14, 409-415.

[31] E. Mary Smallwood, *The Jews Under Roman Rule*, Studies in Judaism in Late Antiquity, ed. J. Neusner (Leiden: Brill, 1976) 140-41, 227-35; Applebaum, "The Legal Status of the Jewish Communities in the Diaspora," 449, 451.

[32] The Jewish association at Sardis may have been called a *synodos*: Applebaum, "The Organization of the Jewish Communities in the Diaspora," 478.

[33] Applebaum, "The Legal Status of the Jewish Communities in the Diaspora," 452-53.

In both new and old cities in the region, therefore, the Jews formed a special group with a status between that of the citizens and that of resident aliens without status or privileges.[34] Because at least some of the Jews' *politeumata* enjoyed autonomy and extensive privileges, many Jews may have felt that they had the equivalent of citizenship. Membership in the *politeuma* may have seemed equivalent to membership in the *polis*. Such an attitude would explain why Josephus and Philo could speak of the Jewish *politeia* in Greek cities, refer to Jews of the Diaspora as *politai* in the cities where they resided, and call them by the name of the city (e.g. "Alexandrians"), a designation usually reserved for citizens.[35]

In cities where the relations between Jews and Greco-Asiatics were not harmonious, such assumptions could arouse tension. When the influence of the Hellenistic kings weakened, some cities attempted to abolish Jewish privileges. During Augustus' reign, Jews living in the cities of Ionia (such as Smyrna, Priene, Ephesus and Miletus) appeared before Marcus Agrippa protesting the abolition of their privileges by the citizens where they were residing.[36] In one of his accounts of this incident, Josephus says the issue was citizenship.[37] If the Jews were claiming citizenship at this time, Agrippa's decision did not confirm it or award it to them, but it did confirm their traditional privileges. These privileges allowed them to observe their own customs without being mistreated.[38] The confirmation of their privileges probably involved affirmation of their right to have an organization to administer their *politeuma*. The specific privileges granted in each city would have varied from place to place and would have been confirmed by Roman officials on an ad hoc basis, thus becoming part of the body of Roman law.[39]

It is well known that the Jews in Alexandria and Caesarea Maritima attempted to win civic equality as a group during the early Roman period. If Jews in western Anatolia aspired to the same goal,

---

[34] In some cites the Jews may have had a status between that of citizens and that of metics; Strabo is quoted by Josephus as saying that there were four groups in the city of Cyrene: citizens, peasants, metics, and Jews: *Ant.* 14. 7. 2 (115); see Applebaum, "The Legal Status of the Jewish Communities in the Diaspora," 445-46.

[35] Applebaum, "The Legal Status of the Jewish Communities in the Diaspora," 435, 439-40, 450-54.

[36] Josephus *Ant.* 16. 2. 3 (27-28); Smallwood, *The Jews Under Roman Rule*, 140-41.

[37] Josephus *Ant.* 12. 3. 2 (125-26).

[38] Ibid., 16. 2. 5 (60).

[39] Applebaum, "The Legal Status of the Jewish Communities in the Diaspora," 460.

Agrippa's ruling near the end of the first century B.C.E. seems to have put an end to such aspirations.[40]

Yet a small but significant body of evidence exists which indicates that some individual Jews in western Anatolia were granted Roman citizenship. Josephus has presented documents recording the decrees of Roman officials releasing Jews in Ephesus who are Roman citizens from military service. These documents date from about 49 to 45 B.C.E.[41] The reason for the exemption stated in the decrees is the Jews' religious scruples—presumably their food laws and their reluctance to bear arms or march on the sabbath.[42] Shimon Applebaum suggested that the underlying reason for their exemption may have been previous military service, for example with Pompey, in his actions against the pirates. Citizenship may have been granted them in return for their service to Pompey.[43]

Other evidence suggests that individual Jewish families were allowed citizenship in certain cities of western Anatolia. Inscriptions from Acmonia in Phrygia indicate that a woman by the name of Julia Severa founded or built (*kataskeuazō*) a synagogue there during the reign of Nero. She was also high priestess of the city.[44] Her name indicates that she was a Roman citizen.[45] Her priestly office is evidence of citizenship in the city of Acmonia. It is possible that she was a Greek, Greco-Asiatic or a Gentile of some other ethnic origin who was favorably disposed toward Judaism. She may, on the other hand, have been Jewish. There is some evidence that her family was distantly related to the Herods. Her second husband, Tyronius Rapo, was evidently of Jewish origin, although he was also a priest of a non-Jewish cult. His Jewish origin is supported by an inscription about his relative, G. Tyronius Cladus.[46]

This body of evidence suggests that local citizenship implied acknowledgement of local gods, but not necesarily rejection of the Jewish way of life entirely. Further, an inscription from Iasos in Caria, dating to the first century C.E., contains a list of ephebes eight of which are certainly or probably Jewish. One of these is Judah. The implication is that some Jewish families were wealthy enough to be able to enroll their sons in the gymnasium of their city.[47] Claudius'

---

[40] Ibid., 452.
[41] Josephus *Ant.* 14. 10. 16, 19 (234, 240).
[42] Compare ibid., 14. 10. 12 (226-27).
[43] Applebaum, "The Legal Status of the Jewish Communities in the Diaspora," 459.
[44] Ibid., 443.
[45] Ramsay, *The Social Basis of Roman Power in Asia Minor*, 6, 209-210.
[46] Applebaum, "The Legal Status of the Jewish Communities in the Diaspora," 443.
[47] Stern, "The Jewish Diaspora," 149; Applebaum, "The Legal Status of the Jewish

rescript indicates that there was a very close relationship between
registration as an ephebe, that is, gymnasium education, and admission to the body of citizens.[48] The gymnasium education was naturally
closely linked to the worship of the city's gods. It is unlikely that an
ephebe of Jewish origin could have avoided at least being present at
rituals in honor of these gods. That some sort of participation in these
rituals was acceptable to at least some Jews in Iasos is indicated by
inscriptions from that city recording donations by a Jew for the
Dionysia.[49]

A second- or third-century C.E. inscription from Hypaepa in
Lydia contains a list of "young Jews," *Ioudaioi neōteroi; neōteroi* was
the name of one of the three age-groups into which gymnasium pupils
were divided.[50] This inscription may indicate Jewish participation in
the city's gymnasium or it may be interpreted as evidence that the
Jews in Hypaepa organized their own gymnasium.[51]

The legal status of the Jews in western Anatolia was thus at least
as secure as that of the metics during the Hellenistic and early Roman
periods. Before the Jewish War in 66-72 C.E., Jews in the region were
allowed to collect the half-shekel donation and to send it to the
authorities of the temple in Jerusalem. After the War, this donation
was converted into the Jewish tax, collected by the Romans and used
for the maintenance of the temple of Jupiter Capitolinus in Rome.
This tax was the only significant change in the Jews' legal status in the
Diaspora after 70 C.E., a fact which Josephus emphasizes.[52] This legal
status placed Jews as a group on the boundary between insiders and
outsiders. The degree to which they were accepted as insiders as a
group increased with the degree of mutual influence and tolerance.
Certain individual Jews became insiders to a greater degree by
achieving citizenship in the city where they resided. These would
more likely count as insiders than those who were awarded Roman
citizenship without local citizenship.

Toward the end of the first century, it is quite credible that in
western Anatolia there were Christians who were virtually indistin-

Communities in the Diaspora," 447; idem, "The Social and Economic Status of the
Jews in the Diaspora," 716.

[48] Tcherikover, *Hellenistic Civilization and the Jews*, 313-14.

[49] Michael Avi-Yonah, "Archaeological Sources," *The Jewish People in the First
Century*, 1. 57.

[50] Ibid.; Stern, "The Jewish Diaspora," 151; Applebaum, "The Legal Status of the
Jewish Communities in the Diaspora," 447 (CII 755).

[51] Applebaum, "The Organization of the Jewish Communities in the Diaspora," 478.

[52] Josephus *Ant.* 12. 3. 1-2 (121-24, 127-28); Applebaum, "The Legal Status of the
Jewish Communities in the Diaspora," 461-62.

guishable from Jews. These would have been as observant (or non-observant) as their Jewish neighbors and have had a Christology which did not offend them. They would have had their own gatherings, but would have participated in those of the local synagogue or synagogues as well. Such Christians would also have shared in the legal status of the local Jews. They would have been outsiders or insiders to the same degree.

Near the "outside" end of the spectrum would be resident aliens without the legal status of metics and without privileges. As indicated above, they had virtually no civil rights and certainly no political rights. The rural Asiatics would also have been virtual outsiders. They produced the agricultural surplus and got in return the means of a subsistence and, usually, protection from violence and war. In the Hellenistic period, those who cultivated royal lands and the estates of landlords were serfs; that is, while their persons were not owned by the proprietors, they were themselves attached to the land and paid rent in money or in kind. There was, however, a tendency toward the establishment of a free peasantry and the appointment of legal officials for their benefit. By the Roman period most peasants were free, but they had virtually no political rights.[53] They spoke a different language from at least the upper classes of the cities, and they offered their real devotion to their own gods.[54]

Christians in western Anatolia toward the end of the first century were still an emerging group. Converts to the Christian way of life among Romans, Greeks, Greco-Asiatics and Asiatics would immediately have become outsiders because they necessarily rejected the worship of the traditional gods. Those among the Jews who believed in Jesus as God's anointed, son of God or some such, would have shared the Jews' legal and social status, insofar as they continued to participate in the life of the local Jewish community and to be accepted by it. The "outsiderhood" of Gentile converts would have been more a matter of attitude and social status than legal status.[55] Presumably, they would continue to enjoy or suffer from whatever status they were born to or relegated to by law, unless legal action were brought against them. The position of male heads of household would have been more secure than that of dependent males, wives, daughters, freedpeople and slaves. If a dependent converted and the

---

[53] Magie, *Roman Rule in Asia Minor*, 143-44; Jones, *The Greek City from Alexander to Justinian*, 160-2, 172-73.
[54] Jones, *The Greek City from Alexander to Justinian*, 295-98.
[55] Ramsay MacMullen, *Paganism in the Roman Empire* (New Haven: Yale University Press, 1981) 62, 176 note 2.

head of his or her household did not, the superior party could put pressure on, withhold benefits and make life difficult in a variety of ways.

Jews who became Christians and who separated voluntarily from the local Jewish community or were rejected by it were in a precarious legal situation. Their Christian associations would no longer be viewed by the authorities as part of the Jewish *politeuma* of their city. They would be viewed as religious associations (*thiasoi*).[56] These were founded for the worship of gods whose cults were not part of the religion of the city. Usually, they were established by the city's resident aliens who had brought their traditional rites with them, as were, for example, the cults of Sarapis and Isis.[57] In Rome itself such *thiasoi* were tolerated, but strict limits were set and enforced.[58] In the provinces the status of these associations usually depended on the action of the city authorities. Permission had to be granted, for example, to establish temples.[59] In many cases, privileges had already been granted to such *thiasoi* during the Hellenistic period. The precarious situation of Christian *thiasoi* arose because, while most religious associations could claim to be continuing as ancient tradition linked to a particular family, city or ethnic group, and while such ancient traditions were respected, the only ancient traditions the Christians could claim were those of the Jews. If the local Jewish community disassociated itself from the Christians the cult would appear to be a new and probably deceptive superstition. It may be that already by the end of the second century, Christian associations were suspected of having the same promiscuous and orgiastic features which the Romans associated with the Dionysiac cult and other mysteries.[60]

Insofar as the Christians met for common meals and their associations appeared to have a social character, they would have been viewed as *collegia* or *hetaeriae*. These terms included a variety of associations or clubs from organizations of artisans to burial societies. Julius Caesar outlawed all *collegia* other than those founded in

---

[56] See Helmut Koester, *Introduction to the New Testament* (2 vols., Hermeneia, Foundations and Facets (Philadelphia: Fortress, 1982) 1. 65-67 and the bibliography on p. 65.

[57] MacMullen, *Paganism in the Roman Empire*, 112-14.

[58] Koester, *Introduction to the New Testament*, 1. 362-65.

[59] Ibid., 365.

[60] Robert L. Wilken, *The Christians As the Romans Saw Them* (New Haven: Yale University Press, 1984) 16-21.

ancient times.[61] His reason for doing so was apparently related to the fact that such clubs had the potential of organizing the voting power of the lower orders, i.e., the poor citizens. The Romans preferred to consolidate power in the hands of the wealthy aristocracies.[62] Claudius and Nero amended the *Lex Iulia de Collegiis* to exempt *collegia tenuiorum,* poor people's clubs. Apparently the latter were not felt to be as significant a political factor as the organizations of artisans.[63]

It is questionable whether Caesar's ban on associations was enforced in western Anatolia in the first century C.E. The inscriptions show that organizations of artisans flourished in the cities of the region not only in the first century but on into the third and fourth.[64] It may be that the *Lex Iulia de Collegiis* was not enforced in the first century, but then was enforced, at least in Bithynia, under Trajan and gradually in other provinces in the second century. Or, it may be that certain organizations in western Anatolia were excepted because of their political and economic power and influence.[65]

Therefore Christian groups which separated definitively from civic institutions and from Jewish associations (*politeumata* or *synodoi*) would have become outsiders socially and legally. If they caused noticeable unrest or disturbances, they would have come to the attention of the Roman governor. They could also have been accused before the governor by Romans, Greeks, Greco-Asiatics or Jews. Motivations for such accusations would have varied, but would have included atheism, that is, the impious rejection of the traditional gods, on the part of Gentiles, and infringement of Jewish tradition and laws, on the part of Jews. If brought to trial, they could have been punished by beating with rods, whipping, simple expulsion from the city, relegation or deportation, which may have involved confiscation of property, or execution.[66]

From the Perspective of Jews

Not much can be said with precision about the attitudes of Jews toward insiders and outsiders in western Anatolia. Evidence is too scarce. The Jews produced very little literature which has survived and can be linked definitively or even tentatively to the region. As far

---

[61] Stern, "The Jewish Diaspora," 163; Applebaum, "The Organization of the Jewish Communities in the Diaspora," 481.

[62] Jones, *The Greek City From Alexander to Justinian*, 134, 271.

[63] Applebaum, "The Organization of the Jewish Communities in the Diaspora," 481.

[64] Ibid., 480-81; Magie, *Roman Rule in Asia Minor*, 1. 46.

[65] Applebaum, "The Organization of the Jewish Communities in the Diaspora," 481.

[66] Koester, *Introduction to the New Testament*, 1. 365-66; on the use of rods and whips see Applebaum, "The Legal Status of the Jewish Communities in the Diaspora," 440.

as I know, the only Jewish writing assigned by a consensus of scholars to western Anatolia in the Hellenistic and early Roman periods is the Jewish substratum of books one and two of the Sybilline Oracles, which form a unified work. Lines 1-323 of book one are surely Jewish, as are 2:6-33. Certain portions are clearly Christian, but in many cases it is difficult to separate the original Jewish oracle from the Christian redaction.[67] The Jewish oracle is assigned to Phrygia because of that region's prominent role in the work. Phrygia is the first land to appear after the flood, and the place where the new generation of humanity will begin. "O Phrygia . . . You will be nurse for all" (*Sib. Or.* 1:196-98). Mount Ararat is located in Phrygia instead of the more usual Armenia (1:261-62).

Noah and the flood story play a prominent role in book one. In the third century C.E., Noah and the Sibyl appear on coins from Apamea, a city of Phrygia.[68] J. Geffcken dated *Sibylline Oracles* 1-2 to the third century on this basis, but more recent studies have dated the Jewish oracle to the time of Augustus.[69] The work organizes history into ten generations. Its prominent themes are ethical exhortation and eschatological expectation. The work also reflects a certain interpenetration or rapprochement of Jewish and Hellenistic myths.

Epigraphical and architectural evidence for Jews in western Anatolia is richer than the literary, but its interpretation is sometimes controversial. Some scholars have argued that many Jews of Anatolia were apostate or syncretistic. Others have emphasized their traditional Jewish character. A. T. Kraabel has addressed this issue in his dissertation and several articles. He will no doubt give it systematic treatment in his forthcoming book, *The Jews of Western Asia Minor.*[70]

Provisionally, it can be said that the boundaries between outsiders and insiders from a Jewish perspective probably varied from place to place. Indeed, there may well have been disagreement among Jews in a particular locality on this issue, for the definition of insiders and

---

[67] John J. Collins, "Sibylline Oracles," *The Old Testament Pseudepigrapha*, ed. James H. Charlesworth (Garden City: Doubleday, 1983) 330-32; the translation given above of *Sib. Or.* 1:196-98 is from this work.

[68] Ibid., 331; Stern, "The Jewish Diaspora," 150; A. Thomas Kraabel, "Impact of the Discovery of the Sardis Synagogue," *Sardis from Prehistoric to Roman Times: Results of the Archaeological Exploration of Sardis 1958-1975*, ed. George M. A. Hanfmann (Cambridge: Harvard University Press, 1983) 181.

[69] Collins, "Sibylline Oracles," 331.

[70] A. Thomas Kraabel, "Judaism in Western Asia Minor Under the Roman Empire," Diss., Harvard University, 1968); idem, "The Roman Diaspora: Six Questionable Assumptions," *Essays in Honor of Yigael Yadin*, ed. G. Vermes and J. Neusner, *Journal of Jewish Studies* 33 (1982) 449-51; idem, "Impact of the Discovery of the Sardis Synagogue," 185-86; see also Ramsay, *The Letters to the Seven Churches of Asia*, 155.

outsiders is, of course, closely bound up with the question of how the Jews in this region understood themselves as a group. One possibility is that they viewed themselves as members of the nation of Judea and citizens of the cities and villages of that nation. They would thus have seen themselves as emigrants or exiles from Judea. Another possibility is that they understood themselves as members of a particular ethnic group, like the Lydians or Carians, or, more assertively, like the Greeks. In this case they would have considered themselves to be a distinct but settled group with as much right to be where they were as anyone else.

It is more likely that, as a group, the Jews considered themselves to be a people or ethnic group rather than emigrants or exiles from a nation.[71] There would of course have been a difference between Jews whose families had been in Anatolia for generations and those recently displaced by the Jewish War. Some of the latter are probably reflected in the second century inscription from Smyrna which refers to a contribution made for public works by a group called *hoi pote Ioudaioi*.[72] This phrase should probably be translated "the former Judeans" rather than "the former Jews."

One became a member of the local Jewish community either by birth, by becoming a proselyte, or by immigrating and being accepted. The way of life adhered to may have varied widely. Perhaps the strictest criterion which would have defined the purest insider was the worship of the God of the Jews combined with the rejection of any other claims to divinity and worship. Another criterion would have been observance in accordance with a generally accepted standard. In the first century B.C.E., the Council, People and Magistrates of Sardis passed a decree relating to Jewish privileges which included a provision that the market officials of the city were to bring in suitable food for them.[73] Another document preserved by Josephus suggests that Jews in Ephesus refused to bear arms or march on the Sabbath, observed food laws, met regularly for worship, and sent money regularly to Jerusalem in the first century B.C.E.[74] At about the same time, Jews in Laodicea (Phrygia) were observing Sabbaths and performing other rites in accordance with their laws.[75] In Miletus (Ionia)

---

[71] S. Applebaum concludes that the Romans viewed Jews outside Judea as an ethnic rather than a national group in "The Legal Status of the Jewish Communities in the Diaspora," 455-60.

[72] Kraabel, "The Roman Diaspora: Six Questionable Assumptions," 455.

[73] Josephus *Ant.* 14. 10. 24 (261); see Kraabel, "Impact of the Discovery of the Sardis Synagogue," 179.

[74] Josephus *Ant.* 14. 10. 12 (226); see also ibid., 14. 10. 25 (263-64).

[75] Ibid., 14. 10. 20 (241-42).

they observed Sabbaths, other rites, and tithed their produce.[76] In Halicarnassus (Caria) they observed festivals, Sabbaths, and built places of prayer near the sea.[77] It is likely that these observances persisted among many Jews in the first century C.E., except that the half-shekel would have been sent to Rome instead of to Jerusalem after 70 C.E. Circumcision is not explicitly mentioned. It is probable that at least some Anatolian Jews practiced the rite.

None of the criteria of observance alone is a sufficient criterion for distinguishing insiders and outsiders. The payment of the Jewish tax, attendance at synagogue, circumcision, observance of Sabbaths, festivals and food laws could all have been combined with tolerance of and even participation in Gentile worship. The only criterion sure to create a clear division between insiders and outsiders would have been strict monotheism and the rejection of the Gentile gods. From the perspective of an insider so defined, the outsiders would have been Roman, Greek, Greco-Asiatic and other polytheists. Included among the outsiders would probably have been Christians who worshipped Jesus Christ as a god or as God.

From the Perspective of Christians

Toward the end of the first century, Christians were still an emergent group. There was great diversity in the formulation of their beliefs and in the organization of their local communities.[78] There was plenty of conflict, to be sure, and no lack of leaders attempting to make their points of view dominant. But it was not yet clear which points of view would win out. We should probably not think of the adherents of various points of view as organized in their separate groups under their leaders and having nothing to do with one another.[79] The earliest evidence of such a schism is in 1 John 2:19 and 2 John 10-11. Raymond Brown dates 1 John and 2 John to about 100 C.E. He places them both in western Anatolia.[80] Apart from that situation, however, we should envisage diverse house churches and occasional larger assemblies in which intense controversy at times broke out and attempts were made to influence the opinions of those present.

Given the emergent and diverse character of the early Christian

---

[76] Ibid., 14. 10. 21 (245).

[77] Ibid., 14. 10. 23 (256-58).

[78] See Walter Bauer, *Orthodoxy and Heresy in Earliest Christianity* (Philadelphia: Fortress, 1971) 61-94; Ulrich B. Müller, *Zur frühchristlichen Theologiegeschichte* (Gütersloh: Mohn, 1976).

[79] Bauer, *Orthodoxy and Heresy in Earliest Christianity*, 70.

[80] Raymond E. Brown, *The Epistles of John* (AB; Garden City: Doubleday, 1982) 101-103.

movement at this time, conclusions about insiders and outsiders can be drawn only cautiously and in general terms. The major criterion for Christian insiders would have been the acknowledgement of Jesus as the anointed of God, as son of God, or as one in some other terms having a key role in relating humanity to the divine realm. Other beliefs and practices were fluid or matters of controversy. The nature of Jesus and the significance of his life and death were emerging as matters of contention, as the Gospel of John, 1 and 2 John, and the letters of Ignatius show.[81] If 3 John was written in western Anatolia, as Brown argues, it provides evidence for some conflict in this region on organization, leadership and authority among Christians. Brown dates the letter to 100-110 C.E.[82] A number of scholars have interpreted the conflict as one between the older authority of itinerant apostles, teachers and prophets and the emerging authority of bishops.[83]

Whether and to what degree Christians needed to conform to Jewish observances was also a controversial issue. Paul's letter to the Galatians reflects a difference of opinion on circumcision (Gal 5:2) and possibly on Sabbaths and festivals (4:10). The letter to the Colossians provides evidence for disagreement on food and drink, festivals, new moons and Sabbaths (Col 2:16). "Food and drink" may refer to Jewish dietary regulations or only to the matter of abstinence (for example, from meat and wine). The so-called Apostolic Decree of Acts 15:20,29 reflects a first-century compromise on the issue.[84] In the early second century, that matter is being hotly disputed in western Anatolia, as Ignatius' letters show.[85]

From the Christian perspective, all who were ignorant of Jesus and his work would have counted as outsiders. Nevertheless, such people would have been seen as potential insiders to be sought out and informed of the gospel. The extreme outsiders would have been those who rejected Jesus as a criminal or a charlatan. Also counting as outsiders were those who assigned too limited an importance to Jesus, such as one healer, teacher or prophet among many.

Outsiders in the Book of Revelation

The purpose of the first part of this essay has been to clarify the range of meanings which the terms "outsider" and "insider" would

---

[81] Ign. *Smyrn.* 2-7; see also Pol. *Phil.* 7.

[82] Brown, *The Epistles of John*, 101-103.

[83] Ibid., 717.

[84] Marcel Simon, "The Apostolic Decree and Its Setting in the Ancient Church," *Bulletin of the John Rylands Library* 52 (1970) 437-60.

[85] Ign. *Magn.* 8-10, *Phld.* 6.

have had in western Anatolia toward the end of the first century C.E. This second part now turns to the attitudes toward outsiders reflected in the book of Revelation. The nearest outsiders will be treated first, namely the Jews.[86] Local polytheists and Christians too close to them will be discussed next. Finally the extreme outsiders, the Romans, will be taken up.

A Synagogue of Satan (Attitude to Jews)

The body of the message to the angel of the Church in Smyrna is as follows:

> I know your tribulation and poverty, but you are rich; and I know the blasphemy of those who call themselves Jews and are not, but are rather a synagogue of Satan. Do not fear what you are about to suffer. Behold, the devil is about to throw some of you into prison, in order that you may be tested, and you will have tribulation in the course of ten days. Be faithful unto death and I shall give you the crown of life.

In this message "tribulation" (*thlipsis*) refers to persecution. Prison, of course, here does not refer to a punishment, but to detention pending trial. "I know your tribulation," therefore, probably refers to harassment, rather than to official measures. The second use of *thlipsis*, "you will have tribulation," refers to official proceedings expected in the near future.

The poverty of the Christians in Smyrna is closely linked to harassment and persecution. Their poverty could be a sign that Christian converts in Smyrna came largely from the lower orders (compare 1 Cor 1:26, Jas 2:5). Poverty would not normally be an issue for slaves, so poor citizens, freedpeople, and indigent resident aliens would come into question. At least some Christians in Smyrna may have been refugees of the Jewish War in Galilee and Judea. Their lot would be hard if they had been farmers or laborers in their homeland and did not have a trade which could be practiced in their new location. Another possibility is that they had been persons of some means whose property was pillaged or livelihood threatened in the

---

[86] In one sense, the Nicolaitans and the followers of "Balaam" and "Jezebel" are nearer outsiders than the Jews. The former are still within the Christian group, whereas the Jews who do not believe in Jesus are technically outsiders. I have, nevertheless, chosen to treat the Jews first as the parent-group of Christians in general and as a group from which, in some ways at least, John does not consider Christians to have separated. This last point will be discussed further later in this essay.

course of the harassment they had experienced (compare Heb 10:34).[87]

The identity of "those who call themselves Jews" has been much debated. The majority of commentators conclude that the reference is to the local Jewish community whose right to the name *Ioudaios* is being challenged by John.[88] A few scholars have argued that these so-called Jews were actually Christians. Massey H. Shepherd Jr. identified them with adherents to a Judaizing form of Christianity open to Jew and Gentile alike which advocated practices like circumcision and observance of the Sabbath, but interpreted them in universal terms drawn from Hellenistic cosmology and philosophy. Shepherd found evidence for such a group in the gospel of John and believed that they were the progenitors of the later Gnostic systems.[89] He identified the so-called Jews of Revelation with those in Philadelphia later criticized by Ignatius for preaching Christ yet observing Judaism. Against them, Ignatius says, "it is better to hear Christianity from the circumcised than Judaism from the uncircumcised."[90]

Many commentators have seen "those who call themselves Jews" as the instigators of the harassment and persecution mentioned in the message. Heinrich Kraft has asserted that if they were Jews, the message could not date to the time of Domitian because the Jews

[87] On this point see Henry B. Swete, *The Apocalypse of St. John* (3rd ed. London: Macmillan, 1917) 31.
[88] Wilhelm Bousset, *Die Offenbarung Johannis,* Meyer K, rev. ed. (Göttingen: Vandenhoeck und Ruprecht, 1896) 242-43; Swete, *The Apocalypse of St. John,* 31; Isbon T. Beckwith, *The Apocalypse of John* (New York: Macmillan, 1922) 452-54; R. H. Charles, *A Critical and Exegetical Commentary on the Revelation of St. John* 2 vols., ICC: (New York: Scribner's, 1920) 1. 56-57; E. B. Allo, *Saint Jean: L'Apocalypse,* EBib, 4th ed. (Paris: Gabalda, 1933) 35; Ernst Lohmeyer, *Die Offenbarung des Johannes,* HNT, rev. ed. (Tübingen: Mohr, Siebeck, 1953) 24; George B. Caird, *A Commentary on the Revelation of St. John the Divine,* HNTC (New York: Harper and Row, 1966) 35; Josephine Massyngberde Ford, *Revelation,* AB (Garden City: Doubleday, 1975) 392-95; J. P. M. Sweet, *Revelation* (Philadelphia: Westminster, 1979) 85; Elisabeth Schüssler Fiorenza, "Apocalyptic and Gnosis in the Book of Revelation and Paul," *JBL* 92 (1973) 572; idem, *Invitation to the Book of Revelation* (Garden City: Doubleday, 1981) 63.
[89] Massey H. Shepherd, Jr., "The Gospel of John," *The Interpreter's One-Volume Commentary on the Bible,* ed. C. M. Laymon (New York, 1971) 708; Shepherd is cited favorably by Sherman E. Johnson in "Early Christianity in Anatolia," *Studies in New Testament and Early Christian Literature: Essays in Honor of Allen P. Wikgren,* NovTSup 33, ed. David E. Aune (Leiden: Brill, 1972) 186; and in idem, "Asia Minor and Early Christianity," *Christianity, Judaism, and Other Greco-Roman Cults: Studies for Morton Smith at Sixty,* 4 parts, Studies in Judaism in Late Antiquity 12, ed. J. Neusner (Leiden: Brill, 1975) 111.
[90] Ign. *Phld.* 6. 1; see also *Phld.* 8. 2 and Ign. *Magn.* 8:10.

themselves were being persecuted at that time.[91] Such was not the
case, at least not in western Anatolia. Domitian insisted on a strict
enforcement of the collection of the Jewish tax, but that does not
amount to persecution. In any case, Kraft has argued that John was not
interested in Jews, but in Christians who had enough influence to
corrupt what he saw as the true confession of faith and way of life. The
phrase "synagogue of Satan" reflects a passionate attack on a group
which was a real threat to John's point of view. Kraft defines this group
as Jewish-Christians who were syncretistic and thus ready to compromise with the State and with paganism. Their "blasphemy" consisted
of denying the reality or the saving character of the death and
resurrection of Christ, rejecting the readiness for martyrdom which
John desired, and claiming to be Jews in order to avoid persecution by
the Roman authorities.[92] The view that this group was syncretistic
derives from an implicit identification of them with the Nicolaitans,
the followers of "Balaam" and "Jezebel." There is nothing in the text
to support this identification.[93] Further, if the group was syncretistic,
they would not need to pretend to be Jews in order to avoid
persecution. Pierre Prigent cites Kraft favorably on these issues in his
own commentary.[94] John Gager, in his new book, *The Origins of
Anti-Semitism*, simply assumes that "those who call themselves
Jews" in Rev 2:9 were Gentile Christians. He gives no arguments or
references in support of his assumption.[95]

The conclusion that "those who call themselves Jews" were
actually the local Jewish community is more likely to be correct. John
was concerned about Jews, their beliefs and activities, as well as
about Christians. (His use of *Ioudaios* as an honorable title does not
prove in itself that he was a native Jew, as R. H. Charles thought, but
it is likely that he was on other grounds.)[96] The narrative about the two

---

[91] Heinrich Kraft, *Die Offenbarung des Johannes*, HNT (Tübingen: Mohr, Siebeck,
1974) 61.

[92] Ibid.

[93] See Fiorenza, "Apocalyptic and Gnosis in the Book of Revelation and Paul," 572.

[94] Pierre Prigent, *L'Apocalypse de Saint Jean*, CNT 14 (Lausanne: Delachaux and
Niestlé, 1981) 47.

[95] John G. Gager, *The Origins of Anti-Semitism* (New York: Oxford University Press,
1983) 132.

[96] Agreeing with Lohmeyer (*Die Offenbarung des Johannes*, 24) against Charles (*A
Critical and Exegetical Commentary on the Revelation of St. John*, 1. 57); the other
grounds for concluding that John was a native Jew are his intimate knowledge of Jewish
Scriptures, the similarity of his book to Jewish apocalypses, and the affinities of his work
with the Jewish Sibylline Oracles and the traditions connected with the "fourth
philosophy" of the Jews. See Adela Yarbro Collins, *Crisis and Catharsis: The Power of
the Apocalypse* (Philadelphia: Westminster, 1984) 46-47, 90-94.

witnesses in chapter 11 is set in Jerusalem, which is spiritually called Sodom and Egypt. John apparently viewed the destruction of Jerusalem as punishment for the rejection of Jesus as messiah and for his crucifixion. But the narrative ends with the repentance of those left in the city after a great earthquake: "they were afraid and they gave glory to the God of heaven" (Rev 11:13). This is the only passage in which divine punishment evokes a positive response. It is not said that the Jews will believe in Jesus as the Christ; rather, Jerusalem will be chastised, and will repent and be rehabilitated.

After 70 C.E. claiming the title "Jew" involved the disadvantage of having to pay the Jewish tax. But this disadvantage must have seemed minor to any pious Jew or Jewish-Christian (see, for example, Matt 17:24-27). That the Jews were a recognized group of resident aliens with their own *politeuma* in many cities, that they had Roman support for their various privileges, and that their monotheism was tolerated, was much more important. It was not terribly important to John that Christians escape persecution by claiming to be Jews, as his emphasis on willingness to die for the testimony of Jesus shows. But the question whether Christians could claim to be legitimate heirs of Jewish tradition was important to the formation of Christian identity; this identity involved matters of self-understanding and prestige as well as legal status.

John's positive use of the title "Jew" has often been contrasted with an alleged pejorative use in the gospel of John. For example, Charles called attention to the positive portrayal of Nathanael as a true Israelite in John 1:47 in contrast to the portrayal of the Jews elsewhere in the gospel as the opponents of Christianity.[97] Lohmeyer emphasized that "Jew" is never a pejorative name in the New Testament, not even in the gospel of John.[98] Beckwith and Allo argued that there is no substantial difference between Revelation and the Gospel of John on this issue.[99] The conclusion that *Ioudaios* is never a pejorative term in the New Testament seems to be correct.

It is sometimes said that John was claiming the title "Jew" for Christians by rejecting merely historical, ethnic or fleshly claims to the name, and suggesting that the Christians are the true or spiritual Jews. In this connection, reference is often made to Rom 2:28-29, where Paul distinguishes between physical circumcision and being a Jew outwardly, and circumcision of the heart and being a Jew in a hidden way. Spiritual circumcision is contrasted with literal circum-

---

[97] Charles, *A Critical and Exegetical Commentary on the Revelation of St. John*, 1. 57.
[98] Lohmeyer, *Die Offenbarung des Johannes*, 24.
[99] Beckwith, *The Apocalypse of John*, 453-54; Allo, *Saint Jean: L'Apocalypse*, 35.

cision.[100] The distinction between the spiritual and the literal is not totally foreign to John, as is shown by his reference to Jerusalem: "spiritually Sodom and Egypt" (11:8). In this message to the Smyrnaeans itself he distinguishes implicitly between literal and spiritual wealth and poverty (v 9). This way of thinking may play a role in John's implicit claim of the term *Ioudaioi* for Christians, but it does not tell the whole story.

I have argued elsewhere that the woman in Revelation 12 portrays the heavenly Israel and that John makes no distinction between an old Israel and a new or between Israel and the Church.[101] The vision strongly suggests an assumption of the continuity with Israel of believers in Jesus. There is also, of course, the awareness of something new in the Christian movement. The element of newness or renewal is reflected in the vision of the *new* Jerusalem (chapters 21-22), where the names of the Lamb's twelve apostles are written upon the wall's foundations (Rev 21:14).

John's implicit use of the term *Ioudaioi* for Christians fits with his assumption of continuity. It is anachronistic and misleading with regard to the book of Revelation, as with much of the New Testament, to assume that the author thought of the Church as a new religion and a new institution replacing Judaism. It is more appropriate to see a certain analogy between the perspective of Revelation and that of the writings of the community at Qumran. In both cases, there is a kind of sectarian thinking which views the beliefs and way of life of a particular group to be the only legitimate heir of the great tradition, namely, the Jewish heritage. The polemic against "the synagogue of Satan" in Rev 2:9 must be seen not as a rejection of religious and ethnic Judaism viewed from a distance, but as a passionate polemic against a sibling or parent faith, like the attacks of the Qumran community on all other Jews as virtual apostates.

In the Community Rule, it is said that those (presumably Jews) who wish to join the community shall separate from "the congregation of the men of falsehood," *'adat 'anšê hā 'āwel* (presumably other Jews). All outsiders, that is those not members of the new covenant, are subject to God's wrath, and unclean. No member of the community is to have dealings with them.[102] Outsiders are called "the men of

---

[100] Charles, *A Critical and Exegetical Commentary on the Revelation of St. John*, 1. 57; Beckwith, *The Apocalypse of John* 453; Allo, *Saint Jean: L'Apocalypse*, 35; Swete, *The Apocalypse of St. John*, 31; Lohmeyer, *Die Offenbarung des Johannes*, 24.
[101] Adela Yarbro Collins, *The Combat Myth in the Book of Revelation*, HDR 9 (Missoula: Scholars Press, 1976) 130-35, idem, *The Apocalypse* (New Testament Message 22; Wilmington, Delaware: Michael Glazier, 1982) 84-88.
[102] IQS 5:1-2, 10-20.

the Pit" (*'anšê haššaḥat*).[103] In the Damascus Document, Jews of a different persuasion are called "the congregation of traitors" (*'adat bôgĕdîm*).[104] In the War Scroll the ungodly of the Covenant, presumably Jews who are not members of the community, are portrayed as allies of the army of Belial, a figure equivalent to Satan.[105]

Even closer parallels can be found to the "synagogue of Satan" in Rev 2:9 and its implied opposite, the synagogue of God or of the Lord. In the War Scroll, the community is called "the congregation of God" (*'adat 'ēl*) and "the assembly of God" (*qĕhal 'ēl*).[106] In the hymns, the (Jewish) opponents of the Righteous Teacher or of the community as a whole are called a congregation of Belial.[107]

The boundaries between the Qumran community and other Jews were drawn on the basis of their differing opinions about the legitimacy of the Jewish people's current Judean leadership, the interpretation of Scripture, and the interpretation of oral law. For the author of Revelation, the primary boundary between Christians and other Jews was the question whether messianic expectation had been fulfilled in Christ. Those who have a right to be called Jews, in John's opinion, are those who believe in Jesus as the anointed one of God. The synagogue of Satan are those who claim to be Jews, but who harass and accuse those who follow the Christian way.[108] The "blasphemy" of the so-called Jews may be simply their claim to be Jews. Alternatively, John may have viewed their statements about the person and work of Jesus, made in opposition to Christian claims, as blasphemous. Or members of the local Jewish community may have made informal accusations that the Christian beliefs and way of life were illegitimate or a threat to order. John may have expected such statements to be made as a formal accusation in the near future before the Roman governor. If the latter situation was the case, then John would have seen the Jewish accusers of Christians in Smyrna as the earthly agents of the heavenly *diabolos* (v 10) who accuses Christians in the heavenly court (compare Rev 12:10, where the term *katēgor* is used).

The message to the angel of the Church in Philadelphia reflects a similar situation (Rev 3:7-13). Similar terminology is used: "synagogue of Satan" and "those who call themselves Jews and are not, but

---

[103] IQS 9:16.
[104] CD 1:12.
[105] IQM 1:1.
[106] IQM 4:9-10.
[107] IQH 2:22.
[108] So also Ford, *Revelation*, 395.

lie" (v 9). Rev 3:9 is the only evidence for a Jewish community in
Philadelphia (Lydia) before the third century C.E.[109]

The polemical language used by Christians against Jewish opponents in the first century C.E. is used in the second century by
Christians against other Christians. Ignatius wrote to the Smyrnaeans
that anyone who acts without the knowledge of the bishop is serving
the devil.[110] Polycarp wrote to the Philippians that whoever does not
confess the testimony of the cross is of the devil and that one who
denies resurrection and judgment is the first-born of Satan.[111] Indeed
according to Irenaeus and Eusebius, Polycarp reviled Marcion as the
first-born of Satan.[112]

Food Sacrificed to Idols and Unchastity (Attitude to Polytheists)

In Rev 2:6 the Christians in Ephesus are praised for hating the
works of the Nicolaitans, but no details are given. Those in Pergamum
are told, "But I have a few things against you: that you have there
some who hold the teaching of Balaam, who taught Balak to put a
stumbling block before the sons of Israel, that they might eat food
sacrificed to idols and practice unchastity; thus you also have some
who hold the teaching of the Nicolaitans" (Rev 2:14-15). The message
to those in Thyatira includes the following remarks: "But I have
against you that you tolerate the woman Jezebel, who calls herself a
prophetess, and teaches and leads astray my servants so that they
practice unchastity and eat food sacrificed to idols. . . . But to the rest
of you in Thyatira, who do not hold this teaching, who do not know the
deep things of Satan, as they say, I do not lay upon you any other
burden, only that you hold what you have until I come" (Rev 2:20,
24-25).

Nothing reliable is known about the Nicolaitans beyond what is
said in these passages. Irenaeus and, following him Hippolytus, say
that they were followers of Nicolaus the proselyte from Antioch, who
was one of the seven Hellenists appointed for service in the Church of
Jerusalem according to Acts 6:5. Clement of Alexandria, the Apostolic
Constitutions, and Victorinus qualify this identification.[113] Most commentators agree that the Nicolaitans, the followers of "Balaam" and
the followers of "Jezebel" all belong to the same movement.[114]

[109] Stern, "The Jewish Diaspora," 151.

[110] Ign. *Smyrn.* 9. 1.

[111] Pol. *Phil.* 7. 1.

[112] Bauer, *Orthodoxy and Heresy in Earliest Christianity*, 70.

[113] Charles, *A Critical and Exegetical Commentary on the Revelation of St. John*, 1. 52.

[114] Ibid., 1. 53; Bousset, *Die Offenbarung Johannis*, 239, 248-49, 257; Caird, *A Com-*

"Balaam" and "Jezebel" are criticized for encouraging their followers to eat *eidōlothyta*, sacrifices offered to idols. Romans, Greeks, and Greco-Asiatics would of course have spoken of *hierothyta*, sacrifices offered to a god. The currency of the word *eidōlothyta* shows that eating such sacrifices had already been condemned by at least some Jews of the Diaspora. Such condemnation is reflected in *Joseph and Aseneth* 8.5.

This issue was controversial in Corinth as 1 Corinthians 8-10 shows. Some in Corinth argued that it was permissible to eat sacrifices offered to idols, since idols were nothing and there is only one God (1 Cor 8:4, 10:23). Paul did not directly condemn their point of view, although he qualified it significantly. He did not deny the existence of the gods entirely, but argued that they were demons (1 Cor 10:20). Participation in their worship counted for him as idolatry (10:14, 21-22). His teaching therefore was first of all not to do anything which would offend those who were scrupulous on this issue (1 Cor 8:7-13, 10:23-11:1). As Krister Stendahl would say, he was more concerned about love than personal integrity.[115] That limitation being satisfied, however, those with a strong conscience were free to eat anything they wished, as long as the context did not unavoidably imply worship of any being other than the one God from whom are all things (8:6, 10; 10:20-22, 25-27). Sharing a meal in a temple, other than the temple in Jerusalem, seems to be excluded (8:10, 10:20-21).

A number of scholars have concluded that John's prohibitions against unchastity and eating food sacrificed to idols are based on the so-called Apostolic Decree of Acts (Acts 15:20, 28-29; 21:25).[116] This decree required "those of the Gentiles who turn to God" (15:19) to abstain from food sacrificed to idols, from consuming blood, from eating meat from animals which had been strangled, and from unchastity (15:29). Some manuscripts of Acts omit the reference to what is strangled and thus allow what Christians today would call a purely ethical interpretation of the decree. Some scholars have defended this text and the "ethical" meaning as original.[117] Most scholars today,

---

mentary on the Revelation of St. John the Divine, 38-41; Fiorenza, "Apocalyptic and Gnosis in the Book of Revelation and Paul, 567-68.

[115] Krister Stendahl, *Paul among Jews and Gentiles* (Philadelphia: Fortress, 1976) 52-67.

[116] Bousset, *Die Offenbarung Johannis,* 257; Charles, *A Critical and Exegetical Commentary on the Revelation of St. John,* 1. 74; Simon, "The Apostolic Decree and Its Setting in the Ancient Church," 442.

[117] Some manuscripts omit "what is strangled" and others omit "unchastity"; the original text probably contained all four prohibitions. See Bruce M. Metzger, *A Textual Commentary on the Greek New Testament* (3rd ed.; New York: United Bible Societies,

however, conclude that the ethical version is secondary, because if it were original, it would be hard to explain how the so-called "ritual" or "ceremonial" version arose. The most difficult part of the decree to interpret is the reference to *porneia*.[118] Ernst Haenchen has argued that the Apostolic Decree is based on four prohibitions contained in Leviticus 17-18 which are presented as binding not only for the Jews but also for the sojourners dwelling among the Jews (LXX-*proselutos*). He interprets *porneia* as marriage to near relatives in violation of the commands in Lev 18:6-18.[119] If Haenchen is right that these two chapters in Leviticus constitute the basis for the Apostolic Decree, *porneia* must be defined more broadly. In Leviticus 18, not only marriage to near relatives is forbidden, but also intercourse with a woman who is menstruating, adultery, homosexuality and intercourse with animals. All these prohibitions pertain both to Jews and to sojourners (Lev 18:19-29).

Haenchen makes a credible case for his judgment that the Apostolic Decree in its ceremonial interpretation was living tradition in the community for which Acts was written and that members of that community mistakenly claimed that it originated with the apostles. It is more likely that it originated in a strongly mixed community of the Diaspora in the hope of maintaining fellowship between Jewish and Gentile Christians.[120] Helmut Koester locates the composition of Acts in Antioch, Ephesus, or Rome during the third Christian generation.[121] If the conclusions of these two scholars are correct, and they are quite credible, it is not at all unlikely that John knew nothing about such a decree (if Acts was not composed in Ephesus). It is clear that it was unknown to Paul from his comment that "those of repute" in Jerusalem added nothing to the gospel as he had been preaching it (Gal 2:6). Paul dealt with food sacrificed to idols and unchastity because these were issues of perennial concern in the interaction of Jews or Christians with Gentiles.

Likewise, John seems to be dealing with issues of concern to him and to other Christians in western Anatolia, rather than alluding to the Apostolic Decree.[122] He is closer to the Apostolic Decree than to Paul

---

1971) 429-34; Ernst Haenchen, *The Acts of the Apostles*, (Philadelphia: Westminster, 1971) 449, note 6; Simon, "The Apostolic Decree and Its Setting in the Ancient Church," 438.

[118] Simon, "The Apostolic Decree and Its Setting in the Ancient Church," 440-50.

[119] Haechen, *The Acts of the Apostles*, 469.

[120] Ibid., 470-71.

[121] Koester, *Introduction to the New Testament*, 2. 310.

[122] If he was aware of the Apostolic Decree, John apparently interpreted it selectively and somewhat idiosyncratically.

in his absolute prohibition of eating food sacrificed to idols. Not only are Christians forbidden to share a meal in a temple of Gentiles, according to John and the decree, but they may not buy such food in the market, eat it in the homes of Gentiles, or eat it in any other location. Paul's position is already very restrictive of social relations between Christians and Gentiles. Only the wealthy in the first century had dining rooms in which to entertain their friends. The vast majority played host at sacred tables, that is, in dining rooms opening off the stoas that ran around sacral areas, on stone couches covered by arbors, or on leaves or straw sheltered by a tent or canopy on the temple grounds.[123] The decree and Revelation would also exclude participation in the meals of Gentile clubs, which virtually always had a patron deity.[124] As we have seen, associations of artisans were very widespread in western Anatolia in the first century.

The *politeuma* of the Jews in Alexandria included three types of organization: the Gerousia, the synagogue, and the association of artisans. There is evidence for a Jewish goldsmiths' association at Sardis, and for Jewish associations of purple-dyers and carpet-weavers at Hierapolis (Phrygia). The evidence is from the third century, but it seems likely that such associations were already in existence in the first century.[125] If Christians had separated from the Jewish communities in Ephesus, Pergamum, and Thyatira, the artisans among them would presumably not have the opportunity to affiliate with the Jewish craft-associations in those cities. The Nicolaitans, "Balaam," and "Jezebel" may have encouraged these Christian artisans to join the Gentile associations, discounting their cultic dimension as a matter of indifference.

As in the case of *porneia* in the Apostolic Decree, it is difficult to determine what John had in mind when he condemned the followers of "Balaam" and "Jezebel" for practicing unchastity. There is little evidence, if any, elsewhere in the book that John was concerned about marriage to near relatives, homosexuality, or bestiality. In Rev 9:21 unchastity is mentioned as one of the sins of humankind, along with murders, sorceries and thefts. The statement that the 144,000 have not defiled themselves with women (14:4) could conceivably reflect concern about the purity of sexual relations with regard to menstruation. But the point of the statement is not so much levitical chastity as it is asceticism: "for they are virgins" (*parthenoi*).

---

[123] MacMullen, *Paganism in the Roman Empire*, 36-38.

[124] Ibid., 39; Koester, *Introduction to the New Testament*, 1. 66-67.

[125] Applebaum, "The Organization of the Jewish Communities in the Diaspora," 476, 479-80, 483.

It is likely that the unchastity condemned in the messages to Pergamum and Thyatira is figurative rather than literal. Probably, it is equivalent to idolatry. It is well known that 'playing the harlot," "fornicating," and "committing adultery" are phrases frequently used in the Jewish Scriptures as figurative descriptions of idolatry. The description of the teacher active in Pergamum, called "Balaam" by John, alludes to Num 31:16 and 25:1-2. In Num 25:1-2 it is said that the people of Israel played the harlot (LXX-*ekporneusai*) with the daughters of Moab, ate of the sacrifices offered to their gods, and worshiped their gods (LXX-*eidōlois*). In the original context, intermarriage and idolatry were both involved. In John's situation there is no indication that marriage with non-Christian Gentiles was an issue. The conclusion that unchastity is meant figuratively is supported by the reference to those who commit adultery with "Jezebel" (Rev 2:22). The context suggests that these adulterers and her "children" are her allies and followers in the teaching which John rejects.

This line of interpretation is further supported by the fact that *porneia, porneuō,* and *pornē* are consistently used in a figurative way outside the messages. The only exception is Rev 9:21 where literal unchastity is meant. Even there, the primary sin is idolatry (9:20). The great harlot portrayed in chapter 17 is clearly Rome. She is both the city and the goddess Roma.[126] In Hosea, the people are symbolized by the prophet's harlot-wife Gomer, who abandons her husband to commit adultery with other men (gods). In Revelation, idolatry is focused on a goddess, Roma. The sexual image, therefore, is not so much adultery, or the people playing the harlot, as it is the deity as harlot. The harlot corrupting the earth with her prostitution (*porneia*) is a symbol of the worship of Roma together with the emperor throughout the Roman empire.[127]

The connection of *porneia* with Rome elsewhere in Revelation raises the question of whether the Nicolaitans, "Balaam" and "Jezebel" were advocating Christian participation in the imperial cult. Ephesus had a cult of Roma beginning with the Republican period. Augustus was also worshiped there,[128] and a temple and cult in honor of Domitian was established there during his reign. After Domitian's death and *damnatio memoriae,* the temple was rededi-

---

[126] On the origins, history and cult of the goddess Roma, see Ronald Mellor, "The Goddess Roma," *Aufstieg und Niedergang der römischen Welt* II 17. 2 (ed. Wolfgang Haase; New York: de Gruyter, 1981) 950-1030.

[127] Rev 14:8; 17:2; 18:3, 9; 19:2.

[128] Magie, *Roman Rule in Asia Minor,* 1. 417, 2. 1613-14.

cated to Vespasian.[129] In 29 B.C.E., Augustus named Pergamum as the seat of the provincial cult of Roma and Augustus. In addition to the provincial cult, there was also a civic cult of Roma and Augustus there.[130] Thyatira had a cult of Roma alone in the republic or early empire, and also a cult of Roma and Augustus.[131] So the cities of Greece and western Anatolia venerated Rome and the emperors enthusiastically. They were worshipped in the way that the cities' protecting deities had formerly been honored. The result was that the common life of the cities was focused not so much on the city-state as on the empire.[132] It is conceivable that native Greco-Asiatic Christians in western Anatolia felt that attending banquets or festivals in honor of Roma and the emperors was compatible with Christian faith. They could have conceived of the emperor as the anointed of God, as Josephus declared Vespasian to be, or as God's servant, as Paul implies in Romans 13.[133]

It is unlikely that the movement John opposes in these three messages was deliberately polytheistic. The scarcity of evidence prevents us from reconstructing their understanding of the relation of the one God to the so-called gods. But it is clear that they did not draw so sharp a line as John did between Christians and polytheists.

The Throne of Satan (Attitude to Rome)

The message to Pergamum begins: "So speaks the one who has the sharp two-edged sword: I know where you dwell, where the throne of Satan is; you hold fast my name, and you did not deny my faith even in the days of Antipas, my faithful witness, who was killed among you, where Satan dwells" (Rev 2:12-13). In chapter 12 Satan is portrayed as a great dragon, an ancient serpent (12:9). In chapter 13, it is said that the dragon gave his power, throne and authority to the beast from the sea (13:2). This beast symbolizes at times the Roman empire as a kingdom and at times a particular emperor.[134] These passages suggest that the throne of Satan in 2:13 is a seat of Roman power. It is not necessarily the case that, had John had the judgment seat of a Roman official in mind, he would have used the word "tribunal" (bēma).[135] John is using powerful traditional language to

---

[129] Kenneth Scott, *The Imperial Cult under the Flavians* (Stuttgart: Kohlhammer, 1936; reprinted, New York: Arno Press, 1975) 96-97.

[130] Magie, *Roman Rule in Asia Minor*, 1. 447, 2. 1614.

[131] Ibid., 2. 1613-14.

[132] Fustel de Coulanges, *The Ancient City*, 377.

[133] Josephus *J. W.* 3. 8. 9 (399-402).

[134] Yarbro Collins, *The Combat Myth in the Book of Revelation*, 170-76.

[135] Against Kraft, *Die Offenbarung des Johannes*, 64.

paint a picture and to evoke an emotional response, not giving a technically correct description.

As the capital of the former Attalid kingdom, Pergamum was made the capital of the new Roman province of Asia in the second century B.C.E., that is, the place of landing and residence of the Roman governor. Although Smyrna had erected a temple dedicated to Roma already in 195 B.C.E., Pergamum was the first city to establish a cult of Roma and Augustus, and was the original center of the provincial imperial cult. Under Augustus, the provincial capital was apparently moved to Ephesus.[136] In 26 C.E. Smyrna was allowed to erect a second temple related to the provincial imperial cult, and thereafter the annual festival seems to have rotated among the prominent cities of Asia.[137] It seems that during the first century the governor acted as judge in several large cities, one of which was Pergamum.[138]

The phrase "the throne of Satan" seems to allude to the governor's seat of judgment, on which he, as the agent of the Roman emperor (the beast of 13:1), carried out Satan's will (13:2). This interpretation fits the emphasis on Antipas as a faithful witness of Christ. Before and after mention of his death, Satan is mentioned. John is apparently calling to the first readers' minds the trial and execution in Pergamum of their fellow Christian Antipas.

This passage is one among many in Revelation which express intense antipathy toward Rome. This antipathy had a variety of sources: general resistance to Roman domination and exploitation expressed mostly verbally by representatives of several peoples of the Hellenistic Near East, Jewish resistance against Rome in Judea and Egypt, Nero's police action against Christians in Rome in the sixties, the destruction of Jerusalem and the temple in 70 C.E., and the imperial cult.[139] If, as seems likely, John left Judea during the Jewish War and settled in western Anatolia, the thriving imperial cult in that region must have been a cause of great culture shock for him. His intense antipathy for it is related to his understanding of Jesus as the ruler of the kings on earth (1:5) and as King of kings and Lord of lords (19:16). Like Polycarp and the Christians in Smyrna who wrote the account of his martyrdom in that city in about 155 C.E., John could acknowledge no king but Jesus Christ.[140]

---

[136] David C. Pellett, "Asia," *IDB* 1 (1962) 257-59.

[137] Magie, *Roman Rule in Asia Minor*, 1. 447-48.

[138] A. H. M. Jones, *The Cities of the Eastern Roman Provinces*, 2nd ed. (Oxford: The Clarendon Press, 1971) 61.

[139] Yarbro Collins, *Crisis and Catharsis*, 88-104.

[140] *Mart. Pol.* 9. 2-3; 21.

Conclusion

In his book *The Functions of Social Conflict*, Lewis Coser defines conflict as "a struggle over values and claims to scarce status, power and resources in which the aims of the opponents are to neutralize, injure or eliminate their rivals."[141] He admits that "certain forms of conflict are indeed destructive of group unity" and that "they lead to disintegration of specific social structures."[142] He suggests, however, that contemporary sociologists view social conflict as necessarily destructive, as primarily dysfunctional and even pathological.[143] Such an imbalance in perspective overlooks those functions of conflict which increase the adaptation or adjustment of particular social relationships or groups by, for example, maintaining group boundaries or preventing the withdrawal of members from a group.[144]

The book of Revelation reflects not only attitudes toward outsiders and deviant insiders, but also interaction and conflict between groups and among members of Christian groups.[145] The conflict between Christians and Jews in western Anatolia toward the end of the first century was, in a sense, a struggle for survival. In Coser's terms, it was a struggle for scarce status. If local Jewish communities did not recognize Christians as part of their *politeuma,* the two groups then had to compete for the status of legitimate heirs to the heritage of Israel. There was also a struggle over values between the two groups. Controversies may be inferred over the understanding of messianic elements in the tradition, over whether honoring Jesus as Lord (*kyrios*) was compatible with recognition of the one true God, and over the status of Rome as God's servant or oppressor.

The conflict between John and the Nicolaitans, "Balaam," and "Jezebel" may also be viewed as a conflict over scarce status. The role of the bishop (*episkopos*) is not a matter of explicit exhortation or controversy in the book of Revelation, as it is a decade or two later in the letters of Ignatius.[146] Conflict among various charismatic leaders is, however, explicit. The Ephesians are praised for rejecting false apostles (Rev 2:2). "Jezebel" is said to call herself a prophetess (2:20). It can be inferred that she was recognized as such, at least by her followers. The leader called "Balaam" was probably a prophet, since

---

[141] Lewis A. Coser, *The Functions of Social Conflict* (New York: The Free Press, 1956) 8.

[142] Ibid.

[143] Ibid., 8, 20-29.

[144] Ibid., 8.

[145] See the distinction Coser makes between conflict and hostile sentiments, ibid, 37.

[146] Ign. *Eph.* 3. 2-6. 2, *Magn.* 2. 1-4. 1, 7. 1, *Trall.* 2-3, 7, *Smyrn.* 8-9.

his teaching was similar to "Jezebel's" and since his Scriptural prototype was a seer. John does not explicitly claim the title prophet, but implies that he is such (22:9). If these prophets were itinerant, as seems likely, they would have been competing not only for the leadership of the various congregations, but also for the hospitality of those able to provide it.[147]

The conflict between John and the other prophets may also be seen as a conflict over values. They apparently disagreed over what constituted idolatry. The controversy over idolatry, which included unchastity, symbolically understood, was a controversy involving group boundaries. The process of self-definition raised questions about the overlapping of memberships and roles such as, could a Christian be a member of a Greek or Greco-Asiatic association of artisans; could a Christian express loyalty to Rome by attending a festival or contest sponsored by the provincial imperial priesthood; were Christians bound to avoid virtually all Greco-Asiatic banquets; and finally, if they could afford to purchase meat at all, must they inquire about its origin and strictly avoid sacred meat? John took a strict position on all these issues, anticipating the later orthodox position over against the Gnostics. This strict position tended to support the evolution of Christians into a "third race," neither Jews nor Gentiles.

The conflict with Rome as interpreted by the book of Revelation was not merely a struggle for survival, but a struggle over power. The underlying issue may be articulated as a tension between autonomy and subservience. It was of course also a conflict about values. The Romans and their allies ordered their lives in terms of a symbolic universe based on polytheism. The symbolic universe which both shapes the book of Revelation and is shaped by it is one based on monotheism.[148] One might expect that the key reason for Christian rejection of the imperial cult was its claiming divine status for a human being. That does not seem to be the case. Again, there is a clash of two symbolic universes. They agree in seeing the divine manifested in human form; they disagree on the specific location of that epiphany. The book of Revelation is the first clear articulation in Christian tradition of these interrelated conflicts between the Church and the Roman Empire, conflicts which were not resolved until centuries later, if they have been yet.

---

[147] Yarbro Collins, *Crisis and Catharsis*, 46, 134-38; compare also 2 Corinthians 10-12 and 3 John.

[148] On the notion of a symbolic universe, see Peter L. Berger and Thomas Luckmann, *The Social Construction of Reality* (Garden City: Doubleday, 1966) 95-96, 98-100.

9

Synagoga Caeca: Systematic Distortion in Gentile Interpretations of Evidence for Judaism in the Early Christian Period

A. T. Kraabel
Luther College

I

The Jews of antiquity were not always what they seem. To those of us who study the Greco-Roman world, that has been clear for a long time. It is also widely understood now in New Testament studies—witness the papers touching on the New Testament at this conference. References to Jews and Jewish practices in these first Christian texts may never be taken at face value. In the earliest Christian accounts, the "Jews" in the story fall into three categories: 1) theological phantoms brought in for inner-church reasons, as one group of Christians battles another; 2) political scapegoats, an all-too-familiar role; 3) if they happen to be *real* Jews, they are often under attack from the Christian side, and the picture is necessarily distorted. These Christian texts were never intended to be historical reference works. They were written for more important and immediate reasons than that. Usually, they served theological purposes. So like the rabbinic literature, they must be approached indirectly if we are to draw historical information from them. This characteristic of the sources requires close attention if we are to come to a clear understanding of how Jews and Christians related to those "outside," and particularly how they defined themselves in relation to the other.

This is particularly true for the Greco-Roman world and Diaspora Judaism, where the evidence is not abundant in the first place, and where it may often be mixed up with pagan concerns as well as with the Christian theological agenda. In a recent article in the Yadin *Festschrift,* I discussed the following six questionable assumptions which are part of the "conventional wisdom" in this area: 1) the Mediterranean Diaspora was *syncretistic*; 2) Diaspora Jews were characterized by a great *missionary zeal*; 3) Jews outside Palestine were *aliens* in the Roman world; 4) their social, economic and intellectual *status* was very low; 5) they were a *monolithic* group, interconnected and even directly controlled from Palestine, a kind of "underground" which was feared and alternatively oppressed and appeased by Roman authorities; 6) their activities and the actions toward them by gentiles are best understood on *religious* terms, since Judaism is a religion first of all (Kraabel, 1982). If these assumptions were in fact correct, they would say a great deal about how Diaspora Jews understood themselves in relation to the non-Jewish majority around them. But the assumptions are questionable, and deserve reexamination.

My purpose here is to continue the theme of that paper in a different way, by giving three particular examples of the distortions which concern me.

II

My first example is neither Jewish nor gentile. It is Samaritan, and comes from the middle of the Hellenistic period. It comprises two Samaritan inscriptions that were recently discovered on the island of Delos, which lies just off the Greek mainland and 150 kilometers southeast of Athens. These two texts are now to be added to the Samaritan papyri from the Wadi Daliyeh and the data from the Shechem excavations led by G. E. Wright. (Wright, 1965, 170-184; Purvis, 1975; 101-115). (Shechem was located at the foot of Mount Gerezim, the Samaritan holy mountain; it was the Samaritan center during the Hellenistic period.) All of these discoveries are from the last three decades.

The Samaritans themselves have been studied in their own right, so we have reconstructions of their history and religious thought. In Biblical times they are associated with the Northern Kingdom, Israel, whose capital was Samaria. In 722, that Northern Kingdom was captured by the Assyrians. Then, at some point after the Exile which took place subsequent to the fall of the Southern Kingdom, Judah, and the destruction of Jerusalem in 587, the Samaritans began to take on a separate existence. Without going into the vexed question of "the origins of the Samaritans," it is clear that three later military campaigns had much to do with Samaritan history in Palestine. They are the capture of the area by Alexander the Great in the late fourth century, the conflicts between Judah Maccabee and the forces of Antiochus Epiphanes in the early second century, and the capture of Shechem and the destruction of the Samaritan Temple on Mount Gerezim by John Hyrcanus late in the second century.

The excavation of Shechem showed that the site had been unoccupied during most of the Persian period (fifth-fourth centuries), but that a great number of people lived there in the next two centuries

(Wright, 1965, 170). Archaeologists from the Shechem expedition also excavated the ruins at Tell er-Ras on the top of Mount Gerezim. Under a temple of Zeus Hypsistos (from the second century A.D.) they found a large building complex which include the remains of the Samaritan Temple known from accounts in Josephus (Bull, 1976).

According to Josephus, the Samaritan Temple was built on the model of the Temple in Jerusalem, and stood for two hundred years (AJ 13.256). While they were under the control of Antiochus Epiphanes, the Samaritans sought to adapt themselves to his hellenization program by dedicating the temple to Zeus Xenios.[1] Such accommodation would distinguish them from the Maccabees, who came to power in Palestine soon thereafter. Conflicts arose with the Maccabees, and the temple on Mount Gerezim was finally destroyed by John Hyrcanus in 128 B.C. Josephus' two hundred years begins, then, with Alexander the Great or soon thereafter, and ends with John Hyrcanus.

During these two centuries, the Samaritans gradually become a group separate from the Jews (Purvis, 1976). "The other" was coming more clearly into focus. The building of the Gerezim Temple, the Samaritans' differences with the Maccabees, and finally, John Hyrcanus' attack on the temple, each are points where Samaritan group becomes more clearly demarcated than it had been before. In all of this, Mount Gerezim is the central symbol to the Samaritans themselves and to those outside. Jews and Samaritans may have had much in common in their history and their scripture, but this piece of real estate always signaled their particularity; in the south there was Jerusalem with its Temple Mount, but the Samaritans had Gerezim.

As for the two inscriptions discovered in 1979 (published by Pierre Bruneau, the leader of the Delos excavations; see Bruneau, 1982; Robert, 1983; Kraabel, 1984), the older, dated between 250 and 175 B.C., is fragmentary. But some of the lost sections may be conjectured. It states: "The Israelites on Delos who make offerings to hallowed, consecrated Mount Gerezim honor Menippos of Heraclea, son of Artemidoros, along with his descendants, who, from his own resources, because of a vow to God, constructed/equipped . . . and presented it . . ." The text fails us at that point, but then continues: ". . . and they crown him with a golden crown . . ." The other inscription, dating from between 150 and 50 B.C., is complete. It reads: "The Israelites on Delos who make offerings to hallowed

---

[1] On a similar move, to dedicate the Temple in Jerusalem to Zeus Olympios (supported by "the Hellenizing party of the Jerusalem priesthood,") see Smith 1971, 190, citing 2 Macc 6.

Mount Gerezim crown with a gold crown Sarapion, son of Jason, of Knossos, for his benefactions toward them."

Each inscription is cut into a rectangular shaft of white marble. Above each, a fine wreath is carved in high relief. (Indeed, as a classicist, I was struck by how properly Greek both steles are; the same design is found time and again across the Mediterranean world.) So the honor was a double one, comprising both the gold wreath ceremonially bestowed on the benefactor, and the inscription that records the honor in a public and permanent fashion. Further, "The Israelites on Delos who make offerings to hallowed Mount Gerezim" are surely Samaritans, part of the Samaritan Diaspora at a time when the Samaritan homeland is prospering and there is a substantial temple on Mount Gerezim. At about the same time, the Samaritan author we know as Ps-Eupolemos is writing in Greek about "hallowed Mount Gerezim," while using the Biblical text of Diaspora Jews, the LXX (Collins, 1983, 38-39; Hengel 1974, 1.88-92).

Previous attempts to understand the Samaritans have seen them pretty much as a *Palestine* phenomenon and very much in second place to the Palestinian Jews. This is particularly the case in New Testament studies despite the reference in Josephus to Samaritans outside Palestine and some other evidence from the Mediterranean Diaspora. But there is indication in Luke-Acts that there was a Christian mission to the Samaritans before the mission to the Gentiles began. The resulting Samaritan Christianity is thought to have left its mark on the New Testament itself. Stephen's speech in the seventh chapter of Acts, the Gospel of John and the Letter to the Hebrews, are the texts most frequently seen as linked to Samaritan Christianity in some way (Scobie, 1972; Pummer, 1979; Coggins 1982).

The two Delos inscriptions open this picture up considerably, for they are not what one would expect from reading earlier accounts of the data for the Samaritan Diaspora (Montgomery, 1907, 148-153; Kippenberg, 1971, 145-150). Rather, they constitute clear evidence of a long-lived Samaritan community well before Christian times and outside the Holy Land, in one of the political and economic centers of the Greek world. The Delos Samaritans call themselves "Israelites," but qualify the term thus: they are the *Gerezim* Israelites. Apparently, the break with the Jews is not yet final, but over against other "Israelites," some clear specification is needed as to what kind of "Israelites" these at Delos are.

At the same time, the "Israelites on Delos" are at home in the Greek world. The steles themselves, the form and language of the inscriptions and the honors paid to benefactors all follow the most proper and common Greek style. So do the names: Menippos, son of

Artemidoros, and Sarapion, son of Jason. If the benefactors are themselves Samaritans, then they indicate an even larger Samaritan diaspora. Heracleia and Knossos are close together on the north shore of Crete, a much larger island some 250 kilometers south of Delos. There may have been Samaritan "Israelites" there as well. (The Jewish community on the island of Rhodes apparently had a similar concern for their temple on Mount Zion. A recent inscription from Jerusalem commemorates a gift to the temple there from a Rhodian Jew of the first century B.C., see Isaac 1983.)

But most important in this whole story is the connection with Mount Gerezim. The split between Jews and Samaritans may not have been complete, but these "Israelites" knew precisely how to identify themselves. The center of their world was Gerezim. They must have known well the Samaritan Temple on the mountain and the flourishing Samaritan community below it. Perhaps, like Ps-Eupolemos, they knew how major Biblical stories had been linked to that mountain in the Samaritan tradition. So Gerezim remained central to their lives, the key to their religious identification even while they lived more than 1000 kilometers away from it in the center of the Greek world.

The "Israelites on Delos" typify one point of this paper. They summarize my response to the invitation offered by those who organized this conference. Their inscriptions are a significant example of how new evidence requires review of accepted historical reconstructions not only in the immediately affected area of scholarship, but also in other fields related to it. In this case the second field, New Testament and ancient Christianity, is much larger than the first, Samaritan studies. Such discoveries have a "ripple effect" as they move from the primary field, the point of impact, to secondary areas. Usually those secondary areas are touched only very slowly by the new data. Sometimes they are not reached at all (Smith, 1983).

Before I move to my next example, let me briefly review the implications of these inscriptions for the study of Diaspora Judaism. The most obvious point to make of course is that what can be said for the Samaritan Diaspora might also be true—even more true—for the Jewish Diaspora in the Mediterranean world. The new Samaritan data indicate, first of all, that the Samaritans were at home in the Greek world. Since there are four or five generations between the earlier inscription and the later one, the Samaritans were a permanent settlement on Delos. They knew Greek customs and the Greek language, and the two benefactors and their fathers bore Greek names. But the Samaritans' tie to the Holy Land is just as obvious, and that is the second point. It was Mount Gerezim which was the center of community identification.

In the third place, the evidence does not fit the standard reconstructions of Samaritan religious history. That story always seems to take place in Palestine, and in ancient times in the area west of the Jordan, north of Judah and south of Galilee. The new evidence calls into question the old critical orthodoxy, particularly where that older view has been appropriated for use in other disciplines (in this case, New Testament and ancient Christianity). Topics such as "Samaritan Christianity" or "Samaritan influence on the New Testament" take on a very different perspective if one must factor in relatively early Greek-speaking communities on Greek islands far to the west of Mount Gerezim.

And this is the fourth and final point: it is evidence from the Mediterranean Diaspora that raises new issues and brings the scholarly pot to boiling. Samaritanism, like Judaism, is seen to be in some sense a Hellenistic religion, with all that implies. If Dura and Sardis raise questions for those who study the Jews of late antiquity, the Delos evidence—small as it is—should make a similar difference in Samaritan studies. Further, it suggests that "Samaritan studies" and "Jewish studies" may be related in ways we had not expected, at least in the Greco-Roman world. I say this because the earliest Jewish synagogue found in the Mediterranean Diaspora is also on Delos, only 100 meters away from where these two inscriptions were discovered (Kraabel, 1979, 491-494).

III

My first example dealt with some very new evidence and its implications for a limited area of scholarship. The second is much more complex and much better known. With it, the emphasis shifts from the Hellenistic period of the Delos inscriptions to the time of the early Roman empire, specifically, the first seven or eight decades of the early Christian movement.

What I want to take up now is embedded in the Christianity of those decades. It is part of the following central question in the beginnings of this religion: "how did Christianity move from Palestine to the Mediterranean Diaspora?" While this may seem a historical topic, it is at bottom a theological one. Our answer to that question also reveals our view of the relationship between ancient Christianity and the powerful cultural and religious forces and ideas which surrounded it, both Greco-Roman and Jewish. Our answer to that question also says a great deal about our understanding of the New Testament itself. It reveals much about how we would in fact approach the question of "the other" in Judaism or Christianity in this period.

My subject initially, then, is Christianity. The Jews of the early Roman empire are involved in that story, but in a curious way. They were not of direct interest either to those who created the historical record in the first place or to most of those who have studied it since. Indeed not only was there no concern to create a full and accurate picture of those Jews, there were powerful reasons to falsify the records and to tell a slanted and partial story about them. This biased, ostensibly historical account was essentially theology, or a *piece* of a theology. But it was theology in historical guise it was taken as history almost from the first by Christians writing after the New Testament was completed and also by later scholars right up to our own day.

However this conference is concerned with Jews, not with Christians, and despite what I have just said about Christianity, Jews are my focus also. I want to look again at the image of Roman Empire Jews which was created by certain very influential New Testament texts. I am particularly interested in the Jews of the Mediterranean Diaspora, since it is with them that the distortion has been most severe. In the New Testament the central texts are Acts and the letters of Paul. The examples with which I wish to make my present point are taken from events and issues which Acts and Paul's letters have in common.[2]

Acts

Acts is the longest book in the New Testament. It begins in Jerusalem with the disciples, and ends with Paul in Rome. That makes it a story of movement. First, the Christians move from Palestine to the Mediterranean Diaspora, and thus, second, from the Jewish world to the gentile one. That is, from being a Jewish sect, they become a Greco-Roman cult. But third, this is also, and most importantly, a theological movement, since the author ("Luke") is chiefly concerned to explain and justify Christianity's departure from Judaism and its transformation into a gentile religion. My purpose is to characterize the implications of all of this for the understanding of Jews and Judaism. To do that in brief compass, I will limit myself to an examination of three terms central to what Acts seems to be saying about Jews.

The first term is "synagogue." This word appears nineteen times in Acts. It is used there chiefly as the place where Christian Diaspora missionary preaching begins, and, with one exception (Apollos, in 18:26), Paul is the preacher. Indeed, after his conversion (9:1-19)

---

[2] For the background to what follows, see my more detailed article (Kraabel 1981).

Paul's first act is to preach in a synagogue (9:20). This is striking when one considers Paul's well-deserved reputation as Apostle to the Gentiles. However Paul's mission to the Jews of the Diaspora synagogue soon arouses opposition and is finally all but fruitless; in 19:9 he pulls the disciples out of the synagogue in Ephesus, and after that, no Christian in Acts goes into a synagogue again.

So conflict appeared to be inevitable. Three programmatic statements made by Paul in rejection of Diaspora Jews highlight this situation. First, in chapter thirteen, after a dispute in the synagogue of Antioch in Pisidia on the southeast coast of Asia Minor, Paul is made to say, "It was necessary that the word of God should be spoken first to you. Since you thrust it from you, and judge yourselves unworthy of eternal life, behold, we turn to the gentiles. For so the Lord has commanded us saying, 'I have set you to be a light for the gentiles, that you may bring salvation to the uttermost parts of the earth'" (verses 46-47, citing Isaiah 49:6).

Then in chapter eighteen, there is a similar dispute farther west, in the Greek City Corinth. As a result, Paul says, "Your blood be upon your heads! I am innocent. From now on I will go to the gentiles" (18:6). Despite this declaration, however, Paul returns to preaching in Diaspora synagogues until 19:9.

The third programmatic statement, as I have termed them, comes in Rome at the end of a rather peaceful discussion between Paul and Jewish leaders there. Paul terminates the conversation surprisingly with two blistering verses from Isaiah followed by this final statement of his own: "Let it be known to you then that this salvation of God has been sent to the gentiles; they will listen" (28:25-28). Two verses later Acts ends.

Obviously, despite his title "Apostle to the Gentiles," Paul in Acts has a great deal to do with Jews. Nearly every time the word synagogue is mentioned, he is involved. And the plot is predictable: time after time he enters the Diaspora synagogue to offer the Christian message, and each time the Jews reject him. As a result, as he moves across the Mediterranean world from east to west, from Antioch to Corinth to Rome, having no choice but to disavow the Jews because they first rejected him and his message. But as a reconstruction of the historical situation in Paul's time, this is all highly suspect, as we shall see when we look at the letters of Paul directly.

The second term from Acts is "proselyte." This word occurs three times in Acts, and only once in the rest of the New Testament. It is that fourth occurence, however, which is by far the best known. It is of course the saying in Matthew 23:15 about the scribes and Pharisees who "traverse sea and land to make a single proselyte, and when he becomes a proselyte, you make him twice as much a child of hell as yourselves." A detailed picture of first-century Judaism as an aggressive missionary religion has been anchored in that obviously polemical saying in Matthew. In view of that, it is remarkable how little Acts makes of the idea. Even more remarkable is that the rest of the New Testament omits the term completely.[3]

The third and last term translates as "God-fearer." It is a term which Luke invented, and it is much more frequent than "proselyte." It occurs in the New Testament only in Acts, where it appears eleven times (Kraabel, 1981, 114-115 with notes). The precise word-combinations in Acts which are usually translated "God-fearer" do not occur outside the New Testament at all, in Christian or Jewish texts. A related Greek adjective, *theosebes*, is found in Jewish inscriptions. There its status as a technical term is disputed. It is frequently argued, however, that *theosebes* in the inscriptions means the person in question was in fact a God-fearer.

As used in Acts, "God-fearer" is usually taken to designate gentiles interested in Judaism and frequenting the synagogue, but not yet converts. Converts would be "proselytes." The archetypical God-fearer is Cornelius, a Roman officer in Caesaria. Acts spends a chapter and a half telling his story (10:1–11:18). With the exception of Cornelius, all God-fearers in Acts are associated with the Diaspora synagogue and with Paul.

In ten of the eleven instances in Acts, the God-fearers are sympathetic to Christianity—so much so that they often become a key factor in scholars' accounts of the earliest Greek-speaking Church. Indeed Acts is often used to construct a history of the earliest Christian mission in linear fashion, from Jews in the Holy Land to Diaspora Jews to God-fearers to other Gentiles, those without particular interest in Judaism. This progression often serves to explain why the last group is the largest of the four by the middle of the second century.

The chief problem with the progression idea is that the God-fearers so quickly disappear from Acts. They are out of the picture even before the Diaspora Jews. Not only are there no references to God-fearers elsewhere in the New Testament, they disappear in Acts as well after 19:19, when Paul withdraws permanently from the synagogue. They are found only in the middle third of the book, while the progression hypothesis would imply that, just at that point, God-fearers should appear in the narrative in increasing numbers.

---

[3] On the *crux interpretum* in 13:43, "God-fearing proselytes," see the standard commentaries.

After the rejection of the Jews, the gentiles closest to Diaspora Judaism should next come into consideration. But during Paul's two year sojourns in Ephesus, Caesaria (the home of Cornelius!) and Rome, subsequent to 19:9, while the new religion is spread in these new gentile cities, the God-fearers never appear.

As I indicated, we would not have the term "God-fearer" if it were not for Luke. It is a tribute to his skill as a story teller that the God-fearers have become so much a part of the traditional story of early Christianity and also a part of many histories of Diaspora Judaism. Michael Avi-Yonah called the God-fearers a "numerous class" of gentiles in the time of the Roman empire (Avi-Yonah, 1976, 37). The *Encyclopedia Judaica* states that there were "perhaps millions" of God-fearers by the first century (10:55). Luke's "theology in historical guise" has become religious history for many historians of Judaism, both Jewish and gentile.[4]

Paul

In Acts, "synagogue" and "God-fearer" are almost always associated with Paul. If we examine Paul's own writings, what more do we learn about the Diaspora Judaism which is supposed to be connected with these terms? The answer is, very little. The terms "synagogue," "proselyte" and "God-fearer" never appear in Paul's letters. This is not because Paul is not interested in fellow Jews; that concern is frequent in his letters, and it is immediate and personal. He is earlier than Luke by a generation, and the issue of the non-Christian Jews is very much alive for him. He cannot understand why they cannot accept the Messiah he has found, and their rejection troubles him greatly. Further, he reveals no knowledge of the Lucan idea that Judaism is only a stage which Christianity passes through on its way to the gentile world, quite the contrary. The climax of his profound letter, Romans, is a section of great passion and great pathos in which he insists almost desperately that sometime, somehow Jews and Christians will be a unity again under a common God (Stendahl, 1976: 23-40).

So while the traditional scholarship would tell us three important things about the Jews of the Diaspora which at the same time are said to be very significant to the ministry of Paul, none of the three has left any trace in Paul's letters! All derive wholly from Acts. They are as follows: 1) Christian missionary work in the Mediterranean world began in the Diaspora synagogue—that is the conclusion to be drawn

---

[4] I borrow this useful phrase from J. Neusner, who uses it in a different but related context (Neusner, 1984, 251).

from the story of Paul which is told in Acts. But 2) the Diaspora synagogue had its own missionary activity going. There may not have been many converts, but there were many gentile sympathizers or"God-fearers."

These first two ideas have had great influence on the usual understanding of the Diaspora synagogue and Diaspora Jews. In later centuries, as the Church gains numerical and political power after Constantine, and when the third theme of Luke begins to receive more attention, they become sinister. Luke's third concept is that the rejection of Christianity by the Jews and the movement of Christianity to the gentile world were all part of the plan of God. They were not accidental; they were divinely intended. It became increasingly common to use this piece of Lucan doctrine to justify turning the Jews in the Christian Roman empire into second class citizens wherever possible. Their status could justifiably be held to the lowest level; that was the proper thing to do. Jews had put themselves there by choosing to reject the Christian message when it was first offered them. And there was theological justification for it as well—after all, it was part of what God Himself had planned.

Acts (again)

This view drawn from Acts had a serious negative effect on the relations between Jews and the Christian Roman empire. Jews were the single ethnic group whose low status had a theological warrant.

A review of both the archaeological and literary evidence suggests that this was not at all Luke's intent. He was actually going in a different direction. In fact, the treatment of synagogues and God-fearers in Acts is one more example of theology in historical guise. Luke had two major, related theological issues on his mind which relate directly to the question of "the other." The way he tells his story in *Acts* allows him to address both.

The first, which we have already alluded to, is this: why the split between the Jews and Christianity? Christianity was, after all, a Jewish sect claiming to have discovered the true Jewish Messiah Luke's answer is on two levels: on the surface, the split involved rejection by the Jews, who had been given full access to the new movement and time and again had spurned it. At a deeper level, of course, this rejection was part of that great divine plan—a plan which in Luke, but not in Paul, leaves non-Christian Jews behind forever.

Less commonly recognized is Luke's other major theological issue, that is: what justifies Christians in going to work among gentiles after having left the Jews behind? In the first century, and for two or three centuries after Luke's time, Christianity continued to be attacked by its enemies as a renegade Jewish sect, one which lost any claim to legitimacy when it repudiated its own origins and went after gentiles (Wilken, 1984, 112-117; 184-196). Luke's God-fearers are the first theological response to that charge. Luke says that it was legitimate for Christians to offer their faith to gentiles precisely because of this precedent in Judaism. In Acts, Diaspora Jews are shown to have done exactly the same thing even before Christianity began. The God-fearers were the result. If Jews could make their religion available to gentiles, Christians could as well. The Jewish mission which produced the God-fearers justifies the later Christian mission. This is the part the God-fearers play in Acts. Their theological purpose is to povide a precedent, and thus a justification, for the Christians' gentile mission. The God-fearers are on the stage as needed, off the stage after they have served their purpose in the plot. It is a tribute to Luke's dramatic ability that they have become so alive for the later church, but the evidence from Paul's own letters, and now from archaeology, makes their historicity questionable. Perhaps it cannot be demonstrated conclusively that there was never a circle of God-fearers associated with ancient Judaism. But what I am arguing is rather that, at least for the Roman Diaspora, the evidence presently available is far from convincing proof for the existence of such a class of gentiles.

Further, if we cannot rely on the presence of the God-fearers, then the traditional understanding of the make-up of Diaspora Judaism may need to be reconsidered. I will return to that at the end of this paper.

Excursus: the Aphrodisias Inscription

I want to conclude this section of the paper with a reference to another inscription, this one still unpublished. (Mellink, 1977; Kraabel, 1981, 125 note 26; see also Rajak's paper in the present volume). When it appears, the evidence I have just summarized, both Jewish and Christian, will all be reviewed again, so it is appropriate that I say something about it today.

This Greek inscription, discovered in 1976, dates from the second or third century and comes from Aphrodisias in Caria, in southwestern Asia Minor. The memorial, or monument (*mnema*) of some sort, is the longest Jewish inscription ever to come from Asia Minor, and one of the longest anywhere. It is not clear whether it comes directly from a synagogue. It consists chiefly of a list of names and occupations, some eighty lines of them in all. A great number of men are being recognized for some unclear reason.

The name list is in two parts. The first is the longer and contains such "Biblical" names as Samuel, Benjamin, Joseph and Judas, whereas the names in the second part of the list are nearly all Greek. The second part of the list is headed *kai hosoi theosebis* (sic), translating as: "and (the following) who (are) pious." The word *theosebes*, which I have translated as "pious," is the closest the Jewish inscriptions come to one of the terms in Acts which is usually translated "God-fearer." Thus, as soon as it is published, this inscription will become *the* central piece of epigraphic evidence in the God-fearer discussion.

Is this a list of "gentiles who are sympathetic to Judaism but have not converted"? That is possible. But in literature and inscriptions *theosebes* does not have a single meaning. Sometimes it is used of persons who are clearly Jews. In other texts it just as clearly designates gentiles who have never been in contact with Jews at all; the earliest example in Sardis is Croesus, the sixth century king of Lydia, the one with all the gold (Herodotos calls him *theosebes* in the first book of his *History* 1. 86.2).

Another example, much closer to the date of Acts and of this inscription, is a famous anti-Christian graffito from Rome, from the Paedagogium under the Palatine Hill. It shows a boy kneeling before a crucified figure with the body of a man and the head of a donkey. The legend beneath reads: "Alexamenos worships god," and the vocabulary is precisely that found in Acts (Väänänen, 1966, 209-212, no. 246). Clearly, we are not dealing with an accepted technical term of one and only one meaning.

Let me suggest an alternative explanation for the Aphrodisias inscription, which at the same time will help to illustrate several issues before this conference. The traditional understanding of Diaspora Judaism appears to assume that to be sympathetic to Jews—to be pro-Jewish—means to be interested in the Jews' religion. From this perspective, for gentiles and Jews in the Greco-Roman world the question of "the other" was a religious one, leading perhaps to an interest in conversion. Yet it is possible simply to be friendly toward Jews as one's neighbors or fellow-townspeople. Such, I believe, was the case at Sardis (Kraabel, 1983). The synagogue there suggests Sardis gentiles acknowledged that Jews had a proper place in the city; they belonged there as an ethnic minority. However, persistence in seeing Judaism in antiquity first of all as a religion has made it hard for many people to understand openness towards Jews in anything other than religious terms. But to have Jewish friends or to take a positive toward Jews need not mean—either today or in antiquity—an interest in changing one's religion. If some of Aphrodisias' *theosebeis* are gentiles, as it appears they are, they could be nothing more than gentile "good neighbors" whom the local Jews wanted to honor. That too is a legitimate relationship to "the other."

The inscription is soon to be published by Joyce Reynolds of Cambridge University. One thing is certain: every article written about it thereafter will trot out these eleven texts from Acts, and much of what I have just talked about will be rehearsed again. Indeed, I would predict that most discussions of the Aphrodisias inscription will take Luke's "theology in historical guise" as straight history instead, with predictable results. As Jack Neusner often reminds us, once established, scholarship's critical orthodoxy is very slow to change.

IV

Pascha in the Greek of the Bible may mean "Passover" or "Easter." It was over *pascha* that Christians had one of the longest of their early battles, from the second century until well into the fifth. The dispute is almost forgotten now, but it was one of the two main causes for the very important Council of Nicaea in 325 (Athanasius *Epistula de Synodis* 5 = PG 26.688B). Although this dispute was wholly within the Church and did not involve non-Christians, it is usually linked to another even larger issue, the relation of Christianity to its parent religion, Judaism. From the details of this dispute, many scholars have drawn significant conclusions about Diaspora Judaism. These I wish to examine briefly here.

Socrates, the fifth-century Church historian, introduces a discussion of the *pascha* controversy at the time of Nicaea by making the observance that some eastern Christians "preferred to observe the festival (of Easter) in a more Jewish fashion" than was acceptable to the majority of the Church (Socrates 1.8). If this appears to be something like a rapprochement with Judaism, decisions with reference to *pascha* by the later fourth-century Church Council at Laodicaea have been taken much further, as evidence for "actual religious fellowship" between Jews and Christians; specifically, scholars see Christian participation in Jewish Passover observance. But allusions to Jewish practices and to Jews in the ancient Church are often not what they seem. This is particularly true when the context is some part of the gentile world outside Palestine. Several of the most problematic references to "the Jews" come from two assemblies of bishops in Phrygia, one at Pazos, the other (just mentioned) at Laodicaea. Both occur about a half-century after Nicaea and both have to do with *pascha*.

The synod of Pazos was a local meeting of Novatianist Christian bishops. Bishops of the state church did not attend, nor did Novati-

anist bishops from the west or from Constantinople. These bishops at
Pazos altered their practice in regard to Easter, deciding "to observe
the Jews as they are doing the feast of unleavened bread (*ta azyma*),
and with them to carry out the festival of Easter (*to pascha*)" (Socrates
4.28).

This is striking for the following three reasons: first, if the decision
constitutes a move toward conformity with Judaism, that is a stance
very different from Novatian's own as regards the Jews. Novatian was
a Roman presbyter, and wrote at least three treatises on things Jewish
in the middle of the third century. One concerned the Sabbath,
another circumcision (both lost), and one was about Jewish foods. At
the beginning of the *de cibis Iudaicis* he calls the Jews *perversi . . . et
ab intellectu suae legis alieni*, and attacks their blindness and ignorance. This was apparently the burden of the two lost works, and it
surely characterizes *de cibis Iudaicis*, which goes on to interpret the
Old Testament in allegorical fashion. (Novatian was no heretic; he
and his followers went into schism as the result of what they
considered to be lax treatment of *lapsi* after the Decian persecution.
Nor was he without intellectual gifts; his *de Trinitate* is a major and
wholly orthodox piece of early Latin theology.)

Second, the Pazos decision has been attributed to Montanist
Christian influence. Another fifth century church historian, Sozomen,
links the two splinter groups and makes it clear that, in Phrygia,
Montanists and Novatianists both celebrated Easter on a date different
from that of the state church (7.18). But Montanism is an unlikely
cause of the Novatianist practice. There was little common in the
origins of these two groups beyond an opposition to what both saw as
moral laxity among the majority of Christians. A century before
Novatian, Montanism had begun as an apocalyptic and charismatic
sect within Phrygia itself. It never enjoyed the kind of official
acceptance which—as we shall see—the Novatianists briefly gained in
the fourth century.

Third, the Pazos decision to "celebrate *pascha* with the Jews" was
counter not only to the practice of Novatian himself but also to that of
Novatianists elsewhere in the fourth century (Socrates 4.28). In the
west and in other parts of the Church—Constantinople, for example—
their Easter observances were the same as those of the majority. This
becomes clear in the story of the Novatianist bishop of Constantinople, Acesius, whom Constantine, in an irenic gesture, invited to the
Council of Nicaea. Acesius strongly reasserted the Novatianist position on *lapsi*, but acknowledged that the majority view on the date of
Easter was also his position, one which he considered to have
apostolic warrant (Socrates, 1.10).

Some decades later the Pazos decision gained a new champion, a converted Jew named Sabbatios who had been ordained a priest by the Novatianist bishop Marcian (Andresen, 1971, 280-282). Sabbatios was aggressive (and probably self-serving) in his demand that all Novatianists fall in line with the Pazos decree. In response, another synod of Novatianist bishops was called, not in Phrygia this time, but at Sangarum in Bithynia. There, Sabbatios asserted that it was "mandatory that the festival (i.e. *pascha*) take place when the Jews are holding their observance" (Socrates, 5.21).

The response to Sabbatios by the Novatianist bishops goes a long way toward clarifying just what was at stake. It points the direction toward a correct understanding of what the real issues were. The bishops decided that the matter was an *adiaphoron*, a matter of indifference, for in earlier times Christians had observed Easter in different ways and that had not split the Church. So Novatianist Christians should not divide over the issue now. In observing Easter, then, Christians should follow the practice each preferred. "It ought to make no difference as regards Christian fellowship; those who celebrate in different ways are nevertheless in concord with the Church" (Socrates, 5.21).

Two conclusions may be drawn from the Sangarum decision. The first is that even among the Novatianists the issue was wholly an intra-Christian one about the method for dating Easter. Socrates' reference to the strength of Sabbatios' Jewish preconceptions even after his ordination should be seen as a diversion (Socrates 5.21). No Novatianist had ever been so innovative as to suggest either a common *pascha* celebration between Christians and Jews or, alternatively, Christian participation in Jewish Passover rites. No group of bishops, Novatianist or not, would have called that an *adiaphoron*.

But the important point to observe is that the Novatianists at Sangarum did not demand an end to that form of Easter observance which Pazos had required. Even though the majority of Novatianist and non-Novatianist Christian leaders would not have supported it, even though as we shall see Constantine himself had opposed any form of celebration which might be associated with "the Jews," the Novatianists did not rule out the kind of Easter which Sabbatios had been demanding.

This tolerance has never been satisfactorily explained. What I am suggesting is that the answer to this question lies not in the character of the Diaspora Jews of this area, but in the strength of a particular aberrant Easter tradition in Phrygia and neighboring areas in the interior of Anatolia. I will describe this tradition in a few moments.

The broad-mindedness of the bishops at Pazos would not have

been acceptable to earlier Church leaders in the west. Nor would Constantine have permitted it; to him, divergences on the Easter date were a threat to the unity of the Church. In a united church it was a scandal to have Easter celebrated on different dates in different places. After Nicaea, Constantine addressed a letter to the bishops on precisely this matter (preserved in Eusebius, *Vit. Const.* 3.18). So Pazos particularly would appear to be a direct challenge to the wishes of the Christian state.

It is impossible that Constantine's dictum would not have been known to the bishops at Pazos. How is their decision to be explained then? Well, as so often in the fourth century, the reasons appear to be more political than theological and more internal than external to the Church. After Constantine's death the situation had become more difficult for the Novatianists. First, under Constantine's son Constantius (ruled 337-361), Novatianists and orthodox alike suffered at the hands of Arian Christians supported by the emperor. In one instance the bishop of Constantinople was able to have government troups sent against the Novatianists. (Socrates had it from an eye witness that the Novatianists armed themselves with sickles and hatchets and killed most of the soldiers [Socrates 2.38].) Valens, emperor from 364 to 378, also persecuted the Novatianists (Socrates, 4.9). And it was during the reign of Valens that the Pazos decision was taken. The Novatianists, then, were feeling considerable pressure from the Constantinople government. Their need to gain support against the state Church caused the Pazos bishops to move in a "Jewish" direction. That decision must have strengthened the Novatianists' position in Phrygia and the neighboring parts of inland Anatolia where the "more Jewish" method of Easter dating was favored. For after Pazos, Sabbatios would gain followers particularly in Phrygia and Galatia where his "Jewish" way of observing Easter was the traditional one, according to Sozomen (7.18). Socrates too notes that among Sabbatios' followers were "particularly those who had come from Phrygia and Galatia" (5.21).

Phrygian Novatianists and Montanists must have realized that they could expect only opposition from Constantinople. Both groups, it appears, deliberately underscored the differences between the Constantinople authorities and local Phrygian Christians over Easter practices. Their intent would have been to gain support in the interior of Anatolia by coming out in favor of an ancient and traditional practice which the central authorities, civil and religious, had attacked (Andresen, 1971, 275;280).

However, Constantine's wishes prevailed in the end. He had assured the eventual collapse of their position, and any similar way of dating Easter, by tying them firmly to an unacceptable dependence on the "blind," "sinful" and "wicked" Jews. Given his concerns for unity, as emperor and as Church leader, there may have been no other position for him to take.

In the fourth century, divergence in Easter dating was no small matter. The pressure for uniformity in the state church had begun even before Nicaea. For instance the first canon of the Council of Arles (A.D. 314) is precisely *ut uno die et tempore pascha celebretur*. According to Athanasius there were two chief issues at Nicaea: the Arian controversy and the fact that Christians in Syria, Cilicia and Mesopotamia "customarily observed *pascha* with the Jews" (*Epistula de Synodis* 5 = PG 26.688B). Eusebius, who sided with Constantine on this issue, nevertheless noted that a quarter of the bishops at Nicaea did not (*De solemnitate paschali* 8 = PG 24:701). Nor did the Council settle the matter; six times in the two decades following, Rome and Alexandria celebrated the festival on different dates (Hefele-Leclercq, 1907, I.1.419). While the lack of uniformity between these two major Christian centers was a scandal to those concerned with unity, neither position could be stigmatized as "keeping *pascha* with the Jews." Despite the attack by Constantine, "keeping *pascha* with the Jews" would continue to be popular in the Anatolian interior into the fifth century.

After Sangarum, Sabbatios continued to press for his understanding of Easter. He and his followers began to meet apart from other Novatianists. Finally, at a meeting held in a place called Xerolophos, he tried to insert his position into scripture itself. While reading aloud from a gospel text which referred to Passover, he interpolated, "cursed be the one who celebrates the *pascha* outside (the days of) unleavened bread" (Socrates, 7.5). This put considerable distance between him and the majority of Novatianists. The "followers of Sabbatios" soon became a distinct group, recognized as such by other Christians. Our earliest sure reference to this separation is from the early 390's (Didymus the Blind, *de Trinitate* = PG 39:420A). In a civil law of 413, "deserters and fugitives from the company of the Novatianists" are directly condemned (*CTh* 16.6.6). Other attacks on Sabbatianoi and Novatianists occur in laws of A.D. 423 (*CTh* 16.5.59) and A.D. 435 (*CTh* 16.5.65).

My thesis in this part of the paper is that these condemnations are the proper background for understanding the puzzling references to the Jews in the decrees of the Council of Laodicaea, the later fourth-century meeting mentioned earlier. Marcel Simon has called them "among the most particularly anti-Jewish canons in the entire conciliar literature" (Simon, 1964, 382). James Parke saw them as strong evidence of an "actual religious fellowship" between Christians and Jews which the bishops at Laodicaea intended to bring to an end (Parke, 1934, 176). But the bishops' concern may have been over Christian issues, not with Jews at all. Neither Simon nor Parkes could have known of the strength of Judaism in this part of Asia Minor. The bulk of that evidence has appeared since they wrote; it comes chiefly from Aphrodisias (already discussed) and from Sardis in nearby Lydia. The excavations at Sardis yielded remains of the largest ancient synagogue ever found, and more Jewish inscriptions than had been known from all of Asia Minor previously (Kraabel, 1983). These discoveries prompted a reexamination of all the evidence for the Judaism of western Asia Minor. For Sardis at least, the impression is of self-confident Jews, at home in the gentile world while at the same time quite concerned for the maintenance of their ancestral traditions and piety. The Jewish evidence now suggests much more contact with pagans than with Christians at least until after the reign of Julian (361-363). Since the great majority of Christians in Asia Minor after the second century were gentiles, not converted Jews, there is no reason on the Jewish side for any kind of rapprochement with Christians. This is a point worth emphasizing, since the earlier understanding of the Laodicaea canons assumes in local Jews a propensity, and even an eagerness, for religious interaction with their Christian neighbors.

Here is how the Anatolian "Easter controversy" began. Lydia and Phrygia had been a center of controversy over Easter since the middle of the second century. This was because they were the home of Quartodecimanism, the ancient practice of dating the *pascha* by the Jewish date for Passover, a custom which could correctly be described as "keeping *pascha* with the Jews." Because Passover falls on a fixed date in the first Jewish (lunar) month Nisan, any weekday might be designated for Passover—and for the Quartodeciman Easter which depended on it. Ultimately this practice goes back to the gospel of John (Fischer, 1976; Beckwith, 1979).

The first "council" of Laodicaea occurred about A.D. 164; the only issue had been the dating of Easter, and the big dispute (*zetesis polle*) had been between two kinds of Quartodecimans—what would become the orthodox position in the fourth century and later was not even represented (Eusebius, 4.26; Fischer, 1976: 19-21). Most of the early leaders of the church in this area were Quartodecimans, and the tradition endured into the fifth century (see Socrates, 7.29 about events at Sardis). But being a Quartodeciman most assuredly did not mean being sympathetic to Judaism or to one's Jewish neighbors. Perhaps the best known Quartodeciman of all, the late second-century bishop of Sardis, Melito, is also the author of a decidedly anti-Jewish paschal sermon (Kraabel, 1971). Eric Werner once called him "the first poet of deicide" (Werner, 1966).

In the fourth century, before the Council of Laodicaea, the synod of Pazos and the subsequent successes of Sabbatios suggest that the "Jewish" method of dating Easter remained strong in the area around Laodicaea well after Nicaea. The bishops at Laodicaea, who took a general position against a number of heresies, may have felt the need for caution when it came to the condemnation of traditional local practices. In order to assert the position of the majority in the Church in regard to the *pascha*—a position not popular around Laodicaea—they worked indirectly, attacking "Jewish" practices within the Church. What they were implying, without stating it directly, is that the Quartodeciman Easter must be seen to be wrong despite its antiquity and its support in Phrygia, e.g. at Pazos. It was wrong because it was "Jewish"; it depended on the Jews.

The details in Socrates' accounts lead to this conclusion. Despite a positive attitude toward the Novatianists generally, Socrates had no sympathy for the kind of Novatianists represented by the Pazos bishops and Sabbatios, and he was persistent in his efforts to blacken them by linking them to Judaism. As Socrates describes it, the decision at Pazos was "to celebrate the festival of *pascha* with them," i.e. the Jews (Socrates, 4.28). His concern to tie "Sabbatianism" to Judaism is introduced when he first describes Sabbatios as a convert still dominated by "Jewish preconceptions" (Socrates, 5.21). Immediately before he recounts the events at Xerolophos which will divide the followers of Sabbatios from the rest of the Novatianists, he spends a page telling of a crippled Jew whom Atticus, bishop of Constantinople, had healed in baptism; while this miracle converted pagans, it could not convince other Jews to accept the faith. The point Socrates wishes to make is clear enough.

The language of Socrates probably reflects the usual way these practices were described by their opponents in the fourth century and later. According to Socrates, many Christians in the east favored observing Easter "more Jewishly" (Socrates, 1.8). What they were doing could be described as "following the Jews" or "celebrating the festival with the Jews" (Socrates 5.21 and 5.22). Their partisans were "those who wholeheartedly favored following the Jews now" (5.22). Sabbatios' followers are "those who separated from the Novatians over the Jewish *pascha*" (7.25). It is this issue, then, rather than any accommodation between gentile Christians and non-Christian Jews, which appears to lie behind the rulings of the Council of Laodicaea. Let me conclude this section of the paper by turning to that Council.

Simon identified seven canons of the Council as being concerned with this issue: 7, 16, 29, 35-38; only the last two referred explicitly to Jews (Simon 1964: 382-383). Canon 7 gives the procedures by which Novatianists, Photinians and Quartodecimans may be received into the Church. Simon holds that these are "Judaizing" groups; but "Judaizing" need not imply interaction with Jews or participation with them in Jewish rites. Canon 16 requires that "gospels with other scriptures" be read on the sabbath, Saturday. Those who presupposed Christian participation in Jewish rites in the Phrygia of this period suggested that Christians and Jews were holding religious observances on Saturdays at which only the Old Testament was read; this canon then would have forced the use of Christian texts at those meetings, and presumably made it impossible for Jews to participate. But Saturday and Sunday were the two days of the week recognized by the Council for Christian religious observance (see canons 49 and 51); so this canon is more likely to be concerned to assure a service with scripture readings on Saturday as well as on Sunday. The canons closest to it are also concerned with the proper conduct of services.

Canon 29 goes on to attack "Judaizing," specifically, refraining from work on Saturday. The bishops hold that Christians should observe Sundays as a rest day "if possible," but should work on Saturday in any case. Again, their target is a "Jewish" practice, not association with Jews.

Then canon 35 forbids, as "secret idolatry," the cult of angels. This had been a problem in the area around Laodicaea since the first century—witness the New Testament letter *Colossians* 2:18 (Simon 1971, 126-128. Colossae is some ten miles east of Laodicaea.) The pagan cult of angels is well attested in Phrygia; it developed into the cult of Saint Michael the Archangel, which has its beginning in this area in the fourth century and then moves west (Rohland, 1977, 69-73; Sheppard, 1982).

As for canon 36, it prohibits the making of *phylakteria* by priests; nor are they to be *magoi*, enchanters, *mathematikoi* or astrologers. While *phylakteria* recalls the "phylacteries" worn by Jews in the New Testament, it here has its more common meaning of "amulet." Again, no mention is made of Jews.

Canon 37-39 appear to go together, though Simon did not include the last one on his list. Their general theme is the avoidance of contact with three groups of unacceptable persons: pagans, heretics and Jews. Forbidden are "holding festivals together with" Jews or heretics (canon 37) or pagans (canon 39), and "participating in" Jewish impieties (canon 38) or pagan atheism (canon 39). More particularly, Christians are not to receive "festival gifts" from Jews or pagans (canon 37). Specifically, in what appears to be an extension of this canon, they are not to accept "unleavened bread" from Jews (canon 38).

It is canon 38, of course, which has been used to suggest that Christians had been joining in Passover observances with Jews. But this now seems unlikely for at least three reasons: 1) from what we know now about Phrygian and Lydian Jewish communities, it is improbable that such an invitation would come from the Jewish side; 2) the chief concern of the Council is not with pagans (mentioned once) or Jews (mentioned twice) but with heretics (canons 7, 8, 9, 31, 32, 33, 34 and 37). This is the situation generally in the church after Nicaea: the enemy is not outside but within. 3) In the heavily gentile Christianity of fourth-century Asia Minor, something as bizarre as Christian participation in the Jewish Passover would surely have occasioned a much more explicit and elaborate protest than the half-dozen words in canon 39. Constantine's dictum on the Easter controversy indicates how devastating it could be to be associated with the Jews merely in the dating of a purely Christian festival. Joining in a Passover observance would have gone far beyond that, and surely called for a thunderous response from the Council of Laodicaea and beyond.

If this reconstruction is correct, then the bishops at Laodicaea were not facing the issue of Jewish and Christian joint rites, or of Christian participation in Jewish Passover ceremonies. There is no evidence here for Christian relations with non-Christian Jews. Something which we thought we knew about Anatolian Judaism turns out to be without documentation; a significant point in the old hypothetical reconstruction of Diaspora Judaism needs to be corrected. The problem at the Council was rather to assert the orthodox position on the dating of Easter in a part of Anatolia where an alternative method was quite deeply embedded. Montanists and Novatianists had appropriated local Easter customs as their own, and had gained temporary support thereby. Sabbatios would continue the same line in a decade or two at Sangarum, and take it much farther at Xerolophos.

In Phrygia in the late fourth century it is highly unlikely that Christians would be treated so obliquely if they were in "actual religious fellowship" with the local Jews, as Parkes thought. What the Council of Laodicaea did was to tie Jews, pagans and heretics together in a joint condemnation in order to undercut a "Jewish" practice regarding Easter. This way of dating Easter had to be attacked because it was at variance with the State church and thus divisive. But the attack had to be made indirectly; the practice itself was old and deeply embedded in local Christianity. The subject was a volatile one, and worse, it was open to exploitation by non-orthodox groups.

Pazos had already shown that, and before long Sabbatios would do it again.

V

Let me draw some conclusions quickly. The *pascha* controversy in the fourth century illustrates four things. 1) It indicates how "Jews" in older reconstructions of the history of that period in the Mediterranean Diaspora are often phantoms, fictional characters in disputes taking place between Christian groups. The archaeological evidence for western Asia Minor shows substantial Jewish communities there, but they did not always conduct themselves in the way later historians had assumed. The *pascha* controversy also illustrates (2) that references to "Jewish" practices do not necessarily indicate the presence either of Jews or of non-Jews sympathetic to Judaism. The "others" are not what they seem.

References to Jews occur in many places in the Christian literature of this period: in the sermons and theological treatises of course, but also in the martyr-acts and in that genre called *adversus Judaeos* literature.[5] Yet there was little interest on the part of non-Jews in studying these Jews dispassionately or in portraying them objectively. This leads to two further conclusions: 3) the "information" which we thought we had about these Jews and their Judaism must now be viewed with great skepticism, for from the Christian sources at least, we really know less than we think we know; 4) but that also requires taking a second look at what is sometimes called the "anti-Semitism" of this period (Sandmel, 1978; Gager, 1983). The tensions between Jews and gentiles may have been greater or less than they appear. There was no uniformity of treatment, and it would be misleading to assume that what held for one period or location was true necessarily for another. There is no way to tell until each source has been tested first for its inner biases.

It was somewhere between the time of Luke and the time of the historian Socrates that the general racism of the Roman empire became refined into the theological anti-Judaism well known in later Christian history (Sherwin-White, 1970; Balsdon, 1979). Such events as the *pascha* controversy help it along even though "real Jews" were not involved in that battle between Christians. That is a point of some significance for a proper understanding of this period in the history of Judaism!

---

[5] A more detailed study of this literature, against the background of new methods and data for ancient Judaism, is being prepared by Robert S. MacLennan, doctoral candidate in Ancient Studies, University of Minnesota.

In the texts from the New Testament, however, the Jews are real enough. They are a matter of great concern, to Paul in one way, to Luke in another. Here it is possible to see the beginnings of the theological manipulation of the story of the Jews from the Christian standpoint.[6] Paul has a personal concern for Jews which is also theological. Luke, on the other hand, presents stylized Jews, characters in a story which has already moved some distance away from him and into the past. Neither author is concerned to present a full and unbiased picture, and perhaps no one expects that. But Luke's God-fearers are just one more example of how quickly the Christian movement could begin to embellish and transform its image of the Jews of the recent past even when there were still eyewitnesses alive who—had they been so minded—could have set the story straight.

I included the Samaritan evidence from Delos first because it was so recently discovered. More important, it is an example of how one piece of new information can help to shift an entire field to new level of complexity and clarity. In this case the evidence comes from the Mediterranean Diaspora, a circumstance which gives it a larger place in the historical record. For Samaritans as well as for Jews, it is the happenings in Palestine which are the better known. Because the Diaspora is much less well attested, the historical reconstructions of it which are commonly used must often be highly hypothetical. Any new evidence from that direction must receive particularly careful scrutiny because of its potential for rearranging the entire construct. That occurred with Dura and it is happening with Sardis in relation to the Jewish Diaspora. The Delos discoveries will have a comparable impact on Samaritan studies.

One of the best known images of Judaism for the medieval church was a figure of a blindfolded woman, *synagoga caeca*, the "unseeing synagogue" unable to perceive the truth of the Christian message. But if the synagogue was "unseeing," it was just as much *unseen*, unclear and obscured to those outside.[7] The Diaspora synagogue is still unclear in many ways. Diaspora Judaism plays all too small a part in the history of Judaism in late antiquity. In the first and second centuries, the situation must have looked very different. The best pattern for success would have been someone like Josephus. He attached himself to one of the most powerful of Romans, was removed

---

[6] A study of the history of interpretation of Acts in this regard is being prepared by Paul Stuehrenberg, doctoral candidate in Ancient Studies, University of Minnesota.
[7] See Klein (1978) and Kraabel (1982, 460-464), and also recent summaries of the anti-Jewish bias in the most influential of ancient church historians, Eusebius, by Grant (1980, 97-113) and Barnes (1981, 169-172, 181-186).

from Palestine, and began writing in Rome in Greek for a Diaspora audience of gentiles and Greek-speaking Jews.

In this period many more Jews lived outside the Holy Land than within it. If you were a young Jew living, say, in the time of Akiba, wondering where your future would be the brightest, the cities of the Mediterranean Diaspora would have been much more desirable than anything in Palestine. Indeed they were more promising, and remained so for several centuries thereafter. For the reasons I have illustrated, the story of these millions of Jews has not been well told in the sources available. That record was compiled almost exclusively by non-Jews. Not only was it incomplete, it was also completely overshadowed by the abundance of rabbinic literature from farther east, much of it indeed from outside the Roman world completely. Now there are new sources—from archaeology primarily—and, more important, new methods and a clearer view of the problem. They must have their impact on the conventional view of the subject.[8]

I polished the conclusions of this paper while on an extended vacation trip through the west coast of the United States by train. My other companion was Eberhard Busch's 1976 biography of the Swiss theologian Karl Barth. As I got the last form of these sentences ready for the word processor, I also observed my fellow passengers—nearly all of them non-Jews—and I read about Barth's career in Germany, and then in Switzerland after his dismissal by the Nazis. I could not help wondering what Europeans between the Wars and Americans in the 1980's—and the hosts of other gentiles before them—would have thought "a Jew" to be if the Mediterranean Diaspora had had its fair share of coverage in the historical record along with Babylonia and Palestine in late antiquity. When the Diaspora synagogue of late antiquity became invisible to the non-Jewish world in the West, the negative effects went far beyond the realm of scholarship. Correction of those distortions, even as late as this, can have unusually broad salutary effects.

Bibliography

Andresen, C.
1971   *Die Kirchen der alten Christenheit*. Stuttgart.

---

[8] To give just one example: in the Mediterranean Diaspora, at least, it seems likely that the major "Jewish symbol" was not any particular form, such as the *menorah* or the lion, but the building itself and the Torah (shrine) within it. On the general subject, and especially on the work of Erwin R. Goodenough, see Smith 1967, Neusner 1981, and Neusner 1984, 143-180.

Avi-Yonah, M.
1976 *The Jews of Palestine.* Oxford.
Balsdon, J. P. V. D.
1979 *Romans and Aliens.* Chapel Hill.
Barnes, T. D.
1981 *Constantine and Eusebius.* Cambridge MA.
Beckwith, R. T.
1979 "The Origin of the Festivals Easter and Whitsun." *Studia Liturgica* 13: 1-20.
Bruneau, P.
1982 "Les Israélites de Delos et la juiverie délienne." *Bulletin de Correspondance Hellénistique* 106: 465-504.
Bull, R. J.
1976 "Gerizim, Mount". IDBS 361.
Busch, E.
1976 *Karl Barth.* Philadelphia.
Coggins, R. J.
1975 *Samaritans and Jews.* Atlanta.
1982 "The Samaritans and *Acts.*" *New Testament Studies* 28: 423-434.
Collins, J. J.
1983 *Between Athens and Jerusalem.* New York.

Encyclopedia Judaica. Jerusalem, 1971.

Fischer, J. A.
1976 "Die Synoden im Osterfeststreit des 2. Jahrhunderts." *Annuarium Historiae Conciliorum* 8: 15-29.
Gager, J. G.
1983 *The Origins of Anti-Semitism.* Oxford.
Grant, R. M.
1980 *Eusebius as Church Historian.* Oxford.
Hefele, K. J. and Leclercq, H.
1907 *Histoire des conciles.* I. 1. Paris.
Hengel,
1974 *Judaism and Hellenism.* London.
Isaac, B.
1983 "A Donation for Herod's Temple in Jerusalem." *Israel Exploration Journal* 33: 86-92.
Kippenberg, H. G.
1971 *Garizim und Synagoge.* Berlin.
Klein, C.
1978 *Anti-Judaism in Christian Theology.* Philadelphia.

Kraabel, A. T.

1971 "Melito the Bishop and the Synagogue at Sardis: Text and Context." *Studies Presented to George M. A. Hanfmann.* Edited by D. G. Mitten, J. G. Pedley and J. A. Scott. Cambridge MA. Pages 77-85.

1979 "The Diaspora Synagogue." *Aufstieg und Niedergang der romischen Welt: Geschichte und Kultur Roms im Spiegel der neueren Forschung,* II.19.1: 477-510.

1981 "The Disappearance of the 'God-fearers'." *Numen* 28: 113-126.

1982 "The Roman Diaspora: Six Questionable Assumptions." *Journal of Jewish Studies* 33:445-64 (special number in honor of Yigael Yadin).

1983 "Impact of the Discovery of the Sardis Synagogue." *Sardis from Prehistoric to Roman Times.* Edited by G. M. A. Hanfmann. Cambridge MA. Pages 178-190.

1984 "New Evidence of the Samaritan Diaspora has been Found of Delos." *Biblical Archaeologist* 47: 44-46.

Mellink, M.

1977 "Archaeology in Asia Minor." *American Journal of Archaeology* 81: 306 (on the Aphrodisias inscription).

Montgomery, J. A.

1907 *The Samaritans.* Philadelphia.

Neusner, J.

1981 "The Symbolism of Ancient Judaism: The Evidence of the Synagogue." *Ancient Synagogues: The State of Research.* Edited by J. Gutmann. Chico CA. Pages 7-17.

1984 *Ancient Judaism: Debates and Disputes.* Chico CA.

Pummer, R.

1979 "New Evidence for Samaritan Christianity?" *Catholic Biblical Quarterly* 41: 98-117.

Purvis, J. D.

1976 "Samaritans." IDBS 776-777.

Robert, J. and L.

1983 "Bulletin épigraphique." *Revue des études grecques,* pages 123-124, no. 281 (on Bruneau 1982).

Rohland, J. P.

1977 *Der Erzengel Michael, Arzt und Feldherr.* Leiden.

Sandmel, S.

1978 *Anti-Semitism in the New Testament?* Philadelphia.

Scobie, C. H. H.

1972 "The Origins and Development of Samaritan Christianity." *New Testament Studies* 19: 390-414.

Sheppard, A. R. R.
 1982 "Pagan Cults of Angels in Roman Asia Minor." *Talanta* 12-13:77-101.
Sherwin-White, A. N.
 1970 *Racial Prejudice in Imperial Rome.* Cambridge UK.
Simon, M.
 1964 *Verus Israel.* Paris.
 1971 "Remarques sur l'Angélolatrie Juive au Début de l'Ere Chrétienne." *Comptes rendus de l'Académie des Inscriptions & Belles-Lettres.* Pages 120-134.
Smith, M.
 1967 "Goodenough's *Jewish Symbols* in Retrospect." *Journal of Biblical Literature* 86: 53-68.
 1971 *Palestinian Parties and Politics that Shaped the Old Testament.* New York.
 1983 "Terminological Boobytraps and Real Problems in Second-Temple Judaeo-Christian Studies." *Traditions in Contact and Change. . . Proceedings of the XIV Congress IAHR.* Edited by P. Slater and D. Wiebe. Winnipeg. Pages 295-306.
Stendahl, K.
 1976 *Paul among Jews and Gentiles.* Philadelphia.
Väänänen, V.
 1966 *Graffiti del Palatino, I: Paedagogium.* Helsinki. No. 246, pages 209-212 (the Alexamenos inscription).
Werner, E.
 1966 "Melito of Sardis, the First Poet of Deicide." *Hebrew Union College Annual* 37: 191-210.
Wilken, R. L.
 1984 *The Christians as the Romans Saw Them.* New Haven.
Wright, G. E.
 1965 *Shechem: The Biography of a Biblical City.* New York.

10
Jews and Christians as Groups in a Pagan World

Tessa Rajak
University of Reading

"The other" is certainly most threatening when he is proximate. But there is also a force of attraction: while the two sides fend one another off (not necessarily in a balanced or equal way), they are also drawn together. I am concerned less with theories of "the other," as such, than with theory as expressed in values and in behaviour—the patterns of life of people or groups of people. But the two—theory and action—have, of course, an intimate (if not a parasitic) relationship, and when we know how people act we can find a new meaning in their theories. The main theme at this point is Jewish groups, with the early Christians figuring by way of comparison and contrast, in respect of the way they face a pagan outside world and refer both inwards and outwards. Although Jewish-Christian relations have been a leading theme in our conference, this paper casts the pagan Gentile in the role of outsider, looking at the Jewish Diaspora in the Greek world of the first centuries A.D.

A Greek synagogue inscription found in 1931 by excavation at Stobi in Macedonia, and dating, it seems, from some time in the third century A.D. records the benefaction of one Claudius Tiberius Polycharmus, son of Achyrios. In fulfillment of a personal vow, this man, by his name a Roman citizen but evidently a Jew, has apparently donated a building he owns for use as a synagogue. The institution will have a dining room and meeting hall attached (τρίκλεινον = triclinium, and τετραστοόν), and he and his heirs will retain the upper storey for their own purposes. No one is to interfere with these arrangements, on pain of being fined by the "patriarch".[1]

Perhaps the most revealing and unexpected statement is Polycharmus's opening description of himself—ὁ πατὴρ τῆς ἐν Στόβοις

---

[1] *CIJ* I, 694; see M. Hengel, "Die Synagogeninschrift von Stobi", *ZNTW* 57 (1966), 145-183; also in J. Gutmann (ed)., *The Synagogue* (1975), 110 ff; for further bibliography, see Hengel n. 2, and (especially on the site), A. T. Kraabel in *ANRW* II, 19, 1 (1979), 495.

συναγωγῆς ὃς πολιτευσάμενος πᾶσαν πολειτέιαν κατὰ τὸν Ἰουδαϊσμὸν. This is not readily translatable, but in the light of Martin Hengel's interpretation, it might be rendered as "father of the Stobi synagogue, who has been fully active in communal affairs for the purposes of Judaism". Of course, the word used for the man's sphere of operation, πολιτέια, has deeper implications than are suggested by the English. Though it can have both a strong and a weaker sense, the connection with *polis* is inescapable, and the connotation of an independent, self-contained and constitutionally-defined unit is always there.

I am not going to make assertions now about Jewish citizenship, at Stobi or elsewhere, or to put forward claims about a separate and autonomous Jewish political body, the so-called πολιτεύμα, which has become a popular subject for scholarly theorizing.[2] Incidentally, Hengel too avoids putting his feet into that morass. I am not concerned here with the technical question of Jewish status at all. But what Hengel has established leads to other interesting implications and consequences; that is, that the sentence must at any rate be a way of referring to the donor's involvement with the Jewish religion and not at all a matter of acting in the interests of Judaism within the larger *politeia,* the city in which Polycharmus lives. There is no very close verbal parallel to be cited for this use of the term *politeia,* but the sense should not be doubted. The expression is in fact somewhat clumsy. Nonetheless, there is significance in the odd choice of words, for a *politeia* is a complete political and moral framework for a citizen, not just a set of external rules, and to be engaged in "politics" is part of the fabric of the life of a Greek. Here, therefore, "Judaism" appears as an alternative framework, as it were, supplying a Jew with a substitute *polis.*

How far in the Stobi case that *politeia* is to be identified as resting on the single institution of the Stobi synagogue is not clear, though what does emerge from the inscription is that the synagogue was (or was claiming to be) the only establishment of the kind in that city and that, with its eating facilities and hall, it was considerably more than just a place of worship. This corporate body, then, would appear to constitute a primary group affiliation for Polycharmus, to the exclusion, we might be tempted to think, of the pagan city around him.

Such an impression is derived in less vivid but equally distinct ways from a multitude of Diaspora Jewish inscriptions coming from

---

[2] See A. Kasher, *The Jews in Hellenistic and Roman Egypt* (1978; Hebrew with English summary); S. Applebaum in *CRINT* I, 1 (1974), chap. 9; E. M. Smallwood, *The Jews under Roman Rule* (1976), 359-361 etc.

the Greek-speaking east of the Roman empire (Stobi, incidentally, is somewhat anomalous in being, as Hengel points out, a primarily Latin-speaking town, in spite of the Greek language of our inscription). One thinks of graves, for example, which bear a valedictory formula such as τῷ λαῷ χαίρειν, hailing the deceased's co-religionists and identifying him until the end, or rather, beyond it, as a member of that "people" (a group of whom—not all, even within his own city—must of course have been personally known to him).[3] One thinks, too, of the separate and explicit hierarchy of status and office associated with a community or an individual synagogue, and of the way an individual's place within it is so often attached to his name, for example: *archisynagogus, archon, prostates,* or perhaps "father of the synagogue" as in the case of Polycharmus. These partly honorific titles may even be assigned to women or small children, and in that respect they operate in a manner strikingly analogous to the titles of civic office in the Greek city at large.[4] The appearance is therefore one of a parallel alternative society. It is a phenomenon which can be more fully delineated within another, not unrelated grouping, that of Pauline Christianity. Indeed, this has recently attracted interest, especially that of Wayne Meeks in *The First Urban Christians.* Meeks writes of the Christian groups' conception of themselves as an *ekklesia*—a term, in fact, scarcely found within Diaspora Judaism or paganism—and studies the "language of separation" which Pauline groups used to distinguish those who did not belong from those who did.[5]

But there are revealing differences. It is paradoxical that while Christianity discarded the (supposed) rigours of the law and of Jewish purity requirements (I shall come back shortly to some doubts about these), it was among Pauline Christians that the drawing of boundaries appears sharper and more complete, the alternative language, value-system and structure more overwhelming. That, at any rate, is the impression we get, although we do have to make allowances for the imbalance of our sources, since we possess a Pauline literature, but virtually no Diaspora-Jewish one for this period. The second apparent difference is also difficult to assess, and for the same reason. The Pauline communities seem often to be most conscious of themselves not so much as part of a big movement, but as small sub-groups,

---

[3] See L. Robert, *Hellenica* III (1946), 103.
[4] See now B. J. Brooten, *Women Leaders in the Ancient Synagogue*, Brown Judaic Studies 36 (1982).
[5] W. A. Meeks, *The First Urban Christians: The Social World of the Apostle Paul* (1983), 84-96.

especially as individual households or families. This division into
small units or cells is entirely intelligible in terms of the way
Christianity grew from small beginnings and spread in the cities. And
in these terms, too, it makes sense that Jewish groups should be more
centralized. Still, the pattern was probably quite varied among the
Jews, and larger cities such as Antioch certainly had more than one
synagogue; in that instance, we do not know whether the worshippers' basis of distribution was purely geographical or not.[6]

My purpose, however, is to try to correct another imbalance
brought about by our sources. For these are produced in and for
sectarian contexts, and aim, broadly, at mutual encouragement (what
today might be called "consciousness-raising"). So they deliberately
stress self-differentiation and group identity. What they are responding to, in fact, is a contrary pull which is always there—that exerted
from the outside by the wider community. Again, this must have
affected Christians and Jews in contrasting ways, for among the early
Christians, most would have come directly out of the world of the
Gentile city and have been linked with it by many ties of affinity, habit
and sentiment. This is perhaps why they need stronger marks of
separation. The Jews, apart from proselytes and "God-fearers", have a
different past; theirs goes right back to early Hellenistic times when
the Greek cities were often ethnically exclusive, closed units. There
was a pattern of separate Jewish communal development, but with
inclinations on the part of some to participate in the general community as, for example, those who sought entrance to the gymnasium
(and probably to citizenship) at Alexandria under Claudius. Such
people were probably secure in their identity and had worked out a
balance of loyalties over generations. Still, this same general point
applies to both Jews and Christians: the impression of total apartness
is illusory, so what in fact we must look for is an interplay between
group identity on the one hand and a relationship (perhaps ambivalent) with the Greek city on the other. Clearly, this will not be a
simple matter.

It is the outward-looking tendencies which I wish to explore and,
in particular, one aspect of the relation between monotheists and the
world around them. Let me introduce this by recalling that on the day
of a pagan festival it was considered undesirable for a Jew to banter
with a Gentile (*Tos. Av. Zar.* 1, 2). The rationale, evidently, is that one
thing leads to another and, before he knows where he is, the

---

[6] On households, etc., see Meeks, *op. cit.*, 29-31; 75-77; on the synagogues at Antioch,
W. A. Meeks and R. L. Wilken, *Jews and Christians in Antioch in the First Four
Centuries of the Common Era*, Sources for Biblical Study 13, (1978), 8-9.

gregarious Jew may find himself taken up in the festival crowd. Of course, the recommendation was meant for Eretz Israel and there, in Galilee at least, Jews lived surrounded by a Jewish majority (as Martin Goodman has emphasized).[7] So perhaps it would not have been too difficult to reserve one's humour for one's co-religionists. But in the Diaspora the situation is entirely reversed. Pagans could not be so easily avoided, and it is hard to see how the normal casual intercourse could have been artificially suppressed without grave damage to good manners and good relations.

This is all the more true since the round of festivals was continuous, and pagan occasions were woven thickly into the fabric of the Greek city's year, especially during the period of the Roman empire. One could not put it better than Gibbon does, writing about the predicament of the Christian (in his 15th chapter): "the innumerable deities and rites of polytheism were closely interwoven with every circumstances of business or pleasure, of public or private life; and it seemed impossible to escape the observance of them without, at the same time, renouncing the commerce of mankind and all the offices and amusements of society." And again, "the dangerous temptations which on every side lurked in ambush to surprise the unguarded, he (the Christian) believed, assailed him with redoubled violence on the days of solemn festivals."[8] It was not merely a question of temple ceremonial; athletic and musical contests for professionals and for locals, oratory and theatrical performances, clowning and pantomime, public feasts and processions, all were included among the festivities dedicated to the local deities, to major gods, or to the divine emperor—or to all three. Not only temples, theatres and stadia, but even the town squares would be taken over. Sacrifice was an integral part of these public celebrations, just as libation was part of any private festive occasion. With the latter, too, Gibbon has some fun at the expense of early Christian Puritanism (such disapproving attitudes were, be it noted, rarely shared by the Jews, though the pressures were the same for both groups): "The Christian, who with pious horror avoided the abominations of the circus or the theatre, found himself encompassed with infernal snares in every convivial entertainment, as often as his friends, invoking the hospitable deities, poured out libations to each other's happiness."

Festivals dominated the city. In one way, this had a symbolic value. In the 2nd century A.D. the orator Dio of Prusa, in a speech to the Rhodians, could say that the celebration of civic festivals (along

---

[7] M. Goodman, *State and Society in Roman Galilee* (1983), chap. 4.

[8] Edward Gibbon, *The Decline and Fall of the Roman Empire*, chap. 15.

with sitting in council) was part of the Greeks' traditional way of life
and by it, they could show themselves better than the rest of the
world. This was best of all if the games made their city dignified
(σεμνήν), with the spectators watching quietly and applauding only
by smacking their lips (ποππυσμός, *Oration* 31, 162-3); for cities were
represented at one another's festivals and also competed in the
splendour of these occasions.[9] Festivals were also of material importance. They generated market trade (this earned Olympia the name
mercatus Olympicus);[10] they occasioned distribution of money and
(sacrificial) meat; and at least until the third century A.D., they
stimulated the flow of funds from the community's benefactors, who
received in exchange personal prominence and prestigious office. In
the case of competitive games, a special official (often called the
agōnothetēs) administered and presided; on other occasions city
magistrates, who were in many ways involved with the local cults,
were in the forefront. For such people, these were highly significant
opportunities to make grand appearances.[11]

To be outside all this was to be effectively outside the city—which
is exactly how some of the early churchmen, especially Tertullian,
exhorted their flocks to see themselves. Is that where we are to locate
the Jewish communities of the Diaspora of the Hellenistic-Roman
world?

While it was utterly incompatible with Judaism to participate in a
sacrifice, let alone to touch sacrificial meat, what did being present as
an uninvolved spectator signify? What if one was present as a
dignitary? What if one was a performer in a contest ultimately
dedicated to a deity? Are we to interpret the familiar cry of misan-
thropy found in so many pagan authors to mean that the Jews utterly
absented themselves from the city's best moments, that they substi-
tuted the rhythms of their own calendar and their own ritual, and
operated purely as self-contained groups?

If the Rabbis of Palestine and their emissaries (*shelikhim*) were
influential, then the answer is to an extent determined. For the aims
and presuppositions of the code in Mishnah and Tosefta, *Avodah
Zarah*, are to create not, admittedly, hostility to idolatry, but still a
clear distancing from anything associated with it or the appearance of
it.[12] This extremely protective form of separation was built, as usual,

---

[9] S. Price, *Rituals and Power: The Roman Imperial Cult in Asia Minor* (1984), 128.
[10] R. MacMullen, *Paganism in the Roman Empire* (1981), 26.
[11] Price, *loc. cit.* (n.9), 122.
[12] See W. A. L. Elmsley, *The Mishna on Idolatry: 'Aboda Zara* (Cambridge, 1911); M. Hadas-Lebel, *ANRW* II, 19, 2 (1979), 397-485, esp. 426-441.

into an intricate system of purity regulations, whose dynamic we are beginning to grasp through the work of Jacob Neusner.[13] The Rabbis were not in entire agreement, but the differences between the milder opinion and the more severe on any issue was only a matter of degree, with the premises unchanged. Thus, while it will have made a substantial difference to trade which view prevailed: either R. Ishmael's view that "for three days before their festivals and for three days after them it is forbidden [to have any business with them]" or the Sages' (*hakhamim*) view that "before their festivals it is forbidden, but after their festivals it is not forbidden"—either way it was transparently clear that the objective was this: to give the festival a wide berth and avoid being pulled into it (M. Av. Zar. 1, 2). Likewise, the necessity of avoiding contact with libation wine was overriding, leading to the rule that "if libation wine fell into the vat, it is forbidden to have any benefit at all from any of it" (M. Av. Zar. 5, 10), and the concession of Rabban Simeon b. Gamaliel, that "it may all be sold to the Gentiles excepting the value of the libation wine that is in it" was no more than a slight softening.

We may be disposed to believe the stories about the travels of Rabban Gamaliel and his fellow scholars from Jamnia, but even if we do, and are prepared to accept the pleasant notion that they preached and argued *halakhah* in the synagogues of Rome (Ex. Rabbah 30, 9 etc.) there is still, I think, no reason to take it that outside Israel those same stringent standard of purity were set, or that the Rabbinic *halakhah*, so far as it had been formed, was transferred there.[14]

It is interesting that the Mishnah has a provocative question on idolatry put to the "elders in Rome" (M. Av. Zar. 4, 7). "If God does not wish an idol to exist, why does He not destroy it?" suggests, perhaps, that the Roman Jews tossed aside Rabbinic ideas on the subject. The answer was as follows: "If idolators worshipped an object not essential to the world, He would destroy the idol. But they worship the Sun, Moon, Stars and Planets. Is He to destroy the world because of fools?" And there was more, for even that did not, apparently, put an end to the interrogation: "Even if it be so, He ought to destroy those objects which are not essential to the world and leave those which it requires." They replied, "Then He would just be supporting the beliefs of the worshippers of these things, in that they would say 'Know that these are gods, for look, they are not destroyed.'"

---

[13] See *The Idea of Purity in Ancient Judaism* (1973), together with *A History of the Mishnaic Law of Purities*, vols. I-XXII (1974-1977).
[14] See S. Safrai in *CRINT* I, 1 (1974), 209.

Tessa Rajak

Judaism in the Hellenized Diaspora can have been adequately
defined by the cult's basic components—Sabbath observance (of one
kind or another),[15] circumcision (though even this, perhaps, with
reservations).[16] study of the Torah, the keeping of the feasts, and ritual
washing.[17]

The evidence of the Pauline Epistles (together with Acts), while
putting a heavy stress on the burdensome aspects of the law of Moses,
in fact does not suggest that the observance of Diaspora Jews
amounted to more than the essentials. These basic requirements in
themselves, had they been imposed on Christians, would have been
trouble enough for a Gentile convert. It is true that Paul's complex
instructions about the consumption of meat from idols, which he did
not ban for Christians but from which they were none the less
exhorted to abstain for the sake of the weaker brethren,[18] make great
play with stressing the more restrictive approach of the Jews (I Cor. 9,
20-25). But it is not surprising for us to learn that such meat (or any
un-kosher meat) was strictly forbidden to Jews. What we should note
is rather that nothing further is suggested by Paul about Jews shun-
ning the many manifestations of paganism around them. Yet I suspect
that at the same time, the *Tendenz* of these Christian texts is in fact the
cause, or part cause, of the vague but widespread notion that Diaspora
Jews led rigidly closed-in lives, separating themselves uncompromis-
ingly from the normal forms of existence.

Whether the Palestinian Rabbis perceived the adherents of such a
basic Judaism as *minim* (heretics) or as mere *ammei ha-aretz* (uneducated peasants) I would not venture to say, but, at any rate, a baraita in
the name of either R. Ishmael or R. Simeon ben Eleazar makes it clear
that the opinion was not favourable. "Israel outside the land (of Israel)
are idolators. In what way? If a gentile held a banquet for his son and
invited all the Jews in his town . . . notwithstanding that they eat their
own food and drink their own wine and are served by their own
servant, the scripture charges them, as if they had eaten of the
sacrifices to the dead, as it is written (Ex. 34, 15): 'And they call thee
and then eat of their sacrifice' " (*T. B. Av. Zar.* 8a; *Tos. Av. Zar.* 4(5),

---

[15] On the question of the Sabbath, see R. Goldenberg, "The Jewish Sabbath in the
Roman World", *ANRW* II, 19, 1 (1979), 414-447, especially 429.
[16] So J. J. Collins in this volume.
[17] On these components, see Goodman, *op. cit.* (n.7), 102, where he neatly cites
Mekhilta together with Justin Martyr.
[18] See G. Theissen, "The Strong and the Weak in Corinth: a Sociological Analysis of a
Theological Quarrel", *The Social Setting of Pauline Christianity: Essays on Corinth*
(transl. J. H. Schutz, 1982).

6).[19] It may, further, be the case that we should read the iconographic remains of this Diaspora Jewry as suggesting special leanings to symbolic mysticism, in the way that E. R. Goodenough did. (This is a question which deserves more attention than it has received, but which is now beyond my scope.) Here I wish to see what light is shed by epigraphic evidence, not directly on the beliefs of those who produced the inscriptions, but simply on their behaviour within the city.

I am not presenting any entirely new material and much of what is relevant has long been available. But let me turn first to a major document which is not yet widely known but which has circulated in unpublished form and already excited discussion and disagreement.[20] This is the long dedicatory inscription of a memorial (μνῆμα) invoking divine aid (θεὸς βοηθός) erected by a society (πάτελλα) of Jews and sympathizers or God-worshippers (θεοσεβεῖς) from Aphrodisias in Caria. These men (and one woman–Yael α προστάτης, "leader") are in some sense responsible to (ὑποτεταγμένοι) a further grouping, a δεκανία), (*minyan?*), of those described as φιλομαθῶν (hakhamim?) and παντευλογ(ητῶν). (The import of that is less clear.) They are, it would appear, an exclusive and inward-looking group, with their own values and, almost, a sub-language; they have made this dedication out of their own funds, and it is an entirely private phenomenon. We do not know where the stone originally stood, nor do we know its date, though it has to come from after the middle of the second century and may belong to the early third (with the reverse possibly added even later). This uncertainty is unfortunate; still, even for a late inscription, what we have here is noteworthy as evidence not only of the separate corporate identity (for certain activities) of a group of Aphrodisian Jews and quasi-Jews, but also for its opposite—their involvement in the city. This emerges not only from the first list of subscribers, who appear to be full Jews, together with three proselytes and two isolated *theosebeis* (for some reason), but also from the second section, headed καὶ ὅσοι θεοσεβῖς (sic). In this group, none of whose names are markedly Jewish, we have no fewer than nine individuals labelled as councillors (βουλευτής). As befits their importance, they appear at the head of the list. Further down we have what seems to be a boxer (Ἀλέξανδρος πύ [κτης]), though some have doubted the supplement,

---

[19] Cf. the Christian discussions at the Ancyra Council of A.D. 314 (can. 7): see Y. Baer, *Scripta Hierosolymitana* 7 (1961), 90 and n.38.

[20] Shortly to be published by Joyce Reynolds (with others) as a Cambridge Philological Society monograph. I am very grateful to her for allowing me to use her transcription and comment.

and a man whose profession is certainly listed as athlete. (For reasons which are uncertain, some but not all of those listed are given a professional description.)

While it may be significant that no councillors or sportsmen are to be found among the fully committed, it is to my mind equally deserving of comment that, together with Jews, we find here registered as participating members of one and the same organization (for study, prayer, eating or burial?) a number of "Sympathizers"—outsiders who have simply attached themselves to Judaism. For there can be no doubt that at the very least the "God-worshippers" named in the first list have been allowed to belong. And it is probable that those of the second list are also a part of the club since, after all, they contribute to the same private memorial. Yet the second list contains men who still describe themselves proudly as city councillors, and presumably operate as such. It also contains men who perform professionally in the games. And all this, it should not be forgotten, was in a city dedicated to and enthusiastic about the cult of the goddess after whom it was named, a city which in the second century A.D. boasted a great number of traditional agonistic events. Nor does there appear to be any embarrassment or difficulty for the councillors about identifying themselves openly with a Jewish group.[21] We should remember that in a Greek city the council house itself might well contain an imperial altar (as at Miletus and Ephesus).

There exist other known cases of persons who have names usually regarded as Jewish and who are councillors and city officials—again mostly from the first half of the third century A.D. In the Sardis synagogue were found several fragmentary inscriptions recording the fulfilment of vows by men who are titled βουλευταί and, in two cases, also Σαρδιανοί, citizens of Sardis.[22] Unfortunately, many other inscriptions from the Sardis synagogue remain unpublished. For Corycus, Cilicia, there is a sarcophagus bearing an incised menorah and the name Αὐρ (ηλίου) Εὐσανβατίου Μενάνδρου Κωρυκιώτου Βουλευτοῦ. This could be dated after A.D. 212, because of the name "Aurelius". And here too the man is not only citizen but also councillor.[23]

Two Phrygian tombs, which Robert traces back to the Jewish community of Acmonia in Phrygia, are identified as Jewish by the imprecations they carry. The first calls down "the curses of Deu-

---

[21] As pointed out by Joyce Reynolds.
[22] L. Robert, *Nouvelles inscriptions de Sardes* (1964), 55-6.
[23] Robert, *loc. cit.* (n.22); *CIJ* II, 788, corrected slightly in *Bulletin épigraphique*, 24, (1954), 103-4.

teronomy" on anyone who tries to intrude upon the burial.[24] It
belongs to Aurelius Phrougianus son of Menocritus and his wife. His
offices are listed at the side as *agoranomos, sitones, paraphylax,
strategos,* and furthermore, "he has carried out all the magistracies
and liturgies." The second is also erected for a couple, and the man
has been a councillor and archon and has lived virtuously (ζήσας
καλῶς). Since it is not the custom for Jews to identify themselves
verbally on such monuments as Jews, it is theoretically possible that
all these individuals were *theosebeis,* like the Aphrodisias councillors—though to my knowledge this has not been suggested. Against
this view, a name like Eusambatios is parallelled by similar constructions among the Jews in the Aphrodisias inscription but not among the
God-worshippers. The councillors with Jewish names are probably,
then, Jews. How many God-fearers or sympathizers might figure in
the epigraphic records, as councillors and in other capacities, without
being identifiable as such, we cannot tell, but we should remember
that in this direction our knowledge is seriously incomplete.

A wholly Jewish official is the "curialis" (πολιτευόμενος) spoken of
by Malalas (290), one Asabinus, who, around A.D. 190, sold his
property so that a municipal building could be erected on it. Here the
obvious fact is underlined that he, like all the councillors and city
dignitaries we have mentioned, was a man of means. In fact, that may
have been partly why these people were pressed into service at a time
when there were fewer public benefactors coming forward in the
cities. It has even been suggested to me that some of these individuals
may have made the liturgical (in the Greek sense) contributions
appropriate to their office without actually performing as officials—in
the way that some Christians appear to have done for pagan priest-
hoods in early fourth century Spain, as we learn from the records of
the Council of Elvira.[25] Whether there were corresponding developments in the integration of non-élite Jews, indeed whether we are to
see them as sharing the same circumstances at all, is probably an
unanswerable question.

With the problem of the Sympathizers, and their relation to the
proper Jews, we may perhaps hope for some further advance. For it
will by now have become evident that the Aphrodisias inscription
sheds new light on the meaning of that problematic term θεοσεβῖς.
There is no doubt that what they are here is a separate and distinct
category of people, less fully Jewish than the others (it is not merely

[24] *Hellenica* X, (1955), 249-51.
[25] In A.D. 306; see E. J. Jonkers (ed), *Acta et symbola conciliorum quae saeculo quarto
habita sunt* (1974), no. 1, can. 3. I owe this suggestion to A. E. Wardman.

a question of origins, for the proselytes have evidently taken new Jewish names) and bearing the epithet as a special label. Yet this is exactly the sense of the term which has been disputed by those who wished to see it merely as a description which might be used to qualify "Jews" by stressing their monotheistic piety.[26] It has to be admitted that at least sometimes the word means more—or rather less—than that, and that there exists such a thing as a semi-proselyte. It is reasonable to go further and take it that the "God-fearers" referred to eleven times in Acts(as φοβούμενοι or σεβόμενοι τὸν θεον) are members of that same class of the partially-committed, in spite of the minor divergence in terminology.

This takes us straight to the inscription, found many years ago *in situ* on the seats of the theatre at Miletus, which comes from the Roman period but cannot be closely dated (a dating of second to third century A.D. would seem right on epigraphic grounds). Here, Schürer's idea that in τόπος Εἰουδέων τῶν καὶ θεοσεβίον (sic), which strictly means "place of the Jews who also are called God-worshipp-ers," we should read τόπος Εἰουδέων καὶ τῶν θεοσεβίον—"place of the Jews and of the God-worshippers"—now gains in appeal.[27] There are two sub-groups named here. Although the Greek, taken as it stands, is incorrectly formulated for this meaning, it is not unusual to find ungrammatical constructions, improper idioms and simple errors of word transposition in this kind of provincial notice. In my view, the text should be interpreted in the light of parallel evidence and especially, now, of the clear statement from Aphrodisias. These few Milesian words offer, in a way, almost as much food for thought as the longer inscription. For again, we have the two groups taken as one, this time not by self-identification but by the external agency which allocated to them the privilege of special seats in the civic theatre. And we have unequivocal testimony to the fact that both groups were regular, prominent and respected among the theatre audiences. They would of course have watched not only plays embodying pagan mythological scenes, but also mime, farce and dance of every kind. Sometimes they would have seen gladiatorial shows (Dio of Prusa, *Or.* 31, 121), sometimes pagan religious ceremonial as well. And all were dedicated, as Tertullian insisted (*de Spect.* 95 ff.) to "those degenerate

---

[26] As L. H. Feldman, "Jewish 'Sympathizers' in Classical Literature and Inscriptions", *TAPA* 81 (1950), 200-208; L. Robert, op. cit. (n.22), 41-45; A. T. Kraabel, "The Disappearance of the God-fearers", *Numen* 28 (1981), 113-26. For bibliography on the subject, see Kraabel, 124 n.7.

[27] *CIJ* 748; E. Schürer, *Geschichte des jüdischen Volkes im Zeitalter Jesu Christi*[4] (1909), III, 174; H. Hommel, *Istanbuler Mitteilungen* 25 (1975), 167-95.

gods, Venus and Liber", with the path to the theatre coming directly
"from the temples and altars, from that miserable mess of incense and
blood, to the tune of flutes and trumpets".[28]

An even more telling association of the two groups (the Jews and
God-fearers), in actual worship can also be demonstrated, though it
appears in an inscription which originates in a part of the empire more
remote from Mediterranean custom. One of the interesting first
century A.D. Jewish manumission inscriptions from Panticapaeum on
the North coast of the Black Sea (part of the Pontic kingdom, and once
Mithridates' stronghold, but also subject to Hellenic influence since
the days of early Greek colonization) concludes with the usual
formula that the freed slave, who is to be untrammelled by any
obligation except to continue with Jewish worship, will be under the
care of the synagogue of the Jews and God-fearers (ἐπιτροπευούους τῆς
συναγωγῆς τῆς Ἰουδαίων καὶ θεὸν σέβων).[29] Whether this is the same
institution as the one mentioned in other inscriptions[30] and described
as just τῆς συναγωγῆς τῶν Ἰουδαίων, we cannot say.

It is worth mentioning at this point that two other Bosphoran
inscription (of A.D. 41) from Gorgippia, appear to show Jewish
manumitters subscribing to the customary pagan oath formula, "by
Zeus, earth and sun."[31] But we should not lean too heavily on this
testimony, first because the text of the first was apparently tampered
with at some stage and, secondly, because the dedication is always to
the Most High, Omnipotent God, who may or may not be a version of
the Jewish deity; even the reference in the first inscription to a house
of prayer (usually a synagogue) is quite compatible with this being at
the very least a pagan production written "under the influence of
Judaism" as Schürer thought, rather than a truly Jewish inscription.
Still, it should be registered that the latter explanation is generally
favored, and rightly so, insofar as the distinction is an operable one.[32]

Moreover, we do know that city Jews were not always averse from
associating themselves with a pagan oath. This emerges strikingly
from the important Cyrene ephebic inscription, and, even though
there it is a case of passive association with, rather than active
adoption of a formula, still it goes well beyond what we might have

<hr/>

[28] Loeb translation.

[29] *CIRB* no. 71.

[30] *Ibid.* nos. 70, 72, 73.

[31] Ibid. 1123 = *CIJ* 690; B. Lifschit₃, *Rivista di Filologia* 92 (1964), 157-161.

[32] Schürer⁴, III, 24, A.D. Nock, who minimizes the Jewish connection, still sees the
epithets *pantokrator* and especially *eulogetos*, as decisive in favour of Jewishness in
this case: *Essays on Religion and the Ancient World* (Oxford, 1972), 474. So also
M. Stem, *CRINT* I, 1(1974), 156, n.4.

expected a priori. This document[33] is part of a list of ephebes—young men in training—attached to the gymnasium of the major city of Cyrene in the years A.D. 3/4, and carries with it some additional graffiti. It contains Jewish names of a kind which seem not open to argument—'Ιούλιος 'Ιησουτος, 'Ελασζαρ 'Ελαζαρος, Χαιρέας 'Ιουδα, 'Αγαθοκλῆς 'Ελαζαρος—and there are also three or four such in the graffiti. It is evident that at the end of the second column came the customary dedication to the gods of the gymnasium, Hermes and Heracles. It is not much consolation to remember that, according to 2 Maccabees, the Hellenizing high priest Jason had been keen to send ambassadors and contributions to the five-yearly festival of Heracles-Melkart at Tyre, nor to note, with Hengel, that the Hellenistic-Jewish historian Cleodemus-Malchus made Heracles marry a granddaughter of Abraham.[34] Applebaum[35] believed that the Jewish ephebes of Cyrene were bent primarily on securing a special half-way-house brand of citizenship, not on sport. Still the gymnasium's simple pleasures, if not its educational centrality, should not be overlooked, especially in the light of two more distinctly Jewish names in fragmentary ephebic lists—'Ιουδας from Iasos in Caria, noted by Robert, and Αὐρ. 'Ιωσης from a third century A.D., list from Coronea, Messenia (in mainland Greece).[36] In addition, H. A., Harris speaks of a possible Menorah scratched on the wall of what was probably the gymnasium changing room, and found by excavation at Priene, but he does not give chapter and verse and, in any case, one can conceive of many possible explanations of this figure–it looks to me more like a fir-tree.[37]

The Sardis synagogue's topography is equivocal in a different way. The synagogue was built (probably towards the end of the second century A.D., though it was much refurbished afterwards), to adjoin the *palaestra*, on a prime site in the centre of the city.[38] We cannot infer a common clientèle, but we must suppose at least that such a degree of external contact was not offensive to the founders or to the worshippers, and that this was so although (as has been shown, once more, by excavation) an institution of this sort could well contain

---

[33] See now G. Lüderitz, *Corpus jüdischer Zeugnisse aus der Cyrenaika* (1983), no. 7.
[34] M. Hengel, *Judaism and Hellenism* (transl. J. Bowden, 1974), I, 74; Cleodemus-Malchus–*FGrH*, no. 727 = C. R. Holladay (ed), *Fragments from Hellenistic Jewish Authors* I (1983), frag. I B, 1.20.
[35] S. Applebaum, *Parola del Passato* 19 (1964), 291-307.
[36] *Hellenica* I (1940), 29; *REJ* 101 (1937), 80; *IG* V, 1, 1398.
[37] H. A. Harris, *Greek Athletics and the Jews* (1976), 93 and Plate I.
[38] For assessment and bibliography, see A. T. Kraabel in *ANRW* XIX, 1 (1979), 83-8; also, A. P. Seager, "The Building History of the Sardis Synagogue", *AJA* 76 (1972), 425-435.

within it rooms housing cult statues—including those of the divine emperor, as at Pergamum.

From one point of view, to be among the ephebes was already an achievement. We can see this in the emperor Claudius's injunction to the Alexandrian Jews "not to intrude themselves into the games presided over by the *gymnasiarchoi* and the *kosmetai*".[39] But eventually—though not until A.D. 304–a man with a Jewish name becomes himself a gymnasiarch in Egypt. An Egyptian woman issues a tax receipt on papyrus, and is represented by her husband, Joannes Aurelius, who is described as γυμν (ασίαρχος).[40] The editors comment "to judge from his name, Joannes was a Jew, though, as it seems, a lax one, if indeed he acted as gymnasiarch, a post hardly compatible with strict adherence to the Jewish faith"! The question is, which brand of the Jewish faith.

If this is the first gymnasiarch to appear so far in surviving records, it does not, of course, follow that there were none before. Another point to bear in mind is that change is likely to have occurred at different rates in different places—the relatively early date of the Cyrene ephebe list deserves emphasis.

It is at Cyrene, interestingly enough, that we find also a Jewish city official of the first century (A.D. 59-61). He thus precedes the Asian councillors by almost two hundred years. So let us leave the gymnasium to cast a concluding eye over the Cyrenaic list of the law-guardians (*nomophylakes*).[41] (This was studied fully by Applebaum.)[42] Among the names is an unequivocal Ἐλαζα(ρ) (Ἰ)ασονος. So this man, presumably a Jew, figures among a small number of officers who supervised law-enforcement and the constitution for a now aristocratic government. Other inscriptions erected by the people of Cyrene are dedicated to Good Fortune, Apollo Nomios, Homonoia (Concord) and Aphrodite. Robert[43] accepts Ἐλαζα(ρ) as Jewish. I suppose it remains theoretically possible that such characters had in fact abandoned their faith but, in the then not wholly unfriendly atmosphere of Cyrene, felt no need to alter their names. Yet that they were Jews, of one kind or another, is the more natural explanation. Were they uneasy about what they were doing? Or was it entirely acceptable within the terms of the Judaism they practised? Among their other limitations, inscriptions are poor evidence for the subtler

---

[39] *CPJ* II, no. 153, ll. 92-3 = P. Lond 1912.
[40] *CPJ* III, no. 474, ll. 1-3.
[41] *CJZC* no. 8.
[42] *Loc. cit.* (no. 35).
[43] Robert, *REG* 75 (1962), 218.

nuances of personal attitude. Perhaps, after all, it was the former; and perhaps the compromise was not without certain tensions. We may fancy that our law guardians and ephebes might be the ancestors of some of those desperate people who were eventually driven, during the Jewish revolt under Trajan, to set upon and vandalize the temples of Hecate, Apollo and Zeus, as well as that of the imperial cult, and probably those of Artemis, Demeter, Isis and the Dioscuri too,[44] and who thus express an underlying resentment about the pagan cults which had formerly been allowed to encroach upon their lives. In their iconoclasm, they may have been taking literally the Deuteronomic injunction—"and ye shall overthrow their altars and break their pillars" (11, 3); yet, after centuries of co-existence, such an outburst must be taken above all as expressing pent-up fury, as the eventual product of old restraints and tensions.

List of Abbreviations Used in the Notes

AJA   *American Journal of Archaeology*
ANRW   H. Temporini and W. Haase, (ed), *Aufstieg und Niedergang der römischen Welt* (1972)
CIJ   *Corpus Inscriptionum Judaicarum*, ed. J. B. Frey (1936-52)
CIRB   *Corpus Insciptionum Regni Bosporani* (1965)
CJZC   G. Lüderitz (ed), with Joyce Reynolds, *Corpus jüdischer Zeugnisse aus der Cyrenaika* (1983)
CRINT   S. Safrai and M. Stern, (eds), *The Jewish People in the First Century: Compendia Rerum Iudaicarum ad Novum Testamentum*, Section 1, 2 vols (1974-6)
FGrH   F. Jacoby, *Die Fragmente der griechischen Historiker* (1940)
IG   *Inscriptiones Graecae*
REG   *Revue des études grecques*
REJ   *Revue des études juives*
ZNTW   *Zeitschrift für die neutestamentliche Wissenschaft*

---

[44] The evidence is mainly archaeological; see S. Applebaum, *Jews and Greeks in Ancient Cyrene* (1979), 272-285; M. Pucci, *La Rivolta ebraica al tempo di Traiano* (1981), 45-46; and for an excellent summary of the evidence, with references, E. M. Smallwood, *The Jews under Roman Rule* (1976), 397-398, with n. 25.

11

"Disaffected Judaism" and Early Christianity: Some Predisposing Factors

Robert Murray, S.J.
Heythrop College, University of London

It is proposed to try to clarify our understanding of early Judaism and Christianity, in the centuries of their formation and growing apart, by using the polarities "insider/outsider" and "self/other" with reference to consciousness, judgment and action. Once Christianity is a distinct entity, it becomes possible to apply these polarized categories clearly and fruitfully. But how are we to analyse the milieu in which Christianity arose? We have come to recognize how mistaken it was to read the characteristics of rabbinic Judaism back into the period before the rise of the School of Jamnia. But every student soon learns how hard it remains to reconstruct—even hypothetically—the movements in Judaism between the two destructions of Jerusalem in 586 B.C.E. and 70 C.E.

How are we to apply our polarities to the Jewish world which was the matrix of Christianity? The gospels picture Jesus as appealing now to "outsiders," now (less often, perhaps) to "insiders." What mutual attitudes were already determining people's reactions to Jesus? Who viewed whom as what in contemporary Judaism, and what effect may these views and feelings have had on the new movement?

What follows is a personal attempt to sketch a picture of some factors which, we may reasonably suspect, affected the self-understanding of Christianity. To some extent, this paper continues a line of thought first explored in public two years ago, in an article entitled "Jews, Hebrews and Christians: some needed distinctions."[1] That piece, admittedly speculative and provisional, arose from longstanding dissatisfaction with the way most writers who consider religious movements in the last centuries B.C.E. and the first centuries C.E. seem content with undifferentiated senses of "Jewish/Judaism" and "Jewish Christian[-ity]." Both the origin of the term *Ioudaios* and its eventually accepted denotation make it uneasily applicable to move-

---

[1] *Novum Testamentum* 24 (1982), 194-208.

ments (however disparate) which rejected the Jerusalem temple and
its "establishment" of priesthood and schools. Despite the light
thrown on this crucial period by many scholars, dissatisfaction with
the terminology and classification for kinds of "Judaism" and "Christianity" continues, as my previous article began by documenting and
trying to analyse.[2] My tentative advocacy of "dissident Hebrews"
(suggested by Josephus, AJ XI, 8, 6) has won no public acclaim; no
doubt "Hebrew" has already caused quite enough trouble in early
Christian sources. There is no doubt that we must stay with "Jewish"
and "Judaism"; that family was and remains so elastic and inclusive
that even its most non-conformist branches should not be excluded
from the name. But we constantly need qualifying and differentiating
adjectives—above all when talking about movements of the kinds just
referred to. To some extent, these involve traditional northern sentiment vis-à-vis Judaea. Of late, H.L. Ginsberg has expressed his sense
of need for a term distinct from "Israelite" or "Jewish," namely
"Israelian,"[3] to refer to Israel in the restricted sense of the old
northern kingdom, and to characteristics of its religious understanding
which continued to be influential when the heritage of the greater
Israel was claimed by Judah. Ginsberg sees that his insight entails
further discussion about the meaning and origin of "Judaism," and
about how other more open concepts of the heritage were repressed in
Nehemiah's time (op. cit., 3-18).

It seems likely, as several scholars have supposed, that anger on
the part of those disqualified, further intensified by other motives
such as repugnance to the new calendar of the restored cult, lies not
only at the root of various movements hostile to the Judaean "establishment," but also behind much of the literature which that establishment could not possibly canonize. How that literature may best be
designated remains disputable. In this paper I look not so much at
questions of genre as of *Tendenz*, especially that which I call "disaffected." The literature has at its head that great monument of vision
and theological reflection, 1 Enoch; it is this, rather than the pious
Jewish book of Daniel, which is the archetypal apocalypse, systematically working out a vision inspired by ancient religious traditions[4] in

---

[2] See, for example, R. E. Brown, "Not Jewish Christianity and Gentile Christianity but
types of Jewish/Gentile Christianity" CBQ 45 (1983), 74-79, though he does not attempt
to locate the sources of confusion as or where I do.

[3] *The Israelian Heritage of Judaism* (New York: Jewish Theological Seminary of
America, 1982), 1-2.

[4] This is increasingly recognized for 1 Enoch. See James C. VanderKam, *Enoch and the
Growth of the Apocalyptic Tradition*, CBQ Monograph Series 16, (Washington, D.C.:
1984); John J. Collins, *The Apocalyptic Imagination* (New York: Crossroad, 1984), chs.

order to make unbearable evils explicable, and hope for the future conceivable.

In my article of 1982 I argued that "Jewish Christianity" could never be understood unless "Jewish" is differentiated so as to allow for at least the following two kinds of background: the first is "Jewish" in the proper sense, that is, accepting the Jerusalem establishment's terms of reference; the second inherits old quarrels with Jerusalem— either that going back to early opposition to the new calendar and temple, or the later quarrel which led to the secession to Qumran.[5] I briefly sketched the lines on which the various New Testament books might be classified in this regard, and hinted at how this differentiation might fruitfully be extended into the developing history of the early Church. I asked finally "Is it possible that the charge against the Jews that they crucified Jesus (very explicit in Melito and early Syriac writers) was formulated by angry Galileans before ever it was by non-Israelite Gentiles?"

This is the starting-point for the present paper. Unfortunately circumstances have not permitted me to undertake the detailed research which I proposed as desirable in the previous article, nor to correlate my hunches with all the relevant work of other scholars. This sequel is again speculative and provisional. Nonetheless, it suggests lines along which to follow up my suggestion.

Given that the early Church's quarrel with "Judaism" was focused on the interpretation of Jesus, we might naturally suppose it was essentially, even entirely, about the refusal to accept him as a prophet and God-sent Messiah, and the charge that the Jewish leaders had

---

1 and 2. While agreeing with those who emphasize the ancient Mesopotamian sources, however, it will be clear that my inclination to see the power of myth still working from the old royal cult puts me in the tradition of Frank Moore Cross. I have been especially stimulated by Jonathan Z. Smith's article "Wisdom and Apocalyptic" (1975), reprinted in Paul D. Hanson (ed.), *Visionaries and their Apocalypses* (Philadelphia: Fortress, 1983) as ch. 6, and also by Margaret Barker's "Some Reflections upon the Enoch Myth", JSOT 15 (1980), 7-29.

[5] In saying "at least two kinds," my aim is only to avoid complexity at this point. My 1982 article was open to the criticism made by W.L.Horbury in JSNT 19 (1983), 48, that I exaggerate the incidence of dissident movements, and also assimilate known ones to each other too much. This is far from my intention, which is to clarify, not to blur the picture. Nevertheless, if various movements arise in opposition to the same institution, they may show certain similarities, may influence each other and may gravitate towards each other. Compare, for example, the history of religious dissent from the Anglican Church in England since the sixteenth century. (This suggests the further thought that an undifferentiated use of "Jewish" in the period under study could be compared to using the term "Anglican" to cover not only members of the established Church but also all Protestants in England!)

delivered him to death by the agency of the Romans. But the New Testament and early Christian witness is more complicated. Stephen, arraigned before the Sanhedrin, expounds a lengthy charge sheet against the Jews and against the very idea of a temple before he ever mentions Jesus. Several books of the New Testament and the sub-apostolic period show that Enoch is regarded as equivalent to Scripture, and links with the "disaffected" literature can be multiplied.

But let us return to the central figure of Jesus. The very categories available for interpreting his teaching and nature were multiple and reflected the oppositions which we must consider. There was not one single Messianism, on the Davidic model. Judaism and the opposition movements had different models for conceiving of the saviour expected from God. One model, that of Melchizedek, appears, on the available evidence, to have flourished especially in the circles revealed by the Qumran discoveries. Jesus' conquest of rebellious spirits, both in the synoptics, in Paul, Peter and in Revelation, again suggests the thought-world of Enoch. There is indeed a case to be considered that already existing hostility to Jerusalem Judaism, and ideas developed in terms other than those of its schools, conditioned the new quarrel about the rejection of Jesus.

I propose to sketch such a case by outlining a number of ideas, beliefs, or practical positions and activities, which may link at least parts of the early Church with movements already hostile to Jerusalem Judaism. There is time only for a sketch; part of the case has been well established by others, while part is frankly speculative and may not appeal to many. If it impresses anyone, that will be by virtue of accumulated hints pointing one way, rather than force of certain facts. I do not presume to reconstruct "trajectories"—to use a fashionable but not quite apt metaphor. (Trajectories arise from aimed firing and are determined by ballistic laws.) Rather I may seem like an amateur water-diviner, exploring with forked hazel twig or bent copper rods to trace lost underground channels. Some channels may be verified, some may be possible, others will remain uncertain. Another imaginative model might be the discovery by aerial photography of ancient settlements and earthworks which cannot be seen from the ground. Both this and "dowsing" involve inevitable imprecision, but yet can direct us towards accurate and fruitful investigation later, and eventually help to produce a new map.

Up to now, attempts to sketch the sectarian map have inevitably been dominated by Josephus' four "philosophies." Of course, his account must never be neglected, but it leaves us with acute problems. Only three of his groups are mentioned in the New Testament; the Essenes are never named. While I do not oppose the majority view that the Qumran people were Josephus' Essenes, the books in their library imply things Josephus never tells us. They treasured Enoch and Judilees, both dedicated to an older calendar than that in use in the second temple. The former appeals to astronomy and uses an angelic myth of the origin of evil to attack the "sinners" who were now in control, the latter claims that the old calendar had been revealed to the patriarchs. Here we have evidence of a quarrel with the Jerusalem establishment both distinct from the Samaritan quarrel and earlier than that which brought about the secession to Qumran. But the Qumran people also used a calendar akin to that of Jubilees, even though the *Mōreh ha-ṣedeq* and his followers seem to have come out from the Zadokite temple priesthood who followed the postexilic calendar, while the sect's approach to *halakhah* has seemed near enough to that of the Pharisees to make scholars such as Louis Ginzberg and C. Rabin relate the Damascus document to that movement.[6] The precise location of the Qumran sect (or Essenes) on the map of Palestinian movements still presents baffling problems as regards both its antecedents, its own quarrel with Jerusalem, and what it became or contributed to. It is not new to trace its influence both to some features of early Christianity and to Qara'ism. What is perhaps newer, in relation to the map which I see forming, is the realization that there were more streams leading from the thought-world of Enoch (whatever the name of the group whose dissatisfaction it expressed) to the early Church than has been generally recognized up to now.[7] Even if those streams do not always express actual hostility in every case, the fact that a quarrel lies behind Enoch, and that Christianity has a new quarrel, justifies our examining early Christianity more carefully in the light of "disaffected"Judaism.

1 Enoch uses a myth of angelic rebellion and the consequent disturbance of divine order (both cosmic and in human society) to attack the "sinners," who are not named but are clearly those who have changed the calendar. David Suter takes the function of the myth "as a *paradigm* (rather than an etiology) of the origin of evil . . . . In the

---

[6] L. Ginzberg, *Eine unbekannte jüdische Sekte* (New York: 1922), E.T. *An Unknown Jewish Sect* (New York: 1970); C. Rabin, *Qumran Studies* (Oxford, 1957).

[7] Despite R.H. Charles' judgement that "the influence of 1 Enoch on the New Testament has been greater than that of all the other apocryphal and pseudepigraphical books put together" (*The Book of Enoch* [Oxford, 1912], p. xcv). See W.J.Dalton, *Christ's Proclamation to the Spirits* (Rome: 1965), ch. VI; G.W.E.Nickelsburg, "Riches, the Rich and God's Judgment in 1 Enoch 92-105 and the Gospel According to Luke," NTS 25 (1979), 324-344; "Enoch, Levi and Peter: Recipients of Revelation in Upper Galilee," JBL 100 (1981), 575-600, and his contribution to the present volume; also M. Barker, "Some Reflections. . ." (note 4 above).

Damascus Document, Jude and 2 Peter, the paradigmatic function of
the myth is expanded into a *typology* of the origin of evil in the form
of lists of great sinners in each generation—lists headed by the fallen
angels".[8] The myth works analogically and "possesses a number of
possibilities for meaning that may not be exhausted by any one
version" (ibid.). I believe that the "Parables," though the latest part of
the book, still exemplify this function. They are called as they are
precisely as heavenly visions which can give insight about both the
cosmos and society. Thus in 43: 3-4 Enoch asks about the circulation
of the stars "according to the number of the angels, and [how] they
keep faith with each other," and he is told "The Lord of Spirits hath
showed thee their parable (Charles renders 'parabolic meaning'):
these are the names of the holy who dwell on the earth . . . ." This
scheme of heavenly realities as paradigms to interpret earthly events
is, surely, the key to interpreting the Book of Revelation. Indeed, it
makes me less attracted by appeals to Philonic Platonism as the
thought-world of Hebrews, or of the Odes of Solomon where they say:
"The likeness of that which is below is that which is above" (Od. 34:
4). This whole area of visionary expression is well discussed by
Christopher Rowland, who proposes to define the scope of apocalyptic literature using the formula in M. Hagigah 2.1: "What is above,
what is beneath, what was beforetime and what will be hereafter."[9]

So far I have discussed only the *function* of the Enochic angel
myth and how this kind of thinking continues in early Christianity. To
turn to the content and message, I am attracted (more than the
majority of scholars in this field) by Margaret Barker's thesis that the
story of the angelic rebellion developed from an *older* tradition
concerning rebellious members of the heavenly host, the traces of
which are in Isaiah 14: 12 ff., 24: 21-22, and in Psalms 82 and 58.[10]
Genesis 6 contains a truncated fragment of the myth in a form which
presupposes a fuller form, one containing elements preserved in 1

---

[8] "Fallen Angel, Fallen Priest: The Problem of Family Purity in 1 Enoch," HUCA 50
(1979), 115-35, 116-117.
[9] *The Open Heaven* (London: SPCK, 1982), ch. 2; see also John J. Collins, *The
Apocalyptic Imagination* (n. 4 above), 9-16. On the contrast between cosmic order and
human disorder in 1 Enoch 2-5 and early Christian literature (e.g. 1 Clement and
Aphrahat, Dem XIV), see R. Murray, "Hellenistic-Jewish Rhetoric in Aphrahat," Or.
Chr. An. 221 (1983), 79-85. But this is a widely-based *topos*, present already in Isaiah 1:
1-2 and Jeremiah 5: 22-25, independently developed by Stoic writers, and found in
Jewish as well as Christian literature.
[10] M. Barker, "Some Reflections. . ." (n. 4 above). Her reconstruction of the context,
development and eventual transmutation of the ancient myth is the subject of a whole
book, the publication of which is expected.

Enoch.[11] Genesis 3, reworking and largely demythologizing another rebellion myth, known from Ezekiel 28, is a deliberate *substitute*, pre-emptively given priority, in order to play down any responsibility for evil other than plain human disobedience. (However, it is left unexplained how the serpent, a creature of God, has already become capable of supernatural malice before the story begins!) Mrs Barker believes the original locus of the rebellion myth was in the old royal cult, a major function of which was to maintain control of all hostile forces, both natural and supernatural. The king, as the earthly representative of the "Holy One of Israel," directed the constantly necessary campaign against the other, disorderly, "Holy Ones," and the this-worldly forces under their influence.[12] This hypothesis of the myth's antiquity in its "pre-angelic" form fits with the strong probability that the pentecontad solar calendar, which the authors of Enoch, Jubilees and the Damascus Document insist was divinely revealed, was simply the old Palestinian agrarian calendar as developed in a solar year structure in the first temple. The variants in what we may call the "old calendarist" literature arise from diverging memories of what it was like before the breach of continuity and the introduction of the lunar-solar calendar which Jerusalem's new masters brought back from Babylon.[13]

I am further impressed by Mrs Barker's argument that the revelation of dangerous and corrupting "wisdom" is an integral part of the myth from the beginning, rather than a distinct theme eventually combined with that of rebellion and fall through lust. This is contrary

---

[11] J.T. Milik, *The Books of Enoch: Aramaic Fragments of Qumran Cave 4* (Oxford: Clarendon Press, 1976), 30-32, maintains simply that the Enoch story is older than and implied by the Genesis story. In this bald form his view has not won acceptance. A view as expressed above remains possible and corresponds to the view that the account of Enoch in Gen 5 presupposes a fuller tradition (cf. VanderKam, *Enoch...* [n. 4 above], ch. II).

[12] Cf. J.Z. Smith, "Wisdom and Apocalyptic" (n. 4 above), especially 109, in the reprint. Cf. my interpretation of Isaiah 33: R. Murray, "Prophecy and the Cult," in R.J. Coggins, A. Phillips and M.A. Knibb, eds., *Israel's Prophetic Heritage* (Cambridge: University Press, 1982), 200-216, especially 205-16.

[13] Cf. J. Morgenstern, "The Calendar of the Book of Jubilees: its Origin and its Character" VT 5 (1955), 34-76, summing up his long series of calendar studies in HUCA, 1924-1947. For the recent debate see J. VanderKam, "The Origin, Character and Early History of the 364-Day Calendar," CBQ 41 (1979), 209-217 and "The 364-Day Calendar in the Enochic Literature", in K.H. Richards ed., *SBL 1983 Seminar Papers* (Chico, CA: Scholars Press, 1983), 157-65; P.R. Davies, "Calendrical Change and Qumran Origins: An Assessment of VanderKam's Theory," CBQ 45 (1983), 80-89. It is not necessary here to take sides in this difficult discussion. I wonder if it is possible that the *Mōreh ha-ṣedeq* at some point was converted to "old calendarism", and that this was a major reason why he seceded?

to the current "orthodoxy," which places the revelation story later in the redaction history. Since it is clear that the Enoch tradition grows and develops, the story may be *redactionally* subsequent, but I still want to hold that its substance belongs to the old myth.[14] (Its absence leaves Gen 6:4 with no explanation of how mankind became wicked.)

This rather lengthy discussion of the Enochic angel myth's antiquity may seem remote from my main theme. But it is important if it is true. If 1 Enoch began from one writer's vision, not much before 200 B.C.E., and its influence passed to the Qumran people, it could be a limited phenomenon which eventually touched early Christianity here and there. And such a minimal view used to be common. But if the roots of Enoch are in memories of the ancient cult, preserved by the "people of the land" who had experienced not exile and intensive spiritual development but abandonment, desolation and then ideological oppression by those who returned (breaking up marriages, disqualifying levites and robbing people of the security of their ancestral calendar), then it is likely that disaffection was both widespread and deep, ready for catalysts to organize it into new movements—rather as in northern Europe and Britain there were many disaffected circles all ready to become Protestants when the Reformation finally broke. I believe that in the New Testament, if we do not restrict ourselves to explicit citations of Enoch or implicit allusions, but look for a vision of the cosmos and the whole moral situation of mankind corresponding to that reflected in 1 Enoch, much important evidence points towards that very world-view, rather than towards that of rabbinic Judaism's forefathers.

Altogether, angels and evil spirits play a much more substantial part in the New Testament than is typical, as far as I know, of the approximately contemporary Jewish literature. Mark's presentation of Jesus as demonstrating a new, divine authority, different not only in its basis, but qualitatively different from that of the scribes (Mk 1:22), is substantiated by Jesus' command of all spirits, both the angels who minister to him in the desert (Mk 1:13) and the demons whose power is shown in disease. These last he casts out with absolute authority (Mk 1:27). The spirits acknowledge Jesus by titles belonging both to the king and to his heavenly patron in the ancient royal cult: "Holy

---

[14] J.J. Collins, in his valuable article "The Apocalyptic Technique: Setting and Function in the Book of Watchers," CBQ 44 (1982), 91-111, takes Mrs. Barker to hold a less nuancé position than is actually the case. My own position here is analogous to what I would maintain regarding numerous gospel pericopes, where I accept literary-critical arguments for recognizing redactional activity, yet still in many cases judge it more likely that the essentials go back to words and acts of Jesus.

one of God" (Mk 1:24), "Son of God" (Mk 3:11), "Son of the Most High God" (Mk 5:7—El Elyon!).[15] We enlightened moderns have not taken the spirits seriously enough. That insoluble problem for the redaction critics, the Marcan Messianic secret, may find its solution also here. Jesus "would not allow the demons to speak, because they knew him" (Mk 1:34). Part of Jesus' strategy was to keep the advantage of surprise over the hostile spirits till his victory was complete— as Ignatius recognized (Eph 19).[16]

At the time of Jesus' appearance, though the rebel spirits have been cast down by God and imprisoned (Isai 24: 22; most fully, 1 Enoch 10, 18, 21 etc.; Jude 6; 2 Peter 2: 4), they have power over vulnerable victims whom they "bind" by disease (Lk 13: 16). But Jesus is the stronger one who comes, releases the victims, and binds their oppressors (Mk 3: 27). The power of binding and loosing, which he gives to his disciples, was the power of exorcism (Mk 3: 15) before it was translated by Jewish Christians into anything like rabbinic authority (Mt 16: 19; 18: 18). The latter, according to the picture in the gospels, is not so much evil as superseded. If Jesus attacks the scribes and pharisees as blind leaders of the blind, he is seen to be speaking for a public which expects something else of God than a blessing on the institutions which maintain and develop a safe *halakhah* to live by. But if that public breathed an air constantly contested by angels and demons, and was acquainted with the Qumran covenanters' conviction of being involved in a cosmic war between the sons of light, allied with the angels, and the sons of darkness, the lot of Belial, then much in the New Testament clicks into place. Indeed, there is a cosmic war in progress, but the meaning of Jesus' life, death and resurrection is that through him, victory for God has already been definitively won. He has triumphed over the demonic powers controlling the world (Col 2: 15) and announced his victory, immediately after the paradox of his death, to the imprisoned disobedient spirits (1 Peter 3: 19). The Enochic myth provides the seer John with the means of interpreting both the challenge realized immediately in the birth of

---

[15] These occur also, of course, on the lips of a good angel in the Lukan Annunciation narrative (Lk 1:32-35)!

[16] Cf. J.M. Hull, *Hellenistic Magic and the Synoptic Tradition* (London: SCM, 1974), especially p. 69. Significant also for my argument for ancient roots is Josephus' belief that exorcism went back to Solomon, a feature not preserved in canonical Scripture (AJ VIII,45; Hull, p. 34). I disagree with Hull's view, however, that the "magical" element in Mark and Luke represents the infiltration of alien, Hellenistic ideas. If Matthew has the least "magical" ideas, that is because it is the most "Jewish" gospel (in the restricted sense of that term); Mark and Luke reflect circles open to other religious concepts.

the Messiah (Rev 12: 7-9) and the future final stages of the cosmic drama (Rev 20).

Meanwhile, till the rebellious spirits are finally bound and destroyed, all who have recognized Jesus as God's son, sent from heaven to rally the sons of light (1 Thess. 5: 5; Col 1: 12-13) are engaged in a battle which consists in a day-to-day ascetical struggle, but which is their part in the cosmic war (1 Thess. 5: 8-9, Eph 6: 10-17). The kind of imagery which expresses this vision links the Qumran Community Rule (1QS 3-4) and the War Scroll, through the New Testament passages just alluded to and the "Two Ways" catechesis in Barnabas (18-20) and the Didache (1-6), to the early Syriac ascetical literature. This forms one of our most clearly traceable underground streams— even if decisive proof is still lacking that these ideas, together with the consecrated celibacy of ascetics stripped for action, go back behind Christianity to the Qumran Covenanters.[17]

Likewise, besides the symbolism of participation in spiritual warfare, the claim to live and worship in fellowship with the angels of God may well be another stream joining early Christianity to the world of Enoch and the Qumran people. For the latter, this claim is expressed e.g. in 1QS 17:7-8, 1QSa 2:8-9 and 1QM 12. In early Christianity the ascetical life soon came to be regarded as a *vita angelica* on earth.[18] But already, in the New Testament, Christians see themselves as united with the heavenly worshipping community (Heb 12: 22-24 and, implicitly, in all the visions of heavenly cult in the book of Revelation).[19] The same book sees churches as having presiding angels (chs. 2-3). The Sanctus, the angelic hymn which proves its antiquity by its similarity in all early eucharistic anaphoras, has its most probable immediate antecedents in the Qumran "Angelic Liturgy" and the Parables of Enoch;[20] its remoter roots are, of course, in Isaiah's vision in the first temple.

In all this, the pre-Christian antecedents seem to point mainly towards "disaffected" groups, behind which we may recognize attach-

---

[17] Cf. R. Murray, "The Exhortation to Candidates for Ascetical Vows at Baptism in the Ancient Syriac Church," NTS 21 (1974-5), 59-80.
[18] Cf. P. Nagel, *Die Motivierung der Askese in der alten Kirche und der Ursprung des Mönchtums*, TU 95 (1966), 34-48.
[19] Cf. E. Peterson, *Das Buch von den Engeln*, E.T. *The Angels and the Liturgy*, (London; Darton, Longman and Todd, 1964), ch.1. More speculatively, G. Dautzenberg in his *Urchristliche Prophetie* (Stuttgart: Kohlhammer, 1975) finds the possible antecedents of early Christian glossolalia (236), which Paul apparently understood as the language of the angels, in the Testament of Job, assigned by both Philonenko and Dautzenberg to the Therapeutae (ibid., 108-118).
[20] Cf. B.D. Spinks, "The Jewish Sources for the Sanctus", HeyJ 21 (1980), 168-79.

ment to features remembered from the old temple cult. Such an appeal to the past of Israel will have taken various forms: not only the way of transformation by canonization on the part of the Jerusalem scribes, but also ways that expressed claims to inheritance on the part of disaffected groups. What are we to say of Merkavah mysticism, whose roots have been thought to lie not far from those who composed the "Angelic Liturgy"? Are we entitled to imagine that a kind of spirituality which was born in sectarian circles later flourished (however suspect) in contact with rabbinic Judaism, as well as influencing Christianity? If we could reach any safe conclusions about the Therapeutae, who may (if certain works are justifiably ascribed to them) have claimed to live in fellowship with angels,[21] this would make it more possible to chart our hidden streams. Philo does not present the Therapeutae as sectarian or as anything other than admirable to him as a good Jew.

When we consider Messianism, the expectation of an anointed agent through whom it was hoped that God would again act to deliver Israel and institute his kingdom on earth, and when likewise we consider the ways in which the early Christians saw Jesus as fulfilling such expectations, then (as I observed above) we must recognize several models of Messianism. One approach is to consider what functions in the Lord's service were understood to require anointing. Obviously, these were kingship, priesthood and prophethood. Evidently, the royal messianism in the Davidic tradition (and therefore beloved of Jerusalem Judaism, inspiring texts such as the Psalms of Solomon 17-18) is claimed for Jesus, for example in the infancy narratives, Romans 1:3 and carries over into Ignatius (Rom 7) and the Didache (9). A priestly messiah appears to be expected at Qumran (1QS 9:11), though this remains obscure; the expectation is clearer in the Testament of Levi (18),[22] which of course reflects at least redaction by Christians. Along this line, we may remember some Syrian Christians' concern to give Jesus a title to priesthood through the hands of John the Baptist[23]; this claim is hardly compatible with the way in which Hebrews ascribes priesthood to Jesus. With the idea of a priestly messiah we are, if not among sects, at least moving farther (if

---

[21] Not explicit in Philo, De Vita Contemplativa (our main source); but cf. Testament of Job (n. 19 above), in J.H. Charlesworth ed., *The Old Testament Pseudepigrapha* I (Garden City, N.Y.: Doubleday, 1984), translation, introduction and commentary, 829-68; cf. also the Apocalypse of Zosimus or History of the Rechabites, ibid., vol. II.

[22] For a recent summary of the position on the data from Qumran and on Test. Levi, see J.J. Collins, *The Apocalyptic Imagination* (n. 4 above), 111-112,122-126.

[23] Cf. R. Murray, *Symbols of Church and Kingdom: A Study in Early Syriac Tradition* (Cambridge: University Press, 1975), 178-80.

I am not mistaken) from the preferred concepts of Jerusalem Judaism. Finally, an eschatological prophet was expected in the light of Deut 18:15 ff., as is referred to, apparently, in 1QS 9:11, and in the questions to John the Baptist (Jn 1:21). This kind of figure appears to occupy the Messianic role for the Samaritans, even though they rejected the prophets canonized by the Jerusalem tradition. Among the reactions to Jesus was to acclaim him as a prophet (Lk 7: 16), but this does not necessarily point to messianic expectations. However, in John 6, the cry that Jesus is "*the* prophet who is to come into the world" leads immediately to an attempt to make him king, a proceeding which Jesus decisively forestalls (Jn 6: 14-15). Would any of this have happened in a world of religion safely controlled by the Jerusalem scribes and rabbis?

Another approach to Messianism is to ask what kind of person, possessed of what nature, was expected as messiah. All the models of messiah-ship summarized in the previous paragraph remain within the human sphere. But there is a range of data which reveals the expectation that a divine figure will exercise messianic functions. Modern New Testament scholarship has conspired to play down the existence of any 'Jewish' background for the early Christian conviction of the preexistence of the Messiah, Holy One and Son of the Most High God, whose incarnation the angel announces to Mary (Lk 1:32-35). But the tide is turning from "hellenistic" theories, as Martin Hengel's *The Son of God* illustrates.[24] Further, the Qumran Melchizedek fragments reveal a figure who functions in the heavenly order, who judges on terms drawn from Ps 82, and for whom is the "day of favor" (which in Isa 61:2 is the Lord's). That passage in Isaiah is spoken by one anointed by YHWH, and in Lk 4:18-19, Jesus claims to be the one signified. The figure named Melchizedek in the fragments is to vanquish Belial, the leader of the forces of evil (Melchireshà in 4Q 'Amram[b]).[25]

Not only these texts are fragmentary; so must be my argument. Still it seems to come together to establish the theme of a figure active in the heavenly sphere whose functions are closely associated with God himself. This figure bears the name used in Hebrews as the basis for a different kind of argument, one concerning the kind of priesthood which can appropriately serve as a model for speaking of Jesus' death as salvific. I see no link, beyond the name, between the Melchizedek

---

[24] *Der Sohn Gottes* (Tübingen, 1975); English Trans. London: SCM, 1976.
[25] See Paul J. Kobelski, *Mechizedek and Melchireša*, CBQ Monograph Series 10 (1981); for a summary of the position, J.J. Collins, *The Apocalyptic Imagination* (n. 4 above), 132.

figure in Hebrews and the Qumran figure, who seems to be identified with Michael. It is different, however, when we turn back to the source of the name. The biblical Melchizedek was a priest-king (therefore presumably with a double title to be anointed) in Salem (understood to be Jerusalem), so the Davidic king could be addressed as "a priest for ever according to the order of Melchizedek" (Ps 110). If the same name was believed to be borne by a heavenly figure, surely this suggested some kind of identity, representative or symbolic, between the king and a heavenly patron bearing the same name as the supposed founder of his line of royal priesthood.

Once again we are led back, by yet another path, from ideas apparently used by early Christianity, to aspects of the royal cult in the first temple. These the redactors of the canonical Tanach did not wish to emphasize, though they let traces remain, especially in the royal covenant tradition as we see it in Ps 89, with its close parallelism between the sovereignty of YHWH and that of the king, or in that remarkable phrase in 1 Chron 29:23, "Solomon sat on the throne of YHWH as king instead of David". Do we need to look further for the model for the Elect One sitting on God's throne in Parables of Enoch 51:3? Is there, even, a simpler or more plausible background for the "Son of Man" in Dan 7? Whether, or how much, Jesus may have meant people to understand his self-designation as "Son of Man" on these lines is an unanswerable question. It is not clear even that the early Church understood it in such a way (unless perhaps Stephen did in his dying vision, Acts 7: 56). But I propose it as a hypothesis worth considering, that the memory of the old "royal theology" which linked the king especially to YHWH as *his* patron, flowed into the early Christian belief in the glorification of Jesus as the Christ. If this could be true, once again it looks as if the streams had flowed through terrain not perfectly controlled by those who had taken over the hierarchical functions in Jerusalem.

Before turning to subjects nearer to actual quarrels with the latter, however, I would like to conclude this section with a suggestion about the background of the christological "hymn" in Philippians 2. The favoured sources seem to be Adam and the Isaian Servant, or the Isaian Servant mediated through Wisdom of Solomon 2-5, as is argued by Dieter Georgi.[26] But none of these options seem to me to fit well

---

[26] "Der vorpaulinische Hymnus Phil 2,6-11," in E. Dinkler (ed.), *Zeit und Geschichte* (Tübingen: Mohr, 1964), 263-93; on Wisdom 2-5 in relation to the Isaian Servant, see G.W.E. Nickelsburg, *Resurrection, Immortality and Eternal Life in Intertestamental Judaism*, Harvard Theological Studies 26 (Cambridge, MA: Harvard University Press, 1972), ch. 2, especially 62-66.

enough as regards either sharing the divine nature or an actual attempt to usurp equality with God. The story in Genesis 3 never says that Adam and Eve actually formed the desire to become like gods. Surely the most appropriate place to look is the use in Isaiah 14:12-15 of the myth of a star-god who tried to usurp the throne of El, but was cast down and imprisoned; variants of the myth doubtless underlie Ezekiel 28 and Isai 24:21-22, and I suppose the Enochic rebellion story to be also related to it. The "hymn" in Philippians (the inverted commas reflect an abiding lack of conviction about this fashionable identification of the genre) pictures Jesus as actually having the right, but renouncing the claim, to equality. His self-abasement, rewarded by exaltation, exactly reverses the pattern of the old myth with an elegance which makes me, at least, feel no need to look further elsewhere. On this view, the other suggestions may still find a place in the creative mixture; Adam has a certain aura of royal wisdom, and the Isaian Servant (which I see as a figure like T.S. Eliot's "familiar compound ghost" in *Little Gidding*) must have, among its components, a lot to do with sacral kingship.

Again, we are fed back to the sort of background for apocalypticism variously proposed by Jonathan Z. Smith and Margaret Barker.[27] And we are looking for the roots of at least some early christology in a direction to which Martin Hengel points (without pursuing it). The same, perhaps, might be true of E.P. Sanders's conclusion that "Paul presents an *essentially different type of religiousness from any found in Palestinian Jewish literature*,"[28] but I believe the essential next step depends on making distinctions in "Jewish" and also between kinds of "apocalyptic" literature, and on searching among heirs of ancient Israel who may have had mixed or negative feelings about being called Jewish. In my previous article I suggested that the Damascus Christians among whom Paul was converted had a dissenting background, and that "his conversion to Jesus. . . also meant making peace with dissenters. This could help to explain his subsequent intense concern with reconciliation."[29]

I have postponed till now the identifiable points at issue between the "disaffected" and Jerusalem, for various reasons. I do not in the least intend to undermine the essential and obvious truth that the new Christian movement had a new quarrel with all elements in the Jerusalem establishment and with anyone else who ought, in Chris-

---

[27] See Smith, "Wisdom and Apocalyptic" and Barker, "Some Reflections. . .", in note 4 above.
[28] *Paul and Palestinian Judaism* (London: SCM, 1977), 543.
[29] Murray, "Jews, Hebrews and Christians" (n. 1 above), 204.

tian eyes, to have been able to recognize Jesus as God's chosen messenger and messiah. What leads the student of Christian origins back to 1 Enoch and the Qumran people is not the survival of their quarrels, as such, but rather of elements of their world-view and "spirituality".

As we have observed, the angelic rebellion myth in 1 Enoch is used to picture disorder on earth as in heaven. Through the abuse of calendrical "wisdom," "sinners" have thrown the seasons into confusion by changing the calendar (1 Enoch 80). As the Enoch tradition develops, further charges become clear. The temple has been polluted by "blinded shepherds" (ibid. 89), and the sinners who are in power exploit the poor (94-104). The same attachment to the old calendar and the same accusations against temple and oppression reappear in the Damascus Document (esp. 2-5). The last two themes are familiar, in various forms, in the preaching of Jesus and his followers, but the devotion to the old calendar cannot be traced into Christianity. Annie Jaubert made an imaginative and exciting attempt to do this, but it has not won credence.[30] There remains the puzzling statement in the third-century *Didascalia* (21) that Jesus and the disciples ate the passover on the third day of the week.[31] This could be explained on Mlle Jaubert's theory, but the theory itself creates too many other problems.

If, however, Enochic and Essene "Old Calendarism" did not pass into Christianity (which too clearly aimed, at first, to relativize the value of almost all religious observances), may we perhaps see a shadow of it in the Colossians' attachment to calendrical concerns as well as to the influence of supernatural powers (Col 2:8-23)? Further, if "Old Calendarism" as such did not survive, Christianity remained vulnerable to outbreaks of this kind of conservatism—witness the Quartodeciman dispute in the second century, the dispute between the Celtic Church and Rome about the reckoning of Easter, Russian Old Calendarism, and other conservative movements such as the "Old Believers," and Catholic reactionary movements such as that which has rejected liturgical change since Vatican II. The last two examples also show how easily the apocalyptic language of Antichrist comes to the lips of those whose sense of an eternally changeless liturgy is threatened.

The Temple is a more fruitful subject for examination. Few would disagree that here, from the prophetic criticism of presumptuous

---

[30] *La Date de la Cène* (Paris: 1957), English Trans. *The Date of the Last Supper* (Staten Island, N.Y.: Alba House, 1965).

[31] *Didascalia Apostolorum*, R.H. Connolly ed (Oxford: Clarendon Press, 1929), 181.

reliance on the temple cult through the Enochic and Essene criticisms to those voiced in early Christianity, we have more of a visible stream than an underground channel. Here a few summary remarks must suffice. Of course there are different attitudes to the Temple in the New Testament. Jesus appears to have respected it and chosen to teach in its courts, but he also relativized its value and foretold its destruction without any sense of final disaster. Among New Testament writers, Luke, especially in Acts, shows a positive attitude to the Temple. This attitude makes his insertion of Stephen's speech all the more striking. Stephen's violent attack (Acts 7), which finally denies the value of a temple as such, has often been analysed as reflecting disaffected, perhaps Samaritan sentiment. Similar hostility can probably be discerned in the Book of Revelation (esp. ch. 11). The Letter to the Hebrews, which I am inclined to see as addressed to readers of "dissident" background, seems curiously unaware of the Temple.[32] The writer's meditation concentrates on the desert tabernacle in a timeless present. This might imply alienation from the actual Temple, but it would be hard, if not impossible, to prove such a case. After all, Josephus discusses the temple cult in the present tense after it has ceased (C. Apionem II, 193-8). Likewise, the activity of the priests is mentioned in the present tense by 1 Clement (40), and the sacrifices by various Christian critics (e.g. Barnabas 2, Ad Diognetum 3) who seem unaware that their mockery no longer has an existing target.

However, apart from attitudes to the Jerusalem Temple itself, there is a particular phenomenon which may even be regarded as a distinct stream. This is the taste for designing "blueprints" for the ideal temple and/or temple city, with the characteristic of more emphasis on squareness than was realized in the second Temple or in that of Herod. This activity begins, to our knowledge, with Ezekiel's visionary plan, which is insistent on squareness (Ez 40-43), 1 Enoch 90:28 looks forward to a new temple brought by God, but does not describe its plan. The most developed "blueprint" for an ideal temple is, of course, the Temple Scroll found at Qumran and possibly referred to in CD 5:2ff.[33] (I cannot discuss here the problems of relationship between these documents and the Qumran community.) As a Mosaic pseudepigraph, the Temple Scroll stands with Jubilees in claiming the authority of Torah. Its reckoning of feasts seems to be by some form of the older calendar, and it proposes a plan of an ideal temple city and temple arranged in concentric squares, on lines nearer to

[32] Murray, "Jews, Hebrews and Christians" (n. 1 above), 205.
[33] Cf. B. Z. Wacholder, *The Dawn of Qumran* (Cincinnati: Hebrew Union College Press, 1983), 112-29.

Ezekiel than to the second Temple. To be sure, much of the scroll consists of detailed *halakhah,* and to that extent, like much in the Qumran documents, is in a different value system from most early Christian teaching. (However, the marriage code for the king in 11Q Temple 57, 15-18, apparently referred to in CD 5:2, can suggest a halachic background for Jesus' teaching on divorce, as J. Fitzmyer has argued.)[34] But to return to the square plan, it is striking that in Revelation 21 the holy city is a perfect cube, with twelve gates commemorating the twelve tribes, as in 11Q Temple 40-41. Yet it contains *no temple,* God and the Lamb being its only temple (Rev 21:22). There could hardly be a more vivid symbolization of early Christianity's claim to need no temple as such (except for metaphors transferring the theme to Christ, the apostles and Christians), nor of the claim that, whatever authority had resided in the Temple, Jesus transcends and supersedes it. Is there, in a way, a "stream" from the authority-claim made by Jubilees and the Temple Scroll to the new movement which acknowledged Jesus as the living and final source of Torah?

The last strand which I wish to mention is that of anger on behalf of the oppressed poor, which comes out so strongly in the Epistle of Enoch and again in New Testament writers, especially Luke. But here it is enough to refer to the work of George Nickelsburg.[35] Of course, anyone can be angry with oppressors, and if this proposed link stood alone it would hardly secure a whole chain. The same might be said of Nickelsburg's suggestion of a significant link, consisting in the location of revelation scenes in Upper Galilee on the slopes of Hermon (where the angels had conspired to rebel, 1 Enoch 6:6!), which could connect Enoch (ibid. 13:7-9), Levi (Test, Levi 6:6) and Jesus' words to Peter (Mt 16:17-19).[36] But Nickelsburg's arguments do not stand alone as imaginative speculations. They relate to a broader picture which is becoming clearer, and they are confirmed by the convergence of similar interpretations of other phenomena.

I am very conscious of the incompleteness of this sketch. If it takes two to make a quarrel, traditions of hostility need to be traced from both ends of the relationship, and I have consistently neglected any approach from what I have called the "establishment" side. I must leave that to others, especially those trained by Jacob Neusner. If

---

[34] "The Matthean Divorce Texts and some New Testament Evidence", TS 37 (1976), 197-226.

[35] *Resurrection.* . . (n. 26 above), ch. 4; "Riches, the Rich and God's Judgment. . ." (n. 7 above).

[36] G. W. E. Nickelsburg, "Enoch, Peter and Levi. . ." (n. 7 above).

there is any merit in the approach adopted in this paper, I hope it will
be tested from the side of the Judaism which was the object of the
disaffection discussed here—the Judaism which was rallied and
reorganized by the rabbis of Jamnia to become the dominant surviving
form. I have sketched a case for an alternative and partially distinct
development from the religion of ancient Israel—an alternative which
had its own attitudes to the works canonized by the Jews as *Tanach,*
and which also treasured other expressions of a heritage believed to
be older, and to have a higher authority than the reconstruction in
force in Jerusalem. I have proposed the hypothesis that significant
features of early Christianity reflect this alternative and disaffected
background, and can be ascribed partly to its influence.

E.P. Sanders quotes approvingly "Schweitzer's argument that a
theme cannot be central which does not explain anything else".[37] I
suggest that the hypothesis explored in this paper can explain far more
about early Christianity than scholars have been able to see, as long as
they were tied to a set of fixed assumptions about Judaism, apocalypticism, Hellenism and several other problematical categories. It has
been assumed that the early Christians created new theological
insights by interaction with the hellenistic world. But who *knows* that
that is the dominant influence, rather than older religious ideas and
traditions which had come down in Israel and, in related forms, in the
whole near East? Why should this material not have been at hand in
already formed complexes, ready to facilitate that extraordinary burst
of theologizing about Jesus which Martin Hengel insists was so early,
and not merely the product of the interaction between the Christian
message and the hellenistic world?[38]

To appreciate this hypothesis, we must rethink assumptions about
the relationship of early Christianity to "Jewish" sources, and about
that of the un-canonized literature to canonical *Tanach.* I Enoch and
the works related to it have been interpreted mainly with regard to
Mesopotamian sources and the canonical *Tanach.* But, by looking
beside and behind the latter within Israelite tradition, it may be
possible to discover an alternative tradition which did not win. There
are abundant points of contact between that alternative tradition and
the canonical Scriptures, but they are points of contact, not necessarily
indications of simple dependence. Many features of the alternative
tradition favored the new Christian movement as the Jerusalem
establishment could not, and those whose dreams were formed by the

---

[37] *Paul and Palestinian Judaism* (n. 28 above), 441.
[38] *The Son of God* (n. 24 above), especially p. 2, but this is the thesis of the whole book.

alternative tradition could have reasons to recognize Jesus different from those which a Jerusalem priest or rabbi might formulate.

And so back to our key categories in this conference. I suggest that Christianity inherited older ways of being "outsiders" in the Jewish family, ant that early Christian ideas of "self" and "other" had a complex prehistory. I suggest that an ironically and tragically fateful scenario for the future of the Israelite family was scripted when the exiled élite returned from Babylon under the Persians, and imposed their revision of religion on brethren stubbornly attached to other and older ways of thinking about the powers of heaven and earth.

THREE
Sorting Out Difference: From the Second to the Fourth Century

12

The Triumphant Majority as Seen by a Dwindled Minority: The Outsider According to the Insider of the Jewish Apocalypses, 70–130

James H. Charlesworth
Princeton Theological Seminary

Introduction

The community, the other, and the individual are the three social elements operating in dynamic contiguity as an organic religious phenomenon develops (a full discussion would demand, *inter alia*, inclusion of the world and sacra, for us usually texts). At times, one of these factors becomes too dominant and oppresses at least one of the other two. During the middle of the second century B.C.E., after the initial successes of the Hasmoneans, the community became extremely powerful, momentarily defeating "the other," and beginning to suppress the individual. The result was the decrees recorded in 1 Maccabees 14:41-49, "the unanimous decision of the people" (the community) which was enforced by severe punishments. This dominance by the community produced the explosion of dissidents within, notably the priests who withdrew in exile to found another community that would not obliterate the individual. This exodus produced the Essene *yaḥad* at what is now called Qumran.

During the persecutions of Antiochus IV Epiphanes, "the other" literally obliterated all the individual's cherished rights and, through wars and persecutions, his life. The result was a disintegration in the community—a process which had commenced even previously.

In turn, the individual became too dominant in the middle of the first century C.E. This caused a breakdown of community life as the corporate unity of Judaism was ripped by factions. This collapse was caused by more than the excesses by the sicarii, revolutionary groups, and Zealots (see the major studies by M. Hengel, D. Rhoads; and H. Guevana's dissertation).[1] But "the other" was too powerful to be obliterated; the Romans wiped out both the individual and the community. The burning of the Temple, the death of thousands, the

---

[1] H. Guevana, "La resistencia judia contra Roma en la epoca de Jesus," Diss. Neitingen 1981.

deportation of the valued and the pollution of the land marked the end of the nation that had become so prominent in world politics. This end, placarded in Titus' column in the Roman forum, was reconfirmed by the defeat of the Bar Cochba forces in 135.

The three elements not only must be held in some healthy relationship, but also must be prevented from subdividing. Indeed, the invitation to the Romans to come to Jerusalem was given precisely because the community had lost its centripetal cohesiveness. Yet "the other" can be ineffective as a force when, as in the times of the Seleucids, the threat from within or without (here, especially from the Parthians) pulls it away from involvement within Palestinian Judaism. Later, the rift between Octavius, Anthony and Cleopatra produced a clever opportunist, Herod the Great, who from 40 to 37 B.C.E. astutely forced Palestinian Jews to live under, if not to accept, the rule of an Idumean.

Further, the individual can fracture, producing, for example, young men who wish to undergo an operation to produce epispasm (1 Macc 1:15, Josephus, *Ant.* 12.241). This particular phenomenon occured not only during the time of Jason the high priest, but virtually throughout the entire period of Early Judaism after Jason.[2]

Hence, during the period of Early Judaism (250 B.C.E. to 200 C.E), the religious phenomenon glibly labeled "Judaism" continued healthy only in so far as community, "the other", and individual were in a meaningful relationship. When one element was too dominant or recessive, then the other two factors, held together because of their dynamic cohesion, tended to suffer.

"The other" is the least easily defined of these three elements, hence some taxonomic observations are imperative. It is ambiguously amorphous and can be extracted out of our paradigm and inserted into each of the other factors producing, besides the non-Jews as "other," two dissimilar factors: the community as "other," and the individual as "other." The Essenes and the Samaritans—clearly "Jews" before 135—saw the community (especially the Jerusalem cultus, the heart of the community for many Jews) as the other. Jannaeus was seen as the other by a large segment of the community, and he himself turned ferociously on those Jews who told him to go kill himself. As in Freudian psychology, the individual can bifurcate normally into the super ego versus the id. This division is reminiscent both of the

---

[2] See T. Mos. 8:3; 1 Cor. 7:18; Soranus, *Gynecology* 2.34; Discorides, *De Materia Medica* 4.15; Celsus, *De Medicina* 7.25; Epiphanius, *De Mensuris et Ponderibus* 16; Martial, *Epigrams* 7.35 and 7.82; and the "Gymnasium Text" in Tcherikover, *Corpus Papyrorum Judaicarum*, vol. 3, 416.

cosmic dualism in the Essene scrolls, with the *beni or* versus the *beni hoshek*, and of the rabbinic and earlier *yetzer ha-tob* versus the *yetzer ha-ra*. In abnormal situations, the split personality becomes directed against the other within the individual. (This phenomenon only partly explains the demon possessions abundant in the time of Jesus of Nazareth.) Similarly, there is a tortured struggle for integration of ideals in the individual (placarded in many passages in Early Jewish literature, especially in the Hodayoth, the Prayer of Manasseh, and the early version of the Shemone Esreh).

The eschatological bifurcation of time so fecund and paradigmatic for Early Judaism, especially during the period we have chosen to study, leads to another potential perception of "the other:" the coming militant "other," the present community versus the coming other community, and the individual versus the eschatological, hopefully paradisiac, other self. This understanding serves as a caveat: all our inquiries must be multi-dimensional.

The purpose of the present paper is to discern how "the other," in all its potential meanings, is perceived and portrayed in the Jewish apocalypses that postdate the burning of the Temple in 70 and predate the defeat of Simon Bar Cochba in 135. So articulated, our purpose elicits three questions: 1) Why this period? 2) Why this literature? 3) Why this question?

First, the period is chosen because it is a pivotal one in the history of Judaism and, of course, one which I have been trying to master. In the decades chosen for our focus, the well-defined time of Second-Temple Judaism comes to an end. With 135 and, only to a certain extent, earlier in 70, the history of Israel and Early Judaism comes to a definitive telos, a clear breaking point from which rabbinic Judaism develops (although it is adumbrated in much that precedes both 135 and 70). This period of history is chosen also because here in this period of lost dreams—indeed the Temple and nation were lost—we might well catch a glimpse of "the other" as it was understood by a defeated people. Here, perhaps, we may find frank statements unadulterated by concessions and balanced tact, although now we must be alert for the distorting emotions of the time and the obvious logical bent towards polemics. Yet, it is precisely in such religious documents that we will find both the deep roots of culture and the definitive configuration of "the other."

Second, the literature has been chosen because along with Josephus' books and the non-redacted portions of the Mishnah, the Jewish apocalypses are major sources for perceiving the thought-world of Judaism from 70 to 135. It is also propitious to focus upon this literature because for the first time in the history of scholarship, the

Jewish apocalypses are now gathered together for review with reliable English translations and introductions in *The Old Testament
Pseudepigrapha: Apocalyptic Literature & Testaments*.[3] Further, a
guide to recent debates and publications can be found in *The
Pseudepigrapha and Modern Research with a Supplement*.[4] Moreover, a good collection of essays with varied opinions has just been
edited by Paul D. Hanson in *Visionaries and their Apocalypses*, and
a symposium of scholarly papers has been edited by David Hellholm
in *Apocalypticism in the Mediterranean World and the Near East*.[5]
Last year, 1983, witnessed a major shift in the availability of sources
for the study of the literature we have chosen for examination.

Now we are left with the third of our initial questions: Why ask
how "the other" is portrayed? Without any doubt, the question is
major and neglected, even if it is anachronistic to the periods under
discussion—(A fact witnessed to by the constellation of scholars who
have chosen to frequent these dusty halls of academia when the
mountains nearby and the beaches to the east and south are so much
more inviting.) But wherein lies the essential depth behind the
question?

Every endeavor has essentially one and the same purpose. The
herculean efforts to scale our highest peak, Mt. Everest, are identical
to the Olympic drive—now going on—to be the best in the present
and perhaps in history. The struggle of the author of 4 Ezra is the same
pilgrimage taken by the so-called Zosimus in the History of the
Rechabites, the astronauts, Carl Lewis, and ourselves. Our publications, if they are good ones, are parallel to the space shuttle. The drive
is essentially the same. In the last analysis, we are searching the
universe in quest of the definition and limits of *homo sapiens*; and
when the pen is laid down from the weary hand, the search has been
for the self which, as Kant knew, is that mysterious dynamo that moves
so rapidly during life it remains eternally elusive. And that is the
essence of all which has been rapidly reviewed in this paragraph.
Behind even *fides quaerens intellectum* lies the yearning to return
home through the Hominidae to oneself in an exploration of the
"I"–which even gramatically resists being viewed objectively.

In the process of the ego's search for the self, no other element

---

[3] J. H. Charlesworth, ed., *The Old Testament Pseudepigrapha*: *Apocalyptic Literature
& Testaments* (Garden City, New York: 1983).
[4] J. H. Charlesworth, *The Pseudepigrapha and Modern Research With a Supplement*,
Septuagint and Cognate Studies 7S (Chico, California: 1981).
[5] P. D. Hanson, *Visionaries and their Apocalypses*, Issues in Religion and Theology,
No. 2 (London and Philadelphia: 1983); D. Hellholm, *Apocalypticism in the Mediterranean World and the Near East* (Tübingen: 1983).

looms so large as the effectively catalytic and formative force from and of "the other." This factor alone protects us from taking up a stance whereby we are lost in discourses with ourselves—and none are madder than they who speak only to themselves. The whole dimension of intentionality and transference which is the essence of language is aborted.

In searching for "the other" and the idea of the other in the Jewish apocalypses composed between 70 and 135, we are on the way towards grasping the Jews' search for Jewishness. We may begin to perceive the footprints of the early wandering Jew who seeks a somatic, psychic, intellectual and religious home in a land of burned maps.

It is only in the deeply serious and intensely emotional documents (that is, religious texts) that we shall find answers to our search for our past *via*, with ourselves as a *viator*. Here is the *viaticum* for self-discovery within a context in which there is only one ultimate OTHER, Yahweh, who wills us to grasp the meaning of *imago dei* in a covenantal circumcised form, and with the *cor malignum* (cf. 4Ezra 3: 20-27, cf. 7:(62)-(74) and 46 [=116]−61[=131]). The evolution of the self is never so clearly revealed in any theory or in any myriad of relics in the biological evolution of mankind as it is in religious writings. Here we find, most sensitively and accurately articulated, the poetic vision of the self. The "I" begins to see past "me" to the "I," if only in a mirrored realm. It was along these lines of discourse, I am convinced, that Jacob Neusner was moving when he wrote the following:

> In the humanistic study of religions, we seek those intellectually sound methods for description, analysis, and interpretation that permit us to see the other in ourselves, and ourselves in the other. These all provide examples of a shared existence. When the humanistic study of religions succeeds, the alien seems less strange. Then, too, the self seems more strange. The alien is within. It is when we understand that we remain perpetually outsiders in our own richly complex, astonishing traditions, strangers where we feel most at home, that the humanistic study of religions begins.
>
> (*Take Judaism*, p. xvii)

Perhaps it is such thoughts as these, in Neusner's *Take Judaism, for Example: Studies Toward the Comparison of Religions,* that served as the intellectual precursor to the present colloquium.[6]

---

[6] J. Neusner, *Take Judaism, for Example: Studies Towards the Comparison of Religions.* Chicago Studies in the History of Judaism. (Chicago and London: 1983).

Methodology

Having come to the end of the introduction, we now confront a major caveat regarding methodology. We cannot merely proceed to the texts that were written with the explicit purpose of explaining the Jewish view of the other. No documents were written with that as the primary purpose. We must proceed, therefore, so as first to understand the date, likely provenience, original language and, especially, original intent of the document. Only when we have heard what the author intended to say can we begin to discern—perhaps only to speculate— what may have been the view concerning the other. Images may have to be decoded and assessed for their relevance, symbolic power, and implicit connotations.

In order to avoid eisegesis, and letting our main question reshape and distort the original thoughts of an author, ten questions will be asked of each document. These methodological questions are the following:

1 What is the original intent of the author or authors?
2 How is this purpose helpful in our search for the author's concept of the other?
3 How does the social situation shape or distort the author's view of the other?
4 Who is the other?
5 Is the other too dominant or recessive, thereby undermining community and individual?
6 What are the author's linguistic means of defining the other?
7 What are the functions of the author's use of symbolic language to express and categorize the other?
8 What is present or absent impressively?
9 How does the search for the author's view of the other help clarify the meaning of the document?
10 If the author is deeply religious, how is the other perceived in terms of God as OTHER?

Obviously these questions are each important, but to proceed with a document applying each question in the above order would produce a mechanical and lifeless product. The following essay is the result of keeping these questions in mind when reading and re-reading each document and then organizing the observations into a meaningful summary. The questions evoke a sensitivity in us which produces a more accurate assessment of an author's view of the other.

The Jewish apocalypses composed between 70 and 135 are to be studied in three categories. First, are those for which we have reliable texts, namely 4 Ezra and 2 Baruch. Second, are those which are preserved only in much later, redacted, and unreliable Slavonic recensions. These are 2 Enoch and the Apocalypse of Abraham. Third, are apocalypses fraught with problems regarding dates and character. These are the Apocalypse of Zephaniah, 3 Baruch, the so-called Apocalypse of Adam, and the Apocalypse of Elijah. The first category alone provides our major sources, for only 4 Ezra and 2 Baruch are clearly Jewish apocalypses and date within our chosen chronological framework. Our exempla, therefore, will be only these two apocalypses, 4 Ezra and 2 Baruch.

At the outset it is pertinent and instructive rapidly to review the attitude to the other in the well-researched Christian apocalypse, the Apocalypse of John. This apocalypse was written in the last decade of the first century C.E. It may come from Asia Minor, perhaps Ephesus, and was written by a Jew converted to Christianity who thought in a Semitic language but wrote in a Semitized Greek. The author's major purpose was to encourage the Christian individuals and communities fearing martyrdom or decimation by the other—clearly Rome and Domitian's self-deific cultus—to persevere. The author accomplishes this task by transporting the reader from his contemplations of the seemingly invincible might of Rome and her armies to a vision of a heavenly realm. There, the attentive reader sees the source of all power graphically displayed. This source of all power is the one who alone is powerful; only the lamb, the crucified Christ, can open the cosmic seals. He alone is addressed as *kurios: Amēn, erchou, kurie Iēsou* (ApJn 22:20). The twofold technique—the transference of the reader to the heavenly realm and the pictorial disclosure (*apokalypsis*) of eternal majesty and power—reveals the essence of apocalyptic thought.

The other in the Apocalypse of John is almost always Rome, and she is consistently viewed as demonic. Antipas has already been martyred in Pergamum, in which ὁ θρόνος τοῦ Σατανᾶ has been placed (2:13), an apt description of the first center for the Roman cult in Asia Minor. The beast described in 13:11-18 is Nero, as R.H. Charles suggested in his commentary (vol. I, p. 367). We now know this identification more certainly thanks to the discovery of a Dead Sea Scroll fragment which preserves a fuller spelling of Nero's name in Hebrew, ‏נרון קסר‎ . Numerically, this name adds up to 666 (cf. DJD, vol. II, p. 100; plate XXIX). Rome is Babylon the great, who forces the people to drink impurities (14:8), and whom the angel proclaims as fallen. In an amazing flash of unexpected clarity the author presents a pellucid portrayal of Rome: She is the great whore, opulent and debauched; she is ἡ μήτηρ τῶν πορνῶν καὶ τῶν βδελυγμάτων τῆς γῆς (17:5). The source of her drunkenness is now crystal clear: μεθύουσαν ἐκ τοῦ αἵματος τῶν ἁγίων καὶ ἐκ τοῦ αἵματος τῶν μαρτύρων Ἰησοῦ (17:6).

With an aside to the well-known Nero redivivus myth in 17:8 (cf. SibOr 5.33-34), the author explains that the great whore sits on seven hills (17:9). He concludes: Καὶ ἡ γυνὴ ἥν εἶδες ἔστιν ἡ πόλις ἡ μεγάλη ἡ ἔχουσα βασιλείαν ἐπὶ τῶν βασιλέων τῆς γῆς (17:18). Her doom is sealed; the international merchants who sold their luxuries in Rome will stand far off and weep over her and lament her demise. The saints, apostles and prophets, however, shall rejoice over her just end because ἐν αὐτῇ αἷμα προφητῶν καὶ ἁγίων εὑρέθη (18:24). Moreover, in heaven a hallelujah is sung because God has judged the great whore and avenged τὸ αἷμα τῶν δούλων αὐτου (19:2).

The theme of Rome as the other who stands against God's holy ones is pervasive in the Apocalypse of John. This emphasis is so thoroughgoing that it produces an excessive concept that is misrepresentative of Christian theology. Only the souls who have been beheaded for their witness to Jesus and refused to worship the emperor (the beast) will be resurrected and reign with Christ for a thousand years (19:1-6). Obviously, this promise leaves out a majority of the Christians who lived in the first century.

This portrayal of Rome may be called the concept of the demonic other. It would be difficult to conceive of a more devasting portrayal of the other. Rome is symbolized through the most disgusting and despicable image—she is a bloody whore, and that is a shocking concept even to our modern (non-Victorian) ears. Our usual terms, like "harlot," do only partial justice to the author's symbolism. She is despised because, as the other, she devours the individual in the author's community. I disagree with G.B. Caird's argument in his *The Revelation of St. John the Divine* that Antipas "must" have been "the only martyr" and that he may have died as a result of "mob violence."[7] While, in the past, scholars have certainly exaggerated Domitian's persecution of Christians, Antipas is probably symbolic of those who were put to death because of their witness to Jesus and refusal to worship Domitian and *Dea roma*.

"The demonic other" will be one possible perspective on Rome for authors of Jewish apocalypses who were contemporaries of the author of the Apocalypse of John. And it is a significant factor in Early Judaism. It is representative of the erosion in relations between

---

[7] G. B. Caird, *The Revelation of St. John the Divine*, Harper New Testament Commentaries (New York and London: 1966), p. 38.

so-called pagans and Jews in Judea—a factor which U. Rappaport calls "the essential reason" for the open rebellion of the late sixties.[8]

There are other possibilities including the reverse, "the benevolent other." This conceptual possibility will seem remote to specialists who know how Rome is portrayed in works like the Sibylline Oracles (Books 3 and 5), the Psalms of Solomon (esp. Psalm 2), the Qumranic War Scroll, and Sepher Zerubbabel. As G. Stemberger demonstrates in *Die Römische Herrschaft im Urteil der Juden*, there was a wide spectrum of Jewish attitudes to Rome,[9] including the contradictory or ambiguous statements in Josephus and Philo. For perceptual clarification, it is important to look at I Maccabees 8.

In 1 Maccabees 8 we do not find anti-Roman propaganda. It is antithetical to the writings of Mithridates VI of Pontus. Rome's invisible might is acknowledged, but the emphasis falls on her loyalty to friends: μετὰ δὲ τῶν φίλων αὐτῶν καὶ τῶν ἐπανπαυομένων αὐτοῖς συνετήρησαν φιλίαν.[10] For those of us who stand on this side of 70 and 135, it is surprising that for the author of 1 Maccabees 8, Rome is the Jew's best friend. Rome is the other who will protect the Jews; she is in covenant relationship with the Jewish people. Rome informs King Demetrius: "Why have you made your yoke heavy upon *our friends* and allies the Jews? If now they appeal again for help against you, we will defend their rights and fight you on sea and on land" (8:31-32 RSV; italics mine).

This positive view of the other—the Romans—was widespread in second-century B.C.E. Palestinian Judaism. It never vanished totally—it is evident to some degree both in the friendly portrayal of Vespasian in *Aboth de-R. Nathan* (Recension A, 4; ed. Schechter, p. 22) and in the attitude of Judah ben Elai (B.Shab. 33b). As one can learn from reading G. Vermes' "Ancient Rome in Post-Biblical Jewish Literature" and, especially, J. Neusner's *A Life of Johanan ben Zakkai*, the establishment of the rabbinic academy at Jamnia is related to a pro-Roman faction in Palestinian Judaism.[11]

A positive friendship continued between Rome and the Jews in the late first century B.C.E., but probably only officially (cf. Ps Sol). Rome did honor Herod with the title *Socius et Amicus Populi Romani*, and this recognition may be traced back to Antipater's assistance of

---

[8] U. Rappaport, "Jewish-Pagan Relations and the Revolt against Rome in 66-70 C. E.," *The Jerusalem Cathedra*, L. I. Levine ed. (Jerusalem: 1981), vol. 7, pp. 81-95.

[9] G. Stemberger, *Die Römishche Herrschaft im Urteil der Juden*, Erträge der Forschung 195 (Darmstadt: 1983).

[10] See 8:11 in Greek and 8:12 in the RSV; cf. 8:7, 17, 20, and 37 in the RSV.

[11] G. Vermes, "Ancient Rome in Post-Biblical Jewish Literature," *Post-Biblical Jewish Studies*, SJLA 8 (Leiden: 1975); J. Neusner, *A Life of Johanan ben Zakkai* (Leiden: 1970²).

Julius Caesar in Egypt in 48-47 B.C.E. The relationship between Rome and Judea was complex and not one-sided, as F. F. Bruce illustrates in a marvelously succinct essay titled "The Romans Through Jewish Eyes."[12]

For the author of 4 Ezra and other Jewish apocalypses that postdate 70, there was a spectrum of possibilities for portraying Rome "the other," from the demonic other, as in the Apocalypse of John, to the benevolent other, as in 1 Maccabees 8. These preliminary methodological and perceptual clarifications now prepare us to seek to discern how the other is portrayed and perceived in the Jewish apocalypses written between 70 and 135.

4 Ezra

The Jewish body of the Fourth Book of Ezra, namely chapters three through fourteen, was composed from pre-seventy Jewish traditions within a few decades of the burning of Jerusalem by the Romans under Titus in 70. Since this catastrophic event (which climaxes the defeat of the Jews) is the central issue behind all of Ezra's questions to Uriel, it is reasonable to conclude that this Jewish apocalypse was written in or near Jerusalem. The extant Latin manuscripts undoubtedly go back to a Greek recension, but there is no doubt that behind it and the extant Syriac version lies an original work that was composed in a Semitic language, perhaps Aramaic, but probably Hebrew. The original purpose of this apocalypse is reflected in both Ezra's questions and Uriel's answers. There is no single organized purpose for this writing, it rather reflects the inarticulate anguish and social anomie that logically followed the destruction of God's chosen people and Temple by idolatrous pagans. The social setting of this writing explains why Ezra's queries are so sharp, penetrating and devasting. They had been honed on the anvil of Roman iron.

The other standing against the Jew and his community is obviously Rome. The first two verses in the opening chapters, in veiled apocalyptic language that substitutes Babylon for Rome and Salathiel for Ezra, refer to the destruction of Jerusalem, *ruinae ciuitatis*; Ezra is exasperated because he sees unadulteratedly the desolation of Zion (*uidi desertionem Sion*) and the Romans' riches (*et habundantiam eorum*; cf. Syriac *WKHYNWTHWN*). A major theme is, then, a contrast: the poverty of the Jew and the wealth of the other. Yet readers

---

[12] F. F. Bruce, "The Romans Through Jewish Eyes," in *Paganisme, Judaïsme, Christianisme: Mélanges offerts à Marcel Simon*, A Benoit, M. Philonenko and C. Vagel eds. (Paris: 1978), pp. 3-12.

who assume that the author of 4 Ezra will now seek to embody the demonic other in a particular other will be surprised, as we shall see.

4 Ezra is a narrative by one author, who uses much older traditions.[13] The author arranged his thoughts under seven visions which are in dialogue form. In the first vision, 3:1-5:20, Ezra (Salathiel) raises numerous penetrating questions centered on humanity's plight. The individual is uppermost in his mind; Adam was burdened with a *cor malignum* (3:20, 21; cf. 4:30) and so transgressed and was overcome (3:21). This evil inclination, this *granum seminis mali* (4:31) becomes a disease inherited by all Adam's descendants. Only to a certain extent does this evil, obviously in every Jew, explain the loss of Zion and the devastation of the promised land. Ezra asks Uriel why God's enemies (3:21) have been given the Jews' land when they have sinned far more than the inhabitants of Jerusalem.

The community is also foremost in the author's mind. It is called "your people" (God's people), Zion, and Israel. The other is "your enemies" (3:30)—clearly God's enemies—Babylon, which is Rome. A dualism, developed into a paradigm, introduces the author's thought; Israel is contrasted with the gentile (4:23), and "the people whom you loved" is set against the "godless tribes" (4:23). A term later developed under this dualism is the "Many" (4:34), which the author later will contrast with "the one."

Most significantly, the author is not writing from a relaxed, detached perspective. He is "greatly agitated" (3:3). The reason is obvious; from the inhabitants of the world, or earth (3:34-36) comes one nation, whom we shall call "the other." This one defeated the nation God loved. The questions are without doubt superior here in the first vision to the vapid answers. Even Uriel must confess some ignorance (4:52).

In terms of our search for "the other" in the early Jewish apocalypses, the most impressive discovery from the first vision is that the devasting deeds by "the other" have forced a Jew—and certainly also others, perhaps his community—to think about the individual and the community. The burning of the Temple seared the Jewish consciousness so that introspective probes led to a search for the meaning of evil in the world and in each person especially. This quest demanded the interrogative mood. So perspicacious were the reflections from this mood that any answer paled in comparison.

---

[13] The literary unity of 4 Ezra has been recently demonstrated by A. L. Thompson in his *Responsibility for Evil in the Theodicy of IV Ezra*. A. L. Thompson, *Responsibility for Evil in the Theodicy of IV Ezra*, SBL Dissertation Series, No. 29 (Missoula, Montana: 1977).

The other was not the central topic. The other's hostility and destructiveness forced a confrontation with the self. What is the meaning of all this that has transpired through the other for me, the Jew, and the Jewish community? Formerly, we tended to think that the Jewish community ceased to exist in Judea and Jerusalem. Archeological research has now proved that Jerusalem was not razed in 70; moreover, it seems likely that some form of worship (not sacrifice as before) continued in the Temple between 70 and 135. Perhaps the "40,000" Jews allowed to settle anywhere (the figure is probably inflated; *Wars* 6.386) abode in Jerusalem, which had not been made uninhabitable, but which had lost its population from the war (*Wars* 6.420-29). Our reflections on the first vision of 4 Ezra have led us to observe that the meaning of the Roman conquest of Palestine for the community clarifies that there was a community in Judea and that it was searching for answers with regard to a flood of questions related to being God's people with his will, the Torah.

The Jewish community existing in Jerusalem seems to be mirrored in 13:40-45. Representatives from it come to Ezra and say to the visionary "if you forsake us, how much better it would have been for us if we also had been consumed in the burning of Zion!" (Metzger in *OTP*, vol. 1, p. 551).

The second vision of Ezra (5:21-6:34) has little to inform us regarding the author's view of "the other." In this vision the author focuses on questions regarding eschatology, a concern found also in the first vision (cf. 4:26-52). He uses terms such as "the first age" and "the age that follows" (5:7) which reveal how close this writing often is to early rabbinic theology—here to *ha-olam ha-zeh* and *ha-olam ha-ba*.

Developed in this section, however, is the concept of "the many" and "the one." In 5:23-30 the author, in poetic phrases, reviews how God chose from many one: from many lands, one land; from many peoples, one people. Yet this paradigm is used to articulate one question: "And now, O Lord, why have you given over *unum pluribus*" (5:28)?

The many—*plurimus* or *multus* and ܣܓܝ̈ܐܐ —is a reflex of the other that stands opposite "the one:" *unus* and ܚܕ . The essential thought now is a question: Why has God given the one he chose to the many? Why have you, O Lord, dishonored the one "who believed your covenants" (5:29) and punished the one by using the other "who opposed your promises" (5:29)? Opposing the tradition (well known, for example, in 1 Baruch 1) that the Lord chastises his sinful and disobedient nation through another nation (1Bar 1:17-19), the author of 4 Ezra rejects this solution through a question: "If you really hate your people, they should be punished at your own hands" (5:30, *OTP*).

Ezra's anguish is developed further. He refers to his grief and "agonies of heart" (5:34). He suffers in the attempt "to understand the way of the Most High and to search out part of his judgment" (5:34, *OTP*).

Uriel's reply is arrestingly short and sharp: "You cannot" (5:35, *OTP*). Clearly, the author's view is now reflected in Ezra's answers. The force of the other's oppressive presence has caused Ezra to find in himself an opaqueness to answers. His discovery is reminiscent of the more recent perceptions obtained by Immanuel Kant, who argued that the self, the universe, and God are a priori, regulative concepts or realities, and noumena that are ultimately unknown.

The second vision was short, but the third one is long (6:35-9:25). In it, "the other" is noticeably absent, except for an aside in 6:57. The concern is for the damnation of the many, the salvation of the few (7:[47]-[61], 8:1), and the time for the impending judgment. Ezra reiterates his anguish (6:36-37), expresses his consternation over the failure and sin of God's people (7:51 [121], 8:32), and articulates a most penetrating consciousness of interior and inherited sin (7:48 [118], cf. 7: [48]).

The fourth vision (9:26-10:59) re-emphasizes, in Ezra's words, that "we who have received the Law and sinned will perish" (9:36 *OTP*). After eating flowers, a change from his usual habit of fasting between visions, Ezra sees a woman mourning. She is Zion. Ezra also sees the woman transformed gloriously; she represents the heavenly Jerusalem. Obviously, then, the central concern is the destruction of Jerusalem, which is now described in detail (10:19-24). The only reference to "the other" in this vision is the reference to "those that hate us" (10:23, *OTP*).

The concept of the other is developed for the first time in the fifth vision (11:1-12:51). The author allegorically portrays Daniel's fourth kingdom as an eagle which rises out of the sea (cf. 1QpHab 3.6-14 and ApJn 13:1-10): It has twelve large wings, eight small wings, and three heads. The eagle rules over all the earth (11:2, cf. 11:5) and no other nation shall rule the earth so long—a reference apparently to Augustus, as G. H. Box long ago thought and as M. A. Knibb now argues.[14]

The view of "the other" is found in the lion's speech to the eagle. According to the interpretation of the vision in 12:4-39, these sym-

---

[14] G. H. Box, *APOT* Vol. 2, p 610; M. A. Knibb with R. J. Coggins, *The First and Second Books of Esdras*, The Cambridge Bible Commentary on the NEB (Cambridge: 1979), p. 240.

bolic figures are inversely Daniel's fourth kingdom, here the Roman
empire, and the Davidic Messiah. The interpretation clarifies, *inter
alia*, that the eagle's twelve wings are twelve kings, the eight little
wings are eight kings with short reigns, and the three heads are three
kings who will reign more oppressively in the last days. The interpretation stresses Rome's ungodliness, wickedness, contemptuous
dealings, and warranted destruction by the Messiah.

The Messiah begins his words with a prophetic formula: *dicit
altissimus tibi*, i.e ܐܡܪ ܠܟ ܡܪܝܐ (11:38). In the following
speech we catch a glimpse of the author's view of "the other." The
Messiah's report of God's message deserves to be quoted in full:

> saying, •"Listen and I will speak to you. The Most High says to you,
> •'Are you not the one that remains of the four beasts which I had
> made to reign in my world, so that the end of my times might come
> through them? •You, the fourth that has come, have conquered all the
> beasts that have gone before; and you have held sway over the world
> with much terror, and over all the earth with grievous oppression;
> and for so long you have dwelt on the earth with deceit. •And you
> have judged the earth, but not with truth; •for you have afflicted the
> meek and injured the peaceable; you have hated those who tell the
> truth, and have loved liars; you have destroyed the dwellings of those
> who brought forth fruit, and have laid low the walls of those who did
> you no harm. •And so your insolence has come up before the Most
> High, and your pride to the Mighty One. •And the Most High has
> looked upon his times, and behold, they are ended, and his ages are
> completed! Therefore you will surely disappear, you eagle, and your
> terrifying wings, and your most evil little wings, and your malicious
> heads, and your most evil talons, and your whole worthless body, •so
> that the whole earth, freed from your violence, may be refreshed and
> relieved, and may hope for the judgment and mercy of him who made
> it.' "
>   (11:38-46; Metzger in *OTP*)

According to God's words, Rome is indicted for terror, oppression,
deceit, judging without the truth, and, with thoughts of Palestine and
Jerusalem, destroying dwellings of "those who brought forth fruit"
and demolishing the walls of "those who did you no harm" (11:42).

The author's attitude to this "other" is innocuous compared to the
devastation and destruction it has brought on the author and his
community. Certainly, the opinion of Rome is not as caustic as that of
the author of the Apocalypse of John. In 4 Ezra, the other is not to be
categorized as "the demonic other;" 4 Ezra is less harsh.

The sixth vision (13:1-58) contains virtually no information regarding the author's view of the other. His concern is "something like the
figure of a man who arises out of the sea" (13:3), who is later identified

as God's son. He will reprove, reproach and destroy the ungodly nations. He will also gather to himself the lost ten tribes.

The seventh vision (14:1-48) contains admonitions to God's people through Ezra, and describes how five skilled scribes wrote 94 books of which 24 were made public; the others were to be reserved for those with wisdom. Here the concern for "the other" gravitates to God as *the* OTHER. He is a righteous judge (*Iustus iudex*) because he took Zion away from Israel who had transgressed the Torah. Either his thought has now changed or developed, but there is no reason to assume the author must be consistent. After all, he is torn apart by what he has experienced.

Summary

Our research discloses two insights. First, without a doubt, Ezra is depressed and exasperated because "the other" destroyed God's people whom he loved, and burned the Temple (cf. esp. 12:44). Secondly, there are only a few comments about Rome "the other." This discovery is surprising in light of the attitude to "the other" in the Apocalypse of John and the pessimistic tone of 4 Ezra which is caused by the other's diabolic actions. Our author's tolerance contrasts categorically with the intolerance for the outside in such authors as Milto of Sardis and Ephrem Syrus (see the papers in this volume by Wilson and Hayman).

Explorations for causes behind this surprising position must take into account the following aspects of 4 Ezra: 1) God is ultimately the one who is behind the loss of Zion and his actions are justified because of the unfaithfulness of those who were given Torah. This explanation, of course, ignores the problem that this idea is sometimes contradicted in the work itself. 2) "The other" has driven the author from extrospection to introspection, and he sees a *cor malignum* that is inveterate and inherited. Humanity was created in the image of God (*imago dei*), but Adam's willful transgression produces blindness and an inability to comprehend the truth, especially God's ways.

The other forced the Jew—in the words of this symposium—to see ourselves as others see us. Introspection lead to perspicacity.

In another sense, the author of 4 Ezra does not have the freedom of options available to the author of the Apocalypse of John, who can look around and never see a burned Temple. That author looks toward the coming descent of the heavenly Jerusalem. The author of 4 Ezra, on the other hand, still smells the smoke of Jerusalem; he remembers the Zealots' fierce hatred for the Romans, and he knows this concept, "the demonic other," caused the end of the Second Temple period. History prevented him from portraying Rome as a bloody whore.

In my estimation, 4 Ezra's hostility to Rome is not only less than that in the Apocalypse of John, but even less than the animosity found in a Jewish writing contemporaneous with it. In the Oracle against Rome in Sibylline Oracles 5.162-75 we find the following words:[15]

> Alas, city of the Latin land, unclean in all things, maenad, rejoicing in vipers, as a widow you will sit by the banks, and the river Tiber will weep for you, its consort. You have a murderous heart and impious spirit. (SibOr 5.168-71; Collins in *OTP* Vol. 1, p. 397).

John Collins, whose translation we have cited, argues that these verses against Rome are "unparalleled in bitterness anywhere in the Sibylline Oracles" (*OTP*, vol. 1, p. 391).

A final reason why the author of 4 Ezra is not excessively hostile to Rome may be his theological perception of the history of salvation. According to 11:44-45, all events are determined: *Et respexit altissimus super sua tempora, et ecce finita sunt, et saecula eius conpleta sunt* (11:44). This point is not to be developed or emphasized as other than a possibility; the Apocalypse of John is also deterministic.

Finally, in light of the debate about whether the author's position should be located in the questions or in the answers, it is apparent that truth is not to be found in an abstracted either or. It is to be found in the questions and the answers, and, fundamentally, not so much in both as in the dynamic unity of dialogue and anguished searching. In this sense, then, the real brilliance and penetrating insights are in the frank questions that at once defy answering and, as we have seen, are conditioned by a chaotic social setting full of bruised (if not aborted) traditions. Ezra's exasperation is the Jew's consternation over the loss of land and Temple; it is generated not so much from mind or heart as from *pneuma* and *Geist*. Hence, it is appropriate that the view of "the other" comes to the fore most clearly not in sections which contain questions or answers, but in a burst of prophetic words from God, through his Messiah. The OTHER (God) articulates the other's future damnation.

2 Baruch

The second major text we shall look at in depth is 2 (Syriac Apocalypse of) Baruch. It was composed a few years after 4 Ezra. Once again the central, formative, underlying force is the shock wave from the fall of the Temple's stones and from the wails of those being slaughtered, raped or carried away as slaves. 2 Baruch was composed in Palestine, perhaps in Jerusalem, but at least not far from there. The

---

[15] Cf. also 5. 386-95, 397-413.

extant Arabic manuscript derives from a Syriac manuscript, and the lone Syriac manuscript of chapters 1 through 77 (of the sixth or seventh century) reveals that the original language of 2 Baruch is Hebrew. Hence, 2 Baruch shares with 4 Ezra the same provenience, theological agenda centered on the issue of theodicy, original language, and social experience of alienation. The differences are, however, more impressive than the similarities.

P. M. Bogaert, in *Apocalypse de Baruch: Introduction, traduction du syriaque et commentaire,* and G. B. Sayler in her dissertation *Have the Promises Failed? A Literary Analysis of 2 Baruch,* have examined R. H. Charles' argument that 2 Baruch is merely a collection of sources.[16] They correctly show that 2 Baruch is a literary unity. In contrast to 4 Ezra's disorganized, anguished search for meaning in a chaotic and virtually nihilistic world, 2 Baruch moves in a narrative form—albeit disjointedly—in a circuitous fashion around one central thought: God is a true and just judge; because the Jerusalemites were faithless and evil, the loss of Zion was inevitable. The main purpose of this apocalypse is to strengthen the Jewish people—"your people"—by giving them a letter of instruction (or guidance) and a scroll of hope (cf. 2 Bar 78:12 in which the reflective ܐܪ appears twice).

The contradictions, for example the apparently conflicting disposition of the Temple's vessels and correlative views regarding a possible restoration of the earthly Temple, which A. F. J. Klijn emphasizes in *OTP,* should be explained in terms of the repetitive, unsystematic flow of narratives in apocalyptic literature.[17] Precisely the same style characterices the Apocalypse of John. (Scholars now rightly reject Charles' theory of sources and redaction.)

The structure of 2 Baruch must be ascertained before we can examine the theme of "the other." Only to a certain extent is 2 Baruch, like 4 Ezra, structured by transitions which describe the seer fasting.[18] For years I have argued that 2 Baruch is organized narratively under seven sections. (A somewhat similar division is defended by Bogaert in *Apocalypse de Baruch* and now followed by M. de Goeij in *De Pseudepigrafen,* volume 2.)[19] Now, under the stimulus from Sayler's literary analysis of 2 Baruch, I have re-examined my own understanding of 2 Baruch, and suggest the following tentative outline:

---

[16] P. M. Bogaert, *Apocalypse de Baruch: Introduction, traduction du syriaque et commentaire,* 2 vols, SC 144 and 145 (Paris: 1969). G. B. Sayler, *Have the Promises Failed? A Literary Analysis of 2 Baruch,* SBL Dissertation Series, No. 72 (Chico, California: 1984).

[17] A. F. J. Klijn, *OTP,* vol. 1, p. 617.

[18] See 2 Bar 5:7, 12:5, 20:5, 47:1-2; but also cf. 9:1 and 43:1.

[19] M. de Goeij, *De Pseudepigrafen,* (Kampen: 1981), vol. 2, pp. 63-66.

I	1-5	beg. 1:1 "And it happened in . . . that . . ."
		end. 5:7 "And we sat there and fasted . . . ."
II	6-12	beg. 6:1 "Now it happened on . . . that, behold . . . ."
		end. 12:5 "I fasted for seven days . . . ."
III	13-20	beg. 13:1 "And after these things, it happened that . . . and behold . . . ."
		end. 20:5 a reference to fasting (divine instruction to Baruch)
IV	21-34	beg. 21:1f. "I went from there and sat . . . And after this . . . ."
		end. 34:1 Baruch leaves his people
V	35-47	beg. 35:1 "And I, Baruch, went to . . . ."
		end. 47:1f. ". . . and I sat there and fasted seven days."
VI	48-52	beg. 48:1 "And it happened after seven days that I . . . ."
		end. 52:7 "And when I had said this I fell asleep there."
VIII	53-77	beg. 53:1 "And I saw a vision. And behold . . . ."
		end. 77:16ff. "And it happened on . . . that I, Baruch, came and sat down under the oak . . . ."

In the first section, 1-5, the author argues that the "evil things" were not done by the other but by "the two tribes." He emphasizes that no other nation or king forced them to sin (1:3). The burned Jerusalem, moreover, is not the real Jerusalem; the true Jerusalem is yet to be revealed, is primordial, was seen by Adam before he sinned, and "is preserved with" God (4:6).

In chapter five, "the other" appears clearly. It is "your haters" (ܣܢܐ̈ܝܟ) who came to Jerusalem and polluted "your sanctuary," carried off "your heritage into captivity," and ruled "over them whom you love" (5:1). They boast before their idols (5:1). The other is "the enemy"; but it "shall not destroy Zion and burn Jerusalem . . ." (ܢܚܪܒ ܠܨܗܝܘܢ ܘܠܐ ܗܘܐ ܠܐܘܪܫܠܡ, 5:3). Clearly, "the other" is Rome. But Zion is not—as one might expect—the heavenly, primordial Jerusalem.

All of these words regarding "the other" lack the fire and anguish of 4 Ezra. The other's categorical acts of hostility against the individual, Baruch, and his community are intellectualized. The other becomes impotent by a transference from the earthly to the ideal. The author of 2 Baruch, who is gifted, has withdrawn into an intellectual realm where "the other" cannot enter. Reality is denied by redefining the real. As we shall see, the incredible is conceived. The Roman armies are not the ones who demolish the walls of Jerusalem.

The second section, 6-12, has numerous references to "the other." It comprises "an army of Chaldeans," that is, the Romans. But, because an angel from heaven has already hidden the treasures, the Romans do not recover the spoils from the Temple. "The other"—the enemies of the Jews—does not destroy the walls of Jerusalem. Four angels demolish them. "The other" is allowed to enter the Temple only after a voice is heard saying: "Enter, enemies, and come, adversaries, because he who guarded the house has left it" (8:2; Klijn in *OTP*). "The other" is Babylon, who is happy, but "Zion has been destroyed" (11:2).

The import of these verses becomes clear when we ask two simple questions: 1) what would Titus have thought about this scenario? 2) has the realism so important to the Heilsgeschichte of the Bible been seriously compromised by this redefinition of the land, the city, and the Temple?

The thrust of these chapters is to affirm that no nation can subdue or conquer God's people. However, the chosen nation has sinned against God; hence God has withdrawn from his earthly house, ordered his messengers to remove the Temple treasures, destroyed the walls, and invited the enemy to enter. God alone is powerful. The author of 4 Baruch later even stresses that the Lord destroyed the Temple with his own hands (ἐκ τῶν χειρῶν σου, 1:6), and Josephus claimed that God was Titus' assistant (*Wars* 5.1.3, 6.9.1).

The thought in 2 Baruch is poetically expressed by a contemporary, the author of the Odes of Solomon, who wrote the following:

> No man can pervert Thy holy place, O my God;
> Nor can he change it, and put it in another place.
>
> Because (he has) no power over it;
> For Thy sanctuary Thou designedst before Thou didst make special places.
>
> (OdesSol 4:1-2)

A similar thought is also found in the Apocalypse of Abraham, which is contemporaneous with 4 Ezra, 2 Baruch, and the Odes of Solomon. The Jerusalem Temple is "the place prepared beforehand" (ApAb 29:17).

The unique thought of 2 Baruch is impressive. It is very different from the Apocalypse of Abraham 27, which reports that "a crowd of heathens" (the Romans) "burned the Temple with fire" and "plundered the holy things that were in it" (27:3, *OTP*). 2 Baruch is also considerably different from Sibylline Oracle 5.408-13, according to which "a certain insignificant and impious king" (ἀφανὴς βασιλεὺς καὶ ἄναγνος) left Jerusalem in ruins.

In section three the author argues that God's judgment is impartial; hence, "his sons" were punished so that they might be forgiven. "The other" is "the nations" or "gentiles" (ܥܡܡܐ , 13:5), who are guilty (13:11), because they have trampled the earth (.ܐܪܥܐ ܘܕܫܘܗ), used the creation unrighteously, and always denied God's beneficence.

Again, as in 4 Ezra, "the other" is the many who have sinned (cf. 15:2) in contrast with the few, such as Moses (18:1-2) and the righteous (15:2). Also reminiscent of 4 Ezra is the poetic expression of humanity's inability to comprehend the Lord's ways (14:8-9). This thought is also strikingly similar to the Odes of Solomon 26:8-13. It is answered somewhat in 2 Baruch 15:5: Humanity—not just Israel—had been given the Law and instructed "with understanding" so that *all* can "understand my judgment." So the evil person will be punished "because he has understanding" (15:6, *OTP*).

The author of 2 Baruch recognizes a crisis (14:19), but he does not share the brokenness and anguish of the author of 4 Ezra. The unique thrust of 2 Baruch is reiterated, in a different way, through a *verbum domini*: "I now took away Zion to visit the world in its own time more speedily" (20:2). Here we find an elevation of the thought that "the other" did not take Zion away from God's people. The eschatological thrust now becomes clear; "the other" has been totally removed from the scene, but only temporarily. God is about to show his "strong judgment" and "inexplorable ways" (20:4). Exhortatively, our author could have added *verbum sapienti sat est*.

Section four of 2 Baruch (21-34) contains a prayer by Baruch in which many urgent needs are uttered. The author's tribulation shows forth through the plea "reprove the angel of death" (21:23). Baruch concludes his prayer with an eschatological plea "show your glory soon" (21:25). It seems to me that in these verses—as one might expect in a prayer in which sheer honesty reigns—the author lets his defenses down and reveals that in many ways, deep down, he hurts for Zion just as did the author of 4 Ezra.

The most surprising aspect of this section is the paucity of attention given to "the other." "The other" is not seen in an eternal hell, condemned to damnation, or castigated, as one might expect knowing how apocalyptists often describe the tortures of the justly damned. This feature is especially evident in the Apocalypse of Peter, which is a near contemporary of 2 Baruch.[20]

The other is merely contrasted with the beloved people. Baruch's prayer is that God's power may be revealed (hence confirmed) by "those who believe that your long-suffering means weakness" (21:20), indeed, by "those who do not know, but who have seen that which has befallen us and our city, up to now . . ." (21:21; *OTP*).

In these verses, "the other" is more inclusive than the Romans who destroyed Judea and burned the holy city. It is conceivable that those who are ignorant, holding false beliefs, may include also unfaithful Jews, perhaps apostates, as well as other non-Romans (cf.47:3). In either case, it is remarkable how non-judgmental is the author of 2 Baruch.

The insider is contrasted with the outsider as the incorruptible is with the corruptible (28:1-7). Language frequently used with regard to those who are planted in Paradise, the land of eternal life (namely those who are incorruptible),[21] is applied to the sole group protected by the Lord: "But in that time I shall protect only those found in those days in this land" (.ܪܥܐ ܗܕܐ , 29:2). The insiders, encompassed by the hostility of "the other" are now perceived as the Palestinian Jews, and only them. Here we are confronted boldfacedly with the territorial promise so characteristic of the Old Testament and much of the literature in Early Judaism, a theme examined by W. D. Davies in *The Gospel and the Land: Early Christianity and Jewish Territorial Doctrine*.[22]

Concern for the Romans has receded from the author's consciousness. They are present, if at all, only generically. At the coming of the Messiah, the wicked will be tormented (30:4-5), but who the ܪܫܝܥܐ are is not specified.

In line with chapter 29, the thought of 31 is about those in the land. They are the insiders who are exhorted as follows: "Do not forget Zion but remember the distress of Jerusalem" (31:4). Such an exhortation would have been otiose, even unthinkable, to the author of 4 Ezra and his community. It is tempting to speculate that the author, like the Qumran Essenes, has entered into an antechamber of heaven.

The narrative thence continues with the prophecy that Zion will be rebuilt, re-destroyed, and finally rebuilt and "protected into

---

[20] Cf. M. Himmelfarb, *Tours of Hell: An Apocalyptic Form in Jewish and Christian Literature* (Philadelphia: 1983).

[21] Cf. OdesSol 11:1-24, 15:8, 22:11, 38:9-11, 40:6.

[22] W. D. Davies, *The Gospel and the Land: Early Christianity and Jewish Territorial Doctrine* (Berkley, London: 1974).

eternity" (32:4). The community is encouraged; "We should not . . . be so sad regarding the evil which has come now . . ." (32:5). The past is insignificant compared to the eschaton.

Baruch departs for "some days" (32:7). It is singularly important in our search for "the other" to observe that the community is seen wailing and lamenting. But they are not lamenting the loss of Zion; they bewail Baruch's departure.

In section five (35-47) Baruch is portrayed lamenting among the ruins of "the holy place," Jerusalem. He prostrates himself where the high priests offered holy sacrifices. Then he falls asleep and experiences a vision. The interpretation of the vision clarifies, regarding "the other" who has oppressed Baruch and his community, that the kingdom which destroyed Zion "will be destroyed" (39:3), that "a fourth kingdom" will be "harsher and more evil" than those before it, and that the Messiah will convict and slay "the last ruler" (40:1).

Baruch sees "many of your people who separated themselves from your statutes and who have cast away from them the yoke of your Law" (41:3, *OTP*). He also sees "others who left behind their vanity and who have fled under your wings" (41:5). The former are the apostates, the latter the proselytes, as Charles saw long ago. Klijn may be correct to perceive among the former the Christians who had been Jews.[23] If he is correct, then this reference is the only one to Christians in these two apocalypses. That should be surprising, for the non-vitriolic language contrasts with the polemics already in the air by 100 C.E.

As we noted at the outset, the community can divide so as to include "the other". According to 41:5, former members of "the other" have now formed part of the community. The borders between the community and "the other" are far less certain than they were to the author of 4 Ezra. To a certain extent, one can say the walls separating the insider from the outsider have crumbled (in places).

This sociological discovery helps explain a problem that lingers from the preceding probes. The author of Baruch cannot ascribe to "the demonic other," for numerous reasons, including the nature of his community's constituents. "The other"—certainly only an infinitesimal number—is found now within the community, and the community itself has lost some members, perhaps to "the other."

The author's concern is primarily with the insiders, with "those who have believed" (42:2), and who will be rewarded. The outsider, "those who have been treating [your Law] with contempt"[24] (42:2),

---

[23] OTP, vol. 1, p. 633.
[24] Cf. 41:3.

are insignificant, "for that which is now is nothing" (44:8). This opaqueness to "the other" is incommensurate with the catastrophies of seventy. 2 Baruch is phenomenologically and eschatologically divorced from the Roman scourge. In contrast to 4 Ezra, its aloofness is impressive.

Only two perspectives are paramount for our author: God's ways are inscrutable, and "the new world" is coming. The new world is eternal, incorruptible, and full of treasures (44:12-14). Within this ambience, the author of 2 Baruch understandably scarcely sees "the other" whose habitation "will be in the fire" (44:15). Logically, therefore, the author turns to—or returns to (cf. 44:2-3)—admonishing the insider (45:1-46:7).

The sixth section (48-52) begins with a celebration of God's unlimited and cosmic knowledge and wisdom. God is the totally OTHER. As for humanity, it is nothing (48:14). The author again employs the paradigm of the one and the many: "For we are a people of the Name; we, who received one Law from the One" (48:23, OTP).

In this chapter, forty-eight, the author comes down strongly on the solution to all problems: everything conceivable is resolved in the dimension of time, "in those days" (48:32) that are about to dawn. The present time is the prophesied time of affliction, enormous vehemence, God's judgment, loss of wisdom, bloodshed, and weeping (48:30-41). In these verses, the author displays a flash of brilliant insight into human psychology: "jealousy will arise in those who did not think much of themselves" (48:37, OTP).

2 Baruch is a cascade of answers upon answers, whereas 4 Ezra is a mélange of questions upon questions. Baruch's dogmatism contrasts unfavorably with Ezra's interrogativeness. Just about when we are saturated with the insensitiveness to the real problems in the world, we arrive at chapter forty-nine, a series of questions about the new age. As I have noted, these questions, are ultimately incomprehensible.[25] Also, the other is noticeably absent.

In chapter fifty-one "the other" surfaces again, and, as earlier, it is under a generic rubric. It is "those who are found to be guilty" (51:1). "The other" comprises the wicked who will suffer torment (51:2), will be transformed into "horrible shapes" (51:5), and "go away to be tormented" (51:6).

Surely, once again, the author is oblivious of "the other." It is as if "the other" is not a significant factor, as if the Romans burned Jerusalem a long time ago and returned to Rome, and as if all is normal

---

[25] OTP, vol. 1, p. 637.

in the world, as it has been since Adam was expelled from Paradise.
There are simply wicked and righteous people.

2 Baruch certainly postdates 70, but here we find an attitude to
Rome logically, but obviously not phenomenologically, out of character with the times. We must not be guilty of assessing the thought of
2 Baruch from the false logic of *post hoc, ergo propter hoc*. These
passages in 2 Baruch are reminiscent of an earlier time when the
Roman government honored and defended the Jews in Palestine and
elsewhere. This relationship is now less obscure thanks to the
publications of M. Stern and U. Rappaport.[26]

A search for sociological answers to the question of why 2
Baruch's author treats "the other" generically and is oblivious of
Rome must first confront a caveat: The author is shaped initially by a
sociological crisis, but he breathes the fragrance from another ideal
world and another final time of messianic blessedness.

Reflections on the social setting of 2 Baruch do open intriguing
insights into and questions about the author's community. It is
obvious, as we have seen, that the community is not only behind the
document, but also appears through the confrontations between
Baruch and God's people. Similarly, it is evident that this people
mourns for the loss of Zion and Temple, the *axis mundi* for Early
Judaism (cf. esp. Jub). Likewise, it is certain that the Davidic Psalter
had moved from scripture to canon by the time the author of 2 Baruch
wrote his apocalypse. Moreover, it is clear that this Jewish community
was driven deep liturgically into the Psalter in search for the articulate
vehicle for synagogally based Judaism. The Psalter, however, was
Temple-oriented and the apocalyptist and his community recited such
Temple Psalms as Psalm 84 and the opening of Psalm 87, especially
verses 1-3 (RSV):

> On the holy mount stands the city he founded;
>   the Lord loves the gates of Zion
>   more than all the dwelling places of Jacob.
> Glorious things are spoken of you,
>   O city of God.

These observations cumulatively lead to a critical question: How
can the individual and community recite these truths and yet not
share 4 Ezra's psychic anguish over the demolished city and burned
Temple? Is not God's house "forsaken and desolate" (Mt 23)?

---

[26] M. Stern, "Sympathy for the Jews in Roman Senatorial Circles in the Early Empire,"
Zion no. 29 (1964), pp. 155-167. U. Rappaport, in *The Jerusalem Cathedra*, vol. 1, pp.
81-95.

It is tempting to endorse L. Festinger's well-known theory of cognitive dissonance, and there is probably some insight to be garnered from his methodology, but presently I can endorse only one answer, an answer which is twofold. First, apocalyptic thought simultaneously dwells in two foci, the social setting—which is often the catalyst to apocalypticism—and the heavenly world or future age. The apocalyptist's perception shifts the source of all meaning to another realm and dimension. Second, apocalyptic thought is universalistic, cosmic, all-encompassing, and has answers for every conceivable question.

When 4 Ezra's questions appear unanswerable, then one of three factors may be operative: A particular passage has been uncritically ripped out of context and narrative; some sections are only apocalyptic because they are in an apocalypse; the questions are volcanic and primordial, but the drama has a telos in which God proves true on his judgment, כי טוב (Gen 1:25, 31).

Finally, the author and his community were free to re-interpret prophecies and traditions. The celebration of the Temple hence becomes a rejoicing in the eternal Temple shown to Adam, Abraham, and others. The apocalyptist and odist would stand ankle-deep in the rubble of Jerusalem and chant,

> For it suffices to perceive and be satisfied,
> For the odists stand in serenity . . . (OdesSol 26:12)

The contemplative one lives above the finiteness of "the other" in the *mysterium tremendi* of otherliness.

The faithful community, especially the individual, is the author's concern and focus. In exhortatory tones, the author celebrates the rewards of the righteous, of "those who are saved" (51:7) who "will be like the angels" (51:10), even "greater than that of the angels" (51:12). To a certain extent 2 Baruch is similar to the in-group literature of the New Testament; we are told about those who believed, those who are saved, and "the first will receive the last" (51:13). Two strikingly similar groups within Early Judaism will diverge and become labeled "Jewish" and "Christian". Once separate, each will turn and espy the other; then each will degenerate and spew forth invectives that are categorically satanic because "the other" is relegated as "the demonic other."

The final section of the apocalypse proper (53-77) reiterates much that has gone before. The evils in this world are represented in the black waters of Baruch's vision (53:1-12). The author absolves God, angels, or demonic forces of the wickedness in humanity. And unlike the author of 4 Ezra, he does not see Adam's sin as a *cor malignum* in all his descendants. In a poetic phrase, the author's position is articulated: "Adam is, therefore, not the cause, except only for himself, but each of us has become our own Adam" (54:19).

But the author undermines his main view. With Adam's sin, all the illnesses and misfortunes of this world appeared (56:6-16). Covering all bases, the author even refers to the sins associated with the fall of the angels (56:12-16;cf. Gen 6:1-4 and 1 Enoch 1-36). Apparently, the author has only one main concern: He wishes to show that God is perfectly just in his apparently harsh treatment of the chosen few and the coming judgment of the many. Later, in 57:2, the author refers to "the unwritten law" which was known before Moses, and dismisses any claim to innocence by non-Jews.

In this section, the other is visible only intermittently and insignificantly. As a group, it is addressed directly by Baruch. He tells "the unrighteous ones" to prepare for destruction (54:17). Again, "those who sin" are blotted out among the faithful ones. Perhaps the disappearance of the hostile "other" in the eschaton helps to explain why the author of 2 Baruch seldom notices or mentions it.

The division of times and the coming new age explain the apparent unbalance of injustice in the present (56:2). The Messiah, or Anointed One, is coming, and *all* will be delivered into his hands (70:9). He is God's servant who comes, calls *all* nations, spares some, and kills others (72:2). Especially noteworthy for an understanding of the author's view of Rome as "the other," is 72:6: "All those, now, who have ruled over you or have known you, will be delivered up to the sword" (Klijn in *OTP*).

With repeated celebrations of God's grandeur and incomprehensible goodness (75:1) the author concludes by re-emphasizing his opening perspective (cf. 1:2). The catastrophies that have befallen Zion are not caused by "the other;" they have occurred because "the place has sinned" (78:9). The community urges the individual, Baruch, to dispatch to those in Babylon (not Rome) "a letter of instruction (scholarship, doctrine, dogma) and a scroll of hope (ܐܓܪܬܐ ܕܝܘܠܦܢܐ ܘܡܓܠܬܐ ܕܣܒܪܐ. , 77:12). The eagle also takes a copy to the lost tribes. This image may be highly symbolical; the eagle was the symbol of the Roman legions (cf. my comments on 4 Ezra 12:4-39).

Running throughout the narrative of 2 Baruch is the celebration of God as OTHER. In the search for understanding of Zion's defeat, the author repeatedly says to God "You alone know the end of times" (21:8); "O Lord . . . Only you know . . ." (48:2-3); "You alone, O Lord, knew the heights of the world beforehand and that which will happen in the times which you bring about by your word" (51:1). Indeed, for the author of 2 Baruch, only God "knows what will happen in the future" (69:2).

Conclusion

The search for "the other" in 4 Ezra and 2 Baruch produces numerous significant insights which should not be systematized or even summarized. The differences between these two apocalypses are significant, and we must not repeat the common error of talking about apocalyptic thought or apocalypticism as if either was cohesive or unified. These are clearly crisis documents; yet even here 4 Ezra is different from 2 Baruch. Ezra in 4 Ezra is torn with anguish, distraught. He bewails that he ever lived (4:12), and is often seen mourning and weeping. Baruch, on the other hand, often is seen falling asleep (36:1, 52:7), and near the end he sits down to rest (55:1).

This is no place to pick up again the unanswered questions assembled above. The remarkable and significant discovery is that the invincible might of Rome, the horrifying and catastrophic loss of land, nation, and Temple, did not mean the demise of Judaism. It did not lead to the death of the Jewish *Geist* and *ésprit*. It did not produce literature that with promethean arrogance accused God of unfaithfulness. There were no charges similar to those that followed the Nazis' holocaust.

One question alone remains nagging, and must be readdressed. Community and individual have been destroyed by "the other," yet attention given to the other is incommensurate with the force with which it has interpenetrated land, community, and individual. Why did not the author of 4 Ezra, or even the author of 2 Baruch, take up the position of Rabbi Simon ben Yochai (140-163) who advised that we should slay the best of the gentiles? Why is "the other" almost non-existent in 4 Ezra and 2 Baruch?

Perhaps this question is to be explained by human psychology: What cannot be changed must be lived with and ignored as much as possible. This attitude is especially wise if the other continues to be diabolical but ceases to be threateningly destructive. Rome was apparently all-powerful; Judaism—despite its long history of covenantal relationship with God—was not only impotent but ripped apart and defeated. Rome however, was not the proximate other; she was the radical other, and so far removed from the essence of Judaism. Moreover, otherness—real otherness—as J. Z. Smith illustrated in our first paper, denies the possibility of discourse.

Another possible answer lies in the adverb used above. Rome was only apparently all powerful. The appropriate means to move from the apparent to the real in Early Judaism had been developed in and through the symbolisms and pictorial otherliness of the Jewish apocalyptic movements, apocalypticism, and literature (notably the apocalypses). Admittedly, 4 Ezra and 2 Baruch are far less pictorially oriented than the Apocalypse of John. But while no lamb is seen who alone is all powerful, nonetheless in 4 Ezra, for example, a Messiah and the son of God and in Baruch, angels destroying Jerusalem, and black and bright waters, are operative in some graphic detail. And their symbolic meanings against "the other" are unambiguous.

Other answers are possible, and we should now have moved far away from the bankrupt and unperceptive system bequeathed us by the Enlightenment: namely a paradigm that seeks to produce through analysis, abstraction, and systematization only one answer. So, we must confront another answer that complements, even completes, those already articulated.

"The other" is insignificant despite its unparalleled horrendous and catastrophic deeds. Our apocalypses are religious writings; God's Godness, his oneness, his promises and his determination of times are the undergirding presuppositions behind all perceptions, even those that still reek with the stench of burned flesh and dreams. Herein lies the scintillating brilliance of the authors of 4 Ezra and 2 Baruch. Despite the universalism in both documents, we find no questions such as "What is wrong with the other?"

The questions are introspective. Why has mankind been burdened with a *cor malignum* (4 Ezra)? Why have each of us been unfaithful (2 Baruch)? Introspection also leads to the corporate solidarity so ancient in the consciousness of Jews, Israelites and Hebrews. Why have the promises to Ezra, Isaiah, David and Abraham failed? The latter, for example, was promised a special relationship with God, a vast posterity, a land. Now, the land lies in ruins, the chosen nation has been invaded, defeated, and exiled; a special relation with God, placarded in the knowledge of God's will, the Torah, has led to a condemnation that is severe and unparalleled in history and among the nations.

Only the apocalyptic mode of discourse, with its dialogues and visions, enables the authors to see, via pictorial imagery and symbolism, that such a perspective is myopic. A wide view entails inclusion of protology; all was once good and the essential, like Israel's election, remains eternal (cf. esp. R. Akiba and Resh Laqish). The cherished aspects of life were present at the beginning and history is nearly finished. The final drama may not satisfy most Jews, because few were faithful, but it certainly will justly punish "the other," who, for a brief declining moment, was all-powerful.

Through transference (apocalyptically, to another world—*the world*—and another time—the conclusive arc of the eschaton—) the authors of the apocalypses reveal two salubrious insights. The other's might is apparent and ephemeral. The other's time is limited and circumvented. To a certain extent, therefore, "the other" looms insignificant because of the genre of apocalyptic thought. This world and this age in which "the other" exists is not essential or even significant. Commitment to God as OTHER flips all paradigms so that the persecuted Jew is the other in search of meaning and self.

The search continued in Judaism long after the period in which apocalyptic thought dominated. Indeed the focus never changed appreciably; the other was relatively insignificant in comparison to the Jewish community and the individual. Halakoth were designed not out of extrospection but almost exclusively from introspection. To look at Torah was to look within. How can community and individual be more faithful to God's will?

This perspective is prominent, for example, in the Mishnah, Sanhedrin 10.1, which is not only influenced by but indeed shaped by the long centuries of Jewish apocalypticism and apocalyptic thought. Banned from the world to come are six types of individuals—at least half of these within the Jewish community, including the one who reads the heretical books like 4 Ezra and 2 Baruch:

אף הקורג בספרים החיצונים (M.San. 10.1).

Obviously the Jewish apocalypses, such as those examined above, were still being read by Jews and the ideas in them were threatening to R. Akiba, who reputedly added the Hebrew clause above.

The great Tanna, however, was wrestling with problems similar to those of the authors of 4 Ezra and 2 Baruch, his near contemporaries. With them, or in harmony with their positions, he proclaimed that Israel's election is protological, absolute, and free from insidious acts by "the other" on earth.[27]

We now move forward to another overview. In contrast to the conception in the Dead Sea Scrolls, "the other" is not another religious group. As we have seen, when it is mentioned in 4 Ezra and 2 Baruch, it is that outsider to which you can attach buzz words and memorable pictorial symbols (usually reversed as with the eagle).

---

[27] Cf. E. E. Urbach, *The Sages: Their Concepts and Beliefs*, I. Abrahams trans. (Jerusalem: 1979), vol. 1, p. 528.

Only in the Apocalypse of John, however, is this procedure fully developed.

The discovery that "the other" is not another religious group in 4 Ezra and 2 Baruch is significant. The contrast with contemporaneous Christian writings is impressive. Nowhere in these two apocalypses have we found evidence of that horrifying tendency that separated Jew and Christian, that painful history of anti-Semitism equally matched by anti-Christianity which has been documented recently by so many scholars (most recently and pointedly by J. Maier in *Jüdische Auseinandersetzung mit dem Christentum in der Antike,* and R. Kampling in *Das Blut Christi und die Juden*).[28] In terms of the paradigm of tolerance versus intolerance of the outsider, the authors of these two Jewish apocalypses are amazingly gracious and enlightened.

The projections of evil upon pre-exilic, pre-seventy Jerusalemites was the only possible answer in a bifurcated paradigm that saw either God as unjust or the fathers as sinners. As Neusner argues in "The World of Jesus' People: Israel in the Land of Israel—Rome in Palestine," "The choice thus represented no choice at all."[29] The resulting perspective is incredibly important. It does not follow that the pre-exilic community was immoral, as W. Harrelson demonstrates so convincingly in the "Prophetic Eschatological Visions and the Kingdom of God" or that the pre-seventy Jews in Palestine were an evil lot.[30] "It was *not* a sinning generation . . . ." (Neusner, *ibid,* p. 20); at least not in comparison to preceding generations, and especially to "the other." Sociological and theological descriptions of the pre-seventy communities must be informed by the insight that the dire confessions of sin and unworthiness, for example in the Hodayoth and the Prayer of Manasseh, are articulated not by inveterate sinners, but by the pious.

The other's actions drove the individual, Ezra or Baruch, to look to the community, the remnant of the nation of God. The words were addressed to the insider. The message is intwined with a full perspective of the universe, history, and, especially, time. God's drama is not yet finished. Hence the significance and wealth of "the other" is only

---

[28] J. Maier, *Jüdische Auseinandersetzung mit dem Christenum in der Antike,* Erträge der Forschung, no. 177 (Darmstadt: 1982). R. Kampling, *Das Blut Christi und die Juden,* Neutestamentiche Abhandlungen, N. F. 16 (Munster: 1984).

[29] J. Neusner, "The World of Jesus' People: Israel in the Land of Israel–Rome in Palestine" in *Judaism in the Beginning of Christianity* (Philadelphia: 1984), p. 20.

[30] W. Harrelson, "Prophetic Eschatological Visions and the Kingdom of God," in H. B. Huffmon, F. A. Spina and A. R. W. Green eds. *The Quest for the Kingdom of God: Studies in Honor of George E. Mendenhall* (Winona Lake, Indiana: 1983), pp. 117-26.

apparent and palpably ephemeral. "The other" drove the faithful Jew to look deep inside Torah, traditions, and self. The actions of "the other" forced the apocalyptists from extrospection to introspection. Looking inside, the authors found a bifurcated self. Unfaithfulness was inside. This discovery is reminiscent of Pogo's dictum, namely that we have found the enemy and we are he.

13

Forbidden Transactions: Prohibited Commerce with Gentiles in Earliest Rabbinism[1]

Gary G. Porton
University of Illinois at Champaign/Urbana

i

For a week we have focused our attention on the concept of "the other." We opened with the question of how "others" have viewed the Jews, and now we have turned to rabbinic discussions of "the other." When many of us think of the outsider from the point of view of the rabbinic documents, the gentile readily comes to mind. For this reason, it becomes our task to ascertain whether or not Mishnah-Tosefta actually picture the gentile as other, and if they do, how they sketch his profile. Because in our allotted time we cannot review all of the material on the gentile, this essay examines only one aspect of the complex relationship between the Palestinian Israelite and the gentile during the first centuries of the common era: it focuses on the laws in Mishnah-Tosefta which define what the Israelite could *not* buy from or sell to gentiles.

A culture clearly defines itself through prohibited actions. By delineating those things which a member of the group may *not* do with a non-member, a segment of society creates borders which

[1] I wish to express my gratitude to my teacher Professor Jacob Neusner for inviting me to deliver this paper. As will be obvious below much of this paper depends on work he has done on Mishnah-Tosefta, the Tannaim, and the Tannaitic period. I have adopted his methods of textual analysis, and I accept most of his presuppositions about the rabbinic collections. In addition, much of what he has demonstrated about the Tannaitic period is assumed throughout this essay.

Further, this paper owes a great deal to my colleague Professor William S. Green of the University of Rochester. Not only did Professor Green suggest the title of this paper, but also he supplied the theoretical framework for my analyses and asked those questions which forced me to organize my thoughts and pursue my study along lines which have proved most beneficial. Moreover, his careful reading of drafts of this essay and his comments on my writing style have helped me to produce a readable and interesting presentation.

Finally, I am indebted to my colleagues Professor William R. Schoedel of the University of Illinois and Professor Alan Avery-Peck of Tulane University. Both read a draft of this paper and offered many important suggestions which have been included in this final version.

separate it from other societal components. For example the Pharisees
defined themselves in terms of with whom they could or could not eat:
a non-Pharisee was a person with whom another Pharisee could not
break bread; a Pharisee was a person with whom another Pharisee
could share a meal.[2] In the market-place, we would assume that "the
other" is one with whom an Israelite may *not* do business.

The market-place was a complex arena of activity where frequent
contact between Israelites and gentiles occurred. The sources which
treat this subject deal with matters which could have transpired daily,
for an Israelite obviously was more likely to encounter a gentile in the
market-place than in the former's synagogue, Temple, or even living
quarters.[3] In the first centuries of our era, the Israelite majority in
Palestine was surrounded by non-Israelites. Although there were
towns which were primarily gentile in population and others whose
citizens were predominantly Israelite, there were few if any locations
which were exclusively Israelite or gentile.[4] Therefore, Israelites and
gentiles had many opportunities to meet in the markets of most, if not
all, villages and towns in Palestine. While the market-place could be
a "neutral" arena where specifically "religious" concerns need not be
paramount or even considered and where sectarian matters might be
modified or ignored in order to allow for the normal progression of
business, from the perspective of the rabbis, the authors of our
documents, the market-place could be a "dangerous" region of activity, a sphere in which the boundaries between Israelites and gentiles
might be crossed easily. Our problem is this: in the economic realm,
is the gentile perceived as "the other," as one with whom contact
should be limited, or does the concept of "the other" hold little
importance in the economic sphere? Or to put it another way: did the

[2] J. Neusner, *From Politics to Piety: The Emergence of Pharisaic Judaism* (Englewood
Cliffs, New Jersey: 1983), tablefellowship, passim.
[3] Mishnah-Tosefta Erubin contain a good deal of law which indicates that there were
Israelite homes in areas where gentiles also lived.
[4] On the non-Israelite population in Palestine see: M. AviYonah, *The Jews of Palestine:
A Political History from the Bar Kokhba War to the Arab Conquest* (New York: 1976),
15-20; E. Mary Smallwood, *The Jews Under Roman Rule: From Pompey to Diocletian*
(Leiden: 1976), 331-335, 467-538; Y. Cohen, *The Attitude to the Gentile in the
Halakhah and in Reality in the Tannaitic Period*, unpublished doctoral dissertation
(Jerusalem: 1975), 108-123. On non-Israelite culture in Palestine see D. Flusser,
"Paganism in Palestine," S. Safrai and M. Stern (eds.), *The Jewish People in the First
Century: Historical Geography, Political History, Social, Cultural and Religious Life
and Institutions* (Philadelphia: 1976), II, 1065-1100. On Israelites and gentiles in
Palestine see E. Schurer, *The History of the Jewish People in the Age of Jesus Christ
(174 B.C.-A.D. 135)*, revised and edited by G. Vermes, F. Millar, and M. Black
(Edinburgh: 1979), II, 1-199.

earliest rabbis see the market-place as a dangerous arena, one in which the gentiles and Israelites had to be separated, or did they view it as a neutral arena, one in which segregation or integration was of little concern?

Our analysis of the rules in Mishnah-Tosefta is not economic and does not rest on the supposition that what is described is actual commercial behavior. To uncover what actually went on in the market-place would require vastly more evidence than is available. Because we possess virtually nothing which is external to and contemporary with Mishnah-Tosefta which would validate or falsify their claims about the economic interaction of the Israelite and gentile, the first reading of these documents must be in terms of themselves.[5] However, these collections were composed by a closed subsection of Israelite society (the rabbis), for its own purposes, and many of these purposes we do not know.[6] Furthermore, we have no way of knowing who, if anyone, followed the rules set down in these collections.[7] We cannot tell when Mishnah-Tosefta describe things which actually occurred or when they discuss a reality which existed only in the minds of their authors. We cannot easily distinguish between those rulings which were actually enforced and those which the rabbis wished to put into affect but could not. For this reason, the present paper deals only with what these rabbinic texts say. From my perspective, the proper questions to ask of these texts focus on how

---

[5] I wish to make clear that the information for this paper is drawn almost entirely from Mishnah-Tosefta. While there may be relevant information in the other rabbinic collections, I have not attempted to analyze those passages at this point. The discrete rabbinic collection is the largest self-contained rabbinic document, and each document should be understood on its own terms. If we continually interpret one document in terms of another, we violate the primary canons of both literary criticism and historical research. A fourth-century interpretation of a third-century text does not necessarily tell us the meaning of the statement found in a third-century text. Furthermore, as I have demonstrated in my work on Ishmael—*The Traditions of Rabbi Ishmael, Part IV, The Material as a Whole* (Leiden: 1982)—each rabbinic text has its own agenda and employs its own literary conventions. Therefore one cannot simply take a statement from one collection and place it alongside that from another document. One cannot do serious work on rabbinic Judaism by ignoring the chronological and literary differences among the rabbinic texts. See G. Porton, *The Traditions of Rabbi Ishmael, Part I, The Non-exegetical Materials* (Leiden: 1976), 4 and *Ishmael*, IV, 1-4.

[6] W. S. Green, "What's in a Name?—The Problematic of Rabbinic 'Biography,' " W. S. Green (ed.), *Approaches to Ancient Judaism* (Missoula: 1978), 77-96. For a discussion of the make-up and composition of Mishnah see J. Neusner, *Judaism: The Evidence of Mishnah* (Chicago: 1981).

[7] There is a long debate over whether or not Mishnah was designed to be a law code. For a summary of the traditional and scholarly opinions and an evaluation of these theories see J. Neusner, *The Modern Study of the Mishnah* (Leiden: 1973).

they present the rabbinic view of the gentile vis-a-vis the Israelite in the market-place, not on who sold what to whom for what price, or what were the economic results of following this or that ruling. Thus, we shall concentrate on what the rabbis *thought* should happen when a gentile met an Israelite in the market and where they thought the boundaries between Israelites and gentiles should be drawn in this arena, without claiming that the texts reflect a reality outside of themselves.

ii

In each business transaction which we shall discuss there are three essential elements: 1) the gentile, 2) the Israelite and 3) the object which is purchased or sold. Consequently, the reason for the prohibited action can result from a view of the gentile, a concern for the Israelite, or the nature of the object. Because each of these issues is a discrete matter, I have organized the relevant *sugyot* according to the element which generates the prohibition.

Our first set of passages focuses on the gentile. Because the objects can be traded among the Israelites, we must assume that there is nothing inherent in the items themselves which prevents their being sold to or bought from gentiles. It is the fact that the gentile is involved in the transaction which causes the business deal to be prohibited.

T.A.Z. 2:4 forbids an Israelite from selling "a sword or the paraphernalia for a sword ... stocks, neck-chains, ropes, or iron chains" to a gentile.[8] This agrees with Rabbi's comment that it is forbidden to sell implements of war to a gentile.[9] In short, an Israelite should not support the possible enemy by supplying him with items which he could use against the former.

M.A.Z. 1:7 prohibits an Israelite from selling bears or lions to gentiles "or anything which causes damage to many [people]." Ignoring the interesting questions of where the Israelites would have secured these lions or bears, where they would have raised them, or why they would have them to sell, Bartinoro argues that this last clause refers to implements of war and does not modify the first clause,[10] while Rabbenu Hanael reads the last clause as an explanation of the first[11] and explains that one should not supply gentiles with

---

[8] The text also equates the gentile and the Samaritan; cf. B.A.Z. 15b.
[9] T.A.Z. 2:3.
[10] Bartinoro *loc. cit.*
[11] Rabbenu Hanael on B.A.Z. 16a.

animals which could bring harm to Israelites.[12] Following Hanael, I
would argue that this ruling is similar to the above mentioned
prohibition against selling to a gentile any implement of war, for both
prohibit an Israelite from selling to a gentile anything with which the
latter might bring harm to the former.[13]

    M.A.Z. 1:5 states that an Israelite cannot sell fircones, white figs
and their stocks, a white cock, or frankincense to a non-Israelite on the
latter's festivals.[14] Judah states that one may sell a white cock among
a flock of cocks or one white cock whose spur has been mutilated.[15]
Furthermore, we are told that any other item may be sold to a gentile
as long as it is not specifically designated as part of an idolatrous
service. Meir ends by stating that one cannot sell to gentiles fine
dates, Hazab dates, or Nicolaus dates. T.A.Z. 1:2 parallels this
mishnah. In Tosefta, Judah b. Petera states that one may sell no less
than three *maneh* of frankincense to a gentile.[16] Tosefta also states that
an Israelite may sell items to a gentile merchant which the former
would not normally sell to a gentile because the merchant will not use
the items for the worship of an idol; he will merely resell them. If,
however, the Israelite knows that the merchant will worship an idol
with the things he has purchased from an Israelite, the latter may not
sell him anything. In addition, Tosefta rules that "one sells them pigs
and dogs and does not worry that they might offer them up to an idol."
This is curious, because pigs and dogs were often sacrificed by both
Greeks and Romans.[17] Similarly, an Israelite may sell wine to a
gentile without assuming that the wine will be used for a libation to an

---

[12] This is the way the Babylonian *gemara* understands the mishnah; B.A.Z. 16a-16b.

[13] Elmslie suggests that this prohibition is related to the Romans' use of the lion and the
bear as part of the circuses. W. L. Elmslie, *The Mishnah on Idolatry 'Aboda Zara*
(Cambridge: 1911), 12.

[14] Compare the following discussion with Lawrence H. Schiffman, "Legislation Concerning Relations with Non-Jews in the Zadokite Fragments and in Tannaitic Literature," *Revue de Qumran* (December, 1983), 43:11:3, 385.

[15] This would make the cock unfit as a sacrifice.

[16] I have taken *mnyn* in the text as the plural of *mnh* so that the text parallels B.A.Z. 14a.
Hadas-Lebel also reads the text in this manner: M. Hadas-Lebel, "Le paganisme à
travers les sources rabbiniques des IIe et IIIe siècles. Contribution à l'etude du
syncrétisme dans l'empire romain," in H. Temporini and W. Haase (eds.), *Aufstieg und
Niedergang der römischen Welt* (Berlin and New York: 1979), II.19.2, 448. See,
however, J. Neusner, *The Tosefta: Neziqin* (New York: 1981), 315: "R. Judah b. Peterah
says: 'In the case of Frankincense, it is no less than three by number.' " I assume that
Judah considered this to be too large an amount for the gentile to use for the worship
of an idol.

[17] G. Dumezil, *Archaic Roman Religion* (Chicago and London: 1970), pig, passim. On
the sacrifice of dogs see Dumezil, 158, 348. Dumezil mentions the connection of the
dog with the Lares, 344.

idol. This is also curious because elsewhere the rabbis assume that a gentile will make a libation with virtually any wine with which the latter comes into contact.[18] While allowing the sale of pigs, dogs, and wine, objects commonly employed in Roman religious rites, Tosefta forbids the sale of water or salt to a gentile if the latter is going to use them for worshiping an idol. In Tosefta, Judah states that an Israelite may sell to a gentile a white cock in a flock of cocks as long as the gentile does not specify how he is going to use the cock.[19] If the gentile states that he needs the cock because he is ill or because he wishes to hold a feast for his son, the sale is permitted.[20]

These texts clearly prohibit an Israelite's selling almost anything to a gentile which the latter might use as part of an idolatrous ritual. This is emphasized in Mishnah, which specifies that these prohibitions apply on gentiles' festivals. It is interesting that the passage in Tosefta omits the reference to the gentile's festival and emphasizes the issue of the gentile's *intended* use of the item. Tosefta assumes that the gentile would willingly tell the Israelite for what purposes he wanted the items. Intention is an important rabbinic concept in Mishnah-Tosefta, and here the gentile is pictured somewhat like a rabbi whose motives are the definitive factor determining proper action and whose intention can be ascertained.[21] It is also important that Tosefta does not have a clear idea of exactly what the gentiles offered, for it allows the sale of dogs and pigs even though these were common offerings among the non-Israelites. Furthermore, one can sell anything to a gentile merchant, for we assume that he will not personally use the items he has purchased, but will sell them to other

---

[18] Cf. T.A.Z. 7:4, 7:6, 3:16. See also the article on wine in G. Wigoder and C. Roth (eds.), *The Encyclopedia Judaica* (Jerusalem: 1973), XVI, 540.

[19] The text is awkward. Given the flow of the passage perhaps it should read that one cannot sell a white cock among other cocks unless the gentile specifies that he wants the cock for his illness or for a feast for his son.

[20] Hadas-Lebel has connected the items discussed in these texts with Roman religious practice. Hadas-Lebel lists several ancient sources which refer to the offering of cocks, 446-447. She suggests that the cock was frequently offered because it was affordable and that the white cock was offered to the more important deities. She also states that fir-cones played a role in the Dionysius cult and in the Attis cult. In fact, Cybel once took the form of a fir-cone. The cone had curative properties and was also viewed as a fertility symbol. It is connected with Demeter, too. Because figs and dates constituted major crops in Palestine, these were frequently used as offerings to a variety of deities.

S. Lieberman has noted that some Palestinian magical texts refer to pine cones, white cocks and frankincense. S. Lieberman, "Palestine in the Third and Fourth Centuries," *Jewish Quarterly Review*, XXVI (1946), 173-174.

[21] See, for example, A. Peck, *The Priestly Gift in Mishnah* (Chico: 1981), 1-28, where Peck shows that it is the Israelite's intention which is the important factor in making something a heave-offering or not.

gentiles. Our texts seem unconcerned with the fact that these items might eventually find a place in the worship of an idol.

M.A.Z. 1:6 states that in no place may Israelites sell large domesticated animals to gentiles.[22] As early as the fourth century these rules were not understood within the talmudic academies. The *gemara* explains that the Israelites were afraid lest the gentiles would work these animals on days of rest.[23] However, the *gemara* is aware of the fact that a non-Israelite may work an animal on a day of rest, for the obligation to rest on the Sabbath is incumbent on Israelites alone, and an Israelite is not responsible for what a gentile does on the Sabbath.[24] The *gemara* then responds that the author(s) of our mishnah were concerned lest a gentile take an animal on a trial basis on Friday afternoon and work it after the commencement of the Sabbath. Because the animal still belongs to the Israelite, he would be responsible for the animal's violating the Sabbath.[25] These discussions are less than convincing. Several scholars have suggested that these texts are related to the problem of idolatry.[26] Given the fact that the Romans often sacrificed large domestic animals, this text could address that practice.[27] However, the Mishnah itself does not explain

---

[22] Cf., Schiffman, 386-387.

[23] B.A.Z. 14b.

[24] M.Shab. 16:6.

[25] The only basis for the *gemara's* concern with the animal's violating the Sabbath is Ben Petra's comment that one may sell a horse to a gentile because the animal will not perform work on the Sabbath for which it is liable for a Sin-offering. However, the meaning of Ben Petra's comment is far from clear. Blidstein explains that the sale of a horse was permitted because it would not be used for plowing on the Sabbath, an act prohibited in the Bible for which the punishment would have been a Sin-offering. Rather, a horse was used to carry people, which is not biblically prohibited. He suggests, however, that Ben Bethyra "did in fact read the biblical verse [Ex. 20:10] (or extended it to mean) that a Jew who owns cattle is responsible for their not working on the Sabbath, even to the degree that he may not sell them to a gentile who will work them." G. J. Blidstein, "The Sale of Animals to Gentiles in Talmudic Law," *Jewish Quarterly Review*, LXI, 3 (January, 1971), 190-191.

[26] Hadas-Lebel cites this mishnah in her discussion of animals offered by gentiles, 442, and Blidstein lists several authors who have made this suggestion, 189, note 4. Schiffman, following, Ginzberg, favors this explanation; Schiffman, 386-387.

[27] Fowler mentions the sacrifice of cows, dogs, goats, horses, lamb, oxen, pigs, red dogs, sheep, and white heifers; W. Warde Fowler, *The Religious Experience of the Roman People from the Earliest Times to the Age of Augustus* (London: 1911), passim. Compare with Dumezil's discussions of these animals. It is probably significant that the text states calves, foals, and large domesticated animals, whole or maimed, cannot be sold to gentiles. Judah permits the sale of maimed domestic animals, for surely they could not be used for sacrifices. Exactly why Ben Bethyra permits the sale of a horse to a gentile is unclear to me.

why large animals could not be sold to gentiles, and at this time, I am not prepared to offer a conclusive explanation.[28]

M.Git. 4:9 says that if a person sells himself or his children to a gentile (presumably to pay off a debt), the person himself can never be redeemed, and his children cannot be redeemed until after his death. T.A.Z. 3:16 states that if an Israelite sells his slave to a non-Israelite, the slave goes out free. The text is curious, for I find it hard to believe that the rabbis could force a gentile who had just put out good money for a slave to set that slave free simply because the rabbis wished him to do so.[29] Both of these texts probably reflect the rabbis' fear that anyone who comes under the gentile's power will be lost to the Israelite community forever.[30] But they do not reflect the reality of the rabbis' powerlessness within the whole of Palestinian society.

M.A.Z. 1:8 states that an Israelite may not sell gentiles crops which are attached to the ground; however, he may sell them crops which have been harvested.[31] Judah reformulates the ruling to read that crops may be sold on condition that they are harvested. T.A.Z. 2:4 states that only mown fodder, harvested grain, and cut trees may be sold to gentiles. Again, Judah rules that these items may be sold on condition that they are mowed, harvested, or cut.[32] The traditional commentators suggest that the issue revolves around providing the gentiles with a reason for acquiring the right of settlement on the Holy Land.[33] But this explanation is less than certain, for T.Pe. 2:9 and 3:12 assume that Israelites sell fields to gentiles.

An anonymous statement in T.Sheb. 6:20 forbids an Israelite from selling Seventh Year produce to or buying it from a gentile.[34] In short,

---

[28] Cohen 187-188 suggests that this prohibition was a means of decreasing the gentiles' ability to effectively work the land, for these animals were used by farmers.

[29] Cf. T.A.Z. 3:19.

[30] Cohen points to the economic ramifications of the gentiles' use of slaves, 178ff.

[31] Cf. Schiffman, 387-388.

[32] On B.A.Z. 20b, this text is turned into a series of "words-of" disputes between Judah and Meir. Meir states that they may be sold on condition that they are detached from the soil, while Judah rules they may be sold only after they have been detached.

[33] See Bartinoro, Yom Tov, and Rashi. The problem of the Israelites' selling land to gentiles is too complex to detain us here. Most scholars believe that the laws changed during the period from 70 to post 135; however, there is little agreement exactly when or how they changed. Most assume that one could sell land to a gentile before 70 but not after 135; Cohen, 124-157; D. Sperber, *Roman Palestine: 200-400, The Land* (Ramat-Gan: 1978), 160-168; A. Gulak, *Study of the History of Hebrew Law during the Period of the Talmud: 1, Laws of Immovable Property* (Jerusalem: 1929).

[34] "Others" rule that one may sell a Samaritan enough food for four meals, while the anonymous text equates the Samaritan with the gentile.

a gentile may have nothing to do with Seventh Year Produce.[35] While the Israelite may sell this ritually unique produce to Israelites, Samaritans, and even to those Israelites whom one suspects of violating the laws of the Seventh Year, T.Sheb. 6:20, he may not sell them to the gentile. Perhaps the rabbis felt that during the Year of Release, crops would be scarce in Palestine and one should not waste the produce by giving it to non-Israelites. As far as buying Seventh-Year produce from gentiles is concerned, the rabbis forbid it because they assume that the gentile cultivated the produce during the Seventh Year. While the gentile is not subject to the Seventh Year's restrictions, the land he holds in Israel is. Produce grown upon that land, therefore, is in every case forbidden to an Israelite. The text's concern derives from the rabbis' view of the land, not from the gentile's nature.[36] Furthermore, this prohibition emphasizes that the obligations of the Seventh-Year were a means of distinguishing between Israelites and gentiles.

The only other item beside the Seventh-year produce that Mishnah-Tosefta clearly prohibit an Israelite from purchasing from a gentile is an egg cracked in a dish.[37] The fear is that the gentile will sell the Israelite an egg from a prohibited bird.[38] We must imagine, however,

---

[35] Lieberman argues that this parallels the ruling in T.Sheb. 5:21 that an Israelite cannot feed Seventh-Year produce to a gentile; S. Lieberman, *Tosefta Kifshutah: Order Zera'im Part II* (New York: 1955), 565, 560. Lieberman argues that an Israelite cannot transmit Seventh-Year produce to a gentile because the gentile is not a member of an Israelite household.

[36] Lieberman offers two explanations: 1) The rabbis were afraid that the gentile had purchased from an Israelite the latter's Seventh-Year produce. However this would be the case only if the first part of the text were ignored. 2) The gentile's activity with the growing of the produce falls under the class of 'bq sby'yt (cf. T.A.Z. 1:12); however, this means that the Israelite would apply the Seventh-year laws to the gentiles as well as to the Israelites. Lieberman, *Tosefta Kifshutah: Zera'im Part II*, 565.

[37] There is some uncertainty about whether or not the Red Heifer could be purchased from a gentile. In T. and M.Par. 2:1, Eliezer says that the Red Heifer may not be purchased from gentiles, but sages allow such purchases. Sages allow this practice because they assume that no work has been done with her, while Eliezer worries lest the gentile's heifer had borne a yoke. Cf. S. Lieberman, *Tosefeth Rishonim* (Jerusalem: 1938), III, 211-212, and J. Neusner, *Eliezer Ben Hyrcanus: The Tradition and the Man* (Leiden: 1973), I, 301-302.

[38] The matter of an egg cracked in a dish is rather complex and confused. T.Hul. 3:24 opens by stating that an Israelite may buy eggs from any source, and ends by stating that an Israelite may not buy eggs which are cracked in a dish from a gentile. In the context of the *sugya*, cracked eggs were forbidden because if an Israelite sold to a gentile eggs from birds which were carrion or ritually prohibited, the Israelite was to have cracked them in a dish. Thus, if a gentile had eggs cracked in a dish these could have been eggs from prohibited birds which he had purchased from an Israelite. Also, the Israelite could not determine from the shell the type of the bird from which the egg had come.

that there were a number of items which our texts assumed an Israelite could not purchase from a gentile—certain types of food,[39] wine,[40] and anything connected with idolatry.[41] Because any item could be used in idolatrous worship and its prohibition was related to this use, the prohibitions are somehow related to the gentile's use of the items.

These pericopae offer a multi-faceted picture of the gentile. Gentiles are dangerous and blood-thirsty; therefore, they cannot be trusted with arms or dangerous beasts. They worship false gods, and this should not be encouraged or supported. According to the traditional commentators, non-Israelites will take any opportunity to seize control of the Holy Land and to lure Israelites away from the latter's God and people. Because gentiles are not Israelites, they cannot be supported by Seventh Year Produce. On the other hand, a gentile can be trusted to tell an Israelite whether or not he intends to use any given item as part of his religious ritual, and a gentile merchant is not treated in the same manner as are other gentiles. Lastly, our texts demonstrate that the rabbis did not have a clear idea of what occurred in the gentile cult.

The second class of *sugyot* were generated by the concern for the *halakhah,* not by an inherent interest in the non-Israelite. Here, specific characteristics of the gentile are unimportant; the gentile appears only to underscore the fact that the Israelite must scrupulously follow his own ritual requirements. The Israelite's adherence to these ritual requirements is ensured by preventing him from benefitting through the sale of a halakhicly prohibited item.

T.Dem. 1:15 states that if an Israelite buys produce for food and decides to sell it, he may not sell it to a gentile or feed it to a domestic animal without first removing the tithe from it. T.Dem. 1:16 gives a similar rule with regard to produce which the Israelite inherited or received as a gift; neither of these may be given to a gentile. Thus, an Israelite cannot sell *demai*-produce to a gentile.[42] Our texts guarantee

---

[39] For example, T.Toh. 11:8 states that grapes which have been laid out on leaves, whether by Israelites or gentiles, are unclean, presumably because the liquid remains on the leaves and conveys uncleanness. T.Toh. 10:5 explains that certain vats of olives which a gentile produced may be unclean. T.A.Z. 4:11 rules that the red berry of sumac is always deemed unclean.

[40] T.A.Z. 7:6 states that a single drop of wine used for libation is prohibited and that it imparts the prohibition to any wine with which it comes into contact.

[41] T.A.Z. 6:12. Interestingly, one may buy something connected to idol-worship from an idolatrous priest if he stole the item for sale, for it is assumed that the priest would sell only an item which is not fit for the proper worship of the idol.

[42] Lieberman wisely rejects the explanation of Hasdé David that the reason for Tosefta's

that the tithe will be removed from all produce which an Israelite might sell to anyone, either to another Israelite or to a gentile.[43]

T.Kil. 5:19 rules that "a piece of clothing in which a prohibited [thread has been woven but in which] it cannot be discerned easily" cannot be sold to a gentile or be used for a donkey-blanket. Simeon b. Leazar adds that one cannot use it to make a "conspicuous bordered garment"; however, one may make a shroud with it. The standard explanation for this prohibited sale is that the gentile might resell the garment to an unsuspecting Israelite.[44] While the issue of a gentile's reselling a prohibited item to an Israelite is commonly found in the Amoraic stratum, it is not explicitly found in the Tannaitic stratum; therefore, we cannot be certain that this is the reason for the prohibition. The practical result of the ruling is that it would encourage the tailor to scrupulously follow the rules of "mixed-kinds," for he could not sell even a slightly flawed item to anyone, even to a gentile.

T.Kil. 9:2 prohibits selling a gentile a piece of linen which has been dyed black with soot.[45] Because soot was normally used as a dye for wool, this improperly dyed material might cause some difficulty for an Israelite. Exactly why this cloth could not be sold to a gentile is unclear, for surely the gentile would not be concerned with the Israelite's laws of "mixed-kinds," especially with the subtle way in which this incorrectly dyed cloth would be affected by these laws. However, the practical result of the rule would be that the dyer would take care to use the proper dye with the proper cloth.[46] Thus, the issue

---

rules was the fear that the gentile would sell the untithed produce to another, unsuspecting Israelite. S. Lieberman, *Tosefta Kifshutah: Order Zera'im, Part I* (New York: 1955), 201-202.

[43] Sarason argues Tosefta's point is that the person who acquires produce in order to eat it must tithe it; therefore, it is clear that the issue is whether or not the Israelite is allowed to forego his obligation to tithe produce which he has purchased for food. By prohibiting the sale to a gentile, our texts make it clear that the produce purchased for food must be tithed no matter what the Israelite actually does with the food. The issue is a matter of intention when buying the produce, not what is actually done with it. R. Sarason, *A History of the Mishnaic Law of Agriculture, Section Three: A Study of Tractate Demai* (Leiden: 1979), 38-39, 51, 102, 123, 129.

[44] B.Pes. 40b and B.A.Z. 65b. Rashi explains that if he made the forbidden cloth into a saddle-cover, a person might take the saddle-cover and sew it into his clothes or make a garment from it.

[45] Our text does state that it may be used for a mattress cover or a blanket. The prohibition against selling this cloth to a gentile does not occur in Y.Kil. 9:2.

[46] From the Israelite's point of view the issue is not the actual violation of the laws of "mixed-kinds;" rather, it is the possible future violation of the laws or the appearance that they have been violated. If an Israelite wore the improperly dyed linen with a piece of wool he would actually violate the laws of "mixed-kinds." If he wore the improperly dyed linen with another piece of linen, other Israelites might assume that

is neither the gentile nor the cloth. Rather, the concern is that an
Israelite might use this cloth improperly without realizing it.

T.Hul. 7:3 seems to forbid the sale of carrion or *terefah*-meat to a
gentile.[47] However it is not clear why a gentile would care whether or
not the meat he bought from an Israelite conformed to the latter's
ritual laws.[48] The *sugya* assumes that the gentile would have the same
concerns about the meat which he ate as would an Israelite. This
makes sense only from a rabbi's point of view. Arguments to the effect
that the gentile would sell or feed the meat to an unsuspecting
Israelite assume that Israelites bought meat from gentiles which they
then would eat, a curious assumption given the common wisdom
about an Israelite's eating habits.[49] The rule in Tosefta makes sense
only as an attempt to ensure that the Israelite gains no benefit from
ritually prohibited meats by selling them to anyone, even to gentiles.[50]

According to M.A.Z. 2:6 there was no firm rule concerning the sale

---

he has mixed wool with linen in violation of the laws of "mixed-kinds." In either case,
the gentile would not have been concerned with these matters.

[47] There are some problems with this text. It opens by stating that one cannot sell
terefah-meat or carrion to a gentile. It then states that there are two reason that an
Israelite may not sell these forbidden meats to a gentile; however, only one reason
appears: the gentile may feed the meat to another Israelite. Notice that the reason
speaks of feeding, while the text opened with a discussion of an Israelite's selling meat
to a gentile. Lieberman, *Tosefeth Rishonim* (Jerusalem: 1938), II, 237, cites one
manuscript which reads "sells" for "feeds," and Neusner, *A History of the Mishnaic
Law of Holy Things: Part III, Hullin, Bekhorot* (Leiden: 1979), 90, accepts this reading.
[48] The problems found in Tosefta's text have been solved in the version in the
Babylonian *gemara*. On B.Hul. 94a, we read that there are two reasons why an Israelite
cannot sell these forbidden meats to a gentile: 1) the Israelite causes the gentile to err
and 2) the gentile may resell the forbidden meat to another Israelite. Rashi states that
if one sells ritually unfit meat to a gentile, the seller must inform the buyer that the meat
is unfit. However, Rashi does not explain why the gentile would care whether or not the
meat was ritually fit. Similarly, Cashdan writes, "For a gentile when buying meat of a
Jew believes that he is buying the meat of an animal that has been ritually slaughtered,
and it is forbidden to take advantage of his ignorance and to pass on to him
terefah-meat;" E. Cashdan, *Hullin*, in I. Epstein (ed.), *The Babylonian Talmud*
(London: 1948), 529, note 2. I can see that one may not want to deceive a gentile;
however, I cannot understand why a gentile would care whether or not the meat he
bought was slaughtered according to the ritual laws of the Israelites.
[49] Schurer, II, 83-84.
[50] Deut. 14:21 states: *You shall not eat anything that has died a natural death—give it
to the stranger in your community to eat, or you may sell it to a foreigner—for you are
a people consecrated to YHWH, your God.*
    Midrash Tannaim, Hoffman, 75 states that one may sell carrion to gentiles. See also
B.A.Z. 20a-20b; B.Hul. 104b; B.B.Q. 41a.

of small domestic animals to gentiles.[51] Where such sales were usual, they were permitted; where such sales were unusual, they were prohibited.[52] Mishnah's ruling may reflect the concern that small animals interfere with the growing of agricultural products. After the Bar Kokhba War, several sages prohibited the rearing of small animals in Palestine in order to promote the reintroduction of farming in the war devastated country. Therefore, in those areas of Palestine where the rearing of small animals was prohibited, small animals could not be raised by anyone, Israelite or gentile.[53]

T.Sheb. 5:9 states that Israelites may not bring small animals such as village-dogs, cats, porcupines and monkeys in order to sell them or to hire them out to gentiles. In T.A.Z. 2:3, Simeon b. Eleazar seems to disagree and states that these animals, "things which peck about the house," may be sold to gentiles. However the exact reading of this passage is less than certain.[54] As the texts stands before us, we have two different positions concerning the sale of village-dogs, porcupines, cats and monkeys to gentiles.[55] If, however, Simeon's comment

---

[51] The *suqya* is also in M.Pes. 4:3.

[52] Rashi, B.A.Z. 14b, following the *gemara*, B.A.Z. 14b-15a, argues that small domestic animals were sold to gentiles only in places where the latter were not suspected of engaging in sexual acts with the animals. Where the gentiles were suspected of practicing immoral sexual acts, small animals were not sold to them. The authors of our texts often assumed that gentiles regularly engaged in sexual acts with animals. See for example T.A.Z. 2:1.

[53] On the problems connected with the rearing of small animals in Palestine after the Bar Kokhba War see Avi-Yonah, 28. However some claimed that it was profitable to raise small animals. See T. Frank, *An Economic Survey of Ancient Rome* (Baltimore: 1938), IV, 153-154.

[54] In T.A.Z. 2:3, Simeon states that the animals may be sold to gentiles. However, the text next states that "just as they may *not* sell these to them, thus, they may not exchange them." In short, the continuation of Tosefta suggests that Simeon's statement should be read as a negative. T.B.Q. 8:17 poses another problem, for in this text, Simeon permits the raising of the small animals, and he says nothing about selling them to gentiles. If we look at the context of Simeon's two comments, we discover that the verb he employs fits the two contexts in which his comments appear. In T.B.Q. 8:17, the discussion centers around the raising of small domestic animals in the land of Israel. The text states: "Just as [Israelites] may not raise small domesticated animals [in the land of Israel], so also they may not raise small wild animals. R. Simeon b. Eleazar says: 'They may raise village-dogs . . . .'" However, T.A.Z. 2:3 deals with the sale of animals, not their rearing. On the basis of these two texts, it is impossible to determine exactly what Simeon said, for either one of his statements could have been altered to fit its new context. We simply do not know if he discussed the selling or the rearing of small animals, nor do we know if his statement in T.A.Z. 2:3 should be read in the negative or the positive.

[55] Exactly why these animals are listed is unclear. Qohelet Rabbah, a much later text than those with which we are concerned here, states: "*Seeing there are many words*

should be read in the negative, as the rest of T.A.Z. 2:3 implies, the texts are consistent: one cannot sell these small animals to gentiles. Exactly why Israelites would raise either monkeys or porcupines in order to sell them to gentiles or for any other purpose is unclear to me. With the exception of the porcupine,[56] these animals were common pets among the Romans,[57] and many have suggested that this proscription is related to the general prohibition against raising small animals in the land of Israel.[58] Perhaps the rabbis are here discouraging the owning of small animals around the house—neither Israelite nor gentile may keep small animals in their dwellings either because they are small animals or, following what Qohelet Rabbah claims at a latter date, because they are useless and dangerous.

In these passages, the gentile is a generic term, for in the rabbinic view the world is totally populated by two types of people, "us and them," Israelites and gentiles. In order to ensure that an Israelite does not benefit from halakhicly prohibited items, the former cannot sell the products to anyone, even to a gentile. These *sugyot* offer us no insights into the gentile's character—beyond the fact that the gentile is not an Israelite. The prohibitions they contain apply to all people alike; they do not rest on any inherent characteristic of the gentile. The prohibitions derive solely from the particulars of rabbinic law.

Our last division of texts deals neither with the items being sold nor with the gentile's being a non-Israelite. Rather, they focus on the time at which the business transaction takes place. In these passages, the reason the Israelite cannot sell the items to a gentile is that it might appear the former has violated a ritual proscription. Like the *sugyot* in the previous class, these texts focus on the *halakhah*; specifically, they center on the effect which the gentile's actions, unknown to him, would have on the way Israelites view one another.

Our texts regulate the sale of leaven to gentiles; however, as we

---

that increase vanity, what is man the better (Qoh. 6:11)? For instance, they who raise monkeys, cats, porcupines, monkeys, and sea-dogs, of what use are they? [One gets] either a bite or a sting [from them], so of what use are they? [He receives] either a wound or a blow from them." To the author(s) of this text, these animals are useless. Furthermore, one who raised them only would be harmed by them. This would parallel M.A.Z. 1:7 which prohibits the sale to gentiles of bears of lions "or anything that can do harm to the people."
[56] I have no idea why anyone would raise a porcupine.
[57] On Roman pets see H. W. Johnston, *The Private Life of the Romans* (Chicago: 1932), 82-83. On the monkey as a pet see Pauly, *Real-Encyclopadie der Classichen Altertumswissenschaft* (Stuttgard: 1894), I, 707 and Klausner, *Reallexikon für Antike und Christentum* (Leipzig: 1941), I, 158-160. On dogs as pets see Pauly, VIII, 2557-2560. On cats as pets see Pauly, XI, 52-57.
[58] See authorities cited by Lieberman in *Zera'im, Part II*, 552-553.

would expect, they formulate the issue from the Israelite's point of view. T.Pes. 1:7 states that "they used to say" one could not sell leaven to a gentile unless the latter had enough time to eat it before it was time for the Israelites to burn the leaven. Aqiba, however, ruled that an Israelite could sell his leaven even at the time of burning.[59] The point of departure is the prohibition against the Israelite's possessing leaven. By restricting the time for the sale of the leaven to the gentile, our text would discourage the Israelite from waiting to the last minute to divest himself of the forbidden foods.

In M.Shab. 1:7, while the Shammaites forbid selling anything to a gentile on the eve of the Sabbath unless he has time to reach a nearby place before the Sabbath begins, the Hillelites "permit" the sale. Thus, according to the Shammaites, an Israelite may not sell anything to a gentile close to the beginning of the Sabbath.[60] M.Shab. 1:7 reflects the Shammaite-Hillelite dispute over whether or not work begun before the Sabbath may be completed on the Sabbath. If we follow the traditional commentators, the issue is that the gentile will appear to be the Israelite's agent, and thus it will appear that the Israelite is violating the Sabbath through his agent's deeds. In any case, the issue is neither the gentile nor the item, it is the Israelites' concern with their not working on the Sabbath.

There were certain times when an Israelite was forbidden from engaging in business with a gentile. M.A.Z. 1:1 prohibits Israelites from trading with gentiles three days before the latters' festivals, and Ishmael (M.A.Z. 1:2) prohibits business transactions three days before

---

[59] The mishnah ends with Yosah's saying that the anonymous ruling corresponds to the House of Shammai and that Aqiba's statement agrees with the House of Hillel. These Houses' rulings appear on B.Shab. 18b and B.Pes. 21a. See J. Neusner, *The Rabbinic Traditions about the Pharisees Before 70* (Leiden: 1971), II, 143-144.

[60] Mishnah and Tosefta add that the Israelite also may not load anything onto a gentile's work-animal or onto the gentile himself. The *gemara*'s version is considerably different, for it forbids the Israelite from lending an article or money to a gentile or from giving him a gift. Yom Tov, quoting Nissin, argues that the Shammaites were worried lest someone, witnessing the gentile's using on the Sabbath an object he had obtained from the Israelite or the thing which the Israelite had helped him load, would reason that the gentile was working on the Sabbath as the Israelite's agent. Cf., Neusner, *Rabbinic Traditions*, II, 124, and S. Lieberman, *Tosefta Kifshutah, Part III, Order Mo'ed* (New York: 1962), 21. A secondary issue involved in these *sugyot* is the dispute between the Shammaites and the Hillelites concerning whether or not work begun on the eve of the Sabbath can be completed after the Sabbath began. The Shammaites held that one should not begin work on the eve of the Sabbath unless there was sufficient time to complete it before the Sabbath commenced. While the Hillelites permitted one to begin work on the eve of the Sabbath even if there were not sufficient time to complete it before the beginning of the Sabbath.

and three days after gentile festivals.[61] T.A.Z. 3:19 is a long passage
which prohibits an Israelite from doing business at a gentile's fair.
These texts do not want an Israelite to engage in or to appear to
engage in any gentile celebration or activity which is either definitely
or seemingly related to the gentile's worship. Although time is the
crucial factor in this passage, the prohibition also rests on the assumption that doing business with a gentile on his festivals will appear to
be a means of supporting his idolatrous practices.

These last few texts were generated by a fear that the Israelite
would appear to violate the *halakhah* through his business dealings
with a gentile; however neither the gentile's character (except in the
last passages), nor the nature of the item being bought or sold, is the
issue which generated these texts. Rather, they reflect a concern with
the Israelite's appearing to have violated the *halakhah*.

iii

We have seen that there is not a single theory about the gentile
which controls the rabbis' drawing of the borders between Israelite
and non-Israelite in the market-place. While the gentile is pictured as
being different from the Israelite, these differences are not consistent.
For example, the first set of materials draws a generally negative view
of the gentile. However within these texts we also saw that the gentile
could be trusted to be open and honest when expressing his intended
use of an item. Also, although the gentile was seen as dangerous,
greedy and tricky, one still could do business with him, as the long list
of items which an Israelite could purchase from a gentile testifies.[62]

---

[61] Judah, M.A.Z. 1:1, allows one to accept repayment of a loan because it will sadden
the gentile; however, "they" argued that while the gentile might be sad now, he will be
happy at a later time. In M.A.Z. 1:2, sages prohibit doing business with gentiles before
their festivals, but not after them.

[62] Israelites were allowed to purchase a wide range of items from a non-Israelite: grain,
wine (T.Pe. 4:1), eggs which were not cracked in a dish (T.Hul. 3:24), animals to be
slaughtered (T.Hul. 9:3), the embryo of a gentile's ass (M.T.Bekh. 1:10, the embryo of
a gentile's cow (M.T.Bekh. 2:1), beasts (T.Bekh. 2:11), nursing animals (T.Bekh. 2:14),
sheep, cows, asses (M.Bekh. 2:11), clothing (T.Meg. 7:14), vats of olives (T.Toh. 10:5),
grapes (T.Toh. 11:8), raisins (T.Toh. 11:9), slaves (T.A.Z. 2:1, pulse, dried figs, garlic,
onions, cedar (T.A.Z. 4:11), metal filings (T.A.Z. 5:3). In addition to these rather
mundane items, certain ritual items such as scrolls, *tefilin*, and *mezuzot* could be
purchased from gentiles as long as they were properly prepared (T.A.Z. 3:6-7). Even
animals used for sacrifices could be purchased from non-Israelites (T.A.Z. 2:1). It is
interesting to note that although it was assumed gentiles regularly practiced bestiality
and that they would make a libation with virtually any wine with which they came into
contact, both of these assumptions were ignored if the Israelite wished to purchase
these items from gentiles. Furthermore, although matters of purity did concern our

Even though our texts were concerned that the Israelites did not support the gentile's religious activities, the rabbis do not appear to have had a clear idea of what occurred in the gentile cult.[63] Indeed, gentile merchants were above all considered businessmen—and one could assume that they would use purchased items for profit, not for worship.

In the second and third classes of materials, the non-Israelite is not pictured negatively or positively; his character is simply ignored. Here, the issue was the *halakhah*, not the gentile. The gentile was an abstraction, that part of the population which was not Israelite. In the second class, one could not do business with an Israelite or a non-Israelite for the same reason: one could not sell items which were ritually prohibited from the rabbis' point of view. The last set of texts were concerned that the Israelite should not appear to have violated the *halakhah*. This meant that an Israelite had to follow scrupulously the *halakhah*, for he would be unable to derive any benefit either from ritually prohibited items or by procrastinating in his obligations.[64]

Our survey yields several interesting results. First, given the fact that the market-place was the area of the most frequent contact between Israelites and gentiles, it is significant that the earliest rabbis did not attempt to draw sharper borders between the two segments of Palestinian society. Either the economic factors were so important that they superseded any concern for contact, or the rabbis simply ignored or did not consider as significant any threat to the coherence of the Israelite community which might result from the *economic* interaction of Israelite and gentile. Non-Israelites could not be avoided, so one had to make the best of the situation.

Second, these texts do not leave us with the impression that the rabbis had a clear view of the gentile as "other." On the one hand he is "nasty," while on the other he can be trusted. On the one hand he had to be dealt with, while on the other hand, he should be avoided.

---

authors, for the most part things were assumed to be ritually fit so that they might be purchased by an Israelite. In short, with the specific exception of an egg cracked in a dish, an Israelite could buy virtually anything from a gentile. As we noted above, there is some uncertainty about whether or not the Red Heifer could be purchased from a gentile.

[63] Mishnah-Tosefta contain many discussions about the Asherah and the cult of Molech. Both were biblical cults, and it is extremely doubtful that they were active in the rabbinic era.

[64] These rules had a secondary results, for they discouraged the existence of ritually prohibited items. If one were to follow these rules, the Israelite could ensure that he was not responsible for a gentile's coming into possession of small animals, unfit meat, or cloth which violated the laws of "mixed-kinds."

On the one hand he was an idolater, while on the other he was a businessman, a buyer or a seller. The reason for this inconsistency may be that the rabbis are not dealing with gentiles as they existed in the outside world. Rather, it appears that they pictured the gentile as they thought he should appear, and the pericopae are thus constructed in light of the concerns of the authors of Mishnah-Tosefta. For example, although the Torah permits the sale of ritually unfit meat to gentiles, Mishnah-Tosefta prohibit these sales for their own reasons. This is demonstrated by the fact that other rabbinic collections permit such transactions. Similarly, the issues of slavery, intention, and "mixed-kinds" which we encountered above were all framed from the rabbis' point of view with little or no reference to the gentile as an actual entity. Frequently, the gentile's character is ignored, and he is treated merely in the abstract. There is little concern with or knowledge of the realities of the gentile's wishes, expectations, or environment. For example, the rabbis expected gentiles to free slaves which they had purchased from Israelites,[65] and they ruled that an Israelite could purchase almost anything else from a gentile—even scrolls, *tefilin*, and *mezuzot*—as long as they had been properly prepared (T.A.Z. 2:8). This assumes that gentiles were familiar with rabbinic law and that they could produce valid ritual objects.[66] And one is scarcely limited with respect to what one may sell them. In short, the gentile's character changes according to the context and purpose of the rabbinic rulings. While this may reflect how non-Israelites really are—some are good while others are not—there is nothing in our *sugyot* which suggests that the rabbis were dealing with "real" gentiles. I would argue that the bloodthirsty, greedy, nasty gentile is as unreal as the trusted, trusting gentile who would freely make his intentions known to an Israelite when purchasing an item from him. The gentile is always pictured from the rabbis' point of view and described in any context in ways which are consistent with the needs of a given passage or literary form or convention.

Third, the limited texts we have examined do not indicate that the

---

[65] In another context the rabbis attempt to regulate the gentile's business practices by setting the terms by which an Israelite can purchase something from a gentile on a trial basis.

[66] The issue is muddied by the fact that some of these purchases may have been a way of redeeming items which gentiles had illegally obtained from Israelites. M.Git. 4:6 prohibits the purchase of scrolls, *tefilin*, or *mezuzot* from gentiles at more than their market-value. The text also discusses the redemption of slaves from gentiles at a fair price, and Yom Tov cites Maimonides who read the rule concerning the ritual objects as a means of discouraging gentiles from stealing them so that they might resell them at a high price to Israelites.

rabbis had a clear view of gentile cults. While the rabbis wanted to limit the Israelite's direct and indirect contact with foreign cults, the authors of the *sugyot* which we have examined do not have accurate knowledge of the gentile's religion and they seem to be willing to put some economic concerns above their desire to keep the Israelites away from any contact with gentile religious activity.

Fourth, it is clear that regular interaction took place between the gentile and the Israelite in the market-place and that the rabbis put few restrictions in the way of this activity.[67]

We often forget that Mishnah-Tosefta do not contain a sustained discussion of the gentile *qua* gentile. The major topic of Avodah Zarah is idolatry, only one aspect of the gentile's existence.[68] This stands in sharp contrast to the writings of the Church Fathers, many of which contain long discussions of the real or imagined Jew, not only as the practitioner of a despised religion, but also as the quintessential other.[69] Thus, the preoccupation with the gentile may well be ours, and not the rabbis. At least in the area of economic concerns, the area where the most frequent contact between Israelite and gentile occurred, it seems that this is in fact the case.

---

[67] My conclusion is the exact opposite of that reached by Cohen. In his English summary, Cohen writes, "In spite of these economic contracts, however, many difficult restrictions were imposed." (x). On the contrary, I am impressed by the few restrictions and their relatively innocuous nature.

[68] J. Neusner, *Judaism: The Evidence of Mishnah* (Chicago: 1981), 202-203. We should also remember that a good deal of the rabbinic discussion of idolatry centers on Israelites who worship idols, not on gentile practices.

[69] For a discussion of the *Aversos Judaeos* tradition see R. Reuther, *Faith and Fraticide* (New York: 1974), 117-182.

14

Passover, Easter, and Anti-Judaism: Melito of Sardis and Others

S. G. Wilson
Carleton University

It was Jules Isaac who insisted, in the years immediately following World War II, that the prayer for the Jews in the Good Friday service of the Roman liturgy had made a fundamental contribution to the development of Christian anti-Semitism.[1] The prayer, usually referred to as *Pro Perfidis Judaeis*, is the eighth of nine intercessions in the Good Friday liturgy. Not only are the Jews called *perfidi*—a term often understood to mean 'perfidious', 'wicked', or 'malicious', when it seems to mean no more than 'unbelieving'—but the accompanying rubric forbade the congregation to kneel in silent prayer as was the custom with the other eight prayers. The Jews, as subjects of the prayer, were thus singled out both by unusual terminology and by distinctive liturgical gesture—a distinction which was officially banned by Roman authorities in 1955. Marcel Simon took issue with Isaac, arguing that a prayer spoken once a year and in a language most congregations did not understand (Latin, until the introduction of vernacular liturgies) could scarcely be credited with such influence.[2] There is little hard evidence with which to defend either view, but even if Isaac exaggerated the importance of this particular prayer, he nevertheless pointed to a significant broader issue—the impact of the Christian liturgy and catachesis on the development of anti-Semitism.

A better known and less disputed example is the influence of the Passion narratives of the canonical Gospels, which form the backbone of the Easter liturgy in most Churches. Not only do they dominate the lectionaries in the weeks surrounding Easter, they also provide the proof-text for many an Easter sermon. As is well known, the Jews are portrayed in an increasingly negative fashion as one moves from the earlier to the later accounts—a trajectory which extends into the

---

[1] J. Isaac, *Jesus et Israel* (Paris: 1948), 364-5; *Genese de l'Antisemitisme* (Paris: 1956), 296-305.
[2] M. Simon, *Verus Israel* (Paris: 1964), 2nd. edition, 488-90.

apocryphal gospels, such as the Gospel of Peter, and into Easter homilies throughout the early centuries. Moreover, no one who has heard contemporary Easter sermons, which typically exaggerate the already simplified accounts of the Gospels, and thus in casual and unthinking fashion enhance the negative image of the Jews, can doubt the detrimental effect these texts and this festival have had on the Christian view of Judaism. The persistence of the view that the Jews were "Christ-killers" or "'God-killers," and the well documented association of the Easter season with the pogroms, are more than sufficient to demonstrate the point.

A fairly recent innovation in the Easter ceremonies of some Canadian Churches also caught my eye—the celebration of a passover meal on Maundy Thursday. Its prayers and rituals follow as closely as possible the Jewish rite but are constantly interlarded with supersessionary convictions about Jesus as the true paschal sacrifice and the Church as the true Israel. Here are fascinating, if muffled, echoes of early Christian practice, but also some pointed issues. It might be an innocent enough attempt to reenact the last days of Jesus' life, usually pursued by those with a love of all forms of ritual, and it might be thought that it has the advantage of reminding Christians of their Jewish roots, about which they are notoriously ignorant. On the other hand, it might be supposed that the supersessionary thrust of the celebration reinforces a typically negative view of Judaism and that such an adaptation of the great annual festival of the Jewish people could only be matched in insensitivity if Jewish communities decided to celebrate the death of heretics and false Messiahs in their Passover rite.

The main point of these contemporary examples, however, is to illustrate the persistence of at least the following two features of the Christian Easter which can be traced back to the earliest centuries: an intimate, but complex relationship with the Jewish Passover, and an anti-Jewish strain which can be variously shaped and caused, but is always there in some form or another. In the two classic works on early Christian attitudes towards Judaism, by Jean Juster and Marcel Simon, the Christian transformation of Passover is considered to be a prime example of deliberate anti-Judaism.[3] As Christians sought to express their own identity distinct from Judaism, the most sensitive and troublesome issues were those fought over common ground. The more intimate and overt the relationship, the more problematic was the issue. That Easter was one such is shown by the frequent

[3] J. Juster, *Les Juifs dans l'empire romaine*, (Paris: 1914), Vol. 1, 308-15; Simon, *Israel*, 362f.

references to paschal controversies in early Christian writings and by
the persistence of diverse practices at least up to the fifth century C.E.
In the rest of this paper I shall look briefly at the development of the
Easter tradition, and in more detail at a specific text which was not
available when Juster and Simon wrote, Melito's *Paschal Homily*. In
so doing, I shall have a number of questions in mind which it might be
useful to specify at the outset. First, to what extent was the formation
of the Christian calendar both motivated by and a contributor towards
Christian anti-Judaism? As with the analogous but less troublesome
shift from Sabbath to Sunday, proximity to the "other" seems to have
bred unease and, eventually, hostility.[4] Why? Secondly, how does
Melito's *Homily* fit into this broader picture? What are its unique
features and how do we explain them? Answers to these questions
lead naturally to themes whose implications for the broader problems
of Jewish-Christian relations lead well beyond the specific case of
Melito. Thirdly, precisely because it is an Easter sermon, Melito's
work pointedly raises the question of the impact on Christian consciousness of various components of the early Christian liturgy—
hymns, prayers, creeds, scripture readings and homilies—many of
which were given a decidedly anti-Jewish twist. Juster, whose discussion of this matter seems not to have been superseded, concludes
that they made a decisive contribution to anti-Jewish sentiment in the
early centuries—a judgement worthy of further reflection at a later
stage.[5]

The origin and development of paschal celebrations in the early
Church is shrouded in obscurity. One of the clearer accounts takes us
immediately to the end of the second century. Eusebius describes a
dispute between the Roman Church and the Christians of Asia Minor
(*H.E.* 5.24.2-6). In 197 C.E., Victor, bishop of Rome, attempted to
enforce a uniform date for the Christian Pascha; it was to be held on
the Sunday following 14th Nisan. The Christians of Asia Minor,
represented in this conflict by Polycrates, bishop of Ephesus, presently celebrated the Pascha on the same day, though not necessarily
in the same manner, as the Jews (i.e. on 14th Nisan). They are thus
called Quartodecimans. Victor's action was neither uniformly supported nor, it seems, immediately effective. Irenaeus, though not a
Quartodeciman, disapproved of Victor's heavy handed policy (Eus.

---

[4] See S. Bacchiocchi, *Anti-Judaism and the Origin of Sunday* (Rome: 1975).
[5] Juster, *Juifs*, 304-37. He includes consideration of catachesis and later festivals such
as the Ascension.

H.E. 5.24.14) and, if later reports are anything to go by, Quartodeciman practice persisted for a considerable time, at least in Asia Minor.[6]
Working back from this conflict and drawing mainly on Eusebius and
Epiphanius (*H.E.* 5.24.14-16, and *Haer.* 70.9-10), we can surmise the
following:

1. The Quartodecimans presented what in all probability was the
earliest form of the Christian Pascha, with roots stretching back into
the apostolic era, perhaps even to the primitive Palestinian Church.[7]
That their practice rested on ancient tradition was recognized by their
opponents (Irenaeus in Eus. *H.E.* 5.24.16; Theodoret in *Haer.*
Fab.Comp. 3.4) and defenders alike (Polycrates in Eus. *H.E.* 5.24.2-6).
In the first century, as far as we know, this was the only form of
Christian paschal celebration, though how widespread it was we
cannot tell. In common with the Jews, the Quartodecimans celebrated
on 14th Nisan, read and expounded the biblical stories of Passover,[8]
and, in the early years at least, awaited the arrival—or, as Christians
would have it, the return—of the Messiah.[9] Two things, however,
seem to have distinguished them: first, during the time of the passover
meal on 14th Nisan, a fast (broken early in the morning with a
Eucharist) which was both a commemoration of the death of Jesus and
a vicarious fast for the Jews who put him to death (Didascalia 21);[10]
and second, a focus on Jesus as the once and for all true paschal lamb
(I Cor. 5.7). Both elements drew attention to Jesus' death rather than
to his resurrection, in line with most other early paschal traditions.

2. At some point in the second century a decision was taken to
celebrate the Pascha on the Sunday after 14th Nisan. At the latest, it
was introduced into the Jerusalem Church following the debacle of
the Bar Cochba rebellion, circa 135 C.E. (Eus. *H.E.* 4.6.4; Epiph.
Haer. 70.9-10). There, in all probability, it replaced a Quartodeciman
tradition. Whether the paschal-Sunday tradition spread from

---

[6] W. Huber, *Passa und Ostern* (Berlin: 1969), 75f.

[7] Generally on Quartodecimans see B. Lohse, *Das Passa Fest der Quartadecimaner*
(Gutersloh: 1953); Huber, *Passa*—especially the bibliography in the latter.

[8] According to Melito's *Homily*, Ex.12 is read; according to Pes.10:1f, Dt.26:5-11 was
used in the Jewish Passover. See more generally Huber, *Passa*, 3-11; S.G. Hall, "Melito
in the light of the Passover Haggadah," *JTS* N.S. 22 (1971), 219-46.

[9] There is some disagreement between Lohse, *Passafest*, and Huber, *Passa*, partly
because the evidence is obscure, partly because it is not clear what counts as evidence
for the Quartodecimans. In general I am persuaded by Huber's more restrained use of
the evidence, except by his attempt to argue that Melito was not a Quartodeciman.

[10] The Didascalia is the main evidence for this practice together with the related
Diataxis quoted by Epiphanins *Haer.* 70.11.3. Melito's *Homily* provides no evidence for
this.

Jerusalem to Rome[11] or vice-versa[12] is not clear, nor is it certain that there was any paschal festival at all in Rome before the second century.[13] What seems certain is that the shift to Sunday from 14th Nisan was, in part at least, a deliberate move to dissociate Christianity from Judaism. The assertion of a separate identity had, as so often, an anti-Jewish twist.

3. As we move into the third and fourth centuries there is evidence for continuing paschal disputes and an increasing hostility towards those who mingled Jewish and Christian practice. Best known, perhaps, is the decree of the Council of Nicea (325 C.E.) and the accompanying letter from the Emperor Constantine:

> All the brethren who are in the East who formerly celebrated Easter with the Jews will henceforth keep it at the same time as the Romans, with us and with all those who from ancient times have celebrated the feast at the same time as us.[14]

Further:

> It appeared an unworthy thing that in the celebration of this most holy feast we should follow the practice of the Jews, who have impiously defiled their hands with enormous sin and are, therefore, deservedly afflicted with blindness of soul....Let us then have nothing in common with the detestable crowd of Jews; for we have received from our Saviour a different way (Eus. *Life of Const.* 3.18-19).

Whether this and similar evidence refers to a continuing Quartodeciman controversy[15] or to a new dispute over the use of Jewish and non-Jewish calendrical calculations remains unclear.[16] More important for our purposes than a precise demarcation of the disputes is the evidence for a persistent entanglement of Passover and Easter and the various anti-Jewish sentiments it provoked. Sometimes this was the result of long-established tradition (Quartodecimans) and sometimes the result of understandable confusion about the relationship of the two among ordinary Christians who lived in close contact with Jews.

---

[11] Huber, *Passa*, 56-61, places it c.168-76 C.E., under Soter. The dispute hinges on the meaning of *terein/me terein* in Eus. *H.E.* 5.24.14: does it distinguish between keeping a Quartodeciman Easter or 'Roman' Easter, or between keeping a Quartodeciman Easter and keeping no Easter at all? Probably the latter. See literature quoted in Huber, *Passa*, 57f.

[12] Bacchiocchi (*Sunday*, 48-51) places it c.116-125 C.E., under Sixtus.

[13] See Bacchiocchi, *Sunday*, 83f.

[14] Bacchiocchi, *Sunday*, 86 n 256.

[15] Lohse, *Passafest*, 17f.

[16] Huber, *Passa*, 64f.

Thus Aphrahat, speaking of the situation in Syria, notes how "greatly troubled are the minds of foolish and unintelligent folk concerning this great day of festival, as to how they should understand and observe it."[17] The issue could become inflamed, as it did in Chrysostom's Antioch, when judaizing Christians expressed their attraction to Judaism by following the Jewish calendar and, worse still, attending the synagogue for Jewish feasts.[18] To counter this threat a number of arguments were devised. They range from supersessionary theologies, through denial of the legality of the Jewish passover, to outright vilification. The following points are typical:

(a) The true meaning of the Passover is to be found in the sacrifice of Jesus as the Paschal lamb (Justin *Dial* 40.2,46.2; Aphrahat. *Dem.* 12; Chrys. *Jud.* 3; *Chron. Pasch.* 6-7).

(b) Pascha is for Christians a weekly (i.e. eucharistic) as well as an annual feast (Aphrahat *Dem.* 12; Chrys. *Jud.* 3).

(c) The Jews cannot legally celebrate Passover because Jerusalem is destroyed (Aphrahat, *Dem.* 12; Chrys. *Jud.* 3) and the priesthood gone (Chrys. *Jud.* 3).

(d) The precise date of Pascha is insignificant because for Christians the key day is always Friday in remembrance of Jesus' passion (Aphrahat *Dem.* 3) or because it cannot at any rate be securely fixed (Chrys. *Jud.* 3).

(e) Christians who follow the Jewish reckoning or, worse still, join in the Jewish feast give prestige to Jewish rather than Christian leaders, confuse and divide the Church and consort with the killers of Christ:

> After you have gone off and shared with those who shed the blood of Christ, how is it that you do not shudder to come back here and share his sacred banquet, to partake of his precious blood? (Chrys. *Jud.* 2.3.5)

From this brief survey we might draw the following conclusions. Whether we consider the dating, the form or the rationale for the Christian Easter, there seems to be an underlying anti-Jewish motif. The Pascha, it seems, presented the Church with a particularly thorny problem as it strove to establish an identity distinct from Judaism. Chronological coincidence, ritual indebtedness and supersessionary convictions combined to present a complex situation. The earliest and simplest move, found among the Quartodecimans, was to reverse the ritual pattern—fasting when the Jews feasted and celebrating joyfully

---

[17] J. Neusner, *Aphrahat and Judaism* (Leiden: 1971), especially 123-7.
[18] R. Wilken, *John Chrysostom and the Jews* (Berkeley and Los Angeles: 1983), passim.

when they ate unleavened bread. The shift to Sunday from 14th Nisan was a more overt break. True, it may have been natural to combine two feast days which celebrated the resurrection, though early Easter traditions seem to focus more on Jesus' death than on his resurrection, but the desire to disentangle the Christian from the Jewish feast was almost certainly a prominent motive. The third and fourth centuries witness the appearance of conciliar decisions banning association with the Jews, and theological schemes which appropriate Passover traditions for the Church and deny them to the Jews. Passover/Easter was, at the best of times, a sensitive issue whenever Jews and Christians came into contact, and it could quickly become a cause of bitter dispute and inflamed rhetoric when, as in fourth century Antioch, it was one of many features of Jewish life that attracted the attention and allegiance of Christians. Hovering all the while was the potentially explosive issue of Jewish responsibility for Jesus' death, recalled sometimes in a vicarious fast and at all times by the passion stories, which was always liable to flare up when relationships soured. And this, quite naturally, leads us to turn our attention to Melito.[19]

MELITO'S PASCHAL HOMILY

Melito's *Homily,* rediscovered in 1932 and first published in 1940, was composed c.167 C.E. and is the earliest Easter homily known to us.[20] For our purposes, it can be divided into three parts which we shall consider briefly in turn.[21]

The first part, which we might entitle, "From Type to Reality," consists of a typological exposition of the Exodus story (sections 1-45). Following a reading of Ex.12, the preacher declares that he will reveal the 'mystery' of the Pascha. In what follows, the core of the argument is predictable rather than mysterious, for it is christological—the true meaning of the Pascha lies in the sacrificial death of Jesus. In an

---

[19] Anti-Judaism was not, of course, the only motivation for Paschal disputes. As mentioned before, the natural drive to develop a festival expressing Christian realities played its role. An avoidance of unseemly public disagreement is mentioned by Epiphanius. The assertion of Rome's primacy may have motivated Victor as much as a concern for Church unity, while the disruption that judaizing created in the Church was a major theme of Chrysostom.

[20] C. Bonner, *The Homily on the Passion by Melito Bishop of Sardis and some Fragments of the Apocryphal Ezekiel,* (London: 1940).

[21] What follows in this section is an abbreviated version of S. G. Wilson, "Melito and Israel," to appear in *Anti-Judaism in Early Christianity,* ed. by S.G. Wilson with L. Gaston. It will be published by Waterloo University Press in 1985. The text and translation used is that of S. G. Hall, *Melito of Sardis 'On Pascha' and Fragments* (Oxford, 1979).

unusually clear statement of hermeneutical principle, Melito summa-
rizes the contrast between old and new Pascha as follows:

This is just what happens in the case of a
preliminary structure:
it does not arise as a finished work,
but because of what is going to be visible
through its image acting as a model.
For this reason a preliminary sketch is made
of the future thing,
out of wax out of clay or of wood,
in order that what will soon arise
taller in height,
and stronger in power,
and beautiful in form,
and rich in its construction,
may be seen through a small and perishable sketch.

But when that of which it is the model arises,
that which once bore the image of the future thing
is itself destroyed as growing useless
having yielded to what is truly real the image of it;
and what once was precious becomes worthless
when what is truly precious has been revealed.

For to each belongs a proper season:
a proper time for the model,
a proper time for the material,
a proper time for the reality.
                              (Lines 224-244)

As then with the perishable examples,
so also with the imperishable things;
as with the earthly things,
so also with the heavenly.

For the very salvation and reality of the Lord
were prefigured in the people,
and the decrees of the gospel were proclaimed in
advance of the law.

The people then was a model by way of preliminary
sketch,
and the law was the writing of a parable;
the gospel is the recounting and fulfilment
of the law,
and the church is the repository of the reality.

The model then was precious before the reality,
and the parable was marvellous before the
interpretation;
that is, the people was precious before the
church arose,
and the law was marvellous before the gospel was
elucidated.

But when the church arose
and the gospel took precedence,
the model was made void, conceding its power to the
reality,
and the law was fulfilled, conceding its power to the
gospel.

In the same way as the model is made void, conceding
the image to the truly real,
and the parable is fulfilled, being elucidated
by the interpretation,
just so also the law was fulfilled when the
gospel was elucidated,
and the people was made void when the church arose,
and the model was abolished when the Lord was revealed,
and today, things once precious have become worthless,
since the really precious things have been revealed.

(ll. 255-279)

The contrast between model (*typos*) and reality (*aletheia*), between blueprint and artifact, and the unambiguous assertion of the redundancy of the one when the other appears, have self-evident implications of Melito's view of Judaism, but it is worth drawing attention to them nevertheless. First, while the main aim is to lay claim to Israel's Passover traditions—to show how Christ is the true lamb and the Christian feast the true Passover—Melito does not stop there. For in the passages quoted above and elsewhere (ll. 280-300) this claim is expanded in sweeping fashion; not only the Passover, but also the People, the Law, the Holy City, the Temple and the particular Covenant have been superseded. The status of the Passover, in other words, represents the status of Israel and her traditions as a whole.

Secondly, and unlike some other early Christian writers, Melito does assign positive value to Israel's traditions; they were, as the model or sketch, "precious" and "marvellous." By the same token, however, when the artifact appears the model is redundant—it is "abolished," "worthless," "made void," "fulfilled," "useless," to use some of Melito's terms. The many and varied terms, however, thrust toward this singular conclusion: Judaism is defunct. The positive evaluation belongs only to Israel's past, the negative to her present.

Thirdly, while the typological foreshadowing of Jesus in the Scriptures is central to his argument, Melito goes still further. For in Melito's curiously modalistic form of christology, Christ is not only prefigured by, but also a participant in Israel's past. As Abel was murdered, Isaac bound, Joseph sold, Moses exposed and David persecuted (ll. 415-24), so was Christ murdered, bound, sold, exposed and persecuted with them (ll. 479-88). The shift from typological prefigurement to modalist participation strengthens the Christian claim to Israel's tradition and compounds Israel's guilt in rejecting Christ, for he was not just prefigured in their past, he *was* their past.

Fourthly, in the dramatic and powerful evocation of Egypt's fate during the Exodus (sections 1-42), the analogous role the Jews will play in the death of Jesus is foreshadowed (sections 72f). When the miracle of the Passover is reenacted in Jesus' death, those who were once saved from their enemies become, by an ironic twist, the enemies of salvation.

The *Homily's* second part (sections 46-71) can be dealt with briefly, since it is only indirectly related to our theme. It consists of a meditation on the Fall and the arrival of Sin and Death in its wake. Now we might expect the exposition on Jesus' death in the next part of the *Homily* to be related to what precedes it. Of some 250 lines in the final part, however, only the last forty consider the benefits of Christ's death (ll. 763-804). The bulk of them consist of an impassioned denunciation of Israel's crime in rejecting and killing their God (ll. 551-762). The proportions demonstrate clearly where Melito's interest lay.

It is the third part of the *Homily* (sections 72-99) which earned Melito the title, "The First Poet of Deicide."[22] Two samples will give the flavour.

But you did not turn out to be 'Israel';
you did not 'see God',
you did not recognize the Lord.
You did not know, Israel, that he is the firstborn of
God,
who was begotten before the morning star,
who tinted the light, who lit up the day,
who divided off the darkness,
who fixed the first marker,
who hung the earth,

---

[22] E. Werner, "Melito of Sardis: The First Poet of Deicide," *HUCA* 37 (1966), 191-210.

who controlled the deep,
who spread out the firmament,
who arrayed the world,
who fitted the stars in heaven,
who lit up the luminaries,
who made the angels in heaven,
who established the thrones there,
who formed man upon earth.
(ll. 562-608)

An unprecedented murder has occurred in the middle of
Jerusalem,
in the city of the law,
in the city of the Hebrews,
in the city of the prophets,
in the city accounted just.

And who has been murdered? Who is the murderer?
I am ashamed to say and I am obliged to tell.
For if the murder had occurred at night,
or if he had been slain in a desert place
one might have had recourse to silence.
But now, in the middle of the street and in the
middle of the city,
at the middle of the day for all to see,
has occurred a just man's unjust murder.

Just so he has once been lifted up on a tall tree,
and a notice has been attached to show who has
been murdered.
Who is this? To say is hard, and not to say is
too terrible.

Yet listen, trembling at him for whom the earth quaked.
He who hung the earth is hanging;
he who fixed the heavens has been fixed;
he who fastened the universe has been fastened to a
tree;
the Sovereign has been insulted;
the God has been murdered;
the King of Israel has been put to death by an
Israelite right hand.
(ll. 693-716)

The main thrust of Melito's denunciation could scarcely be more
clearly stated. The view that the Jews were responsible for Jesus'

death had, of course, a long pedigree in Christian thinking; Melito
was apparently the first, however, to intensify and expand this into
responsibility for the death of God. In the course of his denunciation
Melito introduces a number of subsidiary themes to vary the rhetorical effect, bolster the accusation against Israel, and compound her
guilt.

It is apparent, for example, that the term "Israel" refers indiscriminately to all Jews. No distinction is made between leaders and
people, between Palestinian and diaspora Jews, or between Jews of
the past and present. The malevolence of the Jews is underlined by
contrasting their behaviour with Gentiles who admired and worshipped Jesus (ll. 671-6) and their perversity is brought to the fore by
the assertion that they rejected Jesus *because* he was just and *because*
he did works of compassion (ll. 505f, 545f). The Jews' vigorous
infliction of the greatest possible agony at the point of death, and their
temerity in crucifying Jesus in broad daylight in the midst of the Holy
City (ll. 693f), while they joyfully celebrated the Passover (ll. 566f), is
only further exaggerated by the almost complete absence of Pilate and
any other Romans from the scene. And should the Jews claim that they
were merely the instruments of divine necessity, Melito counters with
the observation that the deed should have been accomplished by the
hands of godless foreigners, not by those of the elect people (ll.
537-45).

Melito's modalist christology, more fully expressed in this section,
compounds the crime. For not only is Christ prefigured by and a
participant in the history of Israel, he is now also identified with the
God of Israel. In rejecting Christ, Israel rejected God himself, the
author of creation and of their election and salvation. They thus
forfeited their right to be his people, and were punished with
bitterness and death (ll. 680f, 744f).

The first and the third parts of Melito's *Homily* are inextricably
linked. In the one we find a radical and rigorous supersessionary
claim: the Jews, as the erstwhile people of God, are no longer; all that
survives of their tradition is of positive value only insofar as it is
absorbed into the Christian reality. In the other, we find the explanation: in rejecting Christ the Jews rejected their God and he, in turn,
has rejected them. The connection is logical, and is reinforced by
literary echoes such as the one between the role of the Egyptians
during the Exodus and that of the Jews during the crucifixion. The two
parts are mutually supportive and equally important for Melito's view
of Judaism—a theme which, as A. T. Kraabel noted several years ago,

has received remarkably little scholarly attention, and that usually restricted to passing references to the charge of deicide.[23]

How do we explain Melito's view and, in particular, those elements uncommon or absent in other Easter homilies? There is no simple answer to this question; rather, there are a number of factors which need to be brought into play. Moreover, many of them introduce issues of broad significance for the question of Jewish-Christian relations in the early centuries and it is partly with an eye to this that they will be considered.

First, it is obvious, but necessary, to note that Melito's anti-Judaism is, in part, the reverse side of his attempt to articulate Christian belief. The historical relationship between the two traditions made this inevitable, and the attempt to occupy common ground—as with the scriptures, or festivals like Passover—intensified the conflict. It is natural too, following the separation of Church and Synagogue and the increasingly confident claims of a Gentile Church, that the ambivalence of a Paul should be replaced by the categorical claims of a Melito. This explains some of the exegetical procedures in the first part of the *Homily*, but not all of them, and not the charge of deicide. I need scarcely add that the relationship between self-definition and repudiation of the "other," which I am only alluding to here, is central to the theme of this conference.

Second, Melito was a trained and highly regarded rhetorician (Tertullian in Jerome, *De viris illustribus*, 24) in the style of the Second Sophistic.[24] Of this, the *Paschal Homily* provides ample confirmation. Scarcely a paragraph is formulated without resort to rhetorical devices which dramatize and enhance its effect. The use of antithesis, paranomasia and rhetorical questions doubtless exaggerates the contrast between Jewish and Christian Passovers just as the use of repetition, anaphora and oxymoron intensifies the denunciation of the Jews. A sensitivity to language and rhetorical device, recently explored to great effect in R. Wilkins work on Chrysostom, is an important feature of any balanced assessment of early Christian statements on Judaism.[25] Nevertheless, there is more to Melito than mere rhetorical skill.

---

[23] A. T. Kraabel, "Melito the Bishop and the Synagogue at Sardis: Text and Context," in *Studies Presented to George M. A. Hanfmann*, e.d. D. G. Mitten, J. G. Pedlen, J. A. Scott (Mainz: 1972) 72-85, here 81 n.25.

[24] See T. Halton, "Stylistic Device in Melito," ------' in *Kyriakon*, Festschrift for J. Quasten, ed. P. Granfield, J. A. Jungmaun, Vol. 1 (Munster, 1970), 249-55; J. Smit Sibinga, "Melito of Sardis: The Artist and His Text," *VC* 24 (1970), 81-104;A. Wifstrand, "The Homily of Melito on the Passion," *VC* 2 (1948), 201-223.

[25] Wilken, *Chrysostom*, 95-127.

Third, Melito was a Quartodeciman (Eus. *H.E.* 5.24.2-6).[26] As a surviving representative of this tradition in the late second century, he would have been under considerable pressure to distinguish the Christian from the Jewish festival and to avoid the charge of judaizing. Even in earlier days the Quartodecimans felt obliged to develop distinctive traits, but by Melito's day the pressures were even greater. The result was that a closer association with Judaism in one respect led to a determined effort to establish distance in others, to separate the old from the new Passover, the Church from Israel. Whether Melito was representative of other Quartodecimans in his day we cannot tell, but he is at any rate an important specific example of the conflicts surrounding Easter and Passover which we looked at earlier in this paper.

Fourth, the town of Sardis contained a long-established, sizable and influential Jewish population. The evidence for this and its significance for Melito's *Homily* has been most clearly laid out by A. T. Kraabel. From the reports in Josephus and from extensive archeological excavations, it is clear that "the Sardis Jewish community was a large one, with a degree of wealth, social status and political power and that the synagogue, on a choice location in the centre of the Roman City, is by far the largest discovered anywhere in the ancient world."[27] The Jews in Sardis were, in short, a force to be reckoned with, and scarcely to be ignored by a Christian community attempting to establish a distinct identity and political standing.

K. H. Rengstorf has claimed that "nothing would be more mistaken than to reproach the bishop of Sardis with a low-class and malicious anti-Judaism. . . .The Jews he has in mind and accuses are not the Jews of his time, much less the Jews of his diocese, but the Jews of long ago, the Jews of the first Good Friday in Jerusalem."[28] Rengstorf, however, provides no evidence for this assertion. Certainly, the Jews of Jesus' day are those to whom Melito primarily refers, but then the rejection of Jesus, and especially his death, is

---

[26] Contra Huber, *Passa*, 31-44. The argument is flawed and provides only a lame explanation of Polycrates plain testimony to the contrary (Eus. *H.E.* 5.24.2-6).

[27] Kraabel, "Melito," passim; further in "Impact of the Discovery of the Sardis Synagogue," in *Sardis from Prehistoric to Roman Times: Results of the Archeological Exploration of Sardis 1958-1975*, ed. G.A.M. Hanfmann (Cambridge Mass: 1983), 178-90 and 284-5; see also K. W. Noakes, "Melito of Sardis and the Jews," Studia Patristica 13 *TU* 116 (1975), pp. 244-9; R. Wilken, "Melito and the Sacrifice of Isaac," *TS* 37 (1976), 53-69; J. Blank, *Meliton von Sardes VOM PASSA; die älteste christliche Osterpredigt* (Freiburg: 1963), 77-86.

[28] K. H. Rengstorf and S. von Kortzfleisch, *Kirche und Synagoge: Handbuch zur Geschichte von Christen und Juden* (Stuttgart: 1968), Vol. 1, p. 73.

precisely the topic of the last third of the *Homily,* and references to contemporary Jewry would have been anachronistic. It might also be argued that, for Melito, there was no Israel to address after these decisive events: she was no longer Israel (ll. 589-91), she had been 'dashed to the ground' and 'lies dead' (ll. 744-5, cf. 662-4). However, it is improbable that this theologoumenon would lead Melito or his audience to make no connection between the *Homily* and contemporary Jewry. The existence of a prominent Jewish community in Sardis makes this even less likely. Moreover, there are moments in the *Homily* when "Israel" is addressed in a manner which suggests something more than a rhetorical flourish aimed at a deceased generation, in which the boundaries between past and present are consciously blurred (ll. 634-5, 651-6, 678, cf. 73-4, 519-31).

Melito, it seems, had the Jews of his own day in mind. Their very existence would implicitly have challenged Christian claims to the traditions of Israel and would have encouraged extreme language and a strident tone. That Melito had to travel to Judea to clarify the content of the Hebrew Bible may also suggest little formal contact with the Jews of Sardis, and perhaps a degree of animosity (Eus. *H.E.* 4.26.14). Some Christians in Sardis may have been converts from Judaism, or descendants of such. Perhaps, too, there was traffic in the other direction. Earlier documents suggest that Gentile Christians in Asia Minor were fascinated by and attracted to Judaism (Ignatius *Phil.* 6:1; Rev. 2),[29] and I suspect this may have been partly the cause of Marcion's radical separation of Christianity from Judaism.[30] There is also the fascinating allusion in Barn. 4:6 to those who say "the covenant remains theirs (i.e. the Jews) and ours too," which would provide an interesting backdrop to Melito's sermon. We know Chrysostom faced precisely this problem in fourth-century Antioch and that it provoked inflammatory language about Judaizers and Jews. There is no firm evidence that Melito faced the problem of Judaizers, but if he did, it would go a long way towards explaining the content and tone of the *Homily.*

Fifth, there are a number of hints that Melito, like many of his contemporaries, attempted to counter the teaching of Marcion.[31] There is no doubt that Marcion posed some awkward problems, not

[29] Cf. L. Gaston, "Judaism of the Uncircumcised in Ignatius and Related Writers," to appear in *Anti-Judaism in Early Christianity*, Vol. 2, see above n. 21.
[30] S. G. Wilson, "Marcion and the Jews," to appear in *Anti-Judaism in Early Christianity*, Vol. 2, see above n.21.
[31] On Melito's anti-Marcionitism see Blank, *Meliton*, 15-17; Werner "Melito" 206-7; Hall, *On Pascha*, xli.

the least of which was how to retain the Hebrew scriptures and resist the Marcionite charge of "judaizing"—to which, of course, Melito, as a Quartodeciman, would be especially susceptible. It has been argued, too, that Tertullian is more anti-Jewish when writing against Marcion than when writing specifically against the Jews.[32] Could the same be true of Melito? Disputes with Marcionites could have influenced his view of Judaism in two ways. They could have encouraged the retention of the Old Covenant by means of its subordination to and fulfillment in the New, with its inevitable denigration of the Old and those who lived by it, and, in reaction to Marcion's separation of Jesus and the God of the Jews, they might have encouraged a virtual identification of them which, in turn, transforms the murderers of Jesus into the murderers of God.

Sixth: Christology, at any rate, deserves a separate mention. Melito's fluid and not entirely consistent christological statements contribute significantly to his view of Judaism. The typology, the modalism, and finally the identification of Christ with the God of Israel, crescendo inexorably to the charge of deicide, and proclaim the tragedy and guilt of the Jews.[33] R. Ruether, it will be noted, has argued that Christology is at the root of early Christian anti-Judaism, its so-called left-hand.[34] It is not, I believe, a thesis which can in this simple form be sustained; Melito's *Homily*, however, does no harm to her case.

Seventh, the Quartodecimans, so Eusebius reports, claimed John as their apostolic guarantor. It is the Gospel of John that places Jesus' death on 14th Nisan. It is also the Gospel of John which treats "the Jews" in peculiarly antagonistic fashion. We cannot certainly place John in Asia Minor nor confidently accept claims of apostolic imprimatur, but the connection may be there, and John's anti-Judaism may have affected Melito. Thus the question of the Gospels' influence, and especially that of their trial narratives, is again legitimately raised.

Finally, we know that Melito addressed an apology to the Emperor in response to a bout of persecution in Asia Minor (Eus. *H.E.* 4.26.5-11). In an extant fragment Melito claims that "our philosophy first flourished among the barbarians."[35] Are the barbarians the Jews or, as is more likely in an apology, the empires which preceded

[32] D. P. Efroymsen "The Patristic Connection," in *Antisemitism and the Foundations of Christianity* ed. A. T. Davies, (New York/Toronto 1979), 98-117.
[33] On Melito's christology see Hall, *On Pascha*, xliii–xliv; Bonner, *Homily*, 27-8.
[34] R. Ruether, *Faith and Fratricide* (New York: 1974).
[35] Hall, *On Pascha*, 63, Fragment 1.

Rome?[36] If the latter, do we have here a fleeting claim for antiquity by appropriation of the heritage of the Jews? That Christians were often considered to be upstarts and that they responded by claiming Jewish antiquity as their own is known from other sources (Ep. Diog. 1:1). Does this, in part, motivate the reflections on Old and New Covenant in the first part of the *Homily* (sections 1-45)? Perhaps. But at any rate it points to yet another theme whose significance goes beyond the specific case of Melito.

Let me summarize: Melito's *Homily* is a fascinating text in its own right, yet it also encourages us to reflect upon a rich array of pertinent issues—Christian self-definition, rhetorical training, paschal traditions, contemporary Jewry, Gentile judaizers, anti-Marcionitism, christology, Gospel passion narratives, political apologetic—all of which deserve consideration in any subtle and complete account of early Jewish-Christian relations.

CONCLUDING REFLECTIONS

The specific example of Melito's *Homily* confirms many of the observations made about the general development of Easter traditions, in particular, the anti-Jewish strain that seems to go hand in hand with it in one form or another. Melito may, of course, have been eccentric, and we cannot even be sure he was a typical Quartodeciman. Yet he illustrates one second-century response to the anxiety and confusion caused by the chronological and theological proximity of Passover and Easter. His solution was extreme—an absolute denial of the Jewish celebration of Passover together with a selective appropriation of some features on behalf of Christianity, and an unrestrained vilification of the Jews for causing the death of Jesus. Further, his paschal reflections become the context for a more sweeping denial of Israel's existence and the charge of deicide. If he is not typical, at least he shows one direction in which paschal disputes could develop. Above all, he alerts us to the potential mischief in the distortions of even the earliest accounts of Jesus' death. For if we do not go all the way with Paul Winter's seminal work on the trial of Jesus, it can still be said that Melito's claims about Jewish responsibility for the death of Jesus are, with few exceptions, historically indefensible and, without exception, theologically abhorrent.[37] Yet, would it be altogether out of place to suggest that the sheer extremity of Melito's position is the best protection against it? Could it be argued that the more restrained records of the Gospels are more insidious, and not

---

[36] Kraabel, "Melito," 84.
[37] P. Winter, *On the Trial of Jesus* (Berlin: 1961).

just because they are canonical and better known? Is this a case where an outright lie is easier to handle than a half-truth? It is perhaps worth a moment's reflection.

In the introductory comments I raised the question of liturgical anti-Judaism. Juster, for example, notes that the drama and solemnity of liturgical occasions, and their constant repetition, ensure a far more lasting effect on the average Christian than many other expressions of anti-Judaism.[38] He contrasts it with the essentially literary, elitist polemic in pagan writings. Equally, we could contrast it with learned tracts like Justin's *Dialogue* or Tertullian's *Adversus Judaeos*, whose effect was probably just as limited. Melito's text is a sermon, composed and delivered with a rhetor's skill on a key liturgical occasion. Its effect is likely to have been lasting and profound, even when we allow for the convention of rhetorical exaggeration. It is a text which confirms in a dramatic way Juster's suspicions, and invites further exploration along the path he has opened up.

Finally, the purpose of this conference is to explore how Jewish and Christian traditions viewed the "outsider" or the "other" and the practical consequences which ensued—we are not only to lament the negative and polemical, but also to explore the positive and tolerant. As to practical consequences, there is little we can say about how various Paschal disputes or texts like Melito's *Homily* may have contributed to social or political action against the Jews except as part of a larger trend. As to the concept of the "other," however, we can be more certain—it was almost entirely negative and intolerant, having neither the intention nor the effect of leaving any theoretical space for Judaism. True, the early Quartodecimans may initially have adapted the Passover festival to their own needs without denying it to the Jews, but presumably, for them as for proponents of the Roman Easter tradition, the seeds of supersession also were there in the remembrance of Jesus' death and resurrection. For Melito, as for Justin, Origen, Chrysostom and Aphrahat, affirmation of Christian belief and ritual meant denial of the Jewish equivalent. Melito's exposition of Old and New Pascha may be more sharply defined than many, but it merely makes explicit a tacit strain in Christianity which appeared in its earliest days, even if the precise terminology is first used by Justin, that the Church is the "New Israel."[39] This claim need not, of course, be accompanied by vilification of the "Old Israel," but the claim does set the two traditions on a collision course, and the Paschal contro-

---

[38] Juster, *Juifs*, Vol. 1, 304-337.
[39] See G.P. Richardson, *Israel and the Apostolic Church* (Cambridge: 1969) for the development of this concept.

versies show how the one can easily lead to the other. And if we step back and broaden the context, we soon arrive at one of the more obscure and sensitive issues for these two and other religious traditions: how to sustain adherence to a religion without some sense of its special, if not exclusive, truth, while not at the same time denying the privilege to others. That is a question which pushes us, as perhaps we should be pushed, into the broader field of the history and comparison of religions.

15

The Way and the Ways: Religious Tolerance and Intolerance in the Fourth Century A.D.

A. H. Armstrong

The subject I propose may seem to my present audience excessively well-worn. None the less it seems to me of such historical interest and contemporary importance that it is still worth looking carefully again at least at selected themes and moments in the controversies and policies of the period between the recognition of Christianity by Constantine and the final establishment of Christian intolerance under Theodosius. The choice of the way of intolerance by the authorities of Church and Empire in the late fourth century has had some very serious and lasting consequences. The last vestiges of its practical effects, in the form of the imposition of at least petty and vexatious disabilities on forms of religion not approved by the local ecclesiastical establishment, lasted in some European countries well into my lifetime. And theoretical approval of this sort of intolerance has often long outlasted the power to apply it in practice. After all, as late as 1945 many approved Roman Catholic theologians in England, and the Roman authorities, objected to a statement on religious freedom very close to Vatican II's declaration on that subject.[1] In general, I do not think that any Christian body has ever abandoned the power to persecute and repress while it actually had it. The acceptance of religious tolerance and freedom as good in themselves has normally been the belated, though sometimes sincere and wholehearted, recognition and acceptance of a *fait accompli*. This long persistence of Theodosian intolerance in practice and its still longer persistence in theory has certainly been a cause, though not the only cause, of that unique phenomenon of our time, the decline not only of Christianity but of all forms of religious belief and the growth of a totally irreligious and unspiritual materialism. This is something which many people, by no means only committed Christians, continually and rightly lament. But I am more and more convinced that a

---

[1] See Michael J. Walsh "Ecumenism in Wartime Britain (2)" in *Heythrop Journal* XXIII No. 4 (October 1982) 377-394.

principal cause of it has been the general experience of Church teaching and practice and of the behaviour of Christians during the centuries from the imperial establishment of Christianity to our own times. The triumph of Christianity carried in it, as perhaps all such triumphs do, the seeds of future defeat. The Church in the fourth century took what it wanted and has been paying for it, in one way or another, ever since.

It seems also important to examine what happened in the fourth century rather carefully because such an examination may do a good deal to dispel the idea that the triumph of Christian intolerance was the inevitable result of some great spiritual movement sweeping on irresistibly to its goal: or even that it was inevitable given the ancient, and particularly the Roman view of the rights and responsibilities of rulers in matters of religion. I would not deny that what actually occurred was inevitable given the actual balance of forces at the time and the course of preceding events, including the long and, on the whole, successful reign of Constantine and the premature death of Julian: though even so, if Gratian and Theodosius had chosen to continue the religious policy of Jovian and Valentinian I rather than to develop further the intolerance of the sons of Constantine, the triumph of Christianity would have been considerably qualified in ways which might have meant that its consequences for the future would have been less deleterious. But I cannot see any deeper necessity here than that of circumstance and actual balance of forces.

In view of what has just been said, we should clearly start our consideration of tolerance and intolerance in the fourth century by a rather careful general consideration of the ancient world's view of the place of religion in society and of the duties of rulers in matters of religion. The place of religion in society in the later Roman Empire was what it had always been in the Greek and Roman world, as in other traditional societies. Religious cults were all-pervasive and central to the life of society and it was therefore generally agreed, as it had always been, that the maintenance and proper regulation of religious practice was the proper concern of the authorities of the state. Religious concern and anxiety had been deepening and intensifying since the late second century, and this of course made the concern of the authorities, in some cases at least, a good deal more intense. But the line between this late antique period and the centuries immediately preceding it, the age of the Hellenistic kingdoms and the early Roman Empire, should not be drawn too sharply. We may, if we like, speak of the Hellenistic Age as "irreligious" in comparison with archaic Greece or the period with which we are now dealing. But this does not mean that it was irreligious in any modern sense. Old cults, and, for the mass of the population, old beliefs continued: splendid new temples like Didyma were built: new cults, including the very successful one of Serapis, were introduced: and one of the most deeply and passionately religious of philosophies, the Stoic, developed. The massive continuity of the old religion is more impressive than the variations of intensity of religious concern at different periods and in different places and groups. The rise in late antiquity of a new form of sacred absolute monarchy of course intensified the sense of religious consecration and religious responsibility of the ruler, and concentrated it on his single sacred person as representative of the divine on earth, and this is important. In considering the effects on Christianity of what happened in the fourth century we need always to remember that the Church of the Fathers was the Church of the Empire and that its thought and institutions developed in a world in which absolute sacred monarchy claiming universal jurisdiction was the only conceivable form of government. But the Sacred Emperors were exercising essentially the same sort of religious authority, for essentially the same reasons, that the magistrates and assemblies of the city-states, and the archaic kings before them, had exercised from the beginning.

The reasons for this religious concern of ancient authorities should not be misunderstood. There was nothing particularly spiritual or other-worldly about it. The concern of the rulers to keep on the right side of God or the gods, to ensure that the divine-human relationship was as it should be in the societies of which they had charge, was part, and a most important part, of their care for the temporal, this-worldly, well being of their subjects. Divine displeasure might bring pestilence and famine, barbarian invasion, defeat in war, or, perhaps most serious of all from a late antique emperor's point of view, the rise and eventual triumph of a rival claimant to the throne. These temporal consequences were believed to be due to divine displeasure by pagans and Christians alike, and sanctions of this kind could be understood even by the stupidest and most unspiritual of emperors, the sort who, Plotinus ironically suggested, turned into eagles after their death.[2] And even those who did not believe in this sort of divine visitation (and in late antiquity they were probably very few) would inherit from the more sceptical side of the early thought of Greece and Rome a conviction that proper religious observance, whatever that was thought to be, was central and essential to the maintenance of the whole fabric of culture and society.

All ancient rulers, then, considered it part, and a most important

---

[2] Plotinus *Ennead* III 4 [15] 2, 25-6.

part, of their duties, to maintain in their dominions a proper relationship with the divine. This was particularly true of Roman authorities,
with their passion for order and precise regulation and their vivid
sense of the social and political importance of religion. And, as has
already been remarked, the way in which the sacred authority of the
emperors of the fourth century was conceived made their sense of
obligation in religious matters particularly intense. A secular society
was inconceivable and impossible in the ancient world, and never
more inconceivable and impossible than in the fourth century. But
having made these generalizations, we need to consider rather carefully the very various ways in which the general principles were
understood and practical conclusions were drawn from them.

The starting-point here must be the obvious and well studied
contrast between Hellenic and Roman paganism and Christianity.
The old religion was a religion of cult, not of dogmatic belief. This
meant that what was thought of as seriously and dangerously displeas-
ing to the divine was anything which endangered the performance of
the sacred rites or might bring them into disrespect or neglect. But
there was no doctrinal orthodoxy deviation from which might bring
down the divine displeasure. People could, and did, think in a great
variety of incompatible ways about the gods, and could express their
opinions, within rather unpredictable limits set by the prevailing
degree of religious concern and anxiety among the general public or
the ruling classes. I do not propose to go into any disputed questions
concerning the persecution of the Christians. But I may perhaps be
permitted the generalization, that the widespread dislike of the
Christians, which from time to time intensified into a feeling that
something drastic must be done about them, sprang from the awareness of an alien barbarian attack on the sacred rites and the ways of
thinking and feeling bound up with them and so on the whole social
fabric which they permeated and the whole peace and harmony of
human society with the divine. And I can certainly be permitted the
obvious observation that the persecutions were decidedly spasmodic.
From the edict of toleration of Gallienus in 261 to the great persecution which began in 303 the Church had enjoyed peace and a kind of
quasi-recognition sufficient to allow it to acquire and hold property,
always a most important aspect of toleration or recognition from the
point of view of the imperial administration. And even during the
Great Persecution itself there is a good deal of evidence for a marked
lack of enthusiasm among a good many local authorities, who were
very lax in enforcing the imperial edicts, as A. H. M. Jones has noted.[3]

---

[3] See A. H. M. Jones, *The Later Roman Empire* (Oxford 1964) Ch. II.

It seems that, though when Christians were persecuted the motive was the fear of divine displeasure and social disruption noted in my earlier generalization, this fear was not always very strong and compelling. At the time when the dominance of the old religious ways was complete, there seem always to have been plenty of pagans who were willing in practice to grant Christians at least the same sort of hostile and contemptuous tolerance which was always given to Jews. And this suggests that the apophatic or agnostic pluralism put forward as a ground for tolerance by pagans of the late fourth century was not simply an accommodation to circumstances. I believe myself that it has very deep roots in authentically Hellenic intellectual and spiritual tradition. But before discussing this further it will be as well to consider some aspects of the thought and practice of the greatest of fourth-century Hellenes, the Emperor Julian.

To a great extent I share the now widespread admiration for Julian. I find him the only genuinely likeable human being in his very unpleasant family, and one whom his promise and early performance show to have been likely to have been a great and good emperor. And I am inclined to think that, if he had reigned as long as Constantine and trained a reasonably competent successor (or successors) to carry on his religious policy, that policy might have had a considerable measure of success. Historians, of course, should not speculate too much on what might have been. But it is surely not too fanciful to suggest that, if the Empire had been officially pagan in the time of St. Augustine's episcopate, and its Christian period had been a remote and for many people unpleasant memory, subsequent religious history would have been rather different. But, in spite of my admiration, I cannot regard Julian as a typical or normal Hellene or Neoplatonist. There is no need to say much about the un-Hellenic character of Julian's religious policy. Dr. Athanassiadi-Fowden's excellent book[4] has shown clearly how thoroughly Byzantine it was. Nothing could be more un-Hellenic than his conception of a great Hellenic religious institution coterminous with the Empire, with a dogmatic Iamblichean orthodoxy and a teaching hierarchy, under the control and direction of the sacred Emperor. In this he stands firmly in the line of development from Constantine to Justinian and beyond. Even if his reign had been longer and his re-Hellenization of the Empire reasonably successful, his Hellenic church could hardly have survived as more than a formal institutional framework. The essential variety of paganism could not have been constricted into an orthodoxy.

Julian's position as a Neoplatonist needs rather more careful

---

[4] *Julian and Hellenism* (Oxford 1981).

examination than it has always received. The account by Eunapius of his reception by Aedesius and his pupils at Pergamum and his choice of Maximus as spiritual director is well enough known.[5] But its implications deserve consideration. It is true that Julian adopted Neoplatonism in its most theurgic and ritualistic form and that he did so in the school of Aedesius at Pergamum. But it is clear from Eunapius that the attitude of Aedesius to theurgy was decidedly reserved.[6] And the account of Julian's choice of Maximus shows that one of the leading members of the Pergamene group, Eusebius of Myndus, was definitely hostile. It is a mistake, and may lead to considerable distortion of the history of Hellenic Neoplatonism, to speak of an older type of "Plotinian" and "Porphyrian" Neoplatonism and a later "Iamblichean", "theurgic" Neoplatonism as if they were two distinct schools or sects. They were, rather, different tendencies or inclinations (sometimes very definite and passionate) in individuals who continued to feel themselves united in all essentials, which are apparent throughout the history of Neoplatonism from the time of Plotinus to the time of Damascius.[7] The extreme and exaggerated "Iamblichean" concern with sacred rites is likely to be a reason for the un-Hellenically ecclesiastical character of Julian's attempted Hellenic restoration and also for his extreme dogmatic intolerance. Religious hatreds always seem to be deepest and bitterest when forms, ceremonies and institutions come into the dispute. And there is another, less noticed, feature of Julian's Neoplatonism which would have tended the same way. It is quite remarkable in a Neoplatonist that little, if anything, is said in his theological writings about the unknowable God and our passionate aspiration to him. Apophatic theology was certainly important to Iamblichus, and remained centrally and at times painfully important to the great theurgic Neoplatonists of Athens, Proclus and Damascius. But Julian is decidedly a kataphatic theologian. He concentrates his theological attention and

---

[5] Eunapius, *Lives of the Philosophers* VII 1.

[6] Eunapius V 1.

[7] Porphyry calls Amelius, the closest friend and collaborator of Plotinus φιλοθύτης, an epithet which would apply admirably to Julian (*Life of Plotinus* 10): and it is perfectly clear from his biography that though Plotinus refused to join in Amelius' pious practices, he and others always regarded Amelius as the senior member of the group and the one closest to the master. For "Plotinian" attitudes in later Neoplatonism see Damascius *Life of Isidore* fr. 40 pp 35-36 Zintzen and "Ep. Phot." 38 p. 64 Zintzen: cp. my remarks on the difference between the two tendencies in "Tradition, Reason and Experience in the Thought of Plotinus" *Plotino e il Neoplatonismo in Oriente e in Occidente* (Rome 1974) = *Plotinian and Christian Studies* (London 1979) XVII pp. 185-187.

personal devotion on the gods of the Iamblichean noeric order, mediators between the transcendent spiritual world and ours; and above all on his personal patron, Helios-Mithras, that great god of whom the visible sun is sacrament, icon or theophany and Julian himself, the Emperor, the appointed representative on earth. And this again would have influenced him in the direction of dogmatic intolerance. The less one thinks one knows about the God of one's faith and aspiration, the easier it will be to see other people's faiths as true ways towards him. Passionate devotion to a highly personalized deity of well-defined character is more likely both to inspire in oneself and to provoke in others of different devotion a passionate and bitter hostility.

I have spoken of Julian's dogmatic intolerance, which indeed is sufficiently apparent. His language about Christianity is as violent as that of any Father of the Church about paganism and heresy. But in fairness to him one must remark briefly on the very moderate degree in which he translated his theoretical ferocity into practical intolerance: and I do not myself believe that if he had returned victorious from Persia he would have moved further in the direction of persecution, though no doubt his practical tolerance of Christians would have remained thoroughly hostile and discriminatory. He shared to the full the conviction of his Christian contemporaries that forced conversion was not permissible. Insult and invective, adverse discrimination, confiscation of the property of dissident groups and prohibition of their worship were permissible. But, in this century, the line was drawn at forced conversion. This is no sound basis for any degree of practical tolerance which we should regard as tolerable nowadays: and the line between prohibiting all expression of religious dissidence and forcing dissidents into at least outward conformity with the prevailing orthodoxy is very difficult to draw in practice and was sometimes overstepped in the fourth century. But Julian drew the line rather further back on the side of tolerance. He never showed any sign of prohibiting Christian worship and teaching in the churches, and I do not believe that if his reign had continued he would have done so. He seems to have had an authentically Hellenic and philosophical conviction that the way to win a battle of ideas was by example and argument, not coercion.

The most extreme example, in the view of Ammianus, of his practical intolerance was of course the decree prohibiting Christians from teaching the pagan classics, which upset the Christians so remarkably. This has been very extensively discussed, and it is clear that Julian's insistence on excluding Christian teachers, the Christians' indignation, and the more easy-going attitude of most contem-

porary pagans, derive from different ideas about the religious content
of the classics which were the basis of the unquestioned and unchal-
lenged common culture of the *oecumene*. Julian, who saw that
religious content in the light of his own Byzantine Hellenic orthodoxy, and was perhaps thinking in terms of training a devout pagan
ruling elite, naturally wished all classical education to be conducted
by teachers of the true faith. Those Christians who thought at all
seriously about the matter, like St. Basil, believed that by judicious
selection and Christian teaching the classics could be, so to speak,
"decaffeinated", their pernicious pagan content neutralized, and what
was useful in them turned to wholly Christian purposes.[8] The more
easy-going pagans, and probably a good many Christians, most likely
thought simply that teaching and learning the classics could not
possibly do anyone anything but good, and that the only way to a
genuine culture was to get as much of them as one could. It was of
course the last point of view which prevailed, with some varying
admixture of the second, and it was the, on the whole unselfconscious
and easy, acceptance of the ancient classics by Christians from the
fifth century A.D. onwards which ensured their survival through the
Christian centuries and made them the centre of upper-class Christian
education down to my own younger days. But Julian was right in a
way. The Hellenic classics could not be purged of their Hellenism
and domesticated to the service of the Church. They did not transmit
through Christendom a Julianist Hellenic orthodoxy which they did
not contain. But they have transmitted a whole complex of ways of
thinking, feeling and imagining which are not compatible with Bibli-
cist and ecclesiastical Christianity. The Muses and the Lady Philosophy are not to be recommended as priests' housekeepers.

One must begin any discussion of the tolerant, pluralist paganism
of the fourth century with the great statement of Symmachus *Non uno
itinere perveniri potest ad tam grande secretum*.[9] But of course the
place of this in his appeal for tolerance is very modest and incidental.
He bases his main case on good Roman grounds of ancient tradition
and more recent precedent, including the precedents of Christian
emperors. A better representative of this way of thinking is, as Henry
Chadwick has seen,[10] Themistius. The great philosopher-orator to

---

[8] This approach has recently been attracting some needed critical attention: cp. E. L.
Fortin, "Hellenism and Christianity in Basil the Great's Address *Ad Adulescentes*" in
Neoplatonism and Early Christian Thought (London, Variorum 1981) 189-203: P.
Athanassiadi-Fowden, *Julian and Hellenism* (see n. 4) 18-19.
[9] *Relatio* III 10.
[10] See his article *Gewissen* in *Reallexikon für Antike und Christentum* X (1978) viii d
col. 1101-2.

whom even intolerant Christian emperors listened with respect was, unusually for his time, an Aristotelian rather than a Platonist. But he is not unaffected by contemporary Platonism, and the simple theology which is the basis of his appeals for tolerance would have been acceptable, as far as it went, to many Neoplatonists. His surviving oration before Jovian,[11] and the summaries of his even more powerful plea for tolerance to Valens in the church historians,[12] give a good idea of his position. I quote (in my own re-translation from the German) Henry Chadwick's excellent conflation of Socrates and Sozomen[13] (whose summaries differ slightly) as a good statement of the common position of these tolerant pluralist pagans. "The differences of opinion between the Christians are unimportant compared with the three hundred different opinions among the pagans. God's glory is increased by the knowledge that religious differences are only a consequence of his unattainable majesty and of human limitations."

We are considering here a temper of mind rather than a formal, systematic doctrine, and one which can express itself, according to the dispositions and circumstances of different individuals and groups, in a variety of ways from formal scepticism and agnosticism to a passionately apophatic theology. This temper of mind is something which can be clearly detected a very long way back in the history of Hellenic thought. One of the most powerful expressions of diffidence about human knowledge of the divine is also one of the earliest, the lines of that formidable philosophical theologian Xenophanes "No man knows, nor will there be anyone who knows, the truth about the gods and about everything I say: for even if one happened to say the complete truth, yet one does not know it oneself: but seeming is wrought over all things".[14] And anyone who reads Herodotus will be able to see how firmly rooted the *non uno itinere* is in ordinary classical Greek thinking about other people's religions. With more direct relevance to the thought of the fourth century A.D., I would maintain that a great deal can be found in the dialogues of Plato (whether Plato himself intended it to be found there or not) which can lead either towards scepticism or towards apophatic theology. It is easy enough, of course, to find scepticism of different degrees and varieties in the Hellenistic and early Imperial periods: and from the first century B.C., at latest, there begins to develop the apophatic

---

[11] *Or.* 5.
[12] Socrates IV 32: Sozomen VI 6-7. The *Oratio de Religionibus* which purports to be a Latin version of this speech is a post-Renaissance forgery.
[13] H. Chadwick, *art. cit.* col. 1102.
[14] Xenophanes Fragment 34 DK.

theology to which sceptical criticism of earlier dogmatisms about the divine made an important contribution. This is all much too summary to be convincing, and needs far more elaboration and discussion than is possible here. A very good concise account, to be published, it is hoped, soon, has been written by R. T. Wallis.[15] But unless we are aware that we are considering here something very widespread and deeply rooted in the whole Hellenic tradition, and not simply the attitude of a group in the fourth century, we shall find it hard to understand the persistent recurrence of this temper of mind throughout the history of later European thought about the divine, not least evident in our own times.

In considering the tolerant pagan pluralism of the fourth century we need to observe the coming together in it of a number of different forms in which this temper of mind expressed itself. There is the old simple awareness, clearly discernible in Herodotus, that people are different and understand the divine in different ways, and that there is no good reason to suppose that any one tradition or nation has a monopoly of truth about the divine: this is not in itself very sceptical, agnostic or apophatic. It was well expressed in the late second century, in an entirely pagan context and without reference to Christianity, by Maximus of Tyre: "If the art of Pheidias awakes the Greeks to the memory of God, the cult of animals the Egyptians, and a river others, and fire others, I do not resent their disagreement: let them only know him, let them only love him, let them only remember him":[16] a peroration of which one can hear an echo in the late fourth century in the celebrated conclusion of the letter of another Maximus, St. Augustine's elderly pagan correspondent, "May the gods preserve you, through whom all we mortals whom the earth supports venerate and worship in a thousand ways with concordant discord the common father of the gods and of all mortals."[17] Then there is the urbane and moderate Academic scepticism of which in the Latin West Cicero was the principal transmitter, a scepticism always accompanied by a strong traditionalism in practical religious matters which certainly weighed heavily against the Christians but may also have told against the exaggerated ritualism of Julian. Finally there is the faith, based on deep religious experience, of the Neoplatonists in a God who is

---

[15] In an article "The Spiritual Importance of Not Knowing" to be published in Volume 15, *Classical Mediterranean Spirituality of World Spirituality: an Encyclopedic History of the Religious Quest.*
[16] Maximus of Tyre, *Dissertatio* VIII (*On Whether Images should be consecrated to the Gods*), end.
[17] Augustine, *Ep.* XVI.

simply beyond us, too great for speech or thought, formulated, as has already been suggested, partly though by no means wholly under the influence of sceptical attacks on dogmatism about the divine. This is indeed important, but should not be regarded, in and by itself and out of the wider context just sketched, as the principal or sole cause of tolerant pluralism.

When we think about the mentality of these fourth-century pagan pluralists we should also take into account another aspect of the Neoplatonism of Plotinus and Porphyry, in which it differs most sharply from that of Iamblichus and his successors. This is the conviction that the only true religion is philosophical religion, and that the stories and practices of non-philosophical religion are, at the best, no more than helpful popular expressions of philosophic truth for non-philosophers. This sort of Neoplatonism is of course compatible with the hostility shown by Porphyry himself to the alien barbarian Christian attack on the whole of Hellenic thought and culture: but it can also issue in a tolerant pluralism or in considerably more positive attitudes towards Christianity. The kind of probably more or less Porphyrian Neoplatonism which he learnt from Hypatia at Alexandria certainly helped Synesius in his decision to accept episcopal office when that seemed to him the best way of serving the community.[18] And Marius Victorinus moved on from tolerant pluralism to see the post-Nicene theology of the Trinity as the perfect expression of Porphyrian metaphysical religion and so was able to accept Christianity whole-heartedly as the perfection of the ancient philosophy and culture which he loved, in which it could be preserved for the future.[19]

We now pass on to Christian intolerance and tolerance in the fourth century. Here we must return to the difference noted earlier (p. 4) between Hellenic paganism and Christianity. The old religion was one of cult, not of belief. There was no doctrinal orthodoxy deviation from which might bring down the divine displeasure. For Christians dogmatic orthodoxy mattered very much, especially for the bishops who felt themselves responsible for the transmission of the true faith and the preservation in unity of faith of their flocks: and the conclusion was generally drawn that it was an important part of the religious responsibilities of the rulers of the Empire to enforce whatever the bishops of any place or time considered orthodoxy to be,

---

[18] I accept the account of Synesius given by Jay Bregman in the latest and best book on him (J. Bregman, *Synesius of Cyrene*, Berkeley-Los Angeles-London 1982).
[19] Here I follow the account of the conversion of Victorinus given by Pierre Hadot in Chapter XV of his *Marius Victorinus* (Paris, Études Augustiniennes, 1971).

if they χwished to avoid the serious temporal and spiritual consequences for Emperor and Empire of the displeasure of an offended
God. The general fourth-century Christian episcopal attitude was well
summed-up early in the next century by Nestorius in his address to
Theodosius II: Δός μοι, ὦ βασιλεῦ, καθαρὰν τὴν γῆν τῶν αἱρετικῶν,
κἀγώ σοι τὸν οὐρανὸν ἀντιδώσω· συγκάθελέ μοι τοὺς αἱρετικοὺς, κἀγὼ
συγκαθελῶ σοι τοὺς Πέρσας[20] promises which must have a double
tragic irony for later readers when we remember not only Ephesus but
that the great future of the Church of the East which heresiologists
call Nestorian lay not in the Roman Empire but in and beyond the
eastern boundaries of the Persian.

When we turn from Christian bishops to Christian emperors the
picture is rather more interesting and varied. I accept as probable
H. A. Drake's view of the religious policy of Constantine, very fully
expounded and well supported by evidence in his study of *De
Laudibus Constantini*:[21] his case does not by any means wholly
depend on the divsion of Eusebius' panegyric into two separate
orations delivered to different audiences on different occasions,
though this seems a reasonable enough hypothesis. If he is right in
seeing Constantine as a sincere Christian who as emperor was always
more concerned with the religious peace and unity of the empire than
with the triumph of right belief at any cost (and there is a great deal of
evidence which points that way) and one who was prepared to the end
of his life to extend a large tolerance to paganism: then we can see him
as providing a weighty precedent for the policy of the Christian
emperors between Julian and Gratian. This deserves a good deal of
attention. All three of these sincerely Christian emperors, Jovian,
Valentinian I, and Valens, were fully tolerant of paganism. Valens,
unlike his brother, considered it his duty to persecute those Christians
whom he considered as heretics on what he reasonably thought was
the best episcopal advice available to him. This illustrates a point
which is always worth bearing in mind when considering Christian
intolerance. Christians have in general, till very recently, spoken of
and behaved to their brethren with whom they disagreed in matters of

[20] Socrates VII 29. The association here of temporal and spiritual prosperity with
orthodoxy is commonplace. The egocentric use of the first person is less so, but may be
due (if Nestorius is accurately and fairly quoted) rather to rhetorical overexcitement
than spiritual arrogance. Or it may simply be due to the introduction by Nestorius into
his sermon of the figure of Christ addressing the Emperor, so that the "I" is Christ, not
Nestorius. Christian preachers have often put their own words into the mouth of their
Master.
[21] *In Praise of Constantine*: A Historical Study and New Translation of Eusebius'
Tricennial Orations (Berkeley-Los Angeles-London 1976).

faith much worse than they have treated adherents of other religions. Ammianus justly remarks that Christians are worse than wild beasts to each other.[22] He does not say, and would not, at least at the time of writing, have been correct in saying that they are worse than wild beasts to non-Christians.

Valens seems to have agreed fully with his brother, and with Jovian before them, in his tolerance of paganism, and it is in the policy of Valentinian I that we can see fully developed what seems to me a perfectly viable alternative to the Theodosian policy of intolerance, adapted to the conditions of the time and congruous with ancient thought about the religious responsibilities of the ruler. It was, of course, a policy of scrupulous tolerance of paganism, inspired, it seems by a genuine belief that all his subjects ought to enjoy complete freedom of worship,[23] combined with a resolute refusal to intervene in any ecclesiastical disputes or to lend the crushing weight of his authority to any party in the deeply divided Church of his time. Valentinian was a firm believer in Nicene Christianity and a military man of little education, unlikely to be deeply influenced by the ideas of pagan intellectuals (though his brother does seem to have listened with respect to Themistius[24]). And he was certainly not of an easy-going disposition, and showed few signs of benevolence, except to bears.[25] His policy seems very likely to have been prompted, not only by a reasonable belief that it was in the best interests of the peace and unity of the empire but by a confidence that it was according to the will of God, which would have been possible within the limits of the general ancient view of the religious responsibilities of the ruler. And if it had persisted and become the imperial norm followed by rulers of the successor states in the West, its consequences might have been far-reaching. Our religious history would surely have been rather different if in many towns, instead of one great bishop and one great cathedral, there had been in the next few centuries two or three

---

[22] Ammianus XXII 5.4.

[23] Cod. Theod. 9.16.9. issued by Valentinian in the names of himself, Valens and Gratian seems to make this clear. Speaking of his consistent policy the emperor says "Testes sunt leges a me in exordio imperii mei datae, quibus unicuique, quod animo inbibisset, colendi libera facultas tributa est. Nec haruspicinam reprehendimus, sed nocenter exerceri vetamus." This, coupled with the exemption, at the instance of Praetextatus, of the Eleusinian and other ancient rites from the prohibition of nocturnal sacrifices (Cod. Theod. 9.16.7: for the exemption see Zosimus 4.3.2-3), shows a scrupulous tolerance in an area not far removed from the magical practices which the emperors so feared and hated (Ammianus XXVIII 1:XXIX 1-2).

[24] See note 12.

[25] For those charming creatures Mica Aurea and Innocentia, and how good the emperor was to them, see Ammianus XXIX 3.9.

vigorously dissentient bishops and two or three rival cathedrals, together with a pagan temple or two.

The bishops were too strong in the end for a tolerant policy to establish itself. But before concluding I would like to take a look at a very insignificant and, as far as we know, untypical bishop in whom a gleam of tolerance may be discerned. This is Pegasius, Bishop of Ilion in 354, who in 362 applied for and obtained a position in Julian's pagan hierarchy. All we know about his beliefs and practices is contained in a letter of Julian to an unknown correspondent defending his appointment of Pegasius in 362, in which he describes how the bishop had shown him round the holy places of Troy when he visited it in the course of his journey to the court of Constantius in 354.[26] A careful examination of this letter has suggested to me that Pegasius may have been something a good deal more interesting than a cynical opportunist or Vicar of Bray. He said himself in 362 that he had always been a faithful crypto-Hellene, and Julian believed him. But at this point it does seem likely that the opportunity of a dignified and lucrative career under the new régime had considerably coloured Pegasius' presentation, and perhaps his actual recollection, of his earlier position. The letter itself makes clear that there were plenty of people who said that Pegasius had always been a rather bigoted Christian, and threw doubt on the sincerity of his conversion to Hellenism: this in fact seems to be why Julian felt he had to write in defence of his appointment. And it is surely rather unlikely that a Hellenic "mole" should have managed to get himself elected and consecrated bishop even in a small Christian community remote from the centres of Christian life and thought and the attention of the bishops of the great sees. We should also remember that the position of Julian in 354 was very different from his position in 362. On that journey to the court at Milan, soon after the execution of his brother Gallus, he can hardly have seemed a promising patron to anyone. It would have been imprudent to make a large bet on his long survival, and very imprudent to wager anything at all on his chances of succeeding to the throne. It seems, therefore, that we are likely to get as near as we can to the real Pegasius if we do not pay much attention to the way in which he and Julian interpreted his beliefs and behaviour in 362, and attend closely to Julian's very precise account of what he did and said in 354.

When he met Julian at Troy and offered his services as guide he

---

[26] Julian, *Letter* 79 Bidez-Rochefort-Lacombrade (78 Hertlein, 19 W. C. Wright): 451 D. Spanheim.

first conducted him to the shrine of the great local hero, Hector. Here Julian was surprised to find fires alight on the altars and the bronze statue of Hector beautifully anointed with oil. He asked Pegasius "Do the Ilians sacrifice?" to which the bishop replied "καὶ τί τοῦτο ἄτοπον,ἄνδρα ἀγαθὸν ἑαυτῶν πολίτην, ὥσπερ ἡμεῖς" ἔφη, "τοὺς μάρτυρας εἰ θεραπεύουσιν;" on which Julian comments ἡ μὲν οὖν εἰκὼν οὐκ ὑγιής· ἡ δὲ προαίρεσις ἐν ἐκείνοις ἐξεταζομένη τοῖς καιροῖς ἀστεία. I am inclined to think that Pegasius meant exactly what he said and that he made the comparison which offended Julian because he was a Christian and it came naturally to him as a Christian. They continued their tour to the temple of Athena and the shrine of Achilles (which Pegasius was later falsely accused of having destroyed). Here everything was in good order and the images well preserved, but there is no further mention of signs of cult. Julian did however particularly notice in the temple of Athena that the bishop did not hiss and make the sign of the cross against the demons, as the impious (i.e. Christians) were accustomed to do. Another piece of information in the letter, not connected with the meeting in 354, is that Julian says he has heard "from those who are now his enemies" that Pegasius used in secret to pray to and venerate the Sun. This hearsay evidence seems, because of its source (presumably those pagans who were now objecting to Pegasius' appointment) to be as worthy of belief as Julian's eyewitness account.

How then, in the light of this reliable evidence, are we to understand the position of Pegasius in 354? The most reasonable interpretation seems to me that he was a sincere Christian, though perhaps not one of very deep and passionate faith. I do not find any reason to suppose that his Christian fellow-townsmen were grossly mistaken in thinking him suitable to be elected bishop (or neighbouring bishops in consecrating him) or that he did not perform his episcopal functions of celebrating the Eucharist and preaching with sufficient devotion. But he was a Christian who saw no harm in permitting, and perhaps performing, traditional rites in honour of a great, good and famous pagan hero of his community as they had always been performed in that community: and a Christian who did not find it necessary to regard the Hellenic gods as devils or to do anything but preserve and honour the holy places of the old religion. As for his praying to the Sun, we should remember the importance of the Sun as a religious symbol for Christians as well as pagans, and that a century later St. Leo the Great in a Christmas sermon found it necessary to condemn the behaviour of some members of his congregation who before entering St. Peter's turned at the top of the steps to bow to the rising sun.[27] Pegasius' regard for the Hellenic past went beyond a qualified acceptance of Hellenic philosophy and an uneasy acquiescence in the necessity of a classical education to a real love of Hellenic myth and legend and even to some extent ritual observance. What parts were played in this by love of the ancient poetry, especially Homer, by the spirit of place of Ilion, and, perhaps, by the importance of the tourist trade to the economy of his diocese, we shall never know. It makes Pegasius a most untypical and unconventional Christian bishop, as far as we know. But we should remember that we only know anything at all about him by the chance of Julian's visit, and we cannot be sure that there were not a good many Christians of similar outlook existing unobtrusively in various parts of the empire.

We have discovered enough good sense and good feeling, even among Christians, in the fourth century, to have made a solution to its religious dissensions more tolerant and tolerable than the Theodosian both possible in the circumstances of the time and in accordance with ancient views of the place of religion in society and the religious responsibilities of rulers. I have said enough at the beginning of this paper about what I believe to be the negative consequences of the solution adopted. But I would like to conclude by drawing attention to some inevitable consequences for the Church which I do not myself regard as entirely undesirable. The Church was left as, for a time, the sole custodian of the ancient culture, and has therefore since attracted, and even now may continue to attract, some whose real love is for that culture rather than for Christianity. And by successfully suppressing all other living and traditional forms of worship the Church has become the sole institution for public worship within the bounds of European civilization. All those who desire to worship God publicly and communally, however variously they may conceive him, must in practice worship him according to Christian rites. These they will naturally and properly interpret in their own various ways, and have their own requirements of the Church which provides them. This is part of the payment for the Theodosian settlement.

---

[27] St. Leo, *In Nativitate Domini Sermo VII* (PL XXVII) 4. p. 142 Leclercq-Dolle (SC).

16

Stable Symbols in a Shifting Society: The Delusion of the Monolithic Gentile in Documents of Late Fourth-Century Judaism

Jacob Neusner
Brown University

When we examine the principal symbols in that form of Judaism represented by rabbinical writings from the first century through the sixth, we naturally find development and change as we move from one document to the next in line. "Torah," for example, symbolizes some few things at the outset of the rabbinic canon's formation, and many more things at the end. The figure of the messiah also serves in more than a few ways. That fact hardly presents surprises. For in an age of change—over many hundreds of years—it is quite natural for people diversely and creatively to use inherited modes of symbolizing the world. Accordingly, stability in symbols—the repeated reference over a long period to a severely limited repertoire—masks a creative and original use of those symbols which respond to the requirements of an ever-changing social world.

What demands attention is the opposite, people's failure to reimagine a symbol that no longer corresponds to, or conveys, perceived reality. When a critical area of social experience undergoes vast transformation, the symbols also should undergo metamorphosis. The one thing that should change is the character of the symbols through which people mentally portray what is going on in that world that their minds and imaginations propose to mediate and to interpret. When, therefore, people continue to speak in the same language about something that has in fact produced drastic change, we must ask why. For reason implies symbols serve to construct an imaginary world that, for the structure to work, must in some way correspond to the world out there.

To jump ahead in the argument and introduce the problem at hand, I point out that the mode of symbolizing the outsider, perceived as a nation and great power equivalent to Israel, remained stable during that period that marked Israel's complete transformation from one thing to something else. At the outset of the period at hand, before

A.D. 70, Israel in its land constituted a small political entity, a state, like many others of its time and place. It was subordinate to a great empire, but was a distinct and autonomous unit, a part of the political structure of that empire. It had working institutions of self-government and politics. At the end of the same period, by the seventh century, Israel in no way constituted a political entity. Such institutions of a political or juridical character that it had had, had lost the recognition and legitimacy formerly conferred upon them.

Moreover, when Israel looked outward, toward the world beyond its limits, the changes proved no less stunning. At the outset, Rome, and at the end, Rome, but what a different Rome! In the first three centuries, Rome was what it had always been, what its predecessors in the Middle East had always been, that is: pagan, and essentially benign toward Israel in its land. From the fourth century, however, Rome became something unprecedented. It was a kind of Israel and a kin to Israel, a knowledgeable competitor, a powerful and canny enemy, a brother.

The modes by which the Jews or, more to the point, the rabbis whose writings survive, proposed to symbolize the world had therefore to take up two contradictory worlds. On the one hand, these "symbols of the stranger" of Israel's history and destiny, and of Israel's relationship to the outsider, dealt with a world in which Israel was, like the outsider, a nation among nations, a political entity confronting another such entity and thus, history among other histories. At the end, these symbols had to convey the reality of an Israel that was essentially different in genus from the outsider, an Israel no longer a nation in the sense in which other groups constituted a nation, no longer a political entity like others, no longer standing at the end of a history essentially consubstantial with the history of the nations.

What we shall see is the surprising fact that, so far as we are able to tell, the modes of political and social symbolization remained essentially stable in a world of change. More to the point, the outsider remained what he had always been, a (mere) pagan, part of a world demanding from Israel no effort whatsoever at differentiation. The "nations" were all alike, and Israel was still not essentially different from them all. Consubstantial, it was thus judged by the same standards, but, to be sure, it was guiltless while the rest were guilty. What makes so puzzling this stability in the modes of symbolizing Israel and the nations, Israel's history and destiny, and the substance of Israel's doctrine, is the following simple fact: in the interval, Christianity had not only come to full and diverse expression, it also had reached power.

In coming to power, Christianity drew upon essentially the same symbolic heritage to which Israel had long had access. To Christianity as much as to Judaism the pagan was a pagan, not differentiable; history began in Eden and led through Sinai to the end of time; the Messiah stood at the climax and goal of this world's history; revelation ("Torah") came from one God to unique Israel. True, for all forms of Christianity, the values assigned to the repertoire of symbols at hand hardly corresponded to those imputed by the Jews. But the symbols remained the same, and so Israel now resorted to what had become a shared symbolic system and structure to express its history and politics.

Under such circumstances, who would be surprised to learn that deep thought went into the revision of the available symbols, into restatement in such wise as to differentiate what had been treated as uniform, to redefine what had been grasped as settled? Surely the Christian, in the symbolic system of Judaism, should look like something other than the pagan—maybe worse, but at least different. Certainly history as a mode of social symbolization should proceed on a somewhat different path from the one it had taken when the one God had not yet come to rule, and when Israel's ancient Scriptures had not yet come to define the nature and destiny of humanity. Reckoning with the radical political changes at hand, we might imagine, should lead at least some profound thinkers to reconsider the symbolic system that had formerly prevailed or, at the very least, to reconsider the nature and definition of symbols that had gone forward into the new age and remained vivid. After all, social change should generate symbol change; political change should make its mark upon the symbols of politics and society.

But if that is what reason dictates we should expect, it is not how things actually happened. As I shall point out, it would take the rabbis of the canon of Judaism nearly a millenium to take seriously the specific character and claims of Christianity and to begin to counter in a systematic way that religious tradition's concrete assertions. Before the High Middle Ages, Judaism would have nothing to say about, let alone to, Christianity. More probative, Jewish thinkers would maintain the fantastic pretense that nothing important happened in either the first or the fourth century—that is, in either the supernatural or the political world at hand. As we shall now see, one important indicator of that fact is the unwillingness of the fourth and early fifth centuries' rabbinic exegetes to concede that Christians were different from pagans. On the contrary, the rabbinic sources treat all pagans as essentially faceless, and Christianity not at all, except as part of the same, blank wall of hostility to God (and, by the way, to Israel).

Before we proceed, we should take note of a parallel and still more striking case of a nation's incapacity to differentiate among outsiders, aliens or enemies. I refer to Rome, which saw as uniform—as mere barbarians—as all with the same policy and plan, what was in fact a vastly differentiated and diverse world of outsiders.

That fact is brilliantly expounded by Walter Goffart in his "Rome, Constantinople, and the Barbarians" (*American Historical Review*, 1981, 86:275-306). Goffart points out how ancient authors in Rome followed the convention of "portraying the tribes of their time under anachronistic names drawn from Herodotus and Tacitus." Goffart comments, "Precisely because the barbarians were always there, never seeming to contemporary observers from the Mediterranean to acquire new characteristics more dangerous than those of the past, there is little reason to look among them for a clue to their startling career in the fifth and sixth centuries A.D." On the Roman side of the frontier, the terms of the encounter remained stable. More important, the term "barbarian" transformed the Roman Empire's neighbors "into a collectivity" (all quotes: p. 277). Consequently, the Romans tended to see all their enemies as essentially uniform and to assume that all outsiders were enemies.

This fact is contrary to reality for, as Goffart says (p. 279), "At no time in antiquity, early or late, was there a collective hostility of barbarians toward the empire or a collective purpose to tear it down." Goffart makes the case that Roman policy toward "the barbarians" failed to take account of the diversity of the challenges presented to the security of the Empire by diverse enemies. So he asks, "Why did the emperors respond more peacefully to barbarian attacks after 376 and 406 than their predecessors had in the third century?" Following his sequence of related questions, Goffart concludes, "The bond between such questions is that each one forces us to look elsewhere for answers than among the non-literate barbarians." The answer (if I may state matters in a general way) lies in the capacity of the Romans' policy-makers to imagine things through the veil of language—hence, symbols—that obscured change.

Now we need hardly be surprised to find in the formative documents of Judaism an equivalent set of tendencies. These three prove most prominent: first, the repeated recourse to anachronism; second, the insistence that the world beyond was essentially undifferentiated; third, the failure to take account, in the symbolization of the social world, of fundamental change.

To give examples of each tendency at the outset, the Mishnah, for its part, describes a political system for Israel in which the people are ruled by a king and high priest in consultation with a sanhedrin. That quaint portrait, provided by Mishnah-tractate Sanhedrin, not only ignores the political institutions that did exist in the second century, it also evokes a political system that in fact never existed in Israelite history prior to its own time. For we cannot point to a single period in the political history of the Jewish nation in which the government consisted of an independent king, high priest and sanhedrin, conducting affairs in the antiseptic separation of powers fantasized by the authors of the Mishnah-tractate. Indeed, it is probably an understatement to call the portrait a mere anachronism, but from the perspective of the second-century authors, that is what they presented.

The lack of differentiation for the outside world may be conveyed in a simple fact. The entire earth outside the Land of Israel in the Mishnah's law was held to suffer from contamination by corpses. Hence it was unclean with a severe mode of uncleanness, and so inaccessible to the holy and life-sustaining processes of the cult. If an Israelite artist were asked to paint a wall-portrait of the world beyond the Land, he would paint the entire wall white, the color of death. The outside world, in the imagination of the Mishnah's law, was the realm of death. Among corpses, how are we to make distinctions?

The failure of symbols to respond to changes in the very social world that they are meant to convey and express, as is clear, forms the focus for what is to come. For this purpose, we speak of modes of symbolization of the outside world, which is to say, means of differentiation between society and the stranger—ways in which people reckon with "the other" in all the manifold ways in which "the other" makes an impact upon "us."

For the present purpose, we take up the most complex "other" with which Jewish thinkers of late antiquity had to contend, namely, the outsider who was not depraved, not barbarian, not pagan, not beyond the realm of the Torah—but who also was not inside. I refer, of course, to the Christians in their many and rich forms. Obviously, we cannot ask the sages of the rabbinic literature to tell us the difference between Arius and Athanasius, or between Marcion and Orthodox Christianity. But we must wonder whether they knew that a Christian was not some form of pagan and, if they did, how they expressed the difference. For the present purpose, we want to ask not about scattered sayings. Everyone knows, for instance, that to the first-century authority Tarfon, is attributed the angry observation that there were people around who knew the truth of the Torah but rejected it:

The books of the Evangelists and the books of the *minim* they do not save from a fire [on the Sabbath]. They are allowed to burn up where they are, they and [even] the references to the Divine Name that are in them... Said R. Tarfon, "May I bury my sons if such things come into my hands and I do not burn them, and even the references to the Divine Name which are in them. And if someone was running after me, I should escape into a temple of idolatry, but I should not go into their houses of worship. For idolators do not recognize the Divinity in denying him, but these recognize the Divinity and deny him. About them Scripture states, "Behind the door and the doorpost you have set your symbol for deserting me, you have uncovered your bed' (Is. 57:8)." (Tosefta Shabbat 13:5)

This statement has long persuaded scholars that the rabbinic authority recognized the difference between pagans and those *minim* under discussion, reasonably assumed to be Christian. I see no reason to differ from the established consensus.

Yet it does not materially advance our inquiry. For we want to know about the collective and large-scale symbols to which people repeatedly resorted when they wished to speak about the outsider in general or the Christian in particular. For that purpose the well-known passage at hand serves not at all. Rather, we need to turn to passages that speak collectively, and thus for the consensus of the community of sages and as part of its canon. We want to identify not merely explicit sayings, but, for the purpose of this discussion, symbols and (more important) modes of symbolization. That is, we want to find out how people speak of "the outsider" and "the Christian" when they do not wish to refer in a limited way but rather to speak in evocative and powerful symbols. What are these symbols? What are these things that speak of something in terms of something else and serve powerfully to evoke emotion and strong feeling in so doing?

Before proceeding to identify an appropriate symbol and to examine its use, let me restate the argument at hand. I want to know how rabbis of the formative centuries of Judaism symbolized the world beyond, how they spoke about "the other." We know that they saw the whole world as "pagan," so that deep in the rhetorical structures of their language and mode of thought lay embedded the distinction between "Israel" and "everybody else." That is not new or surprising. But how, in particular, did these same thinkers express and convey something more subtle, namely the difference among outsiders, as that difference emerged among people who were not Israel but also not pagan? And, as I have made clear, we wish to identify how in symbolic discourse in particular the formative minds framed issues and phrased matters. For the issue is not what people thought in general but how they cast their thoughts in particular into evocative symbols.

The probative evidence derives from an example of thinking at its most symbolic, that is to say, passages in which discourse repeatedly avoids saying things straight out but rather turns to language and images meant to say something in terms of something else. We have further to identify symbols of the outsider—and of differentiation among outsiders—which occur over and over again, that is, symbols which shout their messages so loud and clear that further exposition proves unnecessary. At the same time, we seek examples of discourse at its most symbolic, so we may see how people were framing one thing in terms of something else.

We further want to find documents that address an age of radical social change, so we may assess the stability or the resilience of a symbolic system put to the test. And, finally, we require a symbolic statement cast in such a way that we may compare how diverse groups, at different times, made use of the same symbols.

These criteria are met by those passages of Leviticus Rabbah that deal with the course of human history and, in particular, that portray in powerful symbols the past and present destiny of the world's great empires. The message in the symbolization of the nations comes through in the choice of animals selected to stand for the several empires under discussion; the beasts of Daniel's vision serve. Leviticus Rabbah came to closure, it is generally agreed, around A.D. 400, approximately a century after the Roman Empire in the east had begun to become Christian, and half a century after the last attempt to rebuild the Temple in Jerusalem had failed—a tumultuous age indeed. Finally, we even have evidence of other ways, besides those we shall review, of making use of these same symbols. Accordingly, we have the chance to see how distinctive and striking are the ways in which, in the text at hand, the symbols of animals that stand for the four successive empires of humanity and point towards the messianic time, serve for the framers' message.

Before we turn to the passage itself, let us turn aside and take up the task of describing the age, that is, the events of the fourth century and the way in which, in rabbinic documents of that time and afterward, these events make their impact.

For nearly everyone in the Roman world the most important events of the fourth and fifth centuries (the period in which the Talmud of the Land of Israel and collections of exegeses such as Leviticus Rabbah were coming into being) were, first, the legalization of Christianity, followed very rapidly by, second, the adoption of Christianity as the state's most favored religion and, third, by the delegitimization of paganism and the systematic degradation of Judaism. The astonishing advent of legitimacy and even power provoked Christian intellectuals to rewrite Christian and world history, and to work out theology as a reflection on this new polity and its meaning in the unfolding of human history. A new commonwealth was coming into being, taking over the old and reshaping it for the new age. In 312 Constantine achieved power in the West. In 323 he took the government of the entire Roman empire into his own hands. He promulgated the edict of Milan in 313, whereby Christianity attained the status of toleration. Christians and all others were given "the free power to follow the religion of their choice." In the next decade Christianity became the most favored religion. Converts from Judaism were protected and could not be punished by Jews; Christians were freed of the obligation to perform pagan sacrifices; priests were exempted from certain taxes; Sunday became an obligatory day of rest, and celibacy was permitted. From 324 onward, Constantine ceased to maintain a formal impartiality. He now intervened in the affairs of the Church, settling quarrels among believers, and calling the Church Council at Nicaea (325) to settle issues of the faith. (He was baptized only on the eve of his death in 337.) And over the next century, the pagan cults were destroyed, their priests deprived of support, their intellectuals bereft of standing.

So far as the Jews of the Land of Israel were concerned, not much changed at the Milvian Bridge in 312, when Constantine conquered in the sign of Christ. The sages' writings nowhere refer explicitly to that event. They scarcely gave testimony to its consequences for the Jews, and continued to harp upon prohibited relationships with "pagans" in general, as though nothing had changed from the third century to the fourth and fifth. Legal changes affecting the Jews under Constantine's rule indeed were not substantial. Jews could not proselytize; they could not circumcise slaves when they bought them; Jews could not punish other Jews who became Christians. Jews, finally, were required to serve on municipal councils wherever they lived, an onerous task involving responsibility for collecting taxes. But those who served synagogues, patriarchs and priests were still exempted from civil and personal obligations. In the reign of Constantius III (337-361), further laws aimed at separating Jews from Christians were enacted in 339 in the Canons of Elvira. These forbade intermarriage between Jews and Christians, further protected converts, and forbade Jews to hold slaves of Christian or other gentile origin.

The reversion to paganism on the part of the emperor Julian, ca. 360, involved a measure of favor to Jews and Judaism. To embarrass

Christianity, he permitted the rebuilding of the Temple at Jerusalem, but he died before much progress could be made. In the aftermath of the fiasco of Julian's reversion to paganism, the Christians, returning to power, determined to make certain such a calamity would never recur. Accordingly, over the next century they undertook a sustained attack on the institutions and personnel of paganism in all its expressions. This long-term and systematic effort in time overspread Judaism as well. From the accession of Theodosius II in 383 to the death of his son Arcadius in 408, Judaism came under attack. In the earlier part of the fifth century, Jews' rights and the standing of their corporate communities were substantially affected. The patriarchate of the Jews of the Land of Israel, the ethnarch and his administration, was abolished. So from the turn of the fifth century, the government policy was meant to isolate Jews, lower their status, and suppress their agencies of self-rule.

Laws against intermarriage posed no problem to the Jews, and the ones limiting proselytism and those protecting converts from Judaism, did not affect many people. But the edicts that reduced Jews to second-class citizenship did matter. Jews were not to hold public office, but still had to sit on city councils responsible for the payment of taxes. Later, they were removed from the councils, though still obligated, of course, to pay taxes. Between 404 and 438, Jews were forbidden to hold office in the civil service, represent cities, serve in the army or at the bar, and they ultimately were evicted from every public office. In all, the later fourth and fifth centuries for Israel in its land marked a time of significant change. Once a mere competing faith, Christianity now became paramount. The period from Julian's fall onward, moreover, presented to Israel problems of a profoundly religious character. To these we now turn.

There were five events of fundamental importance for the history of Judaism in the fourth and fifth centuries. All of them except for the last were well know in their day. These were as follows: (1) the conversion of Constantine; (2) the fiasco of Julian's plan to rebuild the Temple of Jerusalem; (3) the depaganization of the Roman empire, a program of attacks on pagan temples and, along the way, on synagogues; (4) the Christianization of the majority of the population of Palestine; and (5) the creation of the Talmud of the Land of Israel and of compositions of Scriptural exegeses. The Talmud and the exegetical compilations came into being in an age of crisis, high hope, and then disaster. Vast numbers of Jews now found chimerical the messianic expectation as they had framed it around Julian's plan to rebuild the Temple. So it was a time of boundless expectations followed by bottomless despair.

From the present perspective, let us briefly review the four events that framed the setting for the fifth, starting with Constantine's conversion. The first point is that we do not know how Jews responded to Constantine's establishment of Christianity as the most favored religion. But in the Land of Israel itself, his works were well known, since he and his mother purchased many sites believed connected with Israel's sacred history and built churches and shrines at them. They rewrote the map of the Land of Israel. Every time they handled a coin, moreover, Jews had to recognize that something of fundamental importance had shifted, for the old pagan images were blotted out as Christian symbols took their place—public events indeed!

A move of the empire from reverence for Zeus to adoration of Mithra meant nothing; paganism was what it was, lacking all differentiation in the Jewish eye. As I have stressed, Christianity was something else. It was different. It was like Judaism. Christians read the Torah and claimed to declare its meaning. Accordingly, the trend of sages' speculation cannot have avoided the issue of the place, within the Torah's messianic pattern, of the remarkable turn in world history represented by the triumph of Christianity. Since the Christians vociferously celebrated confirmation of their faith in Christ's messiahship and, at the moment, Jews were hardly prepared to concur, it falls surely within known patterns for us to suppose that Constantine's conversion would have been identified with some dark moment to prefigure the dawning of the messianic age.

Second, if people were then looking for a brief dawn, the emperor Julian's plan to rebuild the ruined Temple in Jerusalem must have dazzled their eyes. For while Constantine surely raised the messianic question, for a brief hour Emperor Julian appeared decisively to answer it. In 361 the now-pagan Julian gave permission to rebuild the Temple. Work briefly got underway, but stopped because of an earthquake. The intention of Julian's plan was quite explicit. Julian had had in mind to falsify the prophecy of Jesus that "not one stone of the temple would be left upon another." We may take for granted that, since Christ's prophecy had not been proven false, many surely concluded that it indeed had now been shown true. We do not know that Jews in numbers then drew the conclusion that, after all, Jesus really was the Christ. Many Christians said so. But in the next half century, Palestine gained a Christian majority. Christians were not slow to claim their faith had been proved right. We need not speculate on the depth of disappointment felt by those Jews who had hoped that the project would come to fruition and herald, instead of the Christian one, the Messiah they awaited.

Third, the last pagan emperor's threat to Christianity made urgent the delegitimization of paganism. In the formation of a new and aggressive policy toward outsiders, Judaism, too, was caught in the net. To be sure, Jews were to be protected but degraded. But the sword unsheathed against the pagan cult-places, if sharp, was untutored. It was not capable of discriminating among non-Christian centers of divine service. Nor could those who wielded it, zealots of the faith in church and street, have been expected to. The now-Christian Roman government protected synagogues and punished those who damaged them. Its policy was to extirpate paganism but protect a degraded Judaism. But the faithful of the church had their own ideas. The assault against pagan temples spilled over into an ongoing program of attacking synagogue property.

Still worse from the Jews' viewpoint, a phenomenon lacking much precedent over the antecedent thousand years now came into view. There were random attacks on Jews by reason of their faith, as distinct from organized struggles among contending and equal forces, Jewish and other mobs. The long-established Roman tradition of toleration for Judaism and Jews, extending back to the time of Julius Caesar and applying both in law and in custom, now drew to a close. A new fact, at this time lacking all basis in custom and in the policy of state and Church alike, faced Jews. They suffered physical insecurity in their own villages and towns. So Jews' synagogues and their homes housed the same thing, Judaism, and it was to be eradicated. A mark of exceptional piety came to consist in violence against Jews' holy places, their property and persons. Coming in the aftermath of the triumph of Christianity on the one side, and the decisive disproof of the Jews' hope for the rebuilding of the Temple on the other, was the hitherto unimagined war against the Jews. In the last third of the fourth century and the beginning of the fifth, this war raised once again those questions about the meaning and end of history that Constantine, at the beginning of the age at hand, had forced upon Israel's consciousness.

Fourth, at this time there seems to have been a sharp rise in the numbers of Christians in the Holy Land. Christian refugees from the West accounted for part of the growth, but we have some stories about how Jews converted as well. The number of Christian towns and villages dramatically increased. If Jews did convert in sizable numbers, then we should have to point to the events of the preceding decades as ample validation in their eyes for the Christian interpretation of history. Jews had waited nearly three hundred years, from the destruction in 70 to the promise of Julian. Instead of being falsified, Jesus' prophecy had been validated. No stone had been left on stone in the Temple, not after 70, not after 361, just as Jesus had said. Instead of a rebuilt temple, the Jews looked out on a world in which now even their synagogues came under threat and, along with them, their own homes and persons. What could be more ample proof of the truth of the Christians' claim than the worldly triumph of their Church? Resisted for so long, that claim called into question, as in the time of Bar Kokhba, whether it was worth waiting any longer for a messiah that had not come when he was most needed. With followers proclaiming the messiah who *had* come now possessing the world, the question could hardly be avoided.

Now that we understand the context, we appreciate the issues at hand. What has happened is a world-historical change, one that could not be absorbed into Israel's available system of theories on the outsiders, in general, and the meaning of the history of the great empires, in particular. The Christian empire was fundamentally different from its predecessor in two ways. First, it shared with Israel reverence for exactly the same Holy Scriptures on which Jewry based its existence. So it was no longer a wholly other, entirely alien empire that ruled over the horizon. It was now a monotheist, formerly persecuted, biblical empire, not awfully different from Israel in its basic convictions about all important matters of time and eternity. And it was near at hand, and interested. Second, established policies of more than a half a millenium, from the time of the Maccabees' alliance with Rome to the start of the fourth century, now gave way. Tolerance of Judaism and an accommodation with the Jews in their Land—disrupted only by the Jews' own violation of the terms of the agreement in 70 and 132—now no longer governed. Instead, we find intolerance of Judaism and persecution of Jews through attacks on their persons and property.

Accordingly, we must ask how documents of the age addressed the issue of, first, the course of human events, and, second, the character of Rome in particular. To take up that issue, we turn to the apocalyptic passage of Scripture that served to define the images, Daniel's vision of the nations in terms of various animals. The first use of these symbols shows us a way not taken, that is, how rabbis not interested in the issues—probably living a century or more before world-historical change made an impact on the consciousness of the sages' community—treated these images. Only then shall we turn to the treatment of the animal-symbols in our period.

We take up Tosefta's treatment of the apocalyptic vision of Daniel and find that history happens in what takes place in the sages' debates.

T. Miqvaot 7:11

A. A cow which drank purification-water, and which one slaughtered within twenty-four hours—

B. This was a case, and R. Yose the Galilean did declare it clean, and R. Aqiba did declare it unclean.

C. R. Tarfon supported R. Yose the Galilean. R. Simeon ben Nanos supported R. Aqiba.

D. R. Simeon b. Nanos dismissed [the arguments of] R. Tarfon. R. Yose the Galilean dismissed [the arguments of] R. Simeon b. Nanos.

E. R. Aqiba dismissed [the arguments of] R. Yose the Galilean.

F. After a time, he [Yose] found an answer for him [Aqiba].

G. He said to him, "Am I able to reverse myself?"

H. He said to him, "Not anyone [may reverse himself], but you [may do so], for you are Yose the Galilean."

I. [He said to him,] "I shall say to you: Lo, Scripture states, *And they shall be kept for the congregation of the people of Israel for the water for impurity* (Num. 19:9).

J. "Just so long as they are kept, lo, they are water for impurity—but not after a cow has drunk them."

K. This was a case, and thirty-two elders voted in Lud and declared it clean.

L. At that time R. Tarfon recited this verse:

M. "*I saw the ram goring westward and northward and southward, and all the animals were unable to stand against, it, and none afforded protection from its power, and it did just as it liked and grew great* (Dan. 8:4)—

N. "[This is] R. Aqiba.

O. " '*As I was considering, behold, a he-goat came from the west across the face of the whole earth, without touching the ground; and the goat had a conspicuous horn between his eyes.*

P. " '*He came to the ram with the two horns, which I had seen standing on the bank of the river, and he ran at him in his mighty wrath. I saw him come close to the ram, and he was enraged against him and struck the ram and broke his two horns*'—this is R. Aqiba and R. Simeon b. Nanos.

Q. " '*And the ram had no power to stand before him*'—this is R. Aqiba.

R. " '*But he cast him down to the ground and trampled upon him*'— this is R. Yose the Galilean.

S. " '*And there was no one who could rescue the ram from his power*'—these are the thirty-two elders who voted in Lud and declared it clean."

We shall see the same passage in its own context. I cite it here only to underline the contrast between the usage at hand and the one we find in the late fourth or early fifth century composition, Leviticus Rabbah. What we see here is how sages absorb events into their system of classification. So it is sages that make history through the thoughts they think and the rules they lay down. In such a context, we find no interest either in the outsiders and their powers, or in the history of the empires of the world, or, all the more so, in redemption and the messianic fulfillment of time.

What is the alternative to the use of the sort of symbols just now examined? Let us turn immediately to the relevant passages of Leviticus Rabbah:

XIII:V

1. A. Said R. Ishmael b. R. Nehemiah, "All the prophets foresaw what the pagan kingdoms would do [to Israel].
   B. "The first man foresaw what the pagan kingdoms would do [to Israel].
   C. "That is in line with the following verse of Scripture: 'A river flowed out of Eden [to water the garden, and there it divided and became four rivers]' (Gen. 2:10). [The four rivers stand for the four kingdoms, Babylonia, Media, Greece, and Rome]."
2. A. R. Tanhuma said it, [and] R. Menahema [in the name of] R. Joshua b. Levi: "The Holy One, blessed be he, will give the cup of reeling to the nations of the world to drink in the world to come.
   B. "That is in line with the following verse of Scripture: 'A river flowed out of Eden' (Gen. 2:10), the place from which justice [DYN] goes forth."
3. A. "[There it divided] and became four rivers" (Gen 2:10)—this refers to the four kingdoms.
   B. "The name of the first in Pishon (PSWN); [it is the one which flows around the whole land of Havilah, where there is gold; and the gold of that land is good; bdellium and onyx stone are there]" (Gen 2:11-12).
   C. This refers to Babylonia, on account [of the reference to Babylonia in the following verse:] "And their [the Babylonians'] horsemen spread themselves (PSW)" (Hab. 1:8).
   D. [It is further] on account of [Nebuchadnezzar's being] a dwarf, shorter than ordinary men by a handbreadth.
   E. "[It is the one which flows around the whole land of Havilah]" (Gen. 2:11).
   F. "This [reference to the river's flowing around the whole land] speaks of Nebuchadnezzar, the wicked man, who came up and surrounded the entire Land of Israel, which places its hope in the Holy One, blessed be he.
   G. That is in line with the following verse of Scripture: "Hope in God, for I shall again praise him" (Ps. 42:5).

H. "Where there is gold" (Gen. 2:11)—this refers to the words of Torah, "which are more to be desired than gold, more than much fine gold" (Ps. 19:11).

I. "And the gold of that land is good" (Gen. 2:12).

J. This teaches that there is no Torah like the Torah that is taught in the Land of Israel, and there is no wisdom like the wisdom that is taught in the Land of Israel.

K. "Bdellium and onyx stone are there" (Gen. 2:12)—Scripture, Mishnah, Talmud, and lore.

4. A. "The name of the second river is Gihon; [it is the one which flows around the whole land of Cush]" (Gen. 2:13).

B. This refers to Media, which produced Haman, that wicked man, who spit out venom like a serpent.

C. It is on account of the verse: "On your belly will you go" (Gen. 3:14).

D. "It is the one which flows around the whole land of Cush" (Gen. 2:13).

E. [We know that this refers to Media, because it is said:] "Who rules from India to Cush" (Est. 1:1).

5. A. "And the name of the third river is Tigris (HDQL), [which flows east of Assyria]" (Gen. 2:14).

B. This refers to Greece [Syria], which was sharp (HD) and speedy (QL) in making its decrees, saying to Israel, "Write on the horn of an ox that you have no portion in the God of Israel."

C. "Which flows east (QDMT) of Assyria" (Gen. 2:14).

D. Said R. Huna, "In three aspects the kingdom of Greece was in advance (QDMH) of the present evil kingdom [Rome]: in respect to ship-building, the arrangement of camp vigils, and language."

E. Said R. Huna, "Any and every kingdom may be called 'Assyria' (ashur), on account of all of their making themselves powerful at Israel's expense."

F. Said R. Yose b. R. Hanina, "Any and every kingdom may be called Nineveh (NNWH), on account of their adorning (NWY) themselves at Israel's expense."

G. Said R. Yose b. R. Hanina, "Any and every kingdom may be called Egypt (MSRYM), on account of their oppressing (MSYRYM) Israel."

6. A. "And the fourth river is the Euphrates (PRT)" (Gen. 2:14).

B. This refers to Edom [Rome], since it was fruitful (PRT), and multiplied through the prayer of the elder [Isaac at Gen. 27:39].

C. Another interpretation: It was because it was fruitful and multiplied, and so cramped his world.

D. Another explanation: Because it was fruitful and multiplied and cramped his son.

E. Another explanation: Because it was fruitful and multiplied and cramped his house.

F. Another explanation: "Parat"—because in the end, "I am going to exact a penalty from it (PR^c)."

G. That is in line with the following verse of Scripture: "I have trodden (PWRH) the winepress alone" (Is. 63:3).

7. A. [Gen. R. 42:2:] Abraham foresaw what the evil kingdoms would do [to Israel].

B. "[As the sun was going down,] a deep sleep fell on Abraham; and lo, a dread and great darkness fell upon him]" (Gen. 15:12).

C. "Dread" ('YMH) refers to Babylonia, on account of the statement, "Then Nebuchadnezzar was full of fury (HMH)" (Dan. 3:19).

D. "Darkness" refers to Media, which brought darkness to Israel through its decrees: "to destroy, to slay, and to wipe out all the Jews" (Est. 7:4).

E. "Great" refers to Greece.

F. Said R. Judah b. R. Simon, "The verse teaches that the kingdom of Greece set up one hundred twenty-seven governors, one hundred and twenty-seven hyparchs and one hundred twenty-seven commanders."

G. And rabbis say, "They were sixty in each category."

H. R. Berekhiah and R. Hanan in support of this position taken by rabbis: " 'Who led you through the great terrible wilderness, with its fiery serpents and scorpions and thirsty ground where there was no water]' (Deut. 8:15).

I. "Just as the scorpion produces eggs by sixties, so the kingdom of Greece would set up its administration in groups of sixty."

J. "Fell on him" (Gen. 15:12).

K. This refers to Edom, on account of the following verse: "The earth quakes at the noise of their [Edom's] fall" (Jer. 49:21).

L. There are those who reverse matters.

M. "Fear" refers to Edom, on account of the following verse: "And this I saw, a fourth beast, fearful, and terrible" (Dan. 7:7).

N. "Darkness" refers to Greece, which brought gloom through its decrees. For they said to Israel, "Write on the horn of an ox that you have no portion in the God of Israel."

O. 'Great" refers to Media, on account of the verse: "King Ahasuerus made Haman [the Median] great" (Est. 3:1).

P. "Fell on him" refers to Babylonia, on account of the following verse: "Fallen, fallen is Babylonia" (Is. 21:9).

8. A. Daniel foresaw what the evil kingdoms would do [to Israel].

B. "Daniel said, I saw in my vision by night, and behold, the four winds of heaven were stirring up the great sea. And four great beasts came up out of the sea, [different from one another. The first was like a lion and had eagles' wings. Then as I looked, its wings were plucked off... And behold, another beast, a second one, like a bear... After this I looked, and lo, another, like a leopard... After this I saw in the night visions, and behold, a fourth beast, terrible and dreadful and exceedingly strong; and it had great iron teeth]" (Dan. 7:3-7).

C. If you enjoy sufficient merit, it will emerge from the sea, but if not, it will come out of the forest.

D. The animal that comes up from the sea is not violent, but the one that comes up out of the forest is violent.

E. Along these same lines: "The boar out of the wood ravages it" (Ps. 80:14).

F. If you enjoy sufficient merit, it will come from the river, and if not, from the forest.

G. The animal that comes up from the river is not violent, but the one that comes up out of the forest is violent.

H. "Different from one another" (Dan. 7:3).

I. Differing from [hating] one another.

J. This teaches that every nation that rules in the world hates Israel and reduces them to slavery.

K. "The first was like a lion [and had eagles' wings]" (Dan. 7:14).

L. This refers to Babylonia.

M. Jeremiah saw [Babylonia] as a lion. Then he went and saw it as an eagle.

N. He saw it as a lion: "A lion has come up from his thicket" (Jer. 4:7).

O. And [as an eagle:] "Behold, he shall come up and swoop down as the eagle" (Jer. 49:22).

P. People said to Daniel, 'What do you see?"

Q. He said to them, "I see the face like that of a lion and wings like those of an eagle: 'The first was like a lion and had eagles' wings. Then, as I looked, its wings were plucked off, and it was lifted up from the ground [and made to stand upon two feet like a man and the heart of a man was given to it]' (Dan. 7:4).

R. R. Eleazar and R. Ishmael b. R. Nehemiah:

S. R. Eleazar said "While the entire lion was smitten, its heart was not smitten.

T. "That is in line with the following statement: 'And the heart of a man was given to it' (Dan. 7:4)."

U. And R. Ishmael b. R. Nehemiah said, "Even its heart was smitten, for it is written, 'Let his heart be changed from a man's' (Dan. 4:17).

X. "And behold, another beast, a second one, like a bear. [It was raised up one side; it had three ribs in its mouth between its teeth, and it was told, Arise, devour much flesh]" (Dan. 7:5).

Y. This refers to Media.

Z. Said R. Yohanan, "It is like a bear."

AA. It is written, "similar to a wolf" (DB); thus, "And a wolf was there."

BB. That is in accord with the view of R. Yohanan, for R. Yohanan said,

" 'Therefore a lion out of the forest [slays them]' (Jer. 5:6)—this
refers to Babylonia.

CC. " 'A wolf of the deserts spoils them' (Jer. 5:6) refers to Media.

DD. " 'A leopard watches over their cities' (Jer. 5:6) refers to Greece.

EE. " 'Whoever goes out from them will be savaged' (Jer. 5:6) refers to
Edom.

FF. "How so? 'Because their transgressions are many, and their
backslidings still more' (Jer. 5:6)."

GG. "After this, I looked, and lo, another, like a leopard [with four
wings of a bird on its back; and the beast had four heads; and
dominion was given to it]" (Dan. 7:6).

HH. This [leopard] refers to Greece, which persisted impudently in
making harsh decrees, saying to Israel, "Write on the horn of an ox
that you have no share in the God of Israel."

II. "After this I saw in the night visions, and behold, a fourth beast,
terrible and dreadful and exceedingly strong; [and it had great
iron teeth; it devoured and broke in pieces and stamped the
residue with its feet. It was different from all the beasts that were
before it; and it had ten horns]" (Dan. 7:7).

JJ. This refers to Edom [Rome].

KK. Daniel saw the first three visions on one night, and this one he saw
on another night. Now why was that the case?

LL. R. Yohanan and R. Simeon b. Laqish:

MM. R. Yohanan said, "It is because the fourth beast weighed as much
as the first three."

NN. And R. Simeon b. Laqish said, "It outweighed them."

OO. R. Yohanan objected to R. Simeon b. Laqish, " 'Prophesy, therefore, son of man, clap your hands [and let the sword come down
twice; yea, thrice. The sword for those to be slain; it is the sword
for the great slaughter, which encompasses them]' (Ez. 21:14-15).
[So the single sword of Rome weighs against the three others]."

PP. And R. Simeon b. Laqish, how does he interpret the same
passage? He notes that [the threefold sword] is doubled (Ez.
21:14), [thus outweighs the three swords, equally twice their
strength].

9. A. Moses foresaw what the evil kingdoms would do [to Israel].

B. "The camel, rock badger, and hare" (Deut. 14:7). [Compare:
"Nevertheless, among those that chew the cud or part the hoof,
you shall not eat these: the camel, because it chews the cud but
does not part the hoof, is unclean to you. The rock badger, because
it chews the cud but does not part the hoof, is unclean to you. And
the hare, because it chews the cud but does not part the hoof, is
unclean to you, and the pig, because it parts the hoof and is
cloven-footed, but does not chew the cud, is unclean to you" (Lev.
11:4-8).]

C. The camel (GML) refers to Babylonia, [in line with the following verse of Scripture: "O daughter of Babylonia, you who are to be devastated!] Happy will be he who requites (GML) you, with what you have done to us" (Ps. 147:8).

D. "The rock badger" (Deut. 14:7)—this refers to Media.

E. Rabbis and R. Judah b. R. Simon.

F. Rabbis say, "Just as the rock badger exhibits traits of uncleanness and traits of cleanness, so the kingdom of Media produced both a righteous man and a wicked one."

G. Said R. Judah b. R. Simon, "The last Darius was Esther's son. He was clean on his mother's side and unclean on his father's side."

H. "The hare" (Deut 14:7)—this refers to Greece. The mother of King Ptolemy was named "Hare" [in Greek: *lagos*].

I. "The pig" (Deut. 14:7)—this refers to Edom [Rome].

J. Moses made mention of the first three in a single verse and the final one in a verse by itself [(Deut. 14:7, 8)]. Why so?

K. R. Yohanan and R. Simeon b. Laqish.

L. R. Yohanan said, "It is because [the pig] is equivalent to the other three."

M. And R. Simeon b. Laqish said, "It is because it outweighs them."

N. R. Yohanan objected to R. Simeon b. Laqish, " 'Prophesy, therefore, son of man, clap yours hands [and let the sword come down twice, yea thrice]' (Ez. 21:14)."

O. And how does R. Simeon b. Laqish interpret the same passage? He notes that [the threefold sword] is doubled (Ez. 21:14).

10. A. [Gen. R. 65:1:] R. Phineas and R. Hilqiah in the name of R. Simon: "Among all the prophets, only two of them revealed [the true evil of Rome], Assaf and Moses.

B. "Assaf said, 'The pig out of the wood ravages it' (Ps. 80:14).

C. "Moses said, 'And the pig, [because it parts the hoof and is cloven-footed but does not chew the cud]' (Lev. 11:7).

D. "Why is [Rome] compared to a pig?

E. "It is to teach you the following: Just as, when a pig crouches and produces its hooves, it is as if to say, 'See how I am clean [since I have a cloven hoof],' so this evil kingdom takes pride, seizes by violence, and steals, and then gives the appearance of establishing a tribunal for justice."

F. There was the case of a ruler in Caesarea, who put thieves, adulterers, and sorcerers to death, while at the same time telling his counsellor, "That same man [I] did all these three things on a single night."

11. A. Another interpretation: "The camel" (Lev. 11:4).

B. This refers to Babylonia.

C. "Because it chews the cud (M°LM GRH) [but does not part the hoof]" (Lev. 11:4).

D. For it brings forth praises [with its throat (MQLS)] of the Holy One, blessed be he. [The Hebrew words for "chew the cud"—

bring up cud—are now understood to mean "give praise." GRH is connected with GRWN, throat, hence, "bring forth [sounds of praise through] the throat."

E. R. Berekhiah and R. Helbo in the name of R. Ishmael b. R. Nahman: "Whatever [praise of God] David [in writing a psalm] treated singly [item by item], that wicked man [Nebuchadnezzar] lumped together in a single verse.

F. " 'Now I, Nebuchadnezzar, praise and extol and honor the King of heaven, for all his works are right and his ways are just, and those who walk in pride he is able to abase' (Dan. 4:37).

G. " 'Praise'—'O Jerusalem, praise the Lord' (Ps. 147:12).

H. " 'Extol'—'I shall extol you, O Lord, for you have brought me low' (Ps. 30:2).

I. " 'Honor the king of heaven'—'The Lord reigns, let the peoples tremble! He sits enthroned upon the cherubim, let the earth quake' (Ps. 99:1).

J. " 'For all his works are right'—'For the sake of thy steadfast love and thy faithfulness' (Ps. 115:1).

K. " 'And his ways are just'—'He will judge the peoples with equity' (Ps. 96:10).

L. " 'And those who walk in pride'—'The Lord reigns, he is robed in majesty, the Lord is robed, he is girded with strength' (Ps. 93:1).

M. " 'He is able to abase'—'All the horns of the wicked he will cut off' (Ps. 75:11)."

N. "The rock badger" (Lev. 11:5)—this refers to Media.

O. "For it chews the cud"—for it gives praise to the Holy One, blessed be he: "Thus says Cyrus, king of Persia, 'All the kingdoms of the earth has the Lord, the God of the heaven, given me" (Ezra 1:2).

P. "The hare"—this refers to Greece.

Q. "For it chews the cud"—for its gives praise to the Holy One, blessed be he.

R. Alexander the Macedonian, when he saw Simeon the Righteous, said, "Blessed be the God of Simeon the Righteous."

S. "The pig" (Lev. 11:7)—this refers to Edom.

T. "For it does not chew the cud"—for it does not give praise to the Holy One, blessed be He.

U. And it is not enough that it does not give praise, but it blasphemes and swears violently, saying "Whom do I have in heaven, and with you I want nothing on earth" (Ps. 73:25).

12. A. Another interpretation [of GRH, cud, now with reference to GR, stranger:]

B. "The camel" (Lev. 11:4)—this refers to Babylonia.

C. "For it chews the cud" [now: brings up the stranger]—for it exalts righteous men: "And Daniel was in the gate of the king" (Dan. 2:49).

D. "The rock badger" (Lev. 11:5)—this refers to Media.

E. "For it brings up the stranger"—for it exalts righteous men: "Mordecai sat at the gate of the king" (Est. 2:19).

F. "The hare" (Lev. 11:6)—this refers to Greece.

G. "For it brings up the stranger"—for it exalts the righteous.

H. When Alexander of Macedonia saw Simeon the Righteous, he would rise up on his feet. They said to him, "Can't you see the Jew, that you stand up before this Jew?"

I. He said to them, "When I go forth to battle, I see something like this man's visage, and I conquer."

J. "The pig" (Lev. 11:7)—this refers to Rome.

K. "But it does not bring up the stranger"—for it does not exalt the righteous.

L. And it is not enough that it does not exalt them, but it kills them.

M. That is in line with the following verse of Scripture: "I was angry with my people, I profaned my heritage: I gave them into your hand, you showed them no mercy; on the aged you made your yoke exceedingly heavy" (Is. 47:6).

N. This refers to R. Aqiba and his colleagues.

13. A. Another interpretation [now treating "bring up the cud" (GR) as "bring along in its train" (GRR)]:

B. "The camel" (Lev. 11:4)—this refers to Babylonia.

C. "Which brings along in its train"—for it brought along another kingdom after it.

D. "The rock badger" (Lev. 11:5)—this refers to Media.

E. "Which brings along in its train"—for it brought along another kingdom after it.

F. "The hare" (Lev. 11:6)—this refers to Greece.

G. "Which brings along in its train"—for it brought along another kingdom after it.

H. "The pig" (Lev. 11:7)—this refers to Rome.

I. "Which does not bring along in its train"—for it did not bring along another kingdom after it.

J. And why is it then called "pig" (HZYR)? For it restores (MHZRT) the crown to the one who truly should have it [namely, Israel, whose dominion will begin when the rule of Rome ends].

K. That is in line with the following verse of Scripture: "And saviors will come up on Mount Zion to judge the Mountain of Esau [Rome], and the kingdom will then belong to the Lord" (Ob. 1:21).

To stand back and consider this vast apocalyptic vision of Israel's history, we first review the message of the construction as a whole. This comes in two parts, first the explicit, then the implicit.

As to the former, the first claim is that God had told the prophets what would happen to Israel at the hands of the pagan kingdoms Babylonia, Media, Greece and Rome. These kingdoms are further represented by Nebuchadnezzar, Haman, Alexander for Greece, Edom or Esau, interchangeably, for Rome. The same vision came from Adam, Abraham, Daniel and Moses. The same policy toward Israel—oppression, destruction, enslavement, alienation from the true God—emerged from all four.

How does Romes stand out? First, it was made fruitful through the prayer of Isaac in behalf of Esau. Second, Edom is represented by the fourth and final beast. Rome is related through Esau, as Babylonia, Media, and Greece are not. The fourth beast was seen in a vision separate from the first three. It was worst of all and outweighed the rest. In the apocalypticizing of the animals in Lev. 11:4-8 and Deut. 14:7, the camel, rock badger, hare, and pig, the pig, which stands for Rome, again emerges as different from the others and more threatening than the rest. Just as the pig pretends to be a clean beast by showing the cloven hoof, but in fact is an unclean one, so Rome pretends to be just but in fact governs by thuggery. Edom does not pretend to praise God, it only blasphemes. It does not exalt the righteous but kills them. These symbols concede nothing to Christian monotheism and biblicism.

Of greatest importance, while all the other beasts bring further ones in their wake, the pig does not, "It does not bring another kingdom after it." It will restore the crown to the one who will truly deserve it, Israel. Esau will be judged by Zion, so Obadiah 1:21.

Now how has the symbolization delivered an implicit message? It is in the treatment of Rome as distinct, but essentially equivalent to the former kingdoms. This seems to me a stunning way of saying that the now-Christian empire in no way requires differentiation from its pagan predecessors. Nothing has changed, except matters have become worse. Beyond Rome, standing in a straight line with the others, lies the true shift in history, the rule of Israel and the cessation of the dominion of the (pagan) nations.

The polemic represented by the symbolization of Christian Rome, therefore, makes the simple point that, first, Christians are no different from, and no better than, pagans; they are essentially the same. Second, just as Israel had survived Babylonia, Media, Greece, so would they endure to see the end of Rome (whether pagan, whether Christian). But of course, the symbolic polemic rested on false assumptions, and hence conveyed a message that misled Jews by misrepresenting their new enemy. The new Rome really did differ from the old; Christianity was not merely part of a succession of undifferentiated modes of paganism. True, the symbols assigned to Rome attributed worse, more dangerous traits than those assigned to the earlier empires. The pig pretends to be clean, just as the Christians give the signs of adherence to the God of Abraham, Isaac, and Jacob. That much the passage concedes. But it is not enough. For out of symbols should emerge a useful public policy, and the mode of thought represented by symbols in the end should yield an accurate confrontation with that for which the symbol stands.

In fact it would be many centuries before Jews would take seriously, and in its own terms, Christianity's claim to constitute a kind of Judaism, and not a kind of paganism. It would take a long time for Jews to distinguish the Christian from other outsiders. When that differentiation began to emerge, it would be in Christian Europe, on the part of Joseph Kimhi and Moses Nahmanides, and others who had no choice. By that time, to be sure, "paganism" had long disappeared from the world of Israel's residency, on the one hand, and any expectation that Roman rule would give way to Israelite hegemony had lost all worldly credibility. Then, but only then, we find Jews confronting in a systematic way and with solid knowledge of the other side the facts of history that had emerged many centuries earlier.

Whether a different symbolic system would have produced a more realistic and effective policy for the confrontation with triumphant Christianity, we shall never know. For so long, Israel had pretended nothing happened of any importance—not in the first century, not in the fourth. By the time people came around to concede that, after all, Christianity was here to stay and was essentially different from anything Israel had earlier encountered, it was an awareness too late to make such a difference in Israel's framing of its picture of the outsider and its policy toward the alien.

If we may set into a larger framework the data at hand, we note that Judaism and Christianity in late antiquity present histories that mirror one another. When Christianity began, Judaism was the dominant tradition in the Holy Land and formed its ideas within a political framework until the early fifth century. Christianity there was subordinate, and had to work itself out against the background of a politically definitive Judaism. Elsewhere, of course, Christianity had to work out of its subordinate position as well. From the time of Constantine onward, matters reversed themselves. Now Christianity predominated, expressing it ideas in political and institutional terms. Judaism, by contrast, had lost its political foundations and faced the task of working out its self-understanding in terms of a world defined by Christianity, now everywhere triumphant and in charge of politics. The important shift came in the early fourth century.

In consequence of the original situation, Christians had to attend to the limits of their community, while Jews took for granted they knew their own frontiers. Christians therefore addressed the issue of the outsider and undertook to differentiate one from the next, as early, indeed, as Paul's letter to the Romans, which considers the question of Israel "after the flesh." It would be a thousand years before the Jews would find it urgent to take up the question of Israel "after the spirit," the now-ineluctable claim of Christianity to constitute the heir and successor of the "Old Testament" through the New. To conclude: in future inquiries we wish to ask the framers of the two great traditions to tell us, in a systematic and detailed way, precisely how, in theory at least, they coped with difference within and diversity without. To state matters in the most general way, what theory of "the other" did the great minds of Judaic and Christian antiquity work out in order to make sense of themselves and of outsiders? When we know how people defined the other, of course, we grasp how they understood who they themselves were. So we turn back to the beginnings, not to learn merely from whence we came. Rather, we want to find out how people whom we see as our predecessors worked out problems remarkably congruent to the issues of our own country and age.

In a word, our search for theories of the other encompasses the unfolding consciousness of self, how one group understood itself in the encounter with other groups, how each group made peace, in its own mind, with the presence of many others. When we understand how people made sense of one another and, furthermore, formulated such sense as they made in terms they could hand on to coming generations and even incorporate in law and institutions, then we will grasp what we seek. The results thus far prove negative. But the consequence is stunning. Nothing that happened appears to have changed Israel's sense of itself. The fact that symbols of the other proved unchanging indicates, I think, that Israel's sense of the self had endured and overcome an awful crisis.

FOUR
Coping with Difference: Beyond the Fourth Century

17

The Jewish Community of the Later Roman Empire as Seen in the *Codex Theodosianus*

Bernard S. Bachrach
University of Minnesota

Specialists working in medieval history, and especially in the early Middle Ages, all but ignore the Jewish *gens* in general histories of this period. Those who do comment are usually content with a few derogatory remarks about usury.[1] Indeed, Christianity's overwhelming victory in the battle for Western civilization's spiritual allegiance fought during the millennium following the decline and fall of the Roman Empire seems thoroughly to have dampened any real scholarly interest in the arduous and often unsuccessful struggle that was waged by ecclesiastics and their secular allies to diminish the religious attraction of Judaism, the economic power of the Jews, and the political influence of the Jewish community in the late antique and early medieval periods.[2] The steps by which Christianity is made to appear the ineluctable winner over competing belief systems—as though this victory were part of God's overall plan for mankind—is dutifully traced from the Milvian bridge and the Edict of Toleration through Ambrose's humiliation of Theodosius I, the legislation of the *Codex Theodosianus*, and the anti-Jewish polemics of various church fathers, to the massacres perpetrated by a handful of crusaders and the *acta* of the Fourth Lateran Council in 1215.[3]

This whig approach to the "inevitable" victory of Christianity does not inform the historiography of the Jewish people which, by stark contrast, has been dominated for almost two millennia by the theme of suffering. It is argued that the exile imposed by Titus is an

---

[1] See the review by Gavin Langmuir, "Majority History and Post-Biblical Jews," *Journal of the History of Ideas*, 27 (1966), 343-364.

[2] Some of the problems are discussed in Bernard C. Bachrach, *Early Medieval Jewish Policy in Western Europe* (Minneapolis: 1977).

[3] Accounts like Gavin Langmuir's in "From Ambrose of Milan to Emicho of Leiningen: The Transformation of Hostility Against Jews in Northern Christendom," *Settimane di studio del Centro italiano di studi sull'alto medioevo*, 26 (1980), 313-368, tend to strengthen this view, although the author's aims are not intended to that purpose.

ongoing punishment that will be endured until the coming of the Messiah. Within this framework, in order to sustain this Theology of Exile, disaster and defeat are continually highlighted in a more or less intentional manner, not only in historical works, but also in liturgy. The record of forced baptism, expropriation, expulsion and martyrdom has been effectively marshalled; the result is what Salo Baron has justly called the "lachrymose" interpretation.[4]

However the lachrymose view, which may be thought of as a whig interpretation turned on its head, has a curious theological twist of a redeeming nature. The *gentiles* of the Old Testament have all but disappeared during the past 2,000 years, and many other peoples with whom the Jews have shared the historical stage have faded into oblivion under particularly prejudicial conditions. Yet the adherents of the lachrymose interpretation and proponents of the Theology of Exile do not question the peculiar phenomenon of Jewish survival in historical terms, i.e. why did the Jews keep their heads while all around were losing theirs? To approach this question historically would undermine the lachrymose view and in comparative terms make clear that life in exile was not the disaster that is required by the theologians. Indeed, in as unemotional terms as possible, it is difficult to avoid the conclusion that a people which has survived an attempt or many attempts at extermination has endured a more successful history than one with whom the exterminators have succeeded. With the exception of the efforts of a few noteworthy scholars, attempts to place

---

[4] Baron first presented this idea where he used the term "lachrymose theory" in *The Menorah Journal*, 14 (1928), 515-526. A similar and indeed more thoroughgoing attack on Jewish historiography was levied only a month earlier in the same journal by Cecil Roth (pp. 419-434). It is of some interest that even among non-Jewish historians the selective use of evidence to demonstrate the maltreatment of the Jews is pervasive. Thus, for example, no less subtle a craftsman than Langmuir, "Ambrose to Emicho," 341-348, continues to portray Visigothic Jewish policy as one of unrelieved persecution. He argues that "The kings sought to eliminate Judaic religiosity, unsuccessfully, because their own religiosity supportive of the reconstituted people of their kingdom applied to the Jews as much as to anyone else." He goes on to generalize about "royal intolerance" (p. 387). Langmuir unfortunately fails to inform his readers that his generalizations about the kings' policies and "royal intolerance" are based at most upon the actions of six out of a total of eighteen Visigothic monarchs who ruled during the century and a quarter that spanned the period between their conversion to Orthodox Christianity and the Muslim conquest. Most of the other twelve Visigothic rulers have been shown to have pursued pro-Jewish policies. In addition, those few monarchs who pursued anti-Jewish policies usually succeeded a pro-Jewish ruler and had been opposed by the Jews in Spain. See Bernard S. Bachrach, "A Reassessment of Visigothic Jewish Policy, 589-711," *The American Historical Review*, 78 (1973), 11-34, and Bernard S. Bachrach, "Judacot and Judila: a *mise au point*," *Classical Folia*, 30 (1977), 41-46.

Jewish history in a broader context of general history have generated little interest.[5] The working out of Abraham's covenant with God is the "historical" reality that has dominated and in many ways continues to dominate Jewish historiography. The lachrymose interpretation is comprehensible largely in these terms.[6]

The Christian whig and the Jewish lachrymose views reenforce one another. Thus in the latter, the Jewish people is seen as the innocent victim which as part of a divine plan barely survives the efforts of unworthy persecutors. In the whig view, the insidious Jews are seen as the worthy victims of righteous chastizers who are protecting their flocks from contamination. This unholy historiographical symbiosis has encouraged a highly selective treatment of the evidence. Its result has been a tableau of suffering relieved only by recognizing Jewish religious scholarship's prodigious production.[7] It should be clear to historians, if not to theologians, that both the lachrymose and the whig views are major distortions and must be abandoned. However, because of the great weight of earlier scholarship and the widespread popular acceptance of these insidious dogma, it is necessary to combat these very harmful ideas actively.

It is with these aims in mind that I join with a few colleagues, some of whom are here today, in advocating a reexamination of the Jewish *gens* in the later Roman Empire. In order to see how the imperial government viewed the Jewish communities within the empire, I ask you to look with me now at an important group of imperial acts that are included in the *Codex Theodosianus*.[8] It is important in light of previous scholarship to emphasize the banality that while we may be aware of the subsequent course of Jewish history, the actors on the historical stage of the fourth and fifth centuries were not. The emperors and their officials who developed

---

[5] In an excellent essay Peter Riesenberg, "Jews in the Structure of Western Institutions," *Judaism*, 28 (1979), 402-415 successfully sketches, in outline, a balanced view.

[6] The plea of Yitzhak Baer, "It is the privilege of the oppressed people to arouse the conscience of the victors" epitomizes this view which sees the Jews as the vanquished (*Galut*, [New York: 1947], trans. by R. Warshow, 116).

[7] The most glaring example of this is the prevailing consensus that the redaction of the Jerusalem Talmud is a symptom of the serious and continuous persecutions being suffered by Jews during the first quarter of the fifth century. For a discussion of this view see the literature cited by Jeremy Cohen, "Roman Imperial Policy Toward the Jews from Constantine Until the End of the Palestinian Patriarchate (ca. 429)," *Byzantine Studies*, 3 (1976), 25, n. 195.

[8] *CTh.* for *Theodosiani libri xvi cum constitutionibus Sirmondianis et leges novellae ad Theodosianum pertinentes*, eds. Th. Mommsen and P. Meyer, 2 vols. (Berlin: 1905). All translations unless otherwise indicated are from *The Theodosian Code and Novels, and the Sirmondian Constitutions*, trans. C. Pharr (Princeton: 1952).

various policies (as illustrated by their legislation) were not aware of
the overwhelming victory that Christianity would win during the
subsequent millennium, nor did they know that Jews would be
expelled from England, France, and Spain, suffer pogroms in early
modern Europe, and face anihilation in the Holocaust.

I

From the *Codex Theodosianus* it is clear that the Jews of the
Roman empire enjoyed the right to live under the *lex Judaeorum* with
regard to civil matters and that, perhaps even as late as A.D. 398, they
enjoyed special privileges which exempted them from the jurisdiction
of the imperial government in matters that concerned the "forum, the
statutes, and the law." This partial legal autonomy, moreover, permitted the leaders of the Jewish community to use Roman governmental
machinery to enforce the Jewish courts' decisions.[9] In addition, the
Jewish communities of the empire did not suffer from governmental
efforts to fix prices in their markets or to control trade in which Jews
were engaged. The Jewish communities had the sole power to
regulate their own mercantile affairs.[10] In short, it would seem that the
vast edifice of imperial economic control that had been set in place
during Diocletian's reign and which had been modified in various
ways by his successors did not pertain in a fundamental manner to the
Jews.[11] Other exemptions that various classes of Jews obtained from
time to time and which were not enjoyed by gentiles of similar status
included immunity from the compulsory public services of *curiales*,[12]

---

[9] *CTh.* 2.1.10. It is clear that this law diminishes previous Jewish legal privileges which
were very extensive. However, even the reduced legal privileges that the Jews enjoyed
here were far greater than those enjoyed by other groups within the empire. See the
basic treatment of this by Jean Juster, *Les Juifs dans l'Empire Romain* (Paris: 1914), 2,
101-102, and A. Rabello, "The Legal Condition of the Jews in the Roman Empire,"
Aufstieg und Niedergang der römanischen Welt, II. (1980), 731-733, with a useful
discussion of recent scholarship. Cohen, "Roman Imperial Policy Toward the Jews,"
14-15, makes a good case for showing the continued privileged position of the Jews
relative to other groups.

[10] *CTh.* 16.8.10.

[11] Concerning imperial economic legislation see, for example, A. H. M. Jones, *The
Later Roman Empire, 284-602* (Norman, Okla.: 1964), I: 61-68, for the background
established by Diocletion.

[12] *CTh.* 12.1.99, makes clear that prior to 383 Jewish *curiales* enjoyed substantial if not
complete exemptions from the normal *onera* owed by members of this class. However,
the enforcement of these limitations was no easy matter and substantial numbers of
Jews seem to have avoided their obligations. Thus in 399, the emperor Arcadius
reissued this order, *CTh.* 12.1.165. Cf. Cohen ("Roman Imperial Policy Toward the
Jews," 15), who constructs a chain of events that is not sustained by the wording of the
legislation cited above. Honorius' act of 13 September 398 for the West (*CTh.* 12.1.158)

and exemption for the guilds of Jewish shipmasters from duties owed by non-Jewish shipmasters.[13] Finally, it is clear that prominent Jews enjoyed the *dignitas* of the senatorial aristocracy's highest imperial titles[14] and also the *dignitates* of the urban ruling classes.[15]

However, while individual Jews and the Jewish community within the empire enjoyed exemptions, immunities, and honors, we find Judaism to be the subject of rhetorical abuse in governmental acts. Thus, for example, Judaism is characterized at one time or another during this period as a "superstition", a "pollution", a "contagion", a "nefarius sect", a "feral sect", a "villainy" and a "turpitude". The gatherings of Jews are labeled "sacrilegious."[16] However, it is worth noting that while Judaism is attacked, Jews as a people are not attacked in the legislation.[17]

Several questions naturally arise from this situation. For example, why were the Jews, as descendants of a disgraced remnant that had been scattered throughout the empire by Titus some three centuries earlier, granted privileges in excess of those enjoyed by other Roman citizens of comparable social status?[18] Why did Christian Roman emperors, who appear to have been under great pressure from their influential and ecclesiastically high-ranking co-religionists to take vigorous action against the Jews, fail to crack down on this "superstition" and its adherents? Why was the Roman government satisfied with anti-Jewish rhetoric? Why did it eschew anti-Jewish actions?

Some historians have tried to explain the apparent contradictions that underlie an establishment rhetoric, both governmental and ecclesiastical, that degraded Jewish beliefs while permitting Jews to

---

cannot be proven to have caused *CTh.* 12.1.165, and contrary to the suggestion of Pharr (365, n. 294), *CTh.* 16.8.13, cannot be proven to be the "law that was issued in the Eastern part of the Empire" which is mentioned in *CTh.* 12.1.158 and is asserted to have caused its enactment.

[13] *CTh.* 13.5.18. This text in so far as it is usually understood to mean that the burden cannot be imposed upon the Jews as a group (see Cohen, "Roman Imperial Policy Toward the Jews," 13) only makes sense if a guild of Jewish shipmasters is intended. Clearly, if the Jews in question were not shipmasters, they could not do the service normally owed by such people. The remainder of the act may perhaps suggest that individual Jewish shipmasters were to be lawfully summoned for service.

[14] *CTh.* 16.8.8,11,17.

[15] Ibid., 12.1.99, 157, 158, 165; 16.8.2,3,4,24.

[16] Ibid., 2.1.10; 3.1.5; 16.5.44; 7.3; 8.1,6,7.

[17] The rhetoric is discussed by A. Erhardt, "Constantine, Rome, and the Rabbis," *Bulletin of the John Rylands Library,* 42 (1960), 306-307, whose conclusions sometimes go beyond the facts.

[18] For the earlier period see E. Mary Smallwood, *The Jews under Roman Rule from Pompey to Diocletian* (Leiden: 1976).

enjoy legal privileges.[19] One school of thought is summed up by
A. H. M. Jones, who emphasized the over-arching Roman respect for
long-established laws. He writes: "The Jews had since the days of
Caesar been guaranteed the practice of their ancient religion, and the
government shrank from annulling this ancient privilege."[20]

This Roman attitude identified by Jones as a causal element in the
development of imperial Jewish policy may perhaps explain various
acts that protected Jews in the practice of their religion. Several laws
make it clear that Jews are not to be hailed into court on the Sabbath
or compelled to do work in the public interest on the Sabbath.[21] Also,
Jews were not to be compelled to serve away from home where they
might not be able to observe their dietary laws.[22] It was even
mandated that particularly pious Jews were permitted to avoid various
types of governmental obligations that might offend their more highly
developed religious sensibilities.[23] Imperial legislation ordered that
synagogues might be kept up to the standard of their present condition. If one were destroyed or confiscated for ecclesiastical use, a new
one could be built to replace it. Indeed, these laws tend to sustain the
interpretation that the Roman government was willing to have Judaism and the Jewish community preserved.[24] The same may also be

[19] The basic treatment of these verbal attacks on Judaism by church writers remains S.
Krauss's "The Jews in the Works of the Church Fathers," *The Jewish Quarterly Review*,
OS, 5 (1892), 122-157; 6 (1893), 82-99, 225-261.
[20] *The Later Roman Empire*, 2, 948-949. Jones' view is quoted approvingly by Cohen
("Roman Imperial Policy Toward the Jews," 21).
[21] *CTh.* 2.8.26; 16.8.20.
[22] Ibid., 16.8.2.
[23] Ibid., 12.1.99. The latter part of this act has been the subject of considerable debate
although it seems merely to grant legal permission for a person who is "truly dedicated
to God" to find a substitute for the obligations that he owes to the state. Laws that permit
individuals to commute their public obligations by the means of substitutes or cash
payments are traditionally regarded by historians as special legislation intended to
benefit the rich and the powerful who for whatever reasons might want to avoid such
personal inconveniences as the military draft. It would appear that the rhetoric in which
this act is couched has enabled devotees of the lachrymose view to see this "privilege"
as an effort to hurt the Jews. On this point see, for example, the usually more reasonable
James Parkes, *The Conflict of the Church and the Synagogue* (London: 1934), 181. The
observations by Cohen in "Roman Imperial Policy Toward the Jews" (10-11), constitute
a sound critique of Parkes's failure to see the legal context of the act, but Cohen does
not recognize the fact that the right to find a substitute is in itself a privilege.
[24] *CTh.* 16.8.25,27. Much has been made of this legislation as evidence for official
governmental attacks on the Jews. See, for example, the material discussed by Cohen in
his "Roman Imperial Policy Toward the Jews" (13, n. 83). However, whatever efforts of
a legal nature that may have been made during this period to curtail the building of
synagogues would seem to have been abject failures. Thus it is clear that the Patriarch
Gamaliel as late as October 415 was still ordering or authorizing the building of new

said for an act of the emperor Constantius in 361 which reaffirms the immunity of synagogues from the obligation to sustain the quartering of troops.[25] Imperial threats against Christians and any others who would dare to harm Jews, their synagogues, or any of their other property, may also be seen as part of the defense of the Caesarian tradition.[26]

However, the exemption of synagogue officials from governmental service,[27] the imperial recognition of Jewish courts,[28] and the recognition of the Patriarch's broad powers (including his rights to tax the Jewish communities throughout the empire and to overrule the decisions of imperial judges), may suggest to some observers that the emperors were going somewhat beyond Caesarian guarantees.[29] Finally, while the practice was not directly tied to religious rights, it might be argued that imperial legislation permitting Jews to retain ownership of Christian slaves merely manifests the Romans' enduring desire to guarantee the sanctity of property rights.[30]

In ensemble, these *acta* exhibit an exquisite sensitivity on the part of Christian emperors to the needs of a rhetorically abused Jewish minority. Jones's emphasis upon the Roman government's putative reticence to annul ancient privileges hardly does justice to the thrust of this legislation. His explanation fundamentally fails to take into consideration the various economic immunities and also the honors

---

synagogues (*CTh.* 16.8.22). More impressive, however, is the archaeological record which has conclusively demonstrated the building of monumental synagogues in various parts of the empire during the period. See, for example, V. Corbo, S. Loffreda, and A. Spijkerman, *La sinagoga de Cafarnao* (Jerusalem: 1970). For a more general discussion of several synagogues including some of the archaelogical controversies see Cohen, loc. cit., 28-29; and A. Thomas Kraabel, "Social Systems of Six Diaspora Synagogues," in *Ancient Synagogues: The State of Research*, ed. J. Gutmann (Chico, Calif.: 1981), 79-91.

[25] *CTh.* 7.8.2. This act makes it clear that synagogues like other religious institutions are not to be burdened by the duty of having to quarter troops. This obligation fell on the homes of private citizens (*habitiones*) below the senatorial rank. It may be possible in this context that some Roman commanders who had been quartering their troops in Jewish homes were the subject of complaints to the government because the Jews claimed that their *habitiones* were in fact places of worship. This problem needs further research both in the Hebrew texts of the period and in the archaeological evidence. See, for example, the possibilities in Cassiodorus Senator, *Variae*, ed. Th. Mommsen, *MGH, AA.*, XII (Berlin: 1894), Bk. III, no. 45.

[26] *CTh.* 16.8.9,12,26.

[27] Ibid., 16.8.2,3,4,13. See the discussion by Cohen, "Roman Imperial Policy Toward the Jews," pp. 10-11.

[28] *CTh.* 2.1.10, and above, note 9.

[29] Ibid., 16.8.8,13,15,17,22.

[30] Ibid., 16.9.3,4.

that were received by the Jews both of the provincial aristocracies and in the senatorial class. In addition, one might legitimately register more than a slight demurrer as to the accuracy of Jones's interpretation that the Romans in the fourth and fifth centuries evidenced an enduring respect for ancient law. Such doubt is particularly strong with regard to the sanctity of religious privileges. Surely the Arval Brothers, the Vestal Virgins, the devotees of Mithras, and the keepers of the Sibyline books would find Jones's view of Roman respect for ancient law less than compelling. Indeed, at the same time that the Emperor Honorius ordered the sacred books of the Sibyline Oracle to be burned, he assured the Jews that on the Sabbath "no one of them shall be compelled to do anything or be sued in any way, since it appears that the other days can suffice for fiscal advantages and for private litigation."[31]

Although as recently as 1964 Jones pressed this interpretation to explain the survival of the Jews, Jean Juster had pointed out a half century earlier that if Roman respect for ancient law were a dominant element in policy making, then various pagan cults would have been preserved. By contrast with the legalists, as represented by Jones, Juster argued for a school of interpretation seeing the Jews preservation as the result of a subtle nuance in Christian theology that categorized the Jews as *testes veritatis*.[32] This position is ably summarized by Rabello, who writes that the Jews "by their presence alone proved the antiquity and genuineness of the Old Testament. . . .This being so, it was necessary to preserve Judaism, and there was no other way of doing this than by granting privileges to its adherents. But the same theology upon which this argument rested demanded that the status of the Jews be debased. . . ." Thus it is argued that the Jews "became virtually slaves" and every effort had to be made "to bring home continually the fact that the Jew was considered accursed and subservient to the Christian."[33]

This subtle theological nuance is made to do triple duty in support of the lachrymose interpretation. First, it explains the traditional view of imperial Jewish policy in the late empire. "Since the time of Graetz," Jeremy Cohen has pointed out, "virtually all Jewish historians have viewed the Christian Roman emperors from Constantine to Theodosius II as willing agents of a violently anti-Jewish Catholic

[31] Ibid., 8.8.8.
[32] *Les Juifs dans l'Empire romain*, I, 227-230, and n. 5, 227, which runs to page 229, detailing references in the writings of the church fathers concerning the notion of *testes veritatis*.
[33] "The Legal Condition of the Jews in the Roman Empire," 693.

clergy, who steered the emperors along a policy of active persecution of Jews and Judaism. . . .Fanatical emperors curtailed economic freedoms, religious and judicial autonomy, and basic civil rights. . . ."[34] In addition to accounting for the alleged continual persecution of the Jews, this interpretation highlights the redaction of the Jerusalem Talmud during this period as a monumental religious and social response demonstrating the great vitality of the Jewish faith in a time of adversity.[35] Finally, the Christian admission that the Jews testify to the truth of the Old Testament makes it clear that even the gentiles recognized God's covenant with Abraham as having taken place. The suffering experienced in the *Galut* or exile thus is seen to raise Jewish religious accomplishments to their heights while at the same time affirming the truth of the Jews' belief even in the theology of their adversaries.

Clearly, the explanation that the *testes veritatis* interpretation markedly influenced imperial policy can only be used to account for Jewish survival if indeed the "witnesses of the truth" were at the same time vigorously persecuted as claimed by Graetz and later adherents to the lachrymose view. The mere survival, much less the flourishing of the Jews, does not require the *testes veritatis* theology as an explanation. If there were not an effective policy of persecution at the same time as the theology was expounded, then virtually any combination of historical interactions might serve to provide insight as to why the Jews in the later Roman empire did not meet the same unpleasant fate that overcame contemporary pagans and heretics. Finally, it must be emphasized that the simultaneous existence of the *testes veritatis* theology with a vigorous persecution is merely evidence of correlation and not of cause.

These methodological quibbles, however, are not really necessary. Recent detailed study of imperial Jewish policy from Constantine the Great to the end of the Patriarchate has shown that there was no systematic and vigorous persecution of the Jews in the Roman empire. A reign by reign analysis of imperial acts shows that, on balance, the Jews were the beneficiaries of privileges, immunities, and exemptions, rather than of hostile policies. Whatever efforts the emperors did make which might perhaps be construed by doctrinaire adherents of the lachrymose view as anti-Jewish can, in large meas-

---

[34] "Roman Imperial Policy Toward the Jews," 1-2.
[35] See, above, note 7.

ure, be seen as attempts to protect Christians from a vigorous, powerful, and often aggressive Jewish *gens*.[36]

II

In light of the great fears expressed in the writings of the church fathers concerning the Jews and the abusive governmental rhetoric that appears in the *Theodosian Code*, it seems fair to suggest that neither imperial respect for the antiquity of Roman law nor recondite nuances of Christian theology, singly or taken together, adequately explains why Christian Roman emperors permitted and indeed even encouraged Jews and Judaism not only to survive, but more surprisingly, to flourish during the fourth and early fifth centuries. In the remainder of this study, I will look at three particular imperial acts in their respective historical contexts in order to suggest that the Roman emperors saw the Jews as an aggressive, well organized, wealthy, and powerful minority. I will further suggest that it was this view, which pervaded government circles and was shared by the church fathers, that played an important part in motivating the Roman emperors generally to withstand whatever ecclesiastical pressure was exerted to have the Jews persecuted.

During the conflicts that were ushered in by an *interregnum* of more than three months following the death of Constantine the Great, a band of Jewish missionaries illegally invaded an imperial factory where wool was woven for the production of military and civil service uniforms. The missionaries vigorously preached and proselytized among the female Christian workers who had been assigned there. The efforts of the missionaries were successful among the women who were imperial dependents, i.e. of servile status. Following their conversion to Judaism, the women refused to work in the government factory but remained in the area and practiced their new religion.[37]

---

[36] This is the major thrust of Cohen, "Roman Imperial Policy Toward the Jews" (1-29), and his analysis of imperial legislation is essentially accurate.

[37] We learn of this Jewish missionary effort from a rather cryptic description provided in *CTh*. 16.8.6. Scholars have frequently misunderstood this text and assumed that the Jewish missionaries "married" the women who worked in the factory. *Prima facie* the idea of finding enough missionaries available to marry the imperial dependents who served in the factory would be no small task and the use of marriage on a large scale as a proselytizing tactic would certainly be novel. However, more important is the fact that the operative phrase that has been misunderstood, *turpitudinis suae duxere consortium*, means to convert in context and not to marry, i.e. "to lead into the association of their turpitude" with *turpitudo* meaning Judaism and not marriage. The phrase *suis iungant flagitiis* is to be translated "unite in their villany" with *flagitium* meaning Judaism and *iungere* meaning to join or more precisely to convert. J. E. Seaver, *Persecution of the Jews in the Roman Empire 300-439* (Lawrence: 1952), 33, totally

It is unclear whether well organized and successful missionary operations on a reasonably large scale, such as the one described above, were common during the period under discussion here. It is clear, however, that there was a modicum of halachic authority available to sustain those who wished to engage in these activities.[38] The church fathers appear to have regarded Jewish proselytism as a serious threat to Christians and to the efforts of Christian missionaries to convert pagans.[39] Finally, the imperial government as early as the

---

misconstrued this text, and he is followed by Cohen, "Roman Imperial Policy Toward the Jews," 8. Yet another reason why it is highly unlikely that the missionaries married the Christian workers is that the latter were legally unfree, and to marry them would have impinged upon the freedom of the missionaries and especially of their children. Nothing in the subsequent events suggests that the legal status of the missionaries was in any way diminished by their actions. (See below, note 47 for the adjudication of this case, and concerning the status of the workers see Jones, *The Later Roman Empire*, 2, 836, where it is noted that during the "Great Persecution" Christians were made slaves of the imperial treasury and sent to work in the mills.)

So far as I have been able to ascertain, no one has addressed the question as to what reasons the imperial slaves who were employed in the government weaving factory may have had that led to their refusal to work after they had been converted to Judaism. Certainly there was no law that a Jew could not be a slave or an imperial slave, and there is no evidence of the new converts claiming that as a result of having become Jews they were no longer slaves. However, the imperial law did guarantee to Jews that laws would not be made or enforced that impinged upon the practice of the religion of the Jews. In this context it maybe of some importance that in producing uniforms for the imperial civil service and for the army, governmental factories made a cloth called *linostemus* which was woven from a combination of linen and wool (see *Mediae Latinitatis Lexicon Minus*, ed. J. F. Niermeyer [Leiden: 1957], 7, 614, for a long list of references). The wearing of garments made of such a cloth was of course illegal for Jews under Jewish law, and there were also prohibitions in the Mishnah concerning the tailoring of this cloth. A rather extreme interpretation of Kilayim ch. 9.8,9 may have been used as an argument against working in the factory by spokesmen for the slaves. The fact that the emperor required the slaves to return to work may perhaps be construed to indicate that a more traditional view of Jewish law prevailed at the imperial court.

[38] See, for example, W. G. Braude, *Jewish Proselytizing* (Providence: R.I., 1940).

[39] Christian fears are evidenced most systematically in the enactment of canons at frequent local, regional, and general church councils. A useful though not complete list can be found in Parkes, *The Conflict of the Church and the Synagogue*, 419. However, historical context is provided for these acts by the numerous polemics, sermons and letters penned by Church fathers during this period. A useful guide can be found in the articles by Krauss cited in note 19 above. Perhaps most impressive are the sermons of Chrysostom which attack the Jews from every possible direction. These I would suggest are only understandable if Christianity is seen as thoroughly embattled and not winning in the struggle for religious dominance. Parkes (loc. cit. 163-164), who believes that the Christian victory had already been won, can only explain Chrysostom's efforts with the lame suggestion that there was a "too close fellowship between Jews and Christians in Antioch." The similarity in much of the ecclesiastical legislation and in

reign of Septimius Severus recognized that at least some elements within the Jewish community were inclined toward missionary activity and thus made such efforts illegal.[40] Whatever may have been the state of imperial enforcement of this legislation prior to the Edict of Toleration is not clear, but Constantine found it necessary on at least three occasions to act against Jewish proselytism.[41] That Jewish missionary efforts, though illegal, should have been carried on to the extent that they worked their way through the immense red tape of the imperial bureaucracy and came to the attention of a busy emperor like Constantine is remarkable.[42] However, it is perhaps even more noteworthy that Jewish proselytism continued under Constantine's successors through the fourth and early fifth centuries despite an apparent pattern of escalation in the severity of penalties imposed upon both the Jewish missionaries and their converts.[43]

Perhaps an index to the aggressive nature of Jewish religious activity may be seen in the life-threatening physical attacks made by bands of rock throwing Jews on their former co-religionists who had

---

the attacks by the Church fathers has led some scholars to argue that these are *topoi*, i.e. stock phrases and sentiments that had long ceased to have any real meaning. However, in the century under discussion here, which hardly saw the unrelieved progress of Christianity in its march to victory, the Julien episode certainly was traumatic; there was not enough time for such cliches to take root. Rather, it seems more reasonable to suggest that the repeated laments and attacks by Christian leaders and councils on similar themes identify enduring problems. Later in the Middle Ages some problems relating to *topoi* may come to light. See, for example, Bachrach, *Early Medieval Jewish Policy*, 191, n. 14.

[40] Smallwood, *The Jews Under Roman Rule* (540-543), discusses imperial efforts to limit Jewish activity and suggests that they were ineffective.

[41] *CTh.* 16.8.1; 9.1; Sirmondian Constitutions, 4.

[42] Very useful insights into the problems of communications in relation to the Roman bureaucracy are provided by Fergus Millar, *The Emperor in the Roman World* (Ithaca, N.Y.: 1977).

[43] For example, the emperor Constantius is the first to single out those who convert to Judaism for punishment (probably in 352 while at Milan). He mandated that after the converts had been tried and convicted, their property would revert to the imperial fisc (*CTh.* 16.8.7). Gratian, in 383, withdraws the right of converts to make wills (*CTh.* 16.7.3). Apparently, converts to Judaism had avoided confiscation by transferring their wealth to their heirs. With regard to Jews who buy Christian slaves and then circumcise them, Constantius commanded the death penalty (*CTh.* 16.9.2). (Circumcision was of course the outward sign of conversion—perhaps even conversion by force.) Theodosius I equally wanted Jews who converted Christian slaves to Judaism to receive the appropriate punishment, but then he added the *desideratum* that no Christian slave should be permitted to remain in the possession of Jews for fear that the latter might convert them (*CTh.* 3.1.5). However, since Jewish ownership of Christian slaves was not illegal, Theodosius was merely emphasizing a preference. See on this point Cohen, "Roman Imperial Policy Toward the Jews," 11.

been converted to Christianity.[44] In this same vein, it came to the emperor's attention that crowds of Jews were accustomed to mock Christian symbols in public on the Jewish holiday of Purim and that in general, Jews were engaged in efforts "to throw into confusion the sacraments of the Catholic faith."[45] Seen within this framework, the Jewish missionaries discussed above who converted imperial dependents, breached the security of a governmental installation, and brought production to a halt, had probably been more aggressive than most.

The cessation of work at the weaving factory was an attack on the imperial government. The missionaries were guilty of numerous serious crimes, and the weavers were also guilty of several crimes. However, when the local imperial authorities learned what had been done at the weaving factory they took no remedial action to restore production. Similarly, the *comes sacrarum largitionum*, under whose jurisdiction all of the factories of this type throughout the empire were grouped, did nothing. Neither the missionaries nor the converts were punished.[46] Finally, the case was brought to the attention of the Emperor Constantius at Constantinople. On 13 August 339, Constantius made his decision known to the Praetorian Prefect, Evagrius, that: 1) the women are to be returned to work in the weaving factory; 2) Christian women [who are imperial dependents] in the future are not to be converted to Judaism; and 3) Jewish missionaries who in the future convert Christian women [who are imperial dependents] shall be subject to capital punishment.[47]

---

[44] *CTh.* 16.8.1. Erhardt's conclusion in "Constantine, Rome, and the Rabbis" (307) that violent actions by the Jews against their former co-religionists "cannot have been very numerous" cannot be sustained. The very fact that the emperor found it necessary to act officially in the matter suggests that it was sufficiently widespread to require his attention. The subsequent inclusion of the act in the Theodosian Code suggests that it continued to be a matter of imperial concern. Finally, such hostile and aggressive acts continued and were not unknown even in the barbarian successor states of the Roman Empire. For the later period see Bachrach, *Early Medieval Jewish Policy*. See pages 30-33 for urban violence in which Jews played a noteworthy role, page 56 for explicit attacks by Jews on their former co-religionists.

[45] Concerning Purim see *CTh.* 16.8.18, and 16.5.43 concerning attacks on the "Catholic faith".

[46] Each weaving factory within the empire was under the direction of a *procurator*, and the operation of the ensemble of factories or mills was under the direction of the *comes sacrarum largitionum*. The latter was a member of the inner council of the imperial government and headed on elaborate system of courts. See Jones, *The Later Roman Empire*, 1, 485-486, concerning the court system and 2. 836-837, concerning the factories.

[47] *CTh.* 16.8.6. Concerning Evagrius, see A. H. M. Jones, J. R. Martindale and J. Morris,

It is startling to realize that no punishments were ordered by the emperor for the missionaries or their servile converts despite the many crimes that had been committed. The women were not even ordered to abjure their new religion. Moreover, whatever punishments that were mandated were to be for violations of the law in the future. Finally, the emperor's order was minimalist in its scope and covered only unfree female imperial dependents working in government factories. This imperial decision must be considered one of extreme leniency; Constantius' major interest appears to have been getting the factory working again, since it produced military uniforms. It seems likely that this case was politically explosive, and thus the local officials and the *comes sacrarum largitionum* had refused to become involved. Rather, they sent it on to Constantinople for the emperor to adjudicate.[48] We may ask rhetorically, what kind of government defends its interests with such apparent pusillanimity? And may we not answer rhetorically that Constantius was not blinded to the power and influence of the Jewish community by the tears of "eternal self-pity characteristic of Jewish historiography" in the lachrymose mode.[49]

III

On 15 October 415 the Emperor Theodosius II informed Aurelianus, the praetorian prefect for the East, that he had for the second time sent an order to the master of offices concerning the Patriarch Gamaliel. According to the emperor's rescript, Gamaliel held the erroneous opinion that "he could do wrong with impunity". Theodosius ascribed Gamaliel's attitude to the fact that he had received many and various *dignitates* and *honores* from the emperor, including the title of honory prefect. However, Gamaliel had broken a number of laws among which were included the building of new synagogues, the exercising of judicial powers over Christians, and the converting of freeborn and slave Christians and non-Christians to Judaism. As a punishment for these acts, Theodosius tells Aurelianus that he has instructed the master of offices to take back the "imperial letters

---

The Prosopography of the Later Roman Empire (Cambridge: 1971), 1, 284-285; cf. Jones, *The Later Roman Empire*, 2, 1085, n. 53.

[48] Because the emperor Constantius handled the problem and because Evagrius was given the order, it is clear that the weaving factory was located within the area administered by the praetorian prefect for the East. A good guess would be Antioch since such mills were usually in large cities. See Jones, *The Later Roman Empire*, 2, 836, for the location of various installations.

[49] The quotation is from Salo W. Baron, "The Jewish Factor in Medieval Civilization," *Ancient and Medieval Jewish History* (New Brunswick, N.J.: 1972), 514, n. 55.

patent" by which the title of honorary prefect had been conferred upon Gamaliel and to make it clear to the patriarch that he will have to make do with the honors that had been conferred upon him earlier. In addition, any Christian slaves that illegally were in Gamaliel's possession were to be confiscated. Finally, Aurelianus is informed the master of offices was instructed that "if there are any synagogues in desert places which can be destroyed without sedition, he shall have it done."[50]

Like Constantius, who three quarters of a century earlier had evidenced remarkable restraint in the face of aggressive Jewish missionary activity, Theodosius' reaction to Gamaliel's arrogant flaunting of imperial law is cautious in the extreme. First, it is worth noting that Theodosius' initial effort to deprive Gamaliel of the imperial letters patent and to restrain his illegal behavior had failed; the text under consideration here marks the emperor's second effort. Some hint as to the situation's delicacy is indicated by the emperor's admonition to the master of offices. He is warned that the destruction of what surely were illicit synagogues in areas that were unlikely to be thickly populated, i.e. "desert places", should be carried out only if he were sure that his actions would not cause a revolt among the Jews.[51]

This text provides a picture of an emperor who has bestowed high honors on the patriarch of the Jews. The latter, however, seems to have repeatedly flauted the law while strengthening his own power to the disadvantage of Christians. A prior imperial effort to restrain the patriarch's illegal activities had failed, and now the emperor speaks of his fears of Jewish violence and perhaps even of revolt if adulterine synagogues in largely uninhabited places are torn down. However, despite the apparent seriousness of the situation, the emperor confined his punishment of Gamaliel to the loss of an honorary title. The patriarch was permitted to retain all of the other *honores* that the emperor had bestowed upon him previously. Clearly, there is not even the slightest effort to attack Gamaliel's position as leader of the Jewish *gens*.

Imperial worries concerning the patriarch's power may not have been ill-founded. In the early fifth century, the patriarch administered an empire-wide state within a state and had extensive influence with Jews living in the Persian empire. He controlled well organized legal

---

[50] *CTh.* 16.8.6.

[51] Cohen, "Roman Imperial Policy Toward the Jews," 13, n. 83, raises a question as to when and by whom the building of new synagogues was prohibited. He does not think that Theodosius I was responsible. By the reign of Theodosius II, however, there seems no reason to believe the prohibition was not already in effect. See, above, note 24.

and tax systems. At the local level in cities and towns throughout the empire each synagogue levied taxes upon the members of its congregation who paid the *aurum coronarium* to the patriarch's perigrinating agents. This system was so well developed that imperial officials remarked upon how exactly the Jews met their financial obligations as detailed in the patriarch's tax lists.[52]

The aggressive posture of the empire's Jews and the potential danger they posed, as well as the importance of Jews outside the empire, were the subject of widely known stories in the Roman world. Though perhaps apocryphal in detail, these stories appear to have been widely believed true by the common people. For example, the legend of Constantine's mother, Helena, as recorded in the *Acta Sylvestri*, depicts her as living in Bithynia with Constans and Constantius, two of the emperor's sons; there she is shown to have been very much influenced by Jewish rabbis. According to the story in the *Acta*, she repeatedly urged Constantine to become a Jew and, finally, she went to Rome with a group of rabbis in order to convince him to convert. The head of the Jewish community, presumably the patriarch, is said not to have participated because of illness. In any event, the rabbis debated the issue with Sylvester. In a close contest, Sylvester won, and not only Constantine but Helena and also the rabbis who took part in the exchange were as a result converted to Christianity.[53] Although this story highlights a Christian victory, the very fact that the emperor's mother and Constantine himself could have become Jews, were it not for Sylvester's inspired performance, cannot but have had an impact upon Christian consciousness. One could neither ignore the great danger posed by the Jews, nor could one ignore their closeness to the imperial throne. A comparison of this story with the tale of Little Red Riding Hood hopefully will make this point a bit clearer. The wolf ate the grandmother and was about to devour the young heroine when a hunter fortuitously came by and shot the beast. One might priase the hunter and be relieved that the

---

[52] Concerning the patriarchate see Jones, *The Later Roman Empire*, 2, 944-945.

[53] Ehrhardt, "Constantine, Rome and the Rabbis" (289 ff.), provides a satisfactory account of the text-problems and a useful summary of the Jewish element. His belief in the usefulness of this text insofar as it "may yet be the most informative with regard to Constantine as well as in other directions" is not widely shared. However, if Ehrhardt is correct, then rather than dealing with rumors and legend we are face to face with an historical situation. From the point of view to contemporary Christians who believed these tales, their truth is of little importance as to how they may have viewed Jews. From the point of view of the historian, by contrast, if these stories are true, then they strengthen the argument made here that the Jewish community was aggressive and influential and not merely perceived as such.

little girl was rescued, but no one, however naive, will come away from this story without an awareness of the danger posed by wolves.

In a similar vein, it was widely believed that the mother of the Persian ruler Shahpur II, who was frequently in conflict with Constantine and his son Constantius, was very much under Jewish influence and even accepted instruction from Rabba-bar-Joseph.[54] The tradition that Jews were very close to the center of power in the Persian empire may well go back to the story of Queen Esther.

Stories of this type may be multiplied as, for example, one told by John Cassian (d. ca. 432) in his very popular *Collations*. It concerns a Mesopotamian monk who, in a dream, saw an army of Jews vanquish an army of Christians in battle. Therefore, he had himself circumcised and became a Jew.[55] What is important in the context of this study is not whether these and many similar stories about Jewish influence and power are true, but that, as legends which may well have developed from misunderstandings of historical occurrences, they were widely believed during the period under consideration here. The formation of popular opinion need not be based upon the truth, and often it is not.

IV

Wealth was surely an index of power as viewed by the emperor and by local governments. The third text to be considered here strengthens this impression. Information reached the emperor Honorius, no later than the summer of 398, that most of the local governments throughout Apulia and Calabria were on the verge of bankruptcy. This disasterous financial crisis was precipitated, according to a report made to the emperor, by the failure of the Jews who were members of the local aristocracies in these cities to perform the public services and pay the taxes that were owed by all members of this class. The Jews, it appears, claimed that they were exempt from these burdens as a result of an earlier law, perhaps one issued by the Emperor Arcadius in 397. Thus, they had withheld their support for the upkeep of local government. Upon obtaining information concerning this financial crisis, Honorius commanded that whatever exemptions may have been granted in the East did not obtain in the West and that the local Jewish aristocracy in the municipalities throughout

---

[54] Ehrhardt, "Constantine, Rome and the Rabbis," 310.

[55] J. M. Wallace-Hadrill, *The Frankish Church* (Oxford: 1983), 400, discusses this story and concludes: "This story bore witness to the fact that Judaism was always on the march and always had its attractions."

Apulia and Calabria were to pay and perform all that was owed by members of their class.[56]

This text does not permit us to establish just how wealthy local Jewish aristocrats were in Southern Italy, nor can it be estimated how important Jews of this class were throughout the rest of the empire. However, repeated efforts by various emperors to assure that Jewish municipal senators fulfilled their obligations might well suggest that the descendants of the deportees whom Titus had scattered throughout the empire had not done too poorly in the diaspora during the three centuries following the destruction of the second Temple.[57] Those living in Apulia and in Calabria might not have been among the richest in these regions, but it is safe to conclude that, as a collectivity in each affected municipality, the public services and taxes owed by the local Jewish aristocrats were regarded as constituting the margin of urban financial solvency. Without the contribution of the local Jewish aristocrats the viability of local government was at risk. The imperial government, of course, was dependent for its survival upon the successful functioning of its municipalities. Thus we may suggest that in at least some areas of the empire, the Jews were the margin between imperial success and failure.

V

It has been suggested here that the wealth and organization of the Jewish community within the empire and probably beyond the frontiers as well, coupled with its tendency to be aggressive in the pursuit of its goals, was perceived by Christian Roman emperors from Constantine the Great to Theodosius II, and that these perceptions played an important role in the formation of an imperial Jewish policy. However, it is clear that any impression of wealth, power, and aggressiveness is at base comparative, i.e. in relation to whom was the Jewish community's position gauged by imperial policy makers?

One group that was closely related to the Jews but which was manifestly inferior in numbers, wealth, and organization was the Samaritans. The emperors appear to have counted the Samaritans to be a relatively negligible group and generally loaded them with disabilities while not giving them the exemptions, immunities and lenient treatment accorded to the Jews. However, it has been estimated that the Samaritans numbered in the hundreds of thousands. Their main concentration was in the rural communities of Samaria and in the city of Neapolis at the base of Mt. Gerizim. However, they also

---

[56] *CTh.* 12.1.158.
[57] See, above, note 15.

thrived in cities such as Sebaste, Scythopolis and Caesarea.[58] Despite imperial discrimination, Samaritans played an important role in municipal aristocracies and were awarded imperial honors.[59] Nevertheless, like the Jews, the Samaritans were not reticent to attack Christians when the opportunity presented itself.[60]

During the second half of the fifth century the emperors began to enforce anti-Samaritan legislation that had been enacted earlier but which apparently had been less than enthusiastically pursued in previous decades. That the emperors probably had underestimated the potential opposition that the Samaritans could provide is suggested by the bloody revolts of 484, 529, and 556. In the revolt of 484 the Samaritans were able to capture the city of Caesarea Maritima. It required an army commanded by the *dux Palaestinae* to recover the city and defeat the rebels. In the revolt of 529 the Samaritans captured the city of Neapolis. This revolt seems to have been even more widespread and required not only the troops of the *dux Palaestinae* but also Roman forces and their Arab allies. Although probably exaggerated, the numbers of dead are put by contemporaries and near contemporaries at between 20,000 and 100,000. The chronicler Malalas adds that 50,000 Samaritans fled to Persian territory and that 20,000 young Samaritans were delivered as slaves by the Romans to their Arab allies. In the revolt of 556 the Samaritans seized the city of Caesarea once again, slaughtered the Roman governor and captured the *praetorium*, i.e. the well fortified internal citadel where the imperial garrison was stationed. This revolt required the efforts of the *comes Orientis* to crush it.[61]

We should certainly be struck by the military power that the Samaritans could place in the field. We may also be surprised that it took substantial numbers of well trained Roman troops to crush the rebels. The *dux Palestinae*, for example, commanded thousands of

---

[58] The general works of J. A. Montgomery, *The Samaritans* (Philadelphia: 1907), and M. Gaster, *The Samaritans: Their History, Doctrines and Literature* (London: 1925) are still useful. However, much more up to date is the multi-author "Samaritans," in *Encyclopaedia Judaica*, 14 (Jerusalem: 1972), 726-758, with substantial modern bibliography.

[59] Kenneth G. Holum, "Caesarea and the Samaritans," *City, Town and Countryside in the Early Byzantine Era*, ed. R. L. Hohlfelder, East European Monographs, no. 120, Byzantine Series, no. 1 (Boulder: 1982), 66-67.

[60] Ibid., p. 67, with particular reference to Samaritan "bandits" who preyed on Christian pilgrims.

[61] The latest and best treatment of these revolts is by Holum, "Caesarea and the Samaritans" (67-70), although he may well underestimate the strength of the rebels in 556. Further study of the newly discovered *praetorium* at Caesarea will give us a better idea of the kind of military operations that were required to capture it.

regular troops including at least twelve units of *equites*, six *alae*, and eleven cohorts.[62] This was an impressive force. Moreover, we cannot regard as insignificant the numbers of casualties suffered by the Samaritans and by Christians, as well, even though the chroniclers have probably provided exaggerated accounts. In addition, it is of great importance that the Samaritan leaders Justas, in 484, and Julian, in 529, had themselves crowned as *basileus*, held games, and were regarded by hostile contemporaries as usurpers who sought to establish an *imperium Samaritanum*.[63] Clearly, this relatively small minority was capable of causing the Romans a great deal of trouble which did not end with the abovementioned revolts but saw the Samaritans give their support to the Persians. This would seem to have profoundly upset the balance of power in the region, and has been identified as a major factor in the later loss of Samaria to the Muslims in the seventh century.[64]

Of course, Roman emperors from Constantine the Great to Theodosius II could not have been aware of the bloody results that a vigorous anti-Samaritan policy would produce during the later fifth and sixth centuries. Thus, these emperors could not have benefited from the knowledge of how much trouble a minority which was relatively small and weak by comparison with the Jews could cause. However, it is likely that the emperors of the fourth and early fifth centuries were aware of the Jewish community's strength in the empire of their own day, and it is also likely that the fierce military opposition that Jews had provided in previous centuries had not been completely forgotten. The emperors and their advisors surely knew something of the cost to Rome of Masada, the revolts of A.D. 115-117, and of Bar Cochba. There were also some small and not so small revolts during the period under discussion here.[65]

Indeed, even revolts that were launched without the support of the Patriarch had the potential to cause more than a little trouble for the Romans. In 351, for example, a Jew with the name or perhaps the title of Patricius, and who seems to have had his base of power in the

[62] *Notitia Dignitatum*, ed. O. Seeck (repr. Frankfort am Main: 1962), Or. XXXIV.
[63] This is the major contribution of Holum's study, "Caesarea and the Samaritans" (67-70).
[64] See M. Avi-Yonah, *The Jews of Palestine: A Political History of the Bar Kokhba War to the Arab Conquest* (New York: 1976), 272-275, for the general picture.
[65] These minor revolts are somewhat controversial, not insofar as to whether or not they occurred, but as to their importance and causes. For our purposes it matters little whether the revolt mentioned by Chrysostom took place during the reign of Constantine or Constantius or whether the revolt of 351 was motivated by religious concerns or by secular concerns. Cf. Cohen, "Roman Imperial Policy Toward the Jews," 21-22.

mountains at Diocaesarea, seized that city and took the greater part of Galilee. With these initial successes, Patricius' troops took Lydda and Tiberias, apparently with popular support, and he may even have taken the important port city of Acre which is located forty kilometers north-northeast of Diocaesarea. In the course of this series of victories, Patricius seems to have had himself established as *rex Judaeorum* with the lands that he conquered constituted as a sort of *regnum*.[66] In this regard Patricius would seem to have been a forerunner of the wouldbe Samaritan kings, Justas and Julian, who were discussed above.

The Romans, however, were not prepared to permit Patricius to establish an unauthorized Jewish kingdom in Palestine by force of arms. Indeed, it is likely that the Patriarch, whose position surely was undermined by Patricius' successes, sided with the Romans. In any event, a Roman army of considerable size had to go into the field to win back imperial control of this newly established "Jewish king-dom." Even when account is taken for the propensity of contemporary and near contemporary chroniclers to exaggerate both the level of destruction and the loss of human life, it is clear that Diocaesarea was looted and burned although not totally destroyed. It can also be established that both Tiberias and Lydda were damaged. In addition, numerous villages and towns seem to have suffered. But too exact conclusions cannot be drawn since the archaeological evidence is often ambiguous and the written evidence may be suspect.[67]

Although Patricius' *regnum* fell to superior Roman military might, we must remember, and surely the imperial government was aware,

---

[66] The general treatment of this revolt by Avi-Yonah, *The Jews of Palestine*, 176-181, is basically accurate. See also Jones (*The Later Roman Empire*, 2, 944), who also considers this revolt to have been serious. However, cf. S. Lieberman, "Palestine in the Third and Fourth Centuries," *The Jewish Quarterly Review*, 36 (1946), 337-340; he tends to reject all the sources with the exception of Sextus Aurelius Victor, who discusses the establishment of Patricius in a Jewish kingdom of sorts. Moreover, Lieberman (340) recognizes the possibility that Patricius may be an honorary Roman title rather than a name. Jones et al. (*The Prosopography of the Later Roman Empire*, I, 637), conclude that Patricius was the name of the Jewish usurper. Cohen follows Lieberman's hypercritical treatment of the sources and also underestimates the importance of the revolt ("Roman Imperial Policy Toward the Jews," 22, n. 160). In *A Social and Religious History of the Jews*, 2 (2nd ed. New York and Phila.: 1952), 179, Salo Baron speculates unwisely about the cause of the revolt against Gallus while considering it to have been serious. On p. 398, he is correct in calling attention to the archaeological evidence that tends to support the written sources in indicating the seriousness of the revolt.

[67] Avi-Yonah, *The Jews of Palestine*, 176-181; Baron, *A Social and Religious History*, 2, 398.

that this revolt had not been a broadly based movement that involved all important elements of the Jewish *gens*. It did not have the support of the establishment.[68] Nevertheless, in the aftermath of the Roman reconquest, the imperial authorities recognized that it was necessary to station units of the Eastern field army throughout the newly subdued territory. This occupation in some areas lasted for several years and pinned down valuable manpower that could have been used productively on the other fronts.[69]

In the writings of Christian chroniclers during the later fourth and fifth centuries, there appears to have been manifested a tendency to exaggerate the scope of Jewish military success in the revolt of 351 and at the same time to magnify the threat of such victories to Christians.[70] In the same vein, an apocryphal story came to be widely spread shortly after the reconquest. It concerns the Roman general Ursicinus, who administered the occupation of Patricius' erstwhile *regnum Judaeorum* from imperial headquarters at Antioch. As the tale is told, Ursicinus received a delegation of Jewish dignitaries and rose up to meet them when they entered his presence. His courtiers were astonished at his actions and asked him why he paid such honor to Jews. Ursicinus, who is known through the writings of Ammianus Marcellinus as a military commander of the highest quality and as an honorable man, is said to have replied concerning the Jews "I have seen their faces as victors in war."[71] Such exaggerations or perhaps even accurate characterizations of Jewish military prowess in sources

---

[68] The suggestion by H. Mantel ("Studies in the History of the Sanhedrin," *Harvard Semitic Series*, 17 [Cambridge, Mass.: 1961], 242, n. 507) that "Patricius" is Aurelius' way of indicating the patriarch, is criticised on philological grounds by Cohen ("Roman Imperial Policy Toward the Jews," 22, n. 160). Cohen's philological point is well taken, but his argument assumes that a late Roman writer such as Aurelius Victor knew the correct term in Latin and that, in addition, subsequent copyists did not alter the original text. A far more telling criticism of Mantel's speculation is the fact that the Jewish establishment did not support the revolt (as is shown by Baron, *A Social and Religious History*, 2, 398) and that no punitive action was taken by the Romans against the Patriarch in the wake of the revolt. Concerning the aftermath of the revolt see Avi-Yonah, *The Jews of Palestine*, 180-181.

[69] Avi-Yonah, *The Jews of Palestine*, 180-181.

[70] Cohen does a good job of showing the tendency of Christian chroniclers to elaborate on the details of the revolt ("Roman Imperial Policy Toward the Jews," 22, note 160). This leads Cohen to believe that they are exaggerating. Whether their putative exaggerations are sufficient to discount the revolt as unimportant is unlikely (see, above, note 66) and beside the point here. Whether exaggerations or not, Christians who believed these reports surely would be led to worry about future revolts.

[71] Concerning Ursicinus and Ammianus see Jones et al., *The Prosopography of the Later Roman Empire*, I, 985-986. Ursicinus' interaction with the Jews is treated well by Avi-Yonah (*The Jews of Palestine*, 181).

of the later fourth and early fifth centuries would seem to reflect an atmosphere of rumor and legend that enveloped the society. It would be a mistake to underestimate the importance of such tales as representing the *opinio popularis*.

It does not seem unfair to suggest that when Christian Roman emperors of this period considered the possibility of pursuing a vigorous anti-Jewish policy such as those that were advocated by various church fathers, the spectre of problems not dissimilar to those which had faced pagan emperors of the past served to deter them. The history of Patricius' revolt in the mid-fourth century and of the Samaritan revolts in the fifth and sixth centuries clearly illustrates what kind of opposition minorities unsupported by the establishment in Jerusalem could present to an empire that was considerably weaker, following the crash of the third century, than it had been during the reigns of Titus, Trajan, and Hadrian.[72] In conclusion, I would suggest that an anti-Jewish policy was not pursued during the first century and a half following the Edict of Toleration because the imperial government had a sound understanding of political realities. It saw the potential cost, in terms of social dislocation, economic decline, and military conflict, that the Jewish *gens* could impose if it were attacked.

---

[72] The evidence provided by Jones suggests that during the Severan period the *dux Palaestinae* commanded two legions while in the early fifth century he commanded only one (*The Later Roman Empire*, 2, 1943). This weakened imperial military position in the Jewish heartland surely meant that both the Jews and the Samaritans could pose an even greater threat than was the case earlier.

18

The Image of the Jew in the Syriac Anti-Jewish Polemical Literature

A. P. Hayman
University of Edinburgh

This paper is the by-product of an attempt to understand the interaction between a Syriac-speaking ascetic, a stylite, and a Jew who, attracted by the stylite's reputation, came to observe him on his column.[1] The encounter took place somewhere between 730 and 770 C.E. in the village of Gousit, near Homs (Emesa) in Syria. The stylite, named Sergius, subsequently wrote up his side of the debate which he had had with the Jew. As Sergius sat on his column, what did he see when he looked at the Jew standing before him? What image of the Jews inherited from his Christian culture made it inevitable that this encounter would lead only to mutual incomprehension and bitter recrimination? Was there any possibility in the eighth century of a real debate between Jews and Christians in which either might acknowledge that the other had a point? These are some of the questions raised by the attempt to understand Sergius's document and, as we shall see, it offers some wholly expected answers, but also some surprisingly unexpected ones.

The image of the Jews in Syriac Christian literature depends, in the first place, upon a common Christian attitude which emerges virtually full-fledged during the second century C.E. in Justin Martyr's *Dialogue With Trypho The Jew*, the first anti-Jewish dialogue. But the Syriac tradition has its own particular flavour shaped primarily by two figures who seem to have possessed similar religious attitudes and also comparable, dangerous, rhetorical gifts, Ephraem the Syrian and John Chrysostom. Both these men were possessed of the type of mentality that could not stand opposition to what, for them, was obvious, and their resulting frustration boiled over into bitter recrimination against their enemies. In the torrent of abuse which they heaped on the Jewish people, milder voices such as the Persian

---

[1] See *The Disputation of Sergius the Stylite Against a Jew*, ed. A. P. Hayman, *Corpus Scriptorum Christianorum Orientalium (CSCO)*, vols. 338-9 (Louvain: 1973), 18.15.

Sage Aphrahat's and the *Didascalia's* Syriac version were swamped. It is the voice of Ephraem which dominates the earlier Syriac tradition of anti-Jewish polemic, while the later representatives of this traditon, particularly Sergius the Stylite in the eighth century and Dionysius bar Salibhi in the twelfth, have drunk deep from the poisoned well of Chrysostom's *Eight Homilies Against the Judaizers.*

Ephraem's contribution to this tradition has been clearly mapped out by Stanley Kazan in his series of *Oriens Christianus* articles (1961-65) entitled "Isaac of Antioch's Homily Against the Jews," though I fear that Kazan has not fully plumbed the depths of Ephraem's hatred for the Jews.[2] As for the influence of John Chrysostom's Homilies on the Syriac-speaking Church, it has yet to be traced. I shall make some preliminary remarks on the topic later in this paper. Aphrahat's milder but unfortunately not very influential attitude towards the Jews has been thoroughly studied by Jacob Neusner in his *Aphrahat and Judaism.*[3] Robert Murray, in his *Symbols of Church and Kingdom,* has contributed further valuable studies on the attitude of Aphrahat and Ephraem to the Jews,[4] while in a recent article in the E. I. J. Rosenthal festschrift, *Interpreting the Hebrew Bible,* J. G. Snaith has summed up the state of research on "Aphrahat and the Jews" to date.[5] Consequently, I will deal only cursorily with Aphrahat's contribution to the image of the Jews in the Syriac Church and will concentrate my attention on the legacy of Ephraem and John Chrysostom.

Not much can be said about the attitude of Syriac-speaking Christians to the Jews before the fourth century. Recent scholarship on this period has been steadily accumulating more and more evidence about the Jewish and Jewish-Christian input into the formation of the Syriac Church.[6] Perhaps in line with this input, the Syriac version of the *Odes of Solomon* reveals a pro-Jewish attitude quite out of line with that common in the fourth century after Ephraem.[7]

---

[2] *Oriens Christianus (OC)*, 45(1961), 30-53; 46(1962), 87-98; 47(1963), 89-97; 49(1965), 57-78.

[3] *Studia Post-Biblica*, 19(Leiden, 1971).

[4] *Symbols of Church and Kingdom: A Study in Early Syriac Tradition* (London: 1975). Especially Part I:1.

[5] *Interpreting the Hebrew Bible*, ed. J. A. Emerton and S. C. Reif (Cambridge: 1982), 235-250.

[6] See Murray, *Symbols*, esp. 277-347, and S. P. Brock, "Jewish Traditions in Syriac Sources", *JJS* 30:2(1979), 212-232.

[7] Ode 28 is perhaps the bitterest denunciation of Jesus' crucifiers, but these are not identified as Jews; see *The Odes of Solomon*, ed. J. H. Charlesworth (Missoula, Montana: 1977), 108f. Indeed Ode 29:8 identifies the Gentiles as enemies, which is

However, most Syriac literature coming from the period has little specific to say about the Jews. The third century *Book of the Laws of Countries,* attributed to Bardaisan, reveals no knowledge of Judaism beyond what almost any educated man of the time would possess, and certainly no polemical bias.[8] The *Epistle of Mara bar Serapion* does mention one of the standard anti-Jewish polemical arguments, but in a context which reveals no special anti-Jewish bias.[9] The third century *Acts of Judas Thomas,* so far as I can see, makes no polemical references to the Jews. Nonetheless, as Stanley Kazan has argued, the emergence of a common though independently derived tradition of anti-Jewish polemic in Aphrahat and Ephraem shows that the attitude to the Jews which was by the fourth century universal in the Greco-Roman Church must have been percolating through to Syrian Christians.[10] By what route we do not know.

However one source of the Syriac-speaking Church's attitude to the Jews is well-known, namely, the *Didascalia.*[11] This third-century Syrian document, translated into Syriac perhaps as early as 300 C.E., sprang from a Church that was clearly composed of both Jews and Gentiles but was having considerable difficulty in defining the boundaries between itself and Judaism.[12] Its attitude towards the Jews is, therefore, ambiguous. It repeats the standard accusation that it was the people of the Jews who crucified Jesus and that the destruction of the Temple signifies the end of Judaism:

> Fast then on the Friday, because thereon the People killed themselves in crucifying our Saviour.[13]

But unlike so much later anti-Jewish polemic, the *Didascalia* does not make a point of laying the blame for the death of Jesus on contemporary Jews. In fact its attitude to the Jews of its own time is remarkably friendly:

> For even though they hate you, yet ought we to call them brethren.

and

---

evidence for Charlesworth that the Odes comes from 1st century Palestinian Jewish Christians.

[8] H. J. W. Drijvers ed., (Assen: 1965).

[9] W. Cureton ed., *Spicilegium Syriacum* (London: 1855). Text, 46, trans., 73. Mara uses the same argument, in the same context, against the Athenians and the people of Samos i.e., evil eventually rebounds on the heads of its doers.

[10] *OC* 49, 73f.

[11] The most recent edition of the Syriac version is by Arthur Vööbus, *The Didascalia Apostolorum in Syriac, CSCO,* vols. 401-2 (Louvain: 1979). My citations are from R. H. Connolly's English translation *Didascalia Apostolorum* (Oxford: 1929).

[12] Connolly, p.xviif; but note the more cautious attitude of Vööbus, vol. 402, p. 28*.

[13] Connolly, 190, ll. 20f; see also 212, ll. 10ff.

> Thus then, because the People were not obedient, they were made darkness; but the hearing of the ear of you who are of the Gentiles was made light. Wherefore, do you pray and intercede for them, and especially in the days of the Pascha, that by your prayers they may be found worthy of forgiveness, and may return to our Lord Jesus Christ.[14]

The *Didascalia* accepts that the Jews, though mistaken, are loyal adherents of their religion[15] and, most remarkably of all, it tells Christians to mourn for the loss of the Temple:

> For their sake therefore, and for the judgment and destruction of the (holy) place, we ought to fast and to mourn.[16]

I know of no parallel to this sentiment in any other Christian anti-Jewish work. All other Christians gloat over the destruction of Jerusalem as a clear vindication of their position and God's definitive judgment on the Jews and Judaism.

The 23 *Demonstrations* of Aphrahat the Persian Sage were written between the years 337 and 344/5, not far from the present day Mosul. Ten of these *Demonstrations* constitute a specific anti-Jewish polemic. They are the earliest writings of this genre produced by the Syriac Church. R. H. Connolly argued that Aphrahat knew and used the Didascalia,[17] while Robert Murray states that "If Aphrahat had one book besides his Bible, it was probably the Didascalia".[18] Aphrahat's *Demonstrations* reveal that, like the Church which produced the *Didascalia*, his community was having great difficulty in defining the boundary between itself and Judaism. Moreover, the fact that Shapur II's fierce persecution of the Church was raging at the time made Jadaism quite an attractive bolthole for Christians who could not clearly see the difference between the two religions.[19] Aphrahat reacts to this situation not like his near contemporary Ephraem by demonizing the image of contemporary Jews, but by engaging in a vigorous polemic based on what the Jews and the Christians had in common—the Old Testament.

There seems to be no attempt on Aphrahat's part unfairly to represent the views of his Jewish opponents or to impugn their moral integrity. As Neusner says, "what is striking is the utter absence of

---

[14] Connolly, 184, ll.31–185, l.1, and 186, l.30–187, l.4. See also 185, l.10f.
[15] Connolly, 126, ll.16ff.
[16] Connolly, 186, ll.3-5.
[17] Connolly, p. xviii.
[18] Murray, *Symbols*, 337.
[19] A factor strongly stressed by Snaith—see note 5.

anti-Semitism from Aphrahat's thought".[20] However, because it presents Aphrahat's reaction to Jewish taunts that Shapur II's perse-cution of the Christians showed God had abandoned them, his 21st *Demonstration* "On Persecution," is indeed bitter. In it, Aphrahat lets fly comments like:

> Daniel also was persecuted, and Jesus was persecuted. Daniel was persecuted by the Chaldeans, the congregation of evil men, and the Jews, the congregation of iniquitous men, persecuted Jesus.[21]
> Jesus lived and went up from the midst of the darkness, and those who accused and crucified him will be burnt in the flame at the end.[22]

But compared to his contemporaries' remarks, this is very mild comment. And Aphrahat is more cautious even than the *Didascalia*. He does not attribute the blame for Jesus' death to all Jews and it is quite clear that it is specifically those Jews alone who accused and crucified Jesus who "burn at the end."

How do we account for the image of the Jew which Aphrahat presents to us? It cannot be caused only by the *Didascalia's* influence. Most other Syriac-speaking theologians knew this work and it affected their attitude to the Jews not a whit! Jacob Neusner thinks that Aphrahat "must be regarded as the example of the shape Christianity might have taken had it been formed in the Semitic-Iranian Orient, a region quite free from the legacy of pagan Greco-Roman anti-Semit-ism."[23] I am afraid that Ephraem proves this not to be the case. He is every bit as representative as Aphrahat of the original semitic stratum of Syriac Christianity. In the last resort, I cannot attribute Aphrahat's attitude to the Jews to anything other than personal temperament and inclination.

Ephraem, the most celebrated of the Syrian Fathers, was Aphrahat's younger contemporary. He spent most of his life in Nisibis, just inside the borders of the Roman Empire, but left in 363 when the Romans ceded it to Shapur II. He eventually settled in Edessa, where he died in 373. His prodigious output of hymns, sermons, and prose writings has been preserved in a multitude of manuscripts, unlike Aphrahat's work for which we have only one complete MS. Ephraem has no one work specifically dedicated to anti-Jewish polemic, though the latter part of his third *Sermon on the Faith* and his lengthy *Sermon on the Holy Festival of Palm Sunday* are close to this literary

---

[20] *Aphrahat and Judaism*, 5.
[21] *Aphraatis Sapientis Persae Demonstrationes*, ed. I.Parisot, *Patrologia Syriaca*, I:1, col. 973, ll. 1-4; Jacob Neusner, *Aphrahat and Judaism*, 107.
[22] Parisot, col.977, ll. 13-16.
[23] *Aphrahat and Judaism*, 5.

category.[24] The specific themes of his anti-Jewish polemic have been summarised by Stanley Kazan and discussed in greater detail by Robert Murray.[25] In this paper, I am not so much concerned about the intellectual content of Ephraem's arguments as with the image of the Jews which he paints for his readers and for those who sang his hymns in church.

Ephraem's gift is a poetic one. Hence the effectiveness with which he puts over standard themes in the Church's anti-Jewish teaching. Take the image of the Synagogue as a harlot, as depicted in the Sermon on Palm Sunday:

> With the honour of their hosannas, the Church of the Peoples eagerly awaited him.
> It worshipped the King of Kings, but the Harlot was enraged at him, the scab-ridden Synagogue.
> She did not accept him with rejoicing, as the prophets proclaimed to her. . . .
> The Harlot did not incline her ear to the youths and the children.
> She did not listen or prepare herself. . . .
> He wrote a writ of divorce and extended it to the Harlot, the Besmirched One.
> He took the veil off her head, modesty from off her forehead.
> He stripped the ornaments off her. . . .
> Like an adulteress and a harlot he drove her out, expelled her from her bedroom.
> And so she sits without a veil, with uncovered head, in disgrace.
>
> (ll. 319-387).

Ephraem then develops the image of the stripped-off garments as he expounds on the traditional theme of how, since she crucified Christ, Israel has lost everything: priesthood, Temple, Land. Earlier on he had painted the picture of Judaism as a ruined vineyard, as an empty shell which no longer has a reason for existence. The whole series of images constitutes a very effective attempt to depict the emptiness and worthlessness of contemporary Judaism. Later on in the Sermon, the average Jew is depicted as, quite simply, thick—he does not understand the Scriptures when he reads them:

---

[24] *Sermones de Fide,* ed. E. Beck, *CSCO,* vols. 212-3 (Louvain: 1961); "Sermon on Palm Sunday," ed. E. Beck, *Des heiligen Ephraem des Syrers Sermones* II, *CSCO,* vol. 311 (Louvain: 1970), 72-98. Beck has doubts about the authenticity of the Sermon on Palm Sunday but, even if it is not by Ephraem, it is closely influenced by him and definitely reflects his attitude to the Jews. I, personally, am not persuaded by the force of Beck's arguments.

[25] Kazan, *OC* 46, 95-98; 47, 89-92; Murray, *Symbols,* Part I:1.

The foolish one reads the prophets, but does not understand their
  words. . . .
For his intelligence is defective—'Israel's heart has become
  fat and its ears heavy' [Is 6:10],
So that he cannot understand what is written or comprehend what is
  said.

(ll. 486-506).[26]

Given Ephraem's overwhelming conviction that all of nature and
the Old Testament is full of symbols and types of Christ and the
economy of salvation, one can understand his intense irritation at a
people which refused to see what to him was so clear. His intense
detestation of the Jews is, in other words, in direct proportion to the
intensity of his faith.

Ephraem's image of Jews leads to an interesting perversion in the
narrative of Jesus' Triumphant Entry into Jerusalem. In Ephraem's
description, the crowds who acclaim Jesus are described as Gentiles,
not Jews.[27] The mental process by which this happens is clear. It
derives from the stereotype of the Jews as those who have always
rejected the Christian message, whereas on the festival of Palm
Sunday, the Church re-enacts the Triumphant Entry with the Christian worshippers playing the part of the crowd. It is, therefore, easy to
retroject the currect situation into the past and to assume that all who
react favourably to Jesus must be Gentiles, while those who reject him
are Jews. Hence the high priestly circle is transmuted into an
amorphous group, "the Jews," and we get statements like:

> By the Evil One he was tempted,
> By the Jewish People he was questioned,
> By Herod he was interrogated.

We have here, in Ephraem's first *Hymn on the Resurrection*, the
apogee of a process which begins in the passion narratives themselves—the attempt to shift onto the Jewish People as a whole the
blame for accusing and condemning Jesus.[28] But look at the company
they keep in Ephraem's poem—Satan and Herod! Not a mention of
the Romans.

This contrast between Jews and Gentiles in their reaction to Jesus

---

[26] See also *Des heiligen Ephraem des Syrers Paschahymnen*, ed. E. Beck, *CSCO*, vol.
248 (Louvain: 1964), 4.20-25.

[27] Cf. Murray, *Symbols*, 46.

[28] E. Beck ed., *CSCO*, vol. 248, 82; trans. by S. P. Brock, *The Harp of the Spirit* in
Studies Supplementary to Sobornost, 4 (1983) 30.

lies behind Ephraem's *Sermon on Jonah and Nineveh*.[29] Here the role of the unrepentant Jews is to serve as a foil for the Ninevites who astounded Jonah by responding favourably to his message of doom:

> Jonah saw and amazement took hold of him
> [But] of his own people he was ashamed. . . .
> He saw the uncircumcized who circumcized the heart
> But the circumcized hardened the heart

(ll. 901-8).

Ostensibly, in this sermon, Ephraem is contrasting the Ninevites with their contemporary Israelites. But within the typology of the sermon, Ninevites = repentant Gentile Christians, Israelites = contemporary unbelieving Jews. Thus, while Ephraem compares Nineveh to the Church (line 1137), in cataloguing Israel's vices—including the standard ones like child sacrifice within the community—he lapses easily from speaking about 'Hebrews' to speaking about 'Jews' (line 1161). The total impression created for Ephraem's listeners comprises a stark contrast between the righteous, repentant Ninevites (= Christians) and the reprobate, hard-hearted, inhuman Israelites (= Jews).

Ephraem's personal bitter animosity towards the Jews is nowhere revealed more clearly than in his 67th *Nisibene Hymn*.[30] Here, his anti-Jewish rhetoric sinks almost as low as anything produced by modern anti-Semites when he openly admits how much he hates Jews:

> Death did not crucify Jesus but the People,
> How hateful, then, is the People, even more than I am

He then proceeds to build up a terrifying image of Jews as less than human beings, the prime example being how Jewish mothers ate their children:

> It [the People] cast Jeremiah into a pit of mire
> It battered Naboth with stones like a dog. . . .
> The hebrew women, from hunger, ate their children. . . .
> The sons of the prophets and the prophets it destroyed and cast away.
> Elijah fled to heaven away from its rabid frenzy.

Ephraem even stoops to using a theme which recurs so fatefully in modern antisemitism, the "special smell" of the Jews. He confesses he is amazed that the Holy Spirit could dwell so long in a people which smelt so much:

---

[29] E. Beck ed., *CSCO*, vol. 311, 1-40.

[30] E. Beck ed., *Des heiligen Ephraem des Syrers Carmina Nisibena*, II, *CSCO*, vol.240 (Louvain: 1963), 106-108.

I am amazed at the Holy Spirit—how long she dwelt in a
People which stinks just like its way of life.

The gratuitousness of Ephraem's anti-Judaism is demonstrated by
the way in which he simply has to throw in anti-Jewish comments in
completely inappropriate contexts. When I read his beautiful *Hymn
on the Faith*, no.82, from the group of five *Hymns on the Pearl*, I was
stopped short by stanza 2.[31] The whole hymn is a marvellous analogy
between the birth of the pearl and the incarnation of Christ. But in
describing the pearl, Ephraem just has to throw in the following line:

Your symbol rebukes the Jewish girls when they wear you.

A similar uncalled for and bitter image occurs in the first of Ephraem's
Hymns on the Unleavened Bread.[32] Alluding to Jesus' blessing of the
children (Mk 10:13-16) and to his betrayal by Judas, Ephraem says:

The Good One embraced the crucifiers in their children whom he took
    in his arms and blessed.
One person [Judas] was a symbol of them all—
When he [Jesus] was kissed, they bit him with a thief's mouth.

It takes some imagination to create a picture of Jewish children biting
the one who lifts them up to bless them.
    Ephraem's incessant need to bring in anti-Jewish themes reveals
how deep-seated was his detestation of the Jews. There can be no
positives in Ephraem's theology without the inevitable negatives. So,
for instance, the refrain of the 18th Hymn on Unleavened Bread reads:

Praise the Son who gave us his body in place of the unleavened bread
    which he gave to the People.

The refrains of the 17th and 19th hymns in this series are wholly
negative:[33]

Blessed be he who rejected the People and its unleavened bread whose
    hands are defiled by the precious blood
Praise to Christ through whose body has come to nought
The unleavened bread of the People together with the People itself

Indeed, these refrains succintly present the basic theme for this set of
hymns each of which derives its force and power from Ephraem's
virulent rejection of the Jewish unleavened bread. The theme in the
17th hymn's refrain is fully worked out in the 19th, as Ephraem

---

[31] E. Beck ed., *CSCO*, vol. 154 (Louvain: 1955), 252; trans. by S. P. Brock, *Harp*, 32.
[32] E. Beck ed., *CSCO* vol. 248, 3.
[33] Refrain of the 17th Hymn in Beck, 31; of the 19th, 34.

attempts to combat the lure for Christians of celebrating Passover with
the Jews:

> The evil People which desires our death
> Entices and gives us death in its food

(19.5)

After references to the stinking smell of Jewish food reminiscent of
Nisibene Hymn 67, Ephraem reaches the height of his rhetorical
appeal to Christians not to eat Jewish unleavened bread:

> Do not take, my brethren, that unleavened bread
> From a People which defiled its hand with blood.
> Perhaps there cleaves to that unleavened bread
> Some of the defilement with which its hands are full.
> How unclean, therefore, is the unleavened bread
> Which was kneaded by the hands which killed the Son.
> Who indeed will take from that hand
> Which is entirely polluted with the blood of the prophets?

(19.16-17,19,21)

Ephraem then follows through his image of the unleavened bread
kneaded by hands stained with Christ's blood in this startling parallel:

> For the blood of Christ is mixed and dwells
> In the unleavened bread of the People and in our Eucharist.
> He who takes it in through our Eucharist, takes the medicine of life;
> He who eats it with the People, takes the medicine of death.

(19.23-4)

Finally comes an allusion to that fateful verse—Mt 27:25.

> For that blood which they cried out *should be upon them*
> Is mixed in their festivals and sabbaths.
> And he who takes part in their festivals
> The sprinkling of the blood comes to him as well.

(19.25-26)

The language, imagery and argument used here by Ephraem is, as
we shall see, very similar to that used by John Chrysostom in a similar
situation at a not very much later period, in Antioch. The argument
has two strings, rational and irrational. The rational argument is that
Christ has fulfilled the symbolism of unleavened bread so the symbol
is no longer necessary. But there is no doubt that the more powerful
argument is the irrational appeal to the deep-seated taboo against
eating blood. The image of Jews kneading the unleavened bread for
the Passover with hands dripping with the blood of Christ and the
prophets is truly terrifying.

The virulence of Ephraem's anti-Judaism can be partly explained—as it has been by Kazan and others—through the strength of
the continuing attraction which Judaism exercised over Christians.[34]
But it also owes a lot to Ephraem's own fiery temperament, for he
reacted to other threats to the Church (from Bardaisanites, Marcionites, Manicheans, etc.), with the same degree of virulence and abuse.
Unfortunately, Ephraem's approach met the Church's organisational
need to draw a firm line between itself and the Jews. As a result, by
the beginning of the fifth century, Ephraem's legacy appears everywhere in Syriac literature. I will quote two examples from opposite
ends of the Syriac Church's sphere of influence. Ephraem's attitude to
the Jews permeates the foundation legend of the Edessene Church,
The Doctrine of Addai. The earlier form of the legend of Addai, as
quoted by Eusebius (*Ecclesiastical History* I:13), has some mild
anti-Jewish statements. But by the time the fuller version was produced c.400 C.E., Ephraem's influence is clearly discernible. Thus,
the crowds who accompany Jesus on his Triumphant Entry are
distinguished from the Jews:

Upon entering Jerusalem they (Abgar's messengers) saw the
Messiah and celebrated with the crowds who were following him.
On the other hand they saw the Jews standing in groups and plotting what
they might do to him."[35]

The epithet *zāqūphē* (crucifiers), first used by Ephraem, is regularly
applied to the Jews, as in Addai's death-bed oration:[36]

"Beware, therefore, of the crucifiers and do not be friends with them,
lest you be responsible with those whose hands are full of the blood
of the Messiah."[37]

That such teaching could leap out of the realm of rhetoric into
action is proved in the *Chronicle of Edessa,* where bishop Rabbula is
stated to have taken a synagogue from the Jews in 412 C.E.[38] Addai's
farewell speech also clearly depicts the identity problem of the early
Syriac Church:

---

[34] Kazan, *OC* 47, 92.

[35] See *The Teaching of Addai,* trans. G. Howard (Chico, Calif.: 1981), 5. The Old Syriac
reading 'Arameans' instead of 'Greeks' in Jn 12:20 may reflect this belief of the Syriac
Church.

[36] See Howard, 25, 87, 97. Note also on 87 the theme of the Jews as the persecutors of
the prophets.

[37] Howard, 87.

[38] I. Guidi, ed., *Chronica Minora, CSCO, Scriptores Syri,* III.4 (Paris, 1903-5), 7 (item
LI).

Do not be a stumbling block before the blind, but make the path and road smooth in a rough place, between the crucifying Jews and the erring pagans.[39]

Life "between the crucifying Jews and the erring pagans" sums up very well how the official leadership of the Syriac Church perceived their situation.

At about the same time that the *Doctrine of Addai* was receiving its final form, the Acts of the martyrs under Shapur II were emerging from the Church in Seleucia-Ctesiphon. The martyrologies of Simeon Bar Sabbā'ē and his sister, Tarbo, were shaped under the influence of an anti-Jewish attitude close to that of Ephraem and including the epithet *zāqūphē*.[40]

The circumstances which led John Chrysostom in 386-7 to deliver his *Eight Homilies Against the Judaizers* are by now well known.[41] The strength of the judaizing movement which he faced and the power of Judaism's attraction in Antioch in the late 4th century have been clearly laid out for us, especially by Robert Wilken in his *John Chrysostom and the Jews* (Berkeley, 1983). A large part of Chrysostom's literary output is available in Syriac translation though nearly all of it is, as yet, unedited. Amongst this material is a manuscript in the British Museum (B.M. Add. 14,623) which contains extracts from his *Eight Homilies Against the Judaizers*. This is a palimpsest ms and the underwriting contains, very appropriately, polemical anti-heretical writings of Ephraem.[42] Clearly, the scribe felt that Chrysostom was updating Ephraem in the perennial battle against the Church's enemies. The MS is dated 822/3. That Chrysostom's anti-Jewish writings were available in Syriac much earlier than this is proved by B.M. Add. 14,604, dated to the 7th c., which contains part of his *Treatise Against the Jews and the Heathen on the Divinity of Christ*.[43]

Almost 350 years after Chrysostom delivered his homilies, Sergius the Stylite found himself in exactly the same situation *viz-a-viz* the Jews. Nothing seems to have changed in the interval. Towards the end of his *Disputation Against a Jew* (22.1), after Sergius has been

---

[39] Howard, 85.

[40] See Jacob Neusner, "Babylonian Jewry and Shapur II's Persecution of Christianity from 339 to 379 A.D.," *HUCA*, 43 (1972), 77-102.

[41] *Patrologia Graeca*, 48 (Paris, 1863), 844-942; trans. by P. W. Harkins, *The Fathers of the Church*, vol. 68 (Washington, D.C.: 1979).

[42] See W. Wright, *A Catalogue of Syriac Manuscripts in the British Museum* (London: 1870-2), no.DCCLXXXI, 5d.

[43] Wright, *Catalogue*, no.DCCLXI.1.

giving the Jew a hard time by quoting extensively from a now lost
Syriac version of Josephus' *The Jewish War*, the Jew throws in the
following comment, which stops him in his tracks:

> But now I am amazed how, after knowing [all] this, there are among
> you some Christians who associate with us in the synagogue, and
> who bring offerings and alms and oil, and at the time of the Passover
> send unleavened bread [and], doubtless, other things also. They are
> not entirely Christians, and some of our men have said that, if they
> were truly Christians, they would not associate with us in our
> synagogue and in our law.

Sergius' response to this is to accuse the Jews of using these Judaizing
Christians as a pretext for avoiding the strength of his arguments:

> So also you, wicked sons of impious fathers, have failed to wonder
> and be amazed at the signs of Jesus, and have seized on a pretext in
> weak Christians who, doubtless, are the children of heathen and their
> mind has not yet been cleansed from the fear of their fathers' idols.
> Or they are the children of Hebrews, and the former custom still
> prevails over them" (22.5).

There may well have been Jewish converts to Christianity
amongst the Judaizers as Sergius suggests, for we have evidence that
many Jews in Syria converted to Christianity in the late 7th century.[44]
Presumably, conversion was a long term result of the Arab invasion.
Jews who had experienced a brief period of autonomy in Jerusalem
after the Persian conquest of 614 were doubly depressed by its loss.
Conversion offered some balm for their injured hopes.[45] However, the
way the Jew in Sergius' *Disputation* speaks about the Judaizers
suggests that at least the bulk of them were Gentiles.

Sergius reacts to the threat of Judaizing Christianity by reinforcing
the arguments derived from the general Syriac anti-Jewish tradition
with fresh material imported from Antioch. His anti-Jewish polemic
has a much broader range than that of Aphrahat and Ephraem. Besides
the Bible, he utilises a Testimony Book which also appears in the 5th
century Greek *Discussion of St. Silvester*.[46] He uses the Syriac
version of Josephus' *War of the Jews* together with Eusebius' *Ecclesiastical History* and *Chronicle*. He represents a Syriac Church which
is now wide open to the influence of Greco-Roman Christianity and
which has travelled a long way from its original semitic base. Pre-

---

[44] Cf. Brock, *JJS* 30:2(1979), 230.

[45] See M. Avi-Yonah, *The Jews of Palestine* (Oxford: 1976), 257-276.

[46] See Hayman, *Disputation of Sergius the Stylite, CSCO*, vol. 339, pp.9*-32*.

cisely the same set of influences played on Dionysius Bar Salibhi when he wrote his treatise *Against the Jews* in 1166/7.[47]

The image of the Jews in both Chrysostom's *Homilies* and Sergius' *Disputation* is created from the prophets' denunciations of the ancient Israelites and is then applied, via the Christ-killing charge, to contemporary Jews. For example, Sergius cites Is 1:15: "When you spread forth your hands, I will avert my eyes from you; and even though you multiply prayer, I will not listen, for your hands are full of blood." And then he continues:

> Now then, you think that the blood of which Isaiah says your hands are full, is the blood of bulls and sheep. The prophet contended with your fathers whose hands were full of the blood of the prophets and the righteous, but he intended the prophecy for you, the children of sinners on whose hands the blood of Christ is spotted.
>
> (22.13).[48]

When Chrysostom, Sergius and Dionysius make such accusations, they do not just talk in historical terms of the prophets' contemporaries or those of Jesus. They use the second person or even, as in Sergius' case, the second person singular. Sergius writes as if he was actually addressing the Jew standing in front of him! The result is that contemporary Jews can be described in the most slanderous terms. Thus Chrysostom:

> Shall I tell you of their plundering, their covetousness, their abandonment of the poor, their thefts, their cheating in trade? The whole day will not be enough to give you an account of these things.
>
> (*Homily* 1.7.1)

And Sergius:

> Sergius [said]: You have forgotten what I told you—that you cleave to unclean and defiled sorcerers, and you are accomplices in their polluted deeds with adulterers, fornicators, murderers, and all evil-doers.
>
> (15.19).

An accusation repeatedly stressed is that Jews are childkillers.[49]

---

[47] J. de Zwaan ed., (Leiden: 1906). An unfortunately rather poor English translation of this text was produced by R. H. Petersen in 1964 (Ph.D. thesis, Duke University). For the relationship between Sergius' *Disputation* and Dionysius' *Treatise*, see Hayman, *CSCO*, vol. 339, pp. 22*-25*.

[48] Comparable material can be found throughout Chrysostom's first *Homily* and in Dionysius' *Treatise*, 3.5-6.

[49] Cf. Chrysostom, *Homily* 1.6.7-8, Sergius, *Disputation*, 5.6, Dionysius, *Treatise*, 8.4.

This starts from Old Testament texts like Ps 106:36, becomes part of a general image of contemporary Jews based on these OT denunciations, and as we all know, after many centuries, leaves the realm of rhetoric and becomes clothed in terrifying reality in the Christian mind. The ritual murder accusation had been gestating in the Christian imagination for a long time before the Middle Ages.

Once this image of contemporary Jews is created by Chrysostom and Sergius, it is turned to the specific task of keeping Christians out of the synagogue. Thus Chrysostom, *Homily* 1.7.5:

> Tell me this. If a man were to have slain your son, would you endure to look upon him, or to accept his greeting? Would you not shun him as a wicked demon, as the devil himself? They slew the Son of your Lord; do you have the boldness to enter with them under the same roof?

And Sergius:

> For would not your wrath be all the more aroused against a man who had killed your son, if, when he drew near to you and you saw on his fingers the blood of your beloved, yet he, in his madness, thought he could appease you? So also you, by your prayer and your sacrifices, arouse the wrath of God against you and against him who associates with you.
>
> (22.13).[50]

The problem with this image which Chrysostom and Sergius created for their hearers and readers, is that it does not conform to any observable social reality. In fact its very truth is denied when they seek to deploy a different line of argument against the Jews. Chrysostom, followed by Jacob of Sarug in the early 6th century[51] and by Sergius and Dionysius, argues throughout his homilies that in Old Testament times, when the Jews regularly broke the Law, God never deprived them of kingship, priesthood, Temple and Land. But now that they keep the Law, he has deprived them of everything. The reason can only be that they are suffering for crucifying Christ:

> When you Jews lived the life of ungodliness before, you got every-

---

[50] Revised translation from that in my edition, 76, where a line has been accidentally dropped out. The following paragraph (22.14) reiterates the point even more explicitly:
And as again, if a man comes with the murderer of your son to make supplication to you wishing to please the murderer; and you, because you see the blood on the murderer's hands, treat with contempt the gifts which they offer you, and look upon them both with one threatening glance full of wrath and indignation; so every Christian who offers anything in your synagogue is regarded before God.

[51] *Homily Five Against the Jews*, ed. M. Albert, *Jacques de Saroug: Homélies contre les Juifs, Patrologia Orientalis*, vol. 38:1 (1976), 137-159.

thing; now, after the cross, although you seem to be living a more
moderate life, you endure a greater vengeance and have none of your
former blessings.

(Homily 6.4.7)

And Sergius:

But because you have seen that the nations have hated the worship of
idols and turned to Christ, you (for your part) have turned to establish
the Law, which in its time you hated, even as you will always be
perverse

(9.4)

Both Sergius and John Chrysostom seem to be unaware that there is
any inconsistency between this line of argument and their attempt to
depict Jews as lawbreakers, magicians, potential murderers, etc.
Chrysostom can even blandly state:

What could be more pitiable than those who provoke God not only by
transgressing the Law but also by keeping it

(Homily 1.2.3)

This second line of argument's importance, for our purposes, is
that it reveals how when they needed, these anti-Jewish polemicists
could recognize that Jews were actually quite unlike their Old
Testament forbears as described by the prophets. And of course, it was
the Jews' adherence to the Law which attracted the Judaizing Christians. Through the distorted lens of this argument, we can see behind
the rhetorical fantasies of our polemicists to the real image of Jews in
Syrian society. What was provoking the wrath of John Chrysostom,
Sergius and the like, was not that Jews were going round sacrificing
children and consorting with demons, but that they were actually
keeping the Old Testament Law and attracting Christian attention for
doing so. Maybe the Judaizers could spot the inconsistency in the
arguments aimed at them. They certainly do not seem to have taken
much notice of the image of the Jews presented to them by Chrysostom and his followers. So here we have the unexpected answer to our
initial question about the image of the Jew in Syrian society; outside
the circles of the ecclesiastical elite, Jews and Judaism were perceived favourably by ordinary Christians.

To fully substantiate my thesis here I would have to pass from
literary interpretation to historical analysis. In particular, it would be
necessary to bring in the increasingly abundant archaeological and
epigraphical evidence from places like Sardis and Aphrodisias. Indeed, this evidence leads me to suggest that the group known before
the 4th century as the *theoseboi* (the god-fearers), the outer circle of
gentile adherents to the synagogue, though nominally Christian from

the 5th century onwards, in fact continued their practices in another guise, that of judaizing Christianity. But that would be another paper. At the moment, I simply wish to point out that the Syriac anti-Jewish polemical literature sets out to tell us one story about the Jews, but inadvertently ends up telling us another—one which in fact conforms much better to the available non-literary data.

A sidelight on this picture of Judaism's powerful attraction for Christians and of Christian propaganda's inability to counteract its pull is provided by Isaac of Antioch's *Homily Against the Jews*. This comes from the first half of the fifth century and is, as Kazan remarks, "in language and tone strongly reminiscent of the polemic of Ephraem Syrus."[52] What is striking about this Homily, however, is the marked inferiority complex which Isaac reveals over against Jews. They present a powerful, self-confident, particularistic image which he deeply resents:

> I have judgement with Jacob,
> And a discourse with the Jews.
> If we all have one Father,
> Why should anyone feel superior to the nations?
>
> (ll. 2-5)
>
> Through the law you (appear) superior to me,
> Through circumcision and the Sabbath which you observe.
>
> (ll. 34-5)

Isaac's reaction is to demonstrate from the Old Testament how God prefers the underdog. Isaac does not confront the image of the humbled Jew, cowering under the weight of the Theodosian Code, but a powerful elder brother who refuses to share his birthright.

One interesting image which Isaac uses is that of Judaism as a sealed, but empty, moneybag:

> There is a sealed moneybag which is empty.
> Is [this] not you, O Jews?
> The treasure is dug out from you.
> Why do you use the seal?
>
> (ll. 289-292)

The seal is circumcision. But this has for Isaac a continuing value as he explains further on:

> For your shame do you carry your stamp,
> That you may indicate to me what you were.

---

[52] *OC* 47, 93f.

From your stamp I recognize
That something great was [once] hidden in you

(ll. 357-360)

Here we see that argument which, above all others, was to keep a space for Judaism to exist within the Christian realm.

In conclusion, I would like to emphasize two points. When the Syriac Christian writers construct their image of "the Jew" they show no awareness that contemporary Jews are any different from biblical Israelites. Not one of them knows anything at all about the specific concerns of rabbinic Judaism. Hence their inability to comprehend how Judaism can keep going after the loss of the Temple. It is only top-rank Christian scholars like Origen and Jerome or the Jewish-Christian sect of the Nazarenes who know that contemporary rabbinic Judaism is not the same as the religion of the Old Testament period.[53] But the Syriac writers never reached this level of cultural awareness. Their view of Judaism was shaped by the Bible (both Testaments), not by intimate contact with contemporary Jewish scholars. Of course, they are not alone in this. The same is exactly true of the average Christian clergyman in present-day Scotland, despite the easy accessibility in our culture of accurate sources of information about the Jews and Judaism after 70.

The second point I would like to emphasize is Sergius the Stylite's testimony that ordinary Syrian Christians, even in the eighth century, could still not distinguish clearly between Judaism and Christianity. We can trace this uncertainty about the exact boundary between the two religions virtually from the emergence of the Syriac-speaking Church right down to its effective demise as a major cultural force in the Middle East. The intellectual elite, the theologians, clergy, and the shock troops of the Syriac Church, the monks, knew where the boundaries lay. But the ordinary laypeople did not. They appear to have taken a more tolerant attitude to the differences between the two religions despite all the attempts of the Christian elite to create an image of the Jews which would frighten laypeople from having any contact with them. The layman, as quoted in Sergius's *Disputation*, says:

If Christianity is good, behold, I am baptised as a Christian. But if Judaism is also useful, behold, I will associate partly with Judaism that I might hold on to the Sabbath.

(22.15)

---

[53] See A. F. J. Klijn & G. J. Reinink, *Patristic Evidence for Jewish-Christian Sects*, (Leiden: 1973), 220-225.

Sergius characterises this attitude as *šānyūthā* (madness) and *hasīruth re'yānā* (lit. deficiency of intelligence). We, from our 20th century perspective, might choose different adjectives to describe such an attitude.

This persistence of a rather easy-going, tolerant attitude to religious differences amongst the uneducated masses in Syria probably goes a long way to account for the speed with which a previously Christian majority was so rapidly islamicized after the battle of Yarmuk. Since even the Christian elite at first perceived Islam as yet another Judeo-Christian heresy, it is no surprise that this syncretistically inclined laity opted so quickly for the evident material advantages of conversion to Islam.[54] But when it did so, there was left behind in the Church that very elite in which anti-Jewish attitudes were so dominant.[55] The image of the Jew created by Ephraem and John Chrysostom won out through force of historical circumstances, not through its own inherent power. And even in our own time, this image partly conditioned the Eastern Churches' response to the Second Vatican Council's attempt to liberalise the official standpoint of the Church toward the Jews.[56] An earlier, more tolerant attitude, had been completely buried.

---

[54] See Daniel J. Sahas, *John of Damascus and Islam* (Leiden: 1972).

[55] For the social composition of the Syriac Church after the Muslim conquests see B. Spuler, "Syrian Christians Amidst Their Muslim Compatriots", in *A Tribute to Arthur Vööbus*, ed. R. H. Fischer (Chicago: 1977), 370.

[56] See *Commentary on the Documents of Vatican II*, ed. Herbert Vorgrimler (London: 1969), vol. 3, 48f.

19

The Restoration of Israel in Biblical Prophecy: Christian and Jewish Responses in the Early Byzantine Period

Robert L. Wilken
University of Notre Dame

For the Jew and the Christian the land of Israel is at once a spiritual ideal and a geographical fact. The two peoples, however, have profoundly different sensibilities about space, and the historical experience of living in the land has marked Christians and Jews in dissimilar ways. In the past 100 years when the idea of a Jewish homeland in Palestine and the establishment of the state of Israel have been so much a part of western consciousness, the link between the Jewish people and the land has seemed inseparable. From the early stirrings of the *Ḥibbat Zion* (Lover of Zion) societies in eastern Europe in the nineteenth century to the young Americans who move to new settlements on the west Bank today, the idea of settling the land, of living in the land, of cultivating the land has stirred the minds and hearts of Jews deeply. The charter of a society in Vilna, in 1881-2, reads: "The aims of the *Oḥavei Zion* society are to spread the idea of the settlement of *Eretz-Israel* for purposes of working its land among the sons of the Diaspora and . . . to put the idea of resettlement of Eretz Israel into practice, to remove it from the realm of ideas into that of reality."[1]

For the Christian the relation between the historical fact and the spiritual ideal is more tenuous. Yet it is evident to any visitor to the middle East that Christianity has a peculiar relation to the lands now occupied by the state of Israel, the West Bank and the Sinai. Christian tourists, often exceeding 500,000 a year, come from all parts of the world to visit those "holy places" associated with the life of Jesus: Bethlehem, Nazareth, the church of the holy Sepulchre, the Mount of Olives, the Sea of Galilee. However few realize or readily comprehend that Christianity's role in Palestine is not restricted to the time

---

[1] David Vital, *The Origins of Zionism* (Oxford: 1975), 151.

of Jesus and Christian origins, though in other ways they may be well
informed about the Middle East. The Christian religion has a long
history in Palestine. It is a history both of indigenous communities
whose fortunes have been linked to the many conquerors (Arab,
Christian, Turk, and Jew) and of ethnic communities from other parts
of the world (Copts from Egypt, Armenians, Syrians, Ethiopians,
Russians, and so on). Some of these have continuous histories from
antiquity to the present. Today Arab Christian communities, whose
histories reach back centuries, exist in Jerusalem, Bethlehem, Nazareth and elsewhere.[2]

For the three hundred years between the end of the fourth century
and the Arab conquest in the middle of the seventh (638 C.E.),
Palestine was a Christian country. During that period Christians first
began to think of the land of Israel as the "holy land" (a term that
originally gained currency among Christians but later passed into
general use to refer to Palestine). During this period the city of
Jerusalem was elevated to the status of a patriarchal see, overshadowing the old metropolitan city of Caesarea. Further, it acquired political
as well as religious significance in an empire ruled from Constantinople by a Christian emperor.[3]

The period of Byzantine (Christian) rule in Palestine is significant
in three areas: first, as Israeli archaeologists have shown in recent
years,[4] in the history of the land of Israel itself; second, in the history

---

[2] A fourteenth century French pilgrim, Ogier VIII, Seigneur d'Anglure, for example,
reports that the village of Beit Jala (two miles from Bethlehem) was populated mainly
by Christians. He reports that on his trip to the Sinai he stopped in Beit Jala to buy wine.
"We laid in a supply of wine which was delivered by the consul at Jerusalem for,
because the Saracens drink no wine, the pilgrims can get it only at a very great danger
and at a high price. Beit Jala is populated more by Christians than by Saracens. The
Christians work the vineyards where these good wines grow and you may be sure that
one can properly call them good wines." See Roland A. Browne, *The Holy Jerusalem
Voyage of Ogier VII, Seigneur D'Anglure* (Gainesville: 1975). Beit Jala is still a
Christian village and its people grow grapes and produce wine.
[3] For the importance of Palestinian Christianity in the Byazantine period, see most
recently Lorzeno Perrone, *La Chiesa di Palestina e le Controversie Cristologiche, Dal
concilio di Efeso (431) al secondo concilio de Constantinopoli (553)*, Teste e ricerche di
Scienze religiose pubblicati a cura dell'Istituto per le Scienze religiose di Bologna, No.
18, (Brescia: 1980); also E. Honigmann, "Juvenal of Jerusalem, *Dumbarton Oaks
Papers* 5 (Washington: 1950), 209-270.
[4] See for example, A. Ovadiah, *Corpus of the Byzantine Churches in the Holy Land*
(Bonn: 1970); Abraham Negev, *Tempel, Kirchen und Zisternen. Ausgrabungen in der
Wueste Negev* (Stuttgart: 1983); Vasilios Tzaferis, *The Christian Holy Place of Gergesa
(Kursi)*, to appear in the Israeli Department of Antiquities publication *Atiqoth*.
Qadmonioth, the Quarterly for the Antiquities of *Eretz-Israel* and Bible Lands has
regular articles dealing with the archaeology of Byzantine Palestine. See particularly

of Christian life and thought (St. Euthymius and St. Sabas gave Palestinian monasticism its distinctive character and made Palestine the rival of the older monastic centers, Egypt and Syria);[5] third, in the way Christians viewed Jews and Jews viewed Christians—the topic of this conference. For the developments in Palestine during this period injected a new element into relations between Christians and Jews. The old symbols of the Bible, the ancient history of Israel and the city of Jerusalem all acquired political overtones. For the first time in its history, Christianity had more than a spiritual interest in the land of Israel and the topography of biblical history.

I

In the fifth century of the common era a Jew living on the island of Crete claimed "he had been sent from heaven" to lead the Jews to the land of Israel. According to the Christian historian Socrates Scholasticus, who records the story, he took the name of Moses and traveled around the island of Crete preaching to the Jews in the cities. "He promised to lead them through a dry sea into the land of promise (εἰς τὴν γῆν τῆς ἐπαγγελίας)." Many were convinced, and some sold their property and neglected their businesses. When the appointed day arrived, he directed his followers to a promontory overlooking the sea and ordered them to fling themselves into the waters below. Those who arrived first leaped off the cliff only to be dashed against the rocks or to be drowned in the sea. Some were rescued, according to Socrates, by Christian fishermen. The imposter, however, slipped away, and when the people realized they had been deceived, they abandoned their Jewish ways and embraced Christianity. (Socrates, *Historia Ecclesiastica* 7.38).

No doubt this story was intended to demonstrate the superiority of Christianity over its rivals. Yet that is not sufficient reason to deny its veracity. Socrates is a careful historian and his information is often corroborated by other sources and historians of this time. In this case, however, he is the sole witness. Yet whatever the historical kernel behind the story, it indicates that a Christian historian in the fifth century thought it reasonable that Jews wanted to return to the land Israel. What Socrates tells us may simply be an isolated event, a sad

---

Vol. 9, No. 1 (1976) devoted exclusively to Byzantine churches in *Eretz Israel*. Also Yoram Tsafrir and Yizhar Hirschfeld, "The Church and Mosaics at Horvat Berachot, Israel," *Dumbarton Oaks Papers* (Washington: 1979), 291-326.
[5] On the monks of Palestine during the Byzantine period, See Derwas Chitty, *The Desert a City: An Introduction to the Study of Egyptian and Palestinian Monasticism under the Christian Empire* (Crestwood New York: 1966).

tale of an imposter who deluded gullible folk, but it may point to more.

The key lies in the phrase "promised land." When used by Jews at this time, this term referred to the land of Israel—to Palestine in the terminology of the Roman world. Early in the fifth century a Roman prefect in Gaul by the name of Dardanus, had written to Jerome asking the meaning of the phrase *"terra repromissionis"* (ep. 129). "The Jews assert that it is this land [the land of Palestine] that is the land of promise" says Jerome in his response (ep. 129.3). He states that they believe the promised land is the actual land of Judaea, "the land which the Jews possessed when they returned from Egypt, which had been possessed by their ancestors previously, and is therefore not promised but restored" (ep. 129:1). Jerome's view is that the term refers to a future heavenly land (ep. 129.3). The land about which the Jews speak is much too small to be considered the promised land, and much of it is a "desolate desert." Yet, Jerome admits, the Jews "glory" in this land and claim that it was promised to them (ep. 129.4).

This is reminiscent of an old debate between Jews and Christians. Almost two centuries earlier, when a similar question had arisen concerning the phrase "holy land," Origen had refused to identify the "earthly land of Judaea" with the promised land spoken of in the Bible, the "pure land that was 'good and large, flowing with milk honey.'" The promises about this good land, says Origen, were "not spoken about the land of Judaea." Judaea and Jerusalem are symbols of the "pure land which is good and large and lies in a pure heaven, in which is the heavenly Jerusalem" (*Contra Celsum*, 7:28-29). Origen, like most other Christians in the first three centuries rejected the idea that the land of Judaea was a holy land. He appeals, here and elsewhere to the New Testament texts Hebrews 12:22 and Gal. 4:26 which speak of a heavenly Jerusalem in contrast to the present city (*de principiis* 4.3.8).

I think it significant that the dispute about the meaning of "promised land" should surface again in the fifth century. For by that time the historical situation had changed considerably and Christianity was no longer as impartial about Palestine as it had been in the second and third centuries. The evidence can be found in commentaries written by Christians on the Hebrew prophets, and the most important writer in this connection is Jerome.

Jerome's commentaries on the prophets were written in Palestine in the early years of the fifth century. In his *Commentary on Ezekiel* and the *Commentary on Isaiah* (but also on Daniel and the minor prophets), Jerome gives unusual attention to those texts that speak about a return of the Jews to the land of Israel and a restoration of Jewish rule in Jerusalem: for example, Isaiah 35:10, "And the ransomed of the Lord shall return, and come to Zion with singing"; Is. 58:12, "Your ancient ruins shall be rebuilt; you shall raise up the foundations of many generations"; Ezekiel 36:8, "But you, O mountains of Israel shall shoot forth your branches, and yield your fruit to my people Israel for they will soon come home . . . ." Jerome's commentaries are verse by verse expositions of the text, based on his own reading of the Hebrew and a comparison of the Greek versions. Whenever he comes to passages such as these that suggest the Jews' possible return to the land of Israel, their restoration of the cities of Judaea and Jerusalem, and the rebuilding of the temple (e.g. in the final chapters of Ezekiel), he takes pains to demonstrate that the texts cannot be understood to refer to an actual return to Jerusalem. The prophets refer either to things that have already happened in the past or to the new spiritual reality that is found in the Christian church.

Let us begin with Isaiah 58, "Your ancient ruins shall be rebuilt." Commenting on this passage, Jerome says "The Jews and friends of the letter that kills refer this to the rebuilding (*instaurationem*) of the cities of Palestine. They claim that this took place under Zerubabel and Ezra and Nehemiah, *or* they refer it to the end of time, to the reconstruction of Jerusalem and the laying of deep foundations around the cities and the building of walls so high that no enemy can enter and all foes will be barred from them." (*Comm. in Esaiam* 58:12, ll. 15-22; see also *Comm. in Hiezech* 29:17-21, ll. 982-984). Now Jerome's own view is that the text must be taken spiritually to refer to the church, but what interests us here is not his interpretation but the interpretations he opposes and rejects.

Of the two possible Jewish interpretations, one historical and the other eschatological, the historical interpretation had long been met by Christian commentators. Eusebius of Caesarea, whose commentary on Isaiah was written in Palestine early in the fourth century, frequently opposes the historical interpretation of the Jews to a spiritual interpretation referring to the church.[6] Jerome, however, knows Jews who take these prophecies eschatologically as predictions about the coming of the Messiah and the establishment of a Messianic age for the Jews in the land of Israel. Commenting on Ezekiel 28:29-26, "I will gather the house of Israel from the peoples among

---

[6] Cf. for example Eusebius's treatment of Isaiah 58:12 (ed. Ziegler, 360ff.). See also Isaiah 35:9-10 (Ziegler, 230). On Eusebius's Commentary on Isaiah see Michael Hollerich, "The History of the Godly Polity in the Light of Prophecy: A Study of Eusebius of Caesarea's Commentary on Isaiah", Diss. University of Chicago 1985.

whom they are scattered, and manifest my holiness to them in the sight of the nations, then they shall dwell in their own land," Jerome says that many refer this to the time of Zerubabel, the return under Ezra and Nehemiah, but others say it will take place in the last time (*in ultimo tempore*) at the establishment of a 1000 year rule. (*In Hiezech.* 28:20-26, ll. 492-4). A similar point arises in his commentary on Ezekiel 16:55, "As for your sisters, Sodom and her daughters shall return to their former estate, and Samaria and her daughters shall return to your former estate." Jews say that at the "coming of their Messiah" (*in adventu Christi sui*) there will be a thousand year reign and a reestablishment of Sodom to its original condition (*restituendam in antiquum statum*), Jerusalem will be rebuilt and her daughters, that is the cities and villages of Israel, will flourish as they formerly flourished (*florituras ut prius floruerint*) and Jerusalem will be built with silver and precious stones. (Jerome, *In Hiezech.* 16:55, ll. 803-823).

As Jerome presents the hope for restoration, it includes the following characteristics: the Jews will return to Judaea; Jerusalem will be rebuilt and the cities of Judaea restored (*In Hiezech.* 16:55, 5.812-816); the temple will be reconstructed (*In Hiezech.* 37:1-14, l. 1371) and sacrifices will again be offered (*In Hiezech.* 36:1-15, l. 655);[7]

---

[7] Other passages in Jerome's commentaries that discuss the eschatological interpretation of restorationist texts in the prophets are as follows: Ezek 28:25, "I will gather the house of Israel from the peoples among whom they are scattered . . . . they shall dwell in their own land which I gave to my servant Jacob." (*Quod multi ad tempus referunt Zorobabel, Ezdrae et Neemiae, quando reversus est populus Israel et habitavit in terra Iudaea; alii vero in ultimo tempore et in mille annis sperant esse complendum, In Hiezech.* 28:2-26, ll. 492-495). See also Jerome, *In Hiezech.* 29:17-21, ll. 980-934). Joel 3:17, "And Jerusalem shall be holy and strangers shall never again pass through it." Jews and Judaizers refer to this to a thousand year rule, when the Messiah will dwell in Zion, a holy people will gather in Jerusalem, (*ut qui in isto saeculo oppressi sunt ab universis gentibus, in hoc eodem cunctis imperent nationibus, In Joel.* 3:16-17, ll. 313-318). Zach. 14:10-11, "[Jerusalem] shall be inhabited, for there shall be no more curse; Jerusalem shall dwell in security." Jews and judaizing Christians refer this to the future age (*ultimo tempore*), *quando rursum exercenda circumcisio sit et immolandae victimae, et omnia legis praecepta seruanda, ut non Iudaei Christiani, sed Christiani Iudaei fiant.* When the Messiah comes he will rule in a golden and jeweled city of Jerusalem, and all things will be restored to their prior state (*in antiquum statum, In Zachariam* 14:10-11; ll. 333-342)

The most extensive material comes from those sections of the book of Ezechiel dealing with the restoration of Israel, chapters 36-39. See Jerome, *In Hiezech.* 36:1-15, ll. 630-638; 36:16-38. *Alii vero ad mille annorum regnum referuent, quando sub Christo, quem putant esse venturum et civitas exstruatur Hierusalem et aedificetur templum de quo in ultima parte huius prophetiae dicturi sumus* (ll. 804-807). *In Hiezech.* 37:1-14, ll. 1367-1375. Also *In Hiezech.* 28:1-23, ll. 1476-83.

all the requirements of the Law will be carried out (*In Hiezech.* 37:1-14, l. 1371), in particular, circumcision will be observed in Israel (*In Zach.* 14:10-11, ll. 335-6) and the Sabbath will be kept (*In Hiezech.* 36:1-15; l. 657); there will be prosperity and long life (*In Hiezech.* 37:1-14 ll. 1373-5); people will build houses and live in them and plant vineyards (*In Hiezech.* 28:20-26, ll. 489-90); the other nations of the world will serve Israel. Commenting on Isaiah 60:13, "Arise shine for your light has come .... And nations will come to your light," Jerome says. "The Jews and our *semiiudaei*, who await a gold and jeweled Jerusalem from heaven, claim that this will take place in a thousand year reign when all the gentiles will serve Israel, camels will come from Midian, Epha and Saba, they will offer gold and incense and all the sheep of Cedar will gather, and the rams of Nabioth will come that they can be offered on the altar of the temple, which will have been reconstructed .... And the walls of Jerusalem will be built by foreigners, among whom will be the kings of the nations, and the gates of the city will be open always day and night and costly victims will be offered in Jerusalem." (*Comm. in Esa.* 60:1-3, ll. 17-23, 25-28).

Christian commentators complained that Jews took the predictions of the prophets to refer to the Jews alone. The text from Isaiah 25 which speaks of a "feast for all peoples on the mountain of the Lord" was taken by the Jews "to be spoken of themselves" (Eusebius, *In Esa.* 25:6-8: Ziegler, 162, l. 23). Jerome says that the Jews referred it "to Israel" (*In Esa.* 25:1-5, l. 31), "to the people of the Jews" instead of to "all peoples" (*In Esa.* 25:6-8, l. 27). The Jews no doubt interpreted Isaiah 25 in light of Ezekiel 39:17-20, which spoke of Israel enjoying a sacrificial feast on the mountains of Israel. When Israel is restored, never again will it be conquered by the nations of the world, for "the spirit of the Lord will be poured out of them that they might dwell in their land (*terra sua*). It is not the nations who will dwell there, but those who belong to the house of Israel (*proprie domus Israel*)." (Comm. *In Hiezech* 39. 17-29, ll. 2021-23).

These are not isolated references. The restoration of *Eretz Israel* to the Jews is a major preoccupation in Jerome's commentaries. From the way he speaks about these prophecies it appears that he is not dealing simply with literary disputes and the meaning of ancient texts. He describes views that are held by people in his own time and expectations that centered on the future, perhaps even the near future. In his Commentary on Daniel he says that the Hebrews understand the passage about the seventy weeks to refer a time when the Messiah will be born and transgressions will come to an end. "Now the city is deserted and the temple destroyed to its very foundations and the nation is in mourning, but after not a very long time (*non post grande tempus*) it will be restored." (*In Danielem* 9:24, ll. 559-63).

II

Jerome says that it was not only Jews, but Christians who held these views. He calls them variously "half Jews" (semiiudaei), juda-izers (iudaizantes), "our judaizers," or Ebionites.[8] He mentions a number of Christian leaders who had similar ideas, among them Tertullian, Irenaeus, Victorinus, Lactantius and, in his own day, Apollinaris. All of these are Christian millenialists or chiliasts. (*In Esa.* prol. book 18; *Corpus Christianorum 73a*, 740-1.) Christian chiliasts took the passage in Rev. 20 about the heavenly Jerusalem and the 1000 year reign to refer to a time when the saints would rule in Jerusalem. This text was not to be allegorized, Irenaeus argued, for it shows that the resurrection would not take place allegorically or spiritually. When all things are renewed mankind would "actually and really inhabit the city of God" (*adversus haereses* 5.35.2). The saints are "to rule in the same world in which they endured slavery" (*a.h.* 5.32.1).[9]

Jerome has the ancient millenarian tradition in mind, as he makes clear at a number of places in his commentaries (*Comm. in Es. prol.* book 18; *Corpus Christianorum 73a*, 740-42; *Comm. in Hiezech.* 36:1-15, ll. 655-666). Christian chiliasm and Jewish Messianism, however, are two sides of a similar phenomenon. Each envisions a future age in which the people of God will rule securely and will enjoy God's bounty. The time of peace and prosperity—the future kingdom—will be established in the world as we know it, in this world. Against this view, either in its Jewish or Christian form, Christian writers such as Origen, Eusebius, Jerome, Tyconius and Augustine argued for a spiritual kingdom, a heavenly Jerusalem which the saints would enjoy in a transformed existence.

Because the views that Jerome combat, in his commentaries are

---

[8] *iuxta nostros Iudaizantes* (*In Esa* 11:11-14, l. 17); *amici occidentis letterae* (*In Esa* 58:12, l. 16); *nostri semiudaei* (*In Esa.* 60:1-3, l. 17), *Ebionitae* (*In Esa* 66:20, l. 96).
[9] On early Christian millenarianism, see L. Atzberger, *Geschichte der chrislichen Eschatologie innerhalb der vornicaenischen Zeit* (1886); L. Gry, *Le millénarisme dans ses origines et son développement* (Paris: 1904); H. Bietenhard, The Millenial Hope in the Early Church," Scottish Journal of Theology 6 (1953), 12-30; Walter Bauer, "Chiliasmus," *Reallexikon fuer Antike und Christentum* 2 (1954), 1073-78. For apoca-lyptic expectations among Christians during the early Byzantine period, see Klaus Berger, *Die griechische Daniel-Exegese: eine altkirchliche Apokalypse, Studia Post Biblica*, No. 27 (Leiden: 1976), and Paul J. Alexander, "The Medieval Legend of the Last Roman Emperor and Its Messianic Origin," *Journal of the Warburg and Courtauld Institute* 41 (1978), 1-15.

attributed to Jews and Christian millenialists (i.e. judaizers), the question must be asked whether in fact Jerome is really speaking about Jews. Are his opponents primarily judaizing Christians? It is certainly unlikely that Jews would appeal to the book of Revelation. Further, much of what Jerome reports about Jewish Messianism in his day can be learned from Christian chiliasts whom he had read. They speak of a thousand year reign, of the rebuilding of Jerusalem, and the rule of the righteous. Two Christian chiliasts, Cerinthus and Nepos, even mention sacrifices, though these features are absent from other writers (Eusebius, *hist. eccl.* 3.28.4-5; 7.25.3-4). Yet what Jerome reports is more extensive than what we learn from Christian chiliasts, and it is more thoroughly Jewish. It is also based on the specifically restorationist passages from the prophets, particularly the latter chapters of the book of Ezekiel. And even though Rev. 20 is cited, details such as the rebuilding of the cities of Judaea cannot be derived from that passage, and are not mentioned by Christian chiliasts.[10] The one Christian writer who cites some of the same prophetic texts is Irenaeus, but he explicitly gives them a universal meaning and rejects the notion that they apply solely to the Jews (*adversus haereses* 5.33; 4.5.35.2). Jerome also distinguishes between the Christian Messiah, Jesus the Christ, and the Jewish Messiah who will come at the end of time. He explicitly says that the Jews claim these things will take place at[11] "the coming of their Messiah" (*Comm. in Hiezech.* 37:1-14, l. 1176: *in praesentia Christi sui quem putant esse venturum*)." For these reasons, I am inclined to think that Jerome is describing authentic Jewish attitudes that existed in his own time and were shared by judaizing Christians. They were not simply a resurgence of earlier Christian millenial beliefs; his descriptions are too concrete and too frequent to be derived from earlier writers he had to come to know through his reading.

One person in the list of Christian chiliasts was contemporary with Jerome. He is Apollinaris, bishop of Laodicea in Syria, known to historians of Christianity as the author of the first major christological heresy. Jerome presents Apollinaris as a judaizing Christian, and his description is confirmed by a number of his contemporaries, notably Basil of Caesarea, Gregory of Nyssa and Gregory Nazianzus.[12] The

---

[10] For example Tertullian, himself a Christian chiliast, says the Jews hope for a "*restitutio* of Judaea," based on the names of the cities (*Adversus Marcionem* 3.24).

[11] See also Jerome, *Comm. in Hiezech.* 16:55, *in adventu Christi sui, quem nos scimus antichristum* (ll. 805-6); *In Hiezech.* 40:5-13, l. 266.

[12] On Apollinaris as a judaizer, see Basil, ep. 265; also Gregory of Nyssa, ep. 3.24; Gregory Nazianzus, ep. 102; Jerome, *Comm. in Esa.* prologue to book 18 (l. 29);

report is puzzling because it is hard to fit in with what we know about Apollinaris from his other writings, preserved only in fragments. What is significant, however, is that Apollinaris was perceived by late fourth and early fifth-century Christian writers to have identified with Jewish Messianic hopes. As a consequence, what is said about Apollinaris helps us to fill out our picture of Jewish Messianism in this period.

Apollinaris had broken with the traditional Christian interpretation of Daniel 9 which took the statements about the "abomination of desolation" to refer to the destruction of the second Jewish temple under Titus in 70 C.E. Jerome reported how Apollinaris departed from the view that thought the text referred to things that had occurred in the past and directed his longing desires toward the future." Apollinaris sees the text as referring to a time in the future [432 C.E.] when Jerusalem and the temple will be rebuilt. This will take place after the coming of Elijah (Jerome, *Comm. in Dan.* 9:24). In his commentary on Ezek. 36:1-15, "exiles will soon come home and not hear the reproach of the nations," Jerome says that Apollinaris shared the Jews' view that the city of Jerusalem would be rebuilt and the temple constructed anew (l. 664).

Basil of Caesarea gives a similar report. He observes that in his book on the Resurrection "composed in the manner of the Jews, [Apollinaris] tells us to return again to their worship which is according to the law and again to be circumcised, to observe the sabbath, and to abstain from foods, to offer sacrifices to God, and to worship in the temple at Jerusalem, and in general to become Jews instead of Christians." (Ep. 263)

These reports from the late fourth century and early fifth century are reiterated and expanded in the middle of the fifth century by Theodoret bishop of Cyrus in northern Syria. Theodoret was a biblical expositor like Jerome and we possess his commentaries on Isaiah, Ezekiel, the minor prophets, Daniel, and so on. He too had met Jews who interpreted the restorationist passages in the prophets to refer to a coming restoration of Jewish rule in Jerusalem. Like Jerome, he links Jewish Messianism and Christian chiliasm, and the one person he singles out is Apollinaris. Theodoret comments on Haggai 2:24: "On that day says the Lord of hosts, I will take you, O Zerubbabel my servant, the son of Shealtiel, says the Lord, and make you like a signet ring; for I have chosen you, says the Lord of hosts." Theodoret believed that this prophecy had already seen its fulfilment. "However

---

Epiphanius says that he has heard the report that Apollinaris was a chiliast, but he does not believe it (*haer.* 77.36).

I am amazed," he writes "at the folly of Apollinaris who attempts to bring forth a contrary meaning to the things that have been prophecied so clearly, saying that the expedition of Gog and Magog has not yet happened, but will happen at the end of this age." Following the Jews, Apollinaris says that there will be "another Zerubbabel" besides the one who was governor of Judaea (PG 81.1872). This Zerubbabel would be a Messianic figure. Theodoret, then, confirms the reports of Jerome that the passages about the restoration under Zerubbabel were taken by some to have a future or eschatological reference. Ezek 29:29: "I will not hide my face any more from them when I pour out my spirit upon the house of Israel," Theodoret comments: "I am amazed not only at the folly of the Jews but of some others who have the name Christian, holding fast to Jewish myths saying that the invasion of Gog and Magog has not taken place but are waiting for it to happen. They ought to understand that this prophecy is linked to the return from Babylon. . ." (PG 81.1216-7).

III

The question must now be asked whether the statements of these Christian authors find any resonance in Jewish texts from this period. Can we confirm what they tell us? Was there a resurgence of Jewish Messianism and Christian chiliasm in Syria and Palestine in the early Byzantine period? This is a difficult question to answer, and any suggestions must be regarded as tentative. But I should like to sketch out some considerations, drawn from Jewish texts from this period and somewhat later, that lead me to think that Christian commentators are not speaking in a vacuum.

First the passages coming from rabbinical literature should be noted. A number of rabbis calculated the coming of the Messiah for the fifth century, because it was four hundred years from the destruction of the second temple in 70 C.E. They reasoned that the first exile, i.e. the captivity in Egypt, lasted for four hundred years and hence, deliverance could be expected in approximately the same period of time (*B. Sanh.* 99a). Rabbi Hanina was reported to have said that if 400 years have passed since the destruction and someone says to you, "Buy a field worth one thousand denarii for only one denar, do not buy it." (*B. Abodah Zarah* 9b). His presumption was that in the Messianic age, Israel would be restored to the land. Hence there was no need to buy land.[13] Though these texts point to our period, they do not give us much help in answering our question. They have the flavor

---

[13] For other texts see H. A. Silver, *A History of Messianic Speculation in Israel* (New York: 1927), 25 ff.

of school discussions, idle musings. They exhibit little sense of urgency.[14]

There is, however, a more fruitful body of material to help us understand Christian commentators' statements about Jewish Messianism. I am thinking in particular of several apocalyptic works, the *Sefer Zerubavel,* and the *Sefer Eliahu.* These works, which were frequently revised and adapted to new historical situations, have long been known to scholars of medieval Jewry. Many different texts have come down to us, and it is difficult to date the works with any confidence. But they seem to have originated in Palestine and present scholarly opinion dates them in the Byzantine period. The Book of Zerubbabel was written in Hebrew probably in the early seventh century around the Persian invasion of Palestine.[15]

Now I am acutely aware of the difficulty in using apocalyptic works to establish historical events or movements. Yet the similarities between the ideas in these texts and the view that Jerome and Theodoret report are striking.[16] There are correspondences in language, thinking, and the use of Biblical texts. Some of the texts that the Christians single out as particularly problematic are the same texts that are cited in these apocalyptic works. The *Sefer Zerubavel* is presented as a vision of the events that will take place at the end of time when the Messiah comes. It is not insignificant that the man who receives the vision is Zerubbabel, the son of Shealtiel, satrap of Judah. Zerubbabel was instrumental in the restoration of Israel after the Babylonian captivity, and he figures large in Jerome's commentaries.[17]

---

[14] For the persistence of hope for the rebuilding of Jerusalem and the restoration of sacrifices in classical Judaism, see M. Pesachim 10.6: "Therefore, O Lord our God and the God of our fathers, bring us in peace to the feasts and pilgrim festivals which are approaching, while we rejoice in the building of your city and rejoice in your worship; and may we eat there from the sacrifices and the Pesach offerings. . . . Blessed are you O Lord who has redeemed Israel."

[15] I cite from the text of Even Shmuel (Kaufmann), *Midreshei Ge'ulah* (Jerusalem: 1953), 71-83. For a discussion of dating, see pp. 61-63; also the articles of Israel Levi, "Apocalypse de Zorababel et le Roi de Perse Siroes," *REJ* 68 (1914), 129-160; 69 (1919), 108-128; 79 (2930), 57-65. Levi dates the work to the early seventh century (*REJ* 69, p. 112).

[16] On the problems of using apocalyptic works as historical sources see the useful article of Paul J. Alexander, "Medieval Apocalypses as Historical Sources," *American Historical Review* 73 (1968), 997-1018.

[17] On Zerubabel as a point of dispute between Jews and Christians, cf. Theodoret of Cyrus. "Jews connect prophecies of this kind [prophecies looking forward to the blessing of all nations] with Solomon and Zerubbabel, in order to exhibit the groundlessness of the Christian position" (*Eranistes,* PG 83. 61 ff.). See C. Thomas McCollough, *Theodoret of Cyrus as Expositor of the Minor Prophets and Judaism* Diss.

The book of Zerubbabel begins as follows: "The word which was addressed to Zerubbabel son of Shealtiel satrap of Judah. On the 24th day of the month of Shevat the Lord showed me this sight, and the sight which I saw on the river Kedar was as a vision. I was praying before the Lord and I said, "Blessed are you O Lord, who gives life to the dead." My heart was groaning within me saying, "What will be the plan of the eternal temple." (Cf. Ezek. 40ff). A voice comes to Zerubbabel and he is lifted up and brought to Nineveh, the great city, the city of blood. He sees a man described as "wounded and despicable" (Is. 53:3) and asks him where he is. He is told "This is great Rome." Zerubbabel asks the man who he is, and he replies "I am the Messiah of the Lord, and I am imprisoned here in this jail until the time of the end." Grieved at this news Zerubbabel remains silent. The Messiah asks why he is silent, and is answered, " 'Because I heard that you are the Messiah of God, the servant of the Lord and the light of Israel.' At once he seemed to me as a young man, beautiful and fair. And I said to him. 'When will the light of Israel be kindled?' " (ll. 27-30) This is the theme of the book. As Zerubbabel puts it several lines later. "When will come the time of deliverance" (l. 31).

Now it is clear from the book that the deliverance spoken of here is the land of Israel's deliverance from foreign rulers and the reestablishment of Jewish rule in the city of Jerusalem and in Palestine. The *Sefer Zerubavel* pictures the land of Israel under the domination of the evil king Armilius, a name for the Christian Rome Emperor [from Romulus]. Armilius was born from a union of a very beautiful woman and Satan. His rule "extends from one end of the earth to the other, and there is no one who can stand up to him, and whoever does not believe in him he will kill with his cruel sword." (83-4) Armilius had set up religious shrines all over the land (he calls them asheroth) and it seems from the description in the book that he is speaking of Christian churches, perhaps even churches dedicated to St. Mary, the beautiful woman who was the mother of Armilius. "And he [Armilius] will begin to plant on the face of the land all the *asheroth* of the *goyim* which the Lord hates, and he will take the stone [the beautiful woman] from which he was born and transport it to [the valley of Arbael] and he will build seven altars for it, and it will be the chief object of idolatry, and all the peoples will come from all places and

University of Notre Dame, 1985. The references in Jerome's commentaries are numerous. Besides those cited in the text, see the following passages: *Comm. in Esa* 1:26 l. 11; *In Esa* 45:9-13, ll. 74-81; *In Esa.* 57:14, ll. 11-15; *Comm in Hiezech.* 40:1-4, ll. 73-84; *Comm. in Osee* 3:14-5 ll. 179-1860; *In Zach.* 2:10-12, ll. 209-215. See also Louis Ginzberg, *The Legends of the Jews* (Philadelphia: 1928), Vol. 6, 438.

worship this stone and offer incense to it and pour libations, and
everyone who lifts up his heart to look at her will not be able to,
because no man is able to look on her face due to her beauty. And
Armilius angered the Lord with his evil deeds." (ll. 116-124)[18].

The book describes Israel's struggle with its enemies, the victory
of the Lord's Messiah with the aid of his mother Hefsi-vah over
Israel's foes, and the joyful return of the people of Israel to Jerusalem.
At that time the Lord will bring down the "temple constructed above
to the earth" and burnt offerings will go up to the Lord. The glory of
the Lord will be revealed and the exiles of Jerusalem will go up to the
mount of Olives. Zion will see and Jerusalem will rejoice, and Zion
will say, "Who begat these for me" and "Who are these?" And
Nehemiah will go up to Jerusalem and say to her, "Behold your sons
which you bore and which were exiled from you. Rejoice exceedingly
daughter of Zion and shout daughter of Jerusalem. Enlarge the place
of your tent, and let them stretch forth the curtains of your habita-
tions." (Is. 54:2, ll. 150-59) The book ends with a description of
Jerusalem filling the whole land and resting on five mountain peaks,
Lebanon, Mt. Moriah, Tabor, Carmel, and Hermon.[19]

Most of the details of Jewish expectation described by Jerome are
found in the book of Zerubbabel. The land is ruled by foreign powers,
the Messiah comes and drives out the intruders, the exiles return to
Jerusalem with rejoicing, they offer sacrifices in the temple, and the
entire land of Israel is restored to the people of Israel. What is not

---

[18] On this passage see Levi, *REJ* 71 (1920), 59. No doubt the building of Christian
churches, especially in Jewish areas, was an affront to Jews. Epiphanius, writing on the
fourth century, speaks of "building churches in honor of Jesus Christ in Jewish towns
and villages." (*haer.* 30.11.9-10; Holl, 347).

[19] For the idea that the city of Jerusalem will fill the whole land see the interesting
passage in *Siphre Deut*, attributed to R. Yose ben Dormaskitti (Chapter one, ed.
Finkelstein, 7-8):

> The land of Israel is destined to be enlarged and spread out on all sides
> like this fig tree which is small at the bottom but broad at the top. And the
> gates of Jerusalem are going to reach to Damascus, as it is written [Song of
> Songs 7:5], 'Your nose is like the tower of Lebanon, which looks toward
> Damascus.' And the exiles shall come and encamp in it, as it is written
> [Zech 9:1], 'And Damascus shall be his resting place' and as it is also
> written [Is. 2:2], 'And it shall come to pass in the end of days that the
> mountain of the Lord's house shall be established as the top of the
> mountains, and shall be exalted above the hills, and all nations shall flow
> to it,' And as it is further written (Is. 2:3), 'And many peoples shall go and
> [say, 'Come you, and let us go up to the mountain of the Lord, to the house
> of the God of Jacob: and He will teach us of his ways, and we will walk in
> his paths.' For out of Zion shall go forth the law, and the word of the Lord
> from Jerusalem.]

mentioned is the 1000 year reign. This was derived from the book of Revelation and enters the discussion because Jerome is not only speaking of Jews but also of Christian judaizers. The one phrase that stands out is taken from the eschatological passage in Isaiah 2 and Micah 4, "in the end of the days". "It shall come to pass in the latter days that the mountain of the house of the Lord shall be established as the highest of the mountains. . . ." In the *Sefer Zerubavel*, the messenger says he will tell Zerubbabel "what will happen to your people 'in the end of days' " 1.44. At that time a mighty battle will take place and the Messianic age will begin. Jerome's point, repeated over and over in the commentary, is precisely this: the Jews take the restorationist prophecies to refer to the "end time" (*Comm. in Esa.* 58.12, 18 *in ultimo tempore* or "at the end of the ages" Comm. in Michaem 4:1-7, 1. 196 *de fine saeculorum*). Put exegetically, then, the book of Zerubbabel gives us evidence of an eschatological interpretation of the prophecies that refers them not to the historical events of rebuilding after the exile but to a future time when the victorious Messiah will lead his people home to dwell again in the land, to worship God in the temple, and to observe all the requirements of the law.

Besides the *Sefer Zerubavel*, the *Sefer Eliahu*, another apocalyptic work from the Byzantine period, also provides parallels to the material found in the Christian commentaries. This book is a vision to Elijah about the end of times, written sometime between the third to the seventh century of the common era.[20] Its theme too is the great battle that will take place at the end of time and the victory of the saints over the forces of evil, Gog and Magog and their hordes.

At several points the *Sefer Eliahu* cites texts that are said by Jerome to be interpreted by the Jews to refer to the Messianic age and the return of the Jews to Jerusalem. One of these is Isaiah 49:22-23: "Behold I will lift up my hand to the nations, and raise my signal to the peoples; and they shall bring you sons in their bosom and your daughters shall be carried on their shoulders. Kings shall be your foster fathers and their queens your nursing mothers. With their faces to the ground they shall bow down to you and lick the dust of your feet." The *Sefer Eliahu* uses this text to support the hope that the exiles will return and the nations will serve Israel. "After this all the

---

[20] Even Shmeul (*Midreshei Ge'ulah*, 37-40) dates the work to the seventh century, as does Buttenwieser, *Die hebraeische Elias-Apokalypse und ihre Stellung in der apokalyptischen Litteratur des rabbinischen Schrifttums unter der Kirche* (Leipzig: 1897). S. Krauss, "Der roemisch-persische Krieg in der juedischen Elia-Apokalypse," *Jewish Quarterly Review* 14 (1902), 359-372. I cite from the text in Even Shmuel, pp. 41-48. I have been aided in my study of the *Sefer Eliahu* by the unpublished translation and notes of David Levenson.

nations will come and prostrate themselves before each one of Israel and will lick the dust of their feet, as it is written: 'Kings shall be your foster-fathers. . .' " (ll. 63-65). This text, says Jerome, should not be taken "in Jewish fashion" (*more Iudaico*) to mean that all the nations will come and prostrate themselves before the people of Israel and will lick the dust of their feet. The text means that the Lord will be worshipped at Jerusalem. (Comm. in Esa. 49:23, ll. 38 and 57).[21]

The *Sefer Eliahu* also cites a number of other texts that Jerome singles out as Messianic. "A kor of wheat will produce about 900 kor and the wine and oil will do likewise, and every single tree will be laden with choice produce and fruit, as it is written: But you, O mountains of Israel, shall shoot forth your branches, and yield your fruit to my people Israel; for they will soon come home. And snail will eat and be happy for forty years" (ll. 66-69). The text of Ezekiel goes on to say, "the cities will be inhabited and the waste places rebuilt" (36:10). This passage, says Jerome, is taken *"more iudaico,"* for the Jews "anticipate a thousand year reign, when they believe the city of Jerusalem and temple will be reconstructed. . . and happiness in all things." (*Comm. in Hiezech.* ll. 633-38)

The *Sefer Eliahu* gives a rather full description of the descent of the heavenly temple, and the language is reminiscent of what we have already noted in Jerome:

> And Elijah said: "I see a beautiful, splendid and great city descending from Jerusalem already built, as it is written; Jerusalem, built as a city which is bound firmly together [Ps. 122:3]—built and perfected with its people dwelling in it. It sits upon 3000 towers and between each tower are 20 stades and between each stade are 25,000 cubits of emeralds and of precious stones and of pearls, as it is written: 'I will make your pinnacles of agate your gates of carbuncles, and all your walls of precious stones' [Is 54:12]." Elijah said; "I see houses and gates of the righteous with their thresholds, and their doorposts [or Mezuzoth] are of precious stones and the treasuries of the temple are opened to their doors. And among them are Torah and peace, as it is written, 'All your sons shall be taught by the Lord [and great shall be the peace of your sons']" (Is. 54:13 ll. 100-109; cf. Jerome, *Comm. in Esa* 60:1-3, ll. 17-23; *Comm. in Zach* 14:10, l. 333-357).

Jerome, commenting on Isaiah 54:12, one of the texts cited here, says that Isaiah is referring not to the "God of one people, but the God

---

[21] In his Commentary on Isaiah written in the fifth century, Cyril of Alexandria says this text should not be taken to refer to Israel alone (PG 70. 1075).

of the whole world," who calls all humankind not only the Jews. This does not refer, as some think, to a thousand year reign, circumcision, the offering of sacrifices, nor the keeping of the sabbath. The Jews, however, refer it exclusively to themselves. They say, "Let us each eat and drink because tomorrow *we* will rule." (l. 56) They expect a city filled with precious stones, foundations of sapphires, crystal gates and "its sons will not have men as teachers but God and they will be called the disciples of God." (ll. 60-65). The text does not refer to a "city on earth," as the "hebrews and half-Jews" think, but to a heavenly city (ll. 204-6).

Yet another point of correspondence between the books of Zerubbabel and Elijah and the Christian commentaries is the great battle with Gog and Magog. Commenting on Ezekiel 39:28-29, "I am the Lord their God because I sent them into exile among the nations, and then gathered them into their own land. I will leave none of them remaining among the nations any more; and I will not hide my face any more from them. . ." As we noted earlier, Theodoret writes, "I am amazed not only at the folly of the Jews but of some others, who bear the name Christian, holding fast to Jewish myths, saying that the invasion of Gog and Magog has not taken place but are waiting for it to happen. They ought to understand that this prophecy is linked to the return from Babylon" (PG 81.1216-7; see also PG 81.1868). In his commentary on Ezekiel 38.1-23, Jerome reports that Jews and juda-izers believe "Gog" refers to the Scythians who, at the end of a thousand year reign, will cross the Caucasus mountains and come to the "land of Israel" to wage war against the saints (*Comm. in Hiezech.* 38:1-3, ll. 1476-1482).

At the end time, according to the *Sefer Eliahu*, "the holy one, blessed be he, will bring up Gog and Magog and all their hordes. After that all the peoples of the earth will be assembled and will encircle Jerusalem for battle. The Messiah will come and the Holy One, blessed be He, with his help will make war against them, as it is written, 'The Lord will go forth and fight against those nations as when he fights on a day of battle' [Zach 14:3]. The holy one blessed be he will gather every bird of the sky and beast of the earth to eat of their flesh and to drink of their blood [cf. Ezek 39:17], as it is written, 'and the birds of prey will summer upon them. . .' (Isa. 18:6). And Israel will light a fire from their weapons for seven years, as it is written,' Then those who dwell in the cities of Israel will return. . .' [Ezek. 39:9. ll. 70-78]."

Similar ideas are also echoed in another work from this period, the *Vision of Zerubbabel,* an apocalyptic poem about the return of the

Jews to Jerusalem.[22] This work too pictures a great battle between Gog and Magog against the people of Israel and the ultimate victory of the Messiah and the deliverance of Israel. It speaks of the coming rule of the Jews in Jerusalem and the establishment of an eternal temple. When the Messiah comes, "the spirit of the Lord will rest on him and foreigners shall be the vinedressers of the people of the Lord. [Is. 61:5]. And they shall say. Come let us go up to the mountain of the Lord [Is. 2:3]. An eternal temple will be built and it will be established to the highest." (ll. 70-75). In that day "The Lord shall be king over all the land. And he will dwell in the land which I gave to my servant to Jacob in which your fathers dwelled. And they will dwell in it, they and their sons and the sons of their sons forever and David my servant will be prince over them forever" (ll. 80-84).

These apocalyptic writings suggest that the Jews and Christians are not simply quarrelling over the meaning of Biblical texts but with the central symbol of the land and the city of Jerusalem. Jews were beginning to realize that the ancient claims to the land were now being appropriated by the Christians. We can gain another glimpse of a Jewish response in the work of Yose ben Yose, the Hebrew poet from this period.[23] Yose ben Yose is the earliest Hebrew liturgical poet we know by name. He is mentioned by Saadia Gaon in the 10th century (Mirsky, p, 14). He lived in *Eretz Isarel* in the fifth or sixth century, i.e. precisely at the time when the Christianization of Palestine was at its height. Several of his poems belong to the type of liturgical prayers known as *malkkuyyot,* prayers which praise God's sovereignty and kingship. The oldest form of these prayers, some of which can still be found in the Jewish prayer book, e.g. the Alenu, come from the late second-temple period or shortly thereafter. They speak of God's sovereignty over the whole earth, over all humankind:

> It is our duty to praise the master of all, to exalt the creator of the universe. . . . We hope Lord our God, soon to behold the majestic glory, when the abominations shall be removed from the earth, and the false gods exterminated; when the world shall be perfected under the reign of the Almighty, and *all* flesh will call upon your name and all the wicked of the earth will be turned to you. May all the inhabitants of the world realize and know that every knee must bend, every tongue must vow allegiance."

The emphasis is on God's universal kingship, his rule over all the

---

[22] Text of the poem and discussion in Joseph Yahalom, "On the Value of Literary Works as Source to elucidate Historical Questions." *Cathedra 11 (1979)*, 125-133 (in Hebrew).
[23] *Aharon Mirsky*, The Poems of Yose ben Yose (*Jerusalem: 1977*) (in Hebrew).

earth, and the prayer asks the God's reign can be recognized and acknowledged by all peoples of the world.

In the poems of Yose ben Yose, however, the emphasis shifts to Israel and the city of Jerusalem. No longer is the poet concerned about idolaters, those who refuse to bend the knee to the God of all creation, the king of the universe. For the rules of the world, i.e. of the empire, are not idolators, but Christians who believe in the one God who rules over all things. Hence, the poems no longer speak of God's universal reign, but of God's reign in Israel and in the City of Jerusalem. Now the faithful pray that God's rule be established in Israel.

> Make for yourself a terrible name.
> As of old, may you prosper in the throne of your kingdom.
> Let the joy of all the land awake and rise up.
> Establish your throne in the city of the kingdom [i.e. Jerusalem]. [24]

In another peom Yose ben Yose is more explicit, mentioning the Byzantine state with the old word of Rome, Edom. Here he prays for vindication against the Christian rulers.

> Let the deliverers take our side.
> Carry off the glory from Edom.
> And place on the Lord the splendor of the kingdom.[25]

Yose says little in his poems about idolatry, the concern of the other *malkhuyyoth*. Yose ben Yose adapts the ancient prayers to the new situation in which *Eretz Israel* is becoming a Christian land.[26]

IV

We have, in the sources cited above, the outlines of a confrontation between Jews and Christians that is quite unprecedented in earlier texts. Even allowing for the difficulties in dating the apocalyptic texts and the problems of drawing direct links between quite disparate material, the parallels are noteworthy. Of course the book of Zerubabel (and possibly the *Sefer Eliahu* as well) describes a later situation in which Jews had taken hope from the Persian victory over the Romans. Yet the ideas these books employ and their interpretation of Biblical texts is close to what Jerome and Theodoret claim to have learned from Jews and judaizing Christians in the fifth century. I am inclined to think there was a genuine exchange between Jews and

---

[24] *Mirsky*, 92.
[25] *Mirsky*, 94.
[26] *Mirsky*, 16-17. Cf. the Vision of Zerubabel. "Kings from the land of Edom will meet their end/ And the inhabitants of Antioch will rebel but makes peace/ Tiberias and Samaria will be comforted/ And Acco and the Galilee will be shown mercy (ll. 17-21).

Christians on the future of the land of Israel. At Isaiah 66.1-2, "heaven is my throne and the earth is my footstool, what is the house which you would build for me, and what is the place of my rest?" Jerome says that the Jews think the "invisible, incorporeal, and limitless God is to be shut up in the temple in Jerusalem" (ll. 228-30). But then he acknowledges that the Jews respond to his charge. "We [say the Jews] are not so foolish as to think that God can be enclosed in a place [*loco*]. However, in a place set apart for sacrifices, we offer to God animal sacrifices which have been prescribed in the law" (*Comm. in Esa.* 60:3, ll. 12-14).

These commentaries suggest that expectations among Jews for a return to the land of Israel were grounded in the biblical prophecies concerning the restoration of Israel. Whether these were the views of a few Jews, or a particular group, we do not know, but they were widespread enough to attract the attention of Christian leaders and to elicit a response in their commentaries on the prophets.

It is possible that Jewish hopes about Jerusalem had been awakened by Julian's effort in the late fourth century to rebuild the temple in Jerusalem and to return the city to the Jews.[27] Even though his effort failed due to his untimely death, the idea lived on. A generation after his death (386 C.E.) Jews in Antioch were still talking about a restoration of the city of Jerusalem to Jews (John Chrysostom, *homilia ad iudaeos* 7.1), and the frequency of references in Christian writers in the generations after Julian indicates the idea did not die with Julian.[28]

But an even more important development was taking place in Palestine at this time, transforming the ancient home of the Jews, *Eretz Israel,* into a Christian land. During the fifth and sixth centuries over 500 Christian churches were built in Palestine, marking the land with the symbols of the new religion.[29] The city of Jerusalem with its churches and monastaries, its bishop and its monks, came to rival the ancient centers of Constantinople, Antioch, Alexandria and Rome. The city, which even Christians recognized as a Jewish city "according to history," was now revered as a Christian captial (John Cassian, *Collationes* 14.8).

From the fourth century onward pilgrims streamed to Jerusalem

---

[27] See Robert L. Wilken, *John Chrysostom and the Jews* (Berkeley: 1983), 228-160.

[28] See David B. Levenson, *A Source and Tradition Critical Study of the Stories of Julian's Attempt to Rebuild the Jerusalem Temple,* Diss. Harvard University, 1979.

[29] Asher Ovadiah, *Corpus of Byzantine Christian Churches* (Bonn: 1970). The Byzantine period was a time of prosperity in Palestine. See M. Avi-Yoush, "The Economics of Byzantine Palestine," *Israel Exploration Journal* 8 (1958), 39-51.

and other places in Palestine to worship at the holy places.[30] In the fifth century Palestinian monasticism blossomed. There had been a few monks in Palestine earlier, but most were solitary figures who tended to live in the costal areas. But now thousands of men and women from all over the Mediterranean world came to the desert of Judaea. Although there were deserts in the lands from which they came, e.g. in Syria, Cappadocia and Egypt, they wanted to live "in this desert," the desert surrounding Jerusalem, the desert of Elijah and the prophets, of John the Baptiser and Jesus (see Cyril of Scythopolis, Vita Euthymii 5, ed. Schwartz, 14). They left their native lands with the ancient word of God to Abraham in their hearts: "Go from your country and your kindred and your father's house to the land that I will show you" (Gen. 12:1).[31] They came, in the words of the great chronicler of Palestinian monasticism, Cyril of Scythopolis, to "colonize" (πολισθῆναι) the desert in fulfillment of the prophecy of Isaiah (Cyril of Scythopolis, Vita Sabas 6, ed. Schwartz, 90). The desert became a city.

During this period Christians began to use the term "holy land" with specifically Christian overtones to describe the actual land of Palestine. As I have already noted, the term had been rejected by earlier Christians as inappropriate. Christian hope was set on a heavenly kingdom. But now, for the first time, Christians began to use the term "holy land" with theological overtones. Not insignificantly, the term first acquires a specifically Christian sense among the monks of Palestine, the men and women who tried by their own labor and prayer to make the land their own. They spoke of themselves as "inhabitants of this holy land." (ὁι τῆς ἀγιᾶς γῆς ταύτης ὁικήτορες).[32] They dug cisterns, built monasteries and churches, and beckoned their fellows from their native lands to follow them. There were so many Armenians among the monks in the fifth century that St. Sabas, the architect of Pastininian monasticism allowed them to worship in Armenian.

For centuries Christians had appealed to the destruction of the second temple as proof of the demise of Judaism and the triumph of Christianity. So Christians eagerly visited Jerusalem to view the ruins of the temple. Theodoret of Cyrus reports that he went to Jerusalem

---

[30] See John Wilkinson, Jerusalem Pilgrims Before the Crusades (Jerusalem: 1977).

[31] This verse is cited in Theodore of Petra's Vita Theodosii 2, and Paul of Elousa's Vita Theognii 5 (Analecta Bollandia 10, p. 82). See also Jerome, ep. 46.2.

[32] See Cyril of Scythopolis, Vita Sabas 57 (Schwartz, pp. 153-5. For the Christian idea of "holy land" see Robert L. Wilken, "Heiliges Land" in Theologische Realenzyklopaedie, ad loc. (with bibliography). For the biblical idea see W. D. Davies, The Gospel and the Land (Berkeley: 1974).

"to see the desolation with my own eyes" and the ruins confirmed for him the ancient prophecies (*cur. affect.* 11.71). In a famous passage in his commentary on Zephaniah, Jerome also describes the pilgrimage of Jews to Jerusalem on 9 Ab to lament the city's destruction, a sight that reassured Christians (*Comm. in Soph.* 1.15-16, ll. 652-692). His point in reporting the Jewish practice was to remind his readers that the Jewish city was in ruins and its desolation was permanent (*non fuerat consumationis et finis*). In Palestine could one "see" (*cernimus*) the destroyed cities of Judaea, a point that is emphasized by other writers of the period (see John Chrysostom, *hom. in Ps.* 109; *Patrologia Graceca* 55. 274).

By the fifth century, however, something new had happened. No longer did Christians come to Jerusalem simply to see the ruins of the ancient temple. They came to see the new buildings that had been erected over the holy places in Jerusalem and Bethlehem and in other cities of the holy land, "to view the places of the saving sufferings" (Theodoret, *Comm. in Zach.* 8:20-22; *Patrologia Graeca* 81. 1918). The holy places themselves were thought to prove the truth of the things that had happened there (cf. Eusebius, *vita Const.*, 3.30-31). As for the new and magnificent buildings that had been constructed, they were glorious and visible symbols of the new religion's power. A new Christian city was set over against the old that had once belonged to the Jews (Eusebius, *vita Const.* 3.33).

In this setting, the very idea of the Jews' return to Jerusalem seemed a threat to Christians. This may seem improbable with our degree of hindsight, but there are enough hints in the sources to suggest that Jewish hopes disquieted Christians, just as Julian's plan had agitated them in the fourth century.[33] As evidence of Christian

---

[33] Contrary to common opinion, Palestinian Jewry thrived in the Byzantine period. The most impressive evidence comes from the many synagogues built during this period, especially in Galilee but also in Judaea and the south. In the recent survey of Palestinian synagogues, Lee Levine writes:

> The developments in the study of ancient synagogues these past few years have suggested a totally new perspective on the history of the Jewish community in late Roman Palestine. Heretofore it has been commonly assued that the late Roman-Byzantine period witnessed a steady decline of Jewish life and the recession into a kind of Dark Age which was to last for centuries. Large-scale emigration, loss of political status, lapse of key communal institutions, economic hardships and religious discrimination bordering at times on persecution, were assumed to have had their cumulative effect, leaving the Jewish community in an improverished state. This perception has been challenged on a number of fronts. The Cairo Geniza has revealed a series of literary works dating from this period, indicating the existence of creative cultural life among Jews. This

concern about Jewish hopes for the city, i.e., over Jewish Messianism, let me cite a striking text from Theodoret of Cyrus's commentary on Ezekiel. He is discussing the final verse Ezekiel 48:35, which read in the LXX "And the name of the city . . . will be his name." The text should be translated "The Lord is there," but the LXX translators pointed the Hebrew incorrectly. (Should read "there" instead of "its name"; Greek is τὸ ὀνομααὐΤῆς).

Theodoret first observes that the city of Jerusalem has been built and rebuilt several times in history, under Zerubabel, Nehemiah, the Maccabees and, most recently, under Herod. Now Apollinaris, following Jewish fables, says "there has been promised another building of Jerusalem and worship according to the Law of the Jews" (*PG* 81, 1248b-c). At that time, the Law "will be proclaimed by Elijah to the Jews and be confirmed by the Lord Messiah himself."[34] Theodoret then proceeds to offer biblical and theological arguments for why the Law cannot be restored, after which he returns to his point about the rebuilding of the temple in Jerusalem:

> "There is today in Jerusalem the church of the cross, the church of the Resurrection, the church of the Ascension, the church on Mt. Sion, the church in Holy Bethlehem, and many other churches. If the temple of the Jews is rebuilt, will these be destroyed, or will they

impression is the result of the now-accepted dating to late antiquity of a series of liturgical, apocalyptic, halakhic, and mystical works, previously thought to be medieval in origin. To these examples can now be added the ever increasing number of Byzantine synagogues being found throughout Israel. Moreover, other synagogues, products of a somewhat earlier age, continued to undergo extensive renovations, and were in use down to the Arab conquest of Palestine and beyond.
Ancient Synagogues Revealed (Detroit: 1982), 9-10. See also Eric Myers, A. T. Kraabel, and J. F. Strange, *Synagogue Excavations at Khirbet Shema, Upper Galilee, Israel, 1970-72* Annual of the American Schools of Oriental Research, 42 (Durham: 1976). For recent developments in the study of the land of Israel in this period, see *Eretz Israel from the Destruction of the Second Temple to the Muslim Conquest*, Vol. 1, ed. Zvi Baras, Shmuel Safrai, Yoram Tzafrir, Menachem Sartan (Jerusalem: 1982) in Hebrew.

[34] This seems to be a reference to the role that Elijah will play as precursor to the Messiah. This idea is mentioned in Mal 3:23-24 and in Mt. 17:10 and Mk:9-11, but as presented here it seems to be part of the Messianic expectation that Christians had learned from Jews in the fifth century. Jerome mentions the idea in his Commentary on Ezekiel 29:17-21 (*alii ad ultimum tempus referunt quando putant et Heliam esse venturum.*), and it provides the framework for the *Sefer Eliahu*. See *Halakoth Gedoloth* in A. Jellinek, *Beit ha-Midrash* 2 (1938), 54-57; also *Sefer Zerubavel*, ll. 140 ff. See Chaim Milikovsky, Elijah and the Messiah, "*Institute for Jewish Studies*, The Hebrew University Jerusalem, Vol. 2 (1983), 491-496 (in Hebrew), and M. M. Faierstein, "Why Do the Scribes Say That Elijah Must Come First?" *JBL* 100 (1981), 75-86.

continue to be held in honor? If they continue to be honored as they have been in the past, will they be revered by the Jews, or will they be dishonored? If the Jews dishonor them and remain in their former madness, they will receive no benefit from the preaching of the great Elijah [presumably because they were already doing the things he came to proclaim]. If they do honor them, to which of the religious buildings will they show greater respect? To that of the cross, to the Anastasis, or to the one that is going to be built? If they do show greater honor to that one, they will do so because they lack perfect knowledge. But if they prefer these [the Christian buildings], then the building of that one [the temple] will be superflous. If on the other hand they assign equal honor to these and to that one, they will offer sacrifices there, but here they will benefit from the divine mysteries. But how is it possible for them to benefit from the divine mysteries with those who are gentile believers since the law prohibits mixing with gentiles? The result would be that in the same temple Christian rites and Jewish rites would be celebrated at the same time. And once again there would inevitably be conflict and strife, we following our way of life according to our beliefs, and they preferring a form of worship according to the Law."

(*PG* 81, 1252a-1253c)[35]

V

The debate I have just outlined over the interpretation of texts from the prophets on the restoration to the Jews of Jerusalem and the land of Israel speaks directly to the theme of this conference. At one level we can see that as late as the fifth century, Christian writers continued to define themselves in relation to Judaism. Even though Christianity had by this time become ideologically and politically dominant in the Roman world, nevertheless Christian perceptions of the Jews continued to play a significant role in shaping the way Christians thought about themselves. Of course, one of the reasons for this was the simple but profoundly important fact that Christians had appropriated the ancient Jewish Scriptures, the Old Testament, and used the Hebrew Bible in its several translations as the foundation for Christian religious and historical claims. The Christian system of belief, way of life, understanding of the past, and view of the church were all dependent on an interpretation of the ancient books of the Jews. "It is one thing," wrote Jerome," to sing the psalms in churches of Christian believers, quite another to make answer to Jews who cavil at the words." (Pref. Psalms, *PL* 28, 1123-8). That the Old Testament

---

[35] Theodoret attributes these views to Apollinaris, but it is clear from other texts in the commentary where he speaks of similar ideas that he is speaking of Jews as well. See *Comm. in Hiezech.* 37:16 (PG 81. 1192); 37:25 (col. 1197); 37:29 (cols. 1216-7).

was open to another interpretation than that of the Christians, and that this interpretation was expressed by articulate spokesmen of a living tradition was, on the one hand, a continuing source of frustration to Christians, and on the other, an impetus to clarify what they thought.

Now, however, Christians had begun to appropriate a new symbol, the land of Israel itself. The earlier debates between Jews and Christians centered on the meaning of the Law, on the interpretation of Christ, on the understanding of Israel in relation to the church and on the significance of the destruction of the second temple.[36] But Christians had made no claim on the land. Indeed they claimed to be devoted only to a heavenly city. Now they had a real interest in the actual city, and the consequences were far reaching. This can perhaps be illustrated by the term Jerome uses to characterize (or caricature) the Jewish interpretation of the restorationist passages in the prophets. He says that the Jews interpret the prophecies *carnaliter,* i.e. in a carnal or earthly manner. This is of course a familiar term in early Christian literature, both in Latin and Greek (σωματικῶ). Commenting on Isaiah 65:21 "They shall build houses and inhabit them; they plant vineyards and eat their fruit. They shall not build and another inhabit; they shall not plan another eat. . . ." Jerome says that the Jews take this prophecy *carnaliter* to mean that the cities of Judaea will be restored to their original condition. (*Comm in Esa.* 65:21, ll. 9-11; see also *in Es.* 11:15-16; cf. also Eusebius, *in Es.* 2:1-4, 16, ll. 12).

How should one translate *carnaliter?* The best translation is "politically." The Jews believed that the prophecies referred to something that would happen in historical time; they point to the actual return of the Jews to the land of Israel, the resettling of the land, and the building of a Jewish kingdom. Against this idea, Christian writers such as Jerome and Theodoret (and of course many others) offer a spiritual reading of the texts, which in this context means either the texts refer to the spiritual redemption in Christ through the church, or to a heavenly kingdom that will be discontinuous with life on this earth.

Jewish Messianism, in contrast to Christian Messianism, has always been political, as Gershen Scholem reminds us.

"Judaism in all of its forms and manifestations, has always maintained a concept of redemption as an event that takes place publicly, on the stage of history and within the community. It is an occurence which takes place in the visible world and which cannot be con-

---

[36] See Marcel Simon, *Verus Israel. Étude sur les Relations Entre Chrétiens et Juifs dans L'Empire Romain* (Paris: 1964), 189-213

ceived of apart from such visible appearance. In contrast, Christianity conceives of redemption as an event in the spiritual and unseen realm, an event which is reflected in the soul, in the private world of each individual, and which effects an inner transformation which need not correspond to anything outside. Even the *civitas dei* of Augustine, which within the confines of Christian dogmatics and in the interest of the church has made the most far-reaching attempt both to retain and to reinterpret the Jewish categories of redemption, is a community of the mysteriously redeemed with an unredeemed world. What for the one stood unconditionally at the end of history as its most distant aim was for the other the true center of the historical process, even if that process was henceforth peculiarly decked out as Heilsgeschichte."[37]

In speaking then of Jewish beliefs as "carnal," Jerome (even by his own caricature) given us an insight into the character of ancient Jewry. As late as the fifth century, five hundred years after the destruction of the city of Jerusalem by the Romans, Jews continued to believe in a redemption that would take place in the realm of history and politics, in this world. They had not given up their national aspirations. Or to put the matter somewhat more precisely, the Jews differed from other ancient peoples in that they identified with a land from which they believed themselves to have been excluded. The land of Israel was a factor in shaping and maintaining Jewish identity. For the Jew Israel was not an Elysian fields or the Islands of the Blessed as the Greek poets had pictured the place reserved for those favored by the gods (*Odyssey* 4.563-59). It was an actual territory with boundaries and cities, with a past and a future.

The emergence of Christian Palestine in the early Byzantine period and the new identification of Christianity with the land of

---

[37] Gershom Scholem, *The Messianic Idea in Judaism* (New York: 1971), 1. On the political character of Jewish Messianism, see H. A. Silver, *A History of Messianic Speculation in Israel:* It should be borne in mind that Messianism was essentially a political idea. It was bound up with the restoration of the Davidic dynasty and with the reconstitution of the independence of Israel. Certain eschatological and supernatural features were combined with it, but essentially it was a remained a this-worldly, temporal, national ideal" (p. 13). See also Joseph Klausner, *The Messianic Idea in Israel* (New York: 1955), quoting Graetz: "[In the second century] people expected of the Messiah that above all he should bring freedom and the restoration of the national life" (p. 395). In his recent article "Messianic Themes in Formative Judaism," *JAAR* 52 (1984), 357-374, Jacob Neusner argues (contra Scholem and Klausner) that there is "no such thing as the Messianic idea." He shows how diverse Messianic conceptions were during the formative period of Jewish history. His point is well taken. In citing Scholem and Klausner et al. I simply wish to underscore that one of the persistent elements of Jewish Messianism, its this—worldly and political character, came to the fore at the time Christianity became dominant in the land of Israel.

Israel introduced a new element in Christianity's relation to Judaism.[38] For now, Christians, who had previously demoted the earthly Jerusalem in favor of the heavenly city (Gal. 4) and appealed to Jesus' words that "neither on his mountain [Gerizim in Samaria] nor in Jerusalem will you worship the Father" against the "carnal" interpretations of the Jews (John),[39] claimed that the grace of God was more abundant in Jerusalem than in any other place (See Gregory of Nyssa, ep. 2). Many believed that their faith would be incomplete if they did not worship Christ in the very places where he lived (Jerome, ep. 46).

Unlike other Christian beliefs (for example the doctrine of the Trinity) or Christian rituals (for example the Eucharist), the spiritual power associated with Jerusalem centered on a place, on soil and rocks and stones. In contrast to the bread and wine in the Eucharist, the water of Baptism or even the bones of the martyrs, all of which were portable, the city of Jerusalem and the other holy places in the land were fixed, bound to the earth, stationary. The Eucharist could be celebrated anywhere, and whether it took place in a magnificent basilica shimmering with gold and sparkling with mosaics, in a simple house, or in a cave in the desert, its efficacy and meaning did not alter. But the tomb of Christ, the cave in Bethlehem and the mountain from which he ascended to heaven could not be transported. Indeed, their religious potency depended on possessing the places where the events had occurred.[40] It was in Jerusalem during this period that the stational liturgies first arose.[41] Pilgrims come to the holy city to celebrate the saving events of Christ's life at the very places where they had taken place centuries earlier. They were thrilled to read the accounts of biblical history, as Egeria reports, "at the very spot" (*ipso loco* Etheria 3.6).

---

[38] On the change in relations between Jews and Christians in Jerusalem during the Byzantine period see Annon Linder, "Jerusalem between Jews and Christians in the Byzantine Period," *Cathedra* II (1979), 109-119, and the articles responding to his essay by Gedalia Strumsa, Josef Yahalom, Yoram Isafrir and Joshua Praver (in Hebrew).

[39] See Robert L. Wilken, *Judaism and the Early Christian Mind. A Study of Cyril of Alexandria's Exegesis and Theology* (New Haven: 1971), 69-92.

[40] For this reason Christians thought the holy places should be in the hands of Christians, a problem which troubled Christians after the Arab conquest. See the comments by Eutychius, the Melkite patriarch of Alexandria (933-940 C.E.) in his *Book of Demonstration* 1.310, *Corpus Scriptorum Christianorum Orientalium* 193, p. 321.

[41] On the stational liturgy in Jerusalem, see G. Kretschmar, "Festkalendar und Memorialstaetten Jerusalems in altkirchlicher Zeit," *Zeitschrift des deutschen Palestina-Vereins* 87 (1971), 168-205. Also John Baldovin, *The Urban Character of Christian Worship in Jerusalem, Rome and Constantinople from the Fourth to the Tenth Centuries: The Origins, Development, and Meaning of Stational Liturgy*, Diss., Yale, 1983.

In the Byzantine period, Christians began to identify with Israel
in a way that was hardly conceivable in the generations before the
Christianization of Palestine. The Jewish Scriptures, the Christian
Old Testament, took on new life. The traditions of ancient Israel need
no longer be simply spirtualized, they could be applied literally, i.e.
politically. When Zacharias, the patriarch of Jerusalem, was taken
captive by the Persian conquerors in 614 C.E., he adopted the
language of the ancient exiles in Babylonia to express his feelings
about the city:

> "May the name of the Lord be blessed because he does not deal with
> us according to our sins nor require us according to our iniquities.
> 'Woe is me that I am so far from Zion and I dwell among the tents of
> Kedar' [Ps. 121:5]. Like David, so I am longing, singing day and
> night, carrying this verse on my lips: 'If I forget you, O Jerusalem, or
> the people which dwells in your midst, let my right hand wither' [Ps.
> 137]. Let it be known to you my brothers that we also sat down there
> by the waters of Babylon and wept when we remembered Zion,
> Golgotha, the life-giving tomb, Bethlehem of everlasting memory.
> Behold brethren, 'we lift up our eyes to the hills of Zion from whence
> comes our help. . . .'Hear my voice, the voice of Zachariah the
> captive." *PG* 86.3230)[42]

The developments in Palestine in the fifth-sixth centuries altered
the way Christians viewed the Jews because Christians now saw
themselves differently. Few Christians of this time would have said,
as Melito of Sardis did in the second century, "the Jerusalem below
was precious, but it is worthless now because of the Jerusalem above"
(Paschal Homily 45). They would have have been more likely to agree
with the view of another outsider group, the Persians. It was reported
that the Persians were intent on capturing Jerusalem "because this
city is the refuge of all Christians and the strength of their empire."[43]
The rebuilder of Jerusalem after the sack of the Persians in 614

---

[42] See also the poems of Sophronius, the patriarch of Jerusalem at the time of the Arab
conquest. "Holy City of God/Jerusalem, how I long to stand/even now at your gates/ and
go in, rejoicing. A divine longing for holy Solyma/presses upon me insistently (*Anacre-
onticon* 20). Translation of Anacreontica 19 and 20 in John Wilkinson, *Jerusalem
Pilgrims*, 91-92. Text in M. Gigante, *Sophronii Anacreontica*, Opuscula: Testi per
esercitazioni accademiche, 10-12 (Rome: 1957). For Sophronius's reaction to the Arab
invasion, see his Christmas sermon of 634, ed. H. Usener, "Weihnachtspredigt des
Sophronos." *Rheinisches Museum fuer Philologie*, n.f. 41 (1886), 506-515; also Walter
Emil Kaegi, "Initial Byzantine Reactions to the Arab Conquest," *Church History* 38
(1969), 139-149.
[43] Strategius, *The Capture of Jerusalem by the Persians*, 8.4 (ed. G. Garitte, 203, 13).
Corpus Scriptorum Christianorum Orientalium

C.E., bishop Modestus, was called a "second Bezaleel, a new Zerubabel"(Pg 89,1421ff.).

Of course, all of this was to change swiftly and dramatically with the arrival of the Muslim armies at the gates of Jerusalem in 638 C.E. The centuries of Christian rule in Palestine came to an abrupt end, and the Christian idea of holy land underwent another transformation. Now it was to be fueled by pilgrims who came in a steady stream during the next five hundred years until the arrival of the crusaders in the 12th century. But the period of Christian rule in Palestine is instructive, for what it can teach us about both Judaism and Christianity. For the two peoples discovered in this period new things about which to quarrel, and thereby learned new things about themselves.[44] Issues which were submerged in earlier centuries, but which have an enduring significance, now surfaced for the first time. The return of the Jews to the land of Israel has been the great theme of modern Jewish history, and in our day, Jews and Christians alike have looked again with fresh eyes at the ancient prophecies of restoration. It may be too much to say that the men and women of the early Byzantine period foreshadowed the debates of modern times, but the things that identified Jews and engaged Christians then, are not unlike the things that do so today.

---

[44] There is a strong strain of anti-Judaism in Palestinian Christianity in the Byzantine period. It focuses, however, on topics that are unique to Jerusalem, e.g. the finding of the true cross, the proto-martyr St. Stephen, the churches of Jerusalem and Bethlehem. See R. Deveesse, "Une collection hierosolymitaine au Sinai," *Revue Biblique* 47 (1938), 555-58. See Hesychius of Jerusalem, Homily on St. Stephen in P. Devos, "Le panegyrique de saint Etienne par Hesychius de Jerusalem," *Analecta Bollandiana* 86 (1968), 151-172; also M. Aubineau, *Les Homilies Festales d'Hesychius de Jerusalem*, Vol. I, *Subsidia hagiographica*, No. 59 (Brussels: 1970).

20

The Conversions of Avitus of Clermont, and Similar Passages in Gregory of Tours

Walter Goffart
University of Toronto

Between Easter and Pentecost of the year 576, Avitus, bishop of Clermont in the Auvergne, induced several hundred Jews to convert to Christianity. It is the one documented case during the early Middle Ages of conversion on a large scale outside Spain. (Clermont was where, five hundred years later, Urban II would first preach the crusade.) The unusual character of what Avitus brought about, and the difficulties with the evidence, are an incentive to further study—even after the searching examinations by Bernard Blumenkranz and other scholars.[1] A little more about the event and its wider context may be learned by focusing closely on the author on whose testimony we chiefly rely.

Unexpectedly for this rather poorly documented period, we have

---

[1] H. Graetz, *Geschichte der Juden von den ältesten Zeiten bis auf die Gegenwart*, V (Magdeburg: 1860), 59-61 (includes a useful partial translation of Fortunatus' poem); Solo Wittmayer Baron, *A Social and Religious History of the Jews*, III, 2d ed. (N.Y.: 1957), 51-53; Solomon Katz, *The Jews in the Visigothic and Frankish Kingdoms of Spain and Gaul* (Cambridge Mass.: 1937) (singularly uninformative about the events at Clermont); Bernard S. Bachrach, *Early Medieval Jewish Policy in Western Europe* (Minneapolis: 1977), 55-56; Bernhard Blumenkranz, *Juifs et Chrétiens dans le monde occidental, 430-1096* (Paris-The Hague: 1960), 34, 89, 93, 98-99, 134 n. 245, 140-41, 378-79, and, *Les auteurs latins chrétiens du moyen âge sur les Juifs et le Judaisme* (Paris-The Hague: 1963), 64-66 no. 50, 70 no. 58. Blumenkranz sets the standard for any account of this episode. If I occasionally take issue with him (while disregarding others), it is out of respect for the authoritativeness of his interpretation. I am much indebted besides to my friend and colleague, Professor Josef Shatzmiller (University of Toronto), for his thoughtful comments.

When this paper was orally delivered, my attention was kindly drawn to Jean Juster, *La condition légale des Juifs sous les rois visigoths* (Paris: 1912), (originally published in *Études d'histoire juridique offertes à Paul Frédéric Girard*), and to its translation and updating with later bibliography by Alfredo M. Rubello in *Israel Law Review*, 11 (1976), 216-87, 391-414, 563-90. Hardly anything in this work bears on conditions in the Frankish kingdom, with the possible exception of Juster's discussion of the laws concerning Jews in the *Breviarium Alaricianum* (*Lex Romana Visigothorum*).

two informants, and they are the best Latin writers of the day. Bishop
Avitus was a teacher and friend of Gregory, bishop of Tours. The
celebrated historian of the Frankish kingdom in the late sixth century
was a native of Clermont and retained a lively interest in the affairs of
his home town.[2] Another good friend of Gregory's was Venantius
Fortunatus, an Italian poet and man of letters who had settled at
Poitiers, not far from Tours. Soon after Avitus' conversions, Gregory
sent Fortunatus a written report of the incident, inviting him to set it
to verse. Fortunatus complied with an epic of 150 lines, prefaced by a
prose dedication to Gregory; he claims to have dashed off the poem in
a few days, presumably within scant weeks after the conversions took
place.[3] Fortunatus' verses survive, but Gregory's original report does
not; what we have from him is a chapter of his famous *Histories*.
Although Gregory's *Ten Books of Histories* and their hagiographic
companion piece the *Eight Books of Miracles* appear to have been
issued only after his death in 594, internal evidence suggests that the
chapter about Avitus and the Jews was composed in the early 580s or
even earlier, in other words, within about five years of the event.
Gregory had Fortunatus' epic at hand when writing his version.[4] As
we shall see, the poem and Gregory's prose embody surprising
differences, yet they can on no account be deemed independent of
each other; Fortunatus knew only what Gregory had told him, and
Gregory could not have diverged from Fortunatus' verse without
being aware of so doing.

   Many subjects interested Gregory more than the Jews. Out of the
several hundred miracle stories that he composed or recorded, only

---

[2] O. M. Dalton, *The History of the Franks, by Gregory of Tours* (Oxford: 1927), I, 6. For
Gregory's interest, see Dalton's index under Clermont-Ferrand (II, 632).

[3] Dalton, *History of the Franks*, I, 15, 21-22, 81-84. Fortunatus, *Carmina* 5. 5, ed. F.
Leo, *Monumenta Germaniae historica* [hereafter MGH], *Auctores antiquissimi*, IV
(Berlin: 1881), 107-12. Fortunatus refers to Gregory's report and his own rapid
versifying (lines 139-43, p. 112).

[4] For convenience, I shall normally cite Gregory after the collective edition of Wilhelm
Arndt and Bruno Krusch, MGH *Scriptores rerum Merovingicarum*, I (Hannover: 1885).
This contains both the *Histories* and the *Miracula*. There is also a 2d MGH edition of
the *Histories*, by Krusch and Wilhelm Levison (Hannover: 1937-51). Blumenkranz,
Auteurs chrétiens, 70 n. 12, conservatively cites 574-593 as the terminal years for
composition of the *Histories*. It is hard to be certain when any particular chapter was
composed; different facts point in different directions—5. 14 seems to date from 582 and
584, 5. 19 before 582; but 5. 3 is from after 588 (ed. Krusch-Levison, xxi-xxii). Greater
certainty about Gregory's chronology of authorship used to be expressed, such as
580-584/5 for books 5 and 6 (ed. Arndt-Krusch, 17). For our purposes, the problem has
little importance. Gregory's echoes of Fortunatus' poem are indicated in the Krusch-
Levison edition of his account in 205 n. 4, and 206 nn. 1-5.

four involve Jews, and of these, a single one takes place in Gaul; the three other stories came to him at second or third hand from the eastern Mediterranean.[5] The summary of biblical history that opens the *Histories* portrays the ancient Israelites as a paradigm of depraved humanity turning away from God, very much as the Bible does.[6] In a fragmentarily preserved *Commentary on the Psalms*, Gregory notes that Jews and gentiles, synagogue and church, have now exchanged places, and that the Bible has to be understood with this modification: if the Israelites were the typical depraved humanity of the past, the Christians play that role today.[7] In the *Histories*, again, Gregory emphasizes how the Jews mocked Christ at the Passion, rejecting Him, just as they had rejected the prophets. But he names Pontius Pilate as the villain of the Crucifixion, and though the destruction of the Temple by Vespasian and the many deaths during the siege of Jerusalem are mentioned, Gregory does not follow the church historian Eusebius in making this disaster a punishment for the treatment of Christ.[8] Elsewhere, however, he is less circumspect, singling out the Jews as Christ's killers.[9]

Gregory's views are conventional. In a miracle story, he has a Jew exclaim while looking at an image of Christ, "Behold the seductor who humbled us and our people."[10] Gregory took for granted the Jews' hostility toward Christianity, and he was well aware of the reason behind it, but he was content that they should be humbled. The Jews would be Christians if a veil did not obscure their inner sight; their religion was *perfidia;* the duties of a good bishop included preaching to the Jews of his city with a view to their conversion.[11]

Gregory's Gaul was not ethnically or linguistically homogeneous, and the bishop of Tours had few illusions about the fervor and conduct of its Christians. Through the pages of the *Histories,* we are conscious of a multiplicity of peoples coexisting under Frankish rule,

---

[5] Summaries and references in Blumenkranz, *Auteurs chrétiens*, 68-69 nos. 54-56, 57 (the only Gallic one). A Greek version of no. 54 was given by Gregory's Greek contemporary, the church historian Evagrius.

[6] Gregory, *Hist.* 1. 12, 14, 15, 16, 40-42.

[7] Ed. Arndt-Krusch, 874 line 12-13.

[8] *Hist.* 1. 20, 24 (Pontius Pilate), 26 (Vespasian); 43, 45, 46. For the account of Eusebius, *Ecclesiastical History* 3. 5. 3, 6, 7. 1, ed. G. Bardy, I (Paris: 1952), 102-04, 110.

[9] Gregory, *Liber in gloria martyrum* 3, ed. Arndt-Krusch, 489.

[10] *Ibid.* 21, p. 501.

[11] *Hist.* 5. 11, 6. 17, 4. 12; 200, 259, 149. Gregory's reference to *perfidia* is standard Christian Latin; see Bernhard Blumenkranz, "Perfidia," *Archivum Latinitatis medii aevi (Bulletin Du Cange),* 22 (1952), 157-70 (with many citations).

and Gregory does not in any way single out the Jews as outsiders.
Indeed, he never gives a name to the most numerous element of the
population (whom we call Gallo-Romans) or implies that they had any
claims to special consideration. Even the government was not united,
owing to the Frankish practice of allocating equal shares in the
kingdom to each royal son. Gregory was sensitive to the presence of
Arian heretics in Visigothic Spain; as for the pagan peoples to the
north and east (many of them within the Frankish orbit) and the
equally pagan Saxons in Britain, he seems to have been almost wholly
unconcerned about their religious condition.[12] Gregory considered
the present to be preferable to the past, in as much as the Catholic
church of Gaul was safe from internal and external enemies, but he
was well aware that most of its members—even clerical ones—had no
idea of what being a Christian meant. A major theme of the *Histories*
is the folly and depravity of unredeemed humanity, "the downfall of
wretched men (*miserorum excidia*)"; Gregory piles scene upon scene
showing men and women striving after the delusive goods and
delights of this world, and pursuing what, in Augustinian terms,
would be called the life of the *civitas terrena*.[13]

Under the circumstances, it is not surprising that on the few
occasions when Gregory mentions Jews, they often appear in neutral
settings. For instance, ship manned by Jews and sailing from Ville-
franche to Marseilles was compelled by a miracle to pull into the
islands of Lerins; an archdeacon at Bourges called in a Jew to apply
cupping-glasses; a Jewish moneylender was secretly murdered by
royal officials in debt to him, and lacking proof, his relatives were
unable to secure an indictment against the culprits; the Jews of
Clermont joined with the other inhabitants in mourning a well-loved
bishop, and they liked his successor because he was a good customer
of theirs.[14] Several of these episodes are to someone's discredit, but
not to the Jews'. What we mainly learn about the latter are their
various occupations. In addition, a number of passages suggest that

---

[12] Walter Goffart, "Foreigners in the *Histories* of Gregory of Tours," *Florilegium*, 4 (1982), 80-99.

[13] For *miserorum excidia*, see *Hist.* 2. praef., 58-59; this preface is Gregory's most important programatic statement. The views of his work given here are developed in my book in preparation, *The Narrators of Barbarian History (A.D. 550-800): Jordanes, Gregory of Tours, Bede, and Paul the Deacon.*

[14] Summaries and references in Blumenkranz, *Auteurs chrétiens*, 69 no. 56 bis; 70 no. 57 ter; 72 no. 61; 70 no. 57 bis; 72 no. 62 bis a.

Marseille was the main center of Gallic Jewry, from which influences radiated northward via the Rhone valley to Paris and, otherwise, overseas to Italy and perhaps to the East.[15]

As for Jewish conversion to Christianity, Gregory reports two cases but judges them in diametrically opposite ways. He applauds the action of Bishop Avitus and portrays it in the colors of a miracle, but the conversions for which King Chilperic (561-584) was responsible were futile and resulted in a pile of corpses. Because the case Gregory deplores features a king whom he loathed, we should first look at a fleeting episode that sets the Jews in relation with the one contemporary king of whom Gregory thought well. Though lacking the drama of the two sets of conversions, the passage goes far toward defining the condition of Judaism in a late sixth-century Catholic kingdom. Predictably, the difference from the situation in the later Roman Empire was faint.

[King Guntram makes a solemn entry into Orleans and is greeted by large delegations from every segment of the population, carrying bells and banners, and intoning acclamations (*laudes*) in their particular languages.] The Jews who participated in these chants of praise said, "All peoples adore you, bend their knees to you, and are subject to you." This was why, after mass was celebrated, when the king sat at the banquet, he said, "Woe to the Jewish people, evil and faithless and always living by craft. If today," he said, "they sang adulatory praises to the effect that all peoples adored me as lord, it is so that I might order the rebuilding at public expense of their synagogue, which was cast down by the Christians a little while ago. By the Lord's command, I shall never do this." How splendidly admirable the king was in discernment! So well did he understand the craftiness of the heretics that they were completely unable to extract from him the favor that they later sought.[16]

King Guntram's remarks are made in the context of the ancient and well documented ritual of an *adventus*. As Gregory outlines it, delegations greeted the king outside the city with liturgical acclamations. Then the royal party processed to the main church for a religious service after which a feast was laid on. Finally, local

---

[15] *Hist.* 5. 11, p. 201; 6. 17 p. 260, as well as Gregory the Great, *Registrum epistolarum* 1. 45, ed. P. Ewald and L. M. Hartmann, MGH *Epistolae* I (Berlin: 1891), 71-72. That Pope Gregory took a hand in checking the zeal of the bishops of Marseilles and Arles is perhaps more significant than the bishops' actions.

[16] *Hist.* 8. 1; 326. My translation. Cf. Blumenkranz, *Auteurs chrétiens*, p. 72 no. 62.

petitioners were admitted to the king's presence to make requests that, under the circumstances, he had a special incentive to grant. A royal visit was costly to the townspeople, but it was welcome because in return, the king incurred an obligation to bestow lucrative favors, and usually did so within reason.[17]

The ominous feature of the passage is its casual report of the destruction of the Orleans synagogue. A subordinate clause is all we shall hear of it, as though Christian violence toward synagogues were too common to rate special notice. Late Roman evidence suggests that this was the case, and Pope Gregory I (590-604) took pains to check such aggressions in the Italy of his time, and even in Marseilles.[18] Where Orleans was concerned, only one point is stressed, namely, that King Guntram, unmoved by Jewish flattery, refused to grant royal funds for reconstruction.

By law, the Jews had a good claim and Guntram the duty, not perhaps to pay the cost, but at least to secure compensation from the parties responsible for the aggression.[19] A well known parallel from Ostrogothic Italy shows the Jews of Ravenna obtaining by legal action a suitable judgment for the rebuilding of their destroyed meeting place. (To be sure, the Christian source asserts that the judge was biased and the award iniquitous.)[20] Roman law, still applicable even in the Frankish kingdom, was on the side of the Jews, guaranteeing the integrity of their synagogues and prescribing compensation for their loss.

Gregory is so fulsome in celebrating King Guntram's ability to recognize and resist flattery that he urges us to look elsewhere for what he, a conscientious churchman, really had in mind. In a partisan Christian perspective, the better (though unstated) reason for him to praise Guntram was that the king had subordinated state law to the higher demands of God. Two centuries before, in the affair of the synagogue at Callinicum, St. Ambrose of Milan had compelled the

---

[17] Fergus Millar, *The Emperor in the Roman World* (Ithaca, N.Y.: 1977), 31-38; Sabine MacCormack, "Change and Continuity in Late Antiquity: the Ceremony of *Adventus*," *Historia*, 21 (1972), 721-52. For a comment of special interest to this occasion, see Noel Coulet, "De l' intégration à l'exclusion: la place des Juifs dans les cérémonies d'entrée solennelle au moyen âge," *Annales: Économies, sociétés, civilisations*, 34 (1979), 672-83 at 674: the words Gregory quotes are adapted from a Jewish prayer.

[18] Jean Juster, *Les Juifs dans l'Empire romain* (Paris: 1914), I, 462-72 with nn.; for the letters of Gregory the Great, Blumenkranz, *Auteurs chrétiens*, 75 nos. 63, 65 (Marseilles), 80-81 nos. 81-82, 85 no. 85.

[19] Juster, *Juifs dans l'Emp. rom.*, I, 459-62.

[20] *Excerpta Valesiana* 81-82, ed. J. Moreau (Leipzig: 1968), 23-24.

emperor Theodosius I to take this course;[21] the Frank, Guntram, however, acted spontaneously.

Needless to say, Gregory's reasoning and Guntram's are deplorable from our standpoint. Yet they have the historical value of illustrating what early medieval (and late Roman) churchmen expected of their kings. The inclination of the Christian majority to persecute the Jews had found dramatic expression ever since the fourth century, but its dynamism was blunted by a state apparatus and a massive law code that were pre-Christian in origin and sluggish in bending to the precepts of the new religion. This inertial force, the residue of Roman legality, was the principal basis for whatever tranquility the Jews enjoyed; toleration of Judaism was grounded in the same code that incorporated all the other rules of social order, and the privileges of Christianity as well.

However inevitable it was that Christians should subscribe to this ancient body of law, their adhesion was not unqualified. There was a Power higher than that of emperors and kings; in Its name, the martyrs had suffered state persecution, and their defiance of the state-sponsored gods was continually recalled.[22] Tutored in these precedents, Christians were not limited to being passively law-abiding citizens. The undermining of law when it seemed to clash with religious imperatives was a competing duty. Gregory of Tours would have been anomalous if he had not favored the bending of state rules and regulations in conformity with what long-held religious opinion deemed to be God's demands—in this case, that Judaism should be curtailed. Guntram was praiseworthy for doing so in a case that involved only the royal purse; unprompted, as it would seem, he understood that the resources of a Christian king should not be spent to rebuild a place of non-Christian worship.[23] It is not implied,

---

[21] Juster, *Juifs dans l'Emp. rom.*, I, 462-63 n. 3; Otto Seeck, *Geschichte des Untergangs der antiken Welt*, V 2d ed., (Stuttgart: n.d.), 222-24; J. R. Palanque, G. Bardy, and P. de Labriolle, *De la paix constantinienne à la mort de Théodose*, A. Fliche and V. Martin, ed., *Histoire de l'Église*, V; (Paris: 1950), 510-11; Jean Gaudemet, *L'Église dans l'Empire romain (IVe-Ve siècle)* (Paris: 1958), 627.

[22] Two books of Gregory's *Miracula* celebrate martyrs (ed. Arndt-Krusch, pp. 484-584). In a more general way, manuscript collections of saints' lives devote, on average, over two-thirds of their space to narratives of martyrdom: Guy Philippart, *Les légendiers latins et autres manuscrits hagiographiques*, L. Genicot, ed., "Typologie des sources du moyen âge occidental," fasc. 24-25, (Turnhout: 1977), 40-44. These *passiones*, often fictional and lurid, were deemed authentic and prized as reading matter by early medieval Christians. Their message surely influenced action.

[23] Cf. the comments of Ambrose in the case of Callinicum: the synagogue should not be rebuilt, even at state expense; doing so would be an impious act, almost a public apostasy (Palanque et al., *De la paix constantinienne*, 510).

however, that the Jews of Orleans would no longer have a synagogue; only that its reconstruction would be at their expense.

There was a great difference between Guntram's action, which Gregory praised, and King Chilperic's, which he execrated, and the difference had a more principled basis than just personal antipathy. Both in his official capacity and personally, Gregory had many reasons to complain of Chilperic, but he also saw in him the arrogance of royal power (typified in the *Histories* by a dramatic passage where Chilperic makes his short-lived attempt to modify the Nicene formula and impose the resultant heterodoxy upon his subjects).[24] Whereas Guntram strove to rule in what he and his counsellors conceived to be a more Christian fashion, Chilperic aspired to be an autocrat in the Byzantine style. Two passages in the *Histories* are concerned with Chilperic and Jewish conversion. The link between them, almost certainly deliberate on Gregory's part, is a merchant named Priscus, who paid for his favor at court with his life.

> King Chilperic, when still at the aforesaid villa [Nogent-sur-Marne], ordered the baggage to move and made to depart for Paris. When I [Gregory] went to take my leave of him, there appeared a certain Jew named Priscus, who was in his service as a purchasing agent. The king gently took him by the hair and said to me, "Come, priest of God, and place your hand on him." Because [Priscus] resisted, the king said, "O hardened spirit and ever unbelieving generation . . ." [and began a discourse on why Jews should convert]. The Jew replied . . . At this the king was silent, so I joined in and said . . . [the disputation continued at greater length between Priscus and Gregory]. Though I said these and other things, the wretch was never goaded into belief. As he stood silent, the king, seeing that [Priscus] was not brought to remorse by these words, turned to me . . . [and he and Gregory took leave of each other].[25]

Gregory, a careful writer, sets a tidy stage. Chilperic had summoned him to join the royal court at Nogent. Gregory had been there a while.[26] The encounter with Priscus unfolds as a long parenthesis in the formalities of Gregory's taking leave of the king.

In Gregory's *Histories*, the debate with Priscus is not an isolated

---

[24] On Gregory and Chilperic, in brief, Dalton, *History of the Franks*, I, 10-11; Chilperic's theological foray, Gregory of Tours, *Hist.* 5. 44; 236-37.
[25] *Hist.* 6. 5; 247-49. My translation omits all the details of the disputation, which, for reasons to be given shortly, seem to be basically irrelevant. The terms of debate are closely examined by Fausto Parente, "La controversia tra Ebrei e Cristiani in Francia e in Spagna dal VI al IX secolo," Centro italiano di studi sull'alto medioevo, *Settimane di studio*, 26 (1980), 529-639 at 543-52.
[26] *Hist.* 6. 2-3; 245-46.

case of religious disputation; it is one of a string of chapters illustrating the pointlessness of theological argument. Chlotild strives learnedly but without success to convince her husband, Clovis, to become a Christian; Gregory himself argues at different times with King Chilperic and with two Arian Visigoths from Spain, as well as with Priscus. Each time the argument is in vain. Some years later, he did manage to talk a Christian out of his heretical doubts concerning bodily resurrection, but the interlocutor was one of his own priests, who presumably had better reasons than Gregory's words for seeing the light.[27] To document his disbelief in the persuasive power of carefully ordered words and plausible expositions, Gregory cited his own case: though he read and learned the Scriptures under the excellent tutelage of Avitus at Clermont, he was unable to live by them.[28] Others (saints excepted) could hardly be expected to do better. If Gregory's own writings eschewed fine style and focused on the portrayal of current events, both miraculous and appalling, it was because the evidence of lived experience had a persuasive force that rhetoric was manifestly unable to equal. The *Miracles* and *Histories* were his alternative to the impotence of ordinary religious discourse.[29]

To this extent, the debate with Priscus is part of an extended joke running through the *Histories*. All the right things are said; the opposition is allowed its lines and not caricatured, but the Catholic case is allocated far more space; strings of scriptural passages are mustered more impeccably than they could possibly be in a casual, conversational encounter; yet nothing happens. In the Priscus passage, the joke also operates on a secondary level. Chilperic initiates the argument, but Priscus basically shuts him up; the king's repertory of apologetic is as quickly exhausted as is his theology elsewhere.[30] Gregory has to step in, pick up the strands, and carry on in the name of Christianity for several more pages. He assures us that he, at least, did not run out of things to say, but it made no difference. Whereas

---

[27] *Hist.* 2. 29, 5. 44, 5. 43, 6. 40, 10. 13; 90-91, 236-37, 234-36, 278-81, 419-23. Blumenkranz, *Auteurs chrétiens,* 107 n. 6, concerning the letter of Pseudo-Severus of Minorca, recognizes a similar skepticism vis-à-vis the possibilities of persuasion, but places it exclusively in a context of Jewish conversion. The contrast between the ineffectuality of words and the potency of miracles (or action) is a common early medieval theme.

[28] *Vita patrum* 2. praef.; 668-69.

[29] I develop these points in the book indicated above n. 13.

[30] *Hist.* 5. 44; 236-37: the very austere and saintly bishop Salvius of Albi simply terrified the king out of his theological novelty.

Priscus had silenced Chilperic, Gregory now silenced Priscus. The sterile outcome was foreordained.

The opening of the scene is designed as an anticipation of Chilperic's forcible conversions. The king took Priscus by the hair—"gently" is a nice touch—and invited Gregory to carry out the gesture of exorcism, to take the devil out of him, as it were, so that he would believe. There is no sign that Gregory was tempted by Chilperic's suggestion. Blumenkranz comments, "[Priscus] repousse la main que Grégoire veut lui imposer"; the text, omitting any reference to Gregory's wishes or his hand, indicates no more than that Priscus wriggled out of the king's grasp and triggered Chilperic's attempt at exhortation.[31] It would have been out of character for Gregory to respond to the king's invitation. Priscus, though long onstage, is not central to the scene.

Besides using the occasion to reiterate the futility of debate, Gregory dramatizes the loathesomeness of Chilperic. At a casual moment, full of ostensible affability, he lays hands on a merchant who enjoys his favor and tries to bend him to his will. As Gregory well knew, the acts of the martyrs often portray affable emperors and governors amicably urging Christians to sacrifice to the gods.[32] Chilperic was a tyrant in that mold. From his amiable urging and argument, there was only a small step to anger at being thwarted and to the use of force:

This year, King Chilperic ordered that many Jews be baptized; he received the greater number of them from the holy font. Quite a few of them, however, were washed in body only, not in their hearts; they lied to God and returned to the same infidelity that they formerly had, with the result that they both observed the Sabbath and honored the Lord's day.

Absolutely no argument, however, could induce Priscus to recognize the truth. The king, enraged, ordered him to be imprisoned, so that he who could not believe voluntarily might, as it were, be made to listen and believe under duress. But [Priscus], by giving gifts to various persons, obtained a delay until his son was married to a Jewess from Marseilles; he promised craftily that, afterwards, he would go through with what the king had ordered.

Meanwhile, a dispute arose between him and Phatir, a convert from Judaism, who now was the king's godson. On the Sabbath day, Priscus, wrapped in a prayer-shawl and carrying nothing made of

---

[31] On the meaning of the gesture, Parente, "Controversia," 545-46. Blumenkranz, *Juifs et Chrétiens*, p. 70.
[32] Hippolyte Delehaye, *Les passions des martyrs et les genres littéraires* (Brussels: 1921), 257-58.

iron, so as to fulfil the law of Moses, proceeded to the place of prayer. As he did so, Phatir suddenly appeared and with a sword butchered [Priscus] and the attendants he had with him. When they were slain, [Phatir] and his slaves, who had been on an adjoining square, fled to the basilica of St. Julian. While there, they learned that [King Chilperic] granted the master [Phatir] his life but ordered that his slaves be dragged from the basilica and put to death as criminals. Then, after the master had fled, one of [the slaves] drew his sword, killed his fellows, and afterwards stepped out of the basilica with his sword: the people rushed forward and cruelly killed him.

Phatir, however, obtained permission to leave and returned to the kingdom of Guntram, from which he had come. Not many days later Priscus's relatives killed him.[33]

The chapter is in the following two parts: a general statement about Chilperic's conversions and their outcome, then, a more particular scene, designed to illustrate the appalling results of Chilperic's initiative. The reference to the church of St. Julian, today St. Julien-le-Pauvre, permits an approximate localization of Phatir's assault on Priscus. St. Julian's was in Paris, on the left bank of the Seine, near the river and the southern gate; the Petit Pont and the intersection of the Roman roads from Orleans and Lyons were nearby. It was a busy quarter of the city.[34] Gregory uses the term *secretiora*, literally "more withdrawn places," to signify Priscus's Sabbath destination; he obviously means a synagogue. Blumenkranz inferred from Gregory's word that this synagogue was "clandestine," driven underground by Chilperic's persecution.[35] His interpretation is virtually irreconcilable with Priscus's ostentatious approach; besides, we are not told that the Jews of Paris were affected by the royal measure. Gregory's word is probably meant sarcastically, to complement the satiric portrayal of Priscus's scrupulous Sabbath observance.

The thematic opening tells us less than we would like to know. Presumably, Chilperic did not order the baptism of all the Jews in his kingdom; "many" stands without any standard of comparison. If he could personally be godfather to the majority, the Jews affected may

---

[33] *Hist.* 6. 17; 259-60. My translation.

[34] May Vieillard-Troiekouroff, *Les monuments religieux de la Gaule d'après les oeuvres de Grégoire de Tours* (Paris: 1976), 208 (map, p. 203).

[35] Blumenkranz, *Juifs et Chrétiens*, p. 105. In support of Blumenkranz's interpretation, Professor Josef Shatzmiller has pointed out to me that (1) Gregory's usage of *secretiora* = "synagogue" is unique; (2) in later centuries, synagogues attended by converted Jews were both secret and well known to everyone. I would only point out that Gregory's passage refers to the very year of forced conversion, and that, within weeks or months of the event, one would not expect the "secret" to be so openly revealed as it was by Priscus, a notorious non-convert. But there is room for uncertainty.

have been a relatively modest group, perhaps those standing in a close
relationship to the king, on the model of Priscus, a merchant doing
business with the court and presumably enjoying royal protection.
Our eventual discovery that Phatir was from Guntram's kingdom, and
therefore not Chilperic's subject, is another inexplicable detail.[36]

Whatever the numbers were, Gregory isolates Chilperic in the
role of converter. No churchman is mentioned. The conversions take
place by the compelling force of royal command, and we are at once
assured that Chilperic's effort was in vain. To be sure, Gregory uses
strong words about the apostates' lying to God and returning to their
perfidia. As a bishop, he could hardly have spoken otherwise. Forcible baptism was reprehensible, but the circumstances of its conferral
did not impair its validity; there were no provisions for undoing what
was wrongfully done.[37] Even so, Gregory stops at strong words; he
does not suggest that the lapsing converts should somehow be made
to be more orthodox Christians than they were.[38] It is enough that the
reader should realize Chilperic's initiative was futile and redounded
to his discredit.

How profoundly discreditable it was is shown by the sequel.
Gregory rarely leaves any doubt as to whether a scene is on a higher
or lower plane than the reader, or at his level. The disputation
involving Chilperic, Priscus and Gregory has the same elevation as
the reader; Guntram's entrance into Orleans is higher, and Avitus's
conversions (as we shall see) even loftier. Chilperic's constraint of the
Jews is obviously lower; the opening part defines its elevation.[39] A
recurrent dramatic pattern in the many scenes of the *Histories* which
we gaze upon from above is the encounter of bad with worse. In a
famous example, a magnate named Munderic revolts against King
Theuderic I, claiming to be king and gathering a small army of
supporters; Theuderic quells this dangerous rebel but by means so
base and treacherous that Munderic, at the moment of his death,

---

[36] Guntram's *Teilreich* included the old Burgundian kingdom, with the upper part of
the Rhone valley. I agree with Blumenkranz in doubting the identification of our
Priscus with a minter of the same name in Chalon-sur-Saône (Guntram's capital):
Auteurs chrétiens, 71 n. 14; in the opposite sense, Parente, "Controversia," 544 n. 20.
[37] Gregory the Great, *Reg. epist.* 1. 45; p. 72; forced baptism was bad, not because
invalid, but because it occasioned greater sin in the baptized who returned to their
former religion. Cf. the case of Visigothic Spain, Blumenkranz, *Juifs et Chrétiens*, 110.
[38] The implied contrast is with the response of the Visigothic bishops to the forced
conversions by King Sisebut: Blumenkranz, *Juifs et Chrétiens*, 110-12.
[39] For the theory (going back to Aristotle's *Poetics*) on which these distinctions are
made, see Northrop Frye, *The Anatomy of Criticism* (Princeton: 1957), 33-34; Alastair
Fowler, *Kinds of Literature. An Introduction to the Theory of Genres and Modes*
(Cambridge, Mass.: 1982), 242.

acquires a touch of heroism or at least the reader's sympathy. The spectacle presented to us is of a deluded protagonist destroyed by adversaries blacker than he; because all the action is on a lower plane, we cannot identify with any of the parties, but are unavoidably moved by the outcome.[40] The implementation of this pattern in the account of Chilperic's conversions is unmistakable.

As delineated by Gregory, Priscus impresses us by the dignity of his resistance and his scrupulous religious observance, as well as by his determination that his son's marriage should go forward. But he is also the proverbial wily Jew, who knows the right men to bribe and has the means to do so. He carries pride to the point of rashness in not appreciating the danger of his position. Gregory briefly injects Chilperic into the story thus: the enraged tyrant orders Priscus's imprisonment so as to make him hear and believe by compulsion what he cannot voluntarily believe. Gregory, far from being naive, expected his audience to realize that what was not voluntarily believed would be even less persuasive in prison; the sentence is in the same class as Voltaire's witticism about its being customary in England to execute an admiral from time to time in order to encourage the others.[41]

Phatir and his quarrel with Priscus materialize, typically, without adequate details; Gregory thinks it enough that Phatir should be recognized as a scoundrel—he was one of the converts whom Chilperic had welcomed out of the baptismal font. No special attention is drawn to the contrast between Phatir's compliance with Chilperic's wishes and Priscus's resistance, but the implication that it motivated the murderous ambush is strong. When the killing takes place, mere description without commentary is deemed sufficient to horrify. The dénouement is pure Gregory. As Phatir makes his getaway from the church, his slave attendants (*pueri*), whom Gregory carefully locates in another square at the time of the crime, are left to contemplate their execution; the best of the lot mercifully kills his companions and in vain braves the fury of the assembled crowd. This pathetic massacre of the innocents, the most vividly drawn carnage, is meant to capture our sympathy and divert it even from Priscus.[42] The main villain, Chilperic, pardons the murderer; Phatir rejoins respectable society and even tries to lead a normal life by going home to Guntram's kingdom. But Francia was not the Roman Empire; Priscus's relatives soon

[40] *Hist.* 3. 14; 120-22.
[41] Voltaire was alluding to the unfortunate Admiral Byng: *Candide* (1759) ch. 23.
[42] Cf. the fate of Chramn's wife and daughters, *Hist.* 4. 20, p. 158; that of Merovech's attendant, Gailen, 5. 18, p. 215; the lamenting wife and children of Waddo, 9. 35; 390-91; and many other innocents.

exacted revenge upon his slayer. There were reasons for Gregory and
his kind not to be invariably hostile to feud.[43]

We are left with a pile of corpses worthy of Renaissance tragedy in
Priscus and his attendants, Phatir's blameless *pueri,* and Phatir
himself. Chilperic ordered many Jews to be baptized and the outcome
was a river of blood. It is beyond doubt that Gregory totally disapproved of the king's action, indeed, its results proved the godlessness
of the command that set the events in motion. Whether Gregory's
disapproval was motivated by principle is less clear. We can only
approach an answer after we have examined the case of Bishop Avitus
at Clermont.

As noted earlier, there are two very different, though not in fact
independent, accounts of this event. Fortunatus' epic, composed
shortly after the conversions and probably years before Gregory's
chapter in the *Histories,* focuses attention on what happened on or
about Ascension day (14 May 576); Gregory's narrative, however,
starts at Easter (5 April) and touches more briskly than the poem on
the next feast. The two converge in a colorful baptism scene at
Pentecost (24 May). Only the essentials of Fortunatus' poem will be
fully quoted:

> [Christ governs his flock as a good shepherd. He works through
> Avitus, inspiring his words for the increase of the flock. The bishop,
> not content with the numbers given him, increased their measure
> twofold.] The people of Clermont, rent in twain by a disturbance,
> was not one in trust (*fides*) though the city remained one. The Jewish
> fragrance recoiled, offended, from the Christians, and the irreverent
> crowd set itself against the pious ceremonies. [Stiffnecked, the Jews
> refused to bear the yoke of the Lord.] The bishop often admonished
> them in the love of God, so that a harvest of converts might go to
> heaven. [But they refused to see.]
>
> Thus, the day came when the Lord returned to heaven, and the
> Crucified One took an astral journey; the people, armed by faith,
> levelled the Judaic temple; a field appeared where there had been a
> synagogue. Nevertheless, the bishop spoke charmingly to the insur-
> gents in the law of Moses whom anger made furious: [Avitus appeals
> to them to be converted, arguing that the God of the O.T. is identical
> to the Christian Trinity.] "We are the creatures of Him Who is God in
> Trinity. You are the sheep of One; alas, why do you not walk as one?
> Let the flock be one, I pray, just as there is one Shepherd. [Further
> argument.] Either grant my entreaty or, I pray, leave this place. No
> force is applied here; consider which alternative you wish: either

---

[43] J. M. Wallace-Hadrill, "The Bloodfeud of the Franks," in his, *The Long-Haired Kings
and Other Studies in Frankish History* (London: 1962), 121-47.

follow me, or go and follow your own wishes. Yield the place, settler, and lead forth your co-religionists with you, or reside here permanently if you hold a single faith [with everyone else]." With a gentle sound, the bishop gave these pious words to the men, that they should travel whichever path their hearts pleased.

But the band of Jews, incensed and rebellious, swept out, went away, and gathered in a house. Then the Christians, when they saw the Jewish band assembling, at once assailed that lurking deceit. If they roared, they would feel just swordstrokes. . . Emissaries rushed to the bishop bearing instructions: "We the Jews are now your sheepfold. Lest they should perish, gain for God those who might live; if there is a delay, we die and your gains vanish. Come in haste: unless you hasten your steps, father, you will have to bewail the death of babes." Overcome by these lamentations, the merciful bishop swept off to bring the gift of salvation to the afflicted.

They arrived where the untamed crowd lurked in an enclosed place. [A Jewish spokesman addressed Avitus on the theme that, though late in the day, they had finally seen the light.] "But finally we follow, shepherd, where you have often urged us [to go, you] who leads his flock with such sweet salt. We seek the font—have a lake ready." . . . Thence [the bishop] drew to the light those who, when they refused, lay in the shade. And the king of a new soldiery opened the way. The formerly separate columns joined in one, and the love of God gave unity to the two parties. [Lines 103-36, the mass baptism at Pentecost. Lines 137-50, closing remarks to Gregory.][44]

As abridged for our purposes, the poem has four parts: 1. the introductory background, which may be interpreted either in a general way, as stating no more than that the city had two religious communities, or, alternatively, as evoking a recent exacerbation of religious sensitivities that set the formerly tranquil townspeople against each other; 2. the synagogue is destroyed, and Avitus calls on the Jews to convert or leave; 3. the Jews, besieged by armed Christians, promise conversion and implore Avitus to rescue them; 4. in Avitus's presence, the Jews ask for baptism and are led out by him to form one community with the Christians. Without specifying numbers, Fortunatus implies that all the Jews of Clermont were converted, and he is fuzzy in time relationships. One might well infer that Avitus personally delivered his ultimatum on the same day that the synagogue was destroyed and that, within a few hours, the besieged Jews reached their decision; but this compression may be poetic license.

Fortunatus's ovine imagery is relentless; it carries right through to

---

[44] *Loc. cit.* above n. 3.

the portrayal of the Jews, after the synagogue destruction, as furious
wild beasts lurking in a den—animals whom the sword-bearing
Christians deservedly contain. Avitus is oddly isolated; when the
circumstances demand his presence, he turns up, innocent, benevolent, and completely detached from whatever the other Christians of
Clermont were doing. Fortunatus clearly does not think it improper
for the bishop to offer the Jews the choice of conversion or exile; as
just noted, nor does he disapprove of the Christian siege of the house
in which the Jews had gathered. It is hard, from where we stand, to
recognize what credit might redound to Avitus for having gathered a
harvest of converts whom he gained, after a mass assault on their
synagogue, by an ultimatum backed by overt threats of force. Gregory
himself, as we shall see, could not quite stomach the armed crowd: he
chose to leave it out. (His omission is the one case of *suppressio veri*
in the *Histories* that may be documented.)[45] It is not only that, as
predictable, our sensitivities clash with Fortunatus', but rather that
the element of force seems too prominent and one-sided to have been
invisible even to someone of the poet's persuasion.

The place in the poem where one might look for extenuating
circumstances is the passage outlining the background. But Fortunatus' language is ambiguous enough to prevent certainty; perhaps he
says only that there were Christians and Jews at Clermont. However
a more ambitious interpretation makes better sense. Something specific had happened in the city to divide the population (*bifido discissa
tumultu*). True to the epic style, Fortunatus begins *in medias res,*
without later making up for our ignorance. Because the Jews obviously had not acquired their religion recently, the statement that
Clermont was one city but not one in *fides* cannot be both a reference
to two religions and the consequence of the *tumultus*; the religious
duality was of long standing (Jews are recorded at Clermont as far
back as a century earlier). The one result the *tumultus* could have had
was to make religion a contentious matter and, in this way, to
undermine the civil "trust" (*fides*) of the population; not only were
normal neighborly and business relations between Jewish and Christian Arvernians jeopardized, but the city was threatened with a
continuing feud between the two elements of the population. Or so at
least we may conjecture on the shaky basis of four verses, supported
by Fortunatus' insistence that the confrontation at the house pitted
armed Christians against furious Jews. It was not a simple case of
conversion being demanded at sword's point; a genuine feud was in

---

[45] Cf. Godefroid Kurth, "De l'autorité de Grégoire de Tours," in his *Études franques*
(Paris: 1919), II, 174-76. Kurth's overindulgent explanation minimizes the omission.

existence. In this way, Avitus's credit might arise, not from the particular steps to the Jews' conversion, but from his having, in due time, pacified and reconciled his city on a basis of religious *fides* and, surprisingly, without loss of population. Something of this sort is suggested by Gregory of Tours' version, but he too is short on details:

> Because our God always deigns to glorify his bishops, I shall relate what happened this year to the Jews at Clermont. The blessed bishop Avitus often admonished them to set aside the veil of the Mosaic law, to understand what they read in its spiritual sense, and, by attending to sacred Scriptures with a pure heart, to see that Christ was the son of the living God promised by the authority of the prophets and the law. But there remained in their hearts not, I would say, that veil which shielded Moses' face, but a wall.
>
> The bishop also prayed that the veil of the letter might be lifted from before them and that they might be converted to the Lord; and one of them asked to be baptized at Easter. Reborn in the Lord by the sacrament of baptism, he and the others, all in white garments, walked in procession. As all the people entered the gate of the city, one of the Jews, inspired by the devil, poured rancid oil over the head of the Jewish convert. All the people, detesting the deed, wished to stone [the perpetrator], but the bishop did not allow this to be done.
>
> On the blessed day, however, when the Lord ascends to the heavens in glory after redeeming man, when the bishop processed with psalm-singing from the cathedral to the basilica [of St. Illidius], the entire crowd following [the procession] fell upon the synagogue of the Jews and levelled it to the ground, so that the spot resembled a bare field. The next day, the bishop sent envoys [to the Jews], saying, "I do not incite you by force to believe in the Son of God, but I preach and convey the salt of wisdom to your hearts. For I am the shepherd set over the Lord's sheep; and that true Shepherd Who died for us said about you that He had other sheep which did not belong to the flock and should be brought into it, so that there might be one flock and one shepherd. Therefore, if you wish to believe as I do, be one flock under my care. But otherwise, leave this place." For a long time, they were moved by conflicting emotions and hesitated, but on the third day [after Ascension]—as I believe, overcome by the bishop—they agreed and sent a reply to him, saying, "We believe that Jesus is the Son of the living God promised us by the prophets, and therefore we beseech that we might be washed by baptism, lest we persist in this fault."
>
> The bishop rejoiced at the message. After celebrating the nocturns of holy Pentecost, he left for the baptistery outside the walls, and there the whole multitude, prostrate before him, asked for baptism. And he, weeping for joy, washed all of them with water, anointed them with chrism, and gathered them into the bosom of

mother church. Candles glimmered, lamps sparkled, the whole city was whitened with a white-clad flock, nor was there less joy in the city than Jerusalem experienced long ago when the Holy Spirit descended upon the apostles.

More than five hundred were baptized. Those, however, who refused baptism left the city and returned to Marseilles.[46]

Gregory's account reads a little better as history than does the poem. The first and second paragraphs hinge on the contrasting effectiveness of exhortation and prayer. The third paragraph uses the technical terminology of diplomatic or judicial negotiations: Avitus *legatos mittit* to the Jews and, by the by, they *mandata remittunt*. The forty days between Easter and Ascension, and the ten between Ascension and Pentecost, are abruptly jumped, but at least a part of the time sequence is systematically noted. The synagogue is destroyed on Ascension day; on the morrow, Avitus sends his ultimatum; and the next day, the Jews reply (14, 15, 16 May).[47] Gregory also estimates the number of converts and specifies that there were holdouts who, in a surprising verb, "returned" to Marseilles. The main departures from Fortunatus's version are the individual conversion at Easter, with its consequences, and—startlingly—the complete omission of the armed Christians threatening the assembled Jews and influencing their decision.

In Gregory's *Histories*, tales of miracles vie for prominence with tales of "slaughter" (such as that of Chilperic's conversions).[48] The events at Clermont are definitely of the miraculous kind, though nothing conspicuously supernatural occurs in their course. Gregory, in the opening sentence, establishes the elevation of what he is about to relate; he even locates Avitus's accomplishment as the fifth in a set of six chapters about wonder-working holy men relevant to the year 576.[49] Many sentences merely describe or comment on religious ceremonies. We begin on the familiar note of the futility of exhortation; Avitus tried and got nowhere, as was to be expected, but he also

---

[46] *Hist.* 5. 11;199-201. My translation.

[47] Gregory's chronology was misunderstood by Blumenkranz, *Juifs et Chrétiens*, 141, and *Auteurs chrétiens*, p. 70 no. 58; taking the three days (Gregory's *tertia die*) to run from Avitus's ultimatum, he counted a total of five days from Ascension to the Jews' decision. For the correct reckoning, see the marginal annotation of *Hist.* 5. 11, ed. Krusch-Levison 205-06.

[48] Cf. above n. 13. In *Hist.* 2. praef., Gregory spells out his view, inspired by the Bible, Orosius, and other Christian histories, that the course of events was a mixture of miracles (*virtutes sanctorum*) and slaughters (*strages* or *excidia*); his own narrative deliberately implements this vision of history.

[49] *Hist.* 5. 7-12; 199-201.

resorted to prayer, a more trustworthy instrument. And a Jew turned up asking for baptism.[50] That in itself, perhaps, was akin to a miracle.

The main axis of Christian Clermont led from the cathedral and bishop's residence inside the walled town out the main gate to a suburb, about three-quarters of a kilometer distant, near the Tiretaine river, where stood the baptistery and the basilica of St. Illidius, the main local saint. The Jewish quarter, with the synagogue, was also in this suburb.[51] Gregory leaves us in no doubt that the Jewish insult to the newly baptized convert was decisive for the unfolding of events. Interpreting this episode, Blumenkranz suggested that the convert was provocatively paraded near Jewish dwellings, but Gregory does not substantiate this view.[52] The city gate was an unavoidable stage in the procession from baptistery to cathedral, and nothing suggests that Jews lived in this vicinity. What seems to have happened is that an individual Jew positioned himself in a suitable spot and threw the rancid oil, which was specially chosen to mock the neophyte's anointing. He may have sought martyrdom, for Jewish insult of a convert was a very serious offense; a law of Constantine prescribed death by fire for the perpetrator.[53] The Christian crowd at Clermont took a similar view, but Bishop Avitus suppressed its impulse. Did he intend to channel its instincts for vengeance in a more ambitious direction? By ignoring the next forty days, Gregory leaves us guessing. Nevertheless, the connection between the first affront and its sequel is strongly implied; the levelling of the synagogue, too thorough for casual aggression, was the premeditated Christian reply to the Easter insult. By saying nothing about preparations for the destruction, both Fortunatus and Gregory indicate their preference for spontaneity and the free operations of the spirit, but at least they

---

[50] The contrast is rightly understood by Blumenkranz, *Juifs et Chrétiens*, 89 (cf. above n. 27). Gregory's reference to Avitus's praying echoes the Good Friday prayer for the conversion of the Jews, but no factual relationship with the following action is implied. Avitus's exhortation and prayer are set at no particular time, without its being suggested that the bishop prayed on Good Friday and, as a result, was rewarded with a convert at Easter.

[51] Vieillard-Troiekouroff, *Monuments religieux*, 85-104.

[52] Blumenkranz, *Juifs et Chrétiens*, 141. Summarizing Gregory, Blumenkranz, *Auteurs chrétiens*, 70 no. 58, says that the oil was poured "d'une des maisons devant lesquelles passait ce cortège"; Gregory's words are, "Ingredientibus populis portam civitatis, unus Iudeorum . . . oleum . . . diffudit."

[53] *Codex Theodosianus* 16. 8. 1 (repeated in *Codex Justinianus* 1. 9. 3), ed. Th. Mommsen (Berlin: 1904), p. 887. The version of this law current in the barbarian kingdoms more vaguely prescribed punishment in accordance with the magnitude of the crime; Bernard S. Bachrach, *Jews in Barbarian Europe* (Lawrence, Kansas: 1977), 45 no. 7, 49 no. 6.

do not pretend, other than by editing the facts, that the act was a sudden impulse.

From our perspective, it is, of course, outrageous that the destruction of the synagogue in retaliation for the misplaced daring of an individual Jew should result in Avitus's ultimatum to all the Jews to convert or be exiled. Blumenkranz identified the period between Easter and Ascension as the time when Avitus, if fair-minded, should have quieted the Christians down and prevented a small conflict from turning into a large one.[54] He may be right, although the oil-spattering should not be unduly minimized. Our judgment of the events depends very much on what Avitus did or did not do in the forty-day interval, and that information our authorities withhold. But if the circumstances are taken as Fortunatus and Gregory present them, namely, an innocent Avitus and a need for him to take positive action on 15 May, then his ultimatum may have been more statesmanlike than despotic. The Christians had been at least symbolically affronted at Easter, and now the Jews in turn had excellent reason to be aroused. The destruction of a synagogue, as at Orleans, had no obligatory consequences other than the need for reconstruction, but the difference at Clermont was that a state of feud between the two religious communities had been in existence ever since Easter. To this point, bloodshed had been averted. To authorize the rebuilding of the synagogue (never mind the question of costs) would implicitly deny the justice of the Christian revenge; to permit injured Jews to remain in the city even without a synagogue would face Clermont with the threat of their righteous vengeance, whenever they chose to take it (Fortunatus stresses their anger). An impartial and effective state apparatus would have been capable of mastering these difficulties and seeing that the law took its course through punishment for the oil-spattering Jew, compensation for the destroyed synagogue, and enforced peace all around. But Frankish Clermont fell short of these conditions; the local count is a notable absentee from the action.[55] In view of the destructive potential an active feud had for the city, Avitus's order of expulsion is perhaps more predictable than his offer of wholesale baptism.

Gregory treated the whole incident as miraculous, and invited

[54] Blumenkranz, *Juifs et Chrétiens*, 379.
[55] Godefroid Kurth, "Les ducs et comtes d'Auvergne au VIe siècle," in his *Études franques*, I, 195; we know the count's name but little else. Bachrach, *Jewish Policy*, 56, rightly points out that the incident at Clermont took place during a virtual interregnum (King Sigibert was murdered late in 575; his successor was a minor, and the reign began in confusion), but the significance of this fact is hard to assess. Gregory, *e silentio*, considered the political circumstances irrelevant.

Fortunatus to celebrate it in verse out of amazement at its result, for most of the Jews of Clermont assented to Avitus' urgings to be converted. Fortunatus wrote unblushingly of armed Christians threatening the Jews, but Gregory was sensitive enough to leave out their coercive force and to substitute "as I believe, overcome by the bishop"; yet either way, the Jews had the alternative, however grievous, of exile, but chose to remain instead. In Gregory's view, that decision could only mean that Avitus had done something right, that he merited divine assistance. The outcome might have been the departure from Clermont of several hundred productive townsmen, yet, unpredictably, they accepted baptism. The very fact that no early medieval parallel exists (outside the royal compulsion of Visigothic Spain) adds point to Gregory's astonishment.

Might the Jewish community of Clermont have harbored an inner division on whose disagreement the outcome depended? One's eye is caught by the statement that the minority refusing baptism "returned" to Marseilles. There had been Jews at Clermont in the days of Sidonius Apollinaris (470-479), and Gregory refers to them there in the early 550s so the community probably dated from at least the late Roman period.[56] Dalton offers the facile comment that Marseilles was "The port at which they [the Jews of 576] had landed in Gaul."[57] This gloss makes little sense if "they" refers to the entire community of Clermont Jews, yet the verb *reddere* is there. A more satisfactory way out of the difficulty would be to imagine that most of the Clermont Jews were long rooted in the city and district (the Easter convert presumably came from among them), whereas a smaller group consisted of comparative newcomers, probably stricter in religious observance, with ties to Marseilles and points east. Justinian's Mediterranean conquests (533-555) may have facilitated a renewal of Jewish immigration into Gaul. Presumably, again, this minority would have included the author of the Easter incident.[58] If the effect of the newcomers was to arrest and reverse the tendency of the long-settled

---

[56] For the evidence, see Blumenkranz, *Auteurs chrétiens*, 43 nos. 25a-c, 70 no. 57bis. Juster's traces of Jews in Gaul (*Juifs dans l'Emp. rom.*, I, 184-86) date for the most part from the late Roman and even Merovingian periods. At the conference, Professor Blanchetière kindly informed me that an inscription which had recently been thought to illustrate the presence of Jews in Provence in the early Imperial period was quickly shown by H. I. Marrou not to do so.

[57] Dalton, *History of the Franks*, II, 537.

[58] Priscus, who took pains to have his son marry a young woman from the Marseilles community, served King Chilperic in the procuring of precious goods from Byzantium (such goods are central to Chilperic's stay at Nogent-sur-Marne: Gregory of Tours, *Hist.* 6. 2, pp. 245-46). Admittedly, these are faint indications, but as many as there are.

majority toward assimilation, then the crisis of 576 came at a point when the two elements could be detached from each other by Avitus's action, with the unusual result we have seen. Even though, on the basis of the information available to us, this reconstruction is speculative, something of the kind is a possibility, and should not be overlooked. However pressured by the Christians of Clermont, the Jews played an active part in the events, and they need not have formed a cohesive block even before being faced with Avitus's ultimatum.

In composing the *Histories,* Gregory focused on "the high exceptions and the low exceptions," miracles and slaughters, and tended systematically to avoid the middle ground.[59] Besides, he spoke as a Christian bishop and illustrated the condition of the Jews in the Frankish kingdom only from that standpoint. Yet a few general ideas emerge from his testimony. He was no more hostile or friendly to the Jews as an element of the population of Gaul than he was to anyone else; only their religion was objectionable. The assumption he shared with his co-religionists was that sooner or later, the Jews were certain to become Christians; their eventual conversion was divinely promised and laid down in Scriptures. On these premises, the idea of religious pluralism was inconceivable.[60] Instead, Judaism benefited from toleration in the strict sense of the term—a concession made temporarily to what was deemed to be obstinacy and blindness. Since the N.T. God was willing to wait, the faithful should share His patience. On the other hand, patience did not mean forgetting that conversion (in other words, the elimination of Judaism) was the ultimate goal; because the presupposition of tolerance was that the Jews were candidates for conversion—catechumens *qui s'ignorent*— they had to be continually reminded of their duty. To this extent, at least in theory the Jews were under continual pressure from the Christian majority, and the only doubtful point was where laudable pressure ended and reprehensible coercion began. Within this context of Christian belief, Gregory narrates and judges the following three specific cases: the events of Clermont met with his unrestrained approval (in Fortunatus's eyes, even the crowd threatening with swords was estimable); the destruction of the Orleans synagogue was commendable enough not to be compensated for by the funds of a

---

[59] The quotation is from Kurth, "Autorité de Grégoire de Tours," 173.

[60] Cf. J. N. Hillgarth, in *Journal of Theological Studies,* N.S. 30 (1978), 349: "Set against this conviction [that religious unity was essential for any country] any tolerance of pluralism could only be a temporary expedient."

Christian king; Chilperic's baptisms by royal command merited the utmost condemnation.

The difficult thing, from our vantage point, is to look with indulgence upon any form of pressure, including the merely verbal one of being periodically preached to by Christian clergy. Our sympathy instinctively inclines in the direction of the bishop who bought goods from the Jews instead of being concerned with their salvation.[61] In Blumenkranz's reading, the events at Clermont turned on Bishop Avitus's ultimatum to accept baptism or depart; Avitus's allegation, that no force compelled the Jews' belief (recorded without question by Fortunatus and Gregory), seemed to be hypocrisy. One cannot go quite this far and expect to do justice to the conditions and mentality of Frankish Gaul.[62]

For a start, the line between right and wrong has to be drawn where our one observer very clearly drew it. Conversion of Jews by royal fiat, backed by the armed force of the government, was an unconscionable intrusion in a matter of faith (or the sphere of the clergy) and was comparable to tampering by fiat with Christian doctrine. Gregory's sensitivity to this rule, which his episcopal colleagues presumably shared, had its value for the Jews, for the role of the state, as conceived by the leaders of the Gallic church, was basically to maintain the toleration laid down in Roman law together, of course, with all its vexatious restrictions on officeholding, owner-

---

[61] Gregory of Tours, *Hist.* 4. 12;149.

[62] Blumenkranz, *Juifs et Chrétiens*, 379; cf. *Auteurs chrétiens*, 65 n. 4. He wished to stress the role of the clergy as distinct from that of the people. One readily admits that, normally, there was no popular hostility to Jews. But after Easter 576, Clermont was abnormal: a feud had broken out, and the people were touched in their religious sensitivities.

A case suggestive of that of Clermont seems to occur in *Vita s. Sulpitii Bituricensis* 4, ed. B. Krusch, MGH, *Script. rer. Merov.*, IV (Hannover-Leipzig: 1902), 374-75. Blumenkranz, *Auteurs chrétiens*, 110 no. 105bis, (and others) may have interpreted it more literally than it deserves to be. The hagiographer, in praising his hero, asserts in succession that Sulpicius would not endure any heretic, pagan, or Jew to live in his city without baptism, and that, by exhortation and prayer, he induced first a few Jews, then all of them to receive baptism. The first statement would be misunderstood if taken to mean that Sulpicius forced all non-Catholics to leave Bourges; nothing is said that would substantiate so severe a course of action. The hagiographer simply emphasizes the bishop's zeal, his determination that Bourges should be all-Catholic led him to make strenuous and ultimately successful efforts to convert all the Jews of the city (but by preaching and prayer alone, without expulsions). Details are singularly lacking. At best, the hagiographer implies that many Christians in the Bourges of his day were descended from Sulpicius's converts. The passage seems a harmless way to praise the bishop, and little more may be inferred from it than that Sulpicius possibly converted some Jews.

ship of slaves, and the rest.[63] The exclusion of the Frankish king from evangelization had the effect of reserving for the clergy (and the faithful) the obligation to take whatever actions seemed appropriate to keep the Jews aware of the place destined for them in the church. For bishops to ignore the religious diversity was neglect of duty, but the decentralization of the church assured that whatever pressure was applied was localized, haphazard, and conditioned by specific circumstances in which Jews as well as Christians had freedom to act. Gregory's silence concerning the way the Orleans synagogue was destroyed suggests that the harassment of Jews did not indiscriminately appeal to him. His enthusiasm about Avitus at Clermont was aroused, not by any particular step in the action, but by a chain of unforeseeable events, in whose complexity he believed he saw the intrusion of the Almighty. For someone committed to the idea that conversion would occur sooner or later, and that it required the active cooperation of men and God, here was a model case of how it should take place.

Nevertheless, the conditions Gregory evokes were more likely to inhibit mass conversions than to foster them. Unconcerted local efforts, detached from the governmental apparatus and heavily dependent on chance occurrences, could shake the resolve of the Jews of Gaul only in unusual circumstances. Nor should their recuperative powers be left out of account. Our Christian informants tend to look only in one direction, at incidents damaging to Jews, such as destructions of synagogues. When the references to aggressions of this sort from the fourth century onward are assembled, as they were by Juster, one is tempted to imagine a relentless tide of Christian outrages spreading unchecked around the Roman and ex-Roman world, sustained in their finality by the exertions of St. Ambrose and his imitators, who set themselves resolutely against enforcement of the laws prescribing compensation and allowing reconstruction.[64] But the imagery of tides and waves tends to be deceptive, especially when applied to periods of centuries; the implied devastation often fails to take place. Judaism may hardly be said to have been swept from the scene between Constantine and Mohamet. The impression that it ran this risk stems in part from informants who saw what they wished to

---

[63] On restrictions, Juster, *Juifs dans l'Emp. rom.*, I, 230-31; Blumenkranz, *Juifs et Chrétiens*, 184-90. It is interesting to contrast Gregory of Tours, who says nothing of these restrictions, to Gregory the Great, whose letters are often concerned with Jewish-owned slaves (texts summarized in Blumenkranz, *Auteurs chrétiens*, 75-83 *passim*).

[64] Juster, as above n. 18.

see, such as synagogue destructions, but kept no record of Jewish comebacks.[65] We never hear of the law being bent to permit the establishment of a new synagogue, yet such privileges were almost certainly granted, perhaps for a price.[66] The Jews were tolerated, both by law and, in the special sense we have seen, by the church. Their tranquility was threatened by paroxisms of zeal, on the part of bishops and their flocks, of kings, and of individual Jews. The outbreaks of persecution occasioned by these impulses were terrible for those who bore them, but because isolated they unfailingly subsided. In their wake, calm returned, the normal rules of toleration regained hold, recovery could take place, and the religious minority endured.

---

[65] E.g., the gradual restoration of a Jewish community at Alexandria after Cyril's expulsions, on which see Andrew Sharf, *Byzantine Jewry from Justinian to the Fourth Crusade* (London: 1971), 27. It is almost superfluous to point out that our documentation is one-sidedly Christian. Whether this is a function of the generally low volume of historical documentation or of other reasons is hard to say.

[66] Whenever Jews settled in localities lacking an ancient community, the establishment of a "new" synagogue had to be authorized sooner or later.

GENERAL INDEX

INDEX TO BIBLICAL AND TALMUDIC REFERENCES

BIBLE

John (*Cont.*):

2:11	126, 136, 139
2:25–3:1	140
Ch. 3	131
3:1–2	94
3:2	126
3:3	136
3:5	127, 136
3:10	126–127
3:16	83
3:19	136
3:20	137
3:22–26	140
Ch. 4	140
4:20	100
4:22	128
5:1–8	98
5:9–18	83
5:9c–16	98
5:10ff	123
5:17	98
5:18	131
5:24	83
5:30–47	83
5:37	126
5:38	137
5:39	125
5:40	125
5:44	127, 137
5:45	125
Ch. 6	247
6:14–15	274
6:30–31	131
6:39	128
6:42f	136
6:60–66	140
6:62	136
6:63	136
6:66–70	139
Chs. 7–8	131
7:1	95
7:3–5	140
7:13	126
7:16–24	83
7:19	126, 137
7:19ff	123
7:24	137
7:35	97
7:48–52	94
7:49	123, 131
7:50–52	127

John (*Cont.*):

7:52	131
8:15	137
8:22f	136
8:23f	136
8:31	140
8:39–44	136
8:42	136
8:44	136
8:48	131
8:52–53	131
8:59	123, 131
Ch. 9	94–96, 103, 131, 135, 140
9:10	123
9:13–14	83
9:14	123
9:20f	129
9:22	123, 126
9:22f	129
9:28	126
9:28f	125
9:39–41	135
9:40	137
10:11	82
10:12	140
10:15	82
10:18	129
10:29	128
10:30–34	123
10:33	98, 131
11:7f	126
11:8	123
11:24	139
11:24–26	83
11:48	131
11:49–52	82
11:52	97, 126
12:13	126
12:20	97
12:24	128
12:31	136
12:34	124
12:41	131
12:42	94, 123, 129
12:43	127, 137
13:34	124
14:15	124
14:21	124
15:10	124
15:12	125

OLD TESTAMENT APOCRYPHA

If such books are to be listed under Bible, they are index on separate pages, or they may be cited under OTHER ANCIENT SOURCES

The pages which can be inserted will be slugged OTA

MIDRASH

OTHER ANCIENT SOURCES